Central Readings in the
History of Modern Philosophy

Descartes to Kant

SECOND EDITION

Edited by

ROBERT CUMMINS
University of California at Davis

and

DAVID OWEN
University of Arizona

Wadsworth Publishing Company
I(T)P® An International Thomson Publishing Company

Belmont, CA • Albany, NY • Boston • Cincinnati • Johannesburg • London • Madrid • Melbourne
Mexico City • New York • Pacific Grove, CA • Scottsdale, AZ • Singapore • Tokyo • Toronto

PHILOSOPHY EDITOR: Peter Adams
ASSISTANT EDITOR: Kerri Abdinoor
EDITORIAL ASSISTANT: Kelly Bush
MARKETING MANAGER: Dave Garrison
PRINT BUYER: Stacey Weinberger
PERMISSIONS EDITOR: Yanna Walters
COPY EDITOR: Coleen O'Brien
COVER DESIGN: Cassandra Chu
COMPOSITOR: G & S Typesetters, Inc.
PRINTER: Transcontinental

Printed in Canada
3 4 5 6 7 8 9 10

For more information, contact Wadsworth Publishing Company, 10 Davis Drive, Belmont, CA 94002, or electronically
at http://www.wadsworth.com/

International Thomson Publishing Europe
Berkshire House
168-173 High Holborn
London, WC1V 7AA, United Kingdom

International Thomson Editores
Seneca, 53
Colonia Polanco
11560 México D.F. México

Nelson ITP, Australia
102 Dodds Street
South Melbourne
Victoria 3205 Australia

International Thomson Publishing Asia
60 Albert Street #15-01
Albert Complex
Singapore 189969

Nelson Canada
1120 Birchmount Road
Scarborough, Ontario
Canada M1K 5G4

International Thomson Publishing Japan
Hirakawa-cho Kyowa Building, 3F
2-2-1 Hirakawa-cho, Chiyoda-ku
Tokyo 102, Japan

International Thomson Publishing Southern Africa
Building 18, Constantia Square
138 Sixteenth Road, P.O. Box 2459
Halfway House, 1685 South Africa

Library of Congress Cataloging-in-Publication Data
Central readings in the history of modern philosophy : Descartes to
   Kant / edited by Robert Cummins and David Owen. — 2nd ed.
       p.   cm.
   Includes bibliographical references.
   ISBN 0-534-52347-1 (alk. paper)
   1. Philosophy. 2. Philosophy, Modern.   I. Cummins, Robert, [date].
II. Owen, David, [date].
B29.C355   1998
190—dc21   98-7760

Contents

Comparative Historical Chart

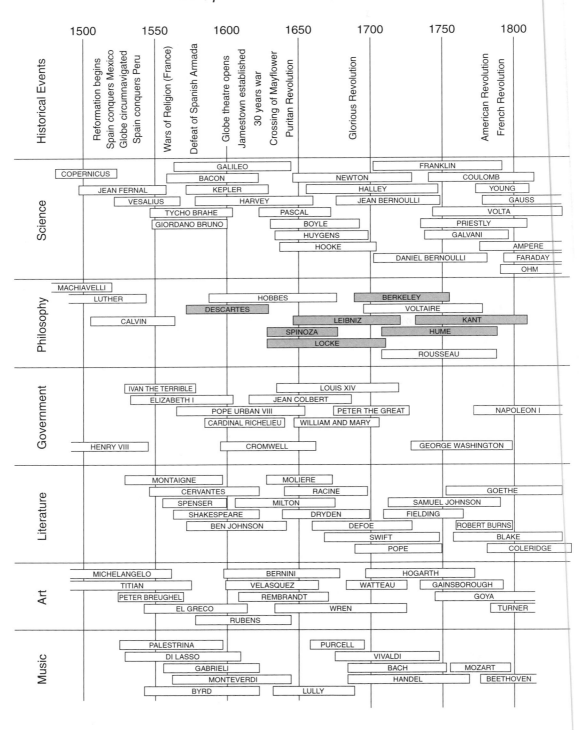

Preface

Almost every philosophy department in America offers a mid-level undergraduate course on the history of early modern philosophy. And yet there is no sensible, single text available for use in such a course. There are, of course, readers consisting of selections from historical texts, but these either cover too wide a range, leaving out too much material relevant to this sort of course, or cover only the Empiricists or only the Rationalists. Even in the latter case, the selections from Locke are always insufficient, and Kant is excluded entirely. Until now, the only alternative has been to build your own text by ordering several individual books. And this alternative has many disadvantages: high cost, multiple book orders with the high risk of at least one of the texts being out of print or late coming into the bookstore, variable editorial policy, and the lack of any reasonable abridgment of Locke's *Essay Concerning Human Understanding* and Kant's *Critique of Pure Reason*.

Our book aims to remedy these defects by providing, in a single volume, the major texts of the most studied figures in the history of early modern philosophy: Descartes's *Meditations,* Spinoza's *Ethics* (Parts I and II), Leibniz's *Discourse on Metaphysics* and *Monadology,* Locke's *Essay Concerning Human Understanding* (abridged), Berkeley's *Principles of Human Knowledge* (abridged) and *Three Dialogues,* Hume's *Enquiry Concerning Human Understanding* and Kant's *Critique of Pure Reason* (abridged). This book provides all the texts necessary for a full year's course in the history of early modern philosophy, and more than enough for a semester- or quarter-length course, giving the instructor the flexibility to tailor the selections to his or her individual preferences. We also think the text could be successfully used in a "topics" based course in metaphysics and epistemology. We provide suggestions for appropriate readings at the end of this preface.

As teachers, each of us must find his or her own style. And so also must we all find our own texts, texts we feel comfortable with and have something to say about, texts we know work for us and our students. Thus, our policy was to include complete texts whenever possible, and when not, always to prefer dropping an entire section or chapter rather than to abridge sections or chapters we did include. Few would dispute the appropriateness of the complete texts of Descartes, Leibniz, Berkeley, and Hume included here. Berkeley's *Dialogues* have been supplemented with the Introduction and first fifty-three sections of the *Principles.* The former contains Berkeley's important attack on abstraction, while the latter contains a concise summary of his entire system.

When forced to abridge, we were guided by the following principles: material dropped should be either (1) tangential to the central metaphysical and epistemological themes that connect all the authors represented, or (2) inappropriate for an undergraduate survey of the modern period. The first policy led us to drop the final three parts of Spinoza's *Ethics,* leaving parts one and two, which contain the material most relevant to the themes that dominate the other major works represented in this volume. The second led us to drop the A-text of the *Critique* as well as many passages in Locke that, like the differences between Kant's editions, are important to scholars but not to undergraduates, many of whom are encountering the texts for the first time.

Locke's *Essay* provided an interesting challenge. In most collections of empiricist writings, Locke is represented mainly by selections from Books II and IV of the *Essay.* Thus, themes considered crucial today—such as the discussions of innateness and concept formation—are entirely absent. In fact, there is no remotely acceptable abridgment under four hundred pages long. We believe we have succeeded in including all the material important for a mid-level course in fewer than two hundred pages.

The lack of any suitable abridgment of Kant's *Critique* has forced most instructors to use his *Prolegomena to Any Future Metaphysics* in undergraduate courses. Abridging Kant's text poses serious difficulties. Though it would be inaccurate to say that most of Locke's discussions can stand on their own, the necessary background can typically be provided in a short lecture. This might be true of Kant's text as well if we understood it better. The fact is, however, that Kant is so difficult that one is often forced to rely on widely distributed passages to interpret any given one. We therefore have provided an unabridged text of the B edition from the preface through the transcendental deduction (that is, through Book I of the Transcendental Analytic). This is then supplemented by those passages that figure most prominently in attempts by recent commentators to explicate Kant's main line of argumentation in the Analytic, namely the Second Analogy and the Refutation of Idealism. (The long footnote from the preface restating the argument of the Refutation is printed with the Refutation rather than in its original place.) This has the advantage, in the context of this book, of focusing on doctrines students will perceive to be directly relevant to Berkeley and Hume, thus helping to maintain a sense of philosophical dialogue. (Further explanation of the relation of the Second Analogy and the Refutation to the rest of the text will be found in the introduction to the Kant section.)

In this (second) edition, we have added a section from the Dialectic, Chapter II (The Antimony of Pure Reason) of Book II (The Dialectical Inferences of Pure Reason). This material puts the rest of the argument in perspective by exposing (but not curing!) the intellectual illusions that arise when the understanding attempts to employ concepts not grounded in experience.

In keeping with the needs of a mid-level undergraduate course, we have aimed at providing accurate texts but without scholarly apparatus. Thus, editor's footnotes and comments have been deleted, and most textual variants have not been included. The text of Descartes's *Meditations* comes from *Descartes: Meditations on First Philosophy,* translated and edited by John Cottingham (Cambridge, 1996) pp. 9–62; Spinoza's *Ethics* from E. Curley, ed., *Collected Works of Spinoza, Vol. 1,* pp. 408–91 (copyright 1985 Princeton University Press); Leibniz's *Discourse on Metaphysics* and *Monadology* from the George Montgomery translation (Open Court Publishing Co., 1990); and the excerpts from Kant's *Critique of Pure Reason,* pp. 17–247, 396–423, 483–84 of the Norman Kemp Smith translation (St. Martin's

Press, 1965). The texts of Locke, Hume, and the Berkeley *Principles* are excerpted with permission from the Past Masters Locke, Berkeley, and Hume text base, InteLex Corp., 1989. Their Locke text is a corrected version of the twelfth edition of *The Works of John Locke,* 1824. The Berkeley *Principles* excerpted here is a corrected version from *The Works of George Berkeley,* Rev. G. N. Wright, ed., 1843. Their Hume text is a corrected version of the text found in *Essays, Moral, Political, and Literary,* T. H. Green and T. H. Grose, eds., 1898. As excerpted here, the Locke text contains Locke's footnotes in square brackets, and transliterated Greek and Hebrew in angle brackets. The Hume text contains some important footnotes and variants in square brackets. We have made some changes to the spelling and punctuation of the InteLex texts. Berkeley's *Dialogues* are reprinted from *Reason and Responsibility,* ed. Joel Feinberg (Belmont, Calif.: Wadsworth, 1985).

Pedagogical Material

Two sample course outlines follow, each suitable for a one-semester or one-quarter course, the first concentrating on epistemology, the second on metaphysics.

Syllabus I: Epistemology

I. Descartes
   A. Meditation I: The method of doubt and the search for certainty.
   B. Meditation II: "I think" is immune to doubt; "What am I? A thing that thinks."
   C. Meditation VI: The existence of the external world.
II. Locke
   A. Book I: No innate ideas.
   B. Book 2: Chapters 1–2, 8, 31.
   C. Book 4: Chapters 1–4, 9, 11, 14–16.

III. Berkeley
   A. Principles 1–33: Critique of realism; Dialogue 1: Naive realism refuted; the distinction between immediate and mediate perception; critique of mediate perception as a basis for realism.
   B. Dialogue 2: Things as collections of ideas; unperceived existence.
IV. Hume: §§1–7.
V. Kant: The Aesthetic, The Deduction, Refutation of Idealism, Second Analogy.

Syllabus II: Metaphysics

I. Descartes: God, Mind and Body: Meditations III–VI
II. Locke: Substance, Causality, Liberty and Necessity, Mind and Body: II.1; II.8; II.21; II.23; III.1–6; IV.3
III. Berkeley
   A. Substance: Dialogues 2–3
   B. Causality, Mind and Body: Principles §§25–33, §65
IV. Hume: Liberty and Necessity, God: §8; §§10–11
V. Leibniz: Substance, Liberty and Necessity, Mind and Body, God: [Discourse,] Monadology
VI. Spinoza: Substance and God, Liberty and Necessity: Part I; Mind and Body: Part II
VII. Kant: The Antinomy of Pure Reason

It is sometimes useful to read the history of philosophy by topics rather than by author. To make this easier to do, and to provide students with some cross-references that will enhance their sense of the philosophical dialogue of the period, we offer here some topic headings together with a list of central texts associated with each. Items in brackets are less central than items not so marked.

Mental Representation

[Descartes: Meditation III]
Locke: II.8–9; II.31; III: IV.7.9
Berkeley: PHK §6–20 (Introduction), §§1–17; First dialogue, 224–end
Spinoza: II, def. 3–4; II, prop 49; II, prop 32–34
Kant: Introduction; Aesthetic; transcendental deduction
Leibniz: Discourse ix, xiv; Monadology §56ff., §61ff.

Innate Ideas

Descartes: Meditation V
Locke: Book I
[Leibniz: Discourse xxiii–xix, Monadology all]
Hume: §2
Kant: Introduction

Types of Knowledge

Locke: IV.1–4
[Leibniz: Discourse xiii, Monadology §§29–35]
Spinoza: II, prop 40ff.
Hume: §4
Kant: Introduction

Knowledge of the External World

Descartes: Meditation VI
Locke: II.31; IV.1–4; IV.11; IV.14–16
[Leibniz: §§56–62]
[Spinoza: Part II]
Berkeley: Principles 1–33; Dialogues
Hume: §12
Kant: Transcendental Deduction, Refutation of
Idealism, Second Analogy

Substance

Locke: II.23; III.3–6
Berkeley: Dialogues 2–3
[Leibniz: Discourse viii–xv, Monadology §§1–13]
Spinoza: Part I

Error and Theodicy

Descartes: Meditations IV and VI
Leibniz: All
Spinoza: I, def 7; prop 36 and appendix
Kant: The Antinomy of Pure Reason

Perception

Locke: II.8–9; IV.11
[Leibniz: Discourse xiv, xxvi, xxxiv, Monadology
§§13–27, 56–62]

Berkeley: First Dialogue
Hume: §12
Kant: Aesthetic

Liberty and Necessity

[Descartes: Meditation IV]
Locke: II.21
[Leibniz: Discourse i–xiii, xxx–xxxi, Monadology
§46ff]
Spinoza: I, def 7; I, props 29–36
Hume: §8

Causality

Locke: II.21.1–4
Berkeley: Principles §§25–33, §65
Hume: §§1–7
Kant: Second Analogy, The Antinomy of Pure
Reason

Mind and Body

Descartes: Meditations IV–VI
Spinoza: Part II
Locke: II.1; II.8; IV.3.6: IV.3.28
[Leibniz: Discourse xxxiii–xxxiv, Monadology §17;
§§63–82]
Berkeley: Principles, §§27–8

God

Descartes: Meditation III
Spinoza: Part I
[Leibniz: All, especially Discourse xxxv–xxxvii,
Monadology §36ff]
Hume: §§10–11
Kant: The Antinomy of Pure Reason

René Descartes
(1596–1650)

Descartes, born in La Haye (now La Haye-Descartes), France, was educated at the Jesuit college in La Flèche. Owing to frail health, he was allowed to stay in bed late into the morning, a habit he found most conducive to philosophizing and kept to all his life. Although the school concentrated on traditional scholastic physics and mathematics, it was forward-looking enough to celebrate Galileo's discovery of the moons of Jupiter in 1611. After leaving La Flèche, Descartes studied law at Poitiers, then traveled throughout Europe for a decade, including three years in Paris, where he met Mersenne, who became his mentor and go-between. In 1629, seeking tranquillity and solitude, he made Holland his permanent home. His major work, *Le Monde*, a scientific work based in part on the Copernican hypothesis, was nearing publication in 1633, when the Inquisition's condemnation of Galileo prompted him to withdraw it. His *Meditations on First Philosophy*, reprinted here, were published in 1641. The *Meditations* resulted from interest in a section of an earlier work, *Discourse on the Method for Conducting One's Reason Rightly,* which contained three scientific essays (on optics, geometry, and meteorology) and a section designed to explain Descartes's method. It was inquiries concerning this section on method that prompted the *Meditations.* Descartes's fame grew, and in 1649 he reluctantly accepted the invitation of Queen Christina of Sweden to join her court. Forced to abandon his lifelong habit of staying in bed in the morning engaged in philosophical reflection, he attended the queen at five o'clock in the morning. Within six months, he caught pneumonia and died.

The *Meditations* do not constitute a systematic treatise on philosophy, nor even a set of rigorous arguments. They are more like a set of mental exercises, as their title suggests, designed to break down the prejudices against accepting the first principles of metaphysics. Such principles had to be seen to be certain and indubitable, if metaphysics, and the new science of Galileo to which Descartes made such an important contribution, were to stand on firm ground and to progress.

Descartes greatly admired mathematics, for its certainty and its clear example of knowledge gained through the understanding rather than the senses. It wasn't the rigor of mathematical proof that inspired Descartes; he was more interested in the discovery of new truths than the proof of old ones. Rather, it was the intellectual certainty of mathematical truths, their clarity and distinctness, that he held in such high regard. He aimed to bring such intellectual certainty to metaphysics and science. The method he used to attain such certainty is called the Method of Doubt. As he put it in the earlier *Discourse on Method,* he resolved "to accept nothing as true which I did not clearly recognize to be so: that is to say, carefully avoid precipitation and prejudice in judgments, and to accept in them nothing more than was presented to my mind so clearly and distinctly that I could have no occasion to doubt it." In the *Meditations,* Descartes shows that, initially, nothing is immune to doubt except the certainty of one's own existence. Using that as the basis for his metaphysical principles, Descartes initiated modern Western philosophy.

Note on the text: Some additions to the original Latin text found in the later French translation are included here in footnotes.

Meditations on First Philosophy

Synopsis of the following six Meditations

In the First Meditation reasons are provided which give us possible grounds for doubt about all things, especially material things, so long as we have no foundations for the sciences other than those which we have had up till now. Although the usefulness of such extensive doubt is not apparent at first sight, its greatest benefit lies in freeing us from all our preconceived opinions, and providing the easiest route by which the mind may be led away from the senses. The eventual result of this doubt is to make it impossible for us to have any further doubts about what we subsequently discover to be true.

In the Second Meditation, the mind uses its own freedom and supposes the non-existence of all the things about whose existence it can have even the slightest doubt; and in so doing the mind notices that it is impossible that it should not itself exist during this time. This exercise is also of the greatest benefit, since it enables the mind to distinguish without difficulty what belongs to itself, i.e. to an intellectual nature, from what belongs to the body. But since some people may perhaps expect arguments for the immortality of the soul in this section, I think they should be warned here and now that I have tried not to put down anything which I could not precisely demonstrate. Hence the only order which I could follow was that normally employed by geometers, namely to set out all the premises on which a desired proposition depends, before drawing any conclusions about it. Now the first and most important prerequisite for knowledge of the immortality of the soul is for us to form a concept of the soul which is as clear as possible and is also quite

Reprinted from *Descartes: Meditations on First Philosophy,* trans. John Cottingham (Cambridge: Cambridge Univ. Press, 1996) pp. 9–62. Reprinted with the permission of Cambridge University Press.

distinct from every concept of body; and that is just what has been done in this section. A further requirement is that we should know that everything that we clearly and distinctly understand is true in a way which corresponds exactly to our understanding of it; but it was not possible to prove this before the Fourth Meditation. In addition we need to have a distinct concept of corporeal nature, and this is developed partly in the Second Meditation itself, and partly in the Fifth and Sixth Meditations. The inference to be drawn from these results is that all the things that we clearly and distinctly conceive of as different substances (as we do in the case of mind and body) are in fact substances which are really distinct one from the other; and this conclusion is drawn in the Sixth Meditation. This conclusion is confirmed in the same Meditation by the fact that we cannot understand a body except as being divisible, while by contrast we cannot understand a mind except as being indivisible. For we cannot conceive of half of a mind, while we can always conceive of half of a body, however small; and this leads us to recognize that the natures of mind and body are not only different, but in some way opposite. But I have not pursued this topic any further in this book, first because these arguments are enough to show that the decay of the body does not imply the destruction of the mind, and are hence enough to give mortals the hope of an after-life, and secondly because the premises which lead to the conclusion that the soul is immortal depend on an account of the whole of physics. This is required for two reasons. First, we need to know that absolutely all substances, or things which must be created by God in order to exist, are by their nature incorruptible and cannot ever cease to exist unless they are reduced to nothingness by God's denying his concurrence to them. Secondly, we need to recognize that body, taken in the general sense, is a substance, so that it too never perishes. But the human body, in so far as it differs from other bodies, is simply made up of a certain configuration of limbs and other accidents of this sort; whereas the human mind is not made up of any accidents in this way, but is a pure substance. For even if all the accidents of the mind change, so that it has different objects of the understanding and different desires and sensations, it does not on that account become a different mind; whereas a human body loses its identity merely as a result of a change in the shape of some of its parts. And it follows from this that while the body can very easily perish, the mind[1] is immortal by its very nature.

In the Third Meditation I have explained quite fully enough, I think, my principal argument for proving the existence of God. But in order to draw my readers' minds away from the senses as far as possible, I was not willing to use any comparison taken from bodily things. So it may be that many obscurities remain; but I hope they will be completely removed later, in my Replies to the Objections. One such problem, among others, is how the idea of a supremely perfect being, which is in us, possesses so much objective reality that it can come only from a cause which is supremely perfect. In the Replies this is illustrated by the comparison of a very perfect machine, the idea of which is in the mind of some engineer. Just as the objective intricacy belonging to the idea must have some cause, namely the scientific knowledge of the engineer, or of someone else who passed the idea on to him, so the idea of God which is in us must have God himself as its cause.

In the Fourth Meditation it is proved that everything that we clearly and distinctly perceive is true, and I also explain what the nature of falsity consists in. These results need to be known both in order to confirm what has gone before and also to make intelligible what is to come later. (But here it should be noted in passing that I do not deal at all with sin, i.e. the error which is committed in pursuing good and evil, but only with the error that occurs in distinguishing truth from falsehood. And there is no discussion of matters pertaining to faith or the conduct of life, but simply of speculative truths which are known soley by means of the natural light.)

In the Fifth Meditation, besides an account of corporeal nature taken in general, there is a new argument demonstrating the existence of God. Again, several difficulties may arise here, but these are resolved later in the Replies to the Objections. Finally

I explain the sense in which it is true that the certainty even of geometrical demonstrations depends on the knowledge of God.

Lastly, in the Sixth Meditation, the intellect is distinguished from the imagination; the criteria for this distinction are explained; the mind is proved to be really distinct from the body, but is shown, notwithstanding, to be so closely joined to it that the mind and the body make up a kind of unit; there is a survey of all the errors which commonly come from the senses, and an explanation of how they may be avoided; and, lastly, there is a presentation of all the arguments which enable the existence of material things to be inferred. The great benefit of these arguments is not, in my view, that they prove what they establish – namely that there really is a world, and that human beings have bodies and so on – since no sane person has ever seriously doubted these things. The point is that in considering these arguments we come to realize that they are not as solid or as transparent as the arguments which lead us to knowledge of our own minds and of God, so that the latter are the most certain and evident of all possible objects of knowledge for the human intellect. Indeed, this is the one thing that I set myself to prove in these Meditations. And for that reason I will not now go over the various other issues in the book which are dealt with as they come up.

First Meditation: What can be called into doubt

Some years ago I was struck by the large number of falsehoods that I had accepted as true in my childhood, and by the highly doubtful nature of the whole edifice that I had subsequently based on them. I realized that it was necessary, once in the course of my life, to demolish everything completely and start again right from the foundations if I wanted to establish anything at all in the sciences that was stable and likely to last. But the task looked an enormous one, and I began to wait until I should reach a mature enough age to ensure that no subsequent time of life would be more suitable for tackling such inquiries. This led me to put the project off for so long that I would now be to blame if by pondering

---

[1] ". . . or the soul of man, for I make no distinction between them" (added in French version).

over it any further I wasted the time still left for carrying it out. So today I have expressly rid my mind of all worries and arranged for myself a clear stretch of free time. I am here quite alone, and at last I will devote myself sincerely and without reservation to the general demolition of my opinions.

But to accomplish this, it will not be necessary for me to show that all my opinions are false, which is something I could perhaps never manage. Reason now leads me to think that I should hold back my assent from opinions which are not completely certain and indubitable just as carefully as I do from those which are patently false. So, for the purpose of rejecting all my opinions, it will be enough if I find in each of them at least some reason for doubt. And to do this I will not need to run through them all individually, which would be an endless task. Once the foundations of a building are undermined, anything built on them collapses of its own accord; so I will go straight for the basic principles on which all my former beliefs rested.

Whatever I have up till now accepted as most true I have acquired either from the senses or through the senses. But from time to time I have found that the senses deceive, and it is prudent never to trust completely those who have deceived us even once.

Yet although the senses occasionally deceive us with respect to objects which are very small or in the distance, there are many other beliefs about which doubt is quite impossible, even though they are derived from the senses—for example, that I am here, sitting by the fire, wearing a winter dressing-gown, holding this piece of paper in my hands, and so on. Again, how could it be denied that these hands or this whole body are mine? Unless perhaps I were to liken myself to madmen, whose brains are so damaged by the persistent vapours of melancholia that they firmly maintain they are kings when they are paupers, or say they are dressed in purple when they are naked, or that their heads are made of earthenware, or that they are pumpkins, or made of glass. But such people are insane, and I would be thought equally mad if I took anything from them as a model for myself.

A brilliant piece of reasoning! As if I were not a man who sleeps at night, and regularly has all the same experiences[2] while asleep as madmen do when awake—indeed sometimes even more improbable ones. How often, asleep at night, am I convinced of just such familiar events—that I am here in my dressing-gown, sitting by the fire—when in fact I am lying undressed in bed! Yet at the moment my eyes are certainly wide awake when I look at this piece of paper; I shake my head and it is not asleep; as I stretch out and feel my hand I do so deliberately, and I know what I am doing. All this would not happen with such distinctness to someone asleep. Indeed! As if I did not remember other occasions when I have been tricked by exactly similar thoughts while asleep! As I think about this more carefully, I see plainly that there are never any sure signs by means of which being awake can be distinguished from being asleep. The result is that I begin to feel dazed, and this very feeling only reinforces the notion that I may be asleep.

Suppose then that I am dreaming, and that these particulars—that my eyes are open, that I am moving my head and stretching out my hands—are not true. Perhaps, indeed, I do not even have such hands or such a body at all. Nonetheless, it must surely be admitted that the visions which come in sleep are like paintings, which must have been fashioned in the likeness of things that are real, and hence that at least these general kinds of things—eyes, head, hands and the body as a whole—are things which are not imaginary but are real and exist. For even when painters try to create sirens and satyrs with the most extraordinary bodies, they cannot give them natures which are new in all respects; they simply jumble up the limbs of different animals. Or if perhaps they manage to think up something so new that nothing remotely similar has ever been seen before—something which is therefore completely fictitious and unreal—at least the colours used in the composition must be real. By similar reasoning, although these general kinds of things—eyes, head, hands and so on—could be imaginary, it must at least be admitted that certain other even simpler and more universal things are real. These are as it were the real colours from which we form all the images of things, whether true or false, that occur in our thought.

This class appears to include corporeal nature in general, and its extension; the shape of extended things; the quantity, or size and number of these

---

[2] "... and in my dreams regularly represent to myself the same things" (French version).

things; the place in which they may exist, the time through which they may endure,[3] and so on.

So a reasonable conclusion from this might be that physics, astronomy, medicine, and all other disciplines which depend on the study of composite things, are doubtful; while arithmetic, geometry and other subjects of this kind, which deal only with the simplest and most general things, regardless of whether they really exist in nature or not, contain something certain and indubitable. For whether I am awake or asleep, two and three added together are five, and a square has no more than four sides. It seems impossible that such transparent truths should incur any suspicion of being false.

And yet firmly rooted in my mind is the long-standing opinion that there is an omnipotent God who made me the kind of creature that I am. How do I know that he has not brought it about that there is no earth, no sky, no extended thing, no shape, no size, no place, while at the same time ensuring that all these things appear to me to exist just as they do now? What is more, just as I consider that others sometimes go astray in cases where they think they have the most perfect knowledge, how do I know that God has not brought it about that I too go wrong every time I add two and three or count the sides of a square, or in some even simpler matter, if that is imaginable? But perhaps God would not have allowed me to be deceived in this way, since he is said to be supremely good. But if it were inconsistent with his goodness to have created me such that I am deceived all the time, it would seem equally foreign to his goodness to allow me to be deceived even occasionally; yet this last assertion cannot be made.[4]

Perhaps there may be some who would prefer to deny the existence of so powerful a God rather than believe that everything else is uncertain. Let us not argue with them, but grant them that everything said about God is a fiction. According to their supposition, then, I have arrived at my present state by fate or chance or a continuous chain of events, or by some other means; yet since deception and error seem to be imperfections, the less powerful they make my original cause, the more likely it is that I am so imperfect as to be deceived all the time. I have no aswer to these arguments, but am finally compelled to admit that there is not one of my former beliefs about which a doubt may not properly be raised; and this is not a flippant or ill-considered conclusion, but is based on powerful and well thought-out reasons. So in future I must withhold my assent from these former beliefs just as carefully as I would from obvious falsehoods, if I want to discover any certainty.[5]

But it is not enough merely to have noticed this; I must make an effort to remember it. My habitual opinions keep coming back, and, despite my wishes, they capture my belief, which is as it were bound over to them as a result of long occupation and the law of custom. I shall never get out of the habit of confidently assenting to these opinions, so long as I suppose them to be what in fact they are, namely highly probable opinions—opinions which, despite the fact that they are in a sense doubtful, as has just been shown, it is still much more reasonable to believe than to deny. In view of this, I think it will be a good plan to turn my will in completely the opposite direction and deceive myself, by pretending for a time that these former opinions are utterly false and imaginary. I shall do this until the weight of preconceived opinion is counter-balanced and the distorting influence of habit no longer prevents my judgment from perceiving things correctly. In the meantime, I know that no danger or error will result from my plan, and that I cannot possibly go too far in my distrustful attitude. This is because the task now in hand does not involve action but merely the acquisition of knowledge.

I will suppose therefore that not God, who is supremely good and the source of truth, but rather some malicious demon of the utmost power and cunning has employed all his energies in order to deceive me. I shall think that the sky, the air, the earth, colours, shapes, sounds and all external things are merely the delusions of dreams which he has devised to ensnare my judgement. I shall consider myself as not having hands or eyes, or flesh, or blood or senses, but as falsely believing that I have all these things. I shall stubbornly and firmly persist in

---

[3] ". . . the place where they are, the time which measures their duration" (French version).

[4] ". . . yet I cannot doubt that he does allow this" (French version).

[5] ". . . in the sciences" (added in French version).

this meditation; and, even if it is not in my power to know any truth, I shall at least do what is in my power,[6] that is, resolutely guard against assenting to any falsehoods, so that the deceiver, however powerful and cunning he may be, will be unable to impose on me in the slightest degree. But this is an arduous undertaking, and a kind of laziness brings me back to normal life. I am like a prisoner who is enjoying an imaginary freedom while asleep; as he begins to suspect that he is asleep, he dreads being woken up, and goes along with the pleasant illusion as long as he can. In the same way, I happily slide back into my old opinions and dread being shaken out of them, for fear that my peaceful sleep may be followed by hard labour when I wake, and that I shall have to toil not in the light, but amid the inextricable darkness of the problems I have now raised.

Second Meditation: The nature of the human mind, and how it is better known than the body

So serious are the doubts into which I have been thrown as a result of yesterday's meditation that I can neither put them out of my mind nor see any way of resolving them. It feels as if I have fallen unexpectedly into a deep whirlpool which tumbles me around so that I can neither stand on the bottom nor swim up to the top. Nevertheless I will make an effort and once more attempt the same path which I started on yesterday. Anything which admits of the slightest doubt I will set aside just as if I had found it to be wholly false; and I will proceed in this way until I recognize something certain, or, if nothing else, until I at least recognize for certain that there is no certainty. Archimedes used to demand just one firm and immovable point in order to shift the entire earth; so I too can hope for great things if I manage to find just one thing, however slight, that is certain and unshakeable.

I will suppose then, that everything I see is spurious. I will believe that my memory tells me lies, and that none of the things that it reports ever happened. I have no senses. Body, shape, extension, movement and place are chimeras. So what remains true? Perhaps just the one fact that nothing is certain.

Yet apart from everything I have just listed, how do I know that there is not something else which does not allow even the slightest occasion for doubt? Is there not a God, or whatever I may call him, who puts into me[7] the thoughts I am now having? But why do I think this, since I myself may perhaps be the author of these thoughts? In that case am not I, at least, something? But I have just said that I have no senses and no body. This is the sticking point: what follows from this: Am I not so bound up with a body and with senses that I cannot exist without them? But I have convinced myself that there is absolutely nothing in the world, no sky, no earth, no minds, no bodies. Does it now follow that I too do not exist? No: if I convinced myself of something[8] then I certainly existed. But there is a deceiver of supreme power and cunning who is deliberately and constantly deceiving me. In that case I too undoubtedly exist, if he is deceiving me; and let him deceive me as much as he can, he will never bring it about that I am nothing so long as I think that I am something. So after considering everything very thoroughly, I must finally conclude that this proposition, *I am, I exist*, is necessarily true whenever it is put forward by me or conceived in my mind.

But I do not yet have a sufficient understanding of what this "I" is, that now necessarily exists. So I must be on my guard against carelessly taking something else to be this "I," and so making a mistake in the very item of knowledge that I maintain is the most certain and evident of all. I will therefore go back and meditate on what I originally believed myself to be, before I embarked on this present train of thought. I will then subtract anything capable of being weakened, even minimally, by the arguments now introduced, so that what is left at the end may be exactly and only what is certain and unshakeable.

What then did I formerly think I was? A man. But what is a man? Shall I say "a rational animal"? No; for then I should have to inquire what an animal

---

[6] ". . . nevertheless it is in my power to suspend my judgment" (French version).

[7] ". . . puts into my mind" (French version).

[8] ". . . or thought anything at all" (French version).

is, what rationality is, and in this way one question would lead me down the slope to other harder ones, and I do not now have the time to waste on subtleties of this kind. Instead I propose to concentrate on what came into my thoughts spontaneoulsy and quite naturally whenever I used to consider what I was. Well, the first thought to come to mind was that I had a face, hands, arms and the whole mechanical structure of limbs which can be seen in a corpse, and which I called the body. The next thought was that I was nourished, that I moved about, and that I engaged in sense-perception and thinking; and these actions I attributed to the soul. But as to the nature of this soul, either I did not think about this or else I imagined it to be something tenuous, like a wind or fire or ether, which permeated my more solid parts. As to the body, however, I had no doubts about it, but thought I knew its nature distinctly. If I had tried to describe the mental conception I had of it, I would have expressed it as follows: by a body I understand whatever has a determinable shape and a definable location and can occupy a space in such a way as to exclude any other body; it can be perceived by touch, sight, hearing, taste or smell, and can be moved in various ways, not by itself but by whatever else comes into contact with it. For, according to my judgement, the power of self-movement, like the power of sensation or of thought, was quite foreign to the nature of a body; indeed, it was a source of wonder to me that certain bodies were found to contain faculties of this kind.

But what shall I now say that I am, when I am supposing that there is some supremely powerful and, if it is permissible to say so, malicious deceiver, who is deliberately trying to trick me in every way he can? Can I now assert that I possess even the most insignificant of all the attributes which I have just said belong to the nature of a body? I scrutinize them, think about them, go over them again, but nothing suggests itself; it is tiresome and pointless to go through the list once more. But what about the attributes I assigned to the soul? Nutrition or movement? Since now I do not have a body, these are mere fabrications. Sense-perception? This surely does not occur without a body, and besides, when asleep I have appeared to perceive through the senses many things which I afterwards realized I did not perceive through the senses at all. Thinking?

At last I have discovered it—thought; this alone is inseparable from me. I am, I exist—that is certain. But for how long? For as long as I am thinking. For it could be that were I totally to cease from thinking, I should totally cease to exist. At present I am not admitting anything except what is necessarily true. I am, then, in the strict sense only a thing that thinks; that is, I am a mind, or intelligence, or intellect, or reason—words whose meaning I have been ignorant of until now. But for all that I am a thing which is real and which truly exists. But what kind of a thing? As I have just said—a thinking thing.

What else am I? I will use my imagination.[9] I am not that structure of limbs which is called a human body. I am not even some thin vapour which permeates the limbs—a wind, fire, air, breath, or whatever I depict in my imagination; for these are things which I have supposed to be nothing. Let this supposition stand;[10] for all that I am still something. And yet may it not perhaps be the case that these very things which I am supposing to be nothing, because they are unknown to me, are in reality identical with the "I" of which I am aware? I do not know, and for the moment I shall not argue the point, since I can make judgements only about things which are known to me. I know that I exist; the question is, what is this "I" that I know? If the "I" is understood strictly as we have been taking it, then it is quite certain that knowledge of it does not depend on things of whose existence I am as yet unaware; so it cannot depend on any of the things which I invent in my imagination. And this very word "invent" shows me my mistake. It would indeed be a case of fictitious invention if I used my imagination to establish that I was something or other; for imagining is simply contemplating the shape or image of a corporeal thing. Yet now I know for certain both that I exist and at the same time that all such images and, in general, everything relating to the nature of body, could be mere dreams ⟨and chimeras⟩. Once

---

[9] ". . . to see if I am not something more" (added in French version).

[10] Lat. *maneat* ("let it stand"), first edition. The second edition has the indicative *manet*: "The proposition still stands, *viz.* that I am nonetheless something." The French version reads: "without changing this supposition, I find that I am still certain that I am something."

this point has been grasped, to say "I will use my imagination to get to know more distinctly what I am" would seem to be as silly as saying "I am now awake, and see some truth; but since my vision is not yet clear enough, I will deliberately fall asleep so that my dreams may provide a truer and clearer representation." I thus realize that none of the things that the imagination enables me to grasp is at all relevant to this knowledge of myself which I possess, and that the mind must therefore be most carefully diverted from such things[11] if it is to perceive its own nature as distinctly as possible.

But what then am I? A thing that thinks. What is that? A thing that doubts, understands, affirms, denies, is willing, is unwilling, and also imagines and has sensory perceptions.

This is a considerable list, if everything on it belongs to me. But does it? Is it not one and the same "I" who is now doubting almost everything, who nonetheless understands some things, who affirms that this one thing is true, denies everything else, desires to know more, is unwilling to be deceived, imagines many things even involuntarily, and is aware of many things which apparently come from the senses? Are not all these things just as true as the fact that I exist, even if I am asleep all the time, and even if he who created me is doing all he can to deceive me? Which of all these activities is distinct from my thinking? Which of them can be said to be separate from myself? The fact that it is I who am doubting and understanding and willing is so evident that I see no way of making it any clearer. But it is also the case that the "I" who imagines is the same "I." For even if, as I have supposed, none of the objects of imagination are real, the power of imagination is something which really exists and is part of my thinking. Lastly, it is also the same "I" who has sensory perceptions, or is aware of bodily things as it were through the senses. For example, I am now seeing light, hearing a noise, feeling heat. But I am asleep, so all this is false. Yet I certainly *seem* to see, to hear, and to be warmed. This cannot be false; what is called "having a sensory perception" is strictly just this, and in this restricted sense of the term it is simply thinking.

From all this I am beginning to have a rather better understanding of what I am. But it still appears— and I cannot stop thinking this—that the corporeal things of which images are formed in my thought, and which the senses investigate, are known with much more distinctness than this puzzling "I" which cannot be pictured in the imagination. And yet it is surely surprising that I should have a more distinct grasp of things which I realize are doubtful, unknown and foreign to me, than I have of that which is true and known—my own self. But I see what it is: my mind enjoys wandering off and will not yet submit to being restrained within the bounds of truth. Very well then; just this once let us give it a completely free rein, so that after a while, when it is time to tighten the reins, it may more readily submit to being curbed.

Let us consider the things which people commonly think they understand most distinctly of all; that is, the bodies which we touch and see. I do not mean bodies in general—for general perceptions are apt to be somewhat more confused—but one particular body. Let us take, for example, this piece of wax. It has just been taken from the honeycomb; it has not yet quite lost the taste of the honey; it retains some of the scent of the flowers from which it was gathered; its colour, shape and size are plain to see; it is hard, cold and can be handled without difficulty; if you rap it with your knuckle it makes a sound. In short, it has everything which appears necessary to enable a body to be known as distinctly as possible. But even as I speak, I put the wax by the fire, and look: the residual taste is eliminated, the smell goes away, the colour changes, the shape is lost, the size increases; it becomes liquid and hot; you can hardly touch it, and if you strike it, it no longer makes a sound. But does the same wax remain? It must be admitted that it does; no one denies it, no one thinks otherwise. So what was it in the wax that I understood with such distinctness? Evidently none of the features which I arrived at by means of the senses; for whatever came under taste, smell, sight, touch or hearing has now altered—yet the wax remains.

Perhaps the answer lies in the thought which now comes to my mind; namely, the wax was not after all the sweetness of the honey, or the fragrance of the flowers, or the whiteness, or the shape, or the sound, but was rather a body which presented itself

---

[11] ". . . from this manner of conceiving things" (French version).

to me in these various forms a little while ago, but which now exhibits different ones. But what exactly is it that I am now imagining? Let us concentrate, take away everything which does not belong to the wax, and see what is left: merely something extended, flexible and changeable. But what is meant here by "flexible" and "changeable"? Is it what I picture in my imagination: that this piece of wax is capable of changing from a round shape to a square shape, or from a square shape to a triangular shape? Not at all; for I can grasp that the wax is capable of countless changes of this kind, yet I am unable to run through this immeasurable number of changes in my imagination, from which it follows that it is not the faculty of imagination that gives me my grasp of the wax as flexible and changeable. And what is meant by "extended"? Is the extension of the wax also unknown? For it increases if the wax melts, increases again if it boils, and is greater still if the heat is increased. I would not be making a correct judgement about the nature of wax unless I believed it capable of being extended in many more different ways than I will ever encompass in my imagination. I must therefore admit that the nature of this piece of wax is in no way revealed by my imagination, but is perceived by the mind alone. (I am speaking of this particular piece of wax; the point is even clearer with regard to wax in general.) But what is this wax which is perceived by the mind alone?[12] It is of course the same wax which I see, which I touch, which I picture in my imagination, in short the same wax which I thought it to be from the start. And yet, and here is the point, the perception I have of it[13] is a case not of vision or touch or imagination—nor has it ever been, despite previous appearances—but of purely mental scrutiny; and this can be imperfect and confused, as it was before, or clear and distinct as it is now, depending on how carefully I concentrate on what the wax consists in.

But as I reach this conclusion I am amazed at how ⟨weak and⟩ prone to error my mind is. For although I am thinking about these matters within myself, silently and without speaking, nonetheless the actual words bring me up short, and I am almost

tricked by ordinary ways of talking. We say that we see the wax itself, if it is there before us, not that we judge it to be there from its colour or shape; and this might lead me to conclude without more ado that knowledge of the wax comes from what the eye sees, and not from the scrutiny of the mind alone. But then if I look out of the window and see men crossing the square, as I just happen to have done, I normally say that I see the men themselves, just as I say that I see the wax. Yet do I see any more than hats and coats which could conceal automatons? I *judge* that they are men. And so something which I thought I was seeing with my eyes is in fact grasped solely by the faculty of judgement which is in my mind.

However, one who wants to achieve knowledge above the ordinary level should feel ashamed at having taken ordinary ways of talking as a basis for doubt. So let us proceed, and consider on which occasion my perception of the nature of the wax was more perfect and evident. Was it when I first looked at it, and believed I knew it by my external senses, or at least by what they call the "common" sense—that is, the power of imagination? Or is my knowledge more perfect now, after a more careful investigation of the nature of the wax and of the means by which it is known? Any doubt on this issue would clearly be foolish; for what distinctness was there in my earlier perception? Was there anything in it which an animal could not possess? But when I distinguish the wax from its outward forms—take the clothes off, as it were, and consider it naked—then although my judgement may still contain errors, at least my perception now requires a human mind.

But what am I to say about this mind, or about myself? (So far, remember, I am not admitting that there is anything else in me except a mind.) What, I ask, is this "I" which seems to perceive the wax so distinctly? Surely my awareness of my own self is not merely much truer and more certain than my awareness of the wax, but also much more distinct and evident. For if I judge that the wax exists from the fact that I see it, clearly this same fact entails much more evidently that I myself also exist. It is possible that what I see is not really the wax; it is possible that I do not even have eyes with which to see anything. But when I see, or think I see (I am not here distinguishing the two), it is simply not possible that I who am now thinking am not something. By the same token, if I judge that the wax ex-

---

[12] ". . . which can be conceived only by the understanding or the mind" (French version).

[13] ". . . or rather the act whereby it is perceived" (added in French version).

ists from the fact that I touch it, the same result follows, namely that I exist. If I judge that it exists from the fact that I imagine it, or for any other reason, exactly the same thing follows. And the result that I have grasped in the case of the wax may be applied to everything else located outside me. Moreover, if my perception of the wax seemed more distinct[14] after it was established not just by sight or touch but by many other considerations, it must be admitted that I now know myself even more distinctly. This is because every consideration whatsoever which contributes to my perception of the wax, or of any other body, cannot but establish even more effectively the nature of my own mind. But besides this, there is so much else in the mind itself which can serve to make my knowledge of it more distinct, that it scarcely seems worth going through the contributions made by considering bodily things.

I see that without any effort I have now finally got back to where I wanted. I now know that even bodies are not strictly perceived by the senses or the faculty of imagination but by the intellect alone, and that this perception derives not from their being touched or seen but from their being understood; and in view of this I know plainly that I can achieve an easier and more evident perception of my own mind than of anything else. But since the habit of holding on to old opinions cannot be set aside so quickly, I should like to stop here and meditate for some time on this new knowledge I have gained, so as to fix it more deeply in my memory.

Third Meditation: The existence of God

I will now shut my eyes, stop my ears, and withdraw all my senses. I will eliminate from my thoughts all images of bodily things, or rather, since this is hardly possible, I will regard all such images as vacuous, false and worthless. I will converse with myself and scrutinize myself more deeply; and in this way I will attempt to achieve, little by little, a more intimate knowledge of myself. I am a thing that thinks: that is, a thing that doubts, affirms, denies, understands a few things, is ignorant of many things,[15] is willing, is unwilling, and also which imagines and has sensory perceptions; for as I have noted before, even though the objects of my sensory experience and imagination may have no existence outside me, nonetheless the modes of thinking which I refer to as cases of sensory perception and imagination, in so far as they are simply modes of thinking, do exist within me—of that I am certain.

In this brief list I have gone through everything I truly know, or at least everything I have so far discovered that I know. Now I will cast around more carefully to see whether there may be other things within me which I have not yet noticed. I am certain that I am a thinking thing. Do I not therefore also know what is required for my being certain about anything? In this first item of knowledge there is simply a clear and distinct perception of what I am asserting; this would not be enough to make me certain of the truth of the matter if it could ever turn out that something which I perceived with such clarity and distinctness was false. So I now seem to be able to lay it down as a general rule that whatever I perceive very clearly and distinctly is true.[16]

Yet I previously accepted as wholly certain and evident many things which I afterwards realized were doubtful. What were these? The earth, sky, stars, and everything else that I apprehended with the senses. But what was it about them that I perceived clearly? Just that the ideas, or thoughts, of such things appeared before my mind. Yet even now I am not denying that these ideas occur within me. But there was something else which I used to assert, and which through habitual belief I thought I perceived clearly, although I did not in fact do so. This was that there were things outside me which were the sources of my ideas and which resembled them in all respects. Here was my mistake; or at any rate, if my judgement was true, it was not thanks to the strength of my perception.[17]

But what about when I was considering something very simple and straightforward in arithmetic

---

[14] The French version has "more clear and distinct" and, at the end of this sentence, "more evidently, distinctly and clearly."

[15] The French version here inserts "loves, hate."
[16] ". . . all the things which we conceive very clearly and very distinctly are true" (French version).
[17] ". . . it was not because of any knowledge I possessed" (French version).

or geometry, for example that two and three added together make five, and so on? Did I now see at least these things clearly enough to affirm their truth? Indeed, the only reason for my later judgement that they were open to doubt was that it occurred to me that perhaps some God could have given me a nature such that I was deceived even in matters which seemed most evident. But whenever my preconceived belief in the supreme power of God comes to mind, I cannot but admit that it would be easy for him, if he so desired, to bring it about that I go wrong even in those matters which I think I see utterly clearly with my mind's eye. Yet when I turn to the things themselves which I think I perceive very clearly, I am so convinced by them that I spontaneously declare: let whoever can do so deceive me, he will never bring it about that I am nothing, so long as I continue to think I am something; or make it true at some future time that I have never existed, since it is now true that I exist; or bring it about that two and three added together are more or less than five, or anything of this kind in which I see a manifest contradiction. And since I have no cause to think that there is a deceiving God, and I do not yet even know for sure whether there is a God at all, any reason for doubt which depends simply on this supposition is a very slight and, so to speak, metaphysical one. But in order to remove even this slight reason for doubt, as soon as the opportunity arises I must examine whether there is a God, and, if there is, whether he can be a deceiver. For if I do not know this, it seems that I can never be quite certain about anything else.

First, however, considerations of order appear to dictate that I now classify my thoughts into definite kinds,[18] and ask which of them can properly be said to be the bearers of truth and falsity. Some of my thoughts are as it were the images of things, and it is only in these cases that the term "idea" is strictly appropriate—for example, when I think of

a man, or a chimera, or the sky, or an angel, or God. Other thoughts have various additional forms: thus when I will, or am afraid, or affirm, or deny, there is always a particular thing which I take as the object of my thought, but my thought includes something more than the likeness of that thing. Some thoughts in this category are called volitions or emotions, while others are called judgements.

Now as far as ideas are concerned, provided they are considered solely in themselves and I do not refer them to anything else, they cannot strictly speaking be false; for whether it is a goat or a chimera that I am imagining, it is just as true that I imagine the former as the latter. As for the will and the emotions, here too one need not worry about falsity; for even if the things which I may desire are wicked or even non-existent, that does not make it any less true that I desire them. Thus the only remaining thoughts where I must be on my guard against making a mistake are judgements. And the chief and most common mistake which is to be found here consists in my judging that the ideas which are in me resemble, or conform to, things located outside me. Of course, if I considered just the ideas themselves simply as modes of my thought, without referring them to anything else, they could scarcely give me any material for error.

Among my ideas, some appear to be innate, some to be adventitious,[19] and others to have been invented by me. My understanding of what a thing is, what truth is, and what thought is, seems to derive simply from my own nature. But my hearing a noise, as I do now, or seeing the sun, or feeling the fire, comes from things which are located outside me, or so I have hitherto judged. Lastly, sirens, hippogriffs and the like are my own invention. But perhaps all my ideas may be thought of as adventitious, or they may all be innate, or all made up; for as yet I have not clearly perceived their true origin.

But the chief question at this point concerns the ideas which I take to be derived from things existing outside me: what is my reason for thinking that they resemble these things? Nature has apparently taught me to think this. But in addition I know by experience that these ideas do not depend on my

---

[18] The opening of this sentence is greatly expanded in the French version: "In order that I may have the opportunity of examining this without interrupting the order of meditating which I have decided upon, which is to start only from those notions which I find first of all in my mind and pass gradually to those which I may find later on, I must here divide my thoughts. . . ."

---

[19] ". . . foreign to me and coming from outside" (French version).

will, and hence that they do not depend simply on me. Frequently I notice them even when I do not want to: now, for example, I feel the heat whether I want to or not, and this is why I think that this sensation or idea of heat comes to me from something other than myself, namely the heat of the fire by which I am sitting. And the most obvious judgement for me to make is that the thing in question transmits to me its own likeness rather than something else.

I will now see if these arguments are strong enough. When I say "Nature taught me to think this," all I mean is that a spontaneous impulse leads me to believe it, not that its truth has been revealed to me by some natural light. There is a big difference here. Whatever is revealed to me by the natural light—for example that from the fact that I am doubting it follows that I exist, and so on—cannot in any way be open to doubt. This is because there cannot be another faculty[20] both as trustworthy as the natural light and also capable of showing me that such things are not true. But as for my natural impulses, I have often judged in the past that they were pushing me in the wrong direction when it was a question of choosing the good, and I do not see why I should place any greater confidence in them in other matters.[21]

Then again, although these ideas do not depend on my will, it does not follow that they must come from things located outside me. Just as the impulses which I was speaking of a moment ago seem opposed to my will even though they are within me, so there may be some other faculty not yet fully known to me, which produces these ideas without any assistance from external things; this is, after all, just how I have always thought ideas are produced in me when I am dreaming.

And finally, even if these ideas did come from things other than myself, it would not follow that they must resemble those things. Indeed, I think I have often discovered a great disparity ⟨between an object and its idea⟩ in many cases. For example, there are two different ideas of the sun which I find within me. One of them, which is acquired as it were from the senses and which is a prime example of an idea which I reckon to come from an external source, makes the sun appear very small. The other idea is based on astronomical reasoning, that is, it is derived from certain notions which are innate in me (or else it is constructed by me in some other way), and this idea shows the sun to be several times larger than the earth. Obviously both these ideas cannot resemble the sun which exists outside me; and reason persuades me that the idea which seems to have emanated most directly from the sun itself has in fact no resemblance to it at all.

All these considerations are enough to establish that it is not reliable judgement but merely some blind impulse that has made me believe up till now that there exist things distinct from myself which transmit to me ideas or images of themselves through the sense organs or in some other way.

But it now occurs to me that there is another way of investigating whether some of the things of which I possess ideas exist outside me. In so far as the ideas are ⟨considered⟩ simply ⟨as⟩ modes of thought, there is no recognizable inequality among them: they all appear to come from within me in the same fashion. But in so far as different ideas ⟨are considered as images which⟩ represent different things, it is clear that they differ widely. Undoubtedly, the ideas which represent substances to me amount to something more and, so to speak, contain within themselves more objective[22] reality than the ideas which merely represent modes or accidents. Again, the idea that gives me my understanding of a supreme God, eternal, infinite, ⟨immutable,⟩ omniscient, omnipotent and the creator of all things that exist apart from him, certainly has in it more objective reality than the ideas that represent finite substances.

Now it is manifest by the natural light that there must be at least as much ⟨reality⟩ in the efficient and

---

[20] ". . . or power for distinguishing truth from falsehood" (French version).

[21] ". . . concerning truth and falsehood" (French version).

[22] ". . . i.e., participate by representation in a higher degree of being or perfection" (added in French version). According to the scholastic distinction invoked in the paragraphs that follow, the "formal" reality of anything is its own intrinsic reality, while the "objective" reality of an idea is a function of its representational content. Thus if an idea *A* represents some object *X* which is *F*, then *F*-ness will be contained "formally" in *X* but "objectively" in *A*.

total cause as in the effect of that cause. For where, I ask, could the effect get its reality from, if not from the cause? And how could the cause give it to the effect unless it possessed it? It follows from this both that something cannot arise from nothing, and also that what is more perfect—that is, contains in itself more reality—cannot arise from what is less perfect. And this is transparently true not only in the case of effects which possess ⟨what the philosophers call⟩ actual or formal reality, but also in the case of ideas, where one is considering only ⟨what they call⟩ objective reality. A stone, for example, which previously did not exist, cannot begin to exist unless it is produced by something which contains, either formally or eminently everything to be found in the stone;[23] similarly, heat cannot be produced in an object which was not previously hot, except by something of at least the same order ⟨degree or kind⟩ of perfection as heat, and so on. But it is also true that the *idea* of heat, or of a stone, cannot exist in me unless it is put there by some cause which contains at least as much reality as I conceive to be in the heat or in the stone. For although this cause does not transfer any of its actual or formal reality to my idea, it should not on that account be supposed that it must be less real.[24] The nature of an idea is such that of itself it requires no formal reality except what it derives from my thought, of which it is a mode.[25] But in order for a given idea to contain such and such objective reality, it must surely derive it from some cause which contains at least as much formal reality as there is objective reality in the idea. For if we suppose that an idea contains something which was not in its cause, it must have got this from nothing; yet the mode of being by which a thing exists objectively ⟨or representatively⟩ in the intellect by way of an idea, imperfect though it may be, is certainly not nothing, and so it cannot come from nothing.

And although the reality which I am considering in my ideas is merely objective reality, I must not on that account suppose that the same reality need not exist formally in the causes of my ideas, but that it is enough for it to be present in them objectively. For just as the objective mode of being belongs to ideas by their very nature, so the formal mode of being belongs to the causes of ideas—or at least the first and most important ones—by *their* very nature. And although one idea may perhaps originate from another, there cannot be an infinite regress here; eventually one must reach a primary idea, the cause of which will be like an archetype which contains formally ⟨and in fact⟩ all the reality ⟨or perfection⟩ which is present only objectively ⟨or representatively⟩ in the idea. So it is clear to me, by the natural light, that the ideas in me are like ⟨pictures, or⟩ images which can easily fall short of the perfection of the things from which they are taken, but which cannot contain anything greater or more perfect.

The longer and more carefully I examine all these points, the more clearly and distinctly I recognize their truth. But what is my conclusion to be? If the objective reality of any of my ideas turns out to be so great that I am sure the same reality does not reside in me, either formally or eminently, and hence that I myself cannot be its cause, it will necessarily follow that I am not alone in the world, but that some other thing which is the cause of this idea also exists. But if no such idea is to be found in me, I shall have no argument to convince me of the existence of anything apart from myself. For despite a most careful and comprehensive survey, this is the only argument I have so far been able to find.

Among my ideas, apart from the idea which gives me a representation of myself, which cannot present any difficulty in this context, there are ideas which variously represent God, corporeal and inanimate things, angels, animals and finally other men like myself.

As far as concerns the ideas which represent other men, or animals, or angels, I have no difficulty in understanding that they could be put together from the ideas I have of myself, of corporeal things and of God, even if the world contained no men besides me, no animals and no angels.

As to my ideas of corporeal things, I can see nothing in them which is so great ⟨or excellent⟩ as to make it seem impossible that it originated in myself.

---

[23] "... i.e., it will contain in itself the same things as are in the stone or other more excellent things" (added in French version). In scholastic terminology, to possess a property "formally" is to possess it literally, in accordance with its definition; to possess it "eminently" is to possess it in some higher form.

[24] "... that this cause must be less real" (French version).

[25] "... i.e. a manner or way of thinking" (added in French version).

For if I scrutinize them thoroughly and examine them one by one, in the way in which I examined the idea of the wax yesterday, I notice that the things which I perceive clearly and distinctly in them are very few in number. The list comprises size, or extension in length, breadth and depth; shape, which is a function of the boundaries of this extension; position, which is a relation between various items possessing shape; and motion, or change in position; to these may be added substance, duration and number. But as for all the rest, including light and colours, sounds, smells, tastes, heat and cold and the other tactile qualities, I think of these only in a very confused and obscure way, to the extent that I do not even know whether they are true or false, that is, whether the ideas I have of them are ideas of real things or of non-things.[26] For although, as I have noted before, falsity in the strict sense, or formal falsity, can occur only in judgements, there is another kind of falsity, material falsity, which occurs in ideas, when they represent non-things as things. For example, the ideas which I have of heat and cold contain so little clarity and distinctness that they do not enable me to tell whether cold is merely the absence of heat or vice versa, or whether both of them are real qualities, or neither is. And since there can be no ideas which are not as it were of things,[27] if it is true that cold is nothing but the absence of heat, the idea which represents it to me as something real and positive deserves to be called false; and the same goes for other ideas of this kind.

Such ideas obviously do not require me to posit a source distinct from myself. For on the one hand, if they are false, that is, represent non-things, I know by the natural light that they arise from nothing—that is, they are in me only because of a deficiency and lack of perfection in my nature. If on the other hand they are true, then since the reality which they represent is so extremely slight that I cannot even distinguish it from a non-thing, I do not see why they cannot originate from myself.

With regard to the clear and distinct elements in my ideas of corporeal things, it appears that I could have borrowed some of these from my idea of myself, namely substance, duration, number and anything else of this kind. For example, I think that a stone is a substance, or is a thing capable of existing independently, and I also think that I am a substance. Admittedly I conceive of myself as a thing that thinks and is not extended, whereas I conceive of the stone as a thing that is extended and does not think, so that the two conceptions differ enormously; but they seem to agree with respect to the classification "substance."[28] Again, I perceive that I now exist, and remember that I have existed for some time; moreover, I have various thoughts which I can count; it is in these ways that I acquire the ideas of duration and number which I can then transfer to other things. As for all the other elements which make up the ideas of corporeal things, namely extension, shape, position and movement, these are not formally contained in me, since I am nothing but a thinking thing; but since they are merely modes of a substance,[29] and I am a substance, it seems possible that they are contained in me eminently.

So there remains only the idea of God; and I must consider whether there is anything in the idea which could not have originated in myself. By the word "God" I understand a substance that is infinite, ⟨eternal, immutable,⟩ independent, supremely intelligent, supremely powerful, and which created both myself and everything else (if anything else there be) that exists. All these attributes are such that, the more carefully I concentrate on them, the less possible it seems that they[30] could have originated from me alone. So from what has been said it must be concluded that God necessarily exists.

It is true that I have the idea of a substance in me in virtue of the fact that I am a substance; but this would not account for my having the idea of an infinite substance, when I am finite, unless this idea proceeded from some substance which really was infinite.

And I must not think that, just as my conceptions of rest and darkness are arrived at by negating movement and light, so my perception of the

---

[26] ". . . chimerical things which cannot exist" (French version).

[27] "And since ideas, being like images, must in each case appear to us to represent something" (French version).

[28] ". . . in so far as they represent substances" (French version).

[29] ". . . and as it were the garments under which corporeal substance appears to us" (French version).

[30] ". . . that the idea I have of them" (French version).

infinite is arrived at not by means of a true idea but merely by negating the finite. On the contrary, I clearly understand that there is more reality in an infinite substance than in a finite one, and hence that my perception of the infinite, that is God, is in some way prior to my perception of the finite, that is myself. For how could I understand that I doubted or desired—that is, lacked something—and that I was not wholly perfect, unless there were in me some idea of a more perfect being which enabled me to recognize my own defects by comparison?

Nor can it be said that this idea of God is perhaps materially false and so could have come from nothing,[31] which is what I observed just a moment ago in the case of the ideas of heat and cold, and so on. On the contrary, it is utterly clear and distinct, and contains in itself more objective reality than any other idea; hence there is no idea which is in itself truer or less liable to be suspected of falsehood. This idea of a supremely perfect and infinite being is, I say, true in the highest degree; for although perhaps one may imagine that such a being does not exist, it cannot be supposed that the idea of such a being represents something unreal, as I said with regard to the idea of cold. The idea is, moreover, utterly clear and distinct; for whatever I clearly and distinctly perceive as being real and true, and implying any perfection, is wholly contained in it. It does not matter that I do not grasp the infinite, or that there are countless additional attributes of God which I cannot in any way grasp, and perhaps cannot even reach in my thought; for it is in the nature of the infinite not to be grasped by a finite being like myself. It is enough that I understand the infinite, and that I judge that all the attributes which I clearly perceive and know to imply some perfection—and perhaps countless others of which I am ignorant—are present in God either formally or eminently. This is enough to make the idea that I have of God the truest and most clear and distinct of all my ideas.

But perhaps I am something greater than I myself understand, and all the perfections which I attribute to God are somehow in me potentially, though not yet emerging or actualized. For I am now experiencing a gradual increase in my knowledge, and I see nothing to prevent its increasing more and more to infinity. Further, I see no reason why I should not be able to use this increased knowledge to acquire all the other perfections of God. And finally, if the potentiality for these perfections is already within me, why should not this be enough to generate the idea of such perfections?

But all this is impossible. First, though it is true that there is a gradual increase in my knowledge, and that I have many potentialities which are not yet actual, this is all quite irrelevant to the idea of God, which contains absolutely nothing that is potential;[32] indeed, this gradual increase in knowledge is itself the surest sign of imperfection. What is more, even if my knowledge always increases more and more, I recognize that it will never actually be infinite, since it will never reach the point where it is not capable of a further increase; God, on the other hand, I take to be actually infinite, so that nothing can be added to his perfection. And finally, I perceive that the objective being of an idea cannot be produced merely by potential being, which strictly speaking is nothing, but only by actual or formal being.

If one concentrates carefully, all this is quite evident by the natural light. But when I relax my concentration, and my mental vision is blinded by the images of things perceived by the senses, it is not so easy for me to remember why the idea of a being more prefect than myself must necessarily proceed from some being which is in reality more perfect. I should therefore like to go further and inquire whether I myself, who have this idea, could exist if no such being existed.

From whom, in this case, would I derive my existence? From myself presumably, or from my parents, or from some other beings less perfect than God; for nothing more perfect than God, or even as perfect, can be thought of or imagined.

Yet if I derived my existence from myself,[33] then I should neither doubt nor want, nor lack anything at all; for I should have given myself all the perfec-

---

[31] "... i.e. could be in me in virtue of my imperfection" (added in French version).

[32] "... but only what is actual and real" (added in French version).

[33] "... and were independent of every other being" (added in French version).

tions of which I have any idea, and thus I should myself be God. I must not suppose that the items I lack would be more difficult to acquire than those I now have. On the contrary, it is clear that, since I am a thinking thing or substance, it would have been far more difficult for me to emerge out of nothing than merely to acquire knowledge of the many things of which I am ignorant—such knowledge being merely an accident of that substance. And if I had derived my existence from myself, which is a greater achievement, I should certainly not have denied myself the knowledge in question, which is something much easier to acquire, or indeed any of the attributes which I perceive to be contained in the idea of God; for none of them seem any harder to achieve. And if any of them were harder to achieve, they would certainly appear so to me, if I had indeed got all my other attributes from myself, since I should experience a limitation of my power in this respect.

I do not escape the force of these arguments by supposing that I have always existed as I do now, as if it followed from this that there was no need to look for any author of my existence. For a lifespan can be divided into countless parts, each completely independent of the others, so that it does not follow from the fact that I existed a little while ago that I must exist now, unless there is some cause which as it were creates me afresh at this moment—that is, which preserves me. For it is quite clear to anyone who attentively considers the nature of time that the same power and action are needed to preserve anything at each individual moment of its duration as would be required to create that thing anew if it were not yet in existence. Hence the distinction between preservation and creation is only a conceptual one, and this is one of the things that are evident by the natural light.

I must therefore now ask myself whether I possess some power enabling me to bring it about that I who now exist will still exist a little while from now. For since I am nothing but a thinking thing—or at least since I am now concerned only and precisely with that part of me which is a thinking thing—if there were such a power in me, I should undoubtedly be aware of it. But I experience no such power, and this very fact makes me recognize most clearly that I depend on some being distinct from myself.

But perhaps this being is not God, and perhaps I was produced either by my parents or by other causes less perfect than God. No; for as I have said before, it is quite clear that there must be at least as much in the cause as in the effect.[34] And therefore whatever kind of cause is eventually proposed, since I am a thinking thing and have within me some idea of God, it must be admitted that what caused me is itself a thinking thing and possesses the idea of all the perfections which I attribute to God. In respect of this cause one may again inquire whether it derives its existence from itself or from another cause. If from itself, then it is clear from what has been said that it is itself God, since if it has the power of existing through its own might,[35] then undoubtedly it also has the power of actually possessing all the perfections of which it has an idea—that is, all the perfections which I conceive to be in God. If, on the other hand, it derives its existence from another cause, then the same question may be repeated concerning this further cause, namely whether it derives its existence from itself or from another cause, until eventually the ultimate cause is reached, and this will be God.

It is clear enough that an infinite regress is impossible here, especially since I am dealing not just with the cause that produced me in the past, but also and most importantly with the cause that preserves me at the present moment.

Nor can it be supposed that several partial causes contributed to my creation, or that I received the idea of one of the perfections which I attribute to God from one cause and the idea of another from another—the supposition here being that all the perfections are to be found somewhere in the universe but not joined together in a single being, God. On the contrary, the unity, the simplicity, or the inseparability of all the attributes of God is one of the most important of the perfections which I understand him to have. And surely the idea of the unity of all his perfections could not have been placed in me by any cause which did not also provide me with the ideas of the other perfections; for no cause could have made me understand

---

[34] "... at least as much reality in the cause as in its effect" (French version).

[35] Lat. *per se;* literally "through itself."

the interconnection and inseparability of the perfections without at the same time making me recognize what they were.

Lastly, as regards my parents, even if everything I have ever believed about them is true, it is certainly not they who preserve me; and in so far as I am a thinking thing, they did not even make me; they merely placed certain dispositions in the matter which I have always regarded as containing me, or rather my mind, for that is all I now take myself to be. So there can be no difficulty regarding my parents in this context. Altogether then, it must be concluded that the mere fact that I exist and have within me an idea of a most perfect being, that is, God, provides a very clear proof that God indeed exists.

It only remains for me to examine how I received this idea from God. For I did not acquire it from the senses; it has never come to me unexpectedly, as usually happens with the ideas of things that are perceivable by the senses, when these things present themselves to the external sense organs—or seem to do so. And it was not invented by me either; for I am plainly unable either to take away anything from it or to add anything to it. The only remaining alternative is that it is innate in me, just as the idea of myself is innate in me.

And indeed it is no surprise that God, in creating me, should have placed this idea in me to be, as it were, the mark of the craftsman stamped on his work—not that the mark need be anything distinct from the work itself. But the mere fact that God created me is a very strong basis for believing that I am somehow made in his image and likeness, and that I perceive that likeness, which includes the idea of God, by the same faculty which enables me to perceive myself. That is, when I turn my mind's eye upon myself, I understand that I am a thing which is incomplete and dependent on another and which aspires without limit to ever greater and better things; but I also understand at the same time that he on whom I depend has within him all those greater things, not just indefinitely and potentially but actually and infinitely, and hence that he is God. The whole force of the argument lies in this: I recognize that it would be impossible for me to exist with the kind of nature I have—that is, having within me the idea of God—were it not the case that God really existed. By "God" I mean the very being

the idea of whom is within me, that is, the possessor of all the perfections which I cannot grasp, but can somehow reach in my thought, who is subject to no defects whatsoever.[36] It is clear enough from this that he cannot be a deceiver, since it is manifest by the natural light that all fraud and deception depend on some defect.

But before examining this point more carefully and investigating other truths which may be derived from it, I should like to pause here and spend some time in the contemplation of God; to reflect on his attributes, and to gaze with wonder and adoration on the beauty of this immense light, so far as the eye of my darkened intellect can bear it. For just as we believe through faith that the supreme happiness of the next life consists solely in the contemplation of the divine majesty, so experience tells us that this same contemplation, albeit much less perfect, enables us to know the greatest joy of which we are capable in this life.

Fourth Meditation: Truth and falsity

During these past few days I have accustomed myself to leading my mind away from the senses; and I have taken careful note of the fact that there is very little about corporeal things that is truly perceived, whereas much more is known about the human mind, and still more about God. The result is that I now have no difficulty in turning my mind away from imaginable things[37] and towards things which are objects of the intellect alone and are totally separate from matter. And indeed the idea I have of the human mind, in so far as it is a thinking thing, which is not extended in length, breadth or height and has no other bodily characteristics, is much more distinct than the idea of any corporeal thing. And when I consider the fact that I have doubts, or that I am a thing that is incomplete and dependent, then there arises in me a clear and distinct idea of a being who is independent and com-

---

[36] ". . . and has not one of the things which indicate some imperfection" (added in French version).
[37] ". . . from things which can be perceived by the senses or imagined" (French version).

plete, that is, an idea of God. And from the mere fact that there is such an idea within me, or that I who possess this idea exist, I clearly infer that God also exists, and that every single moment of my entire existence depends on him. So clear is this conclusion that I am confident that the human intellect cannot know anything that is more evident or more certain. And now, from this contemplation of the true God, in whom all the treasures of wisdom and the sciences lie hidden, I think I can see a way forward to the knowledge of other things.[38]

To begin with, I recognize that it is impossible that God should ever deceive me. For in every case of trickery or deception some imperfection is to be found; and although the ability to deceive appears to be an indication of cleverness or power, the will to deceive is undoubtedly evidence of malice or weakness, and so cannot apply to God.

Next, I know by experience that there is in me a faculty of judgement which, like everything else which is in me, I certainly received from God. And since God does not wish to deceive me, he surely did not give me the kind of faculty which would ever enable me to go wrong while using it correctly.

There would be no further doubt on this issue were it not that what I have just said appears to imply that I am incapable of ever going wrong. For if everything that is in me comes from God, and he did not endow me with a faculty for making mistakes, it appears that I can never go wrong. And certainly, so long as I think only of God, and turn my whole attention to him, I can find no cause of error or falsity. But when I turn back to myself, I know by experience that I am prone to countless errors. On looking for the cause of these errors, I find that I possess not only a real and positive idea of God, or a being who is supremely perfect, but also what may be described as a negative idea of nothingness, or of that which is farthest removed from all perfection. I realize that I am, as it were, something intermediate between God and nothingness, or between supreme being and non-being: my nature is such that in so far as I was created by the supreme being, there is nothing in me to enable me to go wrong or lead me astray; but in so far as I participate in noth-

ingness or non-being, that is, in so far as I am not myself the supreme being and am lacking in countless respects, it is no wonder that I make mistakes. I understand, then, that error as such is not something real which depends on God, but merely a defect. Hence my going wrong does not require me to have a faculty specially bestowed on me by God; it simply happens as a result of the fact that the faculty of true judgement which I have from God is in my case not infinite.

But this is still not entirely satisfactory. For error is not a pure negation,[39] but rather a privation or lack of some knowledge which somehow should be in me. And when I concentrate on the nature of God, it seems impossible that he should have placed in me a faculty which is not perfect of its kind, or which lacks some perfection which it ought to have. The more skilled the craftsman the more perfect the work produced by him; if this is so, how can anything produced by the supreme creator of all things not be complete and perfect in all respects? There is, moreover, no doubt that God could have given me a nature such that I was never mistaken; again, there is no doubt that he always wills what is best. Is it then better that I should make mistakes than that I should not do so?

As I reflect on these matters more attentively, it occurs to me first of all that it is no cause for surprise if I do not understand the reasons for some of God's actions; and there is no call to doubt his existence if I happen to find that there are other instances where I do not grasp why or how certain things were made by him. For since I now know that my own nature is very weak and limited, whereas the nature of God is immense, incomprehensible and infinite, I also know without more ado that he is capable of countless things whose causes are beyond my knowledge. And for this reason alone I consider the customary search for final causes to be totally useless in physics; there is considerable rashness in thinking myself capable of investigating the ⟨impenetrable⟩ purposes of God.

It also occurs to me that whenever we are inquiring whether the works of God are perfect, we

---

[38] ". . . of the other things in the universe" (French version).

[39] ". . . i.e. not simply the defect or lack of some perfection to which I have no proper claim" (added in French version).

ought to look at the whole universe, not just at one created thing on its own. For what would perhaps rightly appear very imperfect if it existed on its own is quite perfect when its function as a part of the universe is considered. It is true that, since my decision to doubt everything, it is so far only myself and God whose existence I have been able to know with certainty; but after considering the immense power of God, I cannot deny that many other things have been made by him, or at least could have been made, and hence that I may have a place in the universal scheme of things.

Next, when I look more closely at myself and inquire into the nature of my errors (for these are the only evidence of some imperfection in me), I notice that they depend on two concurrent causes, namely on the faculty of knowledge which is in me, and on the faculty of choice or freedom of the will; that is, they depend on both the intellect and the will simultaneously. Now all that the intellect does is to enable me to perceive[40] the ideas which are subjects for possible judgments; and when regarded strictly in this light, it turns out to contain no error in the proper sense of that term. For although countless things may exist without there being any corresponding ideas in me, it should not, strictly speaking, be said that I am deprived of these ideas,[41] but merely that I lack them, in a negative sense. This is because I cannot produce any reason to prove that God ought to have given me a greater faculty of knowledge than he did; and no matter how skilled I understand a craftsman to be, this does not make me think he ought to have put into every one of his works all the perfections which he is able to put into some of them. Besides, I cannot complain that the will or freedom of choice which I received from God is not sufficiently extensive or perfect, since I know by experience that it is not restricted in any way. Indeed, I think it is very noteworthy that there is nothing else in me which is so perfect and so great that the possibility of a further increase in its perfection or greatness is beyond my understanding. If, for example, I consider the faculty of understanding, I im-

mediately recognize that in my case it is extremely slight and very finite, and I at once form the idea of an understanding which is much greater—indeed supremely great and infinite; and from the very fact that I can form an idea of it, I perceive that it belongs to the nature of God. Similarly, if I examine the faculties of memory or imagination, or any others, I discover that in my case each one of these faculties is weak and limited, while in the case of God it is immeasurable. It is only the will, or freedom of choice, which I experience within me to be so great that the idea of any greater faculty is beyond my grasp; so much so that it is above all in virtue of the will that I understand myself to bear in some way the image and likeness of God. For although God's will is incomparably greater than mine, both in virtue of the knowledge and power that accompany it and make it more firm and efficacious, and also in virtue of its object, in that it ranges over a greater number of items, nevertheless it does not seem any greater than mine when considered as will in the essential and strict sense. This is because the will simply consists in our ability to do or not do something (that is, to affirm or deny, to pursue or avoid); or rather, it consists simply in the fact that when the intellect puts something forward, we are moved to affirm or deny or to pursue or avoid it in such a way that we do not feel ourselves to be determined by any external force. For in order to be free, there is no need for me to be capable of going in each of two directions; on the contrary, the more I incline in one direction—either because I clearly understand that reasons of truth and goodness point that way, or because of a divinely produced disposition of my inmost thoughts—the freer is my choice. Neither divine grace nor natural knowledge ever diminishes freedom; on the contrary, they increase and strengthen it. But the indifference I feel when there is no reason pushing me in one direction rather than another is the lowest grade of freedom; it is evidence not of any perfection of freedom, but rather of a defect in knowledge or a kind of negation. For if I always saw clearly what was true and good, I should never have to deliberate about the right judgement or choice; in that case, although I should be wholly free, it would be impossible for me ever to be in a state of indifference.

From these considerations I perceive that the power of willing which I received from God is not, when considered in itself, the cause of my mistakes;

---

[40] ". . . without affirming or denying anything" (added in French version).

[41] ". . . it cannot be said that my understanding is deprived of these ideas, as if they were something to which its nature entitles it" (French version).

for it is both extremely ample and also perfect of its kind. Nor is my power of understanding to blame; for since my understanding comes from God, everything that I understand I undoubtedly understand correctly, and any error here is impossible. So what then is the source of my mistakes? It must be simply this; the scope of the will is wider than that of the intellect; but instead of restricting it within the same limits, I extend its use to matters which I do not understand. Since the will is indifferent in such cases, it easily turns aside from what is true and good, and this is the source of my error and sin.

For example, during these past few days I have been asking whether anything in the world exists, and I have realized that from the very fact of my raising this question it follows quite evidently that I exist. I could not but judge that something which I understood so clearly was true; but this was not because I was compelled so to judge by any external force, but because a great light in the intellect was followed by a great inclination in the will, and thus the spontaneity and freedom of my belief was all the greater in proportion to my lack of indifference. But now, besides the knowledge that I exist, in so far as I am a thinking thing, an idea of corporeal nature comes into my mind; and I happen to be in doubt as to whether the thinking nature which is in me, or rather which I am, is distinct from this corporeal nature or identical with it. I am making the further supposition that my intellect has not yet come upon any persuasive reason in favour of one alternative rather than the other. This obviously implies that I am indifferent as to whether I should assert or deny either alternative, or indeed refrain from making any judgement on the matter.

What is more, this indifference does not merely apply to cases where the intellect is wholly ignorant, but extends in general to every case where the intellect does not have sufficiently clear knowledge at the time when the will deliberates. For although probable conjectures may pull me in one direction, the mere knowledge that they are simply conjectures, and not certain and indubitable reasons, is itself quite enough to push my assent the other way. My experience in the last few days confirms this: the mere fact that I found that all my previous beliefs were in some sense open to doubt was enough to turn my absolutely confident belief in their truth into the supposition that they were wholly false.

If, however, I simply refrain from making a judgement in cases where I do not perceive the truth with sufficient clarity and distinctness, then it is clear that I am behaving correctly and avoiding error. But if in such cases I either affirm or deny, then I am not using my free will correctly. If I go for the alternative which is false, then obviously I shall be in error; if I take the other side, then it is by pure chance that I arrive at the truth, and I shall still be at fault since it is clear by the natural light that the perception of the intellect should always precede the determination of the will. In this incorrect use of free will may be found the privation which constitutes the essence of error. The privation, I say, lies in the operation of the will in so far as it proceeds from me, but not in the faculty of will which I received from God, nor even in its operation, in so far as it depends on him.

And I have no cause for complaint on the grounds that the power of understanding or the natural light which God gave me is no greater than it is; for it is in the nature of a finite intellect to lack understanding of many things, and it is in the nature of a created intellect to be finite. Indeed, I have reason to give thanks to him who has never owed me anything for the great bounty that he has shown me, rather than thinking myself deprived or robbed of any gifts he did not bestow.[42]

Nor do I have any cause for complaint on the grounds that God gave me a will which extends more widely than my intellect. For since the will consists simply of one thing which is, as it were, indivisible, it seems that its nature rules out the possibility of anything being taken away from it. And surely, the more widely my will extends, then the greater thanks I owe to him who gave it to me.

Finally, I must not complain that the forming of those acts of will or judgements in which I go wrong happens with God's concurrence. For in so far as these acts depend on God, they are wholly true and good; and my ability to perform them means that there is in a sense more perfection in me than would be the case if I lacked this ability. As for the privation involved—which is all that the essential defi-

---

[42] ". . . rather than entertaining so unjust a thought as to imagine that he deprived me of, or unjustly withheld, the other perfections which he did not give me" (French version).

nition of falsity and wrong consists in—this does not in any way require the concurrence of God, since it is not a thing; indeed, when it is referred to God as its cause, it should be called not a privation but simply a negation.[43] For it is surely no imperfection in God that he has given me the freedom to assent or not to assent in those cases where he did not endow my intellect with a clear and distinct perception; but it is undoubtedly an imperfection in me to misuse that freedom and make judgements about matters which I do not fully understand. I can see, however, that God could easily have brought it about that without losing my freedom, and despite the limitations in my knowledge, I should nonetheless never make a mistake. He could, for example, have endowed my intellect with a clear and distinct perception of everything about which I was ever likely to deliberate; or he could simply have impressed it unforgettably on my memory that I should never make a judgement about anything which I did not clearly and distinctly understand. Had God made me this way, then I can easily understand that, considered as a totality,[44] I would have been more perfect than I am now. But I cannot therefore deny that there may in some way be more perfection in the universe as a whole because some of its parts are not immune from error, while others are immune, than there would be if all the parts were exactly alike. And I have no right to complain that the role God wished me to undertake in the world is not the principal one or the most perfect of all.

What is more, even if I have no power to avoid error in the first way just mentioned, which requires a clear perception of everything I have to deliberate on, I can avoid error in the second way, which depends merely on my remembering to withhold judgement on any occasion when the truth of the matter is not clear. Admittedly, I am aware of a certain weakness in me, in that I am unable to keep my attention fixed on one and the same item of knowledge at all times; but by attentive and repeated meditation I am nevertheless able to make myself

remember it as often as the need arises, and thus get into the habit of avoiding error.

It is here that man's greatest and most important perfection is to be found, and I therefore think that today's meditation, involving an investigation into the cause of error and falsity, has been very profitable. The cause of error must surely be the one I have explained; for if, whenever I have to make a judgement, I restrain my will so that it extends to what the intellect clearly and distinctly reveals, and no further, then it is quite impossible for me to go wrong. This is because every clear and distinct perception is undoubtedly something,[45] and hence cannot come from nothing, but must necessarily have God for its author. Its author, I say, is God, who is supremely perfect, and who cannot be a deceiver on pain of contradiction; hence the perception is undoubtedly true. So today I have learned not only what precautions to take to avoid ever going wrong, but also what to do to arrive at the truth. For I shall unquestionably reach the truth, if only I give sufficient attention to all the things which I perfectly understand, and separate these from all the other cases where my apprehension is more confused and obscure. And this is just what I shall take good care to do from now on.

Fifth Meditation: The essence of material things, and the existence of God considered a second time

There are many matters which remain to be investigated concerning the attributes of God and the nature of myself, or my mind; and perhaps I shall take these up at another time. But now that I have seen what to do and what to avoid in order to reach the truth, the most pressing task seems to be to try to escape from the doubts into which I fell a few days ago, and see whether any certainty can be achieved regarding material objects.

But before I inquire whether any such things exist outside me, I must consider the ideas of these

---

[43] ". . . understanding these terms in accordance with scholastic usage" (added in French version).

[44] ". . . as if there were only myself in the world" (added in French version).

[45] ". . . something real and positive" (French version).

things, in so far as they exist in my thought, and see which of them are distinct, and which confused.

Quantity, for example, or "continuous" quantity as the philosophers commonly call it, is something I distinctly imagine. That is, I distinctly imagine the extension of the quantity (or rather of the thing which is quantified) in length, breadth and depth. I also enumerate various parts of the thing, and to these parts I assign various sizes, shapes, positions and local motions; and to the motions I assign various durations.

Not only are all these things very well known and transparent to me when regarded in this general way, but in addition there are countless particular features regarding shapes, number, motion and so on, which I perceive when I give them my attention. And the truth of these matters is so open and so much in harmony with my nature, that on first discovering them it seems that I am not so much learning something new as remembering what I knew before; or it seems like noticing for the first time things which were long present within me although I had never turned my mental gaze on them before.

But I think the most important consideration at this point is that I find within me countless ideas of things which even though they may not exist anywhere outside me still cannot be called nothing; for although in a sense they can be thought of at will, they are not my invention but have their own true and immutable natures. When, for example, I imagine a triangle, even if perhaps no such figure exists, or has ever existed, anywhere outside my thought, there is still a determinate nature, or essence, or form of the triangle which is immutable and eternal, and not invented by me or dependent on my mind. This is clear from the fact that various properties can be demonstrated of the triangle, for example that its three angles equal two right angles, that its greatest side subtends its greatest angle, and the like; and since these properties are ones which I now clearly recognize whether I want to or not, even if I never thought of them at all when I previously imagined the triangle, it follows that they cannot have been invented by me.

It would be beside the point for me to say that since I have from time to time seen bodies of triangular shape, the idea of the triangle may have come to me from external things by means of the sense organs. For I can think up countless other shapes which there can be no suspicion of my ever having encountered through the senses, and yet I can demonstrate various properties of these shapes, just as I can with the triangle. All these properties are certainly true, since I am clearly aware of them, and therefore they are something, and not merely nothing; for it is obvious that whatever is true is something; and I have already amply demonstrated that everything of which I am clearly aware is true. And even if I had not demonstrated this, the nature of my mind is such that I cannot but assent to these things, at least so long as I clearly perceive them. I also remember that even before, when I was completely preoccupied with the objects of the senses, I always held that the most certain truths of all were the kind which I recognized clearly in connection with shapes, or numbers or other items relating to arithmetic or geometry, or in general to pure and abstract mathematics.

But if the mere fact that I can produce from my thought the idea of something entails that everything which I clearly and distinctly perceive to belong to that thing really does belong to it, is not this a possible basis for another argument to prove the existence of God? Certainly, the idea of God, or a supremely perfect being, is one which I find within me just as surely as the idea of any shape or number. And my understanding that it belongs to his nature that he always exists[46] is no less clear and distinct than is the case when I prove of any shape or number that some property belongs to its nature. Hence, even if it turned out that not everything on which I have meditated in these past days is true, I ought still to regard the existence of God as having at least the same level of certainty as I have hitherto attributed to the truths of mathematics.[47]

At first sight, however, this is not transparently clear, but has some appearance of being a sophism. Since I have been accustomed to distinguish between existence and essence in everything else, I find it easy to persuade myself that existence can also be separated from the essence of God, and

---

[46] ". . . that actual and eternal existence belongs to his nature" (French version).

[47] ". . . which concern only figures and numbers" (added in French version).

hence that God can be thought of as not existing. But when I concentrate more carefully, it is quite evident that existence can no more be separated from the essence of God than the fact that its three angles equal two right angles can be separated from the essence of a triangle, or than the idea of a mountain can be separated from the idea of a valley. Hence it is just as much of a contradiction to think of God (that is, a supremely perfect being) lacking existence (that is, lacking a perfection), as it is to think of a mountain without a valley.

However, even granted that I cannot think of God except as existing, just as I cannot think of a mountain without a valley, it certainly does not follow from the fact that I think of a mountain with a valley that there is any mountain in the world; and similarly, it does not seem to follow from the fact that I think of God as existing that he does exist. For my thought does not impose any necessity on things; and just as I may imagine a winged horse even though no horse has wings, so I may be able to attach existence to God even though no God exists.

But there is a sophism concealed here. From the fact that I cannot think of a mountain without a valley, it does not follow that a mountain and valley exist anywhere, but simply that a mountain and a valley, whether they exist or not, are mutually inseparable. But from the fact that I cannot think of God except as existing, it follows that existence is inseparable from God, and hence that he really exists. It is not that my thought makes it so, or imposes any necessity on any thing; on the contrary, it is the necessity of the thing itself, namely the existence of God, which determines my thinking in this respect. For I am not free to think of God without existence (that is, a supremely perfect being without a supreme perfection) as I am free to imagine a horse with or without wings.

And it must not be objected at this point that while it is indeed necessary for me to suppose God exists, once I have made the supposition that he has all perfections (since existence is one of the perfections), nevertheless the original supposition was not necessary. Similarly, the objection would run, it is not necessary for me to think that all quadrilaterals can be inscribed in a circle; but given this supposition, it will be necessary for me to admit that a rhombus can be inscribed in a circle—which is pat-

ently false. Now admittedly, it is not necessary that I ever light upon any thought of God; but whenever I do choose to think of the first and supreme being, and bring forth the idea of God from the treasure house of my mind as it were, it is necessary that I attribute all perfections to him, even if I do not at that time enumerate them or attend to them individually. And this necessity plainly guarantees that, when I later realize that existence is a perfection, I am correct in inferring that the first and supreme being exists. In the same way, it is not necessary for me ever to imagine a triangle; but whenever I do wish to consider a rectilinear figure having just three angles, it is necessary that I attribute to it the properties which license the inference that its three angles equal no more than two right angles, even if I do not notice this at the time. By contrast, when I examine what figures can be inscribed in a circle, it is in no way necessary for me to think that this class includes all quadrilaterals. Indeed, I cannot even imagine this, so long as I am willing to admit only what I clearly and distinctly understand. So there is a great difference between this kind of false supposition and the true ideas which are innate in me, of which the first and most important is the idea of God. There are many ways in which I understand that this idea is not something fictitious which is dependent on my thought, but is an image of a true and immutable nature. First of all, there is the fact that, apart from God, there is nothing else of which I am capable of thinking such that existence belongs[48] to its essence. Second, I cannot understand how there could be two or more Gods of this kind; and after supposing that one God exists, I plainly see that it is necessary that he has existed from eternity and will abide for eternity. And finally, I perceive many other attributes of God, none of which I can remove or alter.

But whatever method of proof I use, I am always brought back to the fact that it is only what I clearly and distinctly perceive that completely convinces me. Some of the things I clearly and distinctly perceive are obvious to everyone, while others are discovered only by those who look more closely and investigate more carefully; but once they have

---

[48] ". . . necessarily belongs" (French version).

been discovered, the latter are judged to be just as certain as the former. In the case of a right-angled triangle, for example, the fact that the square on the hypotenuse is equal to the square on the other two sides is not so readily apparent as the fact that the hypotenuse subtends the largest angle; but once one has seen it, one believes it just as strongly. But as regards God, if I were not overwhelmed by preconceived opinions, and if the images of things perceived by the senses did not besiege my thought on every side, I would certainly acknowledge him sooner and more easily than anything else. For what is more self-evident than the fact that the supreme being exists, or that God, to whose essence alone existence belongs,[49] exists?

Although it needed close attention for me to perceive this, I am now just as certain of it as I am of everything else which appears most certain. And what is more, I see that the certainty of all other things depends on this, so that without it nothing can ever be perfectly known.

Admittedly my nature is such that so long as[50] I perceive something very clearly and distinctly I cannot but believe it to be true. But my nature is also such that I cannot fix my mental vision continually on the same thing, so as to keep perceiving it clearly; and often the memory of a previously made judgement may come back, when I am no longer attending to the arguments which led me to make it. And so other arguments can now occur to me which might easily undermine my opinion, if I were unaware of God; and I should thus never have true and certain knowledge about anything, but only shifting and changeable opinions. For example, when I consider the nature of a triangle, it appears most evident to me, steeped as I am in the principles of geometry, that its three angles are equal to two right angles; and so long as I attend to the proof, I cannot but believe this to be true. But as soon as I turn my mind's eye away from the proof, then in spite of still remembering that I perceived it very clearly, I can easily fall into doubt about its truth, if I am unaware of God. For I can convince myself

that I have a natural disposition to go wrong from time to time in matters which I think I perceive as evidently as can be. This will seem even more likely when I remember that there have been frequent cases where I have regarded things as true and certain, but have later been led by other arguments to judge them to be false.

Now, however, I have perceived that God exists, and at the same time I have understood that everything else depends on him, and that he is no deceiver; and I have drawn the conclusion that everything which I clearly and distinctly perceive is of necessity true. Accordingly, even if I am no longer attending to the arguments which led me to judge that this is true, as long as I remember that I clearly and distinctly perceived it, there are no counter-arguments which can be adduced to make me doubt it, but on the contrary I have true and certain knowledge of it. And I have knowledge not just of this matter, but of all matters which I remember ever having demonstrated, in geometry and so on. For what objections can now be raised?[51] That the way I am made makes me prone to frequent error? But I now know that I am incapable of error in those cases where my understanding is transparently clear. Or can it be objected that I have in the past regarded as true and certain many things which I afterwards recognized to be false? But none of these were things which I clearly and distinctly perceived: I was ignorant of this rule for establishing the truth, and believed these things for other reasons which I later discovered to be less reliable. So what is left to say? Can one raise the objection I put to myself a while ago, that I may be dreaming, or that everything which I am now thinking has as little truth as what comes to the mind of one who is asleep? Yet even this does not change anything. For even though I might be dreaming, if there is anything which is evident to my intellect, then it is wholly true.

Thus I see plainly that the certainty and truth of all knowledge depends uniquely on my awareness of the true God, to such an extent that I was incapable of perfect knowledge about anything else until I became aware of him. And now it is possible

---

[49] ". . . in the idea of whom alone necessary and eternal existence is comprised" (French version).

[50] ". . . as soon as" (French version).

[51] ". . . to oblige me to call these matters into doubt" (added in French version).

for me to achieve full and certain knowledge of countless matters, both concerning God himself and other things whose nature is intellectual, and also concerning the whole of that corporeal nature which is the subject-matter of pure mathematics.[52]

Sixth Meditation: The existence of material things, and the real distinction between mind and body[53]

It remains for me to examine whether material things exist. And at least I now know they are capable of existing, in so far as they are the subject-matter of pure mathematics, since I perceive them clearly and distinctly. for there is no doubt that God is capable of creating everything that I am capable of perceiving in this manner; and I have never judged that something could not be made by him except on the grounds that there would be a contradiction in my perceiving it distinctly. The conclusion that material things exist is also suggested by the faculty of imagination, which I am aware of using when I turn my mind to material things. For when I give more attentive consideration to what imagination is, it seems to be nothing else but an application of the cognitive faculty to a body which is intimately present to it, and which therefore exists.

To make this clear, I will first examine the difference between imagination and pure understanding. When I imagine a triangle, for example, I do not merely understand that it is a figure bounded by three lines, but at the same time I also see the three lines with my mind's eye as if they were present before me; and this is what I call imagining. But if I want to think of a chiliagon, although I understand that it is a figure consisting of a thousand sides just as well as I understand the triangle to be a three-sided figure, I do not in the same way imagine the thousand sides or see them as if they were present before me. It is true that since I am in the habit of imagining something whenever I think of a corporeal thing, I may construct in my mind a confused representation of some figure; but it is clear that this is not a chiliagon. For it differs in no way from the representation I should form if I were thinking of a myriagon, or any figure with very many sides. Moreover, such a representation is useless for recognizing the properties which distinguish a chiliagon from other polygons. But suppose I am dealing with a pentagon: I can of course understand the figure of a pentagon, just as I can the figure of a chiliagon, without the help of the imagination; but I can also imagine a pentagon, by applying my mind's eye to its five sides and the area contained within them. And in doing this I notice quite clearly that imagination requires a peculiar effort of mind which is not required for understanding; this additional effort of mind clearly shows the difference between imagination and pure understanding.

Besides this, I consider that this power of imagining which is in me, differing as it does from the power of understanding, is not a necessary constituent of my own essence, that is, of the essence of my mind. For if I lacked it, I should undoubtedly remain the same individual as I now am; from which it seems to follow that it depends on something distinct from myself. And I can easily understand that, if there does exist some body to which the mind is so joined that it can apply itself to contemplate it, as it were, whenever it pleases, then it may possibly be this very body that enables me to imagine corporeal things. So the difference between this mode of thinking and pure understanding may simply be this: when the mind understands, it in some way turns towards itself and inspects one of the ideas which are within it; but when it imagines, it turns towards the body and looks at something in the body which conforms to an idea understood by the mind or perceived by the senses. I can, as I say, easily understand that this is how imagination comes about, if the body exists; and since there is no other equally suitable way of explaining imagination that comes to mind, I can make a probable conjecture that the body exists. But this is only a probability; and despite a careful and comprehensive investigations, I do not yet see how the distinct

---

[52] ". . . and also concerning things which belong to corporeal nature in so far as it can serve as the object of geometrical demonstrations which have no concern with whether that object exists" (French version).

[53] ". . . between the soul and body of a man" (French version).

idea of corporeal nature which I find in my imagination can provide any basis for a necessary inference that some body exists.

But besides that corporeal nature which is the subject-matter of pure mathematics, there is much else that I habitually imagine, such as colours, sounds, tastes, pain and so on—though not so distinctly. Now I perceive these things much better by means of the senses, which is how, with the assistance of memory, they appear to have reached the imagination. So in order to deal with them more fully, I must pay equal attention to the senses, and see whether the things which are perceived by means of that mode of thinking which I call "sensory perception" provide me with any sure argument for the existence of corporeal things.

To begin with, I will go back over all the things which I previously took to be perceived by the senses, and reckoned to be true; and I will go over my reasons for thinking this. Next, I will set out my reasons for subsequently calling these things into doubt. And finally I will consider what I should now believe about them.

First of all then, I perceived by my senses that I had a head, hands, feet and other limbs making up the body which I regarded as part of myself, or perhaps even as my whole self. I also perceived by my senses that this body was situated among many other bodies which could affect it in various favourable or unfavorable ways; and I gauged the favourable effects by a sensation of pleasure, and the unfavourable ones by a sensation of pain. In addition to pain and pleasure, I also had sensations within me of hunger, thirst, and other such appetites, and also of physical propensities towards cheerfulness, sadness, anger and similar emotions. And outside me, besides the extension, shapes and movements of bodies, I also had sensations of their hardness and heat, and of the other tactile qualities. In addition, I had sensations of light, colours, smells, tastes and sounds, the variety of which enabled me to distinguish the sky, the earth, the seas, and all other bodies, one from another. Considering the ideas of all these qualities which presented themselves to my thought, although the ideas were, strictly speaking, the only immediate objects of my sensory awareness, it was not unreasonable for me to think that the items which I was perceiving through the senses were things quite distinct from my thought, namely bodies which produced the ideas. For my experience was that these ideas came to me quite without my consent, so that I could not have sensory awareness of any object, even if I wanted to, unless it was present to my sense organs; and I could not avoid having sensory awareness of it when it was present. And since the ideas perceived by the senses were much more lively and vivid and even, in their own way, more distinct than any of those which I deliberately formed through meditating or which I found impressed on my memory, it seemed impossible that they should have come from within me; so the only alternative was that they came from other things. Since the sole source of my knowledge of these things was the ideas themselves, the supposition that the things resembled the ideas was bound to occur to me. In addition, I remembered that the use of my senses had come first, while the use of my reason came only later; and I saw that the ideas which I formed myself were less vivid than those which I perceived with the senses and were, for the most part, made up of elements of sensory ideas. In this way I easily convinced myself that I had nothing at all in the intellect which I had not previously had in sensation. As for the body which by some special right I called "mine," my belief that this body, more than any other, belonged to me had some justification. For I could never be separated from it, as I could from other bodies; and I felt all my appetites and emotions in, and on account of, this body; and finally, I was aware of pain and pleasurable ticklings in parts of this body, but not in other bodies external to it. But why should that curious sensation of pain give rise to a particular distress of mind; or why should a certain kind of delight follow on a tickling sensation? Again, why should that curious tugging in the stomach which I call hunger tell me that I should eat, or a dryness of the throat tell me to drink, and so on? I was not able to give any explanation of all this; except that nature taught me so. For there is absolutely no connection (at least that I can understand) between the tugging sensation and the decision to take food, or between the sensation of something causing pain and the mental apprehension of distress that arises from that sensation. These and other judgments that I made concerning sensory objects, I was apparently taught to make by nature; for I had already made up my mind that this was how things were, before working out any arguments to prove it.

Later on, however, I had many experiences which gradually undermined all the faith I had had in the senses. Sometimes towers which had looked round from a distance appeared square from close up; and enormous statues standing on their pediments did not seem large when observed from the ground. In these and countless other such cases, I found that the judgments of the external senses were mistaken. And this applied not just to the external senses but to the internal senses as well. For what can be more internal than pain? And yet I had heard that those who had had a leg or an arm amputated sometimes still seemed to feel pain intermittently in the missing part of the body. So even in my own case it was apparently not quite certain that a particular limb was hurting, even if I felt pain in it. To these reasons for doubting, I recently added two very general ones. The first was that every sensory experience I have ever thought I was having while awake I can also think of myself as sometimes having while asleep; and since I do not believe that what I seem to perceive in sleep comes from things located outside me, I did not see why I should be any more inclined to believe this of what I think I perceive while awake. The second reason for doubt was that since I did not yet know the author of my being (or at least was pretending not to), I saw nothing to rule out the possibility that my natural constitution made me prone to error even in matters which seemed to me most true. As for the reasons for my previous confident belief in the truth of the things perceived by the senses, I had no trouble in refuting them. For since I apparently had natural impulses towards many things which reason told me to avoid, I reckoned that a great deal of confidence should not be placed in what I was taught by nature. And despite the fact that the perceptions of the senses were not dependent on my will, I did not think that I should on that account infer that they proceeded from things distinct from myself, since I might perhaps have a faculty not yet known to me which produced them.

But now, when I am beginning to achieve a better knowledge of myself and the author of my being, although I do not think I should heedlessly accept everything I seem to have acquired from the senses, neither do I think that everything should be called into doubt.

First, I know that everything which I clearly and distinctly understand is capable of being created by God so as to correspond exactly with my understanding of it. Hence the fact that I can clearly and distinctly understand one thing apart from another is enough to make me certain that the two things are distinct, since they are capable of being separated, at least by God. The question of what kind of power is required to bring about such a separation does not affect the judgment that the two things are distinct. Thus, simply by knowing that I exist and seeing at the same time that absolutely nothing else belongs to my nature or essence except that I am a thinking thing, I can infer correctly that my essence consists solely in the fact that I am a thinking thing. It is true that I may have (or, to anticipate, that I certainly have) a body that is very closely joined to me. But nevertheless, on the one hand I have a clear and distinct idea of myself, in so far as I am simply a thinking, non-extended thing; and on the other hand I have a distinct idea of body,[54] in so far as this is simply an extended, non-thinking thing. And accordingly, it is certain that I[55] am really distinct from by body, and can exist without it.

Besides this, I find in myself faculties for certain special modes of thinking,[56] namely imagination and sensory perception. Now I can clearly and distinctly understand myself as a whole without these faculties; but I cannot, conversely, understand these faculties without me, that is, without an intellectual substance to inhere in. This is because there is an intellectual act included in their essential definition; and hence I perceive that the distinction between them and myself corresponds to the distinction between the modes of a thing and the thing itself.[57] Of course I also recognize that there are other faculties (like those of changing position, of taking on vari-

---

[54] The Latin term *corpus* as used here by Descartes is ambiguous as between "body" (i.e. corporeal matter in general) and "the body" (i.e., this particular body of mine). The French version preserves the ambiguity.

[55] ". . . that is, my soul, by which I am what I am" (added in French version).

[56] ". . . certain modes of thinking which are quite special and distinct from me" (French version).

[57] ". . . between the shapes, movements and other modes or accidents of a body and the body which supports them" (French version).

ous shapes, and so on) which, like sensory perception and imagination, cannot be understood apart from some substance for them to inhere in, and hence cannot exist without it. But it is clear that these other faculties, if they exist, must be in a corporeal or extended substance and not an intellectual one; for the clear and distinct conception of them includes extension, but does not include any intellectual act whatsoever. Now there is in me a passive faculty of sensory perception, that is, a faculty for receiving and recognizing the ideas of sensible objects; but I could not make use of it unless there was also an active faculty, either in me or in something else, which produced or brought about these ideas. But this faculty cannot be in me, since clearly it presupposes no intellectual act on my part,[58] and the ideas in question are produced without my cooperation and often even against my will. So the only alternative is that it is in another substance distinct from me—a substance which contains either formally or eminently all the reality which exists objectively in the ideas produced by this faculty (as I have just noted). This substance is either a body, that is, a corporeal nature, in which case it will contain formally ⟨and in fact⟩ everything which is to be found objectively ⟨or representatively⟩ in the ideas; or else it is God, or some creature more noble than a body, in which case it will contain eminently whatever is to be found in the ideas. But since God is not a deceiver, it is quite clear that he does not transmit the ideas to me either directly from himself, or indirectly, via some creature which contains the objective reality of the ideas not formally but only eminently. For God has given me no faculty at all for recognizing any such source for these ideas; on the contrary, he has given me a great propensity to believe that they are produced by corporeal things. So I do not see how God could be understood to be anything but a deceiver if the ideas were transmitted from a source other than corporeal things. It follows that corporeal things exist. They may not all exist in a way that exactly corresponds with my sensory grasp of them, for in many cases the grasp of the senses is very obscure and

confused. But at least they possess all the properties which I clearly and distinctly understand, that is, all those which, viewed in general terms, are comprised within the subject-matter of pure mathematics.

What of the other aspects of corporeal things which are either particular (for example that the sun is of such and such a size or shape), or less clearly understood, such as light or sound or pain, and so on? Despite the high degree of doubt and uncertainty involved here, the very fact that God is not a deceiver, and the consequent impossibility of there being any falsity in my opinions which cannot be corrected by some other faculty supplied by God, offers me a sure hope that I can attain the truth even in these matters. Indeed, there is no doubt that everything that I am taught by nature contains some truth. For if nature is considered in its general aspect, then I understand by the term nothing other than God himself, or the ordered system of created things established by God. And by my own nature in particular I understand nothing other than the totality of things bestowed on me by God.

There is nothing that my own nature teaches me more vividly than that I have a body, and that when I feel pain there is something wrong with the body, and that when I am hungry or thirsty the body needs food and drink, and so on. So I should not doubt that there is some truth in this.

Nature also teaches me, by these sensations of pain, hunger, thirst and so on, that I am not merely present in my body as a sailor is present in a ship,[59] but that I am very closely joined and, as it were, intermingled with it, so that I and the body form a unit. If this were not so, I, who am nothing but a thinking thing, would not feel pain when the body was hurt, but would perceive the damage purely by the intellect, just as a sailor perceives by sight if anything in his ship is broken. Similarly, when the body needed food or drink, I should have an explicit understanding of the fact, instead of having confused sensations of hunger and thirst. For these sensations of hunger, thirst, pain and so on are nothing but confused modes of thinking which arise from the union and, as it were, intermingling of the mind with the body.

---

[58] "... cannot be in me in so far as I am merely a thinking thing, since it does not presuppose any thought on my part" (French version).

[59] "... as a pilot in his ship" (French version).

I am also taught by nature that various other bodies exist in the vicinity of my body, and that some of these are to be sought out and others avoided. And from the fact that I perceive by my senses a great variety of colours, sounds, smells and tastes, as well as differences in heat, hardness and the like, I am correct in inferring that the bodies which are the source of these various sensory perceptions possess differences corresponding to them, though perhaps not resembling them. Also, the fact that some of the perceptions are agreeable to me while others are disagreeable makes it quite certain that my body, or rather my whole self, in so far as I am a combination of body and mind, can be affected by the various beneficial or harmful bodies which surround it.

There are, however, many other things which I may appear to have been taught by nature, but which in reality I acquired not from nature but from a habit of making ill-considered judgements; and it is therefore quite possible that these are false. Cases in point are the belief that any space in which nothing is occurring to stimulate my senses must be empty; or that the heat in a body is something exactly resembling the idea of heat which is in me; or that when a body is white or green, the selfsame whiteness or greeness which I perceive through my senses is present in the body; or that in a body which is bitter or sweet there is the selfsame taste which I experience, and so on; or, finally, that stars and towers and other distant bodies have the same size and shape which they present to my senses, and other examples of this kind. But to make sure that my perceptions in this matter are sufficiently distinct, I must more accurately define exactly what I mean when I say that I am taught something by nature. In this context I am taking nature to be something more limited than the totality of things bestowed on me by God. For this includes many things that belong to the mind alone—for example my perception that what is done cannot be undone, and all other things that are known by the natural light;[60] but at this stage I am not speaking of these matters. It also includes much that relates to the body alone, like the tendency to move in a down-ward direction, and so on; but I am not speaking of these matters either. My sole concern here is with what God has bestowed on me as a combination of mind and body. My nature, then, in this limited sense, does indeed teach me to avoid what induces a feeling of pain and to seek out what induces feelings of pleasure, and so on. But it does not appear to teach us to draw any conclusions from these sensory perceptions about things located outside us without waiting until the intellect has examined[61] the matter. For knowledge of the truth about such things seems to belong to the mind alone, not to the combination of mind and body. Hence, although a star has no greater effect on my eye than the flame of a small light, that does not mean that there is any real or positive inclination in me to believe that the star is no bigger than the light; I have simply made this judgment from childhood onwards without any rational basis. Similarly, although I feel heat when I go near a fire and feel pain when I go too near, there is no convincing argument for supposing that there is something in the fire which resembles the heat, any more than for supposing that there is something which resembles the pain. There is simply reason to suppose that there is something in the fire, whatever it may eventually turn out to be, which produces in us the feelings of heat or pain. And likewise, even though there is nothing in any given space that stimulates the senses, it does not follow that there is no body there. In these cases and many others I see that I have been in the habit of misusing the order of nature. for the proper purpose of the sensory perceptions given me by nature is simply to inform the mind of what is beneficial or harmful for the composite of which the mind is a part; and to this extent they are sufficiently clear and distinct. But I misuse them by treating them as reliable touchstones for immediate judgments about the essential nature of the bodies located outside us; yet this is an area where they provide only very obscure information.

I have already looked in sufficient detail at how, notwithstanding the goodness of God, it may happen that my judgments are false. But a further problem now comes to mind regarding those very

---

[60] ". . . without any help from the body" (added in French version).

[61] ". . . carefully and maturely examined" (French version).

things which nature presents to me as objects which I should seek out or avoid, and also regarding the internal sensations, where I seem to have detected errors[62]—e.g. when someone is tricked by the pleasant taste of some food into eating the poison concealed inside it. Yet in this case, what the man's nature urges him to go for is simply what is responsible for the pleasant taste, and not the poison, which his nature knows nothing about. The only inference that can be drawn from this is that his nature is not omniscient. And this is not surprising, since man is a limited thing, and so it is only fitting that his perfection should be limited.

And yet it is not unusual for us to go wrong even in cases where nature does urge us towards something. Those who are ill, for example, may desire food or drink that will shortly afterwards turn out to be bad for them. Perhaps it may be said that they go wrong because their nature is disordered, but this does not remove the difficulty. A sick man is no less one of God's creatures than a healthy one, and it seems no less a contradiction to suppose that he has received from God a nature which deceives him. Yet a clock constructed with wheels and weights observes all the laws of its nature just as closely when it is badly made and tells the wrong time as when it completely fulfills the wishes of the clockmaker. In the same way, I might consider the body of a man as a kind of machine equipped with and made up of bones, nerves, muscles, veins, blood and skin in such a way that, even if there were no mind in it, it would still perform all the same movements as it now does in those cases where movement is not under the control of the will or, consequently, of the mind.[63] I can easily see that if such a body suffers from dropsy, for example, and is affected by the dryness of the throat which normally produces in the mind the sensation of thirst, the resulting condition of the nerves and other parts will dispose the body to take a drink, with the result that the disease will be aggravated. Yet this is just as natural as the body's being stimulated by a similar dryness of the throat to take a drink when there is

no such illness and the drink is beneficial. Admittedly, when I consider the purpose of the clock, I may say that it is departing from its nature when it does not tell the right time; and similarly when I consider the mechanism of the human body, I may think that, in relation to the movements which normally occur in it, it too is deviating from its nature if the throat is dry at a time when drinking is not beneficial to its continued health. But I am well aware that "nature" as I have just used it has a very different significance from "nature" in the other sense. As I have just used it, "nature" is simply a label which depends on my thought; it is quite extraneous to the things to which it is applied, and depends simply on my comparison between the idea of a sick man and a badly-made clock, and the idea of a healthy man and a well-made clock. But by "nature" in the other sense I understand something which is really to be found in the things themselves; in this sense, therefore, the term contains something of the truth.

When we say, then, with respect to the body suffering from dropsy, that it has a disordered nature because it has a dry throat and yet does not need to drink, the term "nature" is here used merely as an extraneous label. However, with respect to the composite, that is, the mind united with this body, what is involved is not a mere label, but a true error of nature, namely that it is thirsty at a time when drink is going to cause it harm. It thus remains to inquire how it is that the goodness of God does not prevent nature, in this sense, from deceiving us.

The first observation I make at this point is that there is a great difference between the mind and the body, inasmuch as the body is by its very nature always divisible, while the mind is utterly indivisible. For when I consider the mind, or myself in so far as I am merely a thinking thing, I am unable to distinguish any parts within myself; I understand myself to be something quite single and complete. Although the whole mind seems to be united to the whole body, I recognize that if a foot or arm or any other part of the body is cut off, nothing has thereby been taken away from the mind. As for the faculties of willing, of understanding, of sensory perception and so on, these cannot be termed parts of the mind, since it is one and the same mind that wills, and understands and has sensory perceptions. By contrast, there is no corporeal or extended thing that I can

---

[62] ". . . and thus seem to have been directly deceived by my nature" (added in French version).

[63] ". . . but occurs merely as a result of the disposition of the organs" (French version).

think of which in my thought I cannot easily divide into parts; and this very fact makes me understand that it is divisible. This one argument would be enough to show me that the mind is completely different from the body, even if I did not already know as much from other considerations.

My next observation is that the mind is not immediately affected by all parts of the body, but only by the brain, or perhaps just by one small part of the brain, namely the part which is said to contain the 'common' sense. Every time this part of the brain is in a given state, it presents the same signals to the mind, even though the other parts of the body may be in a different condition at the time. This is established by countless observations, which there is no need to review here.

I observe, in addition, that the nature of the body is such that whenever any part of it is moved by another part which is some distance away, it can always be moved in the same fashion by any of the parts which lie in between, even if the more distant part does nothing. For example, in a cord ABCD, if one end D is pulled so that the other end A moves, the exact same movement could have been brought about if one of the intermediate points B or C had been pulled, and D had not moved at all. In similar fashion, when I feel a pain in my foot, physiology tells me that this happens by means of nerves distributed throughout the foot, and that these nerves are like cords, which go from the foot right up to the brain. When the nerves are pulled in the foot, they in turn pull on inner parts of the brain to which they are attached, and produce a certain motion in them; and nature has laid it down that this motion should produce in the mind a sensation of pain, as occurring in the foot. But since these nerves, in passing from the foot to the brain, must pass through the calf, the thigh, the lumbar region, the back and the neck, it can happen that, even if it is not the part in the foot but one of the intermediate parts which is being pulled, the same motion will occur in the brain as occurs when the foot is hurt, and so it will necessarily come about that the mind feels the same sensation of pain. And we must suppose the same thing happens with regard to any other sensation.

My final observation is that any given movement occurring in the part of the brain that immediately affects the mind produces just one corresponding sensation; and hence the best system that could be devised is that it should produce the one sensation which, of all possible sensations, is most especially and most frequently conducive to the preservation of the healthy man. And experience shows that the sensations which nature has given us are all of this kind; and so there is absolutely nothing to be found in them that does not bear witness to the power and goodness of God. For example, when the nerves in the foot are set in motion in a violent and unusual manner, this motion, by way of the spinal cord, reaches the inner parts of the brain, and there gives the mind its signal for having a certain sensation, namely the sensation of a pain as occurring in the foot. This stimulates the mind to do its best to get rid of the cause of the pain, which it takes to be harmful to the foot. It is true that God could have made the nature of man such that this particular motion in the brain indicated something else to the mind; it might, for example, have made the mind aware of the actual motion occurring in the brain, or in the foot, or in any of the intermediate regions; or it might have indicated something else entirely. But there is nothing else which would have been so conducive to the continued well-being of the body. In the same way, when we need drink, there arises a certain dryness in the throat; this sets in motion the nerves of the throat, which in turn move the inner parts of the brain. This motion produces in the mind a sensation of thirst, because the most useful thing for us to know about the whole business is that we need drink in order to stay healthy. And so it is in the other cases.

It is quite clear from all this that, notwithstanding the immense goodness of God, the nature of man as a combination of mind and body is such that it is bound to mislead himn from time to time. For there may be some occurrence, not in the foot but in one of the other areas through which the nerves travel in their route from the foot to the brain, or even in the brain itself; and if this cause produces the same motion which is generally produced by injury to the foot, then pain will be felt as if it were in the foot. This deception of the senses is natural, because a given motion in the brain must always produce the same sensation in the mind; and the origin of the motion in question is much more often going to be something which is hurting the foot, rather than something existing elsewhere. So it is reasonable that this motion should always indicate to the mind a pain in the foot rather than in any other part of the body. Again, dryness of the throat may sometimes arise not, as it normally does, from the fact that a drink is necessary to the health of the body, but from some quite opposite cause, as happens in the case of the man with dropsy. Yet it is much better that it should mislead on this occasion than that it should always mislead when the body is in good health. And the same goes for the other cases.

This consideration is the greatest help to me, not only for noticing all the errors to which my nature is liable, but also for enabling me to correct or avoid them without difficulty. For I know that in matters regarding the well-being of the body, all my senses report the truth much more frequently than not. Also, I can almost always make use of more than one sense to investigate the same thing; and in addition, I can use both my memory, which connects present experiences with preceding ones, and my intellect, which has by now examined all the causes of error. Accordingly, I should not have any further fears about the falsity of what my senses tell me every day; on the contrary, the exaggerated doubts of the last few days should be dismissd as laughable. This applies especially to the principal reason for doubt, namely my inability to distinguish between being asleep and being awake. For I now notice that there is a vast difference between the two, in that dreams are never linked by memory with all the other actions of life as waking experiences are. If, while I am awake, anyone were suddenly to appear to me and then disappear immediately, as happens in sleep, so that I could not see where he had come from or where he had gone to, it would not be unreasonable for me to judge that he was a ghost, or a vision created in my brain,[64] rather than a real man. But when I distinctly see where things come from and where and when they come to me, and when I can connect my perceptions of them with the whole of the rest of my life without a break, then I am quite certain that when I encounter these things I am not asleep but awake. And I ought not to have even the slightest doubt of their reality if, after calling upon all the senses as well as my memory and my intellect in order to check them, I receive no conflicting reports from any of these sources. For from the fact that God is not a deceiver it follows that in cases like these I am completely free from error. But since the pressure of things to be done does not always allow us to stop and make such a meticulous check, it must be admitted that in this human life we are often liable to make mistakes about particular things, and we must acknowledge the weakness of our nature.

---

[64] "... like those that are formed in the brain when I sleep" (added in French version).

Benedict *Spinoza* [*Baruch Espinosa*]
(1632–1677)

Spinoza's grandfather came to the Netherlands—a republic recently independent of the Spanish Hapsburg empire—with a group of Jewish refugees from the Inquisition in Portugal. By the time Spinoza was born, a prosperous Jewish community was well established in Amsterdam. It had secured permission to build a synagogue, and opened a Hebrew school in 1638, which Spinoza attended. At the age of twenty, Spinoza began studying with Francis van den Ende, an ex-Jesuit physician who opened a private school in 1652. We know

he studied, among other things, Machiavelli, mathematics, and physics. In 1656 Spinoza was expelled from the Congregation of Israel, apparently for his heterodox opinions. It was at this time that he took the name Benedict, the Latin equivalent of Baruch, meaning blessed.

Although he supported himself throughout his life as a lens grinder, Spinoza seems always to have had a rare talent and reputation as a teacher. He began as a teacher in van den Ende's school the same year as his expulsion from the Jewish community, a position he retained until 1660. At the same time, he went to live with (but never joined) the Collegiants, a group of religious dissenters who favored simple worship and no clergy. He seems to have been a kind of tutor to the group, which he continued to live with until 1663. His first published work, *Principles of Cartesianism Geometrically Demonstrated,* was composed for a Collegiant study group. It is noteworthy that it has the same format as the work reprinted here, the *Ethics.* The *Principles* was critical of Descartes, which shows that the deductive format is, for Spinoza, an expository tool, and does not indicate that Spinoza regards the propositions "demonstrated" as true, or even perfectly clear. Though the *Ethics* certainly does represent Spinoza's considered opinions, the reader should be aware that the deductive format does not necessarily have the significance it may appear to have at first.

The *Principles* earned Spinoza a good deal of hostility from Cartesians—there were many in Holland, Descartes having spent much of his life there—and a good deal of notoriety as well. Indeed, Spinoza seems to have been something of a public figure from early in his life. His scientific connections were enhanced by a friendship and correspondence with Henry Oldenburg, who became first secretary of the influential Royal Society in England. In 1670 the *Theological-Political Treatise* was published anonymously in Hamburg. It was widely known that Spinoza was the author, a fact he never denied, and it created a storm of controversy because of its biblical interpretations and support of democratic institutions.

Spinoza's support of democracy, and his friendship with Jan de Witt, a leading figure in the republican government, proved especially dangerous when Louis XIV of France invaded the Netherlands in 1672. A mob executed Jan de Witt and his brother, apparently blaming them for inadequate defensive measures against the French. When Spinoza was summoned to the French headquarters in the following year, rumors spread that he had been a go-between for de Witt and the French, and Spinoza was widely attacked for suspected disloyalty. Nevertheless, in the same year, Spinoza rejected an offer of a professorship in Germany, preferring to remain in Holland, where, he claimed, religious and political freedom were greater than anywhere else. He accepted a pension from de Witt's will, and this, together with his lens grinding, kept him in comfort until his death.

The *Ethics* was begun as a dialogue during his stay with the Collegiants, but was not completed until late in his life, and not published until after his death by some brave friends, former Collegiants. Spinoza corresponded with Leibniz, who came to meet him in 1676, but these exchanges concerned optics, not the issues of the *Ethics.*

Note on the text: Some of the additional material in the *Nagelate Schriften* is included here in square brackets.

Ethics

First Part of the Ethics. On God

Definitions

D1:

By cause of itself I understand that whose essence involves existence, *or* that whose nature cannot be conceived except as existing.

D2:

That thing is said to be finite in its own kind that can be limited by another of the same nature.

For example, a body is called finite because we always conceive another that is greater. Thus a thought is limited by another thought. But a body is not limited by a thought nor a thought by a body.

D3:

By substance I understand what is in itself and is conceived through itself, i.e., that whose concept does not require the concept of another thing, from which it must be formed.

D4:

By attribute I understand what the intellect perceives of a substance, as constituting its essence.

D5:

By mode I understand the affections of a substance, *or* that which is in another through which it is also conceived.

D6:

By God I understand a being absolutely infinite, i.e., a substance consisting of an infinity of attributes, of which each one expresses an eternal and infinite essence.

Exp.: I say absolutely infinite, not infinite in its own kind; for if something is only infinite in its own kind, we can deny infinite attributes of it [(i.e., we

Reprinted from *Collected Works of Spinoza, Vol. 1*, E. Curley, ed. and trans. (Princeton, N.J.: Princeton University Press, 1985), pp. 408–91. Used by permission.

can conceive infinite attributes which do not pertain to its nature)]; but if something is absolutely infinite, whatever expresses essence and involves no negation pertains to its essence.

D7:

That thing is called free which exists from the necessity of its nature alone, and is determined to act by itself alone. But a thing is called necessary, or rather compelled, which is determined by another to exist and to produce an effect in a certain and determinate manner.

D8:

By eternity I understand existence itself, insofar as it is conceived to follow necessarily from the definition alone of the eternal thing.

Exp.: For such existence, like the essence of a thing, is conceived as an eternal truth, and on that account cannot be explained by duration or time, even if the duration is conceived to be without beginning or end.

Axioms

A1:

Whatever is, is either in itself or in another.

A2:

What cannot be conceived through another, must be conceived through itself.

A3:

From a given determinate cause the effect follows necessarily; and conversely, if there is no determinate cause, it is impossible for an effect to follow.

A4:

The knowledge of an effect depends on, and involves, the knowledge of its cause.

A5:

Things that have nothing in common with one another also cannot be understood through one another, *or* the concept of the one does not involve the concept of the other.

A6:

A true idea must agree with its object.

A7:

If a thing can be conceived as not existing, its essence does not involve existence.

P1:

A substance is prior in nature to its affections.

Dem.: This is evident from D3 and D5.

P2:

Two substances having different attributes have nothing in common with one another.

Dem.: This also evident from D3. For each must be in itself and be conceived through itself, *or* the concept of the one does not involve the concept of the other.

P3:

If things have nothing in common with one another, one of them cannot be the cause of the other.

Dem.: If they have nothing in common with one another, then (by A5) they cannot be understood through one another, and so (by A4) one cannot be the cause of the other, q.e.d.

P4:

Two or more distinct things are distinguished from one another, either by a difference in the attributes of the substances or by a difference in their affections.

Dem.: Whatever is, is either in itself or in another (by A1), i.e. (by D3 and D5), outside the intellect there is nothing except substances and their affections. Therefore, there is nothing outside the intellect through which a number of things can be distinguished from one another except substances, *or* what is the same (by D4), their attributes, and their affections, q.e.d.

P5:

In nature there cannot be two or more substances of the same nature or attribute.

Dem.: If there were two or more distinct substances, they would have to be distinguished from one another either by a difference in their attributes, or by a difference in their affections (by P4). If only by a difference in their attributes, then it will be conceded that there is only one of the same attribute. But if by a difference in their affections, then since a substance is prior in nature to its affections (by P1), if the affections are put to one side and [the substance] is considered in itself, i.e. (by D3 and A6), considered truly, one cannot be conceived to be distinguished from another, i.e. (by P4), there cannot be many, but only one [of the same nature *or* attribute], q.e.d.

P6:

One substance cannot be produced by another substance.

Dem.: In nature there cannot be two substances of the same attribute (by P5), i.e. (by P2), which have something in common with each other. Therefore (by P3) one cannot be the cause of the other, *or* cannot be produced by the other, q.e.d.

Cor.: From this it follows that a substance cannot be produced by anything else. For in nature there is nothing except substances and their affections, as is evident from A1, D3, and D5. But it cannot be produced by a substance (by P6). Therefore, substance absolutely cannot be produced by anything else, q.e.d.

Alternatively: This is demonstrated even more easily from the absurdity of its contradictory. For if a substance could be produced by something else, the knowledge of it would have to depend on the knowledge of its cause (by A4). And so (by D3) it would not be a substance.

P7:

It pertains to the nature of a substance to exist.

Dem.: A substance cannot be produced by anything else (by P6C); therefore it will be the cause of itself, i.e. (by D1), its essence necessarily involves existence, *or* it pertains to its nature to exist, q.e.d.

P8:

Every substance is necessarily infinite.

Dem.: A substance of one attribute does not exist unless it is unique (P5), and it pertains to its nature to exist (P7). Of its nature, therefore, it will exist either as finite or as infinite. But not as finite. For then (by D2) it would have to be limited by something else of the same nature, which would also have to exist necessarily (by P7), and so there would be two substances of the same attribute, which is absurd (by P5). Therefore, it exists as infinite, q.e.d.

Schol. 1: Since being finite is really, in part, a negation, and being infinite is an absolute affirmation of the existence of some nature, it follows from P7 alone that every substance must be infinite. [For if we assumed a finite substance, we would, in part, deny existence to its nature, which (by P7) is absurd.]

Schol. 2: I do not doubt that the demonstration of P7 will be difficult to conceive for all who judge things confusedly, and have not been accustomed to know things through their first causes—because they do not distinguish between the modifications of substances and the substances themselves, nor do they know how things are produced. So it happens that they fictitiously ascribe to substances the beginning which they see that natural things have; for those who do not know the true causes of things confuse everything and without any conflict of mind feign that both trees and men speak, imagine that men are formed both from stones and from seed, and that any form whatever is changed into any other. So also, those who confuse the divine nature with the human easily ascribe human affects to God, particularly so long as they are also ignorant of how those affects are produced in the mind.

But if men would attend to the nature of substance, they would have no doubt at all of the truth of P7. Indeed, this proposition would be an axiom for everyone, and would be numbered among the common notions. For by substance they would understand what is in itself and is conceived through itself, i.e., that the knowledge of which does not require the knowledge of any other thing. But by modifications they would understand what is in another, those things whose concept is formed from the concept of the thing in which they are.

This is how we can have true ideas of modifications which do not exist; for though they do not actually exist outside the intellect, nevertheless their essences are comprehended in another in such a way that they can be conceived through it. But the truth of substances is not outside the intellect unless it is in them themselves, because they are conceived through themselves.

Hence, if someone were to say that he had a clear and distinct, i.e., true, idea of a substance, and nevertheless doubted whether such a substance existed, that would indeed be the same as if he were to say that he had a true idea, and nevertheless doubted whether it was false (as is evident to anyone who is sufficiently attentive). Or if someone maintains that a substance is created, he maintains at the same time that a false idea has become true. Of course nothing more absurd can be conceived. So it must be confessed that the existence of a substance, like its essence, is an eternal truth.

And from this we can infer in another way that there is only one [substance] of the same nature,

which I have considered it worth the trouble of showing here. But to do this in order, it must be noted,

I. that the true definition of each thing neither involves nor expresses anything except the nature of the thing defined.

From which it follows,

II. that no definition involves or expresses any certain number of individuals,

since it expresses nothing other than the nature of the thing defined. E.g., the definition of the triangle expresses nothing but the simple nature of the triangle, but not any certain number of triangles. It is to be noted,

III. that there must be, for each existing thing, a certain cause on account of which it exists.

Finally, it is to be noted,

IV. that this cause, on account of which a thing exists, either must be contained in the very nature and definition of the existing thing (*viz. that it pertains to its nature to exist*) or must be outside it.

From these propositions it follows that if, in nature, a certain number of individuals exists, there must be a cause why those individuals, and why neither more nor fewer, exist.

For example, if 20 men exist in nature (*to make the matter clearer, I assume that they exist at the same time, and that no others previously existed in nature*), it will not be enough (i.e., *to give a reason why 20 men exist*) to show the cause of human nature in general; but it will be necessary in addition to show the cause why not more and not fewer than 20 exist. For (by III) there must necessarily be a cause why each [particular man] exists. But this cause (by II and III) cannot be contained in human nature itself, since the true definition of man does not involve the number 20. So (by IV) the cause why these 20 men exist, and consequently, why each of them exists, must necessarily be outside each of them.

For that reason it is to be inferred absolutely that whatever is of such a nature that there can be many individuals [of that nature] must, to exist, have an external cause to exist. Now since it pertains to the nature of a substance to exist (by what we have already shown in this Scholium), its definition must involve necessary existence, and consequently its existence must be inferred from its definition alone. But from its definition (as we have shown from II and III) the existence of a number of substances cannot follow. Therefore it follows necessarily from this, that there exists only one of the same nature, as was proposed.

P9:

The more reality or being each thing has, the more attributes belong to it.

Dem.: This is evident from D4.

P10:

Each attribute of a substance must be conceived through itself.

Dem.: For an attribute is what the intellect perceives concerning a substance, as constituting its essence (by D4); so (by D3) it must be conceived through itself, q.e.d.

Schol.: From these propositions it is evident that although two attributes may be conceived to be really distinct (i.e., one may be conceived without the aid of the other), we still can not infer from that that they constitute two beings, *or* two different substances. For it is of the nature of a substance that each of its attributes is conceived through itself, since all the attributes it has have always been in it together, and one could not be produced by another, but each expresses the reality, *or* being of substance.

So it is far from absurd to attribute many attributes to one substance. Indeed, nothing in nature is clearer than that each being must be conceived under some attribute, and the more reality, or being it has, the more it has attributes which express necessity, *or* eternity, and infinity. And consequently there is also nothing clearer than that a being absolutely infinite must be defined (as we taught in D6) as a being that consists of infinite attributes, each of which expresses a certain eternal and infinite essence.

But if someone now asks by what sign we shall be able to distinguish the diversity of substances, let him read the following propositions, which show that in Nature there exists only one substance, and that it is absolutely infinite. So that sign would be sought in vain.

P11:

God, or a substance consisting of infinite attributes, each of which expresses eternal and infinite essence, necessarily exists.

Dem.: If you deny this, conceive, if you can, that God does not exist. Therefore (by A7) his essence does not involve existence. But this (by P7) is absurd. Therefore God necessarily exists, q.e.d.

Alternatively: For each thing there must be assigned a cause, *or* reason, as much for its existence as for its nonexistence. For example, if a triangle exists, there must be a reason *or* cause why it exists; but if it does not exist, there must also be a reason *or* cause which prevents it from existing, *or* which takes its existence away.

But this reason, *or* cause, must either be contained in the nature of the thing, or be outside it. E.g., the very nature of a square circle indicates the reason why it does not exist, viz. because it involves a contradiction. On the other hand, the reason why a substance exists also follows from its nature alone, because it involves existence (see P7). But the reason why a circle or triangle exists, or why it does not exist, does not follow from the nature of these things, but from the order of the whole of corporeal Nature. For from this [order] it must follow either that the triangle necessarily exists now or that it is impossible for it to exist now.

These things are evident through themselves, but from them it follows that a thing necessarily exists if there is no reason or cause which prevents it from existing. Therefore, if there is no reason or cause which prevents God from existing, or which takes his existence away, it must certainly be inferred that he necessarily exists.

But if there were such a reason, *or* cause, it would have to be either in God's very nature or outside it, i.e., in another substance of another nature. For if it were of the same nature, that very supposition would concede that God exists. But a substance which was of another nature [than the divine] would have nothing in common with God (by P2), and therefore could neither give him existence nor take it away.

Since, then, there can be, outside the divine nature, no reason, *or* cause, which takes away the divine existence, the reason will necessarily have to be in his nature itself, if indeed he does not exist. That is, his nature would involve a contradiction [as in our second Example]. But it is absurd to affirm this of a Being absolutely infinite and supremely perfect. Therefore, there is no cause, *or* reason, either in God or outside God, which takes his existence away. And therefore, God necessarily exists, q.e.d.

Alternatively: To be able not to exist is to lack power, and conversely, to be able to exist is to have power (as is known through itself). So, if what now necessarily exists are only finite beings, then finite beings are more powerful than an absolutely infinite Being. But this, as is known through itself, is absurd. So, either nothing exists or an absolutely infinite Being also exists. But we exist, either in ourselves, or in something else, which necessarily exists (see A1 and P7). Therefore an absolutely infinite Being—i.e. (by D6), God—necessarily exists, q.e.d.

Schol.: In this last demonstration I wanted to show God's existence a posteriori, so that the demonstration would be perceived more easily— but not because God's existence does not follow a priori from the same foundation. For since being able to exist is power, it follows that the more reality belongs to the nature of a thing, the more powers it has, of itself, to exist. Therefore, an absolutely infinite Being, *or* God, has, of himself, an absolutely infinite power of existing. For that reason, he exists absolutely.

Still, there may be many who will not easily be able to see how evident this demonstration is, because they have been accustomed to contemplate only those things that flow from external causes. And of these, they see that those which quickly come to be, i.e., which easily exist, also easily perish. And conversely, they judge that those things to which they conceive more things to pertain are more difficult to do, i.e., that they do not exist so easily. But to free them from these prejudices, I have no need to show here in what manner this proposition—*what quickly comes to be, quickly perishes*—is true, nor whether or not all things are equally easy in respect to the whole of Nature. It is sufficient to note only this, that I am not here speaking of things that come to be from external causes, but only of substances that (by P6) can be produced by no external cause.

For things that come to be from external causes—whether they consist of many parts or of few—owe all the perfection or reality they have to the power of the external cause; and therefore their existence arises only from the perfection of their external cause, and not from their own perfection. On the other hand, whatever perfection substance has is not owed to any external cause. So its existence must follow from its nature alone; hence its existence is nothing but its essence.

Perfection, therefore, does not take away the existence of a thing, but on the contrary asserts it. But imperfection takes it away. So there is nothing of whose existence we can be more certain than we are of the existence of an absolutely infinite, *or* perfect, Being—i.e., God. For since his essence excludes all imperfection, and involves absolute perfection, by that very fact it takes away every cause of doubting his existence, and gives the greatest certainty concerning it. I believe this will be clear even to those who are only moderately attentive.

P12:
No attribute of a substance can be truly conceived from which it follows that the substance can be divided.

Dem.: For the parts into which a substance so conceived would be divided either will retain the nature of the substance or will not. If the first [viz. they retain the nature of the substance], then (by P8) each part will have to be infinite, and (by P7) its own cause, and (by P5) each part will have to consist of a different attribute. And so many substances will be able to be formed from one, which is absurd (by P6). Furthermore, the parts (by P2) would have nothing in common with their whole, and the whole (by D4 and P10) could both be and be conceived without its parts, which is absurd, as no one will be able to doubt.

But if the second is asserted, viz. that the parts will not retain the nature of substance, then since the whole substance would be divided into equal parts, it would lose the nature of substance, and would cease to be, which (by P7) is absurd.

P13:
A substance which is absolutely infinite is indivisible.

Dem.: For if it were divisible, the parts into which it would be divided will either retain the nature of an absolutely infinite substance or they will not. If the first, then there will be a number of substances of the same nature, which (by P5) is absurd. But if the second is asserted, then (as above [P12]), an absolutely infinite substance will be able to cease to be, which (by P11) is also absurd.

Cor.: From these [propositions] it follows that no substance, and consequently no corporeal substance, insofar as it is a substance, is divisible.

Schol.: That substance is indivisible, is understood more simply merely from this, that the nature of substance cannot be conceived unless as infinite, and that by a part of substance nothing can be understood except a finite substance, which (by P8) implies a plain contradiction.

P14:

Except God, no substance can be or be conceived.

Dem.: Since God is an absolutely infinite being, of whom no attribute which expresses an essence of substance can be denied (by D6), and he necessarily exists (by P11), if there were any substance except God, it would have to be explained through some attribute of God, and so two substances of the same attribute would exist, which (by P5) is absurd. And so except God, no substance can be or, consequently, be conceived. For if it could be conceived, it would have to be conceived as existing. But this (by the first part of this demonstration) is absurd. Therefore, except for God no substance can be or be conceived, q.e.d.

Cor. 1: From this it follows most clearly, first, that God is unique, i.e. (by D6), that in Nature there is only one substance, and that it is absolutely infinite (as we indicated in P10S).

Cor. 2: It follows, second, that an extended thing and a thinking thing are either attributes of God, or (by A1) affections of God's attributes.

P15:

Whatever is, is in God, and nothing can be or be conceived without God.

Dem.: Except for God, there neither is, nor can be conceived, any substance (by P14), i.e. (by D3), thing that is in itself and is conceived through itself. But modes (by D5) can neither be nor be conceived without substance. So they can be in the divine nature alone, and can be conceived through it alone. But except for substances and modes there is nothing (by A1). Therefore, [everything is in God and] nothing can be or be conceived without God, q.e.d.

Schol.: [I.] There are those who feign a God, like man, consisting of a body and a mind, and subject to passions. But how far they wander from the true knowledge of God, is sufficiently established by what has already been demonstrated. Them I dis-

miss. For everyone who has to any extent contemplated the divine nature denies that God is corporeal. They prove this best from the fact that by body we understand any quantity, with length, breadth, and depth, limited by some certain figure. Nothing more absurd than this can be said of God, viz. of a being absolutely infinite.

But meanwhile, by the other arguments by which they strive to demonstrate this same conclusion they clearly show that they entirely remove corporeal, *or* extended, substance itself from the divine nature. And they maintain that it has been created by God. But by what divine power could it be created? They are completely ignorant of that. And this shows clearly that they do not understand what they themselves say.

At any rate, I have demonstrated clearly enough—in my judgment, at least—that no substance can be produced or created by any other (see P6C and P8S2). Next, we have shown (P14) that except for God, no substance can either be or be conceived, and hence [in P14C2] we have concluded that extended substance is one of God's infinite attributes. But to provide a fuller explanation, I shall refute my opponents' arguments, which all reduce to these.

[II.] *First,* they think that corporeal substance, insofar as it is substance, consists of parts. And therefore they deny that it can be infinite, and consequently, that it can pertain to God. They explain this by many examples, of which I shall mention one or two.

[i] If corporeal substance is infinite, they say, let us conceive it to be divided in two parts. Each part will be either finite or infinite. If the former, then an infinite is composed of two finite parts, which is absurd. If the latter [i.e., if each part is infinite], then there is one infinite twice as large as another, which is also absurd. [ii] Again, if an infinite quantity is measured by parts [each] equal to a foot, it will consist of infinitely many such parts, as it will also, if it is measured by parts [each] equal to an inch. And therefore, one infinite number will be twelve times greater than another [which is no less absurd]. [iii] Finally, if we conceive that from one point of a certain infinite quantity two lines, say AB and AC, are extended to infinity, it is certain that, although in the beginning they are a certain, determinate distance apart, the distance between B and C is continuously increased, and at last, from being determinate, it

will become indeterminable. Since these absurdities follow—so they think—from the fact that an infinite quantity is supposed, they infer that corporeal substance must be finite, and consequently cannot pertain to God's essence.

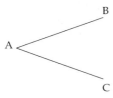

[III.] Their *second* argument is also drawn from God's supreme perfection. For God, they say, since he is a supremely perfect being, cannot be acted on. But corporeal substance, since it is divisible, can be acted on. It follows, therefore, that it does not pertain to God's essence.

[IV.] These are the arguments which I find authors using, to try to show that corporeal substance is unworthy of the divine nature, and cannot pertain to it. But anyone who is properly attentive will find that I have already replied to them, since these arguments are founded only on their supposition that corporeal substance is composed of parts, which I have already (P12 and P13C) shown to be absurd. And then anyone who wishes to consider the matter rightly will see that all those absurdities (*if indeed they are all absurd, which I am not now disputing*), from which they wish to infer that extended substance is finite, do not follow at all from the fact that an infinite quantity is supposed, but from the fact that they suppose an infinite quantity to be measurable and composed of finite parts. So from the absurdities which follow from that they can infer only that infinite quantity is not measurable, and that it is not composed of finite parts. This is the same thing we have already demonstrated above (P12, etc.). So the weapon they aim at us, they really turn against themselves.

If, therefore, they still wish to infer from this absurdity of theirs that extended substance must be finite, they are indeed doing nothing more than if someone feigned that a circle has the properties of a square, and inferred from that the circle has no center, from which all lines drawn to the circumference are equal. For corporeal substance, which cannot be conceived except as infinite, unique, and indivisible (see P8, 5 and 12), they conceive to be composed of finite parts, to be many, and to be divisible, in order to infer that it is finite.

So also others, after they feign that a line is composed of points, know how to invent many arguments, by which they show that a line cannot be divided to infinity. And indeed it is no less absurd to assert that corporeal substance is composed of bodies, *or* parts, than that a body is composed of surfaces, the surfaces of lines, and the lines, finally, of points.

All those who know that clear reason is infallible must confess this—particularly those who deny that there is a vacuum. For if corporeal substance could be so divided that its parts were really distinct, why, then, could one part not be annihilated, the rest remaining connected with one another as before? And why must they all be so fitted together that there is no vacuum? Truly, of things which are really distinct from one another, one can be, and remain in its condition, without the other. Since, therefore, there is no vacuum in nature (a subject I discuss elsewhere), but all its parts must so concur that there is no vacuum, it follows also that they cannot be really distinguished, i.e., that corporeal substance, insofar as it is a substance, cannot be divided.

[V.] If someone should now ask why we are, by nature, so inclined to divide quantity, I shall answer that we conceive quantity in two ways: abstractly, *or* superficially, as we [commonly] imagine it, or as substance, which is done by the intellect alone [without the help of the imagination]. So if we attend to quantity as it is in the imagination, which we do often and more easily, it will be found to be finite, divisible, and composed of parts; but if we attend to it as it is in the intellect, and conceive it insofar as it is a substance, which happens [seldom and] with great difficulty, then (as we have already sufficiently demonstrated) it will be found to be infinite, unique, and indivisible.

This will be sufficiently plain to everyone who knows how to distinguish between the intellect and the imagination—particularly if it is also noted that matter is everywhere the same, and that parts are distinguished in it only insofar as we conceive matter to be affected in different ways, so that its parts are distinguished only modally, but not really.

For example, we conceive that water is divided and its parts separated from one another—insofar as it is water, but not insofar as it is corporeal substance. For insofar as it is substance, it is neither separated nor divided. Again, water, insofar as it is water, is generated and corrupted, but insofar as it is substance, it is neither generated nor corrupted.

[VI.] And with this I think I have replied to the second argument also, since it is based on the supposition that matter, insofar as it is substance, is divisible, and composed of parts. Even if this [reply] were not [sufficient], I do not know why [divisibility] would be unworthy of the divine nature. For (by P14) apart from God there can be no substance by which [the divine nature] would be acted on. All things, I say, are in God, and all things that happen, happen only through the laws of God's infinite nature and follow (as I shall show) from the necessity of his essence. So it cannot be said in any way that God is acted on by another, or that extended substance is unworthy of the divine nature, even if it is supposed to be divisible, so long as it is granted to be eternal and infinite. But enough of this for the present.

P16:

From the necessity of the divine nature there must follow infinitely many things in infinitely many modes, (i.e., everything which can fall under an infinite intellect.)

Dem.: This Proposition must be plain to anyone, provided he attends to the fact that the intellect infers from the given definition of any thing a number of properties that really do follow necessarily from it (i.e., from the very essence of the thing); and that it infers more properties the more the definition of the thing expresses reality, i.e., the more reality the essence of the defined thing involves. But since the divine nature has absolutely infinite attributes (by D6), each of which also expresses an essence infinite in its own kind, from its necessity there must follow infinitely many things in infinite modes (i.e., everything which can fall under an infinite intellect), q.e.d.

Cor. 1: From this it follows that God is the efficient cause of all things which can fall under an infinite intellect.

Cor. 2: It follows, secondly, that God is a cause through himself and not an accidental cause.

Cor. 3: It follows, thirdly, that God is absolutely the first cause.

P17:

God acts from the laws of his nature alone, and is compelled by no one.

Dem.: We have just shown (P16) that from the necessity of the divine nature alone, or (what is the same thing) from the laws of his nature alone, absolutely infinite things follow, and in P15 we have demonstrated that nothing can be or be conceived without God, but that all things are in God. So there can be nothing outside him by which he is determined or compelled to act. Therefore, God acts from the laws of his nature alone, and is compelled by no one, q.e.d.

Cor. 1: From this it follows, first, that there is no cause, either extrinsically or intrinsically, which prompts God to action, except the perfection of his nature.

Cor. 2: It follows, secondly, that God alone is a free cause. For God alone exists only from the necessity of his nature (by P11 and P14C1), and acts from the necessity of his nature (by P17). Therefore (by D7) God alone is a free cause, q.e.d.

Schol.: [I.] Others think that God is a free cause because he can (so they think) bring it about that the things which we have said follow from his nature (i.e., which are in his power) do not happen or are not produced by him. But this is the same as if they were to say that God can bring it about that it would not follow from the nature of a triangle that its three angles are equal to two right angles; *or* that from a given cause the effect would not follow—which is absurd.

Further, I shall show later, without the aid of this Proposition, that neither intellect nor will pertain to God's nature. Of course I know there are many who think they can demonstrate that a supreme intellect and a free will pertain to God's nature. For they say they know nothing they can ascribe to God more perfect than what is the highest perfection in us.

Moreover, even if they conceive God to actually understand in the highest degree, they still do not believe that he can bring it about that all the things he actually understands exist. For they think that in that way they would destroy God's power. If he had created all the things in his intellect (they say), then he would have been able to create nothing more, which they believe to be incompatible with God's omnipotence. So they preferred to maintain that God is indifferent to all things, not creating anything except what he has decreed to create by some absolute will.

But I think I have shown clearly enough (see P16) that from God's supreme power, *or* infinite nature, infinitely many things in infinitely many modes, i.e., all things, have necessarily flowed, or always follow, by the same necessity and in the same way as from the nature of a triangle it follows, from eternity and to eternity, that its three angles are equal to two right angles. So God's omnipotence has been actual from eternity and will remain in the same actuality to eternity. And in this way, at least in my opinion, God's omnipotence is maintained far more perfectly.

Indeed—to speak openly—my opponents seem to deny God's omnipotence. For they are forced to confess that God understands infinitely many creatable things, which nevertheless he will never be able to create. For otherwise, if he created everything he understood [to be creatable] he would (according to them) exhaust his omnipotence and render himself imperfect. Therefore to maintain that God is perfect, they are driven to maintain at the same time that he cannot bring about everything to which his power extends. I do not see what could be feigned which would be more absurd than this or more contrary to God's omnipotence.

[II.] Further—to say something here also about the intellect and will which we commonly attribute to God—if will and intellect do pertain to the eternal essence of God, we must of course understand by each of these attributes something different from what men commonly understand. For the intellect and will which would constitute God's essence would have to differ entirely from our intellect and will, and could not agree with them in anything except the name. They would not agree with one another any more than do the dog that is a heavenly constellation and the dog that is a barking animal. I shall demonstrate this.

If intellect pertains to the divine nature, it will not be able to be (like our intellect) by nature either posterior to (as most would have it), or simultaneous with, the things understood, since God is prior in causality to all things (by P16C1). On the contrary, the truth and formal essence of things is what it is because it exists objectively in that way in God's intellect. So God's intellect, insofar as it is conceived to constitute God's essence, is really the cause both of the essence and of the existence of things. This

seems also to have been noticed by those who asserted that God's intellect, will and power are one and the same.

Therefore, since God's intellect is the only cause of things (viz. as we have shown, both of their essence and of their existence), he must necessarily differ from them both as to his essence and as to his existence. For what is caused differs from its cause precisely in what it has from the cause [for that reason it is called the effect of such a cause]. E.g., a man is the cause of the existence of another man, but not of his essence, for the latter is an eternal truth. Hence, they can agree entirely according to their essence. But in existing they must differ. And for that reason, if the existence of one perishes, the other's existence will not thereby perish. But if the essence of one could be destroyed, and become false, the other's essence would also be destroyed [and become false].

So the thing that is the cause both of the essence and of the existence of some effect, must differ from such an effect, both as to its essence and as to its existence. But God's intellect is the cause both of the essence and of the existence of our intellect. Therefore, God's intellect, insofar as it is conceived to constitute the divine essence, differs from our intellect both as to its essence and as to its existence, and cannot agree with it in anything except in name, as we supposed. The proof proceeds in the same way concerning the will, as anyone can easily see.

P18:
God is the immanent, not the transitive, cause of all things.

Dem.: Everything that is, is in God, and must be conceived through God (by P15), and so (by P16C1) God is the cause of [all] things, which are in him. That is the first [thing to be proven]. And then outside God there can be no substance (by P14), i.e. (by D3), thing which is in itself outside God. That was the second. God, therefore, is the immanent, not the transitive cause of all things, q.e.d.

P19:
God is eternal, or all God's attributes are eternal.

Dem.: For God (by D6) is substance, which (by P11) necessarily exists, i.e. (by P7), to whose nature it pertains to exist, or (what is the same) from whose definition it follows that he exists; and therefore (by D8), he is eternal.

Next, by God's attributes are to be understood what (by D4) expresses an essence of the Divine substance, i.e., what pertains to substance. The attributes themselves, I say, must involve it itself. But eternity pertains to the nature of substance (as I have already demonstrated from P7). Therefore each of the attributes must involve eternity, and so, they are all eternal, q.e.d.

Schol.: This Proposition is also as clear as possible from the way I have demonstrated God's existence (P11). For from that demonstration, I say, it is established that God's existence, like his essence, is an eternal truth. And then I have also demonstrated God's eternity in another way (*Descartes' Principles* IP19), and there is no need to repeat it here.

P20:

God's existence and his essence are one and the same.

Dem.: God (by P19) and all of his attributes are eternal, i.e. (by D8), each of his attributes expresses existence. Therefore, the same attributes of God which (by D4) explain God's eternal essence at the same time explain his eternal existence, i.e., that itself which constitutes God's essence at the same time constitutes his existence. So his existence and his essence are one and the same, q.e.d.

Cor. 1: From this it follows, first, that God's existence, like his essence, is an eternal truth.

Cor. 2: It follows, secondly, that God, *or* all of God's attributes, are immutable. For if they changed as to their existence, they would also (by P20) change as to their essence, i.e. (as is known through itself), from being true become false, which is absurd.

P21:

All the things which follow from the absolute nature of any of God's attributes have always had to exist and be infinite, or are, through the same attribute, eternal and infinite.

Dem.: If you deny this, then conceive (if you can) that in some attribute of God there follows from its absolute nature something that is finite and has a determinate existence, *or* duration, e.g., God's idea in thought. Now since thought is supposed to be an attribute of God, it is necessarily (by P11) infinite by its nature. But insofar as it has God's idea, [thought] is supposed to be finite. But (by D2) [thought] cannot be conceived to be finite unless it is determined through thought itself. But [thought can] not [be determined] through thought itself, insofar as it constitutes God's idea, for to that ex-

tent [thought] is supposed to be finite. Therefore, [thought must be determined] through thought insofar as it does not constitute God's idea, which [thought] nevertheless (by P11) must necessarily exist. Therefore, there is thought which does not constitute God's idea, and on that account God's idea does not follow necessarily from the nature [of this thought] insofar as it is absolute thought (for [thought] is conceived both as constituting God's idea and as not constituting it). [That God's idea does not follow from thought, insofar as it is absolute thought] is contrary to the hypothesis. So if God's idea in thought, or anything else in any attribute of God (for it does not matter what example is taken, since the demonstration is universal), follows from the necessity of the absolute nature of the attribute itself, it must necessarily be infinite. This was the first thing to be proven.

Next, what follows in this way from the necessity of the nature of any attribute cannot have a determinate [existence, *or*] duration. For if you deny this, then suppose there is, in some attribute of God, a thing which follows from the necessity of the nature of that attribute—e.g., God's idea in thought—and suppose that at some time [this idea] did not exist or will not exist. But since thought is supposed to be an attribute of God, it must exist necessarily and be immutable (by P11 and P20C2). So beyond the limits of the duration of God's idea (for it is supposed that at some time [this idea] did not exist or will not exist) thought will have to exist without God's idea. But this is contrary to the hypothesis, for it is supposed that God's idea follows necessarily from the given thought. Therefore, God's idea in thought, or anything else which follows necessarily from the absolute nature of some attribute of God, cannot have a determinate duration, but through the same attribute is eternal. This was the second thing [to be proven]. Note that the same is to be affirmed of any thing which, in some attribute of God, follows necessarily from God's absolute nature.

P22:

Whatever follows from some attribute of God insofar as it is modified by a modification which, through the same attribute, exists necessarily and is infinite, must also exist necessarily and be infinite.

Dem.: The demonstration of this proposition proceeds in the same way as the demonstration of the preceding one.

P23:

Every mode which exists necessarily and is infinite has necessarily had to follow either from the absolute nature of some attribute of God, or from some attribute, modified by a modification which exists necessarily and is infinite.

Dem.: For a mode is in another, through which it must be conceived (by D5), i.e. (by P15), it is in God alone, and can be conceived through God alone. So if a mode is conceived to exist necessarily and be infinite, [its necessary existence and infinitude] must necessarily be inferred, *or* perceived through some attribute of God, insofar as that attribute is conceived to express infinity and necessity of existence, *or* (what is the same, by D8) eternity, i.e. (by D6 and P19), insofar as it is considered absolutely. Therefore, the mode, which exists necessarily and is infinite, has had to follow from the absolute nature of some attribute of God—either immediately (see P21) or by some mediating modification, which follows from its absolute nature, i.e. (by P22), which exists necessarily and is infinite, q.e.d.

P24:

The essence of things produced by God does not involve existence.

Dem.: This is evident from D1. For that whose nature involves existence (considered in itself), is its own cause, and exists only from the necessity of its nature.

Cor.: From this it follows that God is not only the cause of things' beginning to exist, but also of their persevering in existing, *or* (to use a Scholastic term) God is the cause of the being of things. For— whether the things [produced] exist or not so long as we attend to their essence, we shall find that it involves neither existence nor duration. So their essence can be the cause neither of their existence nor of their duration, but only God, to whose nature alone it pertains to exist [,can be the cause] (by P14C1).

P25:

God is the efficient cause, not only of the existence of things, but also of their essence.

Dem.: If you deny this, then God is not the cause of the essence of things; and so (by A4) the essence of things can be conceived without God. But (by P15) this is absurd. Therefore God is also the cause of the essence of things, q.e.d.

Schol.: This Proposition follows more clearly from P16. For from that it follows that from the given divine nature both the essence of things and their existence must necessarily be inferred; and in a word, God must be called the cause of all things in the same sense in which he is called the cause of himself. This will be established still more clearly from the following corollary.

Cor.: Particular things are nothing but affections of God's attributes, *or* modes by which God's attributes are expressed in a certain and determinate way. The demonstration is evident from P15 and D5.

P26:

A thing which has been determined to produce an effect has necessarily been determined in this way by God; and one which has not been determined by God cannot determine itself to produce an effect.

Dem.: That through which things are said to be determined to produce an effect must be something positive (as is known through itself). And so, God, from the necessity of his nature, is the efficient cause both of its essence and of its existence (by P25 & 16); this was the first thing. And from it the second thing asserted also follows very clearly. For if a thing which has not been determined by God could determine itself, the first part of this [proposition] would be false, which is absurd, as we have shown.

P27:

A thing which has been determined by God to produce an effect, cannot render itself undetermined.

Dem.: This proposition is evident from A3.

P28:

Every singular thing, or any thing which is finite and has a determinate existence, can neither exist nor be determined to produce an effect unless it is determined to exist and produce an effect by another cause, which is also finite and has a determinate existence; and again, this cause also can neither exist nor be determined to produce an effect unless it is determined to exist and produce an effect by another, which is also finite and has a determinate existence, and so on, to infinity.

Dem.: Whatever has been determined to exist and produce an effect has been so determined by God (by P26 and P24C). But what is finite and has a determinate existence could not have been produced by the absolute nature of an attribute of God; for whatever follows from the absolute nature of an attribute of God is eternal and infinite (by P21). It had, therefore, to follow either from God or from an attribute of God insofar as it is considered to be affected by some mode. For there is nothing except substance and its modes (by A1, D3, and D5) and modes (by P25C) are nothing but affections of God's attributes. But it also could not follow from God, or from an attribute of God, insofar as it is affected by a modification which is eternal and infinite (by P22). It had, therefore, to follow from, or be determined to exist and produce an effect by God or an attribute of God insofar as it is modified by a modification which is finite and has a determinate existence. This was the first thing to be proven.

And in turn, this cause, *or* this mode (by the same reasoning by which we have already demonstrated the first part of this proposition) had also to be determined by another, which is also finite and has a determinate existence; and again, this last (by the same reasoning) by another, and so always (by the same reasoning) to infinity, q.e.d.

Schol.: Since certain things had to be produced by God immediately, viz. those which follow necessarily from his absolute nature, and others (which nevertheless can neither be nor be conceived without God) had to be produced by the mediation of these first things, it follows:

I. That God is absolutely the proximate cause of the things produced immediately by him, and not [a proximate cause] in his own kind, as they say. For God's effects can neither be nor be conceived without their cause (by P15 and P24C).

II. That God cannot properly be called the remote cause of singular things, except perhaps so that we may distinguish them from those things that he has produced immediately, or rather, that follow from his absolute nature. For by a remote cause we understand one which is not conjoined in any way with its effect. But all things that are, are in God, and so depend on God that they can neither be nor be conceived without him.

P29:

In nature there is nothing contingent, but all things have been determined from the necessity of the divine nature to exist and produce an effect in a certain way.

Dem.: Whatever is, is in God (by P15); but God cannot be called a contingent thing. For (by P11) he exists necessarily, not contingently. Next, the modes of the divine nature have also followed from it necessarily and not contingently (by P16)—either insofar as the divine nature is considered absolutely

(by P21) or insofar as it is considered to be determined to act in a certain way (by P28). Further, God is the cause of these modes not only insofar as they simply exist (by P24C), but also (by P26) insofar as they are considered to be determined to produce an effect. For if they have not been determined by God, then (by P26) it is impossible, not contingent, that they should determine themselves. Conversely (by P27) if they have been determined by God, it is not contingent, but impossible, that they should render themselves undetermined. So all things have been determined from the necessity of the divine nature, not only to exist, but to exist in a certain way, and to produce effects in a certain way. There is nothing contingent, q.e.d.

Schol.: Before I proceed further, I wish to explain here—or rather to advise [the reader]—what we must understand by *Natura naturans* and *Natura naturata*. For from the preceding I think it is already established that by *Natura naturans* we must understand what is in itself and is conceived through itself, *or* such attributes of substance as express an eternal and infinite essence, i.e. (by P14C1 and P17C2), God, insofar as he is considered as a free cause.

But by *Natura naturata* I understand whatever follows from the necessity of God's nature, *or* from any of God's attributes, i.e., all the modes of God's attributes insofar as they are considered as things which are in God, and can neither be nor be conceived without God.

P30:

An actual intellect, whether finite or infinite, must comprehend God's attributes and God's affections, and nothing else.

Dem.: A true idea must agree with its object (by A6), i.e. (as is known through itself), what is contained objectively in the intellect must necessarily be in nature. But in nature (by P14C1) there is only one substance, viz. God, and there are no affections other than those which are in God (by P15) and which can neither be nor be conceived without God (by P15). Therefore, an actual intellect, whether finite or infinite, must comprehend God's attributes and God's affections, and nothing else, q.e.d.

P31:

The actual intellect, whether finite or infinite, like will, desire, love, etc., must be referred to Natura naturata, *not to* Natura naturans.

Dem.: By intellect (as is known through itself) we understand not absolute thought, but only a certain mode of thinking, which mode differs from the others, such as desire, love, etc., and so (by D5) must be conceived through absolute thought, i.e. (by P15 and D6), it must be so conceived through an attribute of God, which expresses the eternal and infinite essence of thought, that can neither be nor be conceived without [that attribute]; and so (by P29S), like the other modes of thinking, it must be referred to *Natura naturata*, not to *Natura naturans*, q.e.d.

Schol.: The reason why I speak here of actual intellect is not because I concede that there is any potential intellect, but because, wishing to avoid all confusion, I wanted to speak only of what we perceive as clearly as possible, i.e., of the intellection itself. We perceive nothing more clearly than that. For we can understand nothing that does not lead to more perfect knowledge of the intellection.

P32:

The will cannot be called a free cause, but only a necessary one.

Dem.: The will, like the intellect, is only a certain mode of thinking. And so (by P28) each volition can neither exist nor be determined to produce an effect unless it is determined by another cause, and this cause again by another, and so on, to infinity. Even if the will be supposed to be infinite, it must still be determined to exist and produce an effect by God, not insofar as he is an absolutely infinite substance, but insofar as he has an attribute that expresses the infinite and eternal essence of thought (by P23). So in whatever way it is conceived, whether as finite or as infinite, it requires a cause by which it is determined to exist and produce an effect. And so (by D7) it cannot be called a free cause, but only a necessary or compelled one, q.e.d.

Cor. 1: From this it follows, first, that God does not produce any effect by freedom of the will.

Cor. 2: It follows, secondly, that will and intellect are related to God's nature as motion and rest are, and as are absolutely all natural things, which (by P29) must be determined by God to exist and produce an effect in a certain way. For the will, like all other things, requires a cause by which it is determined to exist and produce an effect in a certain way. And although from a given will, *or* intellect infinitely many things may follow, God still cannot be said, on that account, to act from freedom of the will, any more than he can be said to act from freedom of motion and rest on account of those things that follow from motion and rest (for infinitely many things also follow from motion and rest). So will does not pertain to God's nature any more than do the other natural things, but is related to him in the same way as motion and rest, and all the other things which, as we have shown, follow from the necessity of the divine nature and are determined by it to exist and produce an effect in a certain way.

P33:

Things could have been produced by God in no other way, and in no other order than they have been produced.

Dem.: For all things have necessarily followed from God's given nature (by P16), and have been determined from the necessity of God's nature to exist and produce an effect in a certain way (by P29). Therefore, if things could have been of another nature, or could have been determined to produce an effect in another way, so that the order of Nature was different, then God's nature could also have been other than it is now, and therefore (by P11) that [other nature] would also have had to exist, and consequently, there could have been two or more Gods, which is absurd (by P14C1). So things could have been produced in no other way and no other order, etc., q.e.d.

Schol. 1: Since by these propositions I have shown more clearly than the noon light that there is absolutely nothing in things on account of which they can be called contingent, I wish now to explain briefly what we must understand by contingent— but first, what [we must understand] by necessary and impossible.

A thing is called necessary either by reason of its essence or by reason of its cause. For a thing's existence follows necessarily either from its essence and definition or from a given efficient cause. And a thing is also called impossible from these same causes—viz. either because its essence, *or* definition, involves a contradiction, or because there is no external cause which has been determined to produce such a thing.

But a thing is called contingent only because of a defect of our knowledge. For if we do not know that the thing's essence involves a contradiction, or if we do know very well that its essence does not involve a contradiction, and nevertheless can affirm nothing certainly about its existence, because the order of causes is hidden from us, it can never seem to us either necessary or impossible. So we call it contingent or possible.

Schol. 2: From the preceding it clearly follows that things have been produced by God with the highest perfection, since they have followed necessarily from a given most perfect nature. Nor does this convict God of any imperfection, for his perfection compels us to affirm this. Indeed, from the opposite, it would clearly follow (as I have just shown), that God is not supremely perfect; because if things had been produced by God in another way, we would have to attribute to God another nature, different from that which we have been compelled to attribute to him from the consideration of the most perfect Being.

Of course, I have no doubt that many will reject this opinion as absurd, without even being willing to examine it—for no other reason than because they have been accustomed to attribute another freedom to God, far different from that we have taught (D7), viz. an absolute will. But I also have no doubt that, if they are willing to reflect on the matter, and consider properly the chain of our demonstrations, in the end they will utterly reject the freedom they now attribute to God, not only as futile, but as a great obstacle to science. Nor is it necessary for me to repeat here what I said in P17S.

Nevertheless, to please them, I shall show that even if it is conceded that will pertains to God's essence, it still follows from his perfection that things could have been created by God in no other way or order. It will be easy to show this if we consider, first, what they themselves concede, viz. that it depends on God's decree and will alone that each thing is what it is. For otherwise God would not be the cause of all things. Next, that all God's decrees have been established by God himself from eternity. For otherwise he would be convicted of imperfection and inconstancy. But since, in eternity, there is neither *when,* nor *before,* nor *after,* it follows, from God's perfection alone, that he can never decree anything different, and never could have, *or* that God was not before his decrees, and cannot be without them.

But they will say that even if it were supposed that God had made another nature of things, or that from eternity he had decreed something else concerning nature and its order, no imperfection in God would follow from that.

Still, if they say this, they will concede at the same time that God can change his decrees. For if God had decreed, concerning nature and its order, something other than what he did decree, i.e., had willed and conceived something else concerning nature, he would necessarily have had an intellect other than he now has, and a will other than he now has. And if it is permitted to attribute to God another intellect and another will, without any change of his essence and of his perfection, why can he not now change his decrees concerning created things, and nevertheless remain equally perfect? For his intellect and will concerning created things and their order are the same in respect to his essence and his perfection, however his will and intellect may be conceived.

Further, all the Philosophers I have seen concede that in God there is no potential intellect, but only an actual one. But since his intellect and his will are not distinguished from his essence, as they all also concede, it follows that if God had had another actual intellect, and another will, his essence would also necessarily be other. And therefore (as I inferred at the beginning) if things had been produced by God otherwise than they now are, God's intellect and his will, i.e. (as is conceded), his essence, would have to be different [from what it now is]. And this is absurd.

Therefore, since things could have been produced by God in no other way, and no other order, and since it follows from God's supreme perfection that this is true, no truly sound reason can persuade us to believe that God did not will to create all the things that are in his intellect, with that same perfection with which he understands them.

But they will say that there is no perfection or imperfection in things; what is in them, on account of which they are perfect or imperfect, and are called good or bad, depends only on God's will. And so, if God had willed, he could have brought it about that what is now perfection would have been the greatest imperfection, and conversely [that what is now an imperfection in things would have been the most perfect]. How would this be different from saying openly that God, who necessarily understands what he wills, can bring it about by his will that he understands things in another way than he does understand them? As I have just shown, this is a great absurdity.

So I can turn the argument against them in the following way. All things depend on God's power. So in order for things to be able to be different, God's will would necessarily also have to be different. But God's will cannot be different (as we have just shown most evidently from God's perfection). So things also cannot be different.

I confess that this opinion, which subjects all things to a certain indifferent will of God, and makes all things depend on his good pleasure, is nearer the truth than that of those who maintain that God does all things for the sake of the good. For they seem to place something outside God, which does not depend on God, to which God attends, as a model, in what he does, and at which he aims, as at a certain goal. This is simply to subject God to fate. Nothing more absurd can be maintained about God, whom we have shown to be the first and only free cause, both of the essence of all things, and of their existence. So I shall waste no time in refuting this absurdity.

P34:

God's power is his essence itself.

Dem.: For from the necessity alone of God's essence it follows that God is the cause of himself (by P11) and (by P16 and P16C) of all things. Therefore, God's power, by which he and all things are and act, is his essence itself, q.e.d.

P35:

Whatever we conceive to be in God's power, necessarily exists.

Dem.: For whatever is in God's power must (by P34) be so comprehended by his essence that it necessarily follows from it, and therefore necessarily exists, q.e.d.

P36:

Nothing exists from whose nature some effect does not follow.

Dem.: Whatever exists expresses the nature, *or* essence of God in a certain and determinate way (by P25C), i.e. (by P34), whatever exists expresses in a certain and determinate way the power of God, which is the cause of all things. So (by P16), from [everything that exists] some effect must follow, q.e.d.

Appendix

With these [demonstrations] I have explained God's nature and properties: that he exists necessarily; that he is unique; that he is and acts from the necessity alone of his nature; that (and how) he is the free cause of all things; that all things are in God and so depend on him that without him they can neither be nor be conceived; and finally, that all things have been predetermined by God, not from freedom of the will *or* absolute good pleasure, but from God's absolute nature, *or* infinite power.

Further, I have taken care, whenever the occasion arose, to remove prejudices that could prevent my demonstrations from being perceived. But because many prejudices remain that could, and can, be a great obstacle to men's understanding the connection of things in the way I have explained it, I considered it worthwhile to submit them here to the scrutiny of reason. All the prejudices I here undertake to expose depend on this one: that men commonly suppose that all natural things act, as men do, on account of an end; indeed, they maintain as certain that God himself directs all things to some certain end, for they say that God has made all things for man, and man that he might worship God.

So I shall begin by considering this one prejudice, asking *first* [I] why most people are satisfied that it is true, and why all are so inclined by nature to embrace it. *Then* [II] I shall show its falsity, and *finally* [III] how, from this, prejudices have arisen concerning *good* and *evil, merit* and *sin, praise* and *blame, order* and *confusion, beauty* and *ugliness,* and other things of this kind.

[I.] Of course this is not the place to deduce these things from the nature of the human mind. It will be sufficient here if I take as a foundation what everyone must acknowledge: that all men are born ignorant of the causes of things, and that they all want to seek their own advantage, and are conscious of this appetite.

From these [assumptions] it follows, *first,* that men think themselves free, because they are conscious of their volitions and their appetite, and do not think, even in their dreams, of the causes by which they are disposed to wanting and willing, because they are ignorant of [those causes]. It follows, *secondly,* that men act always on account of an end, viz. on account of their advantage, which they want. Hence they seek to know only the final causes of what has been done, and when they have heard them, they are satisfied, because they have no reason to doubt further. But if they cannot hear them from another, nothing remains for them but to turn toward themselves, and reflect on the ends by which they are usually determined to do such things; so they necessarily judge the temperament of other men from their own temperament.

Furthermore, they find—both in themselves and outside themselves—many means that are very helpful in seeking their own advantage, e.g., eyes for seeing, teeth for chewing, plants and animals for food, the sun for light, the sea for supporting fish [and so with almost all other things whose natural causes they have no reason to doubt]. Hence, they consider all natural things as means to their own advantage. And knowing that they had found these means, not provided them for themselves, they had reason to believe that there was someone else who had prepared those means for their use. For after they considered things as means, they could not believe that the things had made themselves; but from the means they were accustomed to prepare for themselves, they had to infer that there was a ruler, or a number of rulers of nature, endowed with human freedom, who had taken care of all things for them, and made all things for their use.

And since they had never heard anything about the temperament of these rulers, they had to judge it from their own. Hence, they maintained that the Gods direct all things for the use of men in order to bind men to them and be held by men in the highest honor. So it has happened that each of them has thought up from his own temperament different ways of worshipping God, so that God might love them above all the rest, and direct the whole of Nature according to the needs of their blind desire and insatiable greed. Thus this prejudice was changed into superstition, and struck deep roots in their minds. This was why each of them strove with great diligence to understand and explain the final causes of all things.

But while they sought to show that nature does nothing in vain (i.e., nothing which is not of use to men), they seem to have shown only that nature and the Gods are as mad as men. See, I ask you, how the matter has turned out in the end! Among so many conveniences in nature they had to find many inconveniences: storms, earthquakes, diseases, etc. These, they maintain, happen because the Gods [(whom they judge to be of the same nature as themselves)] are angry on account of wrongs done to them by men, *or* on account of sins committed in their worship. And though their daily experience contradicted this, and though infinitely many examples showed that conveniences and inconveniences happen indiscriminately to the pious and the impious alike, they did not on that account give up their long-standing prejudice. It was easier for them to put this among the other unknown things, whose use they were ignorant of, and so remain in the state of ignorance in which they had been born, than to destroy that whole construction, and think up a new one.

So they maintained it as certain that the judgments of the Gods far surpass man's grasp. This alone, of course, would have caused the truth to be hidden from the human race to eternity, if Mathematics, which is concerned not with ends, but only with the essences and properties of figures, had not shown men another standard of truth. And besides Mathematics, we can assign other causes also (which it is unnecessary to enumerate here), which were able to bring it about that men [—but very few, in relation to the whole human race—] would notice these common prejudices and be led to the true knowledge of things.

[II.] With this I have sufficiently explained what I promised in the first place [viz. why men are so inclined to believe that all things act for an end]. Not many words will be required now to show that Nature has no end set before it, and that all final causes are nothing but human fictions. For I believe I have already sufficiently established it, both by the foundations and causes from which I have shown this prejudice to have had its origin, and also by P16, P32C1 and C2, and all those [propositions] by which I have shown that all things proceed by a certain eternal necessity of nature, and with the greatest perfection.

I shall, however, add this: this doctrine concerning the end turns nature completely upside down. For what is really a cause, it considers as an effect, and conversely [what is an effect it considers as a cause]. What is by nature prior, it makes posterior. And finally, what is supreme and most perfect, it makes imperfect.

For—to pass over the first two, since they are manifest through themselves—as has been established in PP21–23, that effect is most perfect which is produced immediately by God, and the more something requires intermediate causes to produce it, the more imperfect it is. But if the things which have been produced immediately by God had been made so that God would achieve his end, then the last things, for the sake of which the first would have been made, would be the most excellent of all.

Again, this doctrine takes away God's perfection. For if God acts for the sake of an end, he necessarily wants something which he lacks. And though the Theologians and Metaphysicians distinguish between an end of need and an end of assimilation, they nevertheless confess that God did all things for his own sake, not for the sake of the things to be created. For before creation they can assign nothing except God for whose sake God would act. And so they are necessarily compelled to confess that God lacked those things for the sake of which he willed to prepare means, and that he desired them. This is clear through itself.

Nor ought we here to pass over the fact that the Followers of this doctrine, who have wanted to show off their cleverness in assigning the ends of things, have introduced—to prove this doctrine of theirs—a new way of arguing: by reducing things, not to the impossible, but to ignorance. This shows that no other way of defending their doctrine was open to them.

For example, if a stone has fallen from a roof onto someone's head and killed him, they will show, in the following way, that the stone fell in order to kill the man. For if it did not fall to that end, God willing it, how could so many circumstances have concurred by chance (for often many circumstances do concur at once)? Perhaps you will answer that it happened because the wind was blowing hard and the man was walking that way. But they will persist: why was the wind blowing hard at that time? why was the man walking that way at that same time? If you answer again that the wind arose then because on the preceding day, while the weather was still calm, the sea began to toss, and that the man had

been invited by a friend, they will press on—for there is no end to the questions which can be asked: but why was the sea tossing? why was the man invited at just that time? And so they will not stop asking for the causes of causes until you take refuge in the will of God, i.e., the sanctuary of ignorance.

Similarly, when they see the structure of the human body, they are struck by a foolish wonder, and because they do not know the causes of so great an art, they infer that it is constructed, not by mechanical, but by divine, or supernatural art, and constituted in such a way that one part does not injure another.

Hence it happens that one who seeks the true causes of miracles, and is eager, like an educated man, to understand natural things, not to wonder at them, like a fool, is generally considered and denounced as an impious heretic by those whom the people honor as interpreters of nature and the Gods. For they know that if ignorance is taken away, then foolish wonder, the only means they have of arguing and defending their authority, is also taken away. But I leave these things, and pass on to what I have decided to treat here in the *third* place.

[III.] After men persuaded themselves that everything that happens, happens on their account, they had to judge that what is most important in each thing is what is most useful to them, and to rate as most excellent all those things by which they were most pleased. Hence, they had to form these notions, by which they explained natural things: *good, evil, order, confusion, warm, cold, beauty, ugliness.* And because they think themselves free, those notions have arisen: *praise* and *blame, sin* and *merit.* The latter I shall explain after I have treated human nature; but the former I shall briefly explain here.

Whatever conduces to health and the worship of God, they have called *good;* but what is contrary to these, *evil.*

And because those who do not understand the nature of things, but only imagine them, affirm nothing concerning things, and take the imagination for the intellect, they firmly believe, in their ignorance of things and of their own nature, that there is an order in things. For when things are so disposed that, when they are presented to us through the senses, we can easily imagine them, and so can easily remember them, we say that they are well-ordered; but if the opposite is true, we say that they are badly ordered, or confused.

And since those things we can easily imagine are especially pleasing to us, men prefer order to confusion, as if order were anything in nature more than a relation to our imagination. They also say that God has created all things in order, and so, unknowingly attribute imagination to God—unless, perhaps, they mean that God, to provide for human imagination, has disposed all things so that men can very easily imagine them. Nor will it, perhaps, give them pause that infinitely many things are found which far surpass our imagination, and a great many which confuse it on account of its weakness. But enough of this.

The other notions are also nothing but modes of imagining, by which the imagination is variously affected; and yet the ignorant consider them the chief attributes of things, because, as we have already said, they believe all things have been made for their sake, and call the nature of a thing good or evil, sound or rotten and corrupt, as they are affected by it. For example, if the motion the nerves receive from objects presented through the eyes is conducive to health, the objects by which it is caused are called beautiful; those which cause a contrary motion are called ugly. Those which move the sense through the nose, they call pleasant-smelling or stinking; through the tongue, sweet or bitter, tasty or tasteless; through touch, hard or soft, rough or smooth, etc.; and finally, those which move the ears are said to produce noise, sound or harmony. Men have been so mad as to believe that God is pleased by harmony. Indeed there are Philosophers who have persuaded themselves that the motions of the heavens produce a harmony.

All of these things show sufficiently that each one has judged things according to the disposition of his brain; or rather, has accepted affections of the imagination as things. So it is no wonder (to note this, too, in passing) that we find so many controversies to have arisen among men, and that they have finally given rise to Skepticism. For although human bodies agree in many things, they still differ in very many. And for that reason what seems good to one, seems bad to another; what seems ordered to one, seems confused to another; what seems pleasing to one, seems displeasing to another, and so on.

I pass over the [other notions] here, both because this is not the place to treat them at length, and because everyone has experienced this [variability] sufficiently for himself. That is why we have such sayings as "So many heads, so many attitudes," "everyone finds his own judgment more than enough," and "there are as many differences of brains as of palates." These proverbs show sufficiently that men judge things according to the disposition of their brain, and imagine, rather than understand them. For if men had understood them, the things would at least convince them all, even if they did not attract them all, as the example of mathematics shows.

We see, therefore, that all the notions by which ordinary people are accustomed to explain nature are only modes of imagining, and do not indicate the nature of anything, only the constitution of the imagination. And because they have names, as if they were [notions] of beings existing outside the imagination, I call them beings, not of reason, but of imagination. So all the arguments in which people try to use such notions against us can easily be warded off.

For many are accustomed to arguing in this way: if all things have followed from the necessity of God's most perfect nature, why are there so many imperfections in nature? why are things corrupt to the point where they stink? so ugly that they produce nausea? why is there confusion, evil, and sin?

As I have just said, those who argue in this way are easily answered. For the perfection of things is to be judged solely from their nature and power; things are not more or less perfect because they please or offend men's senses, or because they are of use to, or are incompatible with, human nature.

But to those who ask "why God did not create all men so that they would be governed by the command of reason?" I answer only "because he did not lack material to create all things, from the highest degree of perfection to the lowest;" or, to speak more properly, "because the laws of his nature have been so ample that they sufficed for producing all things which can be conceived by an infinite intellect" (as I have demonstrated in P16).

These are the prejudices I undertook to note here. If any of this kind still remain, they can be corrected by anyone with only a little meditation. [And so I find no reason to devote more time to these matters, etc.]

Second Part of the Ethics. On the Nature and Origin of the Mind

I pass now to explaining those things which must necessarily follow from the essence of God, or the infinite and eternal Being—not, indeed, all of them, for we have demonstrated (IP16) that infinitely many things must follow from it in infinitely many modes, but only those that can lead us, by the hand, as it were, to the knowledge of the human Mind and its highest blessedness.

Definitions

D1:
By body I understand a mode that in a certain and determinate way expresses God's essence insofar as he is considered as an extended thing (see IP25C).

D2:
I say that to the essence of any thing belongs that which, being given, the thing is [also] necessarily posited and which, being taken away, the thing is necessarily [also] taken away; or that without which the thing can neither be nor be conceived, and which can neither be nor be conceived without the thing.

D3:
By idea I understand a concept of the Mind that the Mind forms because it is a thinking thing.

Exp.: *I say concept rather than perception, because the word perception seems to indicate that the Mind is acted on by the object. But concept seems to express an action of the Mind.*

D4:
By adequate idea I understand an idea which, insofar as it is considered in itself, without relation to an object, has all the properties, *or* intrinsic denominations of a true idea.

Exp.: *I say intrinsic to exclude what is extrinsic, viz. the agreement of the idea with its object.*

D5:
Duration is an indefinite continuation of existing.

Exp.: *I say indefinite because it cannot be determined at all through the very nature of the existing thing, nor even by the efficient cause, which necessarily posits the existence of the thing, and does not take it away.*

D6:
By reality and perfection I understand the same thing.

D7:
By singular things I understand things that are finite and have a determinate existence. And if a number of Individuals so concur in one action that together they are all the cause of one effect, I consider them all, to that extent, as one singular thing.

Axioms

A1:
The essence of man does not involve necessary existence, i.e., from the order of nature it can happen equally that this or that man does exist, or that he does not exist.

A2:
Man thinks.

A3:
There are no modes of thinking, such as love, desire, or whatever is designated by the word affects of the mind, unless there is in the same Individual the idea of the thing loved, desired, etc. But there can be an idea, even though there is no other mode of thinking.

A4:
We feel that a certain body is affected in many ways.

A5:
We neither feel nor perceive any singular things [or anything of *natura naturata*], except bodies and modes of thinking.
See the postulates after P13.

P1:
Thought is an attribute of God, or God is a thinking thing.

Dem.: Singular thoughts, *or* this or that thought, are modes that express God's nature in a certain and determinate way (by IP25C). Therefore (by ID5) there belongs to God an attribute whose concept all singular thoughts involve, and through which they are also conceived. Therefore, Thought is one of God's infinite attributes, which expresses an eternal and infinite essence of God (see ID6), *or* God is a thinking thing, q.e.d.

Schol.: This Proposition is also evident from the fact that we can conceive an infinite thinking being. For the more things a thinking being can think, the more reality, *or* perfection, we conceive it to contain. Therefore, a being that can think infinitely many things in infinitely many ways is necessarily infinite in its power of thinking. So since we can conceive an infinite Being by attending to thought alone, Thought (by ID4 and D6) is necessarily one of God's infinite attributes, as we maintained.

P2:
Extension is an attribute of God, or *God is an extended thing.*

Dem.: The demonstration of this proceeds in the same way as that of the preceding Proposition.

P3:
In God there is necessarily an idea, both of his essence and of everything that necessarily follows from his essence.

Dem.: For God (by P1) can think infinitely many things in infinitely many modes, *or* (what is the same, by IP16) can form the idea of his essence and of all the things which necessarily follow from it. But whatever is in God's power necessarily exists (by IP35); therefore, there is necessarily such an idea, and (by IP15) it is only in God, q.e.d.

Schol.: By God's power ordinary people understand God's free will and his right over all things which are, things which on that account are commonly considered to be contingent. For they say that God has the power of destroying all things and reducing them to nothing. Further, they very often compare God's power with the power of Kings.

But we have refuted this in IP32C1 and C2, and we have shown in IP16 that God acts with the same necessity by which he understands himself, i.e., just as it follows from the necessity of the divine nature (as everyone maintains unanimously) that God understands himself, with the same necessity it also follows that God does infinitely many things in infinitely many modes. And then we have shown in

IP34 that God's power is nothing except God's active essence. And so it is as impossible for us to conceive that God does not act as it is to conceive that he does not exist.

Again, if it were agreeable to pursue these matters further, I could also show here that that power which ordinary people fictitiously ascribe to God is not only human (which shows that ordinary people conceive God as a man, or as like a man), but also involves lack of power. But I do not wish to speak so often about the same topic. I only ask the reader to reflect repeatedly on what is said concerning this matter in Part I, from P16 to the end. For no one will be able to perceive rightly the things I maintain unless he takes great care not to confuse God's power with the human power or right of Kings.

P4:
God's idea, from which infinitely many things follow in infinitely many modes, must be unique.

Dem.: An infinite intellect comprehends nothing except God's attributes and his affections (by IP30). But God is unique (by IP14C1). Therefore God's idea, from which infinitely many things follow in infinitely many modes, must be unique, q.e.d.

P5:
The formal being of ideas admits God as a cause only insofar as he is considered as a thinking thing, and not insofar as he is explained by any other attribute. I.e., ideas, both of God's attributes and of singular things, admit not the objects themselves, or the things perceived, as their efficient cause, but God himself, insofar as he is a thinking thing.

Dem.: This is evident from P3. For there we inferred that God can form the idea of his essence, and of all the things that follow necessarily from it, solely from the fact that God is a thinking thing, and not from the fact that he is the object of his own idea. So the formal being of ideas admits God as its cause insofar as he is a thinking thing.

But another way of demonstrating this is the following. The formal being of ideas is a mode of thinking (as is known through itself), i.e. (by IP25C), a mode that expresses, in a certain way, God's nature insofar as he is a thinking thing. And so (by IP10) it involves the concept of no other attribute of God, and consequently (by IA4) is the effect of no other attribute than thought. And so the formal being of ideas admits God as its cause insofar as he is considered only as a thinking thing, etc., q.e.d.

P6:

The modes of each attribute have God for their cause only insofar as he is considered under the attribute of which they are modes, and not insofar as he is considered under any other attribute.

Dem.: For each attribute is conceived through itself without any other (by IP10). So the modes of each attribute involve the concept of their own attribute, but not of another one; and so (by IA4) they have God for their cause only insofar as he is considered under the attribute of which they are modes, and not insofar as he is considered under any other, q.e.d.

Cor.: From this it follows that the formal being of things which are not modes of thinking does not follow from the divine nature because [God] has first known the things; rather the objects of ideas follow and are inferred from their attributes in the same way and by the same necessity as that with which we have shown ideas to follow from the attribute of Thought.

P7:

The order and connection of ideas is the same as the order and connection of things.

Dem.: This is clear from IA4. For the idea of each thing caused depends on the knowledge of the cause of which it is the effect.

Cor.: From this it follows that God's [actual] power of thinking is equal to his actual power of acting. I.e., whatever follows formally from God's infinite nature follows objectively in God from his idea in the same order and with the same connection.

Schol.: Before we proceed further, we must recall here what we showed [in the First Part], viz. that whatever can be perceived by an infinite intellect as constituting an essence of substance pertains to one substance only, and consequently that the thinking substance and the extended substance are one and the same substance, which is now comprehended under this attribute, now under that. So also a mode of extension and the idea of that mode are one and the same thing, but expressed in two ways. Some of the Hebrews seem to have seen this, as if through a cloud, when they maintained that God, God's intellect, and the things understood by him are one and the same.

For example, a circle existing in nature and the idea of the existing circle, which is also in God, are one and the same thing, which is explained through different attributes. Therefore, whether we conceive nature under the attribute of Extension, or under the attribute of Thought, or under any other attribute, we shall find one and the same order, *or* one and the same connection of causes, i.e., that the same things follow one another.

When I said [before] that God is the cause of the idea, say of a circle, only insofar as he is a thinking thing, and [the cause] of the circle, only insofar as he is an extended thing, this was for no other reason than because the formal being of the idea of the circle can be perceived only through another mode of thinking, as its proximate cause, and that mode again through another, and so on, to infinity. Hence, so long as things are considered as modes of thinking, we must explain the order of the whole of nature, *or* the connection of causes, through the attribute of Thought alone. And insofar as they are considered as modes of Extension, the order of the whole of nature must be explained through the attribute of Extension alone. I understand the same concerning the other attributes.

So of things as they are in themselves, God is really the cause insofar as he consists of infinite attributes. For the present, I cannot explain these matters more clearly.

P8:

The ideas of singular things, or of modes, that do not exist must be comprehended in God's infinite idea in the same way as the formal essences of the singular things, or modes, are contained in God's attributes.

Dem.: This Proposition is evident from the preceding one, but is understood more clearly from the preceding scholium.

Cor.: From this it follows that so long as singular things do not exist, except insofar as they are comprehended in God's attributes, their objective being, *or* ideas, do not exist except insofar as God's infinite idea exists. And when singular things are said to exist, not only insofar as they are comprehended in God's attributes, but insofar also as they are said to have duration, their ideas also involve the existence through which they are said to have duration.

Schol.: If anyone wishes me to explain this further by an example, I will, of course, not be able to give one which adequately explains what I speak of here, since it is unique. Still I shall try as far as possible to illustrate the matter: the circle is of such a nature that the rectangles formed from the segments of all the straight lines intersecting in it are equal to one another. So in a circle there are contained infinitely many rectangles that are equal to one another. Nevertheless, none of them can be said to exist except insofar as the circle exists, nor also can the idea of any of these rectangles be said to exist except insofar as it is comprehended in the idea of the circle. Now of these infinitely many [rectangles] let two only, viz. [those formed from the segments of lines] D and E, exist. Of course their ideas also exist now, not only insofar as they are only comprehended in the idea of the circle, but also insofar as they involve the existence of those rectangles. By this they are distinguished from the other ideas of the other rectangles.

P9:

The idea of a singular thing which actually exists has God for a cause not insofar as he is infinite, but insofar as he is considered to be affected by another idea of a singular thing which actually exists; and of this [idea] God is also the cause, insofar as he is affected by another third [idea], and so on, to infinity.

Dem.: The idea of a singular thing which actually exists is a singular mode of thinking, and distinct from the others (by P8C and S), and so (by P6) has God for a cause only insofar as he is a thinking thing. But not (by IP28) insofar as he is a thing thinking absolutely; rather insofar as he is considered to be affected by another [determinate] mode of thinking. And God is also the cause of this mode, insofar as he is affected by another [determinate mode of thinking], and so on, to infinity. But the order and connection of ideas (by P7) is the same as the order and connection of causes. Therefore, the cause of one singular idea is another idea, *or* God, insofar as

he is considered to be affected by another idea; and of this also [God is the cause], insofar as he is affected by another, and so on, to infinity, q.e.d.

Cor.: Whatever happens in the singular object of any idea, there is knowledge of it in God, only insofar as he has the idea of the same object.

Dem.: Whatever happens in the object of any idea, there is an idea of it in God (by P3), not insofar as he is infinite, but insofar as he is considered to be affected by another idea of [an existing] singular thing (by P9); but the order and connection of ideas (by P7) is the same as the order and connection of things; therefore, knowledge of what happens in a singular object will be in God only insofar as he has the idea of the same object, q.e.d.

P10:

The being of substance does not pertain to the essence of man, or substance does not constitute the form of man.

Dem.: For the being of substance involves necessary existence (by IP7). Therefore, if the being of substance pertained to the essence of man, then substance being given, man would necessarily be given (by D2), and consequently man would exist necessarily, which (by A1) is absurd, q.e.d.

Schol.: This proposition is also demonstrated from IP5, viz. that there are not two substances of the same nature. Since a number of men can exist, what constitutes the form of man is not the being of substance. Further, this proposition is evident from the other properties of substance, viz. that substance is, by its nature, infinite, immutable, indivisible, etc., as anyone can easily see.

Cor.: From this it follows that the essence of man is constituted by certain modifications of God's attributes.

Dem.: For the being of substance does not pertain to the essence of man (by P10). Therefore, it is something (by IP15) which is in God, and which can neither be nor be conceived without God, *or* (by IP25C) an affection, *or* mode, which expresses God's nature in a certain and determinate way.

Schol.: Everyone, of course, must concede that nothing can either be or be conceived without God. For all confess that God is the only cause of all things, both of their essence and of their existence. I.e., God is not only the cause of the coming to be of things, as they say, but also of their being.

But in the meantime many say that anything without which a thing can neither be nor be conceived pertains to the nature of the thing. And so they believe either that the nature of God pertains to the essence of created things, or that created things can be or be conceived without God—or what is more certain, they are not sufficiently consistent.

The cause of this, I believe, was that they did not observe the [proper] order of Philosophizing. For they believed that the divine nature, which they should have contemplated before all else (because it is prior both in knowledge and in nature) is last in the order of knowledge, and that the things that are called objects of the senses are prior to all. That is why, when they contemplated natural things, they thought of nothing less than they did of the divine nature; and when afterwards they directed their minds to contemplating the divine nature, they could think of nothing less than of their first fictions, on which they had built the knowledge of natural things, because these could not assist knowledge of the divine nature. So it is no wonder that they have generally contradicted themselves.

But I pass over this. For my intent here was only to give a reason why I did not say that anything without which a thing can neither be nor be conceived pertains to its nature—viz. because singular things can neither be nor be conceived without God, and nevertheless, God does not pertain to their essence. But I have said that what necessarily constitutes the essence of a thing is that which, if it is given, the thing is posited, and if it is taken away, the thing is taken away, i.e., the essence is what the thing can neither be nor be conceived without, and vice versa, what can neither be nor be conceived without the thing.

P11:

The first thing that constitutes the actual being of a human Mind is nothing but the idea of a singular thing which actually exists.

Dem.: The essence of man (by P10C) is constituted by certain modes of God's attributes, viz. (by A2) by modes of thinking, of all of which (by A3) the idea is prior in nature, and when it is given, the other modes (to which the idea is prior in nature) must be in the same individual (by A3). And therefore an idea is the first thing that constitutes the be-

ing of a human Mind. But not the idea of a thing which does not exist. For then (by P8C) the idea itself could not be said to exist. Therefore, it will be the idea of a thing which actually exists. But not of an infinite thing. For an infinite thing (by IP21 and 22) must always exist necessarily. But (by A1) it is absurd [that this idea should be of a necessarily existing object]. Therefore, the first thing that constitutes the actual being of a human Mind is the idea of a singular thing which actually exists, q.e.d.

Cor.: From this it follows that the human Mind is a part of the infinite intellect of God. Therefore, when we say that the human Mind perceives this or that, we are saying nothing but that God, not insofar as he is infinite, but insofar as he is explained through the nature of the human Mind, *or* insofar as he constitutes the essence of the human Mind, has this or that idea; and when we say that God has this or that idea, not only insofar as he constitutes the nature of the human Mind, but insofar as he also has the idea of another thing together with the human Mind, then we say that the human Mind perceives the thing only partially, *or* inadequately.

Schol.: Here, no doubt, my readers will come to a halt, and think of many things which will give them pause. For this reason I ask them to continue on with me slowly, step by step, and to make no judgment on these matters until they have read through them all.

P12:

Whatever happens in the object of the idea constituting the human Mind must be perceived by the human Mind, or *there will necessarily be an idea of that thing in the Mind; i.e., if the object of the idea constituting a human Mind is a body, nothing can happen in that body which is not perceived by the Mind.*

Dem.: For whatever happens in the object of any idea, the knowledge of that thing is necessarily in God (by P9C), insofar as he is considered to be affected by the idea of the same object, i.e. (by P11), insofar as he constitutes the mind of some thing. Therefore, whatever happens in the object of the idea constituting the human Mind, the knowledge of it is necessarily in God insofar as he constitutes the nature of the human Mind, i.e. (by P11C), knowledge of this thing will necessarily be in the Mind, *or* the Mind will perceive it, q.e.d.

Schol.: This Proposition is also evident, and more clearly understood from P7S, which you should consult.

P13:

The object of the idea constituting the human Mind is the Body, or *a certain mode of Extension which actually exists, and nothing else.*

Dem.: For if the object of the human Mind were not the Body, the ideas of the affections of the Body would not be in God (by P9C) insofar as he constituted our Mind, but insofar as he constituted the mind of another thing, i.e. (by P11C), the ideas of the affections of the Body would not be in our Mind; but (by A4) we have ideas of the affections of the body. Therefore, the object of the idea that constitutes the human Mind is the Body, and it (by P11) actually exists.

Next, if the object of the Mind were something else also, in addition to the Body, then since (by IP36) nothing exists from which there does not follow some effect, there would necessarily (by P12) be an idea in our Mind of some effect of it. But (by A5) there is no idea of it. Therefore, the object of our Mind is the existing Body and nothing else, q.e.d.

Cor.: From this it follows that man consists of a Mind and a Body, and that the human Body exists, as we are aware of it.

Schol.: From these [propositions] we understand not only that the human Mind is united to the Body, but also what should be understood by the union of Mind and Body. But no one will be able to understand it adequately, *or* distinctly, unless he first knows adequately the nature of our Body. For the things we have shown so far are completely general and do not pertain more to man than to other Individuals, all of which, though in different degrees, are nevertheless animate. For of each thing there is necessarily an idea in God, of which God is the cause in the same way as he is of the idea of the human Body. And so, whatever we have said of the idea of the human Body must also be said of the idea of any thing.

However, we also cannot deny that ideas differ among themselves, as the objects themselves do, and that one is more excellent than the other, and contains more reality, just as the object of the one is more excellent than the object of the other and contains more reality. And so to determine what is the difference between the human Mind and the others, and how it surpasses them, it is necessary for us, as we have said, to know the nature of its object, i.e., of the human Body. I cannot explain this here, nor is that necessary for the things I wish to demonstrate. Nevertheless, I say this in general, that in proportion as a Body is more capable than others of doing many things at once, or being acted on in many ways at once, so its Mind is more capable than others of perceiving many things at once. And in proportion as the actions of a body depend more on itself alone, and as other bodies concur with it less in acting, so its mind is more capable of understanding distinctly. And from these [truths] we can know the excellence of one mind over the others, and also see the cause why we have only a completely confused knowledge of our Body, and many other things which I shall deduce from them in the following [propositions]. For this reason I have thought it worthwhile to explain and demonstrate these things more accurately. To do this it is necessary to premise a few things concerning the nature of bodies.

A1':
All bodies either move or are at rest.

A2':
Each body moves now more slowly, now more quickly.

L1:
Bodies are distinguished from one another by reason of motion and rest, speed and slowness, and not by reason of substance.

Dem.: I suppose that the first part of this is known through itself. But that bodies are not distinguished by reason of substance is evident both from IP5 and from IP8. But it is more clearly evident from those things which are said in IP15S.

L2:
All bodies agree in certain things.

Dem.: For all bodies agree in that they involve the concept of one and the same attribute (by D1), and in that they can move now more slowly, now more quickly, and absolutely, that now they move, now they are at rest.

L3:
A body which moves or is at rest must be determined to motion or rest by another body, which has also been de-

termined to motion or rest by another, and that again by another, and so on, to infinity.

Dem.: Bodies (by D1) are singular things which (by L1) are distinguished from one another by reason of motion and rest; and so (by IP28), each must be determined necessarily to motion or rest by another singular thing, viz. (by P6) by another body, which (by A1') either moves or is at rest. But this body also (by the same reasoning) could not move or be at rest if it had not been determined by another to motion or rest, and this again (by the same reasoning) by another, and so on, to infinity, q.e.d.

Cor.: From this it follows that a body in motion moves until it is determined by another body to rest; and that a body at rest also remains at rest until it is determined to motion by another.

This is also known through itself. For when I suppose that body A, say, is at rest, and do not attend to any other body in motion, I can say nothing about body A except that it is at rest. If afterwards it happens that body A moves, that of course could not have come about from the fact that it was at rest. For from that nothing else could follow but that body A would be at rest.

If, on the other hand, A is supposed to move, then as often as we attend only to A, we shall be able to affirm nothing concerning it except that it moves. If afterwards it happens that A is at rest, that of course also could not have come about from the motion it had. For from the motion nothing else could follow but that A would move. Therefore, it happens by a thing which was not in A, viz. by an external cause, by which [the Body in motion, A] has been determined to rest.

A1":

All modes by which a body is affected by another body follow both from the nature of the body affected and at the same time from the nature of the affecting body, so that one and the same body may be moved differently according to differences in the nature of the bodies moving it. And conversely, different bodies may be moved differently by one and the same body.

A2":

When a body in motion strikes against another which is at rest and cannot give way, then it is reflected, so that it continues to move, and the angle of the line of the reflected motion with the surface of the body at rest which it struck against will be equal to the angle which the line of the incident motion makes with the same surface.

This will be sufficient concerning the simplest bodies, which are distinguished from one another only by motion and rest, speed and slowness. Now let us move up to composite bodies.

Definition: *When a number of bodies, whether of the same or of different size, are so constrained by other bodies that they lie upon one another, or if they so move, whether with the same degree or different degrees of speed, that they communicate their motions to each other in a certain fixed manner, we shall say that those bodies are united with one another and that they all together compose one body* or Individual, *which is distinguished from the others by this union of bodies.*

A3":

As the parts of an Individual, or composite body, lie upon one another over a larger or smaller surface, so they can be forced to change their position with more or less difficulty; and consequently the more or less will be the difficulty of bringing it about that the Individual changes its shape. And therefore the bodies whose parts lie upon one another over a large surface, I shall call *hard;* those whose parts lie upon one another over a small surface, I shall call *soft;* and finally those whose parts are in motion, I shall call *fluid.*

L4:

If, of a body, or of an Individual, which is composed of a number of bodies, some are removed, and at the same time as many others of the same nature take their place, the [body, or the] Individual will retain its nature, as before, without any change of its form.

Dem.: For (by L1) bodies are not distinguished in respect to substance; what constitutes the form of the Individual consists [only] in the union of the bodies (by the preceding definition). But this [union] (by hypothesis) is retained even if a continual change of bodies occurs. Therefore, the Individual will retain its nature, as before, both in respect to substance, and in respect to mode, q.e.d.

L5:

If the parts composing an Individual become greater or less, but in such a proportion that they all keep the same ratio of motion and rest to each other as before, then the Individual will likewise retain its nature, as before, without any change of form.

Dem.: The demonstration of this is the same as that of the preceding Lemma.

L6:

If certain bodies composing an Individual are compelled to alter the motion they have from one direction to another, but so that they can continue their motions and communicate them to each other in the same ratio as before, the Individual will likewise retain its nature, without any change of form.

Dem.: This is evident through itself. For it is supposed that it retains everything which, in its definition, we said constitutes its form. [See the Definition before L4.]

L7:

Furthermore, the Individual so composed retains its nature, whether it, as a whole, moves or is at rest, or whether it moves in this or that direction, so long as each part retains its motion, and communicates it, as before, to the others.

Dem.: This [also] is evident from the definition preceding L4.

Schol.: By this, then, we see how a composite Individual can be affected in many ways, and still preserve its nature. So far we have conceived an Individual which is composed only of bodies which are distinguished from one another only by motion and rest, speed and slowness, i.e., which is composed of the simplest bodies. But if we should now conceive of another, composed of a number of Individuals of a different nature, we shall find that it can be affected in a great many other ways, and still preserve its nature. For since each part of it is composed of a number of bodies, each part will therefore (by L7) be able, without any change of its nature, to move now more slowly, now more quickly, and consequently communicate its motion more quickly or more slowly to the others.

But if we should further conceive a third kind of Individual, composed [of many individuals] of

this second kind, we shall find that it can be affected in many other ways, without any change of its form. And if we proceed in this way to infinity, we shall easily conceive that the whole of nature is one Individual, whose parts, i.e., all bodies, vary in infinite ways, without any change of the whole Individual.

If it had been my intention to deal expressly with body, I ought to have explained and demonstrated these things more fully. But I have already said that I intended something else, and brought these things forward only because I can easily deduce from them the things I have decided to demonstrate.

Postulates

I. The human Body is composed of a great many individuals of different natures, each of which is highly composite.

II. Some of the individuals of which the human Body is composed are fluid, some soft, and others, finally are hard.

III. The individuals composing the human Body, and consequently, the human Body itself, are affected by external bodies in very many ways.

IV. The human Body, to be preserved, requires a great many other bodies, by which it is, as it were, continually regenerated.

V. When a fluid part of the human Body is determined by an external body so that it frequently thrusts against a soft part [of the Body], it changes its surface and, as it were, impresses on [the soft part] certain traces of the external body striking against [the fluid part].

VI. The human Body can move and dispose external bodies in a great many ways.

P14:

The human Mind is capable of perceiving a great many things, and is the more capable, the more its body can be disposed in a great many ways.

Dem.: For the human Body (by Post. 3 and 6) is affected in a great many ways by external bodies, and is disposed to affect external bodies in a great many ways. But the human Mind must perceive everything which happens in the human body (by P12). Therefore, the human Mind is capable of perceiving a great many things, and is the more capable [, as the human Body is more capable], q.e.d.

P15:

The idea that constitutes the formal being [esse] *of the human Mind is not simple, but composed of a great many ideas.*

Dem.: The idea that constitutes the formal being of the human Mind is the idea of a body (by P13), which (by Post. 1) is composed of a great many highly composite Individuals. But of each Individual composing the body, there is necessarily (by P8C) an idea in God. Therefore (by P7), the idea of the human Body is composed of these many ideas of the parts composing the Body, q.e.d.

P16:

The idea of any mode in which the human Body is affected by external bodies must involve the nature of the human Body and at the same time the nature of the external body.

Dem.: For all the modes in which a body is affected follow from the nature of the affected body, and at the same time from the nature of the affecting body (by A1″ [II/99]). So the idea of them (by IA4) will necessarily involve the nature of each body. And so the idea of each mode in which the human Body is affected by an external body involves the nature of the human Body and of the external body, q.e.d.

Cor. 1: From this it follows, first, that the human Mind perceives the nature of a great many bodies together with the nature of its own body.

Cor. 2: It follows, second, that the ideas which we have of external bodies indicate the condition of our own body more than the nature of the external bodies. I have explained this by many examples in the Appendix of Part I.

P17:

If the human Body is affected with a mode that involves the nature of an external body, the human Mind will regard the same external body as actually existing, or as present to it, until the Body is affected by an affect that excludes the existence or presence of that body.

Dem.: This is evident. For so long as the human Body is so affected, the human Mind (by P12) will regard this affection of the body, i.e. (by P16), it will have the idea of a mode that actually exists, an idea that involves the nature of the external body, i.e., an idea that does not exclude, but posits, the existence or presence of the nature of the external body. And so the Mind (by P16C1) will regard the external

body as actually existing, or as present, until it is affected, etc., q.e.d.

Cor.: Although the external bodies by which the human body has once been affected neither exist nor are present, the mind will still be able to regard them as if they were present.

Dem.: While external bodies so determine the fluid parts of the human body that they often thrust against the softer parts, they change (by Post. 5) their surfaces with the result (see A2″ after L3) that they are reflected from it in another way than they used to be before, and still later, when the fluid parts, by their spontaneous motion, encounter those new surfaces, they are reflected in the same way as when they were driven against those surfaces by the external bodies. Consequently, while, thus reflected, they continue to move, they will affect the human Body with the same mode, concerning which the Mind (by P12) will think again, i.e. (by P17), the Mind will again regard the external body as present; this will happen as often as the fluid parts of the human body encounter the same surfaces by their spontaneous motion. So although the external bodies by which the human Body has once been affected do not exist, the Mind will still regard them as present, as often as this action of the body is repeated, q.e.d.

Schol.: We see, therefore, how it can happen (as it often does) that we regard as present things that do not exist. This can happen from other causes also, but it is sufficient for me here to have shown one through which I can explain it as if I had shown it through its true cause; still, I do not believe that I wander far from the true [cause] since all those postulates which I have assumed contain hardly anything that is not established by experience which we cannot doubt, after we have shown that the human Body exists as we are aware of it (see P13C).

Furthermore (from P17C and P16C2), we clearly understand what is the difference between the idea of, say, Peter, which constitutes the essence of Peter's mind, and the idea of Peter which is in another man, say in Paul. For the former directly explains the essence of Peter's body, and does not involve existence, except so long as Peter exists; but the latter indicates the condition of Paul's body more than Peter's nature [see P16C2], and therefore, while that condition of Paul's body lasts, Paul's Mind will still regard Peter as present to itself, even though Peter does not exist.

Next, to retain the customary words, the affections of the human Body whose ideas present external bodies as present to us, we shall call images of things, even if they do not reproduce the [external] figures of things. And when the Mind regards bodies in this way, we shall say that it imagines.

And here, in order to begin to indicate what error is, I should like you to note that the imaginations of the Mind, considered in themselves contain no error, *or* that the Mind does not err from the fact that it imagines, but only insofar as it is considered to lack an idea that excludes the existence of those things that it imagines to be present to it. For if the Mind, while it imagined nonexistent things as present to it, at the same time knew that those things did not exist, it would, of course, attribute this power of imagining to a virtue of its nature, not to a vice—especially if this faculty of imagining depended only on its own nature, i.e. (by ID7), if the Mind's faculty of imagining were free.

P18:

If the human Body has once been affected by two or more bodies at the same time, then when the Mind subsequently imagines one of them, it will immediately recollect the others also.

Dem.: The Mind (by P17C) imagines a body because the human Body is affected and disposed as it was affected when certain of its parts were struck by the external body itself. But (by hypothesis) the Body was then so disposed that the Mind imagined two [or more] bodies at once; therefore it will now also imagine two [or more] at once, and when the Mind imagines one, it will immediately recollect the other also, q.e.d.

Schol.: From this we clearly understand what Memory is. For it is nothing other than a certain connection of ideas involving the nature of things which are outside the human Body—a connection that is in the Mind according to the order and connection of the affections of the human Body.

I say, *first,* that the connection is only of those ideas that involve the nature of things which are outside the human Body, but not of the ideas that explain the nature of the same things. For they are really (by P16) ideas of affections of the human Body which involve both its nature and that of external bodies.

I say, *second,* that this connection happens according to the order and connection of the affections of the human Body in order to distinguish it from the connection of ideas which happens according to the order of the intellect, by which the Mind perceives things through their first causes, and which is the same in all men.

And from this we clearly understand why the Mind, from the thought of one thing, immediately passes to the thought of another, which has no likeness to the first: as, for example, from the thought of the word *pomum* a Roman will immediately pass to the thought of the fruit [viz. an apple], which has no similarity to that articulate sound and nothing in common with it except that the Body of the same man has often been affected by these two [at the same time], i.e., that the man often heard the word *pomum* while he saw the fruit.

And in this way each of us will pass from one thought to another, as each one's association has ordered the images of things in the body. For example, a soldier, having seen traces of a horse in the sand, will immediately pass from the thought of a horse to the thought of a horseman, and from that to the thought of war, etc. But a Farmer will pass from the thought of a horse to the thought of a plow, and then to that of a field, etc. And so each one, according as he has been accustomed to join and connect the images of things in this or that way, will pass from one thought to another.

P19:

The human Mind does not know the human Body itself, nor does it know that it exists, except through ideas of affections by which the Body is affected.

Dem.: For the human Mind is the idea itself, *or* knowledge of the human Body (by P13), which (by P9) is indeed in God insofar as he is considered to be affected by another idea of a singular thing, or because (by Post. 4) the human Body requires a great many bodies by which it is, as it were, continually regenerated; and [because] the order and connection of ideas is (by P7) the same as the order and connection of causes, this idea will be in God insofar as he is considered to be affected by the ideas of a great many singular things. Therefore, God has the idea of the human Body, *or* knows the human Body, insofar as he is affected by a great many other ideas, and not insofar as he constitutes the nature of the human Mind, i.e. (by P11C), the human Mind does not know the human Body.

But the ideas of affections of the Body are in God insofar as he constitutes the nature of the human Mind, *or* the human Mind perceives the same affections (by P12), and consequently (by P16) the human Body itself, as actually existing (by P17).

Therefore to that extent only, the human Mind perceives the human Body itself, q.e.d.

P20:

There is also in God an idea, or *knowledge, of the human Mind, which follows in God in the same way and is related to God in the same way as the idea,* or *knowledge, of the human Body.*

Dem.: Thought is an attribute of God (by P1), and so (by P3) there must necessarily be in God an idea both of [thought] and of all of its affections, and consequently (by P11), of the human Mind also. Next, this idea, *or* knowledge, of the Mind does not follow in God insofar as he is infinite, but insofar as he is affected by another idea of a singular thing (by P9). But the order and connection of ideas is the same as the order and connection of causes (by P7). Therefore, this idea, *or* knowledge, of the Mind follows in God and is related to God in the same way as the idea, *or* knowledge, of the Body, q.e.d.

P21:

This idea of the Mind is united to the Mind in the same way as the Mind is united to the Body.

Dem.: We have shown that the Mind is united to the Body from the fact that the Body is the object of the Mind (see P12 and 13); and so by the same reasoning the idea of the Mind must be united with its own object, i.e., with the Mind itself, in the same way as the Mind is united with the Body, q.e.d.

Schol.: This proposition is understood far more clearly from what is said in P7S; for there we have shown that the idea of the Body and the Body, i.e. (by P13), the Mind and the Body, are one and the same Individual, which is conceived now under the attribute of Thought, now under the attribute of Extension. So the idea of the Mind and the Mind itself are one and the same thing, which is conceived under one and the same attribute, viz. Thought. The idea of the Mind, I say, and the Mind itself follow in God from the same power of thinking and by the same necessity. For the idea of the Mind, i.e., the idea of the idea, is nothing but the form of the idea insofar as this is considered as a mode of thinking without relation to the object. For as soon as someone knows something, he thereby knows that he knows it, and at the same time knows that he knows that he knows, and so on, to infinity. But more on these matters later.

P22:

The human Mind perceives not only the affections of the Body, but also the ideas of these affections.

Dem.: The ideas of the ideas of the affections follow in God in the same way and are related to God in the same way as the ideas themselves of the affections (this is demonstrated in the same way as P20). But the ideas of the affections of the Body are in the human Mind (by P12), i.e. (by P11C), in God, insofar as he constitutes the essence of the human Mind. Therefore, the ideas of these ideas will be in God insofar as he has the knowledge, *or* idea, of the human Mind, i.e. (by P21), they will be in the human Mind itself, which for that reason perceives not only the affections of the Body, but also their ideas, q.e.d.

P23:

The Mind does not know itself, except insofar as it perceives the ideas of the affections of the Body.

Dem.: The idea, *or* knowledge, of the Mind (by P20) follows in God in the same way, and is related to God in the same way as the idea, *or* knowledge, of the body. But since (by P19) the human Mind does not know the human Body itself, i.e. (by P11C), since the knowledge of the human Body is not related to God insofar as he constitutes the nature of the human Mind, the knowledge of the Mind is also not related to God insofar as he constitutes the essence of the human Mind. And so (again by P11C) to that extent the human Mind does not know itself.

Next, the ideas of the affections by which the Body is affected involve the nature of the human Body itself (by P16), i.e. (by P13), agree with the nature of the Mind. So knowledge of these ideas will necessarily involve knowledge of the Mind. But (by P22) knowledge of these ideas is in the human Mind itself. Therefore, the human Mind, to that extent only, knows itself, q.e.d.

P24:

The human Mind does not involve adequate knowledge of the parts composing the human Body.

Dem.: The parts composing the human Body pertain to the essence of the Body itself only insofar as they communicate their motions to one another in a certain fixed manner (see the Definition after L3C), and not insofar as they can be considered as Individuals, without relation to the human Body. For (by Post. 1) the parts of the human Body are highly composite Individuals, whose parts (by L4) can be separated from the human Body and communicate their motions (see A1″ after L3) to other bodies in another manner, while the human Body completely preserves its nature and form. And so the idea, *or* knowledge, of each part will be in God (by P3), insofar as he is considered to be affected by another idea of a singular thing (by P9), a singular thing which is prior, in the order of nature, to the part itself (by P7). The same must also be said of each part of the Individual composing the human Body. And so, the knowledge of each part composing the human Body is in God insofar as he is affected with a great many ideas of things, and not insofar as he has only the idea of the human Body, i.e. (by P13), the idea that constitutes the nature of the human Mind. And so, by (P11C) the human Mind does not involve adequate knowledge of the parts composing the human Body, q.e.d.

P25:

The idea of any affection of the human Body does not involve adequate knowledge of an external body.

Dem.: We have shown (P16) that the idea of an affection of the human Body involves the nature of an external body insofar as the external body determines the human Body in a certain fixed way. But insofar as the external body is an Individual that is not related to the human Body, the idea, *or* knowledge, of it is in God (by P9) insofar as God is considered to be affected with the idea of another thing which (by P7) is prior in nature to the external body itself. So adequate knowledge of the external body is not in God insofar as he has the idea of an affection of the human Body, *or* the idea of an affection of the human Body does not involve adequate knowledge of the external body, q.e.d.

P26:

The human Mind does not perceive any external body as actually existing, except through the ideas of the affections of its own Body.

Dem.: If the human Body is not affected by an external body in any way, then (by P7) the idea of the human Body, i.e. (by P13) the human Mind, is also not affected in any way by the idea of the existence of that body, *or* it does not perceive the existence of that external body in any way. But insofar as the human Body is affected by an external body in some way, to that extent [the human Mind] (by P16 and P16C1) perceives the external body, q.e.d.

Cor.: Insofar as the human Mind imagines an external body, it does not have adequate knowledge of it.

Dem.: When the human Mind regards external bodies through ideas of the affections of its own Body, then we say that it imagines (see P17S); and the Mind cannot in any other way (by P26) imagine external bodies as actually existing. And so (by P25), insofar as the Mind imagines external bodies, it does not have adequate knowledge of them, q.e.d.

P27:

The idea of any affection of the human Body does not involve adequate knowledge of the human body itself.

Dem.: Any idea of any affection of the human Body involves the nature of the human Body insofar as the human Body itself is considered to be affected with a certain definite mode (see P16). But insofar as the human Body is an Individual, which can be affected with many other modes, the idea of this [affection] etc. (See P25D.)

P28:

The ideas of the affections of the human Body, insofar as they are related only to the human Mind, are not clear and distinct, but confused.

Dem.: For the ideas of the affections of the human Body involve the nature of external bodies as much as that of the human Body (by P16), and must involve the nature not only of the human Body [as a whole], but also of its parts; for the affections are modes (by Post. 3) with which the parts of the human Body, and consequently the whole Body, are affected. But (by P24 and P25) adequate knowledge of external bodies and of the parts composing the human Body is in God, not insofar as he is considered to be affected with the human Mind, but insofar as he is considered to be affected with other ideas. Therefore, these ideas of the affections, insofar as they are related only to the human Mind, are like conclusions without premises, i.e. (as is known through itself), they are confused ideas, q.e.d.

Schol.: In the same way we can demonstrate that the idea that constitutes the nature of the human Mind is not, considered in itself alone, clear and distinct; we can also demonstrate the same of the idea of the human Mind and the ideas of the ideas of the human Body's affections [viz. that are confused], insofar as they are referred to the Mind alone. Anyone can easily see this.

P29:

The idea of the idea of any affection of the human Body does not involve adequate knowledge of the human Mind.

Dem.: For the idea of an affection of the human Body (by P27) does not involve adequate knowledge of the Body itself, *or* does not express its nature adequately, i.e. (by P13), does not agree adequately with the nature of the Mind; and so (by IA6) the idea of this idea does not express the nature of the human mind adequately, *or* does not involve adequate knowledge of it, q.e.d.

Cor.: From this it follows that so long as the human Mind perceives things from the common order of nature, it does not have an adequate, but only a confused and mutilated knowledge of itself, of its own Body, and of external bodies. For the Mind does not know itself except insofar as it perceives ideas of the affections of the body (by P23). But it does not perceive its own Body (by P19) except through the very ideas themselves of the affections [of the body], and it is also through them alone that it perceives external bodies (by P26). And so, insofar as it has these [ideas], then neither of itself (by P29), nor of its own Body (by P27), nor of external bodies (by P25) does it have an adequate knowledge, but only (by P28 and P28S) a mutilated and confused knowledge, q.e.d.

Schol.: I say expressly that the Mind has, not an adequate, but only a confused [and mutilated] knowledge, of itself, of its own Body, and of external bodies, so long as it perceives things from the common order of nature, i.e., so long as it is determined externally, from fortuitous encounters with things,

to regard this or that, and not so long as it is determined internally, from the fact that it regards a number of things at once, to understand their agreements, differences, and oppositions. For so often as it is disposed internally, in this or another way, then it regards things clearly and distinctly, as I shall show below.

P30:

We can have only an entirely inadequate knowledge of the duration of our Body.

Dem.: Our body's duration depends neither on its essence (by A1), nor even on God's absolute nature (by IP21). But (by IP28) it is determined to exist and produce an effect from such [other] causes as are also determined by others to exist and produce an effect in a certain and determinate manner, and these again by others, and so to infinity. Therefore, the duration of our Body depends on the common order of nature and the constitution of things. But adequate knowledge of how things are constituted is in God, insofar as he has the ideas of all of them, and not insofar as he has only the idea of the human Body (by P9C). So the knowledge of the duration of our Body is quite inadequate in God, insofar as he is considered to constitute only the nature of the human Mind, i.e. (by P11C), this knowledge is quite inadequate in our Mind, q.e.d.

P31:

We can have only an entirely inadequate knowledge of the duration of the singular things which are outside us.

Dem.: For each singular thing, like the human Body, must be determined by another singular thing to exist and produce effects in a certain and determinate way, and this again by another, and so to infinity (by IP28). But since (in P30) we have demonstrated from this common property of singular things that we have only a very inadequate knowledge of the duration of our Body, we shall have to draw the same conclusion concerning the duration of singular things [outside us], viz. that we can have only a very inadequate knowledge of their duration, q.e.d.

Cor.: From this it follows that all particular things are contingent and corruptible. For we can have no adequate knowledge of their duration (by P31), and that is what we must understand by the contingency of things and the possibility of their corruption (see IP33S1). For (by IP29) beyond that there is no contingency.

P32:

All ideas, insofar as they are related to God, are true.

Dem.: For all ideas which are in God agree entirely with their objects (by P7C), and so (by IA6) they are all true, q.e.d.

P33:

There is nothing positive in ideas on account of which they are called false.

Dem.: If you deny this, conceive (if possible) a positive mode of thinking which constitutes the form of error, *or* falsity. This mode of thinking cannot be in God (by P32). But it also can neither be nor be conceived outside God (by IP15). And so there can be nothing positive in ideas on account of which they are called false, q.e.d.

P34:

Every idea that in us is absolute, or adequate and perfect, is true.

Dem.: When we say that there is in us an adequate and perfect idea, we are saying nothing but that (by P11C) there is an adequate and perfect idea in God insofar as he constitutes the essence of our Mind, and consequently (by P32) we are saying nothing but that such an idea is true, q.e.d.

P35:

Falsity consists in the privation of knowledge which inadequate, or mutilated and confused, ideas involve.

Dem.: There is nothing positive in ideas that constitutes the form of falsity (by P33); but falsity cannot consist in an absolute privation (for it is Minds, not Bodies, which are said to err, or be deceived), nor also in absolute ignorance. For to be ignorant and to err are different. So it consists in the privation of knowledge that inadequate knowledge of things, *or* inadequate and confused ideas, involve, q.e.d.

Schol.: In P17S I explained how error consists in the privation of knowledge. But to explain the matter more fully, I shall give [one or two examples]: men are deceived in that they think themselves free [i.e., they think that, of their own free will, they can either do a thing or forbear doing it], an opinion which consists only in this, that they are conscious of their actions and ignorant of the causes

by which they are determined. This, then, is their idea of freedom—that they do not know any cause of their actions. They say, of course, that human actions depend on the will, but these are only words for which they have no idea. For all are ignorant of what the will is, and how it moves the Body; those who boast of something else, who feign seats and dwelling places of the soul, usually provoke either ridicule or disgust.

Similarly, when we look at the sun, we imagine it as about 200 feet away from us, an error that does not consist simply in this imagining, but in the fact that while we imagine it in this way, we are ignorant of its true distance and of the cause of this imagining. For even if we later come to know that it is more than 600 diameters of the earth away from us, we nevertheless imagine it as near. For we imagine the sun so near not because we do not know its true distance, but because an affection of our body involves the essence of the sun insofar as our body is affected by the sun.

P36:

Inadequate and confused ideas follow with the same necessity as adequate, or clear and distinct ideas.

Dem.: All ideas are in God (by IP15); and, insofar as they are related to God, are true (by P32), and (by P7C) adequate. And so there are no inadequate or confused ideas except insofar as they are related to the singular Mind of someone (see P24 and P28). And so all ideas—both the adequate and the inadequate—follow with the same necessity (by P6C), q.e.d.

P37:

What is common to all things (on this see L2, above) *and is equally in the part and in the whole, does not constitute the essence of any singular thing.*

Dem.: If you deny this, conceive (if possible) that it does constitute the essence of some singular thing, say the essence of B. Then (by D2) it can neither be nor be conceived without B. But this is contrary to the hypothesis. Therefore, it does not pertain to the essence of B, nor does it constitute the essence of any other singular thing, q.e.d.

P38:

Those things which are common to all, and which are equally in the part and in the whole, can only be conceived adequately.

Dem.: Let A be something which is common to all bodies, and which is equally in the part of each body and in the whole. I say that A can only be conceived adequately. For its idea (by P7C) will necessarily be adequate in God, both insofar as he has the idea of the human Body and insofar as he has ideas of its affections, which (by P16, P25, and P27) involve in part both the nature of the human Body and that of external bodies. That is (by P12 and P13), this idea will necessarily be adequate in God insofar as he constitutes the human Mind, *or* insofar as he has ideas that are in the human Mind. The Mind therefore (by P11C) necessarily perceives A adequately, and does so both insofar as it perceives itself and insofar as it perceives its own or any external body. Nor can A be conceived in another way, q.e.d.

Cor.: From this it follows that there are certain ideas, *or* notions, common to all men. For (by L2) all bodies agree in certain things, which (by P38) must be perceived adequately, *or* clearly and distinctly, by all.

P39:
If something is common to, and peculiar to, the human Body and certain external bodies by which the human Body is usually affected, and is equally in the part and in the whole of each of them, its idea will also be adequate in the Mind.

Dem.: Let A be that which is common to, and peculiar to, the human Body and certain external bodies, which is equally in the human Body and in the same external bodies, and finally, which is equally in the part of each external body and in the whole. There will be an adequate idea of A in God (by P7C), both insofar as he has the idea of the human Body, and insofar as he has ideas of the posited external bodies. Let it be posited now that the human Body is affected by an external body through what it has in common with it, i.e., by A; the idea of this affection will involve property A (by P16), and so (by P7C) the idea of this affection, insofar as it involves property A, will be adequate in God insofar as he is affected with the idea of the human Body, i.e. (by P13), insofar as he constitutes the nature of the human Mind. And so (by P11C), this idea is also adequate in the human Mind, q.e.d.

Cor.: From this it follows that the Mind is the more capable of perceiving many things adequately as its Body has many things in common with other bodies.

P40:
Whatever ideas follow in the Mind from ideas that are adequate in the mind are also adequate.

Dem.: This is evident. For when we say that an idea in the human Mind follows from ideas that are adequate in it, we are saying nothing but that (by P11C) in the Divine intellect there is an idea of which God is the cause, not insofar as he is infinite, nor insofar as he is affected with the ideas of a great many singular things, but insofar as he constitutes only the essence of the human Mind [and therefore, it must be adequate].

Schol. 1: With this I have explained the cause of those notions which are called *common*, and which are the foundations of our reasoning.

But some axioms, *or* notions, result from other causes which it would be helpful to explain by this method of ours. For from these [explanations] it would be established which notions are more useful than the others, and which are of hardly any use; and then, which are common, which are clear and distinct only to those who have no prejudices, and finally, which are ill-founded. Moreover, we would establish what is the origin of those notions they call *Second*, and consequently of the axioms founded on them, and other things I have thought about, from time to time, concerning these matters. But since I have set these aside for another Treatise, and do not wish to give rise to disgust by too long a discussion, I have decided to pass over them here.

But not to omit anything it is necessary to know, I shall briefly add something about the causes from which the terms called *Transcendental* have had their origin—I mean terms like Being, Thing and something. These terms arise from the fact that the human Body, being limited, is capable of forming distinctly only a certain number of images at the same time (I have explained what an image is in P17S). If that number is exceeded, the images will begin to be confused, and if the number of images the Body is capable of forming distinctly in itself at once is greatly exceeded, they will all be completely confused with one another.

Since this is so, it is evident from P17C and P18, that the human Mind will be able to imagine distinctly, at the same time, as many bodies as there can be images formed at the same time in its body. But when the images in the body are completely confused, the Mind also will imagine all the bodies confusedly, without any distinction, and comprehend them as if under one attribute, viz. under the attribute of Being, Thing, etc. This can also be deduced from the fact that images are not always equally vigorous and from other causes like these, which it is not necessary to explain here. For our purpose it is sufficient to consider only one. For they all reduce to this: these terms signify ideas that are confused in the highest degree.

Those notions they call *Universal*, like Man, Horse, Dog, etc., have arisen from similar causes, viz. because so many images (e.g., of men) are formed at one time in the human Body that they surpass the power of imagining—not entirely, of course, but still to the point where the Mind can imagine neither slight differences of the singular [men] (such as the color and size of each one, etc.) nor their determinate number, and imagines distinctly only what they all agree in, insofar as they affect the body. For the body has been affected most [forcefully] by [what is common], since each singular has affected it [by this property]. And [the mind] expresses this by the word *man*, and predicates it of infinitely many singulars. For as we have said, it cannot imagine a determinate number of singulars.

But it should be noted that these notions are not formed by all [men] in the same way, but vary from one to another, in accordance with what the body has more often been affected by, and what the Mind imagines or recollects more easily. For example, those who have more often regarded men's stature with wonder will understand by the word *man* an animal of erect stature. But those who have been accustomed to consider something else, will form another common image of men—e.g., that man is an animal capable of laughter, or a featherless biped, or a rational animal.

And similarly concerning the others—each will form universal images of things according to the disposition of his body. Hence it is not surprising that so many controversies have arisen among the philosophers, who have wished to explain natural things by mere images of things.

Schol. 2: From what has been said above, it is clear that we perceive many things and form universal notions:

I. from singular things which have been represented to us through the senses in a way that is mutilated, confused, and without order for the intellect (see P29C); for that reason I have been accustomed to call such perceptions knowledge from random experience;

II. from signs, e.g., from the fact that, having heard or read certain words, we recollect things, and form certain ideas of them, which are like them, and through which we imagine the things (P18S). These two ways of regarding things I shall henceforth call knowledge of the first kind, opinion or imagination.

III. Finally, from the fact that we have common notions and adequate ideas of the properties of things (see P38C, P39, P39C, and P40). This I shall call reason and the second kind of knowledge.

[IV]. In addition to these two kinds of knowledge, there is (as I shall show in what follows) another, third kind, which we shall call intuitive knowledge. And this kind of knowing proceeds from an adequate idea of the formal essence of certain attributes of God to the adequate knowledge of the [formal] essence of things.

I shall explain all these with one example. Suppose there are three numbers, and the problem is to find a fourth which is to the third as the second is to the first. Merchants do not hesitate to multiply the second by the third, and divide the product by the first, because they have not yet forgotten what they heard from their teacher without any demonstration, or because they have often found this in the simplest numbers, or from the force of the Demonstration of P7 in Bk. VII of Euclid, viz. from the common property of proportionals. But in the simplest numbers none of this is necessary. Given the numbers 1, 2, and 3, no one fails to see that the fourth proportional number is 6—and we see this much more clearly because we infer the fourth number from the ratio which, in one glance, we see the first number to have the second.

P41:

Knowledge of the first kind is the only cause of falsity, whereas knowledge of the second and of the third kind is necessarily true.

Dem.: We have said in the preceding scholium that to knowledge of the first kind pertain all those ideas which are inadequate and confused; and so (by P35) this knowledge is the only cause of falsity. Next, we have said that to knowledge of the second and third kinds pertain those which are adequate; and so (by P34) this knowledge is necessarily true.

P42:

Knowledge of the second and third kinds, and not of the first kind, teaches us to distinguish the true from the false.

Dem.: This Proposition is evident through itself. For he who knows how to distinguish between the true and the false must have an adequate idea of the true and of the false, i.e. (P40S2), must know the true and the false by the second or third kind of knowledge.

P43:

He who has a true idea at the same time knows that he has a true idea, and cannot doubt the truth of the thing.

Dem.: An idea true in us is that which is adequate in God insofar as he is explained through the nature of the human Mind (by P11C). Let us posit, therefore, that there is in God, insofar as he is explained through the nature of the human Mind, an adequate idea, A. Of this idea there must necessarily also be in God an idea which is related to God in the same way as idea A (by P20, whose demonstration is universal [and can be applied to all ideas]). But idea A is supposed to be related to God insofar as he is explained through the nature of the human Mind; therefore the idea of idea A must also be related to God in the same way, i.e. (by the same P11C), this adequate idea of idea A will be in the Mind itself which has the adequate idea A. And so he who has an adequate idea, *or* (by P34) who knows a thing truly, must at the same time have an adequate idea, *or* true knowledge, of his own knowledge. I.e. (as is manifest through itself), he must at the same time be certain, q.e.d.

Schol.: In P21S I have explained what an idea of an idea is. But it should be noted that the preceding proposition is sufficiently manifest through itself. For no one who has a true idea is unaware that a true idea involves the highest certainty. For to have a true idea means nothing other than knowing a thing perfectly, *or* in the best way. And of course no one can doubt this unless he thinks that an idea is something mute, like a picture on a tablet, and not a mode of thinking, viz. the very [act of] understanding. And I ask, who can know that he understands some thing unless he first understands it? I.e., who can know that he is certain about some thing unless he is first certain about it? What can there be which is clearer and more certain than a true idea, to serve as a standard of truth? As the light makes both itself and the darkness plain, so truth is the standard both of itself and of the false.

By this I think we have replied to these questions: if a true idea is distinguished from a false one, [not insofar as it is said to be a mode of thinking, but] only insofar as it is said to agree with its object, then a true idea has no more reality or perfection than a false one (since they are distinguished only through the extrinsic denomination [and not through the intrinsic denomination])—and so, does the man who has true ideas [have any more reality or perfection] than him who has only false ideas? Again, why do men have false ideas? And finally, how can someone know certainly that he has ideas which agree with their objects?

To these questions, I say, I think I have already replied. For as far as the difference between a true and a false idea is concerned, it is established from P35 that the true is related to the false as being is to nonbeing. And the causes of falsity I have shown most clearly from P19 to P35S. From this it is also clear what is the difference between the man who has true ideas and the man who has only false ideas. Finally, as to the last, viz. how a man can know that he has an idea that agrees with its object? I have just shown, more than sufficiently, that this arises solely from his having an idea that does agree with its object—*or* that truth is its own standard. Add to this that our Mind, insofar as it perceives things truly, is part of the infinite intellect of God (by P11C); hence, it is as necessary that the mind's clear and distinct ideas are true as that God's ideas are.

P44:

It is of the nature of Reason to regard things as necessary, not as contingent.

Dem.: It is of the nature of reason to perceive things truly (by P41), viz. (by IA6) as they are in themselves, i.e. (by IP29), not as contingent but as necessary, q.e.d.

Cor. 1: From this it follows that it depends only on the imagination that we regard things as contingent, both in respect to the past and in respect to the future.

Schol.: I shall explain briefly how this happens. We have shown above (by P17 and P17C) that even though things do not exist, the Mind still imagines them always as present to itself, unless causes occur which exclude their present existence. Next, we have shown (P18) that if the human Body has once been affected by two external bodies at the same time, then afterwards, when the Mind imagines one of them, it will immediately recollect the other also, i.e., it will regard both as present to itself unless causes occur which exclude their present existence. Moreover, no one doubts but what we also imagine time, viz. from the fact that we imagine some bodies to move more slowly, or more quickly, or with the same speed.

Let us suppose, then, a child, who saw Peter for the first time yesterday, in the morning, but saw Paul at noon, and Simon in the evening, and today again saw Peter in the morning. It is clear from P18 that as soon as he sees the morning light, he will immediately imagine the sun taking the same course through the sky as he saw on the preceding day, *or* he will imagine the whole day, and Peter together with the morning, Paul with noon, and Simon with the evening. That is, he will imagine the existence of Paul and of Simon with a relation to future time. On the other hand, if he sees Simon in the evening, he will relate Paul and Peter to the time past, by imagining them together with past time. And he will do this more uniformly, the more often he has seen them in this same order.

But if it should happen at some time that on some other evening he sees James instead of Simon, then on the following morning he will imagine now Simon, now James, together with the evening time, but not both at once. For it is supposed that he has seen one or the other of them in the evening, but not both at once. His imagination, therefore, will vacillate and he will imagine now this one, now that one, with the future evening time, i.e., he will regard neither of them as certainly future, but both of them as contingently future.

And this vacillation of the imagination will be the same if the imagination is of things we regard in the same way with relation to past time or to present time. Consequently we shall imagine things as contingent in relation to present time as well as to past and future time.

Cor. 2: It is of the nature of Reason to perceive things under a certain species of eternity.

Dem.: It is of the nature of Reason to regard things as necessary and not as contingent (by P44). And it perceives this necessity of things truly (by P41), i.e. (by IA6), as it is in itself. But (by IP16) this necessity of things is the very necessity of God's eternal nature. Therefore, it is of the nature of Reason to regard things under this species of eternity.

Add to this that the foundations of Reason are notions (by P38) which explain those things that are common to all, and which (by P37) do not explain the essence of any singular thing. On that account, they must be conceived without any relation to time, but under a certain species of eternity, q.e.d.

P45:
Each idea of each body, or of each singular thing which actually exists, necessarily involves an eternal and infinite essence of God.

Dem.: The idea of a singular thing which actually exists necessarily involves both the essence of the thing and its existence (by P8C). But singular things (by IP15) cannot be conceived without God—on the contrary, because (by P6) they have God for a cause insofar as he is considered under the attribute of which the things are modes, their ideas must involve the concept of their attribute (by IA4), i.e. (by ID6), must involve an eternal and infinite essence of God, q.e.d.

Schol.: By existence here I do not understand duration, i.e., existence insofar as it is conceived abstractly, and as a certain species of quantity. For I am speaking of the very nature of existence, which is attributed to singular things because infinitely many things follow from the eternal necessity of God's nature in infinitely many modes (see IP16). I am speaking, I say, of the very existence of singular things insofar as they are in God. For even if each one is determined by another singular thing to exist in a certain way, still the force by which each one perseveres in existing follows from the eternal necessity of God's nature. Concerning this, see IP24C.

P46:
The knowledge of God's eternal and infinite essence which each idea involves is adequate and perfect.

Dem.: The demonstration of the preceding Proposition is Universal, and whether the thing is considered as a part or as a whole, its idea, whether of the whole or a part (by P45), will involve God's eternal and infinite essence. So what gives knowledge of an eternal and infinite essence of God is common to all, and is equally in the part and in the whole. And so (by P38) this knowledge will be adequate, q.e.d.

P47:

The human Mind has an adequate knowledge of God's eternal and infinite essence.

Dem.: The human Mind has ideas (by P22) from which it perceives (by P23) itself, (by P19) its own Body, and (by P16C1 and P17) external bodies as actually existing. And so (by P45 and P46) it has an adequate knowledge of God's eternal and infinite essence, q.e.d.

Schol.: From this we see that God's infinite essence and his eternity are known to all. And since all things are in God and are conceived through God, it follows that we can deduce from this knowledge a great many things which we know adequately, and so can form that third kind of knowledge of which we spoke in P40S2 and of whose excellence and utility we shall speak in Part V.

But that men do not have so clear a knowledge of God as they do of the common notions comes from the fact that they cannot imagine God, as they can bodies, and that they have joined the name *God* to the images of things which they are used to seeing. Men can hardly avoid this, because they are continually affected by bodies.

And indeed, most errors consist only in our not rightly applying names to things. For when someone says that the lines which are drawn from the center of a circle to its circumference are unequal, he surely understands (then at least) by a circle something different from what Mathematicians understand. Similarly, when men err in calculating, they have certain numbers in their mind and different ones on the paper. So if you consider what they have in Mind, they really do not err, though they seem to err because we think they have in their mind the numbers which are on the paper. If this were not so, we would not believe that they were erring, just as I did not believe that he was erring whom I recently heard cry out that his courtyard

had flown into his neighbor's hen [although his words were absurd], because what he had in mind seemed sufficiently clear to me [viz. that his hen had flown into his neighbor's courtyard].

And most controversies have arisen from this, that men do not rightly explain their own mind, or interpret the mind of the other man badly. For really, when they contradict one another most vehemently, they either have the same thoughts, or they are thinking of different things, so that what they think are errors and absurdities in the other are not.

P48:

In the Mind there is no absolute, or free, will, but the Mind is determined to will this or that by a cause which is also determined by another, and this again by another, and so to infinity.

Dem.: The Mind is a certain and determinate mode of thinking (by P11), and so (by IP17C2) cannot be a free cause of its own actions, *or* cannot have an absolute faculty of willing and not willing. Rather, it must be determined to willing this or that (by IP28) by a cause which is also determined by another, and this cause again by another, etc., q.e.d.

Schol.: In this same way it is also demonstrated that there is in the Mind no absolute faculty of understanding, desiring, loving, etc. From this it follows that these and similar faculties are either complete fictions or nothing but Metaphysical beings, *or* universals, which we are used to forming from particulars. So intellect and will are to this or that idea, or to this or that volition as "stone-ness" is to this or that stone, or man to Peter or Paul.

We have explained the cause of men's thinking themselves free in the Appendix of Part I. But before I proceed further, it should be noted here that by will I understand a faculty of affirming and denying, and not desire. I say that I understand the faculty by which the Mind affirms or denies something true or something false, and not the desire by which the Mind wants a thing or avoids it.

But after we have demonstrated that these faculties are universal notions which are not distinguished from the singulars from which we form them, we must now investigate whether the volitions themselves are anything beyond the very ideas of things. We must investigate, I say, whether there is any other affirmation or negation in the Mind except that which the idea involves, insofar as it is an idea—on this see the following Proposition and also D3—so that our thought does not fall into pictures. For by ideas I understand, not the images that are formed at the back of the eye (and, if you like, in the middle of the brain), but concepts of Thought [or the objective Being of a thing insofar as it consists only in Thought].

P49:

In the Mind there is no volition, or affirmation and negation, except that which the idea involves insofar as it is an idea.

Dem.: In the Mind (by P48) there is no absolute faculty of willing and not willing, but only singular volitions, viz. this and that affirmation, and this and that negation. Let us conceive, therefore, some singular volition, say a mode of thinking by which the Mind affirms that the three angles of a triangle are equal to two right angles.

This affirmation involves the concept, *or* idea, of the triangle, i.e., it cannot be conceived without the idea of the triangle. For to say that A must involve the concept of B is the same as to say that A cannot be conceived without B. Further, this affirmation (by A3) also cannot be without the idea of the triangle. Therefore, this affirmation can neither be nor be conceived without the idea of the triangle.

Next, this idea of the triangle must involve this same affirmation, viz. that its three angles equal two right angles. So conversely, this idea of the triangle also can neither be nor be conceived without this affirmation.

So (by D2) this affirmation pertains to the essence of the idea of the triangle, and is nothing beyond it. And what we have said concerning this volition (since we have selected it at random), must also be said concerning any volition, viz. that it is nothing apart from the idea, q.e.d.

Cor.: The will and the intellect are one and the same.

Dem.: The will and the intellect are nothing apart from the singular volitions and ideas themselves (by P48 and P48S). But the singular volitions and ideas are one and the same (by P49). Therefore the will and the intellect are one and the same, q.e.d.

Schol.: [I.] By this we have removed what is commonly maintained to be the cause of error. Moreover, we have shown above that falsity consists only in the privation that mutilated and confused ideas in-

volve. So a false idea, insofar as it is false, does not involve certainty. When we say that a man rests in false ideas, and does not doubt them, we do not, on that account, say that he is certain, but only that he does not doubt, or that he rests in false ideas because there are no causes to bring it about that his imagination wavers [or to cause him to doubt them]. On this, see P44S.

Therefore, however stubbornly a man may cling to something false [so that we cannot in any way make him doubt it], we shall still never say that he is certain of it. For by certainty we understand something positive (see P43 and P43S), not the privation of doubt. But by the privation of certainty, we understand falsity.

However, to explain the preceding Proposition more fully, there remain certain things I must warn you of. And then I must reply to the objections that can be made against this doctrine of ours. And finally, to remove every uneasiness, I thought it worthwhile to indicate some of the advantages of this doctrine. Some, I say—for the most important ones will be better understood from what we shall say in Part V.

[II.] I begin, therefore, by warning my Readers, first, to distinguish accurately between an idea, *or* concept, of the Mind, and the images of things that we imagine. And then it is necessary to distinguish between ideas and the words by which we signify things. For because many people either completely confuse these three—ideas, images, and words—or do not distinguish them accurately enough, or carefully enough, they have been completely ignorant of this doctrine concerning the will. But it is quite necessary to know it, both for the sake of speculation and in order to arrange one's life wisely.

Indeed, those who think that ideas consist in images which are formed in us from encounters with [external] bodies, are convinced that those ideas of things [which can make no trace in our brains, or] of which we can form no similar image [in our brain] are not ideas, but only fictions which we feign from a free choice of the will. They look on ideas, therefore, as mute pictures on a panel and preoccupied with this prejudice, do not see that an idea, insofar as it is an idea, involves an affirmation or negation.

And then, those who confuse words with the idea, or with the very affirmation that the idea involves, think that they can will something contrary to what they are aware of, when they only affirm or deny with words something contrary to what they are aware of. But these prejudices can easily be put aside by anyone who attends to the nature of thought, which does not at all involve the concept of extension. He will then understand clearly that an idea (since it is a mode of thinking) consists neither in the image of anything, nor in words. For the essence of words and of images is constituted only by corporeal motions, which do not at all involve the concept of thought.

It should suffice to have issued these few words of warning on this matter, so I pass to objections mentioned above.

[III.A.(i)] The first of these is that they think it clear that the will extends more widely than the intellect, and so is different from the intellect. The reason why they think the will extends more widely than the intellect is that they say they know by experience that they do not require a greater faculty of assenting, *or* affirming, and denying, than we already have, in order to assent to infinitely many other things which we do not perceive—but they do require a greater faculty of understanding. The will, therefore, is distinguished from the intellect because the intellect is finite and the will is infinite.

[III.A.(ii)] Secondly, it can be objected to us that experience seems to teach nothing more clearly than that we can suspend our judgment so as not to assent to things we perceive. This also seems to be confirmed from the fact that no one is said to be deceived insofar as he perceives something, but only insofar as he assents or dissents. E.g., someone who feigns a winged horse does not on that account grant that there is a winged horse, i.e., he is not on that account deceived unless at the same time he grants that there is a winged horse. Therefore, experience seems to teach nothing more clearly than that the will, *or* faculty of assenting, is free, and different from the faculty of understanding.

[III.A.(iii)] Thirdly, it can be objected that one affirmation does not seem to contain more reality than another, i.e., we do not seem to require a greater power to affirm that what is true, is true, than to affirm that something false is true. But [with ideas it is different, for] we perceive that one idea has more reality, *or* perfection, than another. As some objects are more excellent than others, so also

some ideas of objects are more perfect than others. This also seems to establish a difference between the will and the intellect.

[III.A.(iv)] Fourth, it can be objected that if man does not act from freedom of the will, what will happen if he is in a state of equilibrium, like Buridan's ass? Will he perish of hunger and of thirst? If I concede that he will, I would seem to conceive an ass, or a statue of a man, not a man. But if I deny that he will, then he will determine himself, and consequently have the faculty of going where he wills and doing what he wills.

Perhaps other things in addition to these can be objected. But because I am not bound to force on you what anyone can dream, I shall only take the trouble to reply to these objections—and that as briefly as I can.

[III.B.(i)] To the first I say that I grant that the will extends more widely than the intellect, if by intellect they understand only clear and distinct ideas. But I deny that the will extends more widely than perceptions, *or* the faculty of conceiving. And indeed, I do not see why the faculty of willing should be called infinite, when the faculty of sensing is not. For just as we can affirm infinitely many things by the same faculty of willing (but one after another, for we cannot affirm infinitely many things at once), so also we can sense, *or* perceive, infinitely many bodies by the same faculty of sensing (viz. one after another [and not at once]).

If they say that there are infinitely many things which we cannot perceive, I reply that we cannot reach them by any thought, and consequently, not by any faculty of willing. But, they say, if God willed to bring it about that we should perceive them also, he would have to give us a greater faculty of perceiving, but not a greater faculty of willing than he has given us. This is the same as if they said that, if God should will to bring it about that we understood infinitely many other beings, it would indeed be necessary for him to give us a greater intellect, but not a more universal idea of being, in order for us to embrace the same infinity of beings. For we have shown that the will is a universal being, *or* idea, by which we explain all the singular volitions, i.e., it is what is common to them all.

Therefore, since they believe that this common *or* universal idea of all volitions is a faculty, it is not at all surprising if they say that this faculty extends beyond the limits of the intellect to infinity. For the universal is said equally of one, a great many, or infinitely many individuals.

[III.B.(ii)] To the second objection I reply by denying that we have a free power of suspending judgment. For when we say that someone suspends judgment, we are saying nothing but that he sees that he does not perceive the thing adequately. Suspension of judgment, therefore, is really a perception, not [an act of] free will.

To understand this clearly, let us conceive a child imagining a winged horse, and not perceiving anything else. Since this imagination involves the existence of the horse (by P17C), and the child does not perceive anything else that excludes the existence of the horse, he will necessarily regard the horse as present. Nor will he be able to doubt its existence, though he will not be certain of it.

We find this daily in our dreams, and I do not believe there is anyone who thinks that while he is dreaming he has a free power of suspending judgment concerning the things he dreams, and of bringing it about that he does not dream the things he dreams he sees. Nevertheless, it happens that even in dreams we suspend judgment, viz. when we dream that we dream.

Next, I grant that no one is deceived insofar as he perceives, i.e., I grant that the imaginations of the Mind, considered in themselves, involve no error. But I deny that a man affirms nothing insofar as he perceives. For what is perceiving a winged horse other than affirming wings of the horse? For if the Mind perceived nothing else except the winged horse, it would regard it as present to itself, and would not have any cause of doubting its existence, or any faculty of dissenting, unless either the imagination of the winged horse were joined to an idea which excluded the existence of the same horse, or the Mind perceived that its idea of a winged horse was inadequate. And then either it will necessarily deny the horse's existence, or it will necessarily doubt it.

[III.B.(iii)] As for the third objection, I think what has been said will be an answer to it too: viz. that the will is something universal, which is predicated of all ideas, and which signifies only what is common to all ideas, viz. the affirmation, whose adequate essence, therefore, insofar as it is thus conceived abstractly, must be in each idea, and in this way only must be the same in all, but not insofar as it is considered to constitute the idea's essence; for in that regard the singular affirmations differ from one another as much as the ideas themselves do. For example, the affirmation that the idea of a circle involves differs from that which the idea of a triangle involves as much as the idea of the circle differs from the idea of the triangle.

Next, I deny absolutely that we require an equal power of thinking, to affirm that what is true is true, as to affirm that what is false is true. For if you consider the mind, they are related to one another as being to not-being. For there is nothing positive in ideas which constitutes the form of falsity (see P35, P35S, and P47S). So the thing to note here, above all, is how easily we are deceived when we confuse universals with singulars, and beings of reason and abstractions with real beings.

[III.B.(iv)] Finally, as far as the fourth objection is concerned, I say that I grant entirely that a man placed in such an equilibrium (viz. who perceives nothing but thirst and hunger, and such food and drink as are equally distant from him) will perish of hunger and thirst. If they ask me whether such a man should not be thought an ass, rather than a man, I say that I do not know—just as I also do not know how highly we should esteem one who hangs himself, or children, fools, and madmen, etc.

[IV.] It remains now to indicate how much knowledge of this doctrine is to our advantage in life. We shall see this easily from the following considerations:

[A.] Insofar as it teaches that we act only from God's command, that we share in the divine nature, and that we do this the more, the more perfect our actions are, and the more and more we understand God. This doctrine, then, in addition to giving us complete peace of mind, also teaches us wherein our greatest happiness, *or* blessedness, consists: viz. in the knowledge of God alone, by which we are led to do only those things which love and morality advise. From this we clearly understand how far they stray from the true valuation of virtue, who expect to be honored by God with the greatest rewards for their virtue and best actions, as for the greatest bondage—as if virtue itself, and the service of God, were not happiness itself, and the greatest freedom.

[B.] Insofar as it teaches us how we must bear ourselves concerning matters of fortune, *or* things which are not in our power, i.e., concerning things which do not follow from our nature—that we must expect and bear calmly both good fortune and bad. For all things follow from God's eternal decree with the same necessity as from the essence of a triangle it follows that its three angles are equal to two right angles.

[C.] This doctrine contributes to social life, insofar as it teaches us to hate no one, to disesteem no one, to mock no one, to be angry at no one, to envy no one; and also insofar as it teaches that each of us should be content with his own things, and should be helpful to his neighbor, not from unmanly compassion, partiality, or superstition, but from the guidance of reason, as the time and occasion demand. I shall show this in the Fourth Part.

[D.] Finally, this doctrine also contributes, to no small extent, to the common society insofar as it teaches how citizens are to be governed and led, not so that they may be slaves, but that they may do freely the things that are best.

And with this I have finished what I had decided to treat in this scholium, and put an end to this our Second Part. In it I think that I have explained the nature and properties of the human Mind in sufficient detail, and as clearly as the difficulty of the subject allows, and that I have set out doctrines from which we can infer many excellent things, which are highly useful and necessary to know, as will be established partly in what follows.

Gottfried Leibniz
(1646–1716)

Leibniz was born in Leipzig into an academic family: his mother was the daughter of a professor at the University of Leipzig, his father a professor at the same university. He was something of a prodigy. Applying to take the examinations in law at the age of twenty in Leipzig, he was turned down because of his youth, whereupon he went to Altdorf, where he graduated and was offered a professorship. He declined in order to go to Nuremberg to become secretary to the Rosicrucian Society. There he met Johann Christian von Boyneburg, a politically influential former first minister at the court of Mainz. Boyneburg introduced Leibniz to Johann Philipp von Schönborn, elector of Mainz, into whose service he entered, mainly working on legal matters. In 1672 he went to Paris, apparently on personal business of the elector's, where he remained for four years. There he made many important contacts, including Christian Huygens, from whom most of Leibniz's work in physics derives, as well as Antoine Arnauld (famous for his objections to Descartes) and

Nicolas Malebranche, the famous occasional-ist. There he constructed a calculating machine capable of multiplying large numbers, and studied the works of Pascal, Descartes, and Huygens. There also he did the work that entitles him to be cited, with Newton, as co-discoverer of the calculus. An acrimonious (on Newton's part, at least) dispute about priority, exacerbated by another substantive dispute about the proper treatment of force (in which Newton eventually prevailed), plagued Leibniz in his later years.

In 1676 Leibniz, now widely known, went to Hanover to enter the service of the duke, Johann Friedrich. When Johann Friedrich died in 1679, Leibniz stayed on in the service of his son, Ernst August, and then of Georg Ludwig, who became George I of England in 1714. In 1685 Ernst August set Leibniz the task of writing a history of the house of Brunswick, which took Leibniz to Munich, Vienna, and Italy between 1687 and 1690. During his service to the house of Brunswick, Leibniz became close friends with Sophie, the wife of Ernst August, and their daughter Sophie Charlotte. Much of Leibniz's theological writing grew out of discussions with these two. When Sophie Charlotte became queen of Prussia, Leibniz took to visiting her in Berlin, where he helped found, and was appointed president for life to, the Berlin Society of Science (later the Prussian Royal Academy). After Sophie Charlotte's death in 1705, however, his visits were less welcome, and he soon ceased going to Berlin. Though he wanted to go to England with George I, Leibniz was left in Hanover to finish his history, a task unfinished at his death.

Leibniz presents a challenge to scholarship for several reasons. Unlike the other authors reprinted in this volume, Leibniz never wrote anything that can fairly be said to represent all of his central philosophical ideas. Instead of a few definitive works, Leibniz's opus consists of a mass of articles published in a variety of journals, together with a huge correspondence which he kept up throughout his life with persons of every sort. (Many of Leibniz's letters are, in fact, complete essays.) While the *Monadology*, reprinted here, represents his mature metaphysical ideas, it is mainly a position paper, summarizing doctrines, for the most part, rather than arguing for them, and his philosophical views on many topics are not touched on at all. [Our other selection, the *Discourse on Metaphysics*, gives us a little more sense of Leibnizian argumentation. It was written a quarter of a century earlier than the *Monodology* and remained unpublished until long after Leibniz's death. Between the two, we can get some sense of the development of Leibniz's views on a common set of metaphysical problems. The student of Leibniz's metaphysics should also be aware of Leibniz's correspondence with Arnauld, in which the themes of the *Discourse* are further discussed.]

Leibniz's philosophical views changed considerably over the course of his life, and these changes cannot be ignored, given the lack of any definitive work. This was natural for a man whose cast of mind was essentially ecumenical. He defended the scholastics, in much disrepute among the "moderns" of his time, yet held many doctrines, such as the reality of unconscious mental processes and perceptions, and the relativity of space and time, that were justly regarded in his day as extremely radical. He had a lasting interest in formulating a version of Christian doctrine that everyone could accept, and that would put an end to religious disputation and war. He was active in the founding of many scientific societies, and lent his support to various encyclopedia projects designed to bring together in one place technical and scientific knowledge from a variety of sources. He was horrified by what had been lost during the Middle Ages, and hoped to collect and preserve even such things as techniques practiced by craftsmen. Leibniz himself would have been pleased by the idea that readers were led to consult encyclopedia articles and secondary sources in order to prepare for reading the *Monadology*. Students of Locke should also be aware of the *New Essays Concerning Human Understanding*, which Leibniz, moved by Pierre Coste's 1704 French translation of Locke's *Essay Concerning Human Understanding*, wrote as a section-by-section commentary on Locke's masterpiece.

Discourse on Metaphysics

I. Concerning the divine perfection and that God does everything in the most desirable way.

The conception of God which is the most common and the most full of meaning is expressed well enough in the words: God is an absolutely perfect being. The implications, however, of these words fail to receive sufficient consideration. For instance, there are many different kinds of perfection, all of which God possesses, and each one of them pertains to him in the highest degree.

We must also know what perfection is. One thing which can surely be affirmed about it is that those forms or natures which are not susceptible to it to the highest degree, say the nature of numbers or of figures, do not permit of perfection. This is because the number which is the greatest of all (that is, the sum of all the numbers), and likewise the greatest of all figures, imply contradictions. The greatest knowledge, however, and omnipotence contain no impossibility. Consequently power and knowledge do admit of perfection, and in so far as they pertain to God they have no limits.

Reprinted from *Leibniz: Basic Writings*, trans. George Montgomery (1902; reprint, La Salle, Ill.: Open Court, 1990), pp. 3–63.

Whence it follows that God who possesses supreme and infinite wisdom acts in the most perfect manner not only metaphysically, but also from the moral standpoint. And with respect to our selves it can be said that the more we are enlightened and informed in regard to the works of God the more will we be disposed to find them excellent and conforming entirely to that which we might desire.

II. Against those who hold that there is in the works of God no goodness, or that the principles of goodness and beauty are arbitrary.

Therefore I am far removed from the opinion of those who maintain that there are no principles of goodness or perfection in the nature of things, or in the ideas which God has about them, and who say that the works of God are good only through the formal reason that God has made them. If this position were true, God, knowing that he is the author of things, would not have to regard them afterwards and find them good, as the Holy Scripture witnesses. Such anthropological expressions are used only to let us know that excellence is recognized in regarding the works themselves, even if we do not consider their evident dependence on their author. This is confirmed by the fact that it is in reflecting upon the works that we are able to discover the one who wrought. They must therefore bear in themselves his character. I confess that the contrary opinion seems to me extremely dangerous and closely approaches that of recent innovators who hold that the beauty of the universe and the goodness which we attribute to the works of God are chimeras of human beings who think of God in human terms. In saying, therefore, that things are not good according to any standard of goodness, but simply by the will of God, it seems to me that one destroys, without realizing it, all the love of God and all his glory; for why praise him for what he has done, if he would be equally praiseworthy in doing the contrary? Where will be his justice and his wisdom if he has only a certain despotic power, if arbitrary will takes the place of reasonableness, and if in accord with the definition of tyrants, justice consists in that which is pleasing to the most powerful? Besides it seems that every act of willing supposes some reason for the willing and this reason, of course, must precede the act. This is why, accordingly, I find so strange those expressions of certain philosophers who say that the eternal truths of metaphysics and Geometry, and consequently the principles of goodness, of justice, and of perfection, are effects only of the will of God. To me it seems that all these follow from his understanding, which does not depend upon his will any more than does his essence.

III. *Against those who think that God might have made things better than he has.*

No more am I able to approve of the opinion of certain modern writers who boldly maintain that that which God has made is not perfect in the highest degree, and that he might have done better. It seems to me that the consequences of such an opinion are wholly inconsistent with the glory of God. *Uti minus malum habet rationem boni, ita minus bonum habet rationem mali.* I think that one acts imperfectly if he acts with less perfection than he is capable of. To show that an architect could have done better is to find fault with his work. Furthermore this opinion is contrary to the Holy Scriptures when they assure us of the goodness of God's work. For if comparative perfection were sufficient, then in whatever way God had accomplished his work, since there is an infinitude of possible imperfections, it would always have been good in comparison with the less perfect; but a thing is little praiseworthy when it can be praised only in this way.

I believe that a great many passages from the divine writings and from the holy fathers will be found favoring my position, while hardly any will be found in favor of that of these modern thinkers. Their opinion is, in my judgment, unknown to the writers of antiquity and is a deduction based upon the too slight acquaintance which we have with the general harmony of the universe and with the hidden reasons for God's conduct. In our ignorance, therefore, we are tempted to decide audaciously that many things might have been done better.

These modern thinkers insist upon certain hardly tenable subtleties, for they imagine that nothing is so perfect that there might not have been something more perfect. This is an error. They think, indeed, that they are thus safeguarding the liberty of God. As if it were not the highest liberty to act in perfection according to the sovereign reason. For to think that God acts in anything without having any reason for his willing, even if we overlook the fact that such action seems impossible, is an opinion which conforms little to God's glory. For example, let us suppose that God chooses between A and B, and that he takes A without any reason for preferring it to B. I say that this action on the part of God is at least not praiseworthy, for all praise ought to be founded upon reason which *ex hypothesi* is not present here. My opinion is that God does nothing for which he does not deserve to be glorified.

IV. *That love for God demands on our part complete satisfaction with and acquiescence in that which he has done.*

The general knowledge of this great truth that God acts always in the most perfect and most desirable manner possible, is in my opinion the basis of the love which we owe to God in all things; for he who loves seeks his satisfaction in the felicity or perfection of the object loved and in the perfection of his actions. *Idem velle et idem nolle vera amicitia est.* I believe that it is difficult to love God truly when one, having the power to change his disposition, is not disposed to wish for that which God desires. In fact those who are not satisfied with what God does seem to me like dissatisfied subjects whose attitude is not very different from that of rebels. I hold therefore, that on these principles, to act conformably to the love of God it is not sufficient to force oneself to be patient, we must be really satisfied with all that comes to us according to his will. I mean this acquiescence in regard to the past; for as regards the future one should not be a quietist with the arms folded, open to ridicule, awaiting that which God will do; according to the sophism which the ancients called λόγον ἄεργον the lazy reason. It is necessary to act conformably to the presumptive will of God as far as we are able to judge of it, trying with all our might to contribute to the general welfare and particularly to the ornamentation and the perfection of that which touches us, or of that which is nigh and so to speak at our hand. For if the future shall perhaps show that God has not wished our good intention to have its way, it does not follow that he has not wished us to act as we have; on the contrary, since he is the best of all masters, he ever demands only the right intentions, and it is for him to know the hour and the proper place to let good designs succeed.

V. In what the principles of the divine perfection consist, and that the simplicity of the means counterbalances the richness of the effects.

It is sufficient therefore to have this confidence in God, that he has done everything for the best and that nothing will be able to injure those who love him. To know in particular, however, the reasons which have moved him to choose this order of the universe, to permit sin, to dispense his salutary grace in a certain manner,—this passes the capacity of a finite mind, above all when such a mind has not come into the joy of the vision of God. Yet is is possible to make some general remarks touching the course of providence in the government of things. One is able to say, therefore, that he who acts perfectly is like an excellent Geometer who knows how to find the best construction for a problem; like a good architect who utilizes his location and the funds destined for the building in the most advantageous manner, leaving nothing which shocks or which does not display that beauty of which it is capable; like a good householder who employs his property in such a way that there shall be nothing

uncultivated or sterile; like a clever machinist who makes his production in the least difficult way possible; and like an intelligent author who encloses the most of reality in the least possible compass.

Of all beings those which are the most perfect and occupy the least possible space, that is to say those which interfere with one another the least, are the spirits whose perfections are the virtues. That is why we may not doubt that the felicity of the spirits is the principal aim of God and that he puts this purpose into execution, as far as the general harmony will permit. We will recur to this subject again.

When the simplicity of God's way is spoken of, reference is specially made to the means which he employs, and on the other hand when the variety, richness and abundance are referred to, the ends or effects are had in mind. Thus one ought to be proportioned to the other, just as the cost of a building should balance the beauty and grandeur which is expected. It is true that nothing costs God anything, just as there is no cost for a philosopher who makes hypotheses in constructing his imaginary world, because God has only to make decrees in order that a real world come into being; but in matters of wisdom the decrees or hypotheses meet the expenditure in proportion as they are more independent of one another. The reason wishes to avoid multiplicity in hypotheses or principles very much as the simplest system is preferred in Astronomy.

VI. That God does nothing which is not orderly, and that it is not even possible to conceive of events which are not regular.

The activities or the acts of will of God are commonly divided into ordinary and extraordinary. But it is well to bear in mind that God does nothing out of order. Therefore, that which passes for extraordinary is so only with regard to a particular order established among the created things, for as regards the universal order, everything conforms to it. This is so true that not only does nothing occur in this world which is absolutely irregular, but it is even impossible to conceive of such an occurrence. Because, let us suppose for example that some one jots down a quantity of points upon a sheet of paper helter skelter, as do those who exercise the ridiculous art of Geomancy; now I say that it is possible to find a geometrical line whose concept shall be uniform and constant, that is, in accordance with a certain formula, and which line at the same time shall pass through all of those points, and in the same order in which the hand jotted them down; also if a continuous line be traced, which is now straight, now circular, and now of any other description, it is possible to find a mental equivalent, a formula or an equation common to all the points of this line by virtue of which formula the changes in the direction of the line must occur. There is no instance of a face whose contour does not form part of a geometric line and which can not be traced entire by a certain mathematical motion. But when the formula is very complex, that which conforms to it passes for irregular. Thus we may say that in whatever manner God might have created the world, it would always have been regular and in a certain order. God, however, has chosen the most perfect, that is to say the one which is at the same time the simplest in hypotheses and the richest in phenomena, as might be the case with a geometric line, whose construction was easy, but whose properties and effects were extremely remarkable and of great significance. I use these comparisons to picture a certain imperfect resemblance to the divine wisdom, and to point out that which may at least raise our minds to conceive in some sort what cannot otherwise be expressed. I do not pretend at all to explain thus the great mystery upon which depends the whole universe.

VII. That miracles conform to the regular order although they go against the subordinate regulations; concerning that which God desires or permits and concerning general and particular intentions.

Now since nothing is done which is not orderly, we may say that miracles are quite within the order of natural operations. We use the term natural of these operations because they conform to certain subordinate regulations which we call the nature of things. For it can be said that this nature is only a custom of God's which he can change on the occasion of a stronger reason than that which moved him to use these regulations. As regards general and particular intentions, according to the way in which we understand the matter, it may be said on the one hand that everything is in accordance with his most general intention, or that which best conforms to the most perfect order he has chosen; on the other hand, however, it is also possible to say that he has particular intentions which are exceptions to the subordinate regulations above mentioned. Of God's laws, however, the most universal, i.e., that which rules the whole course of the universe, is without exceptions.

It is possible to say that God desires everything which is an object of his particular intention. When we consider the objects of his general intentions, however, such as are the modes of activities of created things and especially of the reasoning creatures with whom God wishes to co-operate, we must make a distinction; for if the action is good in itself, we may say that God wishes it and at times commands it, even though it does not take place; but if it is bad in itself and becomes good only by accident through the course of events and especially after chastisement and satisfaction have corrected its malignity and rewarded the ill with interest in such a way that more perfection results in the whole train of circumstances than would have come if that ill had not occurred,—if all this takes place we must say that God permits the evil, and not that he desired it, although he has co-operated by means of the laws of nature which he has established. He knows how to produce the greatest good from them.

VIII. In order to distinguish between the activities of God and the activities of created things we must explain the conception of an individual substance.

It is quite difficult to distinguish God's actions from those of his creatures. Some think that God does everything; others imagine that he only conserves the force that he has given to created things. How far can we say either of these opinions is right?

In the first place since activity and passivity pertain properly to individual substances (*actiones sunt suppositorum*) it will be necessary to explain what such a substance is. It is indeed true that when several predicates are attributes of a single subject and this subject is not an attribute of another, we speak of it as an individual substance, but this is not enough, and such an explanation is merely nominal. We must therefore inquire what it is to be attribute in reality of a certain subject. Now it is evident that every true predication has some basis in the nature of things, and even when a proposition is not identical, that is, when the predicate is not expressly contained in the subject, it is still necessary that it be virtually contained in it, and this is what the philosophers call *in-esse*, saying thereby that the predicate is in the subject. Thus the content of the subject must always include that of the predicate in such a way that if one understands perfectly the concept of the subject, he will know that the predicate appertains to it also. This being so, we are able to say that this is the nature of an individual substance or of a complete being, namely, to afford a conception so complete that the concept shall be sufficient for the understanding of it and for the deduction of all the predicates of which the substance is or may become the subject. Thus the quality of king, which belonged to Alexander the Great, an abstraction from the subject, is not sufficiently determined to constitute an individual, and does not contain the other qualities of the same subject, nor everything which the idea of this prince includes. God, however, seeing the individual concept, or haeceity, of Alexander, sees there at the same time the basis and the reason of all the predicates which can be truly uttered regarding him; for instance that he will conquer Darius and Porus, even to the point of knowing *a priori* (and not by experience) whether he died a natural death or by poison,—facts which we can learn only through history. When we carefully consider the connection of things we see also the possibility of saying that there was always in the soul of Alexander marks of all that had happened to him and evidences of all that would happen to him and traces even of everything which occurs in the universe, although God alone could recognize them all.

IX. *That every individual substance expresses the whole universe in its own manner and that in its full concept is included all its experiences together with all the attendant circumstances and the whole sequence of exterior events.*

There follow from these considerations several noticeable paradoxes; among others that it is not true that two substances may be exactly alike and differ only numerically, *solo numero,* and that what St. Thomas says on this point regarding angels and intelligences (*quod ibi omne individuum sit species infima*) is true of all substances, provided that the specific difference is understood as Geometers understand it in the case of figures; again that a substance will be able to commence only through creation and perish only through annihilation; that a substance cannot be divided into two nor can one be made out of two, and that thus the number of substances neither augments nor diminishes through natural means, although they are frequently transformed. Furthermore every substance is like an entire world and like a mirror of God, or indeed of the whole world which it portrays, each one in its own fashion; almost as the same city is variously represented according to the various situations of him who is regarding it. Thus the universe is multiplied in some sort as many times as there are substances, and the glory of God is multiplied in the same way by as many wholly different representations of his works. It can indeed be said that every substance bears in some sort the character of God's infinite wisdom and omnipotence, and imitates him as much as it is able to; for it expresses, although confusedly, all that happens in the universe, past, present, and future, deriving thus a certain resemblance to an infinite perception or power of knowing. And since all other substances express this particular substance and accommodate themselves to it, we can say that it exerts its power upon all the others in imitation of the omnipotence of the creator.

X. *That the belief in substantial forms has a certain basis in fact, but that these forms effect no changes in the phenomena and must not be employed for the explanation of particular events.*

It seems that the ancients, able men, who were accustomed to profound meditations and taught theology and philosophy for several centuries and some of whom recommend themselves to us on account of their piety, had some knowledge of that which we have just said and this is why they introduced and maintained the substantial forms so much decried to-day. But they were not so far from the truth nor so open to ridicule as the common run of our new philosophers imagine. I grant that the consideration of these forms is of no service in the details of physics and ought not to be employed in the explanation of particular phenomena. In regard to this last point, the schoolmen were at fault, as were also the physicians of times past who followed their example, thinking they had given the reason for the properties of a body in mentioning the forms and qualities without going to the trouble of examining the manner of operation; as if one should be content to say that a clock had a certain amount of clockness derived from its form, and should not inquire in what the clockness consisted. This is indeed enough for the man who buys it, provided he surrenders the care of it to someone else. The fact, however, that there was this misunderstanding and misuse of the substantial forms should not bring us to throw away something whose recognition is so necessary in metaphysics. Since without these we will not be able, I hold, to know the ultimate principles nor to lift our minds to the knowledge of the incorporeal natures and of the marvels of God. Yet as the geometer does not need to encumber his mind with the famous puzzle of the composition of the continuum, and as no moralist, and still less a jurist or a statesman has need to trouble himself with the great difficulties which arise in conciliating free will with the providential activity of God, (since the geometer is able to make all his demonstrations and the statesman can complete all his deliberations without entering into these discussions which are so necessary and important in Philosophy and Theology), so in the same way the physicist can explain his experiments, now using simpler experiments already made, now employing geometrical and mechanical demonstrations without any need of the general considerations which belong to another sphere, and if he employs the co-operation of God, or perhaps of some soul or animating force, or something else of a similar nature, he goes out of his path quite as much as that man who, when facing an important practical question would wish to enter into profound argumentations regarding the nature of destiny and of our libety; a fault which men quite frequently commit without realizing it when they cumber their minds with considerations regarding fate, and thus they are even sometimes turned from a good resolution or from some necessary provision.

XI. That the opinions of the theologians and of the so-called scholastic philosophers are not to be wholly despised.

I know that I am advancing a great paradox in pretending to resuscitate in some sort the ancient philosophy, and to recall *postliminio* the substantial forms almost banished from our modern thought. But perhaps I will not be condemned lightly when it is known that I have long meditated over the modern philosophy and that I have devoted much time to experiments in physics and to the demonstrations of geometry and that I, too, for a long time was persuaded of the baselessness of those "beings" which, however, I was finally obliged to take up again in spite of myself and as though by force. The many investigations which I carried on compelled me to recognize that our moderns do not do sufficient justice to Saint Thomas and to the other great men of that period and that there is in the theories of the scholastic philosophers and theologians far more solidity than is imagined, provided that these theories are employed *à propos* and in their place. I am persuaded that if some careful and meditative mind were to take the trouble to clarify and direct their thoughts in the manner of analytic geometers, he would find a great treasure of very important truths, wholly demonstrable.

XII. That the conception of the extension of a body is in a way imaginary and does not constitute the substance of the body.

But to resume the thread of our discussion, I believe that he who will meditate upon the nature of substance, as I have explained it above, will find that the whole nature of bodies is not exhausted in their extension, that is to say, in their size, figure and motion, but that we must recognize something which corresponds to soul, something which is commonly called substantial form, although these forms effect no change in the phenomena, any more than do the souls of beasts, that is if they have souls. It is even possible to demonstrate that the ideas of size, figure and motion are not so distinctive as is imagined, and that they stand for something imaginary relative to our perceptions as do, although to a greater extent, the ideas of color, heat, and the other similar qualities in regard to which we may doubt whether they are actually to be found in the nature of the things outside of us. This is why these latter qualities are unable to constitute "substance" and if there is no other principle of identity in bodies than that which has just been referred to a body would not subsist more than for a moment.

The souls and the substance-forms of other bodies are entirely different from intelligent souls which alone know their actions, and not only do not perish through natural means but indeed always retain the knowledge of what they are; a fact which makes them alone open to chastisement or recompense, and makes them citizens of the republic of the universe whose monarch is God. Hence it follows that all the other creatures should serve them, a point which we shall discuss more amply later.

XIII. As the individual concept of each person includes once for all everything which can ever happen to him, in it can be seen, a priori *the evidences or the reasons for the reality of each event, and why one happened sooner than the other. But these events, however certain, are nevertheless contingent, being based on the free choice of God and of his creatures. It is true that their choices always have their reasons, but they incline to the choices under no compulsion of necessity.*

But before going further it is necessary to meet a difficulty which may arise regarding the principles which we have set forth in the preceding. We have said that the concept of an individual substance includes once for all everything which can ever happen to it and that in considering this concept one will be able to see everything which can truly be said concerning the individual, just as we are able to see in the nature of a circle all the properties which can be derived from it. But does it not seem that in this way the difference between contingent and necessary truths will be destroyed, that there will be no place for human liberty, and that an absolute fatality will rule as well over all our actions as over all the rest of the events of the world? To this I reply that a distinction must be made between that which is certain and that which is necessary. Every

one grants that future contingencies are assured since God foresees them, but we do not say just because of that that they are necessary. But it will be objected, that if any conclusion can be deduced infallibly from some definition or concept, it is necessary; and now since we have maintained that everything which is to happen to anyone is already virtually included in his nature or concept, as all the properties are contained in the definition of a circle, therefore, the difficulty still remains. In order to meet the objection completely, I say that the connection or sequence is of two kinds; the one, absolutely necessary, whose contrary implies contradiction, occurs in the eternal verities like the truths of geometry; the other is necessary only *ex hypothesi,* and so to speak by accident, and in itself it is contingent since the contrary is not implied. This latter sequence is not founded upon ideas wholly pure and upon the pure understanding of God, but upon his free decrees and upon the processes of the universe. Let us give an example. Since Julius Caesar will become perpetual Dictator and master of the Republic and will overthrow the liberty of Rome, this action is contained in his concept, for we have supposed that it is the nature of such a perfect concept of a subject to involve everything, in fact so that the predicate may be included in the subject *ut possit inesse subjecto.* We may say that it is not in virtue of this concept or idea that he is obliged to perform this action, since it pertains to him only because God knows everything. But it will be insisted in reply that his nature or form responds to this concept, and since God imposes upon him this personality, he is compelled henceforth to live up to it. I could reply by instancing the similar case of the future contingencies which as yet have no reality save in the understanding and will of God, and which, because God has given them in advance this form, must needs correspond to it. But I prefer to overcome a difficulty rather than to excuse it by instancing other difficulties, and what I am about to say will serve to clear up the one as well as the other. It is here that must be applied the distinction in the kind of relation, and I say that that which happens conformably to these decrees is assured, but that it is not therefore necessary, and if anyone did the contrary, he would do nothing impossible in itself, although it is impossible *ex hypothesi* that that other happen. For if anyone were capable of carrying out a complete demonstration by virtue of which he could prove this connection of the subject, which is Caesar, with the predicate, which is his successful enterprise, he would bring us to see in fact that the future dictatorship of Caesar had its basis in his concept or nature, so that one would see there a reason why he resolved to cross the Rubicon rather than to stop, and why he gained instead of losing the day at Pharsalus, and that it was reasonable and by consequence assured that this would occur, but one would not prove that it was necessary in itself, nor that the contrary implied a contradiction, almost in the same way in which it is reasonable and assured that God will always do what is best although that which is less perfect is not thereby implied. For it would be found that this demonstration of this predicate as belonging to Caesar is not as absolute as are those of numbers or of geometry, but that this predicate supposes a sequence of things which God has shown by his free will. This sequence is based on the first free decree of God which was to do always that which is the most perfect and upon the decree which God made following the first one, regarding human nature, which is that men should always do, although freely, that which appears to be the best. Now every truth which is founded upon this kind of decree is contingent, although certain, for the decrees of God do not change the possibilities of things and, as I have already said, although God assuredly chooses the best, this does not prevent that which is less perfect from being possible in itself. Although it will never happen, it is not its impossibility but its imperfection which causes him to reject it. Now nothing is necessitated whose opposite is possible. One will then be in a position to satisfy these kinds of difficulties, however great they may appear (and in fact they have not been less vexing to all other thinkers who have ever treated this matter), provided that he considers well that all contingent propositions have reasons why they are thus, rather than otherwise, or indeed (what is the same thing) that they have proof *a priori* of their truth, which render them certain and show that the connection of the subject and predicate in these propositions has its basis in the nature of the one and of the other, but he must further remember that such contingent propositions have not the demonstrations of necessity, since their reasons are founded only on the principle of contingency or of the existence of things, that is to say, upon that which is, or which appears to be the best among several things equally possible. Necessary truths, on the other hand, are founded upon the principle of contradiction, and upon the possibility or impossibility of the essences themselves, without regard here to the free will of God or of creatures.

XIV. God produces different substances according to the different views which he has of the world, and by the intervention of God, the appropriate nature of each substance brings it about that what happens to or corresponds to what happens to all the others, without, however, their acting upon one another directly.

After having seen, to a certain extent, in what the nature of substances consists, we must try to explain the dependence they have upon one another and their actions and passions. Now it is first of all very evident that created substances depend upon God who preserves them and can produce them continually by a kind of emanation just as we produce our thoughts, for when God turns, so to say, on all sides and in all fashions, the general system of phenomena which he finds it good to produce for the sake of manifesting his glory, and when he regards all the aspects of the world in all possible manners, since there is no relation which escapes his omniscience, the result of each view of the universe as seen from a different position is a substance which expresses the universe comformably to this view, provided God sees fit to render his thought effective and to produce the substance, and since God's vision is always true, our perceptions are always true and that which deceives us are our judgments, which are of us. Now we have said before, and it follows from what we have just said that each substance is a world by itself, independent of everything else excepting God; therefore, all our phenomena that is all things which are ever able to happen to us, are only consequences of our being. Now as the phenomena maintain a certain order conformably to our nature, or so to speak to the world which is in us (from whence it follows that we can, for the regulation of our conduct, make useful observations which are justified by the outcome of the future phenomena) and as we are thus able often to judge the future by the past without deceiving ourselves, we have sufficient grounds for saying that these phenomena are true and we will not be put to the task of inquiring whether they are outside of us, and whether others perceive them also.

Nevertheless it is most true that the perceptions and expressions of all substances intercorrespond, so that each one following independently certain reasons or laws which he has noticed meets others which are doing the same, as when several have agreed to meet together in a certain place on a set day, they are able to carry out the plan if they wish. Now although all express the same phenomena, this does not bring it about that their expressions are exactly alike. It is sufficient if they are proportional. As when several spectators think they see the same thing and are agreed about it, although each one sees or speaks according to the measure of his vision. It is God alone, (from whom all individuals emanate continually, and who sees the universe not only as they see it, but besides in a very different way from them) who is the cause of this correspondence in their phenomena and who brings it about that that which is particular to one, is also common to all, otherwise there would be no relation. In a way, then, we might properly say, although it seems strange, that a particular substance never acts upon another paticular substance nor is it acted upon by it. That which happens to each one is only the consequence of its complete idea or concept, since this idea already includes all the predicates and expresses the whole universe. In fact nothing can happen to us except thoughts and perceptions, and all our thoughts and perceptions are but the consequence, contingent it is true, of our precedent thoughts and perceptions, in such a way that were I able to consider directly all that happens or appears to me at the present time, I should be able to see all that will happen to me or that will ever appear to me. This future will not fail me, and will surely appear to me even if all that which is outside of me were destroyed, save only that God and myself were left.

Since, however, we ordinarily attribute to other things an action upon us which brings us to perceive things in a certain manner, it is necessary to consider the basis of this judgment and to inquire what there is of truth in it.

XV. The action of one finite substance upon another consists only in the increase in the degrees of the expression of the first combined with a decrease in that of the second, in so far as God has in advance fashioned them so that they shall act in accord.

Without entering into a long discussion it is sufficient for reconciling the language of metaphysics with that of practical life to remark that we preferably attribute to ourselves, and with reason, the phenomena which we express the most perfectly, and that we attribute to other substances those phenomena which each one expresses the best. Thus a substance, which is of an infinite extension in so far as it expresses all, becomes limited in proportion to its more or less perfect manner of expression. It is thus then that we may conceive of substances as interfering with and limiting one another, and hence we are able to say that in this sense they act upon one another, and that they, so to speak, accommodate themselves to one another. For it can happen that a single change which augments the expression of the one may diminish that of the other. Now the virtue of a paticular substance is to express well the glory of God, and the better it expresses it, the less is it limited. Everything when it expresses its virtue or power, that is to say, when it acts, changes to better, and expands just in so far as it acts. When therefore a change occurs by which several substances are affected (in fact every change affects them all) I think we may say that those substances, which by this change pass immediately to a greater degree of perfection, or to a more perfect expression, exert power and act, while those which pass to a lesser degree disclose their weakness and suffer. I also hold that every activity of a substances which has perception implies some pleasure, and every passion some pain, except that it may very well happen that a present advantage will be eventually destroyed by a greater evil, whence it comes that one may sin in acting or exerting his power and in finding pleasure.

XVI. The extraordinary intervention of God is not excluded in that which our particular essences express, because their expression includes everything. Such intervention, however, goes beyond the power of our natural being or of our distinct expression, because these are finite, and follow certain subordinate regulations.

There remains for us at present only to explain how it is possible that God has influence at times upon men or upon other substances by an extraordinary or miraculous intervention, since it seems that nothing is able to happen which is extraordinary or supernatural in as much as all the events which occur to the other substances are only the consequences of their natures. We must recall what was said above in regard to the miracles in the universe. These always conform to the universal law of the general order, although they may contravene the subordinate regulations, and since every person or substance is like a little world which expresses the great world, we can say that this extraordinary action of God upon this substance is nevertheless miraculous, although it is comprised in the general order of the universe in so far as it is expressed by the individual essence or concept of this substance. This is why, if we understand in our natures all that they express, nothing is supernatural in them, because they reach out to everything, an effect always expressing its cause, and God being the veritable cause of the substances. But as that which our natures express the most perfectly pertains to them in a particular manner, that being their special power, and since they are limited, as I have just explained, many things there are which surpass the powers of our natures and even of all limited natures. As a consequence, to speak more clearly, I say that the miracles and the extraordinary interventions of God have this peculiarity that they cannot be foreseen by any created mind however enlightened. This is because the distinct comprehension of the fundamental order surpasses them all, while on the other hand, that which is called natural depends upon less fundamental regulations which the creatures are able to understand. In order then that my words may be as irreprehensible as the meaning I am trying to convey, it will be well to associate certain words with certain significations. We may call that which includes everything that we express and which expresses our union with God himself, nothing going beyond it, our essence. But that which is limited in us may be designated as our nature or our power and in accordance with this terminology that which goes beyond the natures of all created substances is supernatural.

XVII. An example of a subordinate regulation in the law of nature which demonstrates that God always preserves the same amount of force but not the same quantity of motion:— against the Cartesians and many others.

I have frequently spoken of subordinate regulations, or of the laws of nature, and it seems that it will be well to give an example. Our new philosophers are unanimous in employing that famous law that God always preserves the same amount of motion in the universe. In fact it is a very plausible law, and in times past I held it for indubitable. But since then I have learned in what its fault consists. Monsieur Descartes and many other clever mathematicians have thought that the quantity of motion, that is to say the velocity multiplied by the mass* of the moving body, is exactly equivalent to the moving force, or to speak in mathematical terms that the force varies as the velocity multiplied by the mass. Now it is reasonable that the same force is always preserved in the universe. So also, looking to phenomena, it will be readily seen that a mechanical perpetual motion is impossible, because the force in such a machine, being always diminished a little by friction and so ultimately destined to be entirely spent, would necessarily have to recoup its losses,

---

*This term is employed here for the sake of clearness. Leibniz did not possess the concept "mass," which was enunciated by Newton in the same year in which the present treatise was written, 1686. Leibniz uses the terms "body," "magnitude of body," etc. The technical expression "mass" occurs once only in the writings of Leibniz (in a treatise published in 1695), and was there doubtless borrowed from Newton. For the history of the controversy concerning the Cartesian and Leibnizian measure of force, see Mach's *Science of Mechanics,* Chicago, 1893, pp. 272 et seq—*Trans.*

and consequently would keep on increasing of itself without any new impulsion from without; and we see furthermore that the force of a body is diminished only in proportion as it gives up force, either to a contiguous body or to its own parts, in so far as they have a separate movement. The mathematicians to whom I have referred think that what can be said of force can be said of the quantity of motion. In order, however, to show the difference I make two suppositions: in the first place, that a body falling from a certain height acquires a force enabling it to remount to the same height, provided that its direction is turned that way, or provided that there are no hindrances. For instance, a pendulum will rise exactly to the height from which it has fallen, provided the resistance of the air and of certain other small particles do not diminish a little its acquired force.

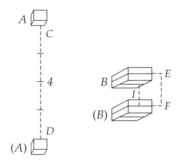

I suppose in the second place that it will take as much force to lift a body A weighing one pound to the height CD, four feet, as to raise a body B weighing four pounds to the height EF, one foot. These two suppositions are granted by our new philosophers. It is therefore manifest that the body A falling from the height CD acquires exactly as much force as the body B falling from the height EF, for the body B at F, having by the first supposition sufficient force to return to E, has therefore the force to carry a body of four pounds to the distance of one foot, EF. And likewise the body A at D, having the force to return to C, has also the force required to carry a body weighing one pound, its own weight, back to C, a distance of four feet. Now by the second supposition the force of these two bodies is equal. Let us now see if the quantity of motion is the same in each case. It is here that we will be surprised to find a very great difference, for it has been proved by Galileo that the velocity acquired by the fall CD is double the velocity acquired by the fall EF, although the height is four times as great. Multiplying, therefore, the body A, whose mass is 1, by its velocity, which is 2, the product or the quantity of movement will be 2, and on the other hand, if we multiply the body B, whose mass is 4, by its velocity which is 1, the product or quantity of motion will be 4. Hence the quantity of the motion of the body A at the point D is half the quantity of motion of the body B at the point F, yet their forces are equal, and there is therefore a great difference between the quantity of motion and the force. This is what we set out to show. We can see therefore how the force ought to be estimated by the quantity of the effect which it is able to produce, for example by the height to which a body of certain weight can be raised. This is a very different thing from the velocity which can be imparted to it, and in order to impart to it double the velocity we must have double the force. Nothing is simpler than this proof and Monsieur Descartes has fallen into error here, only because he trusted too much to his thoughts even when they had not been ripened by reflection. But it astonishes me that his disciples have not noticed this error, and I am afraid that they are beginning to imitate little by little certain Peripatetics whom they ridicule, and that they are accustoming themselves to consult rather the books of their master, than reason or nature.

XVIII. The distinction between force and the quantity of motion is, among other reasons, important as showing that we must have recourse to metaphysical considerations in addition to discussions of existension if we wish to explain the phenomena of matter.

This consideration of the force, distinguished from the quantity of motion is of importance, not only in physics and mechanics for finding the real laws of nature and the principles of motion, and even for correcting many practical errors which have crept into the writings of certain able mathematicians, but also in metaphysics it is of importance for the better understanding of principles. Because motion, if we regard only its exact and formal meaning, that is, change of place, is not something entirely real, and when several bodies change their places reciprocally, it is not possible to determine by considering the bodies alone to which among them movement or repose is to be attributed, as I could demonstrate geometrically, if I wished to stop for it now. But the force, or the proximate cause of these changes is something more real, and there are sufficient grounds for attributing it to one body rather than to another, and it is only through this latter investigation that we can determine to which one the movement must appertain. Now this force is something different from size, from form or from motion, and it can be seen from this consideration that the whole meaning of a body is not exhausted in its extension together with its modifications as our moderns persuade themselves. We are therefore obliged to restore certain beings or forms which they have banished. It appears more and more clear that although all the particular phenomena of nature can be explained mathematically or mechanically by those who understand them, yet nevertheless, the general principles of corporeal nature and even of mechanics are metaphysical rather than geometric, and belong rather to certain indivisible forms or natures as the causes of the appearances, than to the corporeal mass or to extension. This reflection is able to reconcile the mechanical philosophy of the moderns with the circumspection of those intelligent and well-meaning persons who, with a certain justice, fear that we are becoming too far removed from immaterial beings and that we are thus prejudicing piety.

XIX. *The utility of final causes in Physics.*

As I do not wish to judge people in ill part I bring no accusation against our new philosophers who pretend to banish final causes from physics, but I am nevertheless obliged to avow that the consequences of such a banishment appear to me dangerous, especially when joined to that position which I refuted at the beginning of the treatise. That position seemed to go the length of discarding final causes entirely as though God proposed no end and no good in his activity, or as if good were not to be the object of his will. I hold on the contrary that it is just in this that the principle of all existences and of the laws of nature must be sought, hence God always proposes the best and most perfect. I am quite willing to grant that we are liable to err when we wish to determine the purposes or councils of God, but this is the case only when we try to limit them to some particular design, thinking that he has had in view only a single thing, while in fact he regards everything at once. As for instance, if we think that God has made the world only for us, it is a great blunder, although it may be quite true that he has made it entirely for us, and that there is nothing in the universe which does not touch us and which does not accommodate itself to the regard which he has for us according to the principle laid down above. Therefore when we see some good effect or some perfection which happens or which follows from the works of God we are able to say assuredly that God has purposed it, for he does nothing by chance, and is not like us who sometimes fail to do well. Therefore, far from being able to fall into error in this respect as do the extreme statesmen who postulate too much foresight in the designs of Princes, or as do commentators who seek for too much erudition in their authors, it will be impossible to attribute too much reflection to God's infinite wisdom, and there is no matter in which error is less to be feared provided we confine ourselves to affirmations and provided we avoid negative statements which limit the designs of God. All those who see the admirable structure of animals find themselves led to recognize the wisdom of the author of things and I advise those who have any sentiment of piety and indeed of true philosophy to hold aloof from the expressions of certain pretentious minds who instead of saying that eyes were made for seeing, say that we see because we find ourselves having eyes. When one seriously holds such opinions which hand everything over to material necessity or to a kind of chance (although either alternative ought to appear ridiculous to those who understand what we have explained above) it is difficult to recognize an intelligent author of nature. The effect should correspond to its cause and indeed it is best known through the recognition of its cause, so that it is reasonable to introduce a sovereign intelligence ordering things, and in place of making use of the wisdom of this sovereign being, to employ only the properties of matter to explain phenomena. As if in order to account for the capture of an important place by a prince, the historian should say it was because the particles of powder in the cannon having been touched by a spark of fire expanded with a rapidity capable of pushing a hard solid body against the walls of the place, while the little particles which composed the brass of the cannon were so well interlaced that they did not separate under this impact,—as if he should account for it in this way instead of making us see how the foresight of the conqueror brought him to choose the time and the proper means and how his ability surmounted all obstacles.

XX. A noteworthy disquistion in Plato's Phaedo against the philosophers who were too materialistic.

This reminds me of a fine disquisition by Socrates in Plato's Phaedo, which agrees perfectly with my opinion on this subject and seems to have been uttered expressly for our too materialistic philosophers. This agreement has led me to a desire to translate it although it is a little long. Perhaps this example will give some of us an incentive to share in many of the other beautiful and well balanced thoughts which are found in the writings of this famous author.*

XXI. If the mechanical laws depended upon Geometry alone without metaphysical influences, the phenomena would be very difficult from what they are.

Now since the wisdom of God has always been recognized in the detail of the mechanical structures of certain particular bodies, it should also be shown in the general economy of the world and in the constitution of the laws of nature. This is so true that even in the laws of motion in general, the plans of this wisdom have been noticed. For if bodies were only extended masses, and motion were only a change of place, and if everything ought to be and could be deduced by geometric necessity from these two definitions alone, it would follow, as I have shown

---

*There is a gap here in the MS., intended for the passage from Plato, the translation of which Leibniz did not supply.—*Trans.*

elsewhere, that the smallest body on contact with a very large one at rest would impart to it its own velocity, yet without losing any of the velocity that it had. A quantity of other rules wholly contrary to the formation of a system would also have to be admitted. But the decree of the divine wisdom in preserving always the same force and the same total direction has provided for a system. I find indeed that many of the efforts of nature can be accounted for in a twofold way, that is to say by a consideration of efficient causes, and again independently by a consideration of final causes. An example of the latter is God's decree to always carry out his plan by the easiest and most determined way. I have shown this elsewhere in accounting for the catoptric and dioptric laws, and I will speak more at length about it in what follows.

XXII. Reconciliation of the two methods of explanation, the one using final causes, and the other efficient causes, thus satisfying both those who explain nature mechanically and those who have recourse to incorporeal natures.

It is worth while to make the preceding remark in order to reconcile those who hope to explain mechanically the formation of the first tissue of an animal and all the interrelation of the parts, with those who account for the same structure by referring to final causes. Both explanations are good; both are useful not only for the admiring of the work of a great artificer, but also for the discovery of useful facts in physics and medicine. And writers who take these diverse routes should not speak ill of each other. For I see that those who attempt to explain beauty by the divine anatomy ridicule those who imagine that the apparently fortuitous flow of certain liquids has been able to produce such a beautiful variety and that they regard them as over-bold and irreverent. These others on the contrary treat the former as simple and superstitious, and compare them to those ancients who regarded the physicists as impious when they maintained that not Jupiter thundered but some material which is found in the clouds. The best plan would be to join the two ways of thinking. To use a practical comparison, we recognize and praise the ability of a workman not only when we show what designs he had in making the parts of his machine, but also when we explain the instruments which he employed in making each part, above all if these instruments are simple and ingeniously contrived. God is also a workman able enough to produce a machine still a thousand times more ingenious than is our body, by employing only certain quite simple liquids purposely composed in such a way that ordinary laws of nature alone are required to develop them so as to produce such a marvellous effect. But it is also true that this development would not take place if God were not the author of nature. Yet I find that the method of efficient causes, which goes much deeper and is in a measure more immediate and *a priori,* is also more difficult when we come to details, and I think that our philosophers are still very frequently far removed from making the most of this method. The method of final causes, however, is easier and can be frequently employed to find out important and useful truths which we should have to seek for a long time, if we were confined to that other more physical method of which anatomy is able to furnish many examples. It seems to me that Snellius, who was the first discoverer of the laws of refraction would have waited a long time before finding them if he had wished to seek out first how light was formed. But he apparently followed that method which the ancients employed for Catoptrics, that is, the method of final causes. Because, while seeking for the easiest way in which to conduct a ray of light from one given point to another given point by reflection from a given plane (supposing that that was the design of nature) they discovered the equality of the angles of incidence and reflection, as can be seen from a little treatise by Heliodorus of Larissa and also elsewhere. This principle Mons. Snellius, I believe, and afterwards independently of him, M. Fermat, applied most ingeniously to refraction. For since the rays while in the same media always maintain the same proportion of sines, which in turn corresponds to the resistance of the media, it appears that they follow the easiest way, or at least that way which is the most determinate for passing from a given point in one medium to a given point in another medium. That demonstration of this same theorem which M. Descartes has given, using efficient causes, is much less satisfactory. At least we have grounds to think that he would never have found the principle by that

means if he had not learned in Holland of the discovery of Snellius.

XXIII. Returning to immaterial substances we explain how God acts upon the understanding of spirits and ask whether one always keeps the idea of what he thinks about.

I have thought it well to insist a little upon final causes, upon incorporeal natures and upon an intelligent cause with respect to bodies so as to show the use of these conceptions in physics and in mathematics. This for two reasons, first to purge from mechanical philosophy the impiety that is imputed to it, second, to elevate to nobler lines of thought the thinking of our philosophers who incline to materialistic considerations alone. Now, however, it will be well to return from corporeal substances to the consideration of immaterial natures and particularly of spirits, and to speak of the methods which God uses to enlighten them and to act upon them. Although we must not forget that there are here at the same time certain laws of nature in regard to which I can speak more amply elsewhere. It will be enough for now to touch upon ideas and to inquire if we see everything in God and how God is our light. First of all it will be in place to remark that the wrong use of ideas occasions many errors. For when one reasons in regard to anything, he imagines that he has an idea of it and this is the foundation upon which certain philosophers, ancient and modern, have constructed a demonstration of God that is extremely imperfect. It must be, they say, that I have an idea of God, or of a perfect being, since I think of him and we cannot think without having ideas; now the idea of this being includes all perfections and since existence is one of these perfections, it follows that he exists. But I reply, inasmuch as we often think of impossible chimeras, for example of the highest degree of swiftness, of the greatest number, of the meeting of the conchoid with its base or determinant, such reasoning is not sufficient. It is therefore in this sense that we can say that there are true and false ideas according as the thing which is in question is possible or not. And it is when he is assured of the possibility of a thing, that one can boast of having an idea of it. Therefore, the aforesaid argument proves that God exists, if he is possible.

This is in fact an excellent privilege of the divine nature, to have need only of a possibility or an essence in order to actually exist, and it is just this which is called *ens a se*.

XXIV. What clear and obscure, distinct and confused, adequate and inadequate, intuitive and assumed knowledge is, and the definition of nominal, real, causal and essential.

In order to understand better the nature of ideas it is necessary to touch somewhat upon the various kinds of knowledge. When I am able to recognize a thing among others, without being able to say in what its differences or characteristics consist, the knowledge is confused. Sometimes indeed we may know clearly, that is without being in the slightest doubt, that a poem or a picture is well or badly done because there is in it an "I know not what" which satisfies or shocks us. Such knowledge is not yet distinct. It is when I am able to explain the peculiarities which a thing has, that the knowledge is called distinct. Such is the knowledge of an assayer who discerns the true gold from the false by means of certain proofs or marks which make up the definition of gold. But distinct knowledge has degrees, because ordinarily the conceptions which enter into the definitions will themselves have need of definition, and are only known confusedly. When at length everything which enters into a definition or into distinct knowledge is known distinctly, even back to the primitive conception. I call that knowledge adequate. When my mind understands at once and distinctly all the primitive ingredients of a conception, then we have intuitive knowledge. This is extremely rare as most human knowledge is only confused or indeed assumed. It is well also to distinguish nominal from real definition. I call a definition nominal when there is doubt whether an exact conception of it is possible; as for instance, when I say that an endless screw is a line in three dimensional space whose parts are congruent or fall one upon another. Now although this is one of the reciprocal properties of an endless screw, he who did not know from elsewhere what an endless screw was could doubt if such a line were possible, because the other lines whose ends are congruent (there are only two; the circumference of a circle and the straight line) are plane figures, that is to say they can be described *in plano*. This instance enables us to see that any reciprocal property can serve as a nominal definition, but when the property brings us to see the possibility of a thing it makes the definition real, and as long as one has only a nominal definition he cannot be sure of the consequences which he draws, because if it conceals a contradiction or an impossibility he would be able to draw the opposite conclusions. That is why truths do not depend upon names and are not arbitrary, as some of our new philosophers think. There is also a considerable difference among real definitions, for when the possibility proves itself only by experience, as in the definition of quicksilver, whose possibility we know because such a body, which is both an extremely heavy fluid and quite volatile, actually exists, the definition is merely real and nothing more. If, however, the proof of the possibility is *a priori*, the definition is not only real but also causal as for instance when it contains the possible generation of a thing. Finally when the definition, without assuming anything which requires a proof *a priori* of its possibility, carries the analysis clear to the primitive conception, the definition is perfect or essential.

XXV. In what cases knowledge is added to mere contemplation of the idea.

Now that it is manifest that we have no idea of a conception when it is impossible. And in case the knowledge, where we have the idea of it, is only assumed, we do not visualize it because such a conception is known only in like manner as conceptions internally impossible. And if it be in fact possible, it is not by this kind of knowledge that we learn its possibility. For instance, when I am thinking of a thousand or of a chiliagon, I frequently do it without contemplating the idea. Even if I say a thousand is ten times a hundred, I frequently do not trouble to think what ten and a hundred are, because I assume that I know, and I do not consider it necessary to stop just at present to conceive of them. Therefore it may well happen, as it in fact does happen often enough, that I am mistaken in regard to a conception which I assume that I understand, although it is an impossible truth or at least is incompatible with others with which I join it, and whether I am mistaken or not, this way of assuming our knowledge remains the same. It is, then, only when our knowledge is clear in regard to confused conceptions, and when it is intuitive in regard to those which are distinct, that we see its entire idea.

XXVI. Ideas are all stored up within us. Plato's doctrine of reminiscence.

In order to see clearly what an idea is, we must guard ourselves against a misunderstanding. Many regard the idea as the form or the differentiation of our thinking, and according to this opinion we have the idea in our mind, in so far as we are thinking of it, and each separate time that we think of it anew we have another idea although similar to the preceding one. Some, however, take the idea as the immediate object of thought, or as a permanent form which remains even when we are no longer contemplating it. As a matter of fact our soul has the power of representing to itself any form or nature whenever the occasion comes for thinking about it, and I think that this activity of our soul is, so far as it expresses some nature, form or essence, properly the idea of the thing. This is in us, and is always in us, whether we are thinking of it or no. (Our soul expresses God and the universe and all essences as well as all existences.) This position is in accord with my principles that naturally nothing enters into our minds from outside.

It is a bad habit we have of thinking as though our minds receive certain messengers, as it were, or as if they had doors or windows. We have in our minds all those forms for all periods of time because the mind at every moment expresses all its future thoughts and already thinks confusedly of all that which it will ever think distinctly. Nothing can be taught us of which we have not already in our minds the idea. This idea is as it were the material out of which the thought will form itself. This is what Plato has excellently brought out in his doctrine of reminiscence, a doctrine which contains a great deal of truth, provided that it is properly understood and purged of the error of pre-existence, and provided that one does not conceive of the soul as having already known and thought at some other time what it learns and thinks now. Plato has also confirmed his position by a beautiful experiment. He introduces a small boy, whom he leads by short steps, to extremely difficult truths of geometry bearing on incommensurables, all this without teaching the boy anything, merely drawing out replies by a well arranged series of questions. This shows that the soul virtually knows those things, and needs only to be reminded (animadverted) to recognize the truths. Consequently it possesses at least the idea upon which those truths depend. We may say even that it already possesses those truths, if we consider them as the relations of the ideas.

XXVII. In what respect our souls can be compared to blank tablets and how conceptions are derived from the senses.

Aristotle preferred to compare our souls to blank tablets prepared for writing, and he maintained that nothing is in the understanding which does not come through the senses. This position is in accord with the popular conceptions as Aristotle's positions usually are. Plato thinks more profoundly. Such tenets or practicologies are nevertheless allowable in ordinary use somewhat in the same way as those who accept the Copernican theory still continue to speak of the rising and setting of the sun. I find indeed that these usages can be given a real meaning containing no error, quite in the same way as I have already pointed out that we may truly say particular substances act upon one another. In this same sense we may say that knowledge is received from without through the medium of the senses because certain exterior things contain or express more particularly the causes which determine us to certain thoughts. Because in the ordinary uses of life we attribute to the soul only that which belongs to it most manifestly and particularly, and there is no advantage in going further. When, however, we are dealing with the exactness of metaphysical truths, it is important to recognize the powers and independence of the soul which extend infinitely further than is commonly supposed. In order, therefore, to avoid misunderstandings it would be well to choose separate terms for the two. These expressions which are in the soul whether one is conceiving of them or not may be called ideas, while those which one conceives of or consructs may be called conceptions, *conceptus*. But whatever terms are used, it is always false to say that all our conceptions come from the so-called external senses, because those conceptions which I have of myself and of my thoughts, and consequently of being, of substance, of action, of identity, and of many others came from an inner experience.

XXVIII. The only immediate object of our perceptions which exists outside of us is God, and in him alone is our light.

In the strictly metaphysical sense no external cause acts upon us excepting God alone, and he is in immediate relation with us only by virtue of our continual dependence upon him. Whence it follows that there is absolutely no other external object which comes into contact with our souls and directly excites perceptions in us. We have in our souls ideas of everything, only because of the continual action of God upon us, that is to say, because every effect expresses its cause and therefore the essences of our souls are certain expressions, imitations or images of the divine essence, divine thought and divine will, including all the ideas which are there contained. We may say, therefore, that God is for us the only immediate external object, and that we see things through him. For example, when we see the sun or the stars, it is God who gives to us and preserves in us the ideas and whenever our senses are affected according to his own laws in a certain manner, it is he, who by his continual concurrence, determines our thinking. God is the sun and the light of souls, *lumen illuminans omnem hominem venientem in hunc mundum,* although this is not the current conception. I think I have already remarked that during the scholastic period many believed God to be the light of the soul, *intellectus agens animæ rationalis,* following in this the Holy Scriptures and the fathers who were always more Platonic than Aristotelian in their mode of thinking. The Averroists misused this conception, but others, among whom were several mystic theologians, and William of Saint Amour, also I think, understood this conception in a manner which assured the dignity of God and was able to raise the soul to a knowledge of its welfare.

XXIX. Yet we think directly by means of our own ideas and not through God's.

Nevertheless I cannot approve of the position of certain able philosophers who seem to hold that our ideas themselves are in God and not at all in us. I think that in taking this position they have nei-

ther sufficiently considered the nature of substance, which we have just explained, nor the entire extension and independence of the soul which includes all that happens to it, and expresses God, and with him all possible and actual beings in the same way that an effect expresses its cause. It is indeed inconceivable that the soul should think using the ideas of something else. The soul when it thinks of anything must be affected effectively in a certain manner, and it must needs have in itself in advance not only the passive capacity of being thus affected, a capacity already wholly determined, but it must have besides an active power by virtue of which it has always had in its nature the marks of the future production of this thought, and the disposition to produce it at its proper time. All of this shows that the soul already includes the idea which is comprised in any particular thought.

XXX. How God inclines our souls without necessitating them; that there are no grounds for complaint; that we must not ask why Judas sinned because this free act is contained in his concept, the only question being why Judas the sinner is admitted to existence, preferably to other possible persons; concerning the original imperfection or limitation before the fall and concerning the different degrees of grace.

Regarding the action of God upon the human will there are many quite different considerations which it would take too long to investigate here. Nevertheless the following is what can be said in general. God in co-operating with ordinary actions only follows the laws which he has established, that is to say, he continually preserves and produces our being so that the ideas come to us spontaneously or with freedom in that order which the concept of our individual substance carries with itself. In this concept they can be foreseen for all eternity. Furthermore, by virtue of the decree which God has made that the will shall always seek the apparent good in certain particular respects (in regard to which this apparent good always has in it something of reality expressing or imitating God's will), he, without at all necessitating our choice, determines it by that which appears most desirable. For absolutely speaking, our will as contrasted with necessity, is in a state of indifference, being able to act otherwise, or wholly to suspend its action, either alternative being and remaining possible. It therefore devolves upon the soul to be on guard against appearances, by means of a firm will, to reflect and to refuse to act or decide in certain circumstances, except after mature deliberation. It is, however, true and has been assured from all eternity that certain souls will not employ their power upon certain occasions.

But who could do more than God has done, and can such a soul complain of anything except iself? All these complaints after the deed are unjust, inasmuch as they would have been unjust before the deed. Would this soul a little before committing the sin have had the right to complain of God as though he had determind the sin. Since the determinations of God in these matters cannot be foreseen, how would the soul know that it was preordained to sin unless it had already committed the sin? It is merely a question of wishing to or not wishing to, and God could not have set an easier or juster condition. Therefore all judges without asking the reasons which have disposed a man to have an evil will, consider only how far this will is wrong. But, you object, perhaps it is ordained from all eternity that I will sin. Find your own answer. Perhaps it has not been. Now then, without asking for what you are unable to know and in regard to which you can have no light, act according to your duty and your knowledge. But, some one will object; whence comes it then that this man will assuredly do this sin? The reply is easy. It is that otherwise he would not be a man. For God foresees from all time that there will be a certain Judas, and in the concept or idea of him which God has, is contained this future free act. The only question, therefore, which remains is why this certain Judas, the betrayer who is possible only because of the idea of God, actually exists. To this question, however, we can expect no answer here on earth excepting to say in general that it is because God has found it good that he should exist notwithstanding that sin which he foresaw. This evil will be more than overbalanced. God will derive a greater good from it, and it will finally turn out that this series of events in which is included the existence of this sinner, is the most perfect among all the possible series of

events. An explanation in every case of the admirable economy of this choice cannot be given while we are sojourners on earth. It is enough to know the excellence without understanding it. It is here that must be recognized *altitudinem divitiarum*, the unfathomable depth of the divine wisdom, without hesitating at a detail which involves an infinte number of considerations. It is clear, however, that God is not the cause of ill. For not only after the loss of innocence by men, has original sin possessed the soul, but even before that there was an original limitation or imperfection in the very nature of all creatures, which rendered them open to sin and able to fall. There is, therefore, no more difficulty in the supralapsarian view than there is in the other views of sin. To this also, it seems to me can be reduced the opinion of Saint Augustine and of other authors: that the root of evil is in the negativity, that is to say, in the lack or limitation of creatures which God graciously remedies by whatever degree of perfection it pleases him to give. This grace of God, whether ordinary or extraordinary has its degrees and its measures. It is always efficacious in itself to produce a certain proportionate effect and furthermore it is always sufficient not only to keep one from sin but even to effect his salvation, provided that the man co-operates with that which is in him. It has not always, however, sufficient power to ovecome the inclination, for, if it did, it would no longer be limited in any way, and this superiority to limitations is reserved to that unique grace which is absolutely efficacious. This grace is always victorious whether through its own self or through the cognity of circumstances.

XXXI. Concerning the motives of election; concerning faith foreseen and the absolute decree and that it all reduces to the question why God has chosen and resolved to admit to existence just such a possible person, whose concept includes just such a sequence of free acts and of free gifts of grace. This at once puts an end to all difficulties.

Finally, the grace of God is wholly unprejudiced and creatures have no claim upon it. Just as it is not sufficient in accounting for God's choice in his dispensations of grace to refer to his absolute or conditional prevision of men's future actions, so it is also wrong to imagine his decrees as absolute with no reasonable motive. As concerns foreseen faith and good works, it is very true that God has elected none but those whose faith and charity he foresees, *quos se fide donaturum praescivit.* The same question, however, arises again as to why God gives to some rather than to others the grace of faith or of good works. As concerns God's ability to foresee not only the faith and good deeds, but also their material and predisposition, or that which a man on his part contributes to them (since there are as truly diversities on the part of men as on the part of grace, and a man although he needs to be aroused to good and needs to become converted, yet acts in accordance with his temperament),—as regards his ability to foresee there are many who say that God, knowing what a particular man will do without grace, that is without his extraordinary assistance, or knowing at least what will be the human contribution, resolves to give grace to those whose natural dispositions are the best, or at any rate are the least imperfect and evil. But if this were the case then the natural dispositions in so far as they were good would be like gifts of grace, since God would have given advantages to some over others; and therefore, since he would well know that the natural advantages which he had given would serve as motives for his grace or for his extraordinary assistance, would not everything be reduced to his mercy? I think, therefore, that since we do not know how much and in what way God regards natural dispositions in the dispensations of his grace, it would be safest and most exact to say, in accordance with our principles and as I have already remarked, that there must needs be among possible beings the person Peter or John whose concept or idea contains all that particular sequence of ordinary and extraordinary manifestations of grace together with the rest of the accompanying events and circumstances, and that it has pleased God to choose him among an infinite number of persons equally possible for actual existence. When we have said this there seems nothing left to ask, and all difficulties vanish. For in regard to that great and ultimate question why it has pleased God to choose him among so great a number of possible persons, it is surely unreasonable to demand more than the general reasons which we have given. The reasons in detail surpass our ken. Therefore, in-

stead of postulating an absolute decree, which being without reason would be unreasonable, and instead of postulating reasons which do not succeed in solving the difficulties and in turn have need themselves of reasons, it will be best to say with St. Paul that there are for God's choice certain great reasons of wisdom and congruity which he follows, which reasons, however, are unknown to mortals and are founded upon the general order, whose goal is the greatest perfection of the world. This is what is meant when the motives of God's glory and of the manifestation of his justice are spoken of, as well as when men speak of his mercy, and his perfection in general; that immense vastness of wealth, in fine, with which the soul of the same St. Paul was to thrilled.

XXXII. Usefulness of these principles in matters of piety and of religion.

In addition it seems that the thoughts which we have just explained and particularly the great principle of the perfection of God's operations and the concept of substance which includes all its changes with all its accompanying circumstances, far from injuring, serve rather to confirm religion, serve to dissipate great difficulties, to inflame souls with a divine love and to raise the mind to a knowledge of incorporeal substances much more than the present-day hypotheses. For it appears clearly that all other substances depend upon God just as our thoughts emanate from our own substances; that God is all in all and that he is intimately united to all created things, in proportion however to their perfection; that it is he alone who determines them from without by his influence, and if to act is to determine directly, it may be said in metaphysical language that God alone acts upon me and he alone causes me to do good or ill, other substances contributing only because of his determinations; because God, who takes all things into consideration, distributes his bounties and compels created beings to accommodate themselves to one another. Thus God alone constitutes the relation or communication between substances. It is through him that the phenomena of the one meet and accord with the phenomena of the others, so that there may be a reality in our perceptions. In common parlance, however, an action is attributed to particular causes in the sense that I have explained above because it is not necessary to make continual mention of the universal cause when speaking of particular cases. It can be seen also that every substance has a perfect spontaneity (which becomes liberty with intelligent substances). Everything which happens to it is a consequence of its idea or its being and nothing determines it except God only. It is for this reason that a person of exalted mind and revered saintliness may say that the soul ought often to think as if there were only God and itself in the world. Nothing can make us hold to immortality more firmly than this independence and vastness of the soul which protects it completely against exterior things, since it alone constitutes our universe and together with God is sufficient for itself. It is as impossible for it to perish save through annihilation as it is impossible for the universe to destroy itself, the universe whose animate and perpetual expression it is. Furthermore, the changes in this extended mass which is called our body cannot possibly affect the soul nor can the dissipation of the body destroy that which is indivisible.

XXXIII. *Explanation of the relation between the soul and the body, a matter which has been regarded as inexplicable or else as miraculous; concerning the origin of confused perceptions.*

We can also see the explanation of that great mystery "the union of the soul and the body," that is to say how it comes about that the passions and actions of the one are accompanied by the actions and passions or else the appropriate phenomena of the other. For it is not possible to conceive how one can have an influence upon the other and it is unreasonable to have recourse at once to the extraordinary intervention of the universal cause in an ordinary and particular case. The following, however, is the true explanation. We have said that everything which happens to a soul or to any substance is a consequence of its concept; hence the idea itself or the essence of the soul brings it about that all of its appearances or perceptions should be born out of its nature and precisely in such a way that they correspond of themselves to that which happens in the universe at large, but more particularly and more perfectly to that which happens in the body associated with it, because it is in a particular way and only for a certain time according to the relation of other bodies to its own body that the soul expresses the state of the universe. This last fact enables us to see how our body belongs to us, without, however, being attached to our essence. I believe that those who are careful thinkers will decide favorably for our principles because of this single reason, viz., that they are able to see in what consists the relation between the soul and the body, a parallelism which appears inexplicable in any other way. We can also see that the perceptions of our senses even when they are clear must necessarily contain certain confused elements, for as all the bodies in the universe are in sympathy, ours receives the impressions of all the others, and while our senses respond to everything, our soul cannot pay attention to every particular. That is why our confused sensations are the result of a variety of perceptions. This variety is infinite. It is almost like the confused murmuring which is heard by those who approach the shore of a sea. It comes from the continual beatings of innumerable waves. If now, out of many perceptions which do not at all fit together to make one, no particular one perception surpasses the others, and if they make impressions about equally strong or equally capable of holding the attention of the soul, they can be perceived only confusedly.

XXXIV. *Concerning the difference between spirits and other substances, souls or substantial forms; that the immortality which men desire includes memory.*

Supposing that the bodies which constitute a *unum per se,* as human bodies, are substances, and have substantial forms, and supposing that animals have souls, we are obliged to grant that these souls and these substantial forms cannot entirely perish, any more than can the atoms or the ultimate elements of matter, according to the position of other philosophers; for no substance perishes, although it may become very different. Such substances also express the whole universe, although more imperfectly than do spirits. The principle difference, however, is that they do not know that they are, nor what they are. Consequently, not being able to reason, they are unable to discover necessary and universal truths. It is also because they do not reflect regarding themselves that they have no moral qualities, whence it follows that undergoing a thousand transformations, as we see a caterpillar change into a butterfly, the result from a moral or practical standpoint is the same as if we said that they perished in each case, and we can indeed say it from the physical standpoint in the same way that we say bodies perish in their dissolution. But the intelligent soul, knowing that it is and having the ability to say that word "I" so full of meaning, not only continues and exists, metaphysically far more certainly than do the others, but it remains the same from the moral standpoint, and constitutes the same personality, for it is its memory of knowledge of this ego which renders it open to punishment and reward. Also the immortality which is required in morals and in religion does not consist merely in this perpetual existence, which pertains to all substances, for if in addition there were no remembrance of what one had been, immortality would not be at all desirable. Suppose that some individual could suddenly become King of China on condition, however, of forgetting what he had been, as though being born again, would it not amount to the same practically, or as far as the effects could be peceived, as if the individual were annihilated, and a king of China were the same instant created in his place? The individual would have no reason to desire this.

XXXV. The excellence of spirits; that God considers them preferable to other creatures; that the spirits express God rather than the world, while other simple substances express the world rather than God.

In order, however, to prove by natural reasons that God will preserve forever not only our substance, but also our personality, that is to say the recollection and knowledge of what we are (although the distinct knowledge is sometimes suspended during sleep and in swoons) it is necessary to join to metaphysics moral considerations. God must be considered not only as the principle and the cause of all subtances and of all existing things, but also as the chief of all persons or intelligent substances, as the absolute monarch of the most perfect city or republic, such as is constituted by all the spirits together in the universe, God being the most complete of all spirits at the same time that he is greatest of all be-

ings. For assuredly the spirits are the most perfect of substances and best express the divinity. Since all the nature, purpose, virtue and function of substances is, as has been sufficiently explained, to express God and the universe, there is no room for doubting that those substances which give the expression, knowing what they are doing and which are able to understand the great truths about God and the universe, do express God and the universe incomparably better than do those natures which are either brutish and incapable of recognizing truths, or are wholly destitute of sensation and knowledge. The difference between intelligent substances and those which are not intelligent is quite as great as between a mirror and one who sees. As God is himself the greatest and wisest of spirits it is easy to understand that the spirits with which he can, so to speak, enter into converstaion and even into social relations by communicating to them in particular ways his feelings and his will so that they are able to know and love their benefactor, must be nearer to him than the rest of created things which may be regarded as the instruments of spirits. In the same way we see that all wise persons consider far more the condition of a man than of anything else however precious it may be; and it seems that the greatest satisfaction which a soul, satisfied in other respects, can have is to see itself loved by others. However, with respect to God there is this difference that his glory and our worship can add nothing to his satisfaction, the recognition of creatures being nothing but a consequence of his sovereign and perfect felicity and being far from contributing to it or from causing it even in part. Nevertheless, that which is reasonable in finite spirits is found eminently in him and as we praise a king who prefers to preserve the life of a man before that of the most precious and rare of his animals, we should not doubt that the most enlightened and most just of all monarchs has the same preference.

XXXVI. God is the monarch of the most perfect republic composed of all the spirits, and the happiness of this city of God is his principal purpose.

Spirits are of all substances the most capable of perfection and their perfections are different in this that they interfere with one another the least, or rather they aid one another the most, for only the most virtuous can be the most perfect friends. Hence it follows that God who in all things has the greatest perfection will have the greatest care for spirits and will give not only to all of them in general, but even to each one in particular the highest perfection which the universal harmony will permit. We can even say that it is because he is a spirit that God is the originator of existences, for if he had lacked the power of will to choose what is best, there would have been no reason why one possible being should exist rather than any other. Therefore God's being a spirit himself dominates all the consideration which he may have toward created things. Spirits alone are made in his image, being as it were of his blood or as children in the family, since they alone are able to serve him of free will, and to act consciously imitating the divine nature. A single spirit is worth a whole world, because it not only expresses the whole world, but it also knows it and governs itself as does God. In this way we may say that though every substance expresses the whole universe, yet the other substances express the world rather than God, while spirits express God rather than the world. This nature of spirits, so noble that it enables them to approach divinity as much as is possible for created things, has as a result that God derives infinitely more glory from them than from the other beings, or rather the other beings furnish to spirits the material for glorifying him. This moral quality of God which constitutes him Lord and Monarch of spirits influences him so to speak personally and in a unique way. It is through this that he humanizes himself, that he is willing to suffer anthropologies, and that he enters into social relations with us and this consideration is so dear to him that the happy and prosperous condition of his empire which consists in the greatest possible felicity of its inhabitants, becomes supreme among his laws. Happiness is to persons what perfection is to beings. And if the dominant principle in the existence of the physical world is the decree to give it the greatest possible perfection, the primary purpose in the moral world or in the city of God which constitutes the noblest part of the universe ought to be to extend the greatest happiness possible. We must not therefore doubt that God has so ordained everything that spirits not only shall live forever, because this is unavoidable, but that they shall also preserve forever their

moral quality, so that his city may never lose a person, quite in the same way that the world never loses a substance. Consequently they will always be conscious of their being, otherwise they would be open to neither reward nor punishment, a condition which is the essence of a republic, and above all of the most perfect republic where nothing can be neglected. In fine, God being at the same time the most just and the most debonnaire of monarchs, and requiring only a good will on the part of men, provided that it be sincere and intentional, his subjects cannot desire a better condition. To render them perfectly happy he desires only that they love him.

XXXVII. *Jesus Christ has revealed to men the mystery and the admirable laws of the kingdom of heaven, and the greatness of the supreme happiness which God has prepared for those who love him.*

The ancient philosophers knew very little of these important truths. Jesus Christ alone has expressed them divinely as well, and in a way so clear and simple that the dullest minds have understood them. His gospel has entirely changed the face of human affairs. It has brought us to know the kingdom of heaven, or that perfect republic of spirits which deserves to be called the city of God. He it is who has discovered to us its wonderful laws. He alone has made us see how much God loves us and with what care everything that concerns us has been provided for; how God, inasmuch as he cares for the sparrows, will not neglect reasoning beings, who are infinitely more dear to him; how all the hairs of our heads are numbered; how heaven and earth may pass away but the word of God and that which belongs to the means of our salvation will not pass away; how God has more regard for the least one among intelligent souls than for the whole machinery of the world; how we ought not to fear those who are able to destroy the body but are unable to destroy the soul, since God alone can render the soul happy or unhappy; and how the souls of the righteous are protected by his hand against all the upheavals of the universe, since God alone is able to act upon them; how none of our acts are forgotten; how everything is to be accounted for; even careless words and even a spoonful of water which is well used; in fact how everything must result in the greatest welfare of the good, for then shall the righteous become like suns and neither our sense nor our minds have ever tasted of anything approaching the joys which God has laid up for those that love him.

The Monadology

1. The Monad, of which we will speak here, is nothing else than a simple substance, which goes to make up composites; by simple, we mean without parts.

2. There must be simple substances because there are composites; for a composite is nothing else than a collection or *aggregatum* of simple substances.

3. Now, where there are no constituent parts there is possible neither extension, nor form, nor divisibility. These Monads are the true Atoms of nature, and, in fact, the Elements of things.

4. Their dissolution, therefore, is not to be feared and there is no way conceivable by which a simple substance can perish through natural means.

5. For the same reason there is no way conceivable by which a simple substance might, through natural means, come into existence, since it can not be formed by composition.

6. We may say then, that the existence of Monads can begin or end only all at once, that is to say, the Monad can begin only through creation and end only through annihilation. Composites, however, begin or end gradually.

7. There is also no way of explaining how a Monad can be altered or changed in its inner being by any other created thing, since there is no possibility of transposition within it, nor can we conceive of any internal movement which can be produced, directed, increased or diminished there within the substance, such as can take place in the case of composites where a change can occur among the parts. The Monads have no windows through which anything may come in or go out. The Attributes are not liable to detach themselves and make an excursion outside the substance, as could *sensible species* of the Schoolmen. In the same way neither substance nor attribute can enter from without into a Monad.

8. Still Monads must needs have some qualities, otherwise they would not even be existences. And if simple substances did not differ at all in their qualities, there would be no means of perceiving any change in things. Whatever is in a composite can come into it only through its simple elements and the Monads, if they were without qualities, since they do not differ at all in quantity, would be indistinguishable one from another. For instance, if we imagine *a plenum* or completely filled space, where each part receives only the equivalent of its own previous motion, one state of things would not be distinguishable from another.

9. Each Monad, indeed, must be different from every other. For there are never in nature two beings which are exactly alike, and in which it is not possible to find a difference either internal or based on an intrinsic property.

10. I assume it as admitted that every created being, and consequently the created Monad, is subject to change, and indeed that this change is continuous in each.

11. It follows from what has just been said, that the natural changes of the Monad come from an internal principle, because an external cause can have no influence upon its inner being.

12. Now besides this principle of change there must also be in the Monad a manifoldness which changes. This manifoldness constitutes, so to speak,

Reprinted from *Leibniz: Basic Writings*, trans. George Montgomery (1902; reprint, La Salle, Ill.: Open Court, 1990), pp. 251–72.

the specific nature and the variety of the simple substances.

13. This manifoldness must involve a multiplicity in the unity or in that which is simple. For since every natural change takes place by degrees, there must be something which changes and something which remains unchanged, and consequently there must be in the simple substance a plurality of conditions and relations, even though it has no parts.

14. The passing condition which involves and represents a multiplicity in the unity, or in the simple substance, is nothing else than what is called Perception. This should be carefully distinguished from Apperception or Consciousness, as will appear in what follows. In this matter the Cartesians have fallen into a serious error, in that they treat as non-existent those perceptions of which we are not conscious. It is this also which has led them to believe that spirits alone are Monads and that there are no souls of animals or other Entelechies, and it has led them to make the common confusion between a protracted period of unconsciousness and actual death. They have thus adopted the Scholastic error that souls can exist entirely separated from bodies, and have even confirmed ill-balanced minds in the belief that souls are mortal.

15. The action of the internal principle which brings about the change or the passing from one perception to another may be called Appetition. It is true that the desire (*l'appétit*) is not always able to attain to the whole of the perception which it strives for, but it always attains a portion of it and reaches new perceptions.

16. We, ourselves, experience a multiplicity in a simple substance, when we find that the most trifling thought of which we are conscious involves a variety in the object. Therefore all those who acknowledge that the soul is a simple substance ought to grant this multiplicity in the Monad, and Monsieur Bayle should have found no difficulty in it, as he has done in his *Dictionary*, article "Rorarius."

17. It must be confessed, however, that Perception, and that which depends upon it, are inexplicable by mechanical causes, that is to say, by figures and motions. Supposing that there were a machine whose structure produced thought, sensation, and perception, we could conceive of it as increased in size with the same proportions until one was able to enter into its interior, as he would into a mill. Now, on going into it he would find only pieces working upon one another, but never would he find anything to explain Perception. It is accordingly in the simple substance, and not in the composite nor in a machine that the Perception is to be sought. Furthermore, there is nothing besides perceptions and their changes to be found in the simple substance. And it is in these alone that all the internal activities of the simple substance can consist.

18. All simple substances or created Monads may be called Entelechies, because they have in themselves a certain perfection. There is in them a sufficiency which makes them the source of their internal activities, and renders them, so to speak, incorporeal Automatons.

19. If we wish to designate as soul everything which has perceptions and desires in the general sense that I have just explained, all simple substances or created Monads could be called souls. But since feeling is something more than a mere perception I think that the general name of Monad or Entelechy should suffice for simple substances which have only perception, while we may reserve the term Soul for those whose perception is more distinct and is accompanied by memory.

20. We experience in ourselves a state where we remember nothing and where we have no distinct perception, as in periods of fainting, or when we are overcome by a profound, dreamless sleep. In such a state the soul does not sensibly differ at all from a simple Monad. As this state, however, is not permanent and the soul can recover from it, the soul is something more.

21. Nevertheless it does not follow at all that the simple substance is in such a state without perception. This is so because of the reasons given above; for it cannot perish, nor on the other hand would it exist without some affection and the affection is nothing else than its perception. When, however, there are a great number of weak perceptions where nothing stands out distinctively, we are stunned; as when one turns around and around in the same direction, a dizziness comes on, which makes him swoon and makes him able to distinguish nothing. Among animals, death can occasion this state for quite a period.

22. Every present state of a simple substance is a natural consequence of its preceding state, in such a way that its present is big with its future.

23. Therefore, since on awakening after a period of unconsciousness we become conscious of our perceptions, we must, without having been conscious of them, have had perceptions immediately before; for one perception can come in a natural way only from another perception, just as a motion can come in a natural way only from a motion.

24. It is evident from this that if we were to have nothing distinctive, or so to speak prominent, and of a higher flavor in our perceptions, we should be in a continual state of stupor. This is the condition of Monads which are wholly bare.

25. We see that nature has given to animals heightened perceptions, having provided them with organs which collect numerous rays of light or numerous waves of air and thus make them more effective in their combination. Something similar to this takes place in the case of smell, in that of taste and of touch, and perhaps in many other senses which are unknown to us. I shall have occasion very soon to explain how that which occurs in the soul represents that which goes on in the sense-organs.

26. The memory furnishes a sort of consecutiveness which imitates reason but is to be distinguished from it. We see that animals when they have the perception of something which they notice and of which they have had a similar previous perception, are led by the representation of their memory to expect that which was associated in the preceding perception, and they come to have feelings like those which they had before. For instance, if a stick be shown to a dog, he remembers the pain which it has caused him and he whines or runs away.

27. The vividness of the picture, which comes to him or moves him, is derived either from the magnitude or from the number of the previous perceptions. For, oftentimes, a strong impression brings about, all at once, the same effect as a long-continued habit or as a great many re-iterated, moderate perceptions.

28. Men act in like manner as animals, in so far as the sequence of their perceptions is determined only by the law of memory, resembling the *empirical physicians* who practice simply, without any theory, and we are empiricists in three-fourths of our actions. For instance, when we expect that there will be day-light to-morrow, we do so empirically, be-cause it has always happened so up to the present time. It is only the astronomer who uses his reason in making such an affirmation.

29. But the knowledge of eternal and necessary truths is that which distinguishes us from mere animals and gives us reason and the sciences, thus raising us to a knowledge of ourselves and of God. This is what is called in us the Rational Soul or the Mind.

30. It is also through the knowledge of necessary truths and through abstractions from them that we come to perform Reflective Acts, which cause us to think of what is called the I, and to decide that this or that is within us. It is thus, that in thinking upon ourselves we think of *being*, of *substance*, of the *simple* and *composite*, of a *material* thing and of *God* himself, conceiving that what is limited in us is in him without limits. These Reflective Acts furnish the principal objects of our reasonings.

31. Our reasoning is based upon two great principles: first, that of Contradiction, by means of which we decide that to be false which involves contradiction and that to be true which contradicts or is opposed to the false.

32. And second, the principle of Sufficient Reason, in virtue of which we believe that no fact can be real or existing and no statement true unless it has a sufficient reason why it should be thus and not otherwise. Most frequently, however, these reasons cannot be known by us.

33. There are also two kinds of Truths: those of Reasoning and those of Fact. The Truths of Reasoning are necessary, and their opposite is impossible. Those of Fact, however, are contingent, and their opposite is possible. When a truth is necessary, the reason can be found by analysis in resolving it into simpler ideas and into simpler truths until we reach those which are primary.

34. It is thus that with mathematicians the Speculative Theorems and the practical Canons are reduced by analysis to Definitions, Axioms, and Postulates.

35. There are finally simple ideas of which no definition can be given. There are also the Axioms and Postulates or, in a word, the primary principles which cannot be proved and, indeed, have no need of proof. These are identical propositions whose opposites involve express contradictions.

36. But there must be also a sufficient reason for contingent truths or truths of fact; that is to say, for

the sequence of the things which extend throughout the universe of created beings, where the analysis into more particular reasons can be continued into greater detail without limit because of the immense variety of the things in nature and because of the infinite division of bodies. There is an infinity of figures and of movements, present and past, which enter into the efficient cause of my present writing, and in its final cause there are an infinity of slight tendencies and dispositions of my soul, present and past.

37. And as all this detail again involves other and more detailed contingencies, each of which again has need of a similar analysis in order to find its explanation, no real advance has been made. Therefore, the sufficient or ultimate reason must needs be outside of the sequence or series of these details of contingencies, however infinite they may be.

38. It is thus that the ultimate reason for things must be a necessary substance, in which the detail of the changes shall be present merely potentially, as in the fountain-head, and this substance we call God.

39. Now, since this substance is a sufficient reason for all the above mentioned details, which are linked together throughout, *there is but one God, and this God is sufficient.*

40. We may hold that the supreme substance, which is unique, universal and necessary with nothing independent outside of it, which is further a pure sequence of possible being, must be incapable of limitation and must contain as much reality as possible.

41. Whence it follows that God is absolutely perfect, perfection being understood as the magnitude of positive reality in the strict sense, when the limitations or the bounds of those things which have them are removed. There where there are no limits, that is to say, in God, perfection is absolutely infinite.

42. It follows also that created things derive their perfections through the influence of God, but their imperfections come from their own natures, which cannot exist without limits. It is in this latter that they are distinguished from God. An example of this original imperfection of created things is to be found in the natural inertia of bodies.

43. It is true, furthermore, that in God is found not only the source of existences, but also that of essences, in so far as they are real. In other words, he is the source of whatever there is real in the possible. This is because the Understanding of God is in the region of eternal truths or of the ideas upon which they depend, and because without him there would be nothing real in the possibilities of things, and not only would nothing be existent, nothing would be even possible.

44. For it must needs be that if there is a reality in essences or in possibilities or indeed in the eternal truths, this reality is based upon something existent and actual, and, consequently, in the existence of the necessary Being in whom essence includes existence or in whom possibility is sufficient to produce actuality.

45. Therefore God alone (or the Necessary Being) has this prerogative that if he be possible he must necessarily exist, and, as nothing is able to prevent the possibility of that which involves no bounds, no negation, and consequently, no contradiction, this alone is sufficient to establish *a priori* his existence. We have, therefore, proved his existence through the reality of eternal truths. But a little while ago we also proved it *a posteriori,* because contingent beings exist which can have their ultimate and sufficient reason only in the necessary being which, in turn, has the reason for existence in itself.

46. Yet we must not think that the eternal truths being dependent upon God are therefore arbitrary and depend upon his will, as Descartes seems to have held, and after him M. Poiret. This is the case only with contingent truths which depend upon fitness or the choice of the greatest good; necessarily truths on the other hand depend solely upon his understanding and are the inner objects of it.

47. God alone is the ultimate unity or the original simple substance, of which all created or derivative monads are the products, and arise, so to speak, through the continual outflashings (fulgurations) of the divinity from moment to moment, limited by the receptivity of the creature to whom limitation is an essential.

48. In God are present: power, which is the source of everything; knowledge, which contains the details of the ideas; and, finally, will, which changes or produces things in accordance with the principle of the greatest good. To these correspond in the created monad, the subject or basis, the fac-

ulty of perception, and the faculty of appetition. In God these attributes are absolutely infinite or perfect, while in the created monads or in the entelechies (*perfectihabies,* as Hermolaus Barbarus translates this word), they are imitations approaching him in proportion to the perfection.

49. A created thing is said to act outwardly in so far as it has perfection, and to be acted upon by another in so far as it is imperfect. Thus action is attributed to the monad in so far as it has distinct perceptions, and passion or passivity is attributed in so far as it has confused perceptions.

50. One created thing is more perfect than another when we find in the first that which gives an *a priori* reason for what occurs in the second. This is why we say that one acts upon the other.

51. In the case of simple substances, the influence which one monad has upon another is only ideal. It can have its effect only through the mediation of God, in so far as in the ideas of God each monad can rightly demand that God, in regulating the others from the beginning of things, should have regarded it also. For since one created monad cannot have a physical influence upon the inner being of another, it is only through the primal regulation that one can have dependence upon another.

52. It is thus that among created things action and passivity are reciprocal. For God, in comparing two simple substances, finds in each one reasons obliging him to adapt the other to it; and consequently what is active in certain respects is passive from another point of view, active in so far as what we distinctly know in it serves to give a reason for what occurs in another, and passive in so far as the reason for what occurs in it is found in what is distinctly known in another.

53. Now as there are an infinity of possible universes in the ideas of God, and but one of them can exist, there must be a sufficient reason for the choice of God which determines him to select one rather than another.

54. And this reason is to be found only in the fitness or in the degree of perfection which these worlds possess, each possible thing having the right to claim existence in proportion to the perfection which it involves.

55. This is the cause for the existence of the greatest good; namely, that the wisdom of God permits him to know it, his goodness causes him

to choose it, and his power enables him to produce it.

56. Now this interconnection, relationship, or this adaptation of all things to each particular one, and of each one to all the rest, brings it about that every simple substance has relations which express all the others and that it is consequently a perpetual living mirror of the universe.

57. And as the same city regarded from different sides appears entirely different, and is, as it were multiplied respectively, so, because of the infinite number of simple substances, there are a similar infinite number of universes which are, nevertheless, only the aspects of a single one as seen from the special point of view of each monad.

58. Through this means has been obtained the greatest possible variety, together with the greatest order that may be; that is to say, through this means has been obtained the greatest possible perfection.

59. This hypothesis, moreover, which I venture to call demonstrated, is the only one which fittingly gives proper prominence to the greatness of God. M. Bayle recognized this when in his dictionary (article "Rorarius") he raised objections to it; indeed, he was inclined to believe that I attributed too much to God, and more than it is possible to attribute to him: But he was unable to bring forward any reason why this universal harmony which causes every substance to express exactly all others through the relation which it has with them is impossible.

60. Besides, in what has just been said can be seen the *a priori* reasons why things cannot be otherwise than they are. It is because God, in ordering the whole, has had regard to every part and in particular to each monad; and since the monad is by its very nature *representative*, nothing can limit it to represent merely a part of things. It is nevertheless true that this representation is, as regards the details of the whole universe, only a confused representation, and is distinct only as regards a small part of them, that is to say, as regards those things which are nearest or greatest in relation to each monad. If the representation were distinct as to the details of the entire universe, each monad would be a Deity. It is not in the object represented that the monads are limited, but in the modifications of their knowledge of the object. In a confused way they reach out to infinity or to the whole, but are limited

and differentiated in the degree of their distinct perceptions.

61. In this respect composites are like simple substances, for all space is filled up; therefore, all matter is connected. And in a plenum or filled space every movement has an effect upon bodies in proportion to this distance, so that not only is every body affected by those which are in contact with it and responds in some way to whatever happens to them, but also by means of them the body responds to those bodies adjoining them, and their intercommunication reaches to any distance whatsoever. Consequently every body responds to all that happens in the universe, so that he who saw all could read in each one what is happening everywhere, and even what has happened and what will happen. He can discover in the present what is distant both as regards space and as regards time; "All things conspire," as Hippocrates said. A soul can, however, read in itself only what is there represented distinctly. It cannot all at once open up all its folds, because they extend to infinity.

62. Thus although each created monad represents the whole universe, it represents more distinctly the body which specially pertains to it and of which it constitutes the entelechy. And as this body expresses all the universe through the interconnection of all matter in the plenum, the soul also represents the whole universe in representing this body, which belongs to it in a particular way.

63. The body belonging to a monad, which is its entelechy or soul, constitutes together with the entelechy what may be called a *living being*, and with a soul what is called an *animal*. Now this body of a living being or of an animal is always organic, because every monad is a mirror of the universe and is regulated with perfect order there must needs be order also in what represents it, that is to say in the perceptions of the soul and consequently in the body through which the universe is represented in the soul.

64. Therefore every organic body of a living being is a kind of divine machine or natural automaton, infinitely surpassing all artificial automatons. Because a machine constructed by man's skill is not a machine in each of its parts; for instance, the teeth of a brass wheel have parts or bits which to us are not artificial products and contain nothing in themselves to show the use to which the wheel was destined in the machine. The machines of na-

ture, however, that is to say, living bodies, are still machines in their smallest parts *ad infinitum.* Such is the difference between nature and art, that is to say, between divine art and ours.

65. The author of nature has been able to employ this divine and infinitely marvelous artifice, because each portion of matter is not only, as the ancients recognized, infinitely divisible, but also because it is really divided without end, every part in other parts, each one of which has its own proper motion. Otherwise it would be impossible for each portion of matter to express all the universe.

66. Whence we see that there is a world of created things, of living beings, of animals, of entelechies, of souls, in the minutest particle of matter.

67. Every portion of matter may be conceived as like a garden full of plants and like a pond full of fish. But every branch of a plant, every member of an animal, and every drop of the fluids within it, is also such a garden or such a pond.

68. And although the ground and air which lies between the plants of the garden, and the water which is between the fish in the pond, are not themselves plants or fish, yet they nevertheless contain these, usually so small however as to be imperceptible to us.

69. There is, therefore, nothing uncultivated, or sterile or dead in the universe, no chaos, no confusion, save in appearance; somewhat as a pond would appear at a distance when we could see in it a confused movement, and so to speak, a swarming of the fish, without however discerning the fish themselves.

70. It is evident, then, that every living body has a dominating entelechy, which in animals is the soul. The parts, however, of this living body are full of other living beings, plants and animals, which in turn have each one its entelechy or dominating soul.

71. This does not mean, as some who have misunderstood my thought have imagined, that each soul has a quantity or portion of matter appropriated to it or attached to itself for ever, and that it consequently owns other inferior living beings destined to serve it always; because all bodies are in a state of perpetual flux like rivers, and the parts are continually entering in or passing out.

72. The soul, therefore, changes its body only gradually and by degrees, so that it is never deprived all at once of all its organs. There is fre-

quently a metamorphosis in animals, but never metempsychosis or a transmigration of souls. Neither are there souls wholly separate from bodies, nor bodiless spirits. God alone is without body.

73. This is also why there is never absolute generation or perfect death in the strict sense, consisting in the separation of the soul from the body. What we call generation is development and growth, and what we call death is envelopment and diminution.

74. Philosophers have been much perplexed in accounting for the origin of forms, entelechies, or souls. To-day, however, when it has been learned through careful investigations made in plant, insect and animal life, that the organic bodies of nature are never the product of chaos or putrefaction, but always come from seeds in which there was without doubt some preformation, it has been decided that not only is the organic body already present before conception, but also a soul in this body, in a word, the animal itself; and it has been decided that, by means of conception the animal is merely made ready for a great transformation, so as to become an animal of another sort. We can see cases somewhat similar outside of generation when grubs become flies and caterpillars butterflies.

75. These little animals, some of which by conception become large animals, may be called spermatic. Those among them which remain in their species, that is to say, the greater part, are born, multiply, and are destroyed, like the larger animals. There are only a few chosen ones which come out upon a greater stage.

76. This, however, is only half the truth. I believe, therefore, that if the animal never actually commences by natural means, no more does it by natural means come to an end. Not only is there no generation, but also there is no entire destruction or absolute death. These reasonings, carried on *a posteriori* and drawn from experience, accord perfectly with the principles which I have above deduced *a priori*.

77. Therefore we may say that not only the soul (the mirror of the indestructible universe) is indestructible, but also the animal itself is, although its mechanism is frequently destroyed in parts and although it puts off and takes on organic coatings.

78. These principles have furnished me the means of explaining on natural grounds the union, or rather the conformity between the soul and the organic body. The soul follows its own laws, and the body likewise follows its own laws. They are fitted to each other in virtue of the preestablished harmony between all substances, since they are all representations of one and the same universe.

79. Souls act in accordance with the laws of final causes through their desires, ends and means. Bodies act in accordance with the laws of efficient causes or of motion. The two realms, that of efficient causes and that of final causes, are in harmony, each with the other.

80. Descartes saw that souls cannot at all impart force to bodies, because there is always the same quantity of force in matter. Yet he thought that the soul could change the direction of bodies. This was, however, because at that time the law of nature which affirms also that conservation of the same total direction in the motion of matter was not known. If he had known that law, he would have fallen upon my system of preestablished harmony.

81. According to this system bodies act as if (to suppose the impossible) there were no souls at all, and souls act as if there were no bodies, and yet both body and soul act as if the one were influencing the other.

82. Although I find that essentially the same thing is true of all living things and animals, which we have just said (namely, that animals and souls begin from the very commencement of the world and that they no more come to an end than does the world) nevertheless, rational animals have this peculiarity, that their little spermatic animals, as long as they remain such, have only ordinary or sensuous souls, but those of them which are, so to speak, elected, attain by actual conception to human nature, and their sensuous souls are raised to the rank of reason and to the prerogative of spirits.

83. Among the differences that there are between ordinary souls and spirits, some of which I have already instanced, there is also this, that while souls in general are living mirrors or images of the universe of created things, spirits are also images of the Deity himself or of the author of nature. They are capable of knowing the system of the universe, and of imitating some features of it by means of artificial models, each spirit being like a small divinity in its own sphere.

84. Therefore, spirits are able to enter into a sort of social relationship with God, and with respect to them he is not only what an inventor is to

his machine (as in his relation to the other created things), but he is also what a prince is to his subjects, and even what a father is to his children.

85. Whence it is easy to conclude that the totality of all spirits must compose the city of God, that is to say, the most perfect state that is possible under the most perfect monarch.

86. This city of God, this truly universal monarchy, is a moral world within the natural world. It is what is noblest and most divine among the works of God. And in it consists in reality the glory of God, because he would have no glory were not his greatness and goodness known and wondered at by spirits. It is also in relation to this divine city that God properly has goodness. His wisdom and his power are shown everywhere.

87. As we established above that there is a perfect harmony between the two natural realms of efficient and final causes, it will be in place here to point out another harmony which appears between the physical realm of nature and the moral realm of grace, that is to say, between God considered as the architect of the mechanism of the world and God considered as the monarch of the divine city of spirits.

88. This harmony brings it about that things progress of themselves toward grace along natural lines, and that this earth, for example, must be destroyed and restored by natural means at those times when the proper government of spirits demands it, for chastisement in the one case and for a reward in the other.

89. We can say also that God, the Architect, satisfies in all respects God the Law-Giver, that therefore sins will bring their own penalty with them through the order of nature, and because of the very structure of things, mechanical though it is. And in the same way the good actions will attain their rewards in mechanical way through their relation to bodies, although this cannot and ought not always to take place without delay.

90. Finally, under this perfect government, there will be no good action unrewarded and no evil action unpunished; everything must turn out for the well-being of the good; that is to say, of those who are not disaffected in this great state, who, after having done their duty, trust in Providence and who love and imitate, as is meet, the Author of all Good, delighting in the contemplation of his perfections according to the nature of that genuine, pure love which finds pleasure in the happiness of those who are loved. It is for this reason that wise and virtuous persons work in behalf of everything which seems conformable to presumptive or antecedent will of God, and are, nevertheless, content with what God actually brings to pass through his secret, consequent and determining will, recognizing that if we were able to understand sufficiently well the order of the universe, we should find that it surpasses all the desires of the wisest of us, and that it is impossible to render it better than it is, not only for all in general, but also for each one of us in particular, provided that we have the proper attachment for the author of all, not only as the Architect and the efficient cause of our being, but also as our Lord and the Final Cause, who ought to be the whole goal of our will, and who alone can make us happy.

John Locke
(1632–1704)

Locke was born in Wrington, Somerset, England, into a liberal, Puritan family; his father fought against Charles I in the Civil War. He entered Westminster School in 1646, and Christ Church, Oxford, in 1652. He studied traditional logic, grammar, rhetoric, Greek, and moral philosophy. He was elected to a Senior Studentship in 1658, and taught Latin, Greek, and rhetoric. In 1664 he was appointed Censor of Moral Philosophy. About this time, he started work on what would eventually become *An Essay Concerning Human Under-standing*. Apart from his official duties, Locke developed a profound interest in medicine, and it was in a medical capacity that he came to the attention of Lord Ashley, later Earl of Shaftesbury, whose service Locke entered in 1666. While at Oxford, Locke grew to know Robert Boyle, from whom he learned much about the new sciences and the corpuscularian hypothesis. He was elected to the Royal Society in 1668.

With Shaftesbury, Locke entered into the politics of the day. He assisted in framing the constitution of Carolina, and became secretary to the Council of Trade and Plantations. Shaftesbury became chancellor in 1672, and subsequently Locke became embroiled in the attempt to exclude the Catholic Duke of York (later James II) from succeeding to the throne of his brother, Charles II. After Shaftesbury's trial for treason, Locke fled to Holland in 1683. He again took up work on the *Essay.* After the accession of the Protestant William of Orange, Locke returned to England, though now deprived of his studentship. The *Essay* was published in 1690, soon followed by other major works, including *Two Treatises on Government.* He combined this work with public service, serving as Commissioner of Appeals and of the Board of Trade and Plantations.

Locke tells a famous story about the origin of the *Essay:*

> Five or six friends, meeting at my chamber, and discoursing on a subject very remote from this, found themselves quickly at a stand, by the difficulties that arose on every side. After we had awhile puzzled ourselves, without coming any nearer a resolution of those doubts which perplexed us, it came into my thoughts, that we took a wrong course; and that before we set ourselves upon enquiries of that nature, it was necessary to examine our own abilities, and see what objects our understandings were, or were not, fitted to deal with. This I proposed to the company, who all readily assented; and thereupon it was agreed, that this should be our first enquiry.

The *Essay'*s avowed goal became to seek out the limits of what we can understand. Locke thought it important to ascertain the limits of

knowledge, and to search for the boundary between what we can know and what we can only reasonably believe, that is, between knowledge and probable opinion.

In this pursuit Locke thought to oppose excessive skepticism, seen as a threat ever since the rediscovery of the ancient Greek skeptical texts in the previous century. Locke thought that the fact that we cannot know everything is no grounds for thinking we cannot know anything. He uses the metaphor of a sailor's depth-line: "It is of great use to the sailor to know the length of his line, though he cannot with it fathom all the depths of the ocean. It is well he knows that it is long enough to reach the bottom at such places as are necessary to direct his voyage, and caution him against running upon shoals that may ruin him."

Locke starts his task by looking into the origin of all our ideas. Like Descartes, he thought that all knowledge depends on our ideas, what we are immediately aware of. But unlike Descartes, he thought that all our ideas, and hence all knowledge and opinion, come from experience. Book I of the *Essay* is a sustained attack on innate ideas and principles. Book II contains a discussion, conditioned by Locke's central claim that all ideas are derived from experience, of the nature and content of our ideas, or how we mentally represent the world. After a sustained treatment of words and language in Book III, which includes a theory of concept formation as well as warnings not to be misled by words but rather concentrate our attention on ideas, Locke gives his account of knowledge and opinion, in terms of ideas, in Book IV. He also develops an account, again in terms of ideas, of the sorts of reasoning appropriate to knowledge (demonstrative reasoning) and opinion or belief (probable reasoning).

Note on the text: We endeavored to retain the famous passages, and to omit only those passages that do not substantially advance the argument, or that include material of little interest to those encountering the *Essay* for the first time. The omissions are as follows:

- Book I: Chapter 3, [Chapter 4]
- Book II: Chapter 7; Chapter 8, §§ 1–6; Chapter 9, §§ 1–7; Chapter 10, §§ 4–10; [Chapter 11]; Chapter 13, §§ 1–10, 21–27; Chapters 14–20; Chapter 21, §§28–72; Chapter 22 . . .; Chapters 24–26, 28–30, 32–33
- Book III: Chapter 6, §§30–34, 40–43; Chapters 9–11
- Book IV: Chapters . . . [5, 6, 7, 8;] . . . Chapter 10; Chapter 13; Chapter 16; Chapter 17, §§4, 8, 19–24; Chapters 18–20

The text reprinted here contains Locke's footnotes in square brackets, and transliterated Greek and Hebrew in angle brackets.

An *Essay Concerning Human Understanding*

Book I. Of Innate Notions

Chapter I. Introduction

Sections
1. An enquiry into the understanding, pleasant and useful.
2. Design.
3. Method.
4. Useful to know the extent of our comprehension.
5. Our capacity proportioned to our state and concerns, to discover things useful to us.
6. Knowing the extent of our capacities will hinder us from useless curiosity, scepticism, and idleness.
7. Occasion of this essay.
8. What *idea* stands for.

Chapter II. No Innate Principles in the Mind, and Particularly No Innate Speculative Principles

Sections
1. The way shown how we come by any knowledge, sufficient to prove it not innate.
2. General assent, the great argument.
3. Universal consent proves nothing innate.
4. *What is, is;* and, *it is impossible for the same thing to be, and not to be;* not universally assented to.
5. Not on the mind naturally imprinted, because not known to children, idiots, &c.
6, 7. That men know them when they come to the use of reason, answered.
8. If reason discovered them, that would not prove them innate.
9–11. It is false, that reason discovers them.
12. The coming to the use of reason, not the time we come to know these maxims.
13. By this, they are not distinguished from other knowable truths.
14. If coming to the use of reason were the time of their discovery, it would not prove them innate.
15, 16. The steps by which the mind attains several truths.
17. Assenting as soon as proposed and understood proves them not innate.
18. If such an assent be a mark of innate, then that one and two are equal to three; that sweetness is not bitterness; and a thousand the like, must be innate.

Excerpted with permission from the Past Masters Locke text base, InteLex Corp., 1989.

19. Such less general propositions known before these universal maxims.

20. One and one, equal to two, &c. not general,
nor useful, answered.

21. These maxims not being known sometimes
till proposed proves them not innate.

22. Implicitly known before proposing signifies
that the mind is capable of understanding
them, or else signifies nothing.

23. The argument of assenting on first hearing
is upon a false supposition of no precedent
teaching.

24. Not innate, because not universally assented to.

25. These maxims not the first known.

26. And so not innate.

27. Not innate, because they appear least where
what is innate shows itself clearest.

28. Recapitulation.

. . .

Book I. Of Innate Notions

Chapter I. Introduction

1. Since it is the understanding that sets man above
the rest of sensible beings, and gives him all the advantage and dominion which he has over them, it is
certainly a subject, even for its nobleness, worth our
labour to enquire into. The understanding, like the
eye, whilst it makes us see and perceive all other
things, takes no notice of itself; and it requires art
and pains to set it at a distance and make it its own
object. But whatever be the difficulties that lie in the
way of this enquiry; whatever it be that keeps us so
much in the dark to ourselves; sure I am that all the
light we can let in upon our minds, all the acquaintance we can make with our own understandings,
will not only be very pleasant, but bring us great
advantage in directing our thoughts in the search of
other things.

2. This, therefore, being my purpose, to enquire
into the original, certainty, and extent of human
knowledge, together with the grounds and degrees
of belief, opinion, and assent, I shall not at present

meddle with the physical consideration of the mind,
or trouble myself to examine wherein its essence
consists, or by what motions of our spirits, or alterations of our bodies, we come to have any sensation
by our organs, or any ideas in our understandings;
and whether those ideas do, in their formation, any
or all of them, depend on matter or no: These are
speculations which, however curious and entertaining, I shall decline, as lying out of my way in the
design I am now upon. It shall suffice to my present
purpose to consider the discerning faculties of a
man as they are employed about the objects which
they have to do with: And I shall imagine I have not
wholly misemployed myself in the thoughts I shall
have on this occasion if, in this historical, plain
method, I can give any account of the ways whereby
our understandings come to attain those notions of
things we have, and can set down any measures
of the certainty of our knowledge, or the grounds of
those persuasions which are to be found amongst
men, so various, different, and wholly contradictory; and yet asserted somewhere or other, with
such assurance and confidence, that he that shall
take a view of the opinions of mankind, observe
their Opposition, and at the same time consider
the fondness and devotion wherewith they are embraced, the resolution and eagerness wherewith
they are maintained, may perhaps have reason to
suspect that either there is no such thing as truth at
all, or that mankind hath no sufficient means to attain a certain knowledge of it.

3. It is therefore worth while to search out the
bounds between opinion and knowledge, and examine by what measures, in things whereof we have
no certain knowledge, we ought to regulate our
assent, and moderate our persuasions. In order
whereunto, I shall pursue this following method.

First, I shall enquire into the original of those
ideas, notions, or whatever else you please to call
them, which a man observes, and is conscious to
himself he has in his mind; and the ways whereby
the understanding comes to be furnished with
them.

Secondly, I shall endeavour to show what
knowledge the understanding hath by those ideas,
and the certainty, evidence, and extent of it.

Thirdly, I shall make some enquiry into the nature and grounds of faith, or opinion; whereby I

mean that assent which we give to any proposition as true, of whose truth yet we have no certain knowledge; and here we shall have occasion to examine the reasons and degrees of assent.

4. If, by this enquiry into the nature of the understanding, I can discover the powers thereof; how far they reach; to what things they are in any degree proportionate; and where they fail us: I suppose it may be of use to prevail with the busy mind of man to be more cautious in meddling with things exceeding its comprehension; to stop when it is at the utmost extent of its tether; and to sit down in a quiet ignorance of those things which, upon examination, are found to be beyond the reach of our capacities. We should not then perhaps be so forward, out of an affectation of a universal knowledge, to raise questions, and perplex ourselves and others with disputes about things to which our understandings are not suited, and of which we cannot frame in our minds any clear or distinct perceptions, or whereof (as it has perhaps too often happened) we have not any notions at all. If we can find out how far the understanding can extend its view, how far it has faculties to attain certainty, and in what cases it can only judge and guess, we may learn to content ourselves with what is attainable by us in this state.

5. For though the comprehension of our understandings comes exceeding short of the vast extent of things, yet we shall have cause enough to magnify the bountiful author of our being for that proportion and degree of knowledge he has bestowed on us, so far above all the rest of the inhabitants of this our mansion. Men have reason to be well satisfied with what God hath thought fit for them, since he hath given them (as St. Peter says) ⟨*panta pros zoen kai eusebeian*⟩, "whatsoever is necessary for the conveniences of life, and information of virtue"; and has put within the reach of their discovery the comfortable provision for this life, and the way that leads to a better. How short soever their knowledge may come of an universal or perfect comprehension of whatsoever is, it yet secures their great concernments that they have light enough to lead them to the knowledge of their maker, and the sight of their own duties. Men may find matter sufficient to busy their heads, and employ their hands with variety, delight, and satisfaction, if they will not boldly quarrel with their own constitution, and throw away the blessings their hands are filled with, because they are not big enough to grasp everything. We shall not have much reason to complain of the narrowness of our minds if we will but employ them about what may be of use to us; for of that they are very capable: And it will be an unpardonable, as well as childish, peevishness if we undervalue the advantages of our knowledge, and neglect to improve it to the ends for which it was given us, because there are some things that are set out of the reach of it. It will be no excuse to an idle and untoward servant, who would not attend his business by candle-light, to plead that he had not broad sunshine. The candle that is set up in us shines bright enough for all our purposes. The discoveries we can make with this ought to satisfy us; and we shall then use our understandings right when we entertain all objects in that way and proportion that they are suited to our faculties, and upon those grounds they are capable of being proposed to us, and not peremptorily or intemperately require demonstration, and demand certainty, where probability only is to be had, and which is sufficient to govern all our concernments. If we will disbelieve everything because we cannot certainly know all things, we shall do much-what as wisely as he who would not use his legs, but sit still and perish, because he had no wings to fly.

6. When we know our own strength, we shall the better know what to undertake with hopes of success: And when we have well surveyed the powers of our own minds, and made some estimate what we may expect from them, we shall not be inclined either to sit still, and not set our thoughts on work at all, in despair of knowing anything; nor on the other side, question everything, and disclaim all knowledge, because some things are not to be understood. It is of great use to the sailor to know the length of his line, though he cannot with it fathom all the depths of the ocean. It is well he knows that it is long enough to reach the bottom at such places as are necessary to direct his voyage, and caution him against running upon shoals that may ruin him. Our business here is not to know all things, but those which concern our conduct. If we can find out those measures whereby a rational creature, put in that state in which man is in this world, may and ought to govern his opinions, and actions depending thereon, we need not be troubled that some other things escape our knowledge.

7. This was that which gave the first rise to this essay concerning the understanding. For I thought that the first step towards satisfying several enquiries the mind of man was very apt to run into was to take a survey of our own understandings, examine our own powers, and see to what things they were adapted. Till that was done, I suspected we began at the wrong end, and in vain sought for satisfaction in a quiet and sure possession of truths that most concerned us, whilst we let loose our thoughts into the vast ocean of being; as if all that boundless extent were the natural and undoubted possession of our understandings, wherein there was nothing exempt from its decisions, or that escaped its comprehension. Thus men, extending their enquiries beyond their capacities, and letting their thoughts wander into those depths where they can find no sure footing, it is no wonder that they raise questions and multiply disputes, which, never coming to any clear resolution, are proper only to continue and increase their doubts, and to confirm them at last in perfect scepticism. Whereas, were the capacities of our understandings well considered, the extent of our knowledge once discovered, and the horizon found which sets the bounds between the enlightened and dark parts of things, between what is and what is not comprehensible by us, men would perhaps with less scruple acquiesce in the avowed ignorance of the one, and employ their thoughts and discourse with more advantage and satisfaction in the other.

8. This much I thought necessary to say concerning the occasion of this enquiry into human understanding. But, before I proceed on to what I have thought on this subject, I must here in the entrance beg pardon of my reader for the frequent use of the word *idea* which he will find in the following treatise. It being that term which, I think, serves best to stand for whatsoever is the object of the understanding when a man thinks, I have used it to express whatever is meant by *phantasm, notion, species,* or whatever it is which the mind can be employed about in thinking; and I could not avoid frequently using it.

I presume it will be easily granted me that there are such ideas in men's minds; everyone is conscious of them in himself, and men's words and actions will satisfy him that they are in others.

Our first enquiry then shall be how they come into the mind.

Chapter II. No Innate Principles in the Mind

1. It is an established opinion amongst some men that there are in the understanding certain innate principles; some primary notions, ⟨*koinai ennoiai*⟩, characters, as it were, stamped upon the mind of man, which the soul receives in its very first being, and brings into the world with it. It would be sufficient to convince unprejudiced readers of the falseness of this supposition if I should only show (as I hope I shall in the following parts of this discourse) how men, barely by the use of their natural faculties, may attain to all the knowledge they have without the help of any innate impressions; and may arrive at certainty without any such original notions or principles. For I imagine anyone will easily grant that it would be impertinent to suppose the ideas of colours innate in a creature to whom God hath given sight, and a power to receive them by the eyes from external objects: And no less unreasonable would it be to attribute several truths to the impressions of nature, and innate characters, when we may observe in ourselves faculties fit to attain as easy and certain knowledge of them as if they were originally imprinted on the mind.

But because a man is not permitted without censure to follow his own thoughts in the search of truth, when they lead him ever so little out of the common road, I shall set down the reasons that made me doubt of the truth of that opinion, as an excuse for my mistake, if I be in one; which I leave to be considered by those who, with me, dispose themselves to embrace truth, wherever they find it.

2. There is nothing more commonly taken for granted than that there are certain principles, both speculative and practical (for they speak of both), universally agreed upon by all mankind: Which therefore, they argue, must needs be the constant impressions which the souls of men receive in their first beings, and which they bring into the world with them, as necessarily and really as they do any of their inherent faculties.

3. This argument, drawn from universal consent, has this misfortune in it, that if it were true in matter of fact that there were certain truths wherein all mankind agreed, it would not prove them innate, if there can be any other way shown how men may come to that universal agreement in the things they do consent in, which I presume may be done.

4. But, which is worse, this argument of universal consent, which is made use of to prove innate principles, seems to me a demonstration that there are none such; because there are none to which all mankind give an universal assent. I shall begin with the speculative, and instance in those magnified principles of demonstration: "Whatsoever is, is," and "It is impossible for the same thing to be and not to be," which, of all others, I think have the most allowed title to innate. These have so settled a reputation of maxims universally received that it will, no doubt, be thought strange if anyone should seem to question it. But yet I take liberty to say that these propositions are so far from having an universal assent that there are a great part of mankind to whom they are not so much as known.

5. For, first, it is evident that all children and idiots have not the least apprehension or thought of them; and the want of that is enough to destroy that universal assent which must needs be the necessary concomitant of all innate truths: It seeming to me near a contradiction to say that there are truths imprinted on the soul which it perceives or understands not; imprinting, if it signify anything, being nothing else but the making certain truths to be perceived. For to imprint anything on the mind without the mind's perceiving it seems to me hardly intelligible. If therefore children and idiots have souls, have minds, with those impressions upon them, they must unavoidably perceive them, and necessarily know and assent to these truths: Which since they do not, it is evident that there are no such impressions. For if they are not notions naturally imprinted, how can they be innate? And if they are notions imprinted, how can they be unknown? To say a notion is imprinted on the mind, and yet at the same time to say that the mind is ignorant of it, and never yet took notice of it, is to make this impression nothing. No proposition can be said to be in the mind which it never yet knew, which it was never yet conscious of. For if any one may, then, by the

same reason, all propositions that are true, and the mind is capable ever of assenting to, may be said to be in the mind, and to be imprinted: Since, if any one can be said to be in the mind, which it never yet knew, it must be only, because it is capable of knowing it, and so the mind is of all truths it ever shall know. Nay, thus truths may be imprinted on the mind which it never did nor ever shall know: For a man may live long, and die at last in ignorance of many truths which his mind was capable of knowing, and that with certainty. So that if the capacity of knowing be the natural impression contended for, all the truths a man ever comes to know will, by this account, be every one of them innate; and this great point will amount to no more but only to a very improper way of speaking; which, whilst it pretends to assert the contrary, says nothing different from those who deny innate principles. For nobody, I think, ever denied that the mind was capable of knowing several truths. The capacity, they say, is innate, the knowledge acquired. But then to what end such contest for certain innate maxims? If truths can be imprinted on the understanding without being perceived, I can see no difference there can be between any truths the mind is capable of knowing in respect of their original: They must all be innate, or all adventitious: In vain shall a man go about to distinguish them. He therefore that talks of innate notions in the understanding cannot (if he intend thereby any distinct sort of truths) mean such truths to be in the understanding as it never perceived, and is yet wholly ignorant of. For if these words (*to be in the understanding*) have any propriety, they signify to be understood: So that to be in the understanding, and not to be understood; to be in the mind, and never to be perceived; is all one, as to say anything is, and is not, in the mind or understanding. If therefore these two propositions, "Whatsoever is, is," and "It is impossible for the same thing to be and not to be," are by nature imprinted, children cannot be ignorant of them; infants, and all that have souls, must necessarily have them in their understandings, know the truth of them, and assent to it.

6. To avoid this, it is usually answered that all men know and assent to them, when they come to the use of reason, and this is enough to prove them innate. I answer,

7. Doubtful expressions, that have scarce any signification, go for clear reasons, to those who, being prepossessed, take not the pains to examine even what they themselves say. For to apply this answer with any tolerable sense to our present purpose, it must signify one of these two things: either that, as soon as men come to the use of reason, these supposed native inscriptions come to be known and observed by them, or else that the use and exercise of men's reason assists them in the discovery of these principles, and certainly makes them known to them.

8. If they mean that by the use of reason men may discover these principles, and that this is sufficient to prove them innate, their way of arguing will stand thus: (viz.) that whatever truths reason can certainly discover to us, and make us firmly assent to, those are all naturally imprinted on the mind; since that universal assent, which is made the mark of them, amounts to no more but this; that by the use of reason, we are capable to come to a certain knowledge of and assent to them, and, by this means, there will be no difference between the maxims of the mathematicians and theorems they deduce from them; all must be equally allowed innate, they being all discoveries made by the use of reason, and truths that a rational creature may certainly come to know, if he apply his thoughts rightly that way.

9. But how can these men think the use of reason necessary to discover principles that are supposed innate, when reason (if we may believe them) is nothing else but the faculty of deducing unknown truths from principles or propositions that are already known? That certainly can never be thought innate which we have need of reason to discover, unless, as I have said, we will have all the certain truths that reason ever teaches us to be innate. We may as well think the use of reason necessary to make our eyes discover visible objects, as that there should be need of reason, or the exercise thereof, to make the understanding see what is originally engraven on it, and cannot be in the understanding before it be perceived by it. So that to make reason discover those truths, thus imprinted, is to say that the use of reason discovers to a man what he knew before: And if men have those innate impressed truths originally, and before the use of

reason, and yet are always ignorant of them till they come to the use of reason, it is in effect to say that men know, and know them not, at the same time.

10. It will here perhaps be said that mathematical demonstrations, and other truths that are not innate, are not assented to as soon as proposed, wherein they are distinguished from these maxims and other innate truths. I shall have occasion to speak of assent upon the first proposing more particularly by and by. I shall here only, and that very readily, allow that these maxims and mathematical demonstrations are in this different: that the one have need of reason, using of proofs, to make them out, and to gain our assent; but the other, as soon as understood, are, without any the least reasoning, embraced and assented to. But I withal beg leave to observe that it lays open the weakness of this subterfuge, which requires the use of reason for the discovery of these general truths: Since it must be confessed that in their discovery there is no use made of reasoning at all. And I think those who give this answer will not be forward to affirm that the knowledge of this maxim, "That it is impossible for the same thing to be and not to be," is a deduction of our reason. For this would be to destroy that bounty of nature they seem so fond of, whilst they make the knowledge of those principles to depend on the labour of our thoughts. For all reasoning is search, and casting about, and requires pains and application. And how can it with any tolerable sense be supposed that what was imprinted by nature, as the foundation and guide of our reason, should need the use of reason to discover it?

11. Those who will take the pains to reflect with a little attention on the operations of the understanding will find that this ready assent of the mind to some truths depends not either on native inscription, or the use of reason, but on a faculty of the mind quite distinct from both of them, as we shall see hereafter. Reason, therefore, having nothing to do in procuring our assent to these maxims, if by saying that men know and assent to them, when they come to the use of reason, be meant that the use of reason assists us in the knowledge of these maxims, it is utterly false; and were it true, would prove them not to be innate.

12. If by knowing and assenting to them "when we come to the use of reason" be meant that this is the time when they come to be taken notice of by the mind; and that, as soon as children come to the use of reason, they come also to know and assent to these maxims; this also is false and frivolous. First, it is false: Because it is evident these maxims are not in the mind so early as the use of reason: And therefore the coming to the use of reason is falsely assigned, as the time of their discovery. How many instances of the use of reason may we observe in children, a long time before they have any knowledge of this maxim, "That it is impossible for the same thing to be and not to be"? And a great part of illiterate people, and savages, pass many years, even of their rational age, without ever thinking on this, and the like general propositions. I grant, men come not to the knowledge of these general and more abstract truths, which are thought innate, till they come to the use of reason; and I add, nor then neither. Which is so because, till after they come to the use of reason, those general abstract ideas are not framed in the mind, about which those general maxims are, which are mistaken for innate principles; but are indeed discoveries made, and verities introduced and brought into the mind by the same way, and discovered by the same steps, as several other propositions, which nobody was ever so extravagant as to suppose innate. This I hope to make plain in the sequel of this discourse. I allow therefore a necessity, that men should come to the use of reason before they get the knowledge of those general truths; but deny that men's coming to the use of reason is the time of their discovery.

13. In the meantime it is observable that this saying, that men know and assent to these maxims, when they come to the use of reason, amounts in reality of fact to no more but this, That they are never known nor taken notice of before the use of reason, but may possibly be assented to, some time after, during a man's life; but when, is uncertain. And so may all other knowable truths, as well as these; which therefore have no advantage nor distinction from others, by this note of being known when we come to the use of reason; nor are thereby proved to be innate, but quite the contrary.

14. But, secondly, were it true that the precise time of their being known and assented to were when men come to the use of reason, neither would that prove them innate. This way of arguing is as frivolous as the supposition itself is false. For by what kind of logic will it appear that any notion is originally by nature imprinted in the mind in its first constitution, because it comes first to be observed and assented to, when a faculty of the mind which has quite a distinct province begins to exert itself? And therefore, the coming to the use of speech, if it were supposed the time that these maxims are first assented to (which it may be with as much truth as the time when men come to the use of reason), would be as good a proof that they were innate as to say they are innate because men assent to them when they come to the use of reason. I agree then with these men of innate principles, that there is no knowledge of these general and self-evident maxims in the mind till it comes to the exercise of reason: But I deny that the coming to the use of reason is the precise time when they are first taken notice of; and if that were the precise time, I deny that it would prove them innate. All that can with any truth be meant by this proposition, that men assent to them when they come to the use of reason, is no more but this, that the making of general abstract ideas, and the understanding of general names, being a concomitant of the rational faculty, and growing up with it, children commonly get not those general ideas, nor learn the names that stand for them, till, having for a good while exercised their reason about familiar and more particular ideas, they are, by their ordinary discourse and actions with others, acknowledged to be capable of rational conversation. If assenting to these maxims, when men come to the use of reason, can be true in any other sense, I desire it may be shown; or at least, how in this, or any other sense, it proves them innate.

15. The senses at first let in particular ideas, and furnish the yet empty cabinet, and the mind by degrees growing familiar with some of them, they are lodged in the memory, and names got to them. Afterwards the mind, proceeding farther, abstracts them, and by degrees learns the use of general names. In this manner the mind comes to be furnished with ideas and language, the materials about which to exercise its discursive faculty: And the use of reason becomes daily more visible as these materials, that give it employment, increase. But though the having of general ideas, and the use of general words and reason, usually grow together, yet I see

not how this any way proves them innate. The knowledge of some truths, I confess, is very early in the mind; but in a way that shows them not to be innate. For, if we will observe, we shall find it still to be about ideas, not innate, but acquired: It being about those first which are imprinted by external things, with which infants have earliest to do, which make the most frequent impressions on their senses. In ideas thus got, the mind discovers that some agree, and others differ, probably as soon as it has any use of memory; as soon as it is able to retain and perceive distinct ideas. But whether it be then, or no, this is certain, it does so long before it has the use of words, or comes to that which we commonly call "the use of reason." For a child knows as certainly, before it can speak, the difference between the ideas of sweet and bitter (i.e., that sweet is not bitter) as it knows afterwards (when it comes to speak) that wormwood and sugar-plums are not the same thing.

16. A child knows not that three and four are equal to seven till he comes to be able to count seven, and has got the name and idea of equality: And then, upon explaining those words, he presently assents to, or rather perceives the truth of, that proposition. But neither does he then readily assent because it is an innate truth, nor was his assent wanting till then because he wanted the use of reason; but the truth of it appears to him as soon as he has settled in his mind the clear and distinct ideas that these names stand for: And then he knows the truth of that proposition upon the same grounds and by the same means that he knew before, that a rod and a cherry are not the same thing; and upon the same grounds also, that he may come to know afterwards "that it is impossible for the same thing to be and not to be," as shall be more fully shown hereafter. So that the later it is before anyone comes to have those general ideas about which those maxims are; or to know the signification of those general terms that stand for them; or to put together in his mind the ideas they stand for; the later also will it be before he comes to assent to those maxims, whose terms, with the ideas they stand for, being no more innate than those of a cat or a weasel, he must stay till time and observation have acquainted him with them; and then he will be in a capacity to know the truth of these maxims, upon the first occasion that shall make him put together those ideas in his mind, and observe whether they agree or disagree,

according as is expressed in those propositions. And therefore it is that a man knows that eighteen and nineteen are equal to thirty-seven by the same self-evidence that he knows one and two to be equal to three: Yet a child knows this not so soon as the other; not for want of the use of reason, but because the ideas the words *eighteen, nineteen,* and *thirty-seven* stand for are not so soon got as those which are signified by *one, two,* and *three.*

17. This evasion therefore of general assent when men come to the use of reason, failing as it does, and leaving no difference between those supposed innate, and other truths that are afterwards acquired and learnt, men have endeavoured to secure an universal assent to those they call maxims, by saying they are generally assented to as soon as proposed and the terms they are proposed in understood: Seeing all men, even children, as soon as they hear and understand the terms, assent to these propositions, they think it is sufficient to prove them innate. For, since men never fail, after they have once understood the words, to acknowledge them for undoubted truths, they would infer that certainly these propositions were first lodged in the understanding, which, without any teaching, the mind, at the very first proposal, immediately closes with and assents to, and after that never doubts again.

18. In answer to this, I demand "whether ready assent given to a proposition, upon first hearing, and understanding the terms, be a certain mark of an innate principle?" If it be not, such a general assent is in vain urged as a proof of them: If it be said that it is a mark of innate, they must then allow all such propositions to be innate which are generally assented to as soon as heard, whereby they will find themselves plentifully stored with innate principles. For, upon the same ground, viz. of assent at first hearing and understanding the terms, that men would have those maxims pass for innate, they must also admit several propositions about numbers to be innate; and thus, that one and two are equal to three; that two and two are equal to four; and a multitude of other the like propositions in numbers, that everybody assents to at first hearing and understanding the terms, must have a place amongst these innate axioms. Nor is this the prerogative of numbers alone, and propositions made about several of them; but even natural philosophy, and all the other sciences, afford propositions which are sure to meet with assent as soon as they are understood. That two bodies cannot be in the same place is a truth that nobody any more sticks at than at these maxims, that "it is impossible for the same thing to be and not to be"; that "white is not black"; that "a square is not a circle"; that "bitterness is not sweetness": These and a million of such other propositions, as many at least as we have distinct ideas of, every man in his wits, at first hearing, and knowing what the names stand for, must necessarily assent to. If these men will be true to their own rule, and have assent at first hearing and understanding the terms to be a mark of innate, they must allow, not only as many innate propositions as men have distinct ideas; but as many as men can make propositions wherein different ideas are denied one of another. Since every proposition, wherein one different idea is denied of another, will as certainly find assent at first hearing and understanding the terms as this general one, "it is impossible for the same thing to be, and not to be"; or that which is the foundation of it, and is the easier understood of the two, "the same is not different"; by which account they will have legions of innate propositions of this one sort, without mentioning any other. But since no proposition can be innate unless the ideas about which it is be innate, this will be to suppose all our ideas of colours, sounds, tastes, figure, &c. innate; than which there cannot be anything more opposite to reason and experience. Universal and ready assent upon hearing and understanding the terms is (I grant) a mark of self-evidence: But self-evidence, depending not on innate impressions, but on something else (as we shall show hereafter), belongs to several propositions, which nobody was yet so extravagant as to pretend to be innate.

19. Nor let it be said that those more particular self-evident propositions which are assented to at first hearing, as that one and two are equal to three; that green is not red, &c.; are received as the consequences of those more universal propositions, which are looked on as innate principles; since anyone who will but take the pains to observe what passes in the understanding will certainly find that these and the like less general propositions are certainly known, and firmly assented to, by those who are utterly ignorant of those more general maxims;

and so, being earlier in the mind than those (as they are called) first principles, cannot owe to them the assent wherewith they are received at first hearing.

20. If it be said that "these propositions, viz. two and two are equal to four; red is not blue, &c.; are not general maxims, nor of any great use": I answer, that makes nothing to the argument of universal assent upon hearing and understanding. For, if that be the certain mark of innate, whatever proposition can be found that receives general assent as soon as heard and understood, that must be admitted for an innate proposition, as well as this maxim, that "it is impossible for the same thing to be, and not to be"; they being upon this ground equal. And as to the difference of being more general, that makes this maxim more remote from being innate, those general and abstract ideas being more strangers to our first apprehensions than those of more particular self-evident propositions, and therefore it is longer before they are admitted and assented to by the growing understanding. And as to the usefulness of these magnified maxims, that perhaps will not be found so great as is generally conceived, when it comes in its due place to be more fully considered.

21. But we have not yet done with assenting to propositions at first hearing and understanding their terms; it is fit we first take notice that this, instead of being a mark that they are innate, is a proof of the contrary, since it supposes that several who understand and know other things are ignorant of these principles till they are proposed to them; and that one may be unacquainted with these truths till he hears them from others. For, if they were innate, what need they be proposed in order to gaining assent, when by being in the understanding, by a natural and original impression (if there were any such), they could not but be known before? Or doth the proposing them print them clearer in the mind than nature did? If so, then the consequence will be that a man knows them better after he has been thus taught them than he did before. Whence it will follow that these principles may be made more evident to us by others teaching than nature has made them by impression, which will ill agree with the opinion of innate principles, and give but little authority to them; but, on the contrary, makes them unfit to be the foundations of all our other knowledge, as they are pretended to be. This cannot be denied, that men grow first acquainted with many of these self-evident truths upon their being proposed: But it is clear that whosoever does so finds in himself that he then begins to know a proposition which he knew not before, and which, from thenceforth, he never questions: not because it was innate, but because the consideration of the nature of the things contained in those words would not suffer him to think otherwise, how or whensoever he is brought to reflect on them. And if whatever is assented to at first hearing and understanding the terms must pass for an innate principle, every well-grounded observation, drawn from particulars into a general rule, must be innate. When yet it is certain that not all, but only sagacious, heads light at first on these observations, and reduce them into general propositions, not innate, but collected from a preceding acquaintance, and reflection on particular instances. These, when observing men have made them, unobserving men, when they are proposed to them, cannot refuse their assent to.

22. If it be said, "The understanding hath an implicit knowledge of these principles, but not an explicit, before this first hearing" (as they must who will say that they are in the understanding before they are known), it will be hard to conceive what is meant by a principle imprinted on the understanding implicitly; unless it be this, that the mind is capable of understanding and assenting firmly to such propositions. And thus all mathematical demonstrations, as well as first principles, must be received as native impressions on the mind, which I fear they will scarce allow them to be, who find it harder to demonstrate a proposition than assent to it when demonstrated. And few mathematicians will be forward to believe that all the diagrams they have drawn were but copies of those innate characters which nature had engraven upon their minds.

23. There is, I fear, this farther weakness in the foregoing argument, which would persuade us that therefore those maxims are to be thought innate which men admit at first hearing, because they assent to propositions which they are not taught, nor do receive from the force of any argument or demonstration, but a bare explication or understanding of the terms. Under which, there seems to me to lie this fallacy, that men are supposed not to be taught,

nor to learn anything *de novo*; when, in truth, they are taught, and do learn something they were ignorant of before. For first it is evident that they have learned the terms, and their signification; neither of which was born with them. But this is not all the acquired knowledge in the case: The ideas themselves, about which the proposition is, are not born with them, no more than their names, but got afterwards. So that in all propositions that are assented to at first hearing, the terms of the proposition, their standing for such ideas, and the ideas themselves that they stand for, being neither of them innate, I would fain know what there is remaining in such propositions that is innate. For I would gladly have anyone name that proposition whose terms or ideas were either of them innate. We by degrees get ideas and names, and learn their appropriated connexion one with another; and then to propositions, made in such terms, whose signification we have learnt, and wherein the agreement or disagreement we can perceive in our ideas, when put together, is expressed, we at first hearing assent; though to other propositions, in themselves as certain and evident, but which are concerning ideas, not so soon or so easily got, we are at the same time no way capable of assenting. For though a child quickly assents to this proposition, "That an apple is not fire," when, by familiar acquaintance, he has got the ideas of those two different things distinctly imprinted on his mind, and has learnt that the names *apple* and *fire* stand for them; yet it will be some years after, perhaps, before the same child will assent to this proposition, that "it is impossible for the same thing to be and not to be": Because that, though perhaps the words are as easy to be learnt, yet the signification of them being more large, comprehensive, and abstract than of the names annexed to those sensible things the child hath to do with, it is longer before he learns their precise meaning, and it requires more time plainly to form in his mind those general ideas they stand for. Till that be done, you will in vain endeavour to make any child assent to a proposition made up of such general terms: But as soon as ever he has got those ideas, and learned their names, he forwardly closes with the one, as well as the other of the forementioned propositions, and with both for the same reason; viz. because he finds the ideas he has in his mind to agree or disagree, according as the words standing for them, are affirmed or denied one of another in the proposition. But if propositions be brought to him in words, which stand for ideas he has not yet in his mind; to such propositions, however evidently true or false in themselves, he affords neither assent nor dissent, but is ignorant. For words being but empty sounds, any farther than they are signs of our ideas, we cannot but assent to them, as they correspond to those ideas we have, but no farther than that. But the showing by what steps and ways knowledge comes into our minds, and the grounds of several degrees of assent, being the business of the following discourse, it may suffice to have only touched on it here, as one reason that made me doubt of those innate principles.

24. To conclude this argument of universal consent, I agree with these defenders of innate principles that if they are innate, they must needs have universal assent. For that a truth should be innate, and yet not assented to, is to me as unintelligible as for a man to know a truth and be ignorant of it at the same time. But then, by these men's own confession, they cannot be innate; since they are not assented to by those who understand not the terms, nor by a great part of those who do understand them, but have yet never heard nor thought of those propositions; which, I think, is at least one half of mankind. But were the number far less, it would be enough to destroy universal assent, and thereby show these propositions not to be innate, if children alone were ignorant of them.

25. But that I may not be accused to argue from the thoughts of infants, which are unknown to us, and to conclude from what passes in their understandings before they express it, I say next, that these two general propositions are not the truths that first possess the minds of children, nor are antecedent to all acquired and adventitious notions; which, if they were innate, they must needs be. Whether we can determine it or no, it matters not; there is certainly a time when children begin to think, and their words and actions do assure us that they do so. When therefore they are capable of thought, of knowledge, of assent, can it rationally be supposed they can be ignorant of those notions that nature has imprinted, were there any such? Can it be imagined, with any appearance of reason, that they perceive the impressions from things without,

and be at the same time ignorant of those characters which nature itself has taken care to stamp within? Can they receive and assent to adventitious notions, and be ignorant of those which are supposed woven into the very principles of their being, and imprinted there in indelible characters, to be the foundation and guide of all their acquired knowledge, and future reasonings? This would be to make nature take pains to no purpose; or, at least, to write very ill; since its characters could not be read by those eyes, which saw other things very well; and those are very ill supposed the clearest parts of truth, and the foundations of all our knowledge, which are not first known, and without which the undoubted knowledge of several other things may be had. The child certainly knows that the nurse that feeds it is neither the cat it plays with, nor the blackmoor it is afraid of; that the wormseed or mustard it refuses is not the apple or sugar it cries for: This it is certainly and undoubtedly assured of: But will anyone say, it is by virtue of this principle that "it is impossible for the same thing to be and not to be," that it so firmly assents to these and other parts of its knowledge? or that the child has any notion or apprehension of that proposition at an age wherein yet, it is plain, it knows a great many other truths? He that will say, "Children join in these general abstract speculations with their sucking bottles and their rattles," may, perhaps, with justice be thought to have more passion and zeal for his opinion, but less sincerity and truth, than one of that age.

26. Though therefore there be several general propositions that meet with constant and ready assent as soon as proposed to men grown up, who have attained the use of more general and abstract ideas, and names standing for them; yet they not being to be found in those of tender years, who nevertheless know other things, they cannot pretend to universal assent of intelligent persons, and so by no means can be supposed innate: it being impossible that any truth which is innate (if there were any such) should be unknown, at least to anyone who knows anything else: Since, if they are innate truths, they must be innate thoughts: There being nothing a truth in the mind that it has never thought on. Whereby it is evident if there be any innate truths, they must necessarily be the first of any thought on; the first that appear there.

27. That the general maxims we are discoursing of are not known to children, idiots, and a great part of mankind, we have already sufficiently proved; whereby it is evident they have not a universal assent, nor are general impressions. But there is this farther argument in it against their being innate: that these characters, if they were native and original impressions, should appear fairest and clearest in those persons in whom yet we find no footsteps of them: And it is, in my opinion, a strong presumption that they are not innate, since they are least known to those in whom, if they were innate, they must needs exert themselves with most force and vigour. For children, idiots, savages, and illiterate people, being of all others the least corrupted by custom, or borrowed opinions; learning and education having not cast their native thoughts into new moulds, nor, by superinducing foreign and studied doctrines, confounded those fair characters nature had written there; one might reasonably imagine that in their minds these innate notions should lie open fairly to everyone's view, as it is certain the thoughts of children do. It might very well be expected that these principles should be perfectly known to naturals, which being stamped immediately on the soul (as these men suppose), can have no dependence on the constitution or organs of the body, the only confessed difference between them and others. One would think, according to these men's principles, that all these native beams of light (were there any such) should, in those who have no reserves, no arts of concealment, shine out in their full lustre, and leave us in no more doubt of their being there than we are of their love of pleasure, and abhorrence of pain. But alas, amongst children, idiots, savages, and the grossly illiterate, what general maxims are to be found? What universal principles of knowledge? Their notions are few and narrow, borrowed only from those objects they have had most to do with, and which have made upon their senses the frequentest and strongest impressions. A child knows his nurse and his cradle, and by degrees the play-things of a little more advanced age: And a young savage has, perhaps, his head filled with love and hunting, according to the fashion of his tribe. But he that from a child untaught, or a wild inhabitant of the woods, will expect these abstract maxims and reputed principles of science, will, I fear, find himself mistaken. Such kind of general propositions are seldom mentioned in the huts of Indians, much less are they to be found in the thoughts of children, or any impressions of them on the minds of naturals. They are the language and business of the schools and academies of learned nations, accustomed to that sort of conversation or learning where disputes are frequent: these maxims being suited to artificial argumentation and useful for conviction; but not much conducing to the discovery of truth or advancement of knowledge. But of their small use for the improvement of knowledge I shall have occasion to speak more at large, Book IV, Chapter VII.

28. I know not how absurd this may seem to the masters of demonstration, and probably it will hardly go down with anybody at first hearing. I must therefore beg a little truce with prejudice, and the forbearance of censure, till I have been heard out in the sequel of this discourse, being very willing to submit to better judgments. And since I impartially search after truth, I shall not be sorry to be convinced that I have been too fond of my own notions; which I confess we are all apt to be, when application and study have warmed our heads with them.

Upon the whole matter, I cannot see any ground to think these two speculative maxims innate, since they are not universally assented to; and the assent they so generally find is no other than what several propositions, not allowed to be innate, equally partake in with them: and since the assent that is given them is produced another way, and comes not from natural inscription, as I doubt not but to make appear in the following discourse. And if these first principles of knowledge and science are found not to be innate, no other speculative maxims can (I suppose) with better right pretend to be so.

Book II. Of Ideas

Chapter I. Of Ideas in General

Sections
1. Idea is the object of thinking.
2. All ideas come from sensation or reflection.
3. The objects of sensation one source of ideas.
4. The operations of our minds the other source of them.

. . .

Chapter XXXI. Of Adequate and Inadequate Ideas

Book II. Of Ideas

Chapter I. Of Ideas in General, and Their Original

1. Every man being conscious to himself that he thinks, and that which his mind is applied about whilst thinking being the ideas that are there, it is past doubt that men have in their minds several ideas, such as are those expressed by the words *whiteness, hardness, sweetness, thinking, motion, man, elephant, army, drunkenness,* and others. It is in the first place then to be enquired how he comes by them. I know it is a received doctrine that men have native ideas, and original characters, stamped upon their minds, in their very first being. This opinion I have, at large, examined already; and, I suppose, what I have said in the foregoing book will be much more easily admitted when I have shown whence the understanding may get all the ideas it has, and by what ways and degrees they may come into the mind, for which I shall appeal to everyone's own observation and experience.

2. Let us then suppose the mind to be, as we say, white paper, void of all characters, without any ideas; how comes it to be furnished? Whence comes it by that vast store which the busy and boundless fancy of man has painted on it with an almost endless variety? Whence has it all the materials of reason and knowledge? To this I answer, in one word, from *experience;* in that all our knowledge is founded, and from that it ultimately derives itself. Our observation, employed either about external sensible objects, or about the internal operations of our minds, perceived and reflected on by ourselves, is that which supplies our understandings with all the materials of thinking. These two are the fountains of knowledge, from whence all the ideas we have, or can naturally have, do spring.

3. First, Our senses, conversant about particular sensible objects, do convey into the mind several distinct perceptions of things, according to those various ways wherein those objects do affect them: And thus we come by those ideas we have of yellow, white, heat, cold, soft, hard, bitter, sweet, and all those which we call sensible qualities; which when I say the senses convey into the mind, I mean they from external objects convey into the mind what produces there those perceptions. This great source of most of the ideas we have, depending wholly upon our senses, and derived by them to the understanding, I call *sensation.*

4. Secondly, The other fountain from which experience furnisheth the understanding with ideas is the perception of the operations of our own mind within us, as it is employed about the ideas it has got; which operations, when the soul comes to reflect on and consider, do furnish the understanding with another set of ideas, which could not be had from things without. And such are perception, thinking, doubting, believing, reasoning, knowing, willing, and all the different actings of our own minds; which we being conscious of and observing in ourselves, do from these receive into our understandings as distinct ideas, as we do from bodies affecting our senses. This source of ideas every man has wholly in himself; and though it be not sense, as having nothing to do with external objects, yet it is very like it, and might properly enough be called internal sense. But as I call the other *sensation,* so I call this *reflection,* the ideas it affords being such only as the mind gets by reflecting on its own operations within itself. By reflection, then, in the following part of this discourse, I would be understood to mean that notice which the mind takes of its own operations, and the manner of them; by reason whereof there come to be ideas of these operations in the understanding. These two, I say, viz. external material things as the objects of sensation, and the operations of our own minds within as the objects of reflection, are to me the only originals from whence all our ideas take their beginnings. The term *operations* here I use in a large sense, as comprehending not barely the actions of the mind about its ideas, but some sort of passions arising sometimes from them, such as is the satisfaction or uneasiness arising from any thought.

5. The understanding seems to me not to have the least glimmering of any ideas which it doth not receive from one of these two. External objects furnish the mind with the ideas of sensible qualities, which are all those different perceptions they produce in us: And the mind furnishes the understanding with ideas of its own operations.

These, when we have taken a full survey of them, and their several modes, combinations, and relations, we shall find to contain all our whole stock of ideas; and that we have nothing in our minds which did not come in one of these two ways. Let anyone examine his own thoughts, and thoroughly search into his understanding; and then let him tell me whether all the original ideas he has there are any other than of the objects of his senses, or of the operations of his mind, considered as

objects of his reflection; and how great a mass of knowledge soever he imagines to be lodged there, he will, upon taking a strict view, see that he has not any idea in his mind but what one of these two have imprinted; though perhaps with infinite variety compounded and enlarged by the understanding, as we shall see hereafter.

6. He that attentively considers the state of a child at his first coming into the world will have little reason to think him stored with plenty of ideas that are to be the matter of his future knowledge: It is by degrees he comes to be furnished with them. And though the ideas of obvious and familiar qualities imprint themselves before the memory begins to keep a register of time or order, yet it is often so late before some unusual qualities come in the way that there are few men that cannot recollect the beginning of their acquaintance with them: And if it were worth while, no doubt a child might be so ordered as to have but a very few even of the ordinary ideas till he were grown up to a man. But all that are born into the world being surrounded with bodies that perpetually and diversely affect them, variety of ideas, whether care be taken of it or not, are imprinted on the minds of children. Light and colours are busy at hand everywhere when the eye is but open; sounds and some tangible qualities fail not to solicit their proper senses, and force an entrance to the mind; but yet, I think, it will be granted easily that if a child were kept in a place where he never saw any other but black and white till he were a man, he would have no more ideas of scarlet or green than he that from his childhood never tasted an oyster, or a pineapple, has of those particular relishes.

7. Men then come to be furnished with fewer or more simple ideas from without, according as the objects they converse with afford greater or less variety; and from the operations of their minds within, according as they more or less reflect on them. For though he that contemplates the operations of his mind cannot but have plain and clear ideas of them, yet, unless he turn his thoughts that way, and considers them attentively, he will no more have clear and distinct ideas of all the operations of his mind, and all that may be observed therein, than he will have all the particular ideas of any landscape, or of the parts and motions of a clock, who will not turn his eyes to it, and with attention heed all the parts of it. The picture or clock may be so placed that they may come in his way every day; but yet he will have but a confused idea of all the parts they are made up of, till he applies himself with attention to consider them each in particular.

8. And hence we see the reason why it is pretty late before most children get ideas of the operations of their own minds; and some have not any very clear or perfect ideas of the greatest part of them all their lives: Because, though they pass there continually, yet, like floating visions, they make not deep impressions enough to leave in their mind clear, distinct, lasting ideas, till the understanding turns inward upon itself, reflects on its own operations, and makes them the objects of its own contemplation. Children, when they come first into it, are surrounded with a world of new things, which, by a constant solicitation of their senses, draw the mind constantly to them, forward to take notice of new, and apt to be delighted with the variety of changing objects. Thus the first years are usually employed and diverted in looking abroad. Men's business in them is to acquaint themselves with what is to be found without, and so, growing up in a constant attention to outward sensation, seldom make any considerable reflection on what passes within them till they come to be of riper years; and some scarce ever at all.

9. To ask at what time a man has first any ideas is to ask when he begins to perceive; having ideas, and perception, being the same thing. I know it is an opinion that the soul always thinks, and that it has the actual perception of ideas in itself constantly as long as it exists; and that actual thinking is as inseparable from the soul as actual extension is from the body; which, if true, to enquire after the beginning of a man's ideas is the same as to enquire after the beginning of his soul. For by this account soul and its ideas, as body and its extension, will begin to exist both at the same time.

10. But whether the soul be supposed to exist antecedent to, or coeval with, or some time after the first rudiments of organization, or the beginnings of life in the body, I leave to be disputed by those who have better thought of that matter. I confess myself to have one of those dull souls that doth not perceive itself always to contemplate ideas; nor can conceive it any more necessary for the soul always to think than for the body always to move, the perception of ideas being (as I conceive) to the soul what motion is to the body: not its essence, but one of its operations. And therefore, though thinking be supposed never so much the proper action of the soul, yet it is not necessary to suppose that it should be always thinking, always in action. That perhaps is the privilege of the infinite Author and Preserver of all things, "who never slumbers nor sleeps"; but is not competent to any finite being, at least not to the soul of man. We know certainly by experience that we sometimes think; and thence draw this infallible consequence, that there is something in us that has a power to think; but whether that substance perpetually thinks or no, we can be no farther assured than experience informs us. For to say that actual thinking is essential to the soul, and inseparable from it, is to beg what is in question, and not to prove it by reason; which is necessary to be done, if it be not a self-evident proposition. But whether this, that "the soul always thinks," be a self-evident proposition, that everybody assents to at first hearing, I appeal to mankind. It is doubted whether I thought at all last night or no; the question being about a matter of fact, it is begging it to bring, as a proof for it, an hypothesis which is the very thing in dispute: By which way one may prove anything, and it is but supposing that all watches, whilst the balance beats, think; and it is sufficiently proved, and past doubt, that my watch thought all last night. But he that would not deceive himself ought to build his hypothesis on matter of fact, and make it out by sensible experience, and not presume on matter of fact, because of his hypothesis, that is, because he supposes it to be so: Which way of proving amounts to this, that I must necessarily think all last night, because another supposes I always think, though I myself cannot perceive that I always do so.

But men in love with their opinions may not only suppose what is in question, but allege wrong matter of fact. How else could anyone make it an inference of mine that a thing is not, because we are not sensible of it in our sleep? I do not say there is no soul in a man because he is not sensible of it in his sleep: But I do say, he cannot think at any time, waking or sleeping, without being sensible of it.

Our being sensible of it is not necessary to anything but to our thoughts; and to them it is, and to them it always will be, necessary, till we can think without being conscious of it.

11. I grant that the soul in a waking man is never without thought, because it is the condition of being awake: But whether sleeping without dreaming be not an affection of the whole man, mind as well as body, may be worth a waking man's consideration; it being hard to conceive that anything should think and not be conscious of it. If the soul doth think in a sleeping man without being conscious of it, I ask, whether during such thinking it has any pleasure or pain, or be capable of happiness or misery? I am sure the man is not, no more than the bed or earth he lies on. For to be happy or miserable without being conscious of it seems to me utterly inconsistent and impossible. Or if it be possible that the soul can, whilst the body is sleeping, have its thinking, enjoyments and concerns, its pleasures or pain, apart, which the man is not conscious of nor partakes in; it is certain that Socrates asleep and Socrates awake is not the same person: But his soul when he sleeps, and Socrates the man, consisting of body and soul when he is waking, are two persons; since waking Socrates has no knowledge of or concernment for that happiness or misery of his soul which it enjoys alone by itself whilst he sleeps, without perceiving anything of it; no more than he has for the happiness or misery of a man in the Indies, whom he knows not. For if we take wholly away all consciousness of our actions and sensations, especially of pleasure and pain, and the concernment that accompanies it, it will be hard to know wherein to place personal identity.

12. "The soul, during sound sleep, thinks," say these men. Whilst it thinks and perceives, it is capable certainly of those of delight or trouble, as well as any other perceptions; and it must necessarily be conscious of its own perceptions. But it has all this apart; the sleeping man, it is plain, is conscious of nothing of all this. Let us suppose then the soul of Castor, while he is sleeping, retired from his body; which is no impossible supposition for the men I have here to do with, who so liberally allow life, without a thinking soul, to all other animals. These men cannot then judge it impossible, or a contradiction, that the body should live without the soul; nor that the soul should subsist and think, or have perception, even perception of happiness or misery, without the body. Let us then, as I say, suppose the soul of Castor separated, during his sleep, from his body, to think apart. Let us suppose, too, that it chooses for its scene of thinking the body of another man, v.g. Pollux, who is sleeping without a soul: For if Castor's soul can think, whilst Castor is asleep, what Castor is never conscious of, it is no matter what place it chooses to think in. We have here then the bodies of two men with only one soul between them, which we will suppose to sleep and wake by turns; and the soul still thinking in the waking man, whereof the sleeping man is never conscious, has never the least perception. I ask then, whether Castor and Pollux, thus, with only one soul between them, which thinks and perceives in one what the other is never conscious of, nor is concerned for, are not two as distinct persons as Castor and Hercules, or as Socrates and Plato were? And whether one of them might not be very happy, and the other very miserable? Just by the same reason they make the soul and the man two persons, who make the soul think apart what the man is not conscious of. For I suppose nobody will make identity of persons to consist in the soul's being united to the very same numerical particles of matter: For if that be necessary to identity, it will be impossible, in that constant flux of the particles of our bodies, that any man should be the same person two days, or two moments, together.

13. Thus, methinks, every drowsy nod shakes their doctrine who teach that the soul is always thinking. Those, at least, who do at any time sleep without dreaming can never be convinced that their thoughts are sometimes for four hours busy without their knowing of it; and if they are taken in the very act, waked in the middle of that sleeping contemplation, can give no manner of account of it.

14. It will perhaps be said that the soul thinks even in the soundest sleep, but the memory retains it not. That the soul in a sleeping man should be this moment busy a-thinking, and the next moment in a waking man not remember nor be able to recollect one jot of all those thoughts, is very hard to be conceived, and would need some better proof than bare assertion to make it be believed. For who can without any more ado but being barely told so imagine that the greatest part of men do, during all their lives, for several hours every day, think of something which, if they were asked even in the middle of these thoughts, they could remember nothing at all of? Most men, I think, pass a great part of their sleep without dreaming. I once knew a man that was bred a scholar, and had no bad memory, who told me he had never dreamed in his life till he had that fever he was then newly recovered of, which was about the five or six and twentieth year of his age. I suppose the world affords more such instances: At least everyone's acquaintance will furnish him with examples enough of such as pass most of their nights without dreaming.

15. To think often, and never to retain it so much as one moment, is a very useless sort of thinking: And the soul, in such a state of thinking, does very little, if at all, excel that of a looking-glass, which constantly receives variety of images, or ideas, but retains none; they disappear and vanish, and there remain no footsteps of them; the looking-glass is never the better for such ideas, nor the soul for such thoughts. Perhaps it will be said that in a waking man the materials of the body are employed, and made use of, in thinking; and that the memory of thoughts is retained by the impressions that are made on the brain, and the traces there left after such thinking; but that in the thinking of the soul, which is not perceived in a sleeping man, there the soul thinks apart, and making no use of the organs of the body, leaves no impressions on it, and consequently no memory of such thoughts. Not to mention again the absurdity of two distinct persons which follows from this supposition, I answer farther that whatever ideas the mind can receive and contemplate without the help of the body, it is reasonable to conclude, it can retain without the help of the body too; or else the soul, or any separate spirit, will have but little advantage by thinking. If it has no memory of its own thoughts; if it cannot lay them up for its own use, and be able to recall them upon occasion; if it cannot reflect upon what is past, and make use of its former experiences, reasonings, and contemplations: To what purpose does it think? They who make the soul a thinking thing, at this rate, will not make it a much more noble being than those do whom they condemn for allowing it to be nothing but the subtlest parts of

matter. Characters drawn on dust, that the first breath of wind effaces; or impressions made on a heap of atoms, or animal spirits, are altogether as useful, and render the subject as noble, as the thoughts of a soul that perish in thinking; that once out of sight are gone forever, and leave no memory of themselves behind them. Nature never makes excellent things for mean or no uses; and it is hardly to be conceived that our infinitely wise Creator should make so admirable a faculty as the power of thinking, that faculty which comes nearest the excellency of his own incomprehensible being, to be so idly and uselessly employed, at least a fourth part of its time here, as to think constantly, without remembering any of those thoughts, without doing any good to itself or others, or being any way useful to any other part of the creation. If we will examine it, we shall not find, I suppose, the motion of dull and senseless matter, anywhere in the universe, made so little use of and so wholly thrown away.

16. It is true, we have sometimes instances of perception whilst we are asleep; and retain the memory of those thoughts: But how extravagant and incoherent for the most part they are; how little conformable to the perfection and order of a rational being, those who are acquainted with dreams need not be told. This I would willingly be satisfied in, whether the soul, when it thinks thus apart, and as it were separate from the body, acts less rationally than when conjointly with it, or no. If its separate thoughts be less rational, then these men must say that the soul owes the perfection of rational thinking to the body: If it does not, it is a wonder that our dreams should be, for the most part, so frivolous and irrational; and that the soul should retain none of its more rational soliloquies and meditations.

17. Those who so confidently tell us that the soul always actually thinks, I would they would also tell us what those ideas are that are in the soul of a child, before or just at the union with the body, before it hath received any by sensation. The dreams of sleeping men are, as I take it, all made up of the waking man's ideas, though for the most part oddly put together. It is strange, if the soul has ideas of its own that it derived not from sensation or reflection (as it must have, if it thought before it received any impressions from the body), that it should never, in its private thinking (so private that the man himself perceives it not), retain any of them the very moment it wakes out of them, and then make the man glad with new discoveries. Who can find it reason that the soul should, in its retirement, during sleep, have so many hours' thoughts, and yet never light on any of those ideas it borrowed not from sensation or reflection; or at least preserve the memory of none but such, which, being occasioned from the body, must needs be less natural to a spirit? It is strange the soul should never once in a man's whole life recall over any of its pure native thoughts, and those ideas it had before it borrowed anything from the body; never bring into the waking man's view any other ideas but what have a tang of the cask, and manifestly derive their original from that union. If it always thinks, and so had ideas before it was united, or before it received any from the body, it is not to be supposed but that during sleep it recollects its native ideas; and during that retirement from communicating with the body, whilst it thinks by itself, the ideas it is busied about should be, sometimes at least, those more natural and congenial ones which it had in itself, underived from the body, or its own operations about them: Which, since the waking man never remembers, we must from this hypothesis conclude either that the soul remembers something that the man does not, or else that memory belongs only to such ideas as are derived from the body, or the mind's operations about them.

18. I would be glad also to learn from these men who so confidently pronounce that the human soul, or, which is all one, that a man always thinks, how they come to know it; nay, how they come to know that they themselves think, when they themselves do not perceive it. This, I am afraid, is to be sure without proofs, and to know without perceiving. It is, I suspect, a confused notion taken up to serve an hypothesis; and none of those clear truths, that either their own evidence forces us to admit, or common experience makes it impudence to deny. For the most that can be said of it is that it is possible the soul may always think, but not always retain it in memory: And, I say, it is as possible that the soul may not always think, and much more probable that it should sometimes not think, than that it should often think, and that a long while together, and not

be conscious to itself, the next moment after, that it had thought.

19. To suppose the soul to think, and the man not to perceive it, is, as has been said, to make two persons in one man: And if one considers well these men's way of speaking, one should be led into a suspicion that they do so. For they who tell us that the soul always thinks do never, that I remember, say that a man always thinks. Can the soul think, and not the man? Or a man think, and not be conscious of it? This perhaps would be suspected of jargon in others. If they say the man thinks always, but is not always conscious of it, they may as well say his body is extended without having parts. For it is altogether as intelligible to say that a body is extended without parts as that anything thinks without being conscious of it, or perceiving that it does so. They who talk thus may, with as much reason, if it be necessary to their hypothesis, say that a man is always hungry, but that he does not always feel it: Whereas hunger consists in that very sensation, as thinking consists in being conscious that one thinks. If they say that a man is always conscious to himself of thinking, I ask how they know it. Consciousness is the perception of what passes in a man's own mind. Can another man perceive that I am conscious of anything, when I perceive it not myself? No man's knowledge here can go beyond his experience. Wake a man out of a sound sleep, and ask him what he was that moment thinking of. If he himself be conscious of nothing he then thought on, he must be a notable diviner of thoughts that can assure him that he was thinking: May he not with more reason assure him he was not asleep? This is something beyond philosophy; and it cannot be less than revelation that discovers to another thoughts in my mind, when I can find none there myself; and they must needs have a penetrating sight who can certainly see that I think, when I cannot perceive it myself, and when I declare that I do not; and yet can see that dogs or elephants do not think, when they give all the demonstration of it imaginable, except only telling us that they do so. This some may suspect to be a step beyond the Rosicrucians; it seeming easier to make one's self invisible to others than to make another's thoughts visible to me, which are not visible to himself. But it is but defining the soul to be "a substance that always thinks," and the business is done. If such definition be of any authority, I know not what it can serve for, but to make many men suspect that they have no souls at all, since they find a good part of their lives pass away without thinking. For no definitions that I know, no suppositions of any sect, are of force enough to destroy constant experience; and perhaps it is the affectation of knowing beyond what we perceive that makes so much useless dispute and noise in the world.

20. I see no reason therefore to believe that the soul thinks before the senses have furnished it with ideas to think on; and as those are increased and retained, so it comes by exercise to improve its faculty of thinking in the several parts of it, as well as afterwards, by compounding those ideas, and reflecting on its own operations, it increases its stock, as well as facility in remembering, imagining, reasoning, and other modes of thinking.

21. He that will suffer himself to be informed by observation and experience, and not make his own hypothesis the rule of nature, will find few signs of a soul accustomed to much thinking in a new-born child, and much fewer of any reasoning at all. And yet it is hard to imagine that the rational soul should think so much, and not reason at all. And he that will consider that infants, newly come into the world, spend the greatest part of their time in sleep, and are seldom awake, but when either hunger calls for the teat, or some pain (the most importunate of all sensations), or some other violent impression on the body forces the mind to perceive and attend to it: He, I say, who considers this will perhaps find reason to imagine that a foetus in the mother's womb differs not much from the state of a vegetable; but passes the greatest part of its time without perception or thought, doing very little but sleep in a place where it needs not seek for food, and is surrounded with liquor, always equally soft, and near of the same temper; where the eyes have no light, and the ears so shut up, are not very susceptible of sounds; and where there is little or no variety, or change of objects to move the senses.

22. Follow a child from its birth, and observe the alterations that time makes, and you shall find, as the mind by the senses comes more and more to be furnished with ideas, it comes to be more and more awake; thinks more, the more it has matter to think on. After some time it begins to know the objects which, being most familiar with it, have made lasting impressions. Thus it comes by degrees to know the persons it daily converses with, and distinguishes them from strangers; which are instances and effects of its coming to retain and distinguish the ideas the senses convey to it. And so we may observe how the mind, by degrees, improves in these, and advances to the exercise of those other faculties of enlarging, compounding, and abstracting its ideas, and of reasoning about them, and reflecting upon all these; of which I shall have occasion to speak more hereafter.

23. If it shall be demanded, then, when a man begins to have any ideas, I think the true answer is, when he first has any sensation. For since there appear not to be any ideas in the mind before the senses have conveyed any in, I conceive that ideas in the understanding are coeval with sensation; which is such an impression or motion, made in some part of the body, as produces some perception in the understanding. It is about these impressions made on our senses by outward objects that the mind seems first to employ itself in such operations as we call perception, remembering, consideration, reasoning, &c.

24. In time the mind comes to reflect on its own operations about the ideas got by sensation, and thereby stores itself with a new set of ideas, which I call ideas of reflection. These are the impressions that are made on our senses by outward objects that are extrinsical to the mind, and its own operations, proceeding from powers intrinsical and proper to itself; which, when reflected on by itself, become also objects of its contemplation, are, as I have said, the original of all knowledge. Thus the first capacity of human intellect is that the mind is fitted to receive the impressions made on it, either through the senses by outward objects, or by its own operations when it reflects on them. This is the first step a man makes towards the discovery of anything, and the groundwork whereon to build all those notions which ever he shall have naturally in this world. All those sublime thoughts which tower above the clouds, and reach as high as heaven itself, take their rise and footing here: In all that great

extent wherein the mind wanders, in those remote speculations it may seem to be elevated with, it stirs not one jot beyond those ideas which sense or reflection have offered for its contemplation.

25. In this part the understanding is merely passive; and whether or no it will have these beginnings and, as it were, materials of knowledge, is not in its own power. For the objects of our senses do, many of them, obtrude their particular ideas upon our minds whether we will or no; and the operations of our minds will not let us be without at least some obscure notions of them. No man can be wholly ignorant of what he does when he thinks. These simple ideas, when offered to the mind, the understanding can no more refuse to have, nor alter when they are imprinted, nor blot them out and make new ones itself, than a mirror can refuse, alter, or obliterate the images or ideas which the objects set before it do therein produce. As the bodies that surround us do diversely affect our organs, the mind is forced to receive the impressions, and cannot avoid the perception of those ideas that are annexed to them.

Chapter II. Of Simple Ideas

1. The better to understand the nature, manner, and extent of our knowledge, one thing is carefully to be observed concerning the ideas we have; and that is, that some of them are simple, and some complex.

Though the qualities that affect our senses are, in the things themselves, so united and blended that there is no separation, no distance between them; yet it is plain the ideas they produce in the mind enter by the senses simple and unmixed. For though the sight and touch often take in from the same object, at the same time, different ideas; as a man sees at once motion and colour; the hand feels softness and warmth in the same piece of wax; yet the simple ideas thus united in the same subject are as perfectly distinct as those that come in by different senses: The coldness and hardness which a man feels in a piece of ice being as distinct ideas in the mind as the smell and whiteness of a lily; or as the taste of sugar, and smell of a rose. And there is nothing can be plainer to a man than the clear and distinct perception he has of those simple ideas; which, being each in itself uncompounded, contains in it nothing but

one uniform appearance or conception in the mind, and is not distinguishable into different ideas.

2. These simple ideas, the materials of all our knowledge, are suggested and furnished to the mind only by those two ways above-mentioned, viz. sensation and reflection. When the understanding is once stored with these simple ideas, it has the power to repeat, compare, and unite them, even to an almost infinite variety, and so can make at pleasure new complex ideas. But it is not in the power of the most exalted wit, or enlarged understanding, by any quickness or variety of thought, to invent or frame one new simple idea in the mind not taken in by the ways before mentioned: Nor can any force of the understanding destroy those that are there. The dominion of man, in this little world of his own understanding, being much-what the same as it is in the great world of visible things, wherein his power, however managed by art and skill, reaches no farther than to compound and divide the materials that are made to his hand, but can do nothing towards the making the least particle of new matter, or destroying one atom of what is already in being. The same inability will everyone find in himself who shall go about to fashion in his understanding any simple idea not received in by his senses from external objects, or by reflection from the operations of his own mind about them. I would have anyone try to fancy any taste which had never affected his palate; or frame the idea of a scent he had never smelt: And when he can do this, I will also conclude that a blind man hath ideas of colours, and a deaf man true distinct notions of sounds.

3. This is the reason why, though we cannot believe it impossible to God to make a creature with other organs, and more ways to convey into the understanding the notice of corporeal things than those five, as they are usually counted, which he has given to man: Yet I think it is not possible for anyone to imagine any other qualities in bodies, howsoever constituted, whereby they can be taken notice of, besides sounds, tastes, smells, visible and tangible qualities. And had mankind been made but with four senses, the qualities then which are the objects of the fifth sense had been as far from our notice, imagination, and conception as now any belonging to a sixth, seventh, or eighth sense can possibly be:

Which, whether yet some other creatures, in some other parts of this vast and stupendous universe, may not have, will be a great presumption to deny. He that will not set himself proudly at the top of all things, but will consider the immensity of this fabric, and the great variety that is to be found in this little and inconsiderable part of it which he has to do with, may be apt to think that in other mansions of it there may be other and different intelligent beings, of whose faculties he has as little knowledge or apprehension as a worm shut up in one drawer of a cabinet hath of the senses or understanding of a man: Such variety and excellency being suitable to the wisdom and power of the Maker. I have here followed the common opinion of man's having but five senses; though, perhaps, there may be justly counted more: But either supposition serves equally to my present purpose.

Chapter III. Of Ideas of One Sense

1. The better to conceive the ideas we receive from sensation, it may not be amiss for us to consider them in reference to the different ways whereby they make their approaches to our minds, and make themselves perceivable by us.

First, then, There are some which come into our minds by one sense only.

Secondly, There are others that convey themselves into the mind by more senses than one.

Thirdly, Others that are had from reflection only.

Fourthly, There are some that make themselves way, and are suggested to the mind by all the ways of sensation and reflection. We shall consider them apart under these several heads.

First, There are some ideas which have admittance only through one sense, which is peculiarly adapted to receive them. Thus light and colours, as white, red, yellow, blue, with their several degrees or shades and mixtures, as green, scarlet, purple, sea-green, and the rest, come in only by the eyes; all kinds of noises, sounds, and tones, only by the ears; the several tastes and smells, by the nose and palate. And if these organs, or the nerves which are the conduits to convey them from without to their audience in the brain, the mind's presence-room (as I may so call it), are, any of them, so disordered as

not to perform their functions, they have no postern to be admitted by; no other way to bring themselves into view, and be perceived by the understanding.

The most considerable of those belonging to the touch are heat and cold, and solidity: All the rest, consisting almost wholly in the sensible configuration, as smooth and rough, or else more or less firm adhesion of the parts, as hard and soft, tough and brittle, are obvious enough.

2. I think it will be needless to enumerate all the particular simple ideas belonging to each sense. Nor indeed is it possible if we would, there being a great many more of them belonging to most of the senses than we have names for. The variety of smells, which are as many almost, if not more than, species of bodies in the world, do most of them want names. *Sweet* and *stinking* commonly serve our turn for these ideas, which in effect is little more than to call them pleasing or displeasing; though the smell of a rose and violet, both sweet, are certainly very distinct ideas. Nor are the different tastes, that by our palates we receive ideas of, much better provided with names. *Sweet, bitter, sour, harsh,* and *salt* are almost all the epithets we have to denominate that numberless variety of relishes which are to be found distinct, not only in almost every sort of creatures, but all the different parts of the same plant, fruit, or animal. The same may be said of colours and sounds. I shall, therefore, in the account of simple ideas I am here giving, content myself to set down only such as are most material to our present purpose, or are in themselves less apt to be taken notice of, though they are very frequently the ingredients of our complex ideas, amongst which, I think, I may well account solidity; which therefore I shall treat of in the next chapter.

Chapter IV. Of Solidity

1. The idea of solidity we receive by our touch: And it arises from the resistance which we find in body to the entrance of any other body into the place it possesses, till it has left it. There is no idea which we receive more constantly from sensation than solidity. Whether we move or rest, in what posture soever we are, we always feel something under us that supports us, and hinders our farther sinking downwards; and the bodies which we daily handle make us perceive that, whilst they remain between them, they do by an insurmountable force hinder the approach of the parts of our hands that press them. That which thus hinders the approach of two bodies, when they are moved one towards another, I call solidity. I will not dispute whether this acceptation of the word *solid* be nearer to its original signification than that which mathematicians use it in: It suffices that, I think, the common notion of solidity will allow, if not justify, this use of it; but if anyone think it better to call it *impenetrability*, he has my consent. Only I have thought the term *solidity* the more proper to express this idea, not only because of its vulgar use in that sense, but also because it carries something more of positive in it than *impenetrability*, which is negative, and is perhaps more a consequence of solidity than solidity itself. This, of all other, seems the idea most intimately connected with and essential to body, so as nowhere else to be found or imagined, but only in matter. And though our senses take no notice of it, but in masses of matter, of a bulk sufficient to cause a sensation in us; yet the mind, having once got this idea from such grosser sensible bodies, traces it farther; and considers it, as well as figure, in the minutest particle of matter that can exist; and finds it inseparably inherent in body, wherever or however modified.

2. This is the idea which belongs to body, whereby we conceive it to fill space. The idea of which filling of space is that where we imagine any space taken up by a solid substance, we conceive it so to possess it, that it excludes all other solid substances; and will forever hinder any other two bodies that move towards one another in a straight line from coming to touch one another, unless it removes from between them, in a line not parallel to that which they move in. This idea of it the bodies which we ordinarily handle sufficiently furnish us with.

3. This resistance, whereby it keeps other bodies out of the space which it possesses, is so great that no force, how great soever, can surmount it. All the bodies in the world, pressing a drop of water on all sides, will never be able to overcome the resistance which it will make, soft as it is, to their approaching one another, till it be removed out of their way: Whereby our idea of solidity is distinguished both from pure space, which is capable neither of resistance nor motion; and from the ordinary idea of hardness. For a man may conceive two bodies at a distance, so as they may approach one another, without touching or displacing any solid thing, till their superficies come to meet: Whereby, I think, we have the clear idea of space without solidity. For (not to go so far as annihilation of any particular body) I ask whether a man cannot have the idea of the motion of one single body alone without any other succeeding immediately into its place? I think it is evident he can: the idea of motion in one body no more including the idea of motion in another than the idea of a square figure in one body includes the idea of a square figure in another. I do not ask whether bodies do so exist that the motion of one body cannot really be without the motion of another? To determine this either way is to beg the question for or against a vacuum. But my question is, whether one cannot have the idea of one body moved whilst others are at rest? And I think this no one will deny. If so, then the place it deserted gives us the idea of pure space without solidity, whereinto any other body may enter, without either resistance or protrusion of anything. When the sucker in a pump is drawn, the space it filled in the tube is certainly the same whether any other body follows the motion of the sucker or not: Nor does it imply a contradiction that, upon the motion of one body, another that is only contiguous to it should not follow it. The necessity of such a motion is built only on the supposition that the world is full, but not on the distinct ideas of space and solidity, which are as different as resistance and not resistance, protrusion and not protrusion. And that men have ideas of space without a body, their very disputes about a vacuum plainly demonstrate, as is showed in another place.

4. Solidity is hereby also differenced from hardness, in that solidity consists in repletion, and so an utter exclusion of other bodies out of the space it possesses; but hardness, in a firm cohesion of the parts of matter, making up masses of a sensible bulk, so that the whole does not easily change its figure. And indeed, *hard* and *soft* are names that we give to things only in relation to the constitutions of our own bodies; that being generally called hard by us which will put us to pain sooner than change figure by the pressure of any part of our bodies; and that on the contrary soft which changes the situation of its parts upon an easy and unpainful touch.

But this difficulty of changing the situation of the sensible parts amongst themselves, or of the figure of the whole, gives no more solidity to the hardest body in the world than to the softest; nor is an adamant one jot more solid than water. For though the two flat sides of two pieces of marble will more easily approach each other, between which there is nothing but water or air, than if there be a diamond between them, yet it is not that the parts of the diamond are more solid than those of water, or resist more, but because the parts of water being more easily separable from each other, they will, by a side-motion, be more easily removed, and give way to the approach of the two pieces of marble. But if they could be kept from making place by that side-motion, they would eternally hinder the approach of these two pieces of marble as much as the diamond; and it would be as impossible by any force to surmount their resistance as to surmount the resistance of the parts of a diamond. The softest body in the world will as invincibly resist the coming together of any other two bodies, if it be not put out of the way, but remain between them, as the hardest that can be found or imagined. He that shall fill a yielding soft body well with air or water will quickly find its resistance; and he that thinks that nothing but bodies that are hard can keep his hands from approaching one another may be pleased to make a trial with the air enclosed in a foot-ball. The experiment, I have been told, was made at Florence, with a hollow globe of gold filled with water and exactly closed, which farther shows the solidity of so soft a body as water. For the golden globe thus filled being put into a press which was driven by the extreme force of screws, the water made itself way through the pores of that very close metal; and finding no room for a nearer approach of its particles within, got to the outside, where it rose like a dew, and so fell in drops before the sides of the globe could be made to yield to the violent compression of the engine that squeezed it.

5. By this idea of solidity is the extension of body distinguished from the extension of space; the extension of body being nothing but the cohesion or continuity of solid, separable, movable parts; and the extension of space, the continuity of unsolid, inseparable, and immovable parts. Upon the solidity of bodies also depend their mutual impulse, resistance, and protrusion. Of pure space, then, and so-lidity, there are several (amongst which I confess myself one) who persuade themselves they have clear and distinct ideas; and that they can think on space without anything in it that resists or is protruded by body. This is the idea of pure space, which they think they have as clear as any idea they can have of the extension of body: The idea of the distance between the opposite parts of a concave superficies being equally as clear without as with the idea of any solid parts between: And on the other side they persuade themselves that they have, distinct from that of pure space, the idea of something that fills space, that can be protruded by the impulse of other bodies, or resist their motion. If there be others that have not these two ideas distinct, but confound them, and make but one of them, I know not how men who have the same idea under different names, or different ideas under the same name, can in that case talk with one another; any more than a man who, not being blind or deaf, has distinct ideas of the colour of scarlet, and the sound of a trumpet, could discourse concerning scarlet colour with the blind man I mentioned in another place, who fancied that the idea of scarlet was like the sound of a trumpet.

6. If anyone asks me what this solidity is, I send him to his senses to inform him: Let him put a flint or a foot-ball between his hands, and then endeavour to join them, and he will know. If he thinks this not a sufficient explication of solidity, what it is, and wherein it consists, I promise to tell him what it is, and wherein it consists, when he tells me what thinking is, or wherein it consists; or explains to me what extension or motion is, which perhaps seems much easier. The simple ideas we have are such as experience teaches them us, but if, beyond that, we endeavour by words to make them clearer in the mind, we shall succeed no better than if we went about to clear up the darkness of a blind man's mind by talking; and to discourse into him the ideas of light and colours. The reason of this I shall show in another place.

Chapter V. Of Simple Ideas of Divers Senses

The ideas we get by more than one sense are of space, or extension, figure, rest, and motion; for these make perceivable impressions, both on the eyes and touch: And we can receive and convey into our minds the ideas of the extension, figure, motion, and rest of bodies, both by seeing and feeling. But having occasion to speak more at large of these in another place, I here only enumerate them.

Chapter VI. Of Simple Ideas of Reflection

1. The mind, receiving the ideas mentioned in the foregoing chapters from without, when it turns its view inward upon itself, and observes its own actions about those ideas it has, takes from thence other ideas, which are as capable to be the objects of its contemplation as any of those it received from foreign things.

2. The two great and principal actions of the mind, which are most frequently considered, and which are so frequent that everyone that pleases may take notice of them in himself, are these two: *perception* or *thinking*; and *volition* or *willing*.

The power of thinking is called the *understanding*, and the power of volition is called the *will*; and these two powers or abilities in the mind are denominated faculties. Of some of the modes of these simple ideas of reflection, such as are *remembrance, discerning, reasoning, judging, knowledge, faith,* &c., I shall have occasion to speak hereafter.

Chapter VIII. Some Farther Considerations Concerning Our Simple Ideas

7. To discover the nature of our ideas the better, and to discourse of them intelligibly, it will be convenient to distinguish them as they are ideas or perceptions in our minds, and as they are modifications of matter in the bodies that cause such perceptions in us: that so we may not think (as perhaps usually is done) that they are exactly the images and resemblances of something inherent in the subject; most of those of sensation being in the mind no more the likeness of something existing without us than the names that stand for them are the likeness of our ideas, which yet upon hearing they are apt to excite in us.

8. Whatsoever the mind perceives in itself, or is the immediate object of perception, thought, or understanding, that I call *idea*; and the power to produce any idea in our mind I call a *quality* of the subject wherein that power is. Thus a snow-ball having the power to produce in us the ideas of white, cold, and round, the power to produce those ideas in us, as they are in the snow-ball, I call qualities; and as they are sensations or perceptions in our understandings, I call them ideas; which ideas, if I speak of sometimes as in the things themselves, I would be understood to mean those qualities in the objects which produce them in us.

9. Qualities thus considered in bodies are, first, such as are utterly inseparable from the body, in what state soever it be; such as in all the alterations and changes it suffers, all the force can be used upon it, it constantly keeps; and such as sense constantly finds in every particle of matter which has bulk enough to be perceived, and the mind finds inseparable from every particle of matter, though less than to make itself singly be perceived by our senses, v.g. Take a grain of wheat, divide it into two parts, each part has still solidity, extension, figure, and mobility; divide it again, and it retains still the same qualities; and so divide it on till the parts become insensible, they must retain still each of them all those qualities. For division (which is all that a mill, or pestle, or any other body does upon another, in reducing it to insensible parts) can never take away either solidity, extension, figure, or mobility from any body, but only makes two or more distinct separate masses of matter, of that which was but one before: all which distinct masses, reckoned as so many distinct bodies, after division make a certain number. These I call *original* or *primary qualities* of body, which I think we may observe to produce simple ideas in us, viz. solidity, extension, figure, motion or rest, and number.

10. Secondly, such qualities which in truth are nothing in the objects themselves but powers to produce various sensations in us by their primary qualities, i.e. by the bulk, figure, texture, and motion of their insensible parts, as colours, sounds, tastes, &c., these I call *secondary qualities*. To these might be added a third sort, which are allowed to be barely powers, though they are as much real qualities in the subject as those which I, to comply with the common way of speaking, call qualities, but, for distinction, secondary qualities. For the power in fire to produce a new colour or consistency in wax or clay by its primary qualities is as much a quality in fire as the power it has to produce in me a new idea or sensation of warmth or burning, which I felt not before, by the same primary qualities, viz. the bulk, texture, and motion of its insensible parts.

11. The next thing to be considered is how bodies produce ideas in us; and that is manifestly by impulse, the only way which we can conceive bodies to operate in.

12. If, then, external objects be not united to our minds when they produce ideas therein, and yet we perceive these original qualities in such of them as singly fall under our senses, it is evident that some motion must be thence continued by our nerves, or animal spirits, by some parts of our bodies, to the brains or the seat of sensation, there to produce in our minds the particular ideas we have of them. And since the extension, figure, number, and motion of bodies of an observable bigness may be perceived at a distance by the sight, it is evident some singly imperceptible bodies must come from them to the eyes, and thereby convey to the brain some motion which produces these ideas which we have of them in us.

13. After the same manner that the ideas of these original qualities are produced in us, we may conceive that the ideas of secondary qualities are also produced, viz., by the operation of insensible particles on our senses. For it being manifest that there are bodies and good store of bodies, each whereof are so small that we cannot, by any of our senses, discover either their bulk, figure, or motion as is evident in the particles of the air and water, and others extremely smaller than those, perhaps as much smaller than the particles of air and water as the particles of air and water are smaller than peas or hail-stones: Let us suppose at present that the different motions and figures, bulk and number of such particles, affecting the several organs of our senses, produce in us those different sensations which we have from the colours and smells of bodies; v.g. that a violet, by the impulse of such insensible particles of matter of peculiar figures and bulks, and in different degrees and modifications of their motions, causes the ideas of the blue colour and sweet scent of that flower to be produced in our minds; it being no more impossible to conceive that God should annex such ideas to such motions with

which they have no similitude than that he should annex the idea of pain to the motion of a piece of steel dividing our flesh, with which that idea hath no resemblance.

14. What I have said concerning colours and smells may be understood also of tastes and sounds, and other the like sensible qualities; which, whatever reality we by mistake attribute to them, are in truth nothing in the objects themselves but powers to produce various sensations in us, and depend on those primary qualities, viz. bulk, figure, texture, and motion of parts, as I have said.

15. From whence I think it easy to draw this observation, that the ideas of primary qualities of bodies are resemblances of them, and their patterns do really exist in the bodies themselves; but the ideas produced in us by these secondary qualities have no resemblance of them at all. There is nothing like our ideas existing in the bodies themselves. They are, in the bodies we denominate from them, only a power to produce those sensations in us: And what is sweet, blue, or warm in idea is but the certain bulk, figure, and motion of the insensible parts in the bodies themselves, which we call so.

16. Flame is denominated hot and light; snow, white and cold; and manna, white and sweet, from the ideas they produce in us: Which qualities are commonly thought to be the same in those bodies that those ideas are in us, the one the perfect resemblance of the other, as they are in a mirror; and it would by most men be judged very extravagant if one should say otherwise. And yet he that will consider that the same fire that at one distance produces in us the sensation of warmth, does at a nearer approach produce in us the far different sensation of pain, ought to bethink himself what reason he has to say that his idea of warmth, which was produced in him by the fire, is actually in the fire; and his idea of pain, which the same fire produced in him the same way, is not in the fire. Why are whiteness and coldness in snow, and pain not, when it produces the one and the other idea in us, and can do neither, but by the bulk, figure, number, and motion of its solid parts?

17. The particular bulk, number, figure, and motion of the parts of fire or snow are really in them, whether anyone's senses perceive them or no: And therefore they may be called *real qualities*, because they really exist in those bodies: But light, heat, whiteness, or coldness are no more really in them than sickness or pain is in manna. Take away the sensation of them; let not the eyes see light, or colours, nor the ears hear sounds; let the palate not taste, nor the nose smell; and all colours, tastes, odours, and sounds, as they are such particular ideas, vanish and cease, and are reduced to their causes, i.e. bulk, figure, and motion of parts.

18. A piece of manna of a sensible bulk is able to produce in us the idea of a round or square figure, and, by being removed from one place to another, the idea of motion. This idea of motion represents it as it really is in the manna moving: A circle or square are the same, whether in idea or existence, in the mind or in the manna; and this, both motion and figure are really in the manna, whether we take notice of them or no: This everybody is ready to agree to. Besides, manna, by the bulk, figure, texture, and motion of its parts, has a power to produce the sensations of sickness, and sometimes of acute pains or gripings, in us. That these ideas of sickness and pain are not in the manna, but effects of its operations on us, and are nowhere when we feel them not: This also everyone readily agrees to. And yet men are hardly to be brought to think that sweetness and whiteness are not really in manna, which are but the effects of the operations of manna by the motion, size, and figure of its particles on the eyes and palate; as the pain and sickness caused by manna are confessedly nothing but the effects of its operations on the stomach and guts, by the size, motion, and figure of its insensible parts (for by nothing else can a body operate, as has been proved): as if it could not operate on the eyes and palate, and thereby produce in the mind particular distinct ideas which in itself it has not, as well as we allow it can operate on the guts and stomach, and thereby produce distinct ideas which in itself it has not. These ideas, being all effects of the operations of manna on several parts of our bodies, by the size, figure, number, and motion of its parts: Why those produced by the eyes and palate should rather be thought to be really in the manna than those produced by the stomach and guts; or why the pain and sickness, ideas that are the effect of manna, should be thought to be nowhere when they are not felt; and yet the sweetness and whiteness, effects of the same manna on other parts of the body, by ways equally as unknown, should be thought to exist in the manna, when they are not seen or tasted, would need some reason to explain.

19. Let us consider the red and white colours in porphyry: Hinder light from striking on it, and its colours vanish; it no longer produces any such ideas in us. Upon the return of light, it produces these appearances on us again. Can anyone think any real alterations are made in the porphyry by the presence or absence of light, and that those ideas of whiteness and redness are really in porphyry in the light, when it is plain it has no colour in the dark? It has, indeed, such a configuration of particles, both night and day, as are apt, by the rays of light rebounding from some parts of that hard stone, to produce in us the idea of redness, and from others the idea of whiteness; but whiteness or redness are not in it at any time, but such a texture that hath the power to produce such a sensation in us.

20. Pound an almond, and the clear white colour will be altered into a dirty one, and the sweet taste into an oily one. What real alteration can the beating of the pestle make in any body, but an alteration of the texture of it?

21. Ideas being thus distinguished and understood, we may be able to give an account how the same water, at the same time, may produce the idea of cold by one hand and of heat by the other; whereas it is impossible that the same water, if those ideas were really in it, should at the same time be both hot and cold: For if we imagine warmth, as it is in our hands, to be nothing but a certain sort and degree of motion in the minute particles of our nerves, or animal spirits, we may understand how it is possible that the same water may, at the same time, produce the sensations of heat in one hand, and cold in the other; which yet figure never does, that never producing the idea of a square by one hand, which has produced the idea of a globe by another. But if the sensation of heat and cold be nothing but the increase or diminution of the motion of the minute parts of our bodies, caused by the corpuscles of any other body, it is easy to be understood that if that motion be greater in one hand than in the other; if a body be applied to the two hands, which has in its minute particles a greater motion than in those of one of the hands, and a less than in those of the other, it will increase the motion of the one hand, and lessen it in the other, and so cause the different sensations of heat and cold that depend thereon.

22. I have in what just goes before been engaged in physical enquiries a little farther than perhaps I intended. But it being necessary to make the nature of sensation a little understood, and to make the difference between the qualities in bodies, and the ideas produced by them in the mind, to be distinctly conceived, without which it were impossible to discourse intelligibly of them, I hope I shall be pardoned this little excursion into natural philosophy, it being necessary in our present enquiry to distinguish the primary and real qualities of bodies, which are always in them (viz. solidity, extension, figure, number, and motion or rest, and are sometimes perceived by us, viz. when the bodies they are in are big enough singly to be discerned), from those secondary and imputed qualities, which are but the powers of several combinations of those primary ones, when they operate without being distinctly discerned; whereby we may also come to know what ideas are, and what are not, resemblances of something really existing in the bodies we denominate from them.

23. The qualities then that are in bodies, rightly considered, are of three sorts.

First, the bulk, figure, number, situation, and motion or rest of their solid parts; those are in them, whether we perceive them or no; and when they are of that size that we can discover them, we have by these an idea of the thing as it is in itself, as is plain in artificial things. These I call *primary qualities.*

Secondly, the power that is in any body, by reason of its insensible primary qualities, to operate after a peculiar manner on any of our senses, and thereby produce in us the different ideas of several colours, sounds, smells, tastes, &c. These are usually called *sensible qualities.*

Thirdly, the power that is in any body, by reason of the particular constitution of its primary qualities, to make such a change in the bulk, figure, texture, and motion of another body as to make it operate on our senses differently from what it did before. Thus the sun has a power to make wax white, and fire to make lead fluid. These are usually called *powers.*

The first of these, as has been said, I think may be properly called real, original, or primary qualities, because they are in the things themselves, whether they are perceived or no: and upon their different modifications it is that the secondary qualities depend.

The other two are only powers to act differently upon other things, which powers result from the different modifications of those primary qualities.

24. But though these two latter sorts of qualities are powers barely, and nothing but powers, relating to several other bodies, and resulting from the different modifications of the original qualities; yet they are generally otherwise thought of. For the second sort, viz. the powers to produce several ideas in us by our senses, are looked upon as real qualities, in the things thus affecting us: But the third sort are called and esteemed barely powers, v.g. the idea of heat, or light, which we receive by our eyes or touch from the sun, are commonly thought real qualities existing in the sun, and something more than mere powers in it. But when we consider the sun, in reference to wax, which it melts or blanches, we look on the whiteness and softness produced in the wax not as qualities in the sun, but effects produced by powers in it: Whereas, if rightly considered, these qualities of light and warmth, which are perceptions in me when I am warmed, or enlightened by the sun, are no otherwise in the sun than the changes made in the wax, when it is blanched or melted, are in the sun. They are all of them equally powers in the sun, depending on its primary qualities; whereby it is able, in the one case, so to alter the bulk, figure, texture, or motion of some of the insensible parts of my eyes or hands as thereby to produce in me the idea of light or heat; and in the other it is able so to alter the bulk, figure, texture, or motion of the insensible parts of the wax as to make them fit to produce in me the distinct ideas of white and fluid.

25. The reason why the one is ordinarily taken for real qualities, and the other only for bare powers, seems to be because the ideas we have of distinct colours, sounds, &c., containing nothing at all in them of bulk, figure, or motion, we are not apt to think them the effects of these primary qualities, which appear not, to our senses, to operate in their production; and with which they have not any apparent congruity, or conceivable connexion. Hence it is that we are so forward to imagine that those ideas are the resemblances of something really existing in the objects themselves: Since sensation discovers nothing of bulk, figure, or motion of parts in their production; nor can reason show how bodies, by their bulk, figure, and motion, should produce in the mind the ideas of blue or yellow, &c. But in the other case, in the operations of bodies changing the qualities one of another, we plainly discover that the quality produced hath commonly no resemblance with anything in the thing producing it; wherefore we look on it as a bare effect of power. For though receiving the idea of heat, or light, from the sun, we are apt to think it is a perception and resemblance of such a quality in the sun; yet when we see wax, or a fair face, receive change of colour from the sun, we cannot imagine that to be the reception or resemblance of anything in the sun, because we find not those different colours in the sun itself. For our senses being able to observe a likeness or unlikeness of sensible qualities in two different external objects, we forwardly enough conclude the production of any sensible quality in any subject to be an effect of bare power, and not the communication of any quality which was really in the efficient, when we find no such sensible quality in the thing that produced it. But our senses not being able to discover any unlikeness between the idea produced in us, and the quality of the object producing it; we are apt to imagine that our ideas are resemblances of something in the objects, and not the effects of certain powers placed in the modification of their primary qualities, with which primary qualities the ideas produced in us have no resemblance.

26. To conclude, beside those before mentioned primary qualities in bodies, viz. bulk, figure, extension, number, and motion of their solid parts, all the rest whereby we take notice of bodies, and distinguish them one from another, are nothing else but several powers in them depending on those primary qualities; whereby they are fitted, either by immediately operating on our bodies, to produce several different ideas in us, or else by operating on other bodies, so to change their primary qualities, as to render them capable of producing ideas in us, different from what before they did. The former of these, I think, may be called secondary qualities, im-

mediately perceivable: the latter, secondary qualities, mediately perceivable.

Chapter IX. Of Perception

8. We are further to consider concerning perception that the ideas we receive by sensation are often in grown people altered by the judgment, without our taking notice of it. When we set before our eyes a round globe, of any uniform colour, v.g. gold, alabaster, or jet, it is certain that the idea thereby imprinted in our mind is of a flat circle variously shadowed, with several degrees of light and brightness coming to our eyes. But we having by use been accustomed to perceive what kind of appearance convex bodies are wont to make in us, what alterations are made in the reflections of light by the difference of the sensible figures of bodies, the judgment presently, by an habitual custom, alters the appearances into their causes; so that from that which is truly variety of shadow or colour, collecting the figure, it makes it pass for a mark of figure, and frames to itself the perception of a convex figure and an uniform colour; when the idea we receive from thence is only a plane variously coloured, as is evident in painting. To which purpose I shall here insert a problem of that very ingenious and studious promoter of real knowledge, the learned and worthy Mr. Molineaux, which he was pleased to send me in a letter some months since; and it is this: Suppose a man born blind, and now adult, and taught by his touch to distinguish between a cube and a sphere of the same metal, and nighly of the same bigness, so as to tell, when he felt one and the other, which is the cube, which the sphere. Suppose then the cube and sphere placed on a table, and the blind man be made to see: *Quaere,* "whether by his sight, before he touched them, he could now distinguish and tell which is the globe, which the cube?" To which the acute and judicious proposer answers: Not. For though he has obtained the experience of how a globe, how a cube affects his touch; yet he has not yet obtained the experience that what affects his touch so or so must affect his sight so or so: Or that a protuberant angle in the cube, that pressed his hand unequally, shall appear to his eye as it does in the cube. I agree with this thinking gentleman, whom I am proud to call my friend, in his answer to this problem; and am of opinion that the blind man at first sight would not be able with certainty to say which was the globe, which the cube, whilst he only saw them: though he could unerringly name them by his touch, and certainly distinguish them by the difference of their figures felt. This I have set down, and leave with my reader, as an occasion for him to consider how much he may be beholden to experience, improvement, and acquired notions, where he thinks he had not the least use of, or help from, them: and the rather, because this observing gentleman further adds that having, upon the occasion of my book, proposed this to divers very ingenious men, he hardly ever met with one that at first gave the answer to it which he thinks true, till by hearing his reasons they were convinced.

9. But this is not, I think, usual in any of our ideas but those received by sight: because sight, the most comprehensive of all our senses, conveying to our minds the ideas of light and colours, which are peculiar only to that sense; and also the far different ideas of space, figure, and motion, the several varieties whereof change the appearances of its proper object, viz. light and colours; we bring ourselves by use to judge of the one by the other. This, in many cases, by a settled habit, in things whereof we have frequent experience, is performed so constantly and so quick that we take that for the perception of our sensation which is an idea formed by our judgment; so that one, viz. that of sensation, serves only to excite the other, and is scarce taken notice of itself: As a man who reads or hears with attention and understanding takes little notice of the characters, or sounds, but of the ideas that are excited in him by them.

10. Nor need we wonder that this is done with so little notice, if we consider how quick the actions of the mind are performed: For as itself is thought to take up no space, to have no extension, so its actions seem to require no time, but many of them seem to be crowded into an instant. I speak this in comparison to the actions of the body. Anyone may easily observe this in his own thoughts who will take the pains to reflect on them. How, as it were in an instant, do our minds with one glance see all the parts of a demonstration, which may very well be called a long one, if we consider the time it will require to put it into words, and step by step show it

another? Secondly, we shall not be so much surprised that this is done in us with so little notice, if we consider how the facility which we get of doing things, by a custom of doing, makes them often pass in us without our notice. Habits, especially such as are begun very early, come at last to produce actions in us which often escape our observation. How frequently do we, in a day, cover our eyes with our eye-lids, without perceiving that we are at all in the dark? Men that by custom have got the use of a by-word do almost in every sentence pronounce sounds which, though taken notice of by others, they themselves neither hear nor observe. And therefore it is not so strange that our mind should often change the idea of its sensation into that of its judgment, and make one serve only to excite the other without our taking notice of it.

11. This faculty of perception seems to me to be that which puts the distinction betwixt the animal kingdom and the inferior parts of nature. For however vegetables have, many of them, some degrees of motion, and upon the different application of other bodies to them, do very briskly alter their figures and motions, and so have obtained the name of sensitive plants, from a motion which has some resemblance to that which in animals follows upon sensation: Yet I suppose it is all bare mechanism, and no otherwise produced than the turning of a wild oat-beard by the insinuation of the particles of moisture, or the shortening of a rope by the affusion of water. All which is done without any sensation in the subject, or the having or receiving any ideas.

12. Perception, I believe, is in some degree in all sorts of animals; though in some, possibly, the avenues provided by nature for the reception of sensations are so few, and the perception they are received with so obscure and dull, that it comes extremely short of the quickness and variety of sensation which is in other animals; but yet it is sufficient for, and wisely adapted to, the state and condition of that sort of animals who are thus made. So that the wisdom and goodness of the Maker plainly appear in all the parts of this stupendous fabric, and all the several degrees and ranks of creatures in it.

13. We may, I think, from the make of an oyster, or cockle, reasonably conclude that it has not so many nor so quick senses as a man, or several other

animals; nor if it had, would it, in that state and in-capacity of transferring itself from one place to an-other, be bettered by them. What good would sight and hearing do to a creature that cannot move itself to or from the objects wherein at a distance it per-ceives good or evil? And would not quickness of sensation be an inconvenience to an animal that must lie still where chance has once placed it, and there receive the afflux of colder or warmer, clean or foul, water, as it happens to come to it?

14. But yet I cannot but think there is some small dull perception, whereby they are distin-guished from perfect insensibility. And that this may be so, we have plain instances even in man-kind itself. Take one in whom decrepit old age has blotted out the memory of his past knowledge, and clearly wiped out the ideas his mind was formerly stored with; and has, by destroying his sight, hear-ing, and smell quite, and his taste to a great degree, stopped up almost all the passages for new ones to enter; or if there be some of the inlets yet half open, the impressions made are scarce perceived, or not at all retained. How far such an one (notwithstand-ing all that is boasted of innate principles) is in his knowledge, and intellectual faculties, above the condition of a cockle or an oyster, I leave to be con-sidered. And if a man had passed sixty years in such a state, as it is possible he might, as well as three days, I wonder what difference there would have been, in any intellectual perfections, between him and the lowest degree of animals.

15. Perception then being the first step and degree towards knowledge, and the inlet of all the materials of it, the fewer senses any man, as well as any other creature, hath, and the fewer and duller the impressions are that are made by them, and the duller the faculties are that are employed about them, the more remote are they from that knowl-edge which is to be found in some men. But this be-ing in great variety of degrees (as may be perceived amongst men) cannot certainly be discovered in the several species of animals, much less in their par-ticular individuals. It suffices me only to have re-marked here that perception is the first operation of all our intellectual faculties, and the inlet of all knowledge in our minds. And I am apt too to imag-ine that it is perception in the lowest degree of it which puts the boundaries between animals and the

inferior ranks of creatures. But this I mention only as my conjecture by the by, it being indifferent to the matter in hand which way the learned shall deter-mine of it.

Chapter X. Of Retention

1. The next faculty of the mind, whereby it makes a farther progress towards knowledge, is that which I call *retention,* or the keeping of those simple ideas which from sensation or reflection it hath received. This is done two ways: first, by keeping the idea which is brought into it, for some time actually in view, which is called *contemplation.*

2. The other way of retention is the power to revive again in our minds those ideas which after imprinting have disappeared, or have been as it were laid aside out of sight; and thus we do, when we conceive heat or light, yellow or sweet, the object being removed. This is *memory,* which is as it were the store-house of our ideas. For the narrow mind of man not being capable of having many ideas un-der view and consideration at once, it was necessary to have a repository to lay up those ideas which at another time it might have use of. But our ideas being nothing but actual perceptions in the mind, which cease to be anything when there is no percep-tion of them, this laying up of our ideas in the re-pository of the memory signifies no more but this, that the mind has a power in many cases to revive perceptions which it has once had, with this addi-tional perception annexed to them, that it has had them before. And in this sense it is that our ideas are said to be in our memories, when indeed they are actually nowhere but only there is an ability in the mind when it will to revive them again, and as it were paint them anew on itself, though some with more, some with less, difficulty; some more lively, and others more obscurely. And thus it is by the as-sistance of this faculty that we are to have all those ideas in our understandings which, though we do not actually contemplate, yet we can bring in sight, and make appear again, and be the objects of our thoughts, without the help of those sensible quali-ties which first imprinted them there.

3. Attention and repetition help much to the fixing any ideas in the memory; but those which naturally at first make the deepest and most lasting impression are those which are accompanied with pleasure or pain. The great business of the senses being to make us take notice of what hurts or advantages the body, it is wisely ordered by nature (as has been shown) that pain should accompany the reception of several ideas; which supplying the place of consideration and reasoning in children, and acting quicker than consideration in grown men, makes both the old and young avoid painful objects with that haste which is necessary for their preservation; and in both, settles in the memory a caution for the future.

. . .

Chapter XII. Of Complex Ideas

1. We have hitherto considered those ideas in the reception whereof the mind is only passive, which are those simple ones received from sensation and reflection before mentioned, whereof the mind cannot make one to itself, nor have any idea which does not wholly consist of them. But as the mind is wholly passive in the reception of all its simple ideas so it exerts several acts of its own, whereby out of its simple ideas, as the materials and foundations of the rest, the others are framed. The acts of the mind wherein it exerts its power over its simple ideas are chiefly these three: (1) Combining several simple ideas into one compound one, and thus all complex ideas are made. (2) The second is bringing two ideas, whether simple or complex, together, and setting them by one another, so as to take a view of them at once, without uniting them into one; by which way it gets all its ideas of relations. (3) The third is separating them from all other ideas that accompany them in their real existence; this is called abstraction: And thus all its general ideas are made. This shows man's power, and its ways of operation, to be much the same in the material and intellectual world. For the materials in both being such as he has no power over, either to make or destroy, all that man can do is either to unite them together, or to set them by one another, or wholly separate them. I shall here begin with the first of these in the consideration of complex ideas, and come to the other two in their due places. As simple ideas are observed to exist in several combinations united together, so the mind has a power to con-

sider several of them united together as one idea; and that not only as they are united in external objects, but as itself has joined them. Ideas thus made up of several simple ones put together, I call *complex*; such as are beauty, gratitude, a man, an army, the universe; which though complicated of various simple ideas, or complex ideas made up of simple ones, yet are, when the mind pleases, considered each by itself as one entire thing, and signified by one name.

2. In this faculty of repeating and joining together its ideas, the mind has great power in varying and multiplying the objects of its thoughts infinitely beyond what sensation or reflection furnishes it with; but all this still confined to those simple ideas which it received from those two sources, and which are the ultimate materials of all its compositions: For simple ideas are all from things themselves, and of these the mind can have no more, nor other, than what are suggested to it. It can have no other ideas of sensible qualities than what come from without by the senses; nor any ideas of other kind of operations of a thinking substance than what it finds in itself; but when it has once got these simple ideas, it is not confined barely to observation, and what offers itself from without: It can, by its own power, put together those ideas it has, and make new complex ones, which it never received so united.

3. Complex ideas, however compounded and decompounded, though their number be infinite, and the variety endless, wherewith they fill and entertain the thoughts of men, yet, I think, they may be all reduced under these three heads:

1. Modes.

2. Substances.

3. Relations.

4. First, Modes I call such complex ideas which, however compounded, contain not in them the supposition of subsisting by themselves, but are considered as dependences on or affections of substances; such as are the ideas signified by the words *triangle, gratitude, murder,* &c. And if in this I use the word *mode* in somewhat a different sense from its ordinary signification, I beg pardon; it being unavoidable in discourses differing from the ordinary received notions either to make new words, or to use old words in somewhat a new signification: The latter whereof, in our present case, is perhaps the more tolerable of the two.

5. Of these modes, there are two sorts which deserve distinct consideration. First, there are some which are only variations, or different combinations of the same simple idea, without the mixture of any other; as a *dozen* or *score,* which are nothing but the ideas of so many distinct units added together: And these I call *simple modes,* as being contained within the bounds of one simple idea. Secondly, there are others compounded of simple ideas of several kinds, put together to make one complex one; v.g. *beauty,* consisting of a certain composition of colour and figure, causing delight to the beholder; *theft,* which being the concealed change of the possession of anything, without the consent of the proprietor, contains, as is visible, a combination of several ideas of several kinds: And these I call *mixed modes.*

6. Secondly, the ideas of substances are such combinations of simple ideas as are taken to represent distinct particular things subsisting by themselves; in which the supposed or confused idea of substance, such as it is, is always the first and chief. Thus if to substance be joined the simple idea of a certain dull whitish colour, with certain degrees of weight, hardness, ductility, and fusibility, we have the idea of lead; and a combination of the ideas of a certain sort of figure, with the powers of motion, thought, and reasoning, joined to substance, make the ordinary idea of a man. Now of substances also there are two sorts of ideas: one of single substances, as they exist separately, as of a man or a sheep; the other of several of those put together, as an army of men, or flock of sheep: which collective ideas of several substances thus put together are as much each of them one single idea as that of a man, or an unit.

7. Thirdly, the last sort of complex ideas is that we call *relation,* which consists in the consideration and comparing one idea with another. Of these several kinds we shall treat in their order.

8. If we will trace the progress of our minds, and with attention observe how it repeats, adds together, and unites its simple ideas received from sensation or reflection, it will lead us farther than at first, perhaps, we should have imagined. And, I believe, we shall find, if we warily observe the originals of our notions, that even the most abstruse ideas, how remote soever they may seem from sense, or from any operations of our own minds, are yet only such as the understanding frames to itself, by repeating and joining together ideas that it had either from objects of sense, or from its own operations about them: So that those even large and abstract ideas are derived from sensation or reflection, being no other than what the mind, by the ordinary use of its own faculties, employed about ideas received from objects of sense, or from the operations it observes in itself about them, may and does attain unto. This I shall endeavour to show in the ideas we have of space, time, and infinity, and some few others, that seem the most remote from those originals.

Chapter XIII. Of Simple Modes, and First, of the Simple Modes of Space

11. There are some that would persuade us that body and extension are the same thing: Who either change the signification of words, which I would not suspect them of, they having so severely condemned the philosophy of others because it hath been too much placed in the uncertain meaning or deceitful obscurity of doubtful or insignificant terms. If therefore they mean by body and extension the same that other people do, viz. by body something that is solid and extended, whose parts are separable and movable different ways; and by extension, only the space that lies between the extremities of those solid coherent parts, and which is possessed by them, they confound very different ideas one with another. For I appeal to every man's own thoughts, whether the idea of space be not as distinct from that of solidity as it is from the idea of scarlet colour? It is true, solidity cannot exist without extension; neither can scarlet colour exist without extension: But this hinders not but that they are distinct ideas. Many ideas require others as necessary to their existence or conception, which yet are very distinct ideas. Motion can neither be, nor be conceived, without space; and yet motion is not space, nor space motion: Space can exist without it, and they are very distinct ideas; and so, I think, are those of space and solidity. Solidity is so inseparable an idea from body that upon that depends its filling of space, its contact, impulse, and communication of motion upon impulse. And if it be a reason to prove that spirit is different from body, because thinking includes not the idea of extension in it, the same reason will be as valid, I suppose, to prove that space is not body, because it includes not the idea of solidity in it, space and solidity being as distinct ideas as thinking and extension, and as wholly separable in the mind one from another. Body, then, and extension, it is evident, are two distinct ideas. For,

12. First, Extension includes no solidity nor resistance to the motion of body, as body does.

13. Secondly, The parts of pure space are inseparable one from the other; so that the continuity cannot be separated neither really, nor mentally. For I demand of anyone to remove any part of it from another with which it is continued, even so much as in thought. To divide and separate actually, is, as I think, by removing the parts one from another, to make two superficies, where before there was a continuity; and to divide mentally is to make in the mind two superficies, where before there was a continuity, and consider them as removed one from the other; which can only be done in things considered by the mind as capable of being separated; and by separation, of acquiring new distinct superficies, which they then have not, but are capable of; but neither of these ways of separation, whether real or mental, is, as I think, compatible to pure space.

It is true, a man may consider so much of such a space as is answerable or commensurate to a foot, without considering the rest; which is indeed a partial consideration, but not so much as mental separation, or division; since a man can no more mentally divide without considering two superficies separate one from the other than he can actually divide without making two superficies disjoined one from the other: But a partial consideration is not separating. A man may consider light in the sun without its heat; or mobility in body without its extension, without thinking of their separation. One is only a partial consideration, terminating in one alone; and the other is a consideration of both, as existing separately.

14. Thirdly, The parts of pure space are immovable, which follows from their inseparability,

motion being nothing but change of distance between any two things: But this cannot be between parts that are inseparable, which therefore must needs be at perpetual rest one amongst another.

Thus the determined idea of simple space distinguishes it plainly and sufficiently from body; since its parts are inseparable, immovable, and without resistance to the motion of body.

15. If anyone ask me, what this space I speak of is? I will tell him when he tells me what his extension is. For to say, as is usually done, that extension is to have *partes extra partes* is to say only that extension is extension: For what am I the better informed in the nature of extension when I am told that extension is to have parts that are ex tended, exterior to parts that are extended, i.e. extension consists of extended parts? As if one asking, what a fibre was? I should answer him, that it was a thing made up of several fibres: Would he thereby be enabled to understand what a fibre was better than he did before? Or rather, would he not have reason to think that my design was to make sport with him, rather than seriously to instruct him?

16. Those who contend that space and body are the same bring this dilemma: Either this space is something or nothing; if nothing be between two bodies, they must necessarily touch: If it be allowed to be something, they ask whether it be body or spirit? To which I answer, by another question, who told them that there was, or could be, nothing but solid beings, which could not think, and thinking beings that were not extended? which is all they mean by the terms body and spirit.

17. If it be demanded (as usually it is) whether this space, void of body, be substance or accident, I shall readily answer, I know not; nor shall be ashamed to own my ignorance, till they that ask show me a clear distinct idea of substance.

18. I endeavour, as much as I can, to deliver myself from those fallacies which we are apt to put upon ourselves by taking words for things. It helps not our ignorance to feign a knowledge where we have none, by making a noise with sounds, without clear and distinct significations. Names made at pleasure neither alter the nature of things, nor make us understand them but as they are signs of and stand for determined ideas. And I desire those who lay so much stress on the sound of these two syllables, *substance,* to consider whether applying it, as they do, to the infinite incomprehensible God, to finite spirits, and to body, it be in the same sense; and whether it stands for the same idea, when each of those three so different beings are called substances. If so, whether it will not thence follow that God, spirits, and body, agreeing in the same common nature of substance, differ not any otherwise than in a bare different modification of that substance; as a tree and a pebble, being in the same sense body, and agreeing in the common nature of body, differ only in a bare modification of that common matter; which will be a very harsh doctrine. If they say that they apply it to God, finite spirits, and matter, in three different significations, and that it stands for one idea when God is said to be a substance, for another, when the soul is called substance, and for a third when body is called so; if the name *substance* stands for three several distinct ideas, they would do well to make known those distinct ideas, or at least to give three distinct names to them, to prevent in so important a notion the confusion and errours that will naturally follow from the promiscuous use of so doubtful a term; which is so far from being suspected to have three distinct significations that in ordinary use it has scarce one clear distinct signification; and if they can thus make three distinct ideas of substance, what hinders why another may not make a fourth?

19. They who first ran into the notion of accidents, as a sort of real beings that needed something to inhere in, were forced to find out the word *substance* to support them. Had the poor Indian philosopher (who imagined that the earth also wanted something to bear it up) but thought of this word *substance,* he needed not to have been at the trouble to find an elephant to support it, and a tortoise to support his elephant: The word *substance* would have done it effectually. And he that enquired might have taken it for as good an answer from an Indian philosopher that substance, without knowing what it is, is that which supports the earth; as we take it for a sufficient answer, and good doctrine, from our European philosophers that substance, without knowing what it is, is that which supports accidents. So that of substance we have no idea of what it is, but only a confused obscure one of what it does.

20. Whatever a learned man may do here, an intelligent American who enquired into the nature of things would scarce take it for a satisfactory account if, desiring to learn our architecture, he should be told that a pillar was a thing supported by a basis, and a basis something that supported a pillar. Would he not think himself mocked, instead of taught, with such an account as this? And a stranger to them would be very liberally instructed in the nature of books, and the things they contained, if he should be told that all learned books consisted of paper and letters, and that letters were things inhering in paper, and paper a thing that held forth letters: a notable way of having clear ideas of letters and papers! But were the Latin words *inhaerentia* and *substantia* put into the plain English ones that answer them, and were called *sticking on* and *under-propping,* they would better discover to us the very great clearness there is in the doctrine of substance and accidents, and show of what use they are in deciding of questions in philosophy.

Chapter XXI. *Of Power*

1. The mind being every day informed, by the senses, of the alteration of those simple ideas it observes in things without, and taking notice how one comes to an end, and ceases to be, and another begins to exist which was not before; reflecting also on what passes within itself, and observing a constant change of its ideas, sometimes by the impression of outward objects on the senses, and sometimes by the determination of its own choice; and concluding from what it has so constantly observed to have been, that the like changes will for the future be made in the same things by like agents, and by the like ways; considers in one thing the possibility of having any of its simple ideas changed, and in another the possibility of making that change: and so comes by that idea which we call *power.* Thus we say, fire has a power to melt gold, i.e. to destroy the consistency of its insensible parts, and consequently its hardness, and make it fluid; and gold has a power to be melted; that the sun has a power to blanch wax, and wax a power to be blanched by the sun, whereby the yellowness is destroyed, and whiteness made to exist in its room. In which, and the like cases, the power we consider is in reference to the change of perceivable ideas: For we cannot observe any alteration to be made in, or operation upon, anything but by the observable change of its sensible ideas; nor conceive any alteration to be made but by conceiving a change of some of its ideas.

2. Power thus considered is two-fold, viz. as able to make, or able to receive, any change: The one may be called *active,* and the other *passive,* power. Whether matter be not wholly destitute of active power, as its author, God, is truly above all passive power; and whether the intermediate state of created spirits be not that alone which is capable of both active and passive power, may be worth consideration. I shall not now enter into that enquiry, my present business being not to search into the original of power, but how we come by the idea of it. But since active powers make so great a part of our complex ideas of natural substances (as we shall see hereafter) and I mention them as such, according to common apprehension; yet they being not perhaps so truly active powers as our hasty thoughts are apt to represent them, I judge it not amiss, by this intimation, to direct our minds to the consideration of God and spirits, for the clearest idea of active power.

3. I confess power includes in it some kind of relation (a relation to action or change), as indeed which of our ideas, of what kind soever, when attentively considered, does not? For our ideas of extension, duration, and number, do they not all contain in them a secret relation of the parts? Figure and motion have something relative in them much more visibly: And sensible qualities, as colours and smells, &c., what are they but the powers of different bodies, in relation to our perception? And if considered in the things themselves, do they not depend on the bulk, figure, texture, and motion of the parts? All which include some kind of relation in them. Our idea therefore of power, I think, may well have a place amongst other simple ideas, and be considered as one of them, being one of those that make a principal ingredient in our complex ideas of substances, as we shall hereafter have occasion to observe.

4. We are abundantly furnished with the idea of passive power by almost all sorts of sensible things. In most of them we cannot avoid observing their sensible qualities, nay, their very substances, to be in a continual flux: And therefore with reason we look on them as liable still to the same change. Nor have we of active power (which is the more proper signification of the word *power*) fewer instances: Since whatever change is observed, the mind must collect a power somewhere, able to make that change, as well as a possibility in the thing itself to receive it. But yet, if we will consider it attentively, bodies, by our senses, do not afford us so clear and distinct an idea of active power as we have from reflection on the operations of our minds. For all power relating to action, and there being but two sorts of action, whereof we have an idea, viz. thinking and motion; let us consider whence we have the clearest ideas of the powers which produce these actions. (1) Of thinking, body affords us no idea at all; it is only from reflection that we have that. (2) Neither have we from body any idea of the beginning of motion. A body at rest affords us no idea of any active power to move; and when it is set in motion itself, that motion is rather a passion than an action in it. For when the ball obeys the motion of a billiard stick, it is not any action of the ball, but bare passion: Also when by impulse it sets another ball in motion that lay in its way, it only communicates the motion it had received from another, and loses in itself so much as the other received, which gives us but a very obscure idea of an active power of moving in body, whilst we observe it only to transfer but not produce any motion. For it is but a very obscure idea of power which reaches not the production of the action, but the continuation of the passion. For so is motion in a body impelled by another, the continuation of the alteration made in it from rest to motion being little more an action than the continuation of the alteration of its figure by the same blow is an action. The idea of the beginning of motion we have only from reflection on what passes in ourselves, where we find by experience that barely by willing it, barely by a thought of the mind, we can move the parts of our bodies which were before at rest. So that it seems to me, we have from the observation of the operation of bodies by our senses but a very imperfect obscure idea of active power, since they afford us not any idea in themselves of the power to begin any action, either motion or thought. But if, from the impulse bodies are observed to make one upon another, anyone thinks he has a clear idea of power, it serves as well to my purpose, sensation being one of those ways whereby the mind comes by its ideas: Only I thought it worth while to consider here by the way whether the mind doth not receive its idea of active power clearer from reflection on its own operations than it doth from any external sensation.

5. This at least I think evident, that we find in ourselves a power to begin or forbear, continue or end, several actions of our minds, and motions of our bodies, barely by a thought or preference of the mind ordering, or, as it were, commanding, the doing or not doing such or such a particular action. This power which the mind has thus to order the consideration of any idea, or the forbearing to consider it; or to prefer the motion of any part of the body to its rest, and vice versa, in any particular instance, is that which we call the *will*. The actual exercise of that power, by directing any particular action, or its forbearance, is that which we call *volition* or *willing*. The forbearance of that action consequent to such order or command of the mind, is called *voluntary*. And whatsoever action is performed without such a thought of the mind is called *involuntary*. The power of perception is that which we call the *understanding*. Perception, which we make the act of the understanding, is of three sorts: (1) The perception of ideas in our minds. (2) The perception of the signification of signs. (3) The perception of the connexion or repugnancy, agreement or disagreement, that there is between any of our ideas. All these are attributed to the understanding, or perceptive power, though it be the two latter only that use allows us to say we understand.

6. These powers of the mind, viz. of perceiving and of preferring, are usually called by another name: And the ordinary way of speaking is that the understanding and will are two *faculties* of the mind; a word proper enough, if it be used as all words should be, so as not to breed any confusion in men's thoughts, by being supposed (as I suspect it has been) to stand for some real beings in the soul that performed those actions of understanding and volition. For when we say the will is the commanding and superior faculty of the soul; that it is or is not free; that it determines the inferior faculties; that it follows the dictates of the understanding, &c.;

though these, and the like expressions, by those that carefully attend to their own ideas, and conduct their thoughts more by the evidence of things than the sound of words, may be understood in a clear and distinct sense; yet I suspect, I say, that this way of speaking of faculties has misled many into a confused notion of so many distinct agents in us, which had their several provinces and authorities, and did command, obey, and perform several actions, as so many distinct beings; which has been no small occasion of wrangling, obscurity, and uncertainty in questions relating to them.

7. Everyone, I think, finds in himself a power to begin or forbear, continue or put an end to, several actions in himself. From the consideration of the extent of this power of the mind over the actions of the man, which everyone finds in himself, arise the ideas of *liberty* and *necessity*.

8. All the actions that we have any idea of, reducing themselves, as has been said, to these two, viz. thinking and motion; so far as a man has power to think, or not to think; to move, or not to move, according to the preference or direction of his own mind; so far is a man free. Wherever any performance or forbearance are not equally in a man's power; wherever doing or not doing will not equally follow upon the preference of his mind directing it: There he is not free, though perhaps the action may be voluntary. So that the idea of liberty is the idea of a power in any agent to do or forbear any particular action, according to the determination or thought of the mind, whereby either of them is preferred to the other: Where either of them is not in the power of the agent to be produced by him according to his volition, there he is not at liberty; that agent is under necessity. So that liberty cannot be where there is no thought, no volition, no will; but there may be thought, there may be will, there may be volition, where there is no liberty. A little consideration of an obvious instance or two may make this clear.

9. A tennis-ball, whether in motion by the stroke of a racket, or lying still at rest, is not by anyone taken to be a free agent. If we enquire into the reason, we shall find it is because we conceive not a tennis-ball to think, and consequently not to have any volition, or preference of motion to rest, or vice versa; and therefore has not liberty, is not a free agent; but all its both motion and rest come under our idea of necessary, and are so called. Likewise a man falling into the water (a bridge breaking under him) has not herein liberty, is not a free agent. For though he has volition, though he prefers his not falling to falling; yet the forbearance of that motion not being in his power, the stop or cessation of that motion follows not upon his volition; and therefore therein he is not free. So a man striking himself or his friend, by a convulsive motion of his arm, which it is not in his power, by volition or the direction of his mind, to stop, or forbear, nobody thinks he has in this liberty; everyone pities him, as acting by necessity and constraint.

10. Again, suppose a man be carried, whilst fast asleep, into a room where is a person he longs to see and speak with; and be there locked fast in, beyond his power to get out: He awakes, and is glad to find himself in so desirable company, which he stays willingly in, i.e. prefers his stay to going away; I ask, Is not this stay voluntary? I think nobody will doubt it; and yet being locked fast in, it is evident he is not at liberty not to stay, he has not freedom to be gone. So that liberty is not an idea belonging to volition, or preferring; but to the person having the power of doing, or forbearing to do, according as the mind shall choose or direct. Our idea of liberty reaches as far as that power, and no farther. For wherever restraint comes to check that power, or compulsion takes away that indifferency of ability on either side to act, or to forbear acting, there liberty, and our notion of it, presently ceases.

11. We have instances enough, and often more than enough, in our own bodies. A man's heart beats, and the blood circulates, which it is not in his power by any thought or volition to stop; and therefore in respect to these motions, where rest depends not on his choice, nor would follow the determination of his mind, if it should prefer it, he is not a free agent. Convulsive motions agitate his legs, so that though he wills it ever so much, he cannot by any power of his mind stop their motion (as in that odd disease called *chorea sancti Viti*) but he is perpetually dancing; he is not at liberty in this action, but under as much necessity of moving as a stone that falls, or a tennis-ball struck with a racket. On the other side, a palsy or the stocks hinder his legs from obeying the determination of his mind, if it would

thereby transfer his body to another place. In all these there is want of freedom; though the sitting still even of a paralytic, whilst he prefers it to a removal, is truly voluntary. Voluntary then is not opposed to necessary, but to involuntary. For a man may prefer what he can do to what he cannot do; the state he is in to its absence or change, though necessity has made it in itself unalterable.

12. As it is in the motions of the body, so it is in the thoughts of our minds: Where any one is such that we have power to take it up, or lay it by, according to the preference of the mind, there we are at liberty. A waking man being under the necessity of having some ideas constantly in his mind is not at liberty to think, or not to think; no more than he is at liberty whether his body shall touch any other or no: But whether he will remove his contemplation from one idea to another is many times in his choice; and then he is in respect of his ideas as much at liberty as he is in respect of bodies he rests on; he can at pleasure remove himself from one to another. But yet some ideas to the mind, like some motions to the body, are such as in certain circumstances it cannot avoid, nor obtain their absence by the utmost effort it can use. A man on the rack is not at liberty to lay by the idea of pain, and divert himself with other contemplations: And sometimes a boisterous passion hurries our thoughts as a hurricane does our bodies, without leaving us the liberty of thinking on other things, which we would rather choose. But as soon as the mind regains the power to stop or continue, begin or forbear any of these motions of the body without, or thoughts within, according as it thinks fit to prefer either to the other, we then consider the man as a free agent again.

13. Wherever thought is wholly wanting, or the power to act or forbear according to the direction of thought; there necessity takes place. This in an agent capable of volition, when the beginning or continuation of any action is contrary to that preference of his mind, is called *compulsion;* when the hindering or stopping any action is contrary to his volition, it is called *restraint.* Agents that have no thought, no volition, at all are in everything necessary agents.

14. If this be so (as I imagine it is), I leave it to be considered whether it may not help to put an end to that long agitated, and, I think, unreasonable,

because unintelligible, question, viz. Whether man's will be free, or no? For if I mistake not, it follows from what I have said that the question itself is altogether improper; and it is as insignificant to ask whether man's will be free as to ask whether his sleep be swift, or his virtue square, liberty being as little applicable to the will as swiftness of motion is to sleep, or squareness to virtue. Everyone would laugh at the absurdity of such a question as either of these, because it is obvious that the modifications of motion belong not to sleep, nor the difference of figure to virtue: And when anyone well considers it, I think he will as plainly perceive that liberty, which is but a power, belongs only to agents, and cannot be an attribute or modification of the will, which is also but a power.

15. Such is the difficulty of explaining and giving clear notions of internal actions by sounds that I must here warn my reader that ordering, directing, choosing, preferring, &c., which I have made use of, will not distinctly enough express volition, unless he will reflect on what he himself does when he wills. For example, preferring, which seems perhaps best to express the act of volition, does it not precisely. For though a man would prefer flying to walking, yet who can say he ever wills it? Volition, it is plain, is an act of the mind knowingly exerting that dominion it takes itself to have over any part of the man, by employing it in, or withholding it from, any particular action. And what is the will, but the faculty to do this? And is that faculty anything more in effect than a power, the power of the mind to determine its thought, to the producing, continuing, or stopping any action, as far as it depends on us? For can it be denied that whatever agent has a power to think on its own actions, and to prefer their doing or omission either to other, has that faculty called will? Will then is nothing but such a power. Liberty, on the other side, is the power a man has to do or forbear doing any particular action, according as its doing or forbearance has the actual preference in the mind; which is the same thing as to say, according as he himself wills it.

16. It is plain, then, that the will is nothing but one power or ability; and freedom another power or ability: so that to ask whether the will has freedom is to ask whether one power has another power, one ability another ability; a question at first sight too grossly absurd to make a dispute or need an answer. For who is it that sees not that powers belong only to agents, and are attributes only of substances, and not of powers themselves? So that this way of putting the question, viz. Whether the will be free? is in effect to ask, Whether the will be a substance, an agent? or at least to suppose it, since freedom can properly be attributed to nothing else. If freedom can with any propriety of speech be applied to power, or may be attributed to the power that is in a man to produce or forbear producing motion in parts of his body, by choice or preference; which is that which denominates him free, and is freedom itself. But if anyone should ask whether freedom were free, he would be suspected not to understand well what he said; and he would be thought to deserve Midas's ears who, knowing that *rich* was a denomination for the possession of riches, should demand whether riches themselves were rich.

17. However, the name *faculty*, which men have given to this power called the will, and whereby they have been led into a way of talking of the will as acting, may, by an appropriation that disguises its true sense, serve a little to palliate the absurdity; yet the will in truth signifies nothing but a power, or ability, to prefer or choose: And when the will under the name of a faculty is considered as it is, barely as an ability to do something, the absurdity in saying it is free, or not free, will easily discover itself. For if it be reasonable to suppose and talk of faculties as distinct beings that can act (as we do, when we say the will orders, and the will is free), it is fit that we should make a speaking faculty, and a walking faculty, and a dancing faculty, by which these actions are produced, which are but several modes of motion; as well as we make the will and understanding to be faculties, by which the actions of choosing and perceiving are produced, which are but several modes of thinking; and we may as properly say that it is the singing faculty sings, and the dancing faculty dances as that the will chooses, or that the understanding conceives; or as is usual, that the will directs the understanding, or the understanding obeys, or obeys not the will: It being altogether as proper and intelligible to say that the power of speaking directs the power of singing, or the power of singing obeys or disobeys the power of speaking.

18. This way of talking, nevertheless, has prevailed, and, as I guess, produced great confusion. For these being all different powers in the mind, or in the man, to do several actions, he exerts them as he thinks fit: But the power to do one action is not operated on by the power of doing another action. For the power of thinking operates not on the power of choosing, nor the power of choosing on the power of thinking; no more than the power of dancing operates on the power of singing, or the power of singing on the power of dancing; as anyone who reflects on it will easily perceive: And yet this is it which we say when we thus speak that the will operates on the understanding, or the understanding on the will.

19. I grant that this or that actual thought may be the occasion of volition, or exercising the power a man has to choose: or the actual choice of the mind, the cause of actual thinking on this or that thing: as the actual singing of such a tune may be the cause of dancing such a dance, and the actual dancing of such a dance the occasion of singing such a tune. But in all these it is not one power that operates on another: But it is the mind that operates and exerts these powers; it is the man that does the action, it is the agent that has power, or is able to do. For powers are relations, not agents: And that which has the power, or not the power, to operate is that alone which is or is not free, and not the power itself. For freedom, or not freedom, can belong to nothing but what has or has not a power to act.

20. The attributing to faculties that which belonged not to them has given occasion to this way of talking: But the introducing into discourses concerning the mind, with the name of faculties, a notion of their operating has, I suppose, as little advanced our knowledge in that part of ourselves as the great use and mention of the like invention of faculties in the operations of the body has helped us in the knowledge of physic. Not that I deny there are faculties, both in the body and mind: They both of them have their powers of operating, else neither the one nor the other could operate. For nothing can operate that is not able to operate; and that is not able to operate that has no power to operate. Nor do

I deny that those words, and the like, are to have their place in the common use of languages that have made them current. It looks like too much affectation wholly to lay them by: And philosophy itself, though it likes not a gaudy dress, yet when it appears in public must have so much complacency as to be clothed in the ordinary fashion and language of the country, so far as it can consist with truth and perspicuity. But the fault has been that faculties have been spoken of and represented as so many distinct agents. For it being asked, what it was that digested the meat in our stomachs? it was a ready and very satisfactory answer to say that it was the digestive faculty. What was it that made anything come out of the body? the expulsive faculty. What moved? the motive faculty. And so in the mind, the intellectual faculty, or the understanding, understood; and the elective faculty, or the will, willed or commanded. This is in short to say, that the ability to digest, digested; and the ability to move, moved; and the ability to understand, understood. For *faculty, ability,* and *power,* I think, are but different names of the same things; which ways of speaking, when put into more intelligible words, will, I think, amount to thus much: that digestion is performed by something that is able to digest, motion by something able to move, and understanding by something able to understand. And in truth it would be very strange if it should be otherwise; as strange as it would be for a man to be free without being able to be free.

21. To return then to the enquiry about liberty, I think the question is not proper, whether the will be free, but whether a man be free. Thus, I think, **1.** That so far as anyone can, by the direction or choice of his mind, preferring the existence of any action to the non-existence of that action, and vice versa, make it to exist or not exist; so far he is free. For if I can, by a thought directing the motion of my finger, make it move when it was at rest, or vice versa, it is evident that in respect of that I am free: And if I can, by a like thought of my mind, preferring one to the other, produce either words or silence, I am at liberty to speak, or hold my peace: And as far as this power reaches, of acting, or not acting, by the determination of his own thought preferring either, so far is a man free. For how can we think anyone freer than to have the power to do what he will? And so far as anyone can, by preferring any action to its not being, or rest to any action, produce that action or rest, so far can he do what he will. For such a preferring of action to its absence is the willing of it: And we can scarce tell how to imagine any being freer than to be able to do what he wills. So that in respect of actions within the reach of such a power in him, a man seems as free as it is possible for freedom to make him.

22. But the inquisitive mind of man, willing to shift off from himself, as far as he can, all thoughts of guilt, though it be by putting himself into a worse state than that of fatal necessity, is not content with this: Freedom, unless it reaches farther than this, will not serve the turn: And it passes for a good plea, that a man is not free at all, if he be not as free to will as he is to act what he wills. Concerning a man's liberty, there yet therefore is raised this farther question, Whether a man be free to will? which I think is what is meant when it is disputed whether the will be free. And as to that I imagine,

23. 2. That willing, or volition, being an action, and freedom consisting in a power of acting or not acting, a man in respect of willing or the act of volition, when any action in his power is once proposed to his thoughts, as presently to be done, cannot be free. The reason whereof is very manifest: For it being unavoidable that the action depending on his will should exist or not exist; and its existence, or not existence, following perfectly the determination and preference of his will; he cannot avoid willing the existence, or not existence, of that action; it is absolutely necessary that he will the one, or the other; i.e. prefer the one to the other; since one of them must necessarily follow; and that which does follow follows by the choice and determination of his mind, that is, by his willing it; for if he did not will it, it would not be. So that in respect of the act of willing, a man in such a case is not free, liberty consisting in a power to act, or not to act; which, in regard of volition, a man, upon such a proposal, has not. For it is unavoidably necessary to prefer the doing or forbearance of an action in a man's power, which is once so proposed to his thoughts: A man must necessarily will the one or the other of them, upon which preference or volition, the action or its forbearance, certainly follows, and is truly voluntary. But the act of volition, or preferring one of the

two, being that which he cannot avoid, a man in respect of that act of willing is under a necessity, and so cannot be free; unless necessity and freedom can consist together, and a man can be free and bound at once.

24. This then is evident, that in all proposals of present action, a man is not at liberty to will or not to will, because he cannot forbear willing, liberty consisting in a power to act or to forbear acting, and in that only. For a man that sits still is said yet to be at liberty, because he can walk if he wills it. But if a man sitting still has not a power to remove himself, he is not at liberty; so likewise a man falling down a precipice, though in motion, is not at liberty, because he cannot stop that motion if he would. This being so, it is plain that a man that is walking, to whom it is proposed to give off walking, is not at liberty whether he will determine himself to walk, or give off walking, or no: He must necessarily prefer one or the other of them, walking or not walking; and so it is in regard of all other actions in our power so proposed, which are the far greater number. For considering the vast number of voluntary actions that succeed one another every moment that we are awake in the course of our lives, there are but few of them that are thought on or proposed to the will, till the time they are to be done: And in all such actions, as I have shown, the mind in respect of willing has not a power to act, or not to act, wherein consists liberty. The mind in that case has not a power to forbear willing; it cannot avoid some determination concerning them, let the consideration be as short, the thought as quick as it will, it either leaves the man in the state he was before thinking, or changes it; continues the action, or puts an end to it. Whereby it is manifest that it orders and directs one, in preference to or with neglect of the other, and thereby either the continuation or change becomes unavoidably voluntary.

25. Since, then, it is plain that in most cases a man is not at liberty whether he will or no; the next thing demanded is, whether a man be at liberty to will which of the two he pleases, motion or rest? This question carries the absurdity of it so manifestly in itself that one might thereby sufficiently be convinced that liberty concerns not the will. For to ask, whether a man be at liberty to will either motion or rest, speaking or silence, which he pleases, is to ask, whether a man can will what he wills, or be pleased with what he is pleased with? A question which, I think, needs no answer; and they who can make a question of it must suppose one will to determine the acts of another, and another to determine that; and so on *in infinitum.*

26. To avoid these and the like absurdities, nothing can be of greater use than to establish in our minds determined ideas of the things under consideration. If the ideas of liberty and volition were well fixed in the understandings, and carried along with us in our minds, as they ought, through all the questions that are raised about them, I suppose a great part of the difficulties that perplex men's thoughts, and entangle their understandings, would be much easier resolved; and we should perceive where the confused signification of terms or where the nature of the thing caused the obscurity.

73. And thus I have, in a short draught, given a view of our original ideas, from whence all the rest are derived, and of which they are made up; which if I would consider, as a philosopher, and examine on what causes they depend, and of what they are made, I believe they all might be reduced to these very few primary and original ones, viz.

> Extension,
> Solidity,
> Mobility, or the power of being moved;

which by our senses we receive from body;

> Perceptivity, or the power of perception, or
>   thinking;
> Motivity, or the power of moving:

which by reflection we receive from our minds. I crave leave to make use of these two new words, to avoid the danger of being mistaken in the use of those which are equivocal. To which if we add

> Existence,
> Duration,
> Number;

which belong both to the one and the other, we have, perhaps, all the original ideas on which the rest depend. For by these, I imagine, might be explained the nature of colours, sounds, tastes, smells, and all other ideas we have, if we had but faculties acute enough to perceive the severally modified ex-

tensions and motions of these minute bodies which produce those several sensations in us. But my present purpose being only to enquire into the knowledge the mind has of things by those ideas and appearances which God has fitted it to receive from them, and how the mind comes by that knowledge, rather than into their causes, or manner of production, I shall not, contrary to the design of this essay, set myself to enquire philosophically into the peculiar constitution of bodies, and the configuration of parts, whereby they have the power to produce in us the ideas of their sensible qualities: I shall not enter any farther into that disquisition, it sufficing to my purpose to observe that gold or saffron has a power to produce in us the idea of yellow, and snow or milk the idea of white, which we can only have by our sight, without examining the texture of the parts of those bodies, or the particular figures or motion of the particles which rebound from them, to cause in us that particular sensation: Though when we go beyond the bare ideas in our minds, and would enquire into their causes, we cannot conceive anything else to be in any sensible object whereby it produces different ideas in us, but the different bulk, figure, number, texture, and motion of its insensible parts.

. . .

Chapter XXIII. Of Our Complex Ideas of Substances

1. The mind being, as I have declared, furnished with a great number of the simple ideas conveyed in by the senses, as they are found in exterior things, or by reflection on its own operations, takes notice also that a certain number of these simple ideas go constantly together; which being presumed to belong to one thing, and words being suited to common apprehensions, and made use of for quick dispatch, are called, so united in one subject, by one name: Which, by inadvertency, we are apt afterward to talk of and consider as one simple idea, which indeed is a complication of many ideas together; because, as I have said, not imagining how these simple ideas can subsist by themselves, we accustom ourselves to suppose some substratum wherein they do subsist, and from which they do result, which therefore we call *substance.*

2. So that if anyone will examine himself concerning his notion of pure substance in general, he will find he has no other idea of it at all, but only a supposition of he knows not what support of such qualities which are capable of producing simple ideas in us; which qualities are commonly called *accidents.* If anyone should be asked, what is the subject wherein colour or weight inheres, he would have nothing to say, but the solid extended parts: And if he were demanded, what is it that solidity and extension adhere in, he would not be in a much better case than the Indian beforementioned, who, saying that the world was supported by a great elephant, was asked what the elephant rested on; to which his answer was, a great tortoise. But being again pressed to know what gave support to the broad-backed tortoise, replied, something he knew not what. And thus here, as in all other cases where we use words without having clear and distinct ideas, we talk like children; who being questioned what such a thing is, which they know not, readily give this satisfactory answer, that it is *something:* Which in truth signifies no more, when so used either by children or men, but that they know not what; and that the thing they pretend to know and talk of is what they have no distinct idea of at all, and so are perfectly ignorant of it, and in the dark. The idea, then, we have, to which we give the general name *substance,* being nothing but the supposed, but unknown, support of those qualities we find existing, which we imagine cannot subsist *sine re substante,* without some thing to support them, we call that support *substantia;* which, according to the true import of the word, is, in plain English, standing under or upholding.

3. An obscure and relative idea of substance in general being thus made, we come to have the ideas of particular sorts of substances by collecting such combinations of simple ideas as are, by experience and observation of men's senses, taken notice of to exist together, and are therefore supposed to flow from the particular internal constitution or unknown essence of that substance. Thus we come to have the ideas of a man, horse, gold, water, &c., of which substances, whether anyone has any other clear idea, farther than of certain simple ideas coexistent together, I appeal to everyone's own experience. It is the ordinary qualities observable in iron, or a diamond, put together that make the true complex idea of those substances, which a smith or a jeweller commonly knows better than a philosopher; who, whatever substantial forms he may talk of, has no other idea of those substances than what is framed by a collection of those simple ideas which are to be found in them; only we must take notice that our complex ideas of substances, besides all those simple ideas they are made up of, have always the confused idea of something to which they belong, and in which they subsist. And therefore, when we speak of any sort of substance, we say it is a thing having such or such qualities: as body is a thing that is extended, figured, and capable of motion; spirit, a thing capable of thinking; and so hardness, friability, and power to draw iron, we say, are qualities to be found in a lodestone. These and the like fashions of speaking intimate that the substance is supposed always something besides the extension, figure, solidity, motion, thinking, or other observable ideas, though we know not what it is.

4. Hence, when we talk or think of any particular sort of corporeal substances, as horse, stone, &c., though the idea we have of either of them be but the complication or collection of those several simple ideas of sensible qualities which we used to find united in the thing called *horse* or *stone;* yet because we cannot conceive how they should subsist alone, nor one in another, we suppose them existing in and supported by some common subject; which support we denote by the name *substance,* though it be certain we have no clear or distinct idea of that thing we suppose a support.

5. The same thing happens concerning the operations of the mind, viz. thinking, reasoning, fearing, &c., which we concluding not to subsist of themselves, nor apprehending how they can belong to body, or be produced by it, we are apt to think these the actions of some other substance, which we call *spirit;* whereby yet it is evident that, having no other idea or notion of matter but something wherein those many sensible qualities which affect our senses do subsist; by supposing a substance, wherein thinking, knowing, doubting, and a power of moving, &c. do subsist, we have as clear a notion of the substance of spirit as we have of body: the one being supposed to be (without knowing what it is) the substratum to those simple ideas we have from without; and the other supposed (with a like igno-rance of what it is) to be the substratum to those operations we experiment in ourselves within. It is plain, then, that the idea of corporeal substance in matter is as remote from our conceptions and ap-prehensions as that of spiritual substance or spirit; and therefore from our not having any notion of the substance of spirit, we can no more conclude its non-existence than we can for the same reason deny the existence of body; it being as rational to affirm there is no body, because we have no clear and dis-tinct idea of the substance of matter, as to say there is no spirit, because we have no clear and distinct idea of the substance of a spirit.

6. Whatever therefore be the secret, abstract nature of substance in general, all the ideas we have of particular distinct sorts of substances are noth-ing but several combinations of simple ideas, co-existing in such, though unknown, cause of their union, as makes the whole subsist of itself. It is by such combinations of simple ideas, and nothing else, that we represent particular sorts of substances to ourselves: Such are the ideas we have of their several species in our minds; and such only do we, by their specific names, signify to others, v.g. *man, horse, sun, water, iron:* Upon hearing which words, everyone who understands the language frames in his mind a combination of those several simple ideas which he has usually observed or fancied to exist together under that denomination; all which he supposes to rest in, and be, as it were, adherent to that unknown common subject, which inheres not in anything else. Though in the meantime it be manifest, and everyone upon enquiry into his own thoughts will find that he has no other idea of any substance, v.g. let it be gold, horse, iron, man, vitriol, bread, but what he has barely of those sen-sible qualities which he supposes to inhere, with a supposition of such a substratum as gives, as it were, a support to those qualities or simple ideas which he has observed to exist united together. Thus the idea of the sun, what is it but an aggregate of those several simple ideas, bright, hot, roundish, having a constant regular motion, at a certain dis-tance from us, and perhaps some other? As he who thinks and discourses of the sun has been more or less accurate in observing those sensible qualities, ideas, or properties which are in that thing which he calls the sun.

7. For he has the perfectest idea of any of the particular sorts of substances who has gathered and put together most of those simple ideas which do exist in it, among which are to be reckoned its active powers and passive capacities; which though not simple ideas, yet in this respect, for brevity's sake, may conveniently enough be reckoned amongst them. Thus the power of drawing iron is one of the ideas of the complex one of that substance we call a lodestone; and a power to be so drawn is a part of the complex one we call iron: Which powers pass for inherent qualities in those subjects. Because every substance, being as apt, by the powers we observe in it, to change some sensible qualities in other subjects as it is to produce in us those simple ideas which we receive immediately from it, does, by those new sensible qualities introduced into other subjects, discover to us those powers, which do thereby mediately affect our senses, as regularly as its sensible qualities do it immediately: V.g. we immediately by our senses perceive in fire its heat and colour; which are, if rightly considered, nothing but powers in it to produce those ideas in us: We also by our senses perceive the colour and brittle-ness of charcoal, whereby we come by the knowl-edge of another power in fire, which it has to change the colour and consistency of wood. By the former, fire immediately, by the latter, it mediately discov-ers to us these several powers, which therefore we look upon to be a part of the qualities of fire, and so make them a part of the complex idea of it. For all those powers that we take cognizance of, terminat-ing only in the alteration of some sensible qualities in those subjects on which they operate, and so making them exhibit to us new sensible ideas; there-fore it is that I have reckoned these powers amongst the simple ideas which make the complex ones of the sorts of substances; though these powers, con-sidered in themselves, are truly complex ideas. And in this looser sense I crave leave to be understood, when I name any of these potentialities among the simple ideas, which we recollect in our minds when we think of particular substances. For the powers that are severally in them are necessary to be con-sidered, if we will have true distinct notions of the several sorts of substances.

8. Nor are we to wonder that powers make a great part of our complex ideas of substances, since their secondary qualities are those which, in most of them, serve principally to distinguish substances one from another, and commonly make a considerable part of the complex idea of the several sorts of them. For our senses failing us in the discovery of the bulk, texture, and figure of the minute parts of bodies, on which their real constitutions and differences depend, we are fain to make use of their secondary qualities, as the characteristical notes and marks, whereby to frame ideas of them in our minds, and distinguish them one from another. All which secondary qualities, as has been shown, are nothing but bare powers. For the colour and taste of opium are, as well as its soporific or anodyne virtues, mere powers depending on its primary qualities, whereby it is fitted to produce different operations on different parts of our bodies.

9. The ideas that make our complex ones of corporeal substances are of these three sorts. First, the ideas of the primary qualities of things which are discovered by our senses, and are in them even when we perceive them not; such are the bulk, figure, number, situation, and motion of the parts of bodies, which are really in them, whether we take notice of them or no. Secondly, the sensible secondary qualities which, depending on these, are nothing but the powers those substances have to produce several ideas in us by our senses; which ideas are not in the things themselves otherwise than as anything is in its cause. Thirdly, the aptness we consider in any substance to give or receive such alterations of primary qualities, as that the substance so altered should produce in us different ideas from what it did before; these are called active and passive powers: All which powers, as far as we have any notice or notion of them, terminate only in sensible simple ideas. For whatever alteration a lodestone has the power to make in the minute particles of iron, we should have no notion of any power it had at all to operate on iron, did not its sensible motion discover it: And I doubt not but there are a thousand changes that bodies we daily handle have a power to cause in one another, which we never suspect, because they never appear in sensible effects.

10. Powers therefore justly make a great part of our complex ideas of substances. He that will examine his complex idea of gold will find several of its ideas that make it up to be only powers: as the power of being melted, but of not spending itself in the fire; of being dissolved in *aqua regia;* are ideas as necessary to make up our complex idea of gold as its colour and weight, which, if duly considered, are also nothing but different powers. For to speak truly, yellowness is not actually in gold, but is a power in gold to produce that idea in us by our eyes, when placed in a due light: And the heat, which we cannot leave out of our ideas of the sun, is no more really in the sun than the white colour it introduces into wax. These are both equally powers in the sun, operating, by the motion and figure of its sensible parts, so on a man as to make him have the idea of heat; and so on wax as to make it capable to produce in a man the idea of white.

11. Had we senses acute enough to discern the minute particles of bodies, and the real constitution on which their sensible qualities depend, I doubt not but they would produce quite different ideas in us; and that which is now the yellow colour of gold would then disappear, and instead of it we should see an admirable texture of parts of a certain size and figure. This microscopes plainly discover to us; for what to our naked eyes produces a certain colour is, by thus augmenting the acuteness of our senses, discovered to be quite a different thing; and the thus altering, as it were, the proportion of the bulk of the minute parts of a coloured object to our usual sight produces different ideas from what it did before. Thus sand or pounded glass, which is opaque, and white to the naked eye, is pellucid in a microscope; and a hair seen this way loses its former colour, and is in a great measure pellucid, with a mixture of some bright sparkling colours, such as appear from the refraction of diamonds, and other pellucid bodies. Blood to the naked eye appears all red; but by a good microscope, wherein its lesser parts appear, shows only some few globules of red, swimming in a pellucid liquor: And how these red globules would appear, if glasses could be found that could yet magnify them a thousand or ten thousand times more, is uncertain.

12. The infinitely wise Contriver of us, and all things about us, hath fitted our senses, faculties, and organs to the conveniences of life, and the business we have to do here. We are able, by our senses, to know and distinguish things; and to examine them so far as to apply them to our uses, and several ways to accommodate the exigencies of this life. We have insight enough into their admirable contrivances and wonderful effects to admire and magnify the wisdom, power, and goodness of their Author. Such a knowledge as this, which is suited to our present condition, we want not faculties to attain. But it appears not that God intended we should have a perfect, clear, and adequate knowledge of them: That perhaps is not in the comprehension of any finite being. We are furnished with faculties (dull and weak as they are) to discover enough in the creatures to lead us to the knowledge of the Creator, and the knowledge of our duty: And we are fitted well enough with abilities to provide for the conveniences of living: These are our business in this world. But were our senses altered, and made much quicker and acuter, the appearance and outward scheme of things would have quite another face to us; and, I am apt to think, would be inconsistent with our being, or at least well-being, in this part of the universe which we inhabit. He that considers how little our constitution is able to bear a remove into parts of this air, not much higher than that we commonly breathe in, will have reason to be satisfied that in this globe of earth allotted for our mansion, the all-wise Architect has suited our organs, and the bodies that are to affect them one to another. If our sense of hearing were but one thousand times quicker than it is, how would a perpetual noise distract us? And we should in the quietest retirement be less able to sleep or meditate than in the middle of a sea-fight. Nay, if that most instructive of our senses, seeing, were in any man a thousand or a hundred thousand times more acute than it is by the best microscope, things several millions of times less than the smallest object of his sight now would then be visible to his naked eyes, and so he would come nearer to the discovery of the texture and motion of the minute parts of corporeal things; and in many of them, probably get ideas of their internal constitutions. But then he would be in a quite different world from other people: Nothing would appear the same to him, and others; the visible ideas of everything would be different. So that I doubt whether he and the rest of men could discourse concerning the objects of sight, or have any communication about colours, their appearances being so wholly different. And perhaps such a quickness and tenderness of sight could not endure bright

sunshine, or so much as open daylight; nor take in but a very small part of any object at once, and that too only at a very near distance. And if, by the help of such microscopical eyes (if I may so call them), a man could penetrate farther than ordinary into the secret composition and radical texture of bodies, he would not make any great advantage by the change, if such an acute sight would not serve to conduct him to the market and exchange; if he could not see things he was to avoid, at a convenient distance; nor distinguish things he had to do with, by those sensible qualities others do. He that was sharp-sighted enough to see the configuration of the minute particles of the spring of a clock, and observe upon what peculiar structure and impulse its elastic motion depends, would no doubt discover something very admirable: But if eyes so framed could not view at once the hand, and the characters of the hour-plate, and thereby at a distance see what o'clock it was, their owner could not be much benefited by that acuteness; which, whilst it discovered the secret contrivance of the parts of the machine, made him lose its use.

13. And here give me leave to propose an extravagant conjecture of mine, viz. that since we have some reason (if there be any credit to be given to the report of things that our philosophy cannot account for) to imagine that spirits can assume to themselves bodies of different bulk, figure, and conformation of parts, whether one great advantage some of them have over us may not lie in this, that they can so frame and shape to themselves organs of sensation or perception as to suit them to their present design, and the circumstances of the object they would consider. For how much would that man exceed all others in knowledge who had but the faculty so to alter the structure of his eyes, that one sense, as to make it capable of all the several degrees of vision which the assistance of glasses (casually at first lighted on) has taught us to conceive? What wonders would he discover who could so fit his eyes to all sorts of objects as to see, when he pleased, the figure and motion of the minute particles in the blood, and other juices of animals, as distinctly as he does, at other times, the shape and motion of the animals themselves? But to us, in our present state, unalterable organs so contrived as to discover the figure and motion of the minute parts of bodies, whereon depend those sensible qualities we now observe in them, would perhaps be of no advantage. God has, no doubt, made them so, as is best for us in our present condition. He hath fitted us for the neighbourhood of the bodies that surround us, and we have to do with: And though we cannot, by the faculties we have, attain to a perfect knowledge of things, yet they will serve us well enough for those ends abovementioned, which are our great concernment. I beg my reader's pardon for laying before him so wild a fancy, concerning the ways of perception of beings above us; but how extravagant soever it be, I doubt whether we can imagine anything about the knowledge of angels, but after this manner, some way or other in proportion to what we find and observe in ourselves. And though we cannot but allow that the infinite power and wisdom of God may frame creatures with a thousand other faculties and ways of perceiving things without them than what we have, yet our thoughts can go no farther than our own: so impossible it is for us to enlarge our very guesses beyond the ideas received from our own sensation and reflection. The supposition, at least, that angels do sometimes assume bodies needs not startle us; since some of the most ancient and most learned fathers of the church seemed to believe that they had bodies: And this is certain, that their state and way of existence is unknown to us.

14. But to return to the matter in hand, the ideas we have of substances, and the ways we come by them: I say, our specific ideas of substances are nothing else but a collection of a certain number of simple ideas, considered as united in one thing. These ideas of substances, though they are commonly simple apprehensions, and the names of them simple terms; yet in effect are complex and compounded. Thus the idea which an Englishman signifies by the name *swan* is white colour, long neck, red beak, black legs, and whole feet, and all these of a certain size, with a power of swimming in the water, and making a certain kind of noise: and perhaps, to a man who has long observed this kind of birds, some other properties which all terminate in sensible simple ideas, all united in one common subject.

15. Besides the complex ideas we have of material sensible substances, of which I have last spoken, by the simple ideas we have taken from those operations of our own minds, which we experiment daily in ourselves, as thinking, understanding, willing, knowing, and power of beginning motion, &c., co-existing in some substance: We are able to frame the complex idea of an immaterial spirit. And thus by putting together the ideas of thinking, perceiving, liberty, and power of moving themselves, and other things, we have as clear a perception and notion of immaterial substances as we have of material. For putting together the ideas of thinking and willing, or the power of moving or quieting corporeal motion, joined to substance of which we have no distinct idea, we have the idea of an immaterial spirit; and by putting together the ideas of coherent solid parts, and a power of being moved, joined with substance, of which likewise we have no positive idea, we have the idea of matter. The one is as clear and distinct an idea as the other: the idea of thinking, and moving a body, being as clear and distinct ideas as the ideas of extension, solidity, and being moved. For our idea of substance is equally obscure, or none at all in both: It is but a supposed I know not what, to support those ideas we call accidents. It is for want of reflection that we are apt to think that our senses show us nothing but material things. Every act of sensation, when duly considered, gives us an equal view of both parts of nature, the corporeal and spiritual. For whilst I know, by seeing or hearing, &c., that there is some corporeal being without me, the object of that sensation, I do more certainly know that there is some spiritual being within me that sees and hears. This, I must be convinced, cannot be the action of bare insensible matter; nor ever could be, without an immaterial thinking being.

16. By the complex idea of extended, figured, coloured, and all other sensible qualities, which is all that we know of it, we are as far from the idea of the substance of body as if we knew nothing at all: Nor after all the acquaintance and familiarity which we imagine we have with matter, and the many qualities men assure themselves they perceive and know in bodies, will it perhaps upon examination be found that they have any more, or clearer, primary ideas belonging to body than they have belonging to immaterial spirit.

17. The primary ideas we have peculiar to body, as contradistinguished to spirit, are the cohesion of solid, and consequently separable, parts, and a power of communicating motion by impulse. These, I think, are the original ideas proper and peculiar to body; for figure is but the consequence of finite extension.

18. The ideas we have belonging and peculiar to spirit are thinking and will, or a power of putting body into motion by thought, and which is consequent to it, liberty. For as body cannot but communicate its motion by impulse to another body, which it meets with at rest; so the mind can put bodies into motion, or forbear to do so, as it pleases. The ideas of existence, duration, and mobility are common to them both.

19. There is no reason why it should be thought strange that I make mobility belong to spirit: For having no other idea of motion but change of distance with other beings that are considered as at rest; and finding that spirits, as well as bodies, cannot operate but where they are, and that spirits do operate at several times in several places; I cannot but attribute change of place to all finite spirits (for of the infinite Spirit I speak not here). For my soul, being a real being, as well as my body, is certainly as capable of changing distance with any other body, or being as body itself, and so is capable of motion. And if a mathematician can consider a certain distance or a change of that distance between two points, one may certainly conceive a distance and a change of distance between two spirits: and so conceive their motion, their approach or removal, one from another.

20. Everyone finds in himself that his soul can think, will, and operate on his body in the place where that is; but cannot operate on a body, or in a place an hundred miles distant from it. Nobody can imagine that his soul can think, or move a body at Oxford, whilst he is at London; and cannot but know that, being united to his body, it constantly changes place all the whole journey between Oxford and London, as the coach or horse does that carries him, and I think may be said to be truly all that while in motion: Or if that will not be allowed to afford us a clear idea enough of its motion, its being separated from the body in death, I think, will; for to consider it as going out of the body, or leaving it, and yet to have no idea of its motion, seems to me impossible.

21. If it be said by anyone that it cannot change place because it hath none, for the spirits are not *in loco,* but *ubi,* I suppose that way of talking will not now be of much weight to many, in an age that is not much disposed to admire, or suffer themselves to be deceived by, such unintelligible ways of speaking. But if anyone thinks there is any sense in that distinction, and that it is applicable to our present purpose, I desire him to put it into intelligible English; and then from thence draw a reason to show that immaterial spirits are not capable of motion. Indeed motion cannot be attributed to God; not because he is an immaterial, but because he is an infinite Spirit.

22. Let us compare, then, our complex idea of an immaterial spirit with our complex idea of body, and see whether there be any more obscurity in one than in the other, and in which most. Our idea of body, as I think, is an extended solid substance, capable of communicating motion by impulse: And our idea of soul, as an immaterial spirit, is of a substance that thinks, and has a power of exciting motion in body, by willing or thought. These, I think, are our complex ideas of soul and body, as contradistinguished; and now let us examine which has most obscurity in it, and difficulty to be apprehended. I know that people whose thoughts are immersed in matter, and have so subjected their minds to their senses that they seldom reflect on anything beyond them, are apt to say they cannot comprehend a thinking thing, which perhaps is true: But I affirm, when they consider it well, they can no more comprehend an extended thing.

23. If anyone say, he knows not what it is thinks in him; he means, he knows not what the substance is of that thinking thing: No more, say I, knows he what the substance is of that solid thing. Farther, if he says he knows not how he thinks: I answer, neither knows he how he is extended; how the solid parts of body are united, or cohere together to make extension. For though the pressure of the particles of air may account for the cohesion of several parts of matter, that are grosser than the particles of air, and have pores less than the corpuscles of air; yet the weight or pressure of the air will not explain nor can be a cause of the coherence of the particles of air themselves. And if the pressure of the aether, or any subtler matter than the air, may unite, and hold fast together the parts of a particle of air, as well as other bodies; yet it cannot make bonds for itself, and hold together the parts that make up every the least corpuscle of that *materia subtilis.* So that that hypothesis, how ingeniously soever explained, by showing that the parts of sensible bodies are held together by the pressure of other external insensible bodies, reaches not the parts of the aether itself; and by how much the more evident it proves that the parts of other bodies are held together by the external pressure of the aether, and can have no other conceivable cause of their cohesion and union, by so much the more it leaves us in the dark concerning the cohesion of the parts of the corpuscles of the aether itself; which we can neither conceive without parts, they being bodies, and divisible; nor yet how their parts cohere, they wanting that cause of cohesion, which is given of the cohesion of the parts of all other bodies.

24. But, in truth, the pressure of any ambient fluid, how great soever, can be no intelligible cause of the cohesion of the solid parts of matter. For though such a pressure may hinder the avulsion of two polished superficies, one from another, in a line perpendicular to them, as in the experiment of two polished marbles; yet it can never, in the least, hinder the separation by a motion, in a line parallel to those surfaces. Because the ambient fluid, having a full liberty to succeed in each point of space, deserted by a lateral motion, resists such a motion of bodies so joined, no more than it would resist the motion of that body, were it on all sides environed by that fluid, and touched no other body: And therefore, if there were no other cause of cohesion, all parts of bodies must be easily separable by such a lateral sliding motion. For if the pressure of the aether be the adequate cause of cohesion, wherever that cause operates not, there can be no cohesion. And since it cannot operate against a lateral separation (as has been shown), therefore in every imaginary plane, intersecting any mass of matter, there could be no more cohesion than of two polished surfaces, which will always, notwithstanding any imaginable pressure of a fluid, easily slide one from another. So that, perhaps, how clear an idea soever we think we have of the extension of body, which is nothing but the cohesion of solid parts, he that shall well consider it in his mind may have rea-

son to conclude that it is as easy for him to have a clear idea how the soul thinks as how body is extended. For since body is no farther, nor otherwise extended, than by the union and cohesion of its solid parts, we shall very ill comprehend the extension of body without understanding wherein consists the union and cohesion of its parts: Which seems to me as incomprehensible as the manner of thinking, and how it is performed.

25. I allow it is usual for most people to wonder how anyone should find a difficulty in what they think they every day observe. Do we not see, will they be ready to say, the parts of bodies stick firmly together? Is there anything more common? And what doubt can there be made of it? And the like, I say, concerning thinking and voluntary motion: Do we not every moment experiment it in ourselves? And therefore can it be doubted? The matter of fact is clear, I confess; but when we would a little nearer look into it, and consider how it is done, there I think we are at a loss, both in the one and the other; and can as little understand how the parts of body cohere as how we ourselves perceive, or move. I would have anyone intelligibly explain to me how the parts of gold, or brass (that but now in fusion were as loose from one another as the particles of water, or the sands of an hour-glass), come in a few moments to be so united, and adhere so strongly one to another, that the utmost force of men's arms cannot separate them: A considering man will, I suppose, be here at a loss to satisfy his own or another man's understanding.

26. The little bodies that compose that fluid we call water are so extremely small that I have never heard of anyone who by a microscope (and yet I have heard of some that have magnified to ten thousand; nay, to much above a hundred thousand times) pretended to perceive their distinct bulk, figure, or motion: And the particles of water are also so perfectly loose one from another that the least force sensibly separates them. Nay, if we consider their perpetual motion, we must allow them to have no cohesion one with another; and yet let but a sharp cold come, they unite, they consolidate, these little atoms cohere, and are not, without great force, separable. He that could find the bonds that tie these heaps of loose little bodies together so firmly; he that could make known the cement that makes them stick so fast one to another; would discover a great and yet unknown secret: And yet when that was done, would he be far enough from making the extension of body (which is the cohesion of its solid parts) intelligible, till he could show wherein consisted the union, or consolidation of the parts of those bonds, or of that cement, or of the least particle of matter that exists. Whereby it appears that this primary and supposed obvious quality of body will be found, when examined, to be as incomprehensible as anything belonging to our minds, and a solid extended substance as hard to be conceived as a thinking immaterial one, whatever difficulties some would raise against it.

27. For, to extend our thoughts a little farther, that pressure which is brought to explain the cohesion of bodies is as unintelligible as the cohesion itself. For if matter be considered, as no doubt it is, finite, let anyone send his contemplation to the extremities of the universe, and there see what conceivable hoops, what bond he can imagine to hold this mass of matter in so close a pressure together; from whence steel has its firmness, and the parts of a diamond their hardness and indissolubility. If matter be finite, it must have its extremes; and there must be something to hinder it from scattering asunder. If, to avoid this difficulty, anyone will throw himself into the supposition and abyss of infinite matter, let him consider what light he thereby brings to the cohesion of body, and whether he be ever the nearer making it intelligible, by resolving it into a supposition, the most absurd and most incomprehensible of all other: So far is our extension of body (which is nothing but the cohesion of solid parts) from being clearer, or more distinct, when we would enquire into the nature, cause, or manner of it, than the idea of thinking.

28. Another idea we have of body is the power of communication of motion by impulse: and of our souls, the power of exciting motion by thought. These ideas, the one of body, the other of our minds, every day's experience clearly furnishes us with: But if here again we enquire how this is done, we are equally in the dark. For to the communication of motion by impulse, wherein as much motion is lost to one body as is got to the other, which is the ordinariest case, we can have no other conception but of the passing of motion out of one body into

another: Which, I think, is as obscure and unconceivable as how our minds move or stop our bodies by thought, which we every moment find they do. The increase of motion by impulse, which is observed or believed sometimes to happen, is yet harder to be understood. We have by daily experience clear evidence of motion produced both by impulse and by thought; but the manner how hardly comes within our comprehension: We are equally at a loss in both. So that however we consider motion, and its communication, either from body or spirit, the idea which belongs to spirit is at least as clear as that which belongs to body. And if we consider the active power of moving, or, as I may call it, motivity, it is much clearer in spirit than body; since two bodies, placed by one another at rest, will never afford us the idea of a power in the one to move the other, but by a borrowed motion: Whereas the mind, every day, affords us ideas of an active power of moving of bodies; and therefore it is worth our consideration, whether active power be not the proper attribute of spirits, and passive power of matter. Hence may be conjectured that created spirits are not totally separate from matter, because they are both active and passive. Pure spirit, viz. God, is only active; pure matter is only passive; those beings that are both active and passive, we may judge to partake of both. But be that as it will, I think, we have as many and as clear ideas belonging to spirit as we have belonging to body, the substance of each being equally unknown to us, and the idea of thinking in spirit as clear as of extension in body; and the communication of motion by thought, which we attribute to spirit, is as evident as that by impulse, which we ascribe to body. Constant experience makes us sensible of both these, though our narrow understandings can comprehend neither. For when the mind would look beyond those original ideas we have from sensation or reflection, and penetrate into their causes, and manner of production, we find still it discovers nothing but its own shortsightedness.

29. To conclude: Sensation convinces us that there are solid extended substances; and reflection, that there are thinking ones: Experience assures us of the existence of such beings; and that the one hath a power to move body by impulse, the other by thought; this we cannot doubt of. Experience, I say,

every moment furnishes us with the clear ideas, both of the one and the other. But beyond these ideas, as received from their proper sources, our faculties will not reach. If we would enquire farther into their nature, causes, and manner, we perceive not the nature of extension clearer than we do of thinking. If we would explain them any farther, one is as easy as the other; and there is no more difficulty to conceive how a substance we know not should by thought set body into motion than how a substance we know not should by impulse set body into motion. So that we are no more able to discover wherein the ideas belonging to body consist than those belonging to spirit. From whence it seems probable to me that the simple ideas we receive from sensation and reflection are the boundaries of our thoughts; beyond which the mind, whatever efforts it would make, is not able to advance one jot; nor can it make any discoveries when it would pry into the nature and hidden causes of those ideas.

30. So that, in short, the idea we have of spirit, compared with the idea we have of body, stands thus: The substance of spirits is unknown to us; and so is the substance of body equally unknown to us. Two primary qualities or properties of body, viz. solid coherent parts and impulse, we have distinct clear ideas of: So likewise we know, and have distinct clear ideas of, two primary qualities or properties of spirit, viz. thinking and a power of action; i.e. a power of beginning or stopping several thoughts or motions. We have also the ideas of several qualities inherent in bodies, and have the clear distinct ideas of them; which qualities are but the various modifications of the extension of cohering solid parts, and their motion. We have likewise the ideas of the several modes of thinking, viz. believing, doubting, intending, fearing, hoping; all which are but the several modes of thinking. We have also the ideas of willing and moving the body consequent to it, and with the body itself too; for, as has been shown, spirit is capable of motion.

31. Lastly, if this notion of immaterial spirit may have, perhaps, some difficulties in it not easily to be explained, we have therefore no more reason to deny or doubt the existence of such spirits than we have to deny or doubt the existence of body; because the notion of body is cumbered with some difficulties very hard, and perhaps impossible, to be explained or understood by us. For I would

fain have instanced anything in our notion of spirit more perplexed, or nearer a contradiction, than the very notion of body includes in it: The divisibility *in infinitum* of any finite extension involving us, whether we grant or deny it, in consequences impossible to be explicated or made in our apprehensions consistent; consequences that carry greater difficulty, and more apparent absurdity, than anything can follow from the notion of an immaterial knowing substance.

32. Which we are not at all to wonder at, since we having but some few superficial ideas of things, discovered to us only by the senses from without, or by the mind, reflecting on what it experiments in itself within, have no knowledge beyond that, much less of the internal constitution and true nature of things, being destitute of faculties to attain it. And therefore experimenting and discovering in ourselves knowledge, and the power of voluntary motion, as certainly as we experiment or discover in things without us, the cohesion and separation of solid parts, which is the extension and motion of bodies; we have as much reason to be satisfied with our notion of immaterial spirit as with our notion of body, and the existence of the one as well as the other. For it being no more a contradiction that thinking should exist, separate and independent from solidity, than it is a contradiction that solidity should exist, separate and independent from thinking, they being both but simple ideas, independent one from another; and having as clear and distinct ideas in us of thinking as of solidity: I know not why we may not as well allow a thinking thing without solidity, i.e. immaterial, to exist as a solid thing without thinking, i.e. matter, to exist; especially since it is not harder to conceive how thinking should exist without matter than how matter should think. For whensoever we would proceed beyond these simple ideas we have from sensation and reflection, and dive farther into the nature of things, we fall presently into darkness and obscurity, perplexedness and difficulties; and can discover nothing farther but our own blindness and ignorance. But whichever of these complex ideas be clearest, that of body or immaterial spirit, this is evident, that the simple ideas that make them up are no other than what we have received from sensation or reflection: And so is it of all our other ideas of substances, even of God himself.

33. For if we examine the idea we have of the incomprehensible supreme being, we shall find that we come by it the same way; and that the complex ideas we have both of God and separate spirits are made of the simple ideas we receive from reflection: V.g. having, from what we experiment in ourselves, got the ideas of existence and duration; of knowledge and power; of pleasure and happiness; and of several other qualities and powers, which it is better to have than to be without: When we would frame an idea the most suitable we can to the supreme being, we enlarge every one of these with our idea of infinity; and so putting them together, make our complex idea of God. For that the mind has such a power of enlarging some of its ideas, received from sensation and reflection, has been already shown.

34. If I find that I know some few things, and some of them, or all, perhaps imperfectly, I can frame an idea of knowing twice as many; which I can double again, as often as I can add to number; and thus enlarge my idea of knowledge, by extending its comprehension to all things existing, or possible. The same also I can do of knowing them more perfectly; i.e. all their qualities, powers, causes, consequences, and relations, &c., till all be perfectly known that is in them, or can any way relate to them: and thus frame the idea of infinite or boundless knowledge. The same may also be done of power, till we come to that we call infinite; and also of the duration of existence without beginning or end; and so frame the idea of an eternal being. The degrees or extent wherein we ascribe existence, power, wisdom, and all other perfections (which we can have any ideas of) to that sovereign being which we call God, being all boundless and infinite, we frame the best idea of him our minds are capable of: All which is done, I say, by enlarging those simple ideas we have taken from the operations of our own minds, by reflection; or by our senses, from exterior things; to that vastness to which infinity can extend them.

35. For it is infinity, which, joined to our ideas of existence, power, knowledge, &c., makes that complex idea whereby we represent to ourselves, the best we can, the supreme being. For though in his own essence (which certainly we do not know, not knowing the real essence of a pebble, or a fly, or of our own selves) God be simple and uncompounded; yet I think I may say we have no other idea of him but a complex one of existence, knowledge, power, happiness, &c., infinite and eternal: Which are all distinct ideas, and some of them, being relative, are again compounded of others: All which being, as has been shown, originally got from sensation and reflection, go to make up the idea or notion we have of God.

36. This farther is to be observed, that there is no idea we attribute to God, bating infinity, which is not also a part of our complex idea of other spirits. Because being capable of no other simple ideas, belonging to anything but body, but those which by reflection we receive from the operation of our own minds, we can attribute to spirits no other but what we receive from thence: And all the difference we can put between them in our contemplation of spirits is only in the several extents and degrees of their knowledge, power, duration, happiness, &c. For that in our ideas, as well of spirits as of other things, we are restrained to those we receive from sensation and reflection is evident from hence, that in our ideas of spirits, how much soever advanced in perfection beyond those of bodies, even to that of infinite, we cannot yet have any idea of the manner wherein they discover their thoughts one to another: Though we must necessarily conclude that separate spirits, which are beings that have perfecter knowledge and greater happiness than we, must needs have also a perfecter way of communicating their thoughts than we have, who are fain to make use of corporeal signs and particular sounds; which are therefore of most general use, as being the best and quickest we are capable of. But of immediate communication, having no experiment in ourselves, and consequently no notion of it at all, we have no idea how spirits, which use not words, can with quickness, or much less how spirits, that have no bodies, can be masters of their own thoughts, and communicate or conceal them at pleasure, though we cannot but necessarily suppose they have such a power.

37. And thus we have seen what kind of ideas we have of substances of all kinds, wherein they consist, and how we came by them. From whence, I think, it is very evident,

First, That all our ideas of the several sorts of substances are nothing but collections of simple ideas, with a supposition of something to which they belong, and in which they subsist; though of this supposed something we have no clear distinct idea at all.

Secondly, That all the simple ideas that, thus united in one common substratum, make up our complex ideas of several sorts of substances are no other but such as we have received from sensation or reflection. So that even in those which we think we are most intimately acquainted with, and that come nearest the comprehension of our most enlarged conceptions, we cannot go beyond those simple ideas. And even in those which seem most remote from all we have to do with, and do infinitely surpass anything we can perceive in ourselves by reflection, or discover by sensation in other things, we can attain to nothing but those simple ideas which we originally received from sensation or reflection; as is evident in the complex ideas we have of angels, and particularly of God himself.

Thirdly, That most of the simple ideas that make up our complex ideas of substances, when truly considered, are only powers, however we are apt to take them for positive qualities; v.g. the greatest part of the ideas that make our complex idea of gold are yellowness, great weight, ductility, fusibility, and solubility in *aqua regia,* &c., all united together in an unknown substratum: All which ideas are nothing else but so many relations to other substances, and are not really in the gold, considered barely in itself, though they depend on those real and primary qualities of its internal constitution, whereby it has a fitness differently to operate, and be operated on by several other substances.

Chapter XXVII. *Of Identity and Diversity*

1. Another occasion the mind often takes of comparing is the very being of things, when, considering anything as existing at any determined time and place, we compare it with itself existing at another time, and thereon form the ideas of identity and diversity. When we see any thing to be in any place in any instant of time, we are sure (be it what it will) that it is that very thing, and not another, which at that same time exists in another place, how like and undistinguishable soever it may be in all other respects: And in this consists identity, when the ideas it is attributed to vary not at all from what they were that moment wherein we consider their former ex-

istence, and to which we compare the present. For we never finding, nor conceiving it possible, that two things of the same kind should exist in the same place at the same time, we rightly conclude that whatever exists anywhere at any time excludes all of the same kind, and is there itself alone. When therefore we demand whether any thing be the same or no; it refers always to some thing that existed such a time in such a place, which it was certain at that instant was the same with itself, and no other. From whence it follows that one thing cannot have two beginnings of existence, nor two things one beginning; it being impossible for two things of the same kind to be or exist in the same instant, in the very same place, or one and the same thing in different places. That therefore that had one beginning is the same thing; and that which had a different beginning in time and place from that is not the same, but diverse. That which has made the difficulty about this relation has been the little care and attention used in having precise notions of the things to which it is attributed.

2. We have the ideas but of three sorts of substances: (1) God. (2) Finite intelligences. (3) Bodies. First, God is without beginning, eternal, unalterable, and everywhere; and therefore concerning his identity, there can be no doubt. Secondly, finite spirits having had each its determinate time and place of beginning to exist, the relation to that time and place will always determine to each of them its identity, as long as it exists.

Thirdly, the same will hold of every particle of matter, to which no addition or subtraction of matter being made, it is the same. For though these three sorts of substances, as we term them, do not exclude one another out of the same place; yet we cannot conceive but that they must necessarily each of them exclude any of the same kind out of the same place: Or else the notions and names of identity and diversity would be in vain, and there could be no such distinctions of substances, or anything else one from another. For example: Could two bodies be in the same place at the same time, then those two parcels of matter must be one and the same, take them great or little: Nay, all bodies must be one and the same. For by the same reason that two particles of matter may be in one place, all bodies may be in one place: Which, when it can be supposed, takes away the distinction of identity and diversity of one and more, and renders it ridiculous. But it being a contradiction that two or more should be one, identity and diversity are relations and ways of comparing well-founded, and of use to the understanding. All other things being but modes or relations ultimately terminated in substances, the identity and diversity of each particular existence of them too will be by the same way determined: Only as to things whose existence is in succession, such as are the actions of finite beings, v.g. motion and thought, both which consist in a continued train of succession, concerning their diversity, there can be no question: Because each perishing the moment it begins, they cannot exist in different times, or in different places, as permanent beings can at different times exist in distant places; and therefore no motion or thought, considered as at different times, can be the same, each part thereof having a different beginning of existence.

3. From what has been said, it is easy to discover what is so much enquired after, the *principium individuationis;* and that, it is plain, is existence itself, which determines a being of any sort to a particular time and place, incommunicable to two beings of the same kind. This, though it seems easier to conceive in simple substances or modes, yet when reflected on is not more difficult in compound ones, if care be taken to what it is applied: V.g. let us suppose an atom, i.e. a continued body under one immutable superficies, existing in a determined time and place; it is evident that, considered in any instant of its existence, it is in that instant the same with itself. For being at that instant what it is, and nothing else, it is the same, and so must continue as long as its existence is continued; for so long it will be the same, and no other. In like manner, if two or more atoms be joined together into the same mass, every one of those atoms will be the same, by the foregoing rule: And whilst they exist united together, the mass, consisting of the same atoms, must be the same mass, or the same body, let the parts be ever so differently jumbled. But if one of these atoms be taken away, or one new one added, it is no longer the same mass, or the same body. In the state of living creatures, their identity depends not on a mass of the same particles, but on something else. For in them the variation of great parcels of matter alters not the identity: An oak growing from a plant to a great tree, and then lopped, is still the same oak; and a colt grown up to a horse, sometimes fat, sometimes lean, is all the while the same horse: Though in both these cases, there may be a manifest change of the parts; so that truly they are not either of them the same masses of matter, though they be truly one of them the same oak, and the other the same horse. The reason whereof is that in these two cases, a mass of matter and a living body, identity is not applied to the same thing.

4. We must therefore consider wherein an oak differs from a mass of matter, and that seems to me to be in this, that the one is only the cohesion of particles of matter any how united, the other such a disposition of them as constitutes the parts of an oak; and such an organization of those parts as is fit to receive and distribute nourishment, so as to continue and frame the wood, bark, and leaves, &c., of an oak, in which consists the vegetable life. That being then one plant which has such an organization of parts in one coherent body partaking of one common life, it continues to be the same plant as long as it partakes of the same life, though that life be communicated to new particles of matter vitally united to the living plant, in a like continued organization conformable to that sort of plants. For this organization being at any one instant in any one collection of matter is in that particular concrete distinguished from all other, and is that individual life which existing constantly from that moment both forwards and backwards, in the same continuity of insensibly succeeding parts united to the living body of the plant, it has that identity which makes the same plant, and all the parts of it, parts of the same plant, during all the time that they exist united in that continued organization, which is fit to convey that common life to all the parts so united.

5. The case is not so much different in brutes, but that anyone may hence see what makes an animal, and continues it the same. Something we have like this in machines, and may serve to illustrate it. For example, what is a watch? It is plain it is nothing but a fit organization or construction of parts to a certain end, which when a sufficient force is added to it, it is capable to attain. If we would suppose this machine one continued body, all whose organized parts were repaired, increased, or diminished by a

constant addition or separation of insensible parts, with one common life, we should have something very much like the body of an animal; with this difference, that in an animal the fitness of the organization, and the motion wherein life consists, begin together, the motion coming from within; but in machines, the force coming sensibly from without is often away when the organ is in order, and well fitted to receive it.

6. This also shows wherein the identity of the same man consists: viz. in nothing but a participation of the same continued life, by constantly fleeting particles of matter, in succession vitally united to the same organized body. He that shall place the identity of man in anything else, but like that of other animals in one fitly organized body, taken in any one instant, and from thence continued under one organization of life in several successively fleeting particles of matter united to it, will find it hard to make an embryo, one of years, mad and sober, the same man, by any supposition, that will not make it possible for Seth, Ismael, Socrates, Pilate, St. Austin, and Caesar Borgia to be the same man. For if the identity of soul alone makes the same man, and there be nothing in the nature of matter why the same individual spirit may not be united to different bodies, it will be possible that those men living in distant ages, and of different tempers, may have been the same man: Which way of speaking must be, from a very strange use of the word *man,* applied to an idea out of which body and shape are excluded. And that way of speaking would agree yet worse with the notions of those philosophers who allow of transmigration, and are of opinion that the souls of men may, for their miscarriages, be detruded into the bodies of beasts, as fit habitations, with organs suited to the satisfaction of their brutal inclinations. But yet I think nobody, could he be sure that the soul of Heliogabalus were in one of his hogs, would yet say that hog were a man or Heliogabalus.

7. It is not therefore unity of substance that comprehends all sorts of identity, or will determine it in every case: But to conceive and judge of it aright, we must consider what idea the word it is applied to stands for; it being one thing to be the same *substance,* another the same *man,* and a third the same *person,* if *person, man,* and *substance* are three names standing for three different ideas; for such as is the idea belonging to that name, such must be the identity: Which, if it had been a little more carefully attended to, would possibly have prevented a great deal of that confusion which often occurs about this matter, with no small seeming difficulties, especially concerning personal identity, which therefore we shall, in the next place, a little consider.

8. An animal is a living organized body; and consequently the same animal, as we have observed, is the same continued life communicated to different particles of matter, as they happen successively to be united to that organized living body. And whatever is talked of other definitions, ingenuous observation puts it past doubt that the idea in our minds, of which the sound *man* in our mouths is the sign, is nothing else but of an animal of such a certain form: Since I think I may be confident that, whoever should see a creature of his own shape and make, though it had no more reason all its life than a cat or a parrot, would call him still a man; or whoever should hear a cat or a parrot discourse, reason, and philosophize would call or think it nothing but a cat or a parrot; and say the one was a dull, irrational man, and the other a very intelligent rational parrot. A relation we have in an author of great note is sufficient to countenance the supposition of a rational parrot. His words [*Memoirs of What Passed in Christendom from 1672 to 1679,* p. 57/392.] are:

I had a mind to know from Prince Maurice's own mouth the account of a common but much credited story that I had heard so often from many others, of an old parrot he had in Brazil during his government there, that spoke, and asked, and answered common questions like a reasonable creature: So that those of his train there generally concluded it to be witchery or possession; and one of his chaplains, who lived long afterwards in Holland, would never from that time endure a parrot, but said they all had a devil in them. I had heard many particulars of this story, and assevered by people hard to be discredited, which made me ask Prince Maurice what there was of it. He said, with his usual plainness and dryness in talk, there was something true, but a great deal false of what had been reported. I desired to know of him what there was of the first? He told me short and coldly that he had heard of such an old parrot when he had been at Brazil; and though he believed nothing of it, and it was a good way off, yet he had so much curiosity as to send for it: That it was a very great and a very old one; and when it came first into the room where the prince was, with a great many Dutchmen about him, it said presently, What a company of white men are here! They asked it what it thought that man was, pointing to the prince? It answered, some general or other; when they brought it close to him, he asked it, D'où venez vous? It answered, De Marinnan. The Prince, À qui estes vous? The parrot, À un Portugais. Prince, Que fais tu là? Parrot, Je garde les poulles. The prince laughed, and said, Vous gardez les poulles? The parrot answered, Oui, moi; et je scai bien faire; and made the chuck four or five times that people use to make to chickens when they call them. [Whence come ye? It answered, From Marinnan. The Prince, To whom do you belong? The parrot, To a Portugeze. Prince, What do you do there? Parrot, I look after the chickens. The prince laughed and said, You look after the chickens? The parrot answered, Yes I, and I know well enough how to do it.] I set down the words of this worthy dialogue in French, just as prince Maurice said them to me. I asked him in what language the parrot spoke, and he said, in Brasilian. I asked whether he understood Brasilian; he said no, but he had taken care to have two interpreters by him, the one a Dutchman that spoke Brasilian, and the other a Brazilian that spoke Dutch; that he asked them separately and privately, and both of them agreed in telling him just the same thing that the parrot had said. I could not but tell this odd story, because it is so much out of the way, and from the first hand, and what may pass for a good one; for I dare say this prince at least believed himself in all he told me, having ever passed for a very honest and pious man. I leave it to naturalists to reason, and to other men to believe, as they please upon it: However, it is not, per-

haps, amiss to relieve or enliven a busy scene sometimes with such digressions, whether to the purpose or no.

I have taken care that the reader should have the story at large in the author's own words, because he seems to me not to have thought it incredible; for it cannot be imagined that so able a man as he, who had sufficiency enough to warrant all the testimonies he gives of himself, should take so much pains, in a place where it had nothing to do, to pin so close not only on a man whom he mentions as his friend, but on a prince in whom he acknowledges very great honesty and piety, a story, which if he himself thought incredible, he could not but also think ridiculous. The Prince, it is plain, who vouches this story, and our author, who relates it from him, both of them call this talker a parrot: And I ask anyone else who thinks such a story fit to be told, whether if this parrot, and all of its kind, had always talked, as we have a prince's word for it this one did, whether, I say, they would not have passed for a race of rational animals: But yet whether for all that they would have been allowed to be men, and not parrots? For I presume, it is not the idea of a thinking or rational being alone that makes the idea of a man in most people's sense, but of a body, so and so shaped, joined to it: And if that be the idea of a man, the same successive body not shifted all at once must, as well as the same immaterial spirit, go to the making of the same man.

9. This being premised, to find wherein personal identity consists, we must consider what *person* stands for; which, I think, is a thinking intelligent being, that has reason and reflection, and can consider itself as itself, the same thinking thing in different times and places; which it does only by that consciousness which is inseparable from thinking, and, as it seems to me, essential to it: it being impossible for anyone to perceive, without perceiving that he does perceive. When we see, hear, smell, taste, feel, meditate, or will anything, we know that we do so. Thus it is always as to our present sensations and perceptions: And by this everyone is to himself that which he calls *self;* it not being considered in this case whether the same self be continued in the same or divers substances. For since consciousness always accompanies thinking, and it is that which makes everyone to be what he calls *self,* and thereby distinguishes himself from all other thinking things; in this alone consists personal identity, i.e. the sameness of a rational being: And as far as this consciousness can be extended backwards to any past action or thought, so far reaches the identity of that person; it is the same self now it was then; and it is by the same self with this present one that now reflects on it, that that action was done.

10. But it is farther enquired, whether it be the same identical substance? This few would think they had reason to doubt of, if these perceptions, with their consciousness, always remained present in the mind, whereby the same thinking thing would be always consciously present, and, as would be thought, evidently the same to itself. But that which seems to make the difficulty is this, that this consciousness being interrupted always by forgetfulness, there being no moment of our lives wherein we have the whole train of all our past actions before our eyes in one view, but even the best memories losing the sight of one part whilst they are viewing another; and we sometimes, and that the greatest part of our lives, not reflecting on our past selves, being intent on our present thoughts, and in sound sleep having no thoughts at all, or at least none with that consciousness which remarks our waking thoughts: I say, in all these cases, our consciousness being interrupted, and we losing the sight of our past selves, doubts are raised whether we are the same thinking thing, i.e. the same substance or no. Which, however reasonable or unreasonable, concerns not personal identity at all: the question being, what makes the same person, and not whether it be the same identical substance, which always thinks in the same person; which in this case matters not at all: Different substances, by the same consciousness (where they do partake in it), being united into one person, as well as different bodies by the same life are united into one animal, whose identity is preserved, in that change of substances, by the unity of one continued life. For it being the same consciousness that makes a man be himself to himself, personal identity depends on that only, whether it be annexed solely to one individual substance, or can be continued in a succession of several substances. For as far as any intelligent being can repeat the idea of any past action with the same consciousness it had of it at first, and with the same consciousness it has of any present

action: So far it is the same personal self. For it is by the consciousness it has of its present thoughts and actions that it is self to itself now, and so will be the same self, as far as the same consciousness can extend to actions past or to come; and would be by distance of time, or change of substance, no more two persons, than a man be two men by wearing other clothes to-day than he did yesterday, with a long or a short sleep between: the same consciousness uniting those distant actions into the same person, whatever substances contributed to their production.

11. That this is so, we have some kind of evidence in our very bodies, all whose particles, whilst vitally united to this same thinking conscious self, so that we feel when they are touched and are affected by and conscious of good or harm that happens to them, are a part of ourselves; i.e. of our thinking conscious self. Thus the limbs of his body are to everyone a part of himself; he sympathizes and is concerned for them. Cut off a hand, and thereby separate it from that consciousness he had of its heat, cold, and other affections, and it is then no longer a part of that which is himself, any more than the remotest part of matter. Thus we see the substance whereof personal self consisted at one time may be varied at another, without the change of personal identity; there being no question about the same person, though the limbs which but now were a part of it, be cut off.

12. But the question is, whether if the same substance which thinks be changed, it can be the same person; or, remaining the same, it can be different persons?

And to this I answer: First, This can be no question at all to those who place thought in a purely material animal constitution, void of an immaterial substance. For whether their supposition be true or no, it is plain they conceive personal identity preserved in something else than identity of substance; as animal identity is preserved in identity of life, and not of substance. And therefore those who place thinking in an immaterial substance only, before they can come to deal with these men, must show why personal identity cannot be preserved in the change of immaterial substances, or variety of particular immaterial substances, as well as animal identity is preserved in the change of material substances, or variety of particular bodies: Unless they will say, it is one immaterial spirit that makes the same life in brutes as it is one immaterial spirit that makes the same person in men; which the Cartesians at least will not admit, for fear of making brutes thinking things too.

13. But next, as to the first part of the question, whether if the same thinking substance (supposing immaterial substances only to think) be changed, it can be the same person? I answer, that cannot be resolved but by those who know what kind of substances they are that do think, and whether the consciousness of past actions can be transferred from one thinking substance to another. I grant, were the same consciousness the same individual action, it could not: But it being a present representation of a past action, why it may not be possible that that may be represented to the mind to have been, which really never was, will remain to be shown. And therefore how far the consciousness of past actions is annexed to any individual agent, so that another cannot possibly have it, will be hard for us to determine, till we know what kind of action it is that cannot be done without a reflex act of perception accompanying it, and how performed by thinking substances, who cannot think without being conscious of it. But that which we call the same consciousness, not being the same individual act, why one intellectual substance may not have represented to it, as done by itself, what it never did, and was perhaps done by some other agent—why, I say, such a representation may not possibly be without reality of matter of fact, as well as several representations in dreams are, which yet whilst dreaming we take for true, will be difficult to conclude from the nature of things. And that it never is so, will by us, till we have clearer views of the nature of thinking substances, be best resolved into the goodness of God, who as far as the happiness or misery of any of his sensible creatures is concerned in it, will not by a fatal errour of theirs transfer from one to another that consciousness which draws reward or punishment with it. How far this may be an argument against those who would place thinking in a system of fleeting animal spirits, I leave to be considered. But yet to return to the question before us, it must be allowed that if the same consciousness (which, as has been shown, is quite a different thing from the same numerical figure or motion in body) can be transferred from one thinking substance to another, it will be possible that two thinking substances may make but one person. For the same consciousness being preserved, whether in the same or different substances, the personal identity is preserved.

14. As to the second part of the question, whether the same immaterial substance remaining, there may be two distinct persons? which question seems to me to be built on this, whether the same immaterial being, being conscious of the action of its past duration, may be wholly stripped of all the consciousness of its past existence, and lose it beyond the power of ever retrieving it again; and so as it were beginning a new account from a new period, have a consciousness that cannot reach beyond this new state. All those who hold pre-existence are evidently of this mind, since they allow the soul to have no remaining consciousness of what it did in that pre-existent state, either wholly separate from body, or informing any other body; and if they should not, it is plain, experience would be against them. So that personal identity reaching no farther than consciousness reaches, a pre-existent spirit not having continued so many ages in a state of silence, must needs make different persons. Suppose a Christian, Platonist, or Pythagorean should, upon God's having ended all his works of creation the seventh day, think his soul hath existed ever since; and should imagine it has revolved in several human bodies, as I once met with one who was persuaded his had been the soul of Socrates (how reasonably I will not dispute; this I know, that in the post he filled, which was no inconsiderable one, he passed for a very rational man, and the press has shown that he wanted not parts or learning), would anyone say that he being not conscious of any of Socrates's actions or thoughts, could be the same person with Socrates? Let anyone reflect upon himself, and conclude that he has in himself an immaterial spirit, which is that which thinks in him, and in the constant change of his body keeps him the same, and is that which he calls himself: Let him also suppose it to be the same soul that was in Nestor or Thersites, at the siege of Troy (for souls being, as far as we know anything of them in their nature, indifferent to any parcel of matter, the supposition has no apparent absurdity in it), which it may have been, as well as it is now the soul of any other man: But he now having no consciousness of any of the actions either of Nestor or Thersites, does or can he conceive himself the same person with either of them? Can he be concerned in either of their actions? Attribute them to himself, or think them his own more than the actions of any other men that ever existed? So that this consciousness not reaching to any of the actions of either of those men, he is no more one self with either of them than if the soul or immaterial spirit that now informs him had been created, and began to exist, when it began to inform his present body; though it were ever so true that the same spirit that informed Nestor's or Thersites's body were numerically the same that now informs his. For this would no more make him the same person with Nestor than if some of the particles of matter that were once a part of Nestor were now a part of this man; the same immaterial substance, without the same consciousness, no more making the same person by being united to any body than the same particle of matter, without consciousness united to any body, makes the same person. But let him once find himself conscious of any of the actions of Nestor, he then finds himself the same person with Nestor.

15. And thus we may be able, without any difficulty, to conceive the same person at the resurrection, though in a body not exactly in make or parts the same which he had here, the same consciousness going along with the soul that inhabits it. But yet the soul alone, in the change of bodies, would scarce to anyone but to him that makes the soul the man be enough to make the same man. For should the soul of a prince, carrying with it the consciousness of the prince's past life, enter and inform the body of a cobbler, as soon as deserted by his own soul, everyone sees he would be the same person with the prince, accountable only for the prince's actions: But who would say it was the same man? The body too goes to the making of the man, and would, I guess, to everybody determine the man in this case; wherein the soul, with all its princely thoughts about it, would not make another man: But he would be the same cobbler to everyone besides himself. I know that, in the ordinary way of speaking, the same person, and the same man, stand for one and the same thing. And indeed everyone will always have a liberty to speak as he pleases,

and to apply what articulate sounds to what ideas he thinks fit, and change them as often as he pleases. But yet when we will enquire what makes the same spirit, man, or person, we must fix the ideas of spirit, man, or person in our minds; and having resolved with ourselves what we mean by them, it will not be hard to determine in either of them, or the like, when it is the same, and when not.

16. But though the same immaterial substance or soul does not alone, wherever it be, and in whatsoever state, make the same man; yet it is plain consciousness, as far as ever it can be extended, should it be to ages past, unites existences and actions, very remote in time, into the same person, as well as it does the existences and actions of the immediately preceding moment; so that whatever has the consciousness of present and past actions is the same person to whom they both belong. Had I the same consciousness that I saw the ark and Noah's flood as that I saw an overflowing of the Thames last winter, or as that I write now; I could no more doubt that I who write this now, that saw the Thames overflowed last winter, and that viewed the flood at the general deluge, was the same self, place that self in what substance you please, than that I who write this am the same *myself* now whilst I write (whether I consist of all the same substance, material or immaterial, or no) that I was yesterday. For as to this point of being the same self, it matters not whether this present self be made up of the same or other substances; I being as much concerned and as justly accountable for any action that was done a thousand years since, appropriated to me now by this self-consciousness, as I am for what I did the last moment.

17. Self is that conscious thinking thing, whatever substance made up of (whether spiritual or material, simple or compounded, it matters not), which is sensible, or conscious of pleasure and pain, capable of happiness or misery, and so is concerned for itself, as far as that consciousness extends. Thus everyone finds that, whilst comprehended under that consciousness, the little finger is as much a part of himself as what is most so. Upon separation of this little finger, should this consciousness go along with the little finger, and leave the rest of the body, it is evident the little finger would be the person, the same person; and self then would have nothing to do with the rest of the body. As in this case it is the consciousness that goes along with the substance, when one part is separate from another, which makes the same person, and constitutes this inseparable self; so it is in reference to substances remote in time. That with which the consciousness of this present thinking thing can join itself makes the same person, and is one self with it, and with nothing else; and so attributes to itself, and owns all the actions of that thing as its own, as far as that consciousness reaches, and no farther; as everyone who reflects will perceive.

18. In this personal identity is founded all the right and justice of reward and punishment; happiness and misery being that for which everyone is concerned for himself, and not mattering what becomes of any substance not joined to or affected with that consciousness. For as it is evident in the instance I gave but now, if the consciousness went along with the little finger when it was cut off, that would be the same self which was concerned for the whole body yesterday, as making part of itself, whose actions then it cannot but admit as its own now. Though if the same body should still live, and immediately, from the separation of the little finger, have its own peculiar consciousness, whereof the little finger knew nothing; it would not at all be concerned for it, as a part of itself, or could own any of its actions, or have any of them imputed to him.

19. This may show us wherein personal identity consists; not in the identity of substance, but, as I have said, in the identity of consciousness; wherein, if Socrates and the present mayor of Queenborough agree, they are the same person: If the same Socrates waking and sleeping do not partake of the same consciousness, Socrates waking and sleeping is not the same person. And to punish Socrates waking for what sleeping Socrates thought, and waking Socrates was never conscious of, would be no more of right than to punish one twin for what his brother-twin did, whereof he knew nothing, because their outsides were so like that they could not be distinguished; for such twins have been seen.

20. But yet possibly it will still be objected, suppose I wholly lose the memory of some parts of my life beyond a possibility of retrieving them, so that perhaps I shall never be conscious of them again; yet am I not the same person that did those actions, had those thoughts that I once was conscious of, though I have now forgot them? To which I answer, that we must here take notice what the word *I* is applied to: which, in this case, is the man only. And the same man being presumed to be the same person, *I* is easily here supposed to stand also for the same person. But if it be possible for the same man to have distinct incommunicable consciousness at different times, it is past doubt the same man would at different times make different persons; which, we see, is the sense of mankind in the solemnest declaration of their opinions, human laws not punishing the mad man for the sober man's actions, nor the sober man for what the mad man did, thereby making them two persons: Which is somewhat explained by our way of speaking in English, when we say such an one is "not himself," or is "beside himself"; in which phrases it is insinuated, as if those who now or at least first used them thought that self was changed, the self-same person was no longer in that man.

21. But yet it is hard to conceive that Socrates, the same individual man, should be two persons. To help us a little in this, we must consider what is meant by Socrates, or the same individual man.

First, it must be either the same individual, immaterial, thinking substance; in short, the same numerical soul, and nothing else.

Secondly, or the same animal, without any regard to an immaterial soul.

Thirdly, or the same immaterial spirit united to the same animal.

Now take which of these suppositions you please, it is impossible to make personal identity to consist in anything but consciousness, or reach any farther than that does.

For by the first of them, it must be allowed possible that a man born of different women, and in distant times, may be the same man. A way of speaking, which whoever admits, must allow it possible for the same man to be two distinct persons, as any two that have lived in different ages, without the knowledge of one another's thoughts.

By the second and third, Socrates in this life, and after it, cannot be the same man any way but by the same consciousness; and so making human identity to consist in the same thing wherein we place personal identity, there will be no difficulty to allow the same man to be the same person. But then they who place human identity in consciousness only, and not in something else, must consider how they will make the infant Socrates the same man with Socrates after the resurrection. But whatsoever to some men makes a man, and consequently the same individual man, wherein perhaps few are agreed, personal identity can by us be placed in nothing but consciousness (which is that alone which makes what we call self) without involving us in great absurdities.

22. But is not a man drunk and sober the same person? Why else is he punished for the fact he commits when drunk, though he be never afterwards conscious of it? Just as much the same person as a man that walks and does other things in his sleep is the same person, and is answerable for any mischief he shall do in it. Human laws punish both, with a justice suitable to their way of knowledge; because in these cases, they cannot distinguish certainly what is real, what counterfeit: And so the ignorance in drunkenness or sleep is not admitted as a plea. For though punishment be annexed to personality, and personality to consciousness, and the drunkard perhaps be not conscious of what he did; yet human judicatures justly punish him, because the fact is proved against him, but want of consciousness cannot be proved for him. But in the great day, wherein the secrets of all hearts shall be laid open, it may be reasonable to think, no one shall be made to answer for what he knows nothing of; but shall receive his doom, his conscience accusing or excusing him.

23. Nothing but consciousness can unite remote existences into the same person; the identity of substance will not do it. For whatever substance there is, however framed, without consciousness there is no person: And a carcase may be a person, as well as any sort of substance be so without consciousness.

Could we suppose two distinct incommunicable consciousnesses acting the same body, the one constantly by day, the other by night; and, on the other side, the same consciousness acting by intervals two distinct bodies: I ask in the first case, whether the day and the night man would not be two as distinct persons as Socrates and Plato? And whether, in the second case, there would not be one person in two distinct bodies, as much as one man is the same in two distinct clothings? Nor is it at all material to say that this same and this distinct consciousness, in the cases above mentioned, is owing to the same and distinct immaterial substances, bringing it with them to those bodies; which, whether true or no, alters not the case: Since it is evident the personal identity would equally be determined by the consciousness, whether that consciousness were annexed to some individual immaterial substance or no. For granting that the thinking substance in man must be necessarily supposed immaterial, it is evident that immaterial thinking thing may sometimes part with its past consciousness, and be restored to it again; as appears in the forgetfulness men often have of their past actions: And the mind many times recovers the memory of a past consciousness, which it had lost for twenty years together. Make these intervals of memory and forgetfulness, to take their turns regularly by day and night, and you have two persons with the same immaterial spirit, as much as in the former instance two persons with the same body. So that self is not determined by identity or diversity of substance, which it cannot be sure of but only by identity of consciousness.

24. Indeed it may conceive the substance whereof it is now made up to have existed formerly, united in the same conscious being: But, consciousness removed, that substance is no more itself, or makes no more a part of it, than any other substance; as is evident in the instance we have already given of a limb cut off, of whose heat, or cold, or other affections, having no longer any consciousness, it is no more of a man's self than any other matter of the universe. In like manner it will be in reference to any immaterial substance, which is void of that consciousness whereby I am myself to myself: If there be any part of its existence which I cannot upon recollection join with that present consciousness whereby I am now myself, it is in that part of its existence no more myself than any other immaterial being. For whatsoever any substance has thought or done, which I cannot recollect, and

by my consciousness make my own thought and action, it will no more belong to me, whether a part of me thought or did it, than if it had been thought or done by any other immaterial being anywhere existing.

25. I agree, the more probable opinion is that this consciousness is annexed to, and the affection of, one individual immaterial substance.

But let men, according to their divers hypotheses, resolve of that as they please, this every intelligent being, sensible of happiness or misery, must grant, that there is something that is himself that he is concerned for, and would have happy: That this self has existed in a continued duration more than one instant, and therefore it is possible may exist, as it has done, months and years to come, without any certain bounds to be set to its duration, and may be the same self, by the same consciousness, continued on for the future. And thus, by this consciousness, he finds himself to be the same self which did such or such an action some years since, by which he comes to be happy or miserable now. In all which account of self, the same numerical substance is not considered as making the same self; but the same continued consciousness, in which several substances may have been united, and again separated from it; which, whilst they continued in a vital union with that, wherein this consciousness then resided, made a part of that same self. Thus any part of our bodies vitally united to that which is conscious in us makes a part of ourselves: But upon separation from the vital union, by which that consciousness is communicated, that which a moment since was part of ourselves, is now no more so than a part of another man's self is a part of me: and it is not impossible but in a little time may become a real part of another person. And so we have the same numerical substance become a part of two different persons; and the same person preserved under the change of various substances. Could we suppose any spirit wholly stripped of all its memory or consciousness of past actions, as we find our minds always are of a great part of ours, and sometimes of them all; the union or separation of such a spiritual substance would make no variation of personal identity, any more than that of any particle of matter does. Any substance vitally united to the present thinking being is a part of that very same self which

now is: Anything united to it by a consciousness of former actions makes also a part of the same self, which is the same both then and now.

26. *Person*, as I take it, is the name for this self. Wherever a man finds what he calls *himself*, there, I think, another may say is the same person. It is a forensic term appropriating actions and their merit; and so belongs only to intelligent agents capable of a law, and happiness and misery. This personality extends itself beyond present existence to what is past only by consciousness, whereby it becomes concerned and accountable, owns and imputes to itself past actions, just upon the same ground and for the same reason that it does the present. All which is founded in a concern for happiness, the unavoidable concomitant of consciousness; that which is conscious of pleasure and pain, desiring that that self that is conscious should be happy. And therefore whatever past actions it cannot reconcile or appropriate to that present self by consciousness, it can be no more concerned in than if they had never been done: And to receive pleasure or pain, i.e. reward or punishment, on the account of any such action is all one as to be made happy or miserable in its first being, without any demerit at all. For supposing a man punished now for what he had done in another life, whereof he could be made to have no consciousness at all, what difference is there between that punishment and being created miserable? And therefore conformable to this the apostle tells us that at the great day, when everyone shall "receive according to his doings, the secrets of all hearts shall be laid open." The sentence shall be justified by the consciousness all persons shall have, that they themselves, in what bodies soever they appear, or what substances soever that consciousness adheres to, are the same that committed those actions, and deserve that punishment for them.

27. I am apt enough to think I have, in treating of this subject, made some suppositions that will look strange to some readers, and possibly they are so in themselves. But yet, I think, they are such as are pardonable in this ignorance we are in of the nature of that thinking thing that is in us, and which we look on as *ourselves*. Did we know what it was, or how it was tied to a certain system of fleeting animal spirits; or whether it could or could not perform

its operations of thinking and memory out of a body organized as ours is; and whether it has pleased God that no one such spirit shall ever be united to any but one such body, upon the right constitution of whose organs its memory should depend, we might see the absurdity of some of those suppositions I have made. But taking, as we ordinarily now do (in the dark concerning these matters), the soul of a man for an immaterial substance, independent from matter, and indifferent alike to it all, there can from the nature of things be no absurdity at all to suppose that the same soul may, at different times, be united to different bodies, and with them make up, for that time, one man: as well as we suppose a part of a sheep's body yesterday should be a part of a man's body to-morrow, and in that union make a vital part of Meliboeus himself, as well as it did of his ram.

28. To conclude: Whatever substance begins to exist, it must, during its existence, necessarily be the same: Whatever compositions of substances begin to exist, during the union of those substances the concrete must be the same: Whatsoever mode begins to exist, during its existence it is the same: And so if the composition be of distinct substances and different modes, the same rule holds. Whereby it will appear that the difficulty or obscurity that has been about this matter rather rises from the names ill used than from any obscurity in things themselves. For whatever makes the specific idea to which the name is applied, if that idea be steadily kept to, the distinction of anything into the same and divers will easily be conceived, and there can arise no doubt about it.

29. For supposing a rational spirit be the idea of a man, it is easy to know what is the same man; viz. the same spirit, whether separate or in a body, will be the same man. Supposing a rational spirit vitally united to a body of a certain conformation of parts to make a man, whilst that rational spirit, with that vital conformation of parts, though continued in a fleeting successive body, remains, it will be the same man. But if to anyone the idea of a man be but the vital union of parts in a certain shape; as long as that vital union and shape remain, in a concrete no otherwise the same but by a continued succession of fleeting particles, it will be the same man. For whatever be the composition whereof the

complex idea is made, whenever existence makes it one particular thing under any denomination, the same existence, continued, preserves it the same individual under the same denomination.

Chapter XXXI. Of Adequate and Inadequate Ideas

1. Of our real ideas, some are adequate, and some are inadequate. Those I call *adequate* which perfectly represent those archetypes which the mind supposes them taken from; which it intends them to stand for, and to which it refers them. *Inadequate* ideas are such which are but a partial or incomplete representation of those archetypes to which they are referred. Upon which account it is plain,

2. First, that all our simple ideas are adequate. Because being nothing but the effects of certain powers in things, fitted and ordained by God to produce such sensations in us, they cannot but be correspondent and adequate to those powers: And we are sure they agree to the reality of things. For if sugar produce in us the ideas which we call whiteness and sweetness, we are sure there is a power in sugar to produce those ideas in our minds, or else they could not have been produced by it. And so each sensation answering the power that operates on any of our senses, the idea so produced is a real idea (and not a fiction of the mind, which has no power to produce any simple idea); and cannot but be adequate, since it ought only to answer that power: And so all simple ideas are adequate. It is true, the things producing in us these simple ideas are but few of them denominated by us as if they were only the causes of them, but as if those ideas were real beings in them. For though fire be called painful to the touch, whereby is signified the power of producing in us the idea of pain, yet it is denominated also light and hot; as if light and heat were really something in the fire more than a power to excite these ideas in us; and therefore are called qualities in or of the fire. But these being nothing, in truth, but powers to excite such ideas in us, I must in that sense be understood, when I speak of secondary qualities, as being in things; or of their ideas, as being the objects that excite them in us. Such ways of speaking, though accommodated to the vulgar notions, without which one cannot be

well understood, yet truly signify nothing but those powers which are in things to excite certain sensations or ideas in us: Since were there no fit organs to receive the impressions fire makes on the sight and touch, nor a mind joined to those organs to receive the ideas of light and heat by those impressions from the fire or sun, there would yet be no more light or heat in the world than there would be pain, if there were no sensible creature to feel it, though the sun should continue just as it is now, and Mount Aetna flame higher than ever it did. Solidity and extension, and the termination of it, figure, with motion and rest, whereof we have the ideas, would be really in the world as they are, whether there were any sensible being to perceive them or no: And therefore we have reason to look on those as the real modifications of matter, and such as are the exciting causes of all our various sensations from bodies. But this being an enquiry not belonging to this place, I shall enter no farther into it, but proceed to show what complex ideas are adequate, and what not.

3. Secondly, our complex ideas of modes, being voluntary collections of simple ideas which the mind puts together without reference to any real archetypes or standing patterns existing anywhere, are and cannot but be adequate ideas. Because they, not being intended for copies of things really existing, but for archetypes made by the mind to rank and denominate things by, cannot want anything, they having each of them that combination of ideas, and thereby that perfection, which the mind intended they should, so that the mind acquiesces in them, and can find nothing wanting. Thus by having the idea of a figure with three sides meeting at three angles, I have a complete idea, wherein I require nothing else to make it perfect. That the mind is satisfied with the perfection of this its idea is plain in that it does not conceive that any understanding hath or can have a more complete or perfect idea of that thing it signifies by the word *triangle,* supposing it to exist, than itself has in that complex idea of three sides and three angles; in which is contained all that is or can be essential to it, or necessary to complete it, wherever or however it exists. But in our ideas of substances it is otherwise. For there desiring to copy things as they really do exist, and to represent to ourselves that constitution on which

all their properties depend, we perceive our ideas attain not that perfection we intend: We find they still want something we should be glad were in them; and so are all inadequate. But mixed modes and relations, being archetypes without patterns, and so having nothing to represent but themselves, cannot but be adequate, every thing being so to itself. He that at first put together the idea of danger perceived, absence of disorder from fear, sedate consideration of what was justly to be done, and executing that without disturbance, or being deterred by the danger of it, had certainly in his mind that complex idea made up of that combination; and intending it to be nothing else but what is, nor to have in it any other simple ideas but what it hath, it could not also but be an adequate idea: And laying this up in his memory, with the name *courage* annexed to it, to signify to others, and denominate from thence any action he should observe to agree with it, had thereby a standard to measure and denominate actions by, as they agreed to it. This idea thus made, and laid up for a pattern, must necessarily be adequate, being referred to nothing else but itself, nor made by any other original but the good-liking and will of him that first made this combination.

4. Indeed another coming after, and in conversation learning from him the word *courage,* may make an idea to which he gives the name *courage,* different from what the first author applied it to and has in his mind when he uses it. And in this case, if he designs that his idea in thinking should be conformable to the other's idea, as the name he uses in speaking is conformable in sound to his, from whom he learned it, his idea may be very wrong and inadequate: Because in this case, making the other man's idea the pattern of his idea in thinking, as the other man's word or sound is the pattern of his in speaking, his idea is so far defective and inadequate as it is distant from the archetype and pattern he refers it to, and intends to express and signify by the name he uses for it; which name he would have to be a sign of the other man's idea (to which, in its proper use, it is primarily annexed) and of his own, as agreeing to it: To which, if his own does not exactly correspond, it is faulty and inadequate.

5. Therefore these complex ideas of modes, when they are referred by the mind, and intended to correspond to the ideas in the mind of some other intelligent being, expressed by the names we apply to them, they may be very deficient, wrong, and inadequate; because they agree not to that which the mind designs to be their archetype and pattern: In which respect only, any idea of modes can be wrong, imperfect, or inadequate. And on this account our ideas of mixed modes are the most liable to be faulty of any other; but this refers more to proper speaking than knowing right.

6. Thirdly, what ideas we have of substances, I have above showed. Now those ideas have in the mind a double reference: (1) Sometimes they are referred to a supposed real essence of each species of things. (2) Sometimes they are only designed to be pictures and representations in the mind of things that do exist by ideas of those qualities that are discoverable in them. In both which ways, these copies of those originals and archetypes are imperfect and inadequate.

First, it is usual for men to make the names of substances stand for things, as supposed to have certain real essences, whereby they are of this or that species: And names standing for nothing but the ideas that are in men's minds, they must constantly refer their ideas to such real essences as to their archetypes. That men (especially such as have been bred up in the learning taught in this part of the world) do suppose certain specific essences of substances, which each individual in its several kinds is made conformable to and partakes of is so far from needing proof that it will be thought strange if anyone should do otherwise. And thus they ordinarily apply the specific names they rank particular substances under to things, as distinguished by such specific real essences. Who is there almost who would not take it amiss if it should be doubted whether he called himself a man with any other meaning than as having the real essence of a man? And yet if you demand what those real essences are, it is plain men are ignorant, and know them not. From whence it follows that the ideas they have in their minds, being referred to real essences, as to archetypes which are unknown, must be so far from being adequate that they cannot be supposed to be any representation of them at all. The complex ideas we have of substances are, as it has been

shown, certain collections of simple ideas that have been observed or supposed constantly to exist together. But such a complex idea cannot be the real essence of any substance; for then the properties we discover in that body would depend on that complex idea, and be deducible from it, and their necessary connexion with it be known; as all properties of a triangle depend on, and, as far as they are discoverable, are deducible from, the complex idea of three lines, including a space. But it is plain that in our complex ideas of substances are not contained such ideas on which all the other qualities that are to be found in them do depend. The common idea men have of iron is a body of a certain colour, weight, and hardness; and a property that they look on as belonging to it is malleableness. But yet this property has no necessary connection with that complex idea, or any part of it; and there is no more reason to think that malleableness depends on that colour, weight, and hardness than that colour or that weight depends on its malleableness. And yet, though we know nothing of these real essences, there is nothing more ordinary than that men should attribute the sorts of things to such essences. The particular parcel of matter which makes the ring I have on my finger is forwardly, by most men, supposed to have a real essence, whereby it is gold; and from whence those qualities flow which I find in it, viz. its peculiar colour, weight, hardness, fusibility, fixedness, and change of colour upon a slight touch of mercury, &c. This essence, from which all these properties flow, when I enquire into it and search after it, I plainly perceive I cannot discover: The farthest I can go is only to presume that it being nothing but body, its real essence or internal constitution, on which these qualities depend, can be nothing but the figure, size, and connexion of its solid parts; of neither of which having any distinct perception at all can I have any idea of its essence, which is the cause that it has that particular shining yellowness, a greater weight than anything I know of the same bulk, and a fitness to have its colour changed by the touch of quicksilver. If anyone will say that the real essence and internal constitution, on which these properties depend, is not the figure, size, and arrangement or connexion of its solid parts, but something else, called its particular form; I am farther from having any idea of its real essence than I was before: For I have an idea of figure, size, and situation of solid parts in general, though I have none of the particular figure, size, or putting together of parts whereby the qualities above-mentioned are produced; which qualities I find in that particular parcel of matter that is on my finger, and not in another parcel of matter with which I cut the pen I write with. But when I am told that something besides the figure, size, and posture of the solid parts of that body is its essence, something called *substantial form,* of that, I confess, I have no idea at all, but only of the sound *form,* which is far enough from an idea of its real essence, or constitution. The like ignorance as I have of the real essence of this particular substance, I have also of the real essence of all other natural ones; of which essences, I confess, I have no distinct ideas at all; and I am apt to suppose others, when they examine their own knowledge, will find in themselves, in this one point, the same sort of ignorance.

7. Now then, when men apply to this particular parcel of matter on my finger a general name already in use, and denominate it *gold,* do they not ordinarily or are they not understood to give it that name as belonging to a particular species of bodies, having a real internal essence; by having of which essence, this particular substance comes to be of that species, and to be called by that name? If it be so, as it is plain it is, the name, by which things are marked, as having that essence, must be referred primarily to that essence; and consequently the idea to which that name is given, must be referred also to that essence, and be intended to represent it. Which essence, since they who so use the names know not, their ideas of substances must be all inadequate in that respect, as not containing in them that real essence which the mind intends they should.

8. Secondly, those who, neglecting that useless supposition of unknown real essences whereby they are distinguished, endeavour to copy the substances that exist in the world by putting together the ideas of those sensible qualities which are found co-existing in them, though they come much nearer a likeness of them than those who imagine they know not what real specific essences; yet they arrive not at perfectly adequate ideas of those substances they would thus copy into their minds; nor do those copies exactly and fully contain all that is to be found in their archetypes. Because those qualities and powers of substances, whereof we make their complex ideas, are so many and various that no man's complex idea contains them all. That our complex ideas of substances do not contain in them all the simple ideas that are united in the things themselves, it is evident, in that men do rarely put into their complex idea of any substance all the simple ideas they do know to exist in it. Because endeavouring to make the signification of their names as clear and as little cumbersome as they can, they make their specific ideas of the sorts of substance, for the most part, of a few of those simple ideas which are to be found in them: But these having no original precedency, or right to be put in, and make the specific idea more than others that are left out, it is plain that both these ways our ideas of substances are deficient and inadequate. The simple ideas, whereof we make our complex ones of substances, are all of them (bating only the figure and bulk of some sorts) powers, which being relations to other substances, we can never be sure that we know all the powers that are in any one body, till we have tried what changes it is fitted to give to or receive from other substances, in their several ways of application: Which being impossible to be tried upon any one body, much less upon all, it is impossible we should have adequate ideas of any substance made up of a collection of all its properties.

9. Whosoever first lighted on a parcel of that sort of substance we denote by the word *gold* could not rationally take the bulk and figure he observed in that lump to depend on its real essence or internal constitution. Therefore those never went into his idea of that species of body; but its peculiar colour, perhaps, and weight were the first he abstracted from it, to make the complex idea of that species. Which both are but powers; the one to affect our eyes after such a manner, and to produce in us that idea we call yellow; and the other to force upwards any other body of equal bulk; they being put into a pair of equal scales, one against another. Another perhaps added to these the ideas of fusibility and fixedness, two other passive powers, in relation to the operation of fire upon it; another, its ductility

and solubility in *aqua regia,* two other powers relating to the operation of other bodies, in changing its outward figure, or separation of it into insensible parts. These, or part of these, put together usually make the complex idea in men's minds of that sort of body we call gold.

10. But no one who hath considered the properties of bodies in general, or this sort in particular, can doubt that this called gold has infinite other properties not contained in that complex idea. Some who have examined this species more accurately could, I believe, enumerate ten times as many properties in gold, all of them as inseparable from its internal constitution as its colour or weight: And it is probable, if anyone knew all the properties that are by divers men known of this metal, there would be an hundred times as many ideas go to the complex idea of gold as any one man yet has in his; and yet perhaps that not be the thousandth part of what is to be discovered in it. The changes that that one body is apt to receive, and make in other bodies, upon a due application, exceeding far not only what we know, but what we are apt to imagine. Which will not appear so much a paradox to anyone who will but consider how far men are yet from knowing all the properties of that one no very compound figure, a triangle; though it be no small number that are already by mathematicians discovered of it.

11. So that all our complex ideas of substances are imperfect and inadequate. Which would be so also in mathematical figures, if we were to have our complex ideas of them only by collecting their properties in reference to other figures. How uncertain and imperfect would our ideas be of an ellipsis, if we had no other idea of it but some few of its properties? Whereas having in our plain idea the whole essence of that figure, we from thence discover those properties, and demonstratively see how they flow, and are inseparable from it.

12. Thus the mind has three sorts of abstract ideas or nominal essences:

First, simple ideas, which are ⟨*ektupa*⟩, or copies; but yet certainly adequate. Because being intended to express nothing but the power in things to produce in the mind such a sensation, that sensation, when it is produced, cannot but be the effect of that power. So the paper I write on, having the power, in the light (I speak according to the common notion of light), to produce in men the sensation which I call white, it cannot but be the effect of such a power, in something without the mind; since the mind has not the power to produce any such idea in itself; and being meant for nothing else but the effect of such a power, that simple idea is real and adequate; the sensation of white, in my mind, being the effect of that power which is in the paper to produce it, is perfectly adequate to that power; or else, that power would produce a different idea.

13. Secondly, the complex ideas of substances are ectypes, copies too; but not perfect ones, not adequate: Which is very evident to the mind, in that it plainly perceives that whatever collection of simple ideas it makes of any substance that exists, it cannot be sure that it exactly answers all that are in that substance: Since not having tried all the operations of all other substances upon it, and found all the alterations it would receive from, or cause in, other substances, it cannot have an exact adequate collection of all its active and passive capacities; and so not have an adequate complex idea of the powers of any substance existing, and its relations, which is that sort of complex idea of substances we have. And after all, if we would have, and actually had, in our complex idea, an exact collection of all the secondary qualities or powers of any substance, we should not yet thereby have an idea of the essence of that thing. For since the powers or qualities that are observable by us are not the real essence of that substance, but depend on it, and flow from it, any collection whatsoever of these qualities cannot be the real essence of that thing. Whereby it is plain that our ideas of substances are not adequate; are not what the mind intends them to be. Besides, a man has no idea of substance in general, nor knows what substance is in itself.

14. Thirdly, complex ideas of modes and relations are originals, and archetypes; are not copies, nor made after the pattern of any real existence, to which the mind intends them to be conformable, and exactly to answer. These being such collections of simple ideas that the mind itself puts together, and such collections that each of them contains in it precisely all that the mind intends that it should, they are archetypes and essences of modes that may exist; and so are designed only for, and belong only to, such modes as, when they do exist, have an exact conformity with those complex ideas. The ideas therefore of modes and relations cannot but be adequate.

Book III. Of Words

Chapter I. Of Words or Language in General

Sections

Chapter II. Of the Signification of Words

Sections

Chapter III. Of General Terms

Sections

Chapter IV. Of the Names of Simple Ideas

Sections

Chapter V. Of the Names of Mixed Modes and Relations

Sections

Chapter VI. Of the Names of Substances

Sections

Chapter VII. Of Particles

Sections

Chapter VIII. Of Abstract and Concrete Terms

Sections

Book III. *Of Words*

Chapter I. *Of Words or Language in General*

1. God, having designed man for a sociable creature, made him not only with an inclination and under a necessity to have fellowship with those of his own kind; but furnished him also with language, which was to be the great instrument and common tie of society. Man therefore had by nature his organs so fashioned as to be fit to frame articulate sounds, which we call words. But this was not enough to produce language; for parrots, and several other birds, will be taught to make articulate sounds distinct enough, which yet, by no means, are capable of language.

2. Besides articulate sounds, therefore, it was farther necessary that he should be able to use these sounds as signs of internal conceptions; and to make them stand as marks for the ideas within his own mind, whereby they might be made known to others, and the thoughts of men's minds be conveyed from one to another.

3. But neither was this sufficient to make words so useful as they ought to be. It is not enough for the perfection of language that sounds can be made signs of ideas, unless those signs can be so made use of as to comprehend several particular things; for the multiplication of words would have perplexed their use, had every particular thing need of a distinct name to be signified by. To remedy this inconvenience, language had yet a farther improvement in the use of general terms, whereby one word was made to mark a multitude of particular existences: Which advantageous use of sounds was obtained only by the difference of the ideas they were made signs of, those names becoming general which are made to stand for general ideas, and those remaining particular where the ideas they are used for are particular.

4. Besides these names which stand for ideas, there be other words which men make use of, not to signify any idea, but the want or absence of some ideas simple or complex, or all ideas together; such as are *nihil* in Latin, and in English, *ignorance* and *barrenness*. All which negative or privitive words cannot be said properly to belong to or signify no ideas: For then they would be perfectly insignificant sounds; but they relate to positive ideas and signify their absence.

5. It may also lead us a little towards the original of all our notions and knowledge if we remark how great a dependence our words have on common sensible ideas: And how those which are made use of to stand for actions and notions quite re-

moved from sense have their rise from thence, and from obvious sensible ideas are transferred to more abstruse significations; and made to stand for ideas that come not under the cognizance of our senses: v.g. *to imagine, apprehend, comprehend, adhere, conceive, instill, disgust, disturbance, tranquillity,* &c., are all words taken from the operations of sensible things, and applied to certain modes of thinking. *Spirit,* in its primary signification, is breath; *angel* a messenger: And I doubt not but if we could trace them to their sources, we should find, in all languages, the names which stand for things that fall not under our senses to have had their first rise from sensible ideas. By which we may give some kind of guess what kind of notions they were, and whence derived, which filled their minds who were the first beginners of languages: And how nature, even in the naming of things, unawares suggested to men the originals and principles of all their knowledge: Whilst, to give names that might make known to others any operations they felt in themselves, or any other ideas that came not under their senses, they were fain to borrow words from ordinary known ideas of sensation, by that means to make others the more easily to conceive those operations they experimented in themselves which made no outward sensible appearances; and then when they had got known and agreed names, to signify those internal operations of their own minds, they were sufficiently furnished to make known by words all their other ideas; since they could consist of nothing but either of outward sensible perceptions or of the inward operations of their minds about them: We having, as has been proved, no ideas at all but what originally come either from sensible objects without or what we feel within ourselves, from the inward workings of our own spirits, of which we are conscious to ourselves within.

6. But to understand better the use and force of language as subservient to instruction and knowledge, it will be convenient to consider,

First, To what it is that names, in the use of language, are immediately applied.

Secondly, Since all (except proper) names are general, and so stand not particularly for this or that single thing, but for sorts and ranks of things, it will be necessary to consider, in the next place, what the sorts and kinds, or, if you rather like the Latin names, what the species and genera of things are, wherein they consist, and how they come to be made. These being (as they ought) well looked into, we shall the better come to find the right use of words, the natural advantages and defects of language, and the remedies that ought to be used, to avoid the inconveniences of obscurity or uncertainty in the signification of words, without which it is impossible to discourse with any clearness, or order, concerning knowledge: Which being conversant about propositions, and those most commonly universal ones, has greater connexion with words than perhaps is suspected.

These considerations therefore shall be the matter of the following chapters.

Chapter II. Of the Signification of Words

1. Man, though he has great variety of thoughts, and such, from which others, as well as himself, might receive profit and delight; yet they are all within his own breast, invisible and hidden from others, nor can of themselves be made to appear. The comfort and advantage of society not being to be had without communication of thoughts, it was necessary that man should find out some external sensible signs whereof those invisible ideas, which his thoughts are made up for, might be made known to others. For this purpose nothing was so fit, either for plenty or quickness, as those articulate sounds which with so much ease and variety he found himself able to make. Thus we may conceive how words which were by nature so well adapted to that purpose came to be made use of by men, as the signs of their ideas; not by any natural connexion that there is between particular articulate sounds and certain ideas, for then there would be but one language amongst all men; but by a voluntary imposition, whereby such a word is made arbitrarily the mark of such an idea. The use then of words is to be sensible marks of ideas; and the ideas they stand for are their proper and immediate signification.

2. The use men have of these marks being either to record their own thoughts for the assistance of their own memory, or, as it were, to bring out their ideas, and lay them before the view of others; words in their primary or immediate signification stand for nothing but the ideas in the mind of him that uses them, how imperfectly soever or carelessly those ideas are collected from the things which they are supposed to represent. When a man speaks to another, it is that he may be understood; and the end of speech is that those sounds, as marks, may make known his ideas to the hearer. That then which words are the marks of are the ideas of the speaker: Nor can anyone apply them as marks immediately to anything else but the ideas that he himself hath. For this would be to make them signs of his own conceptions, and yet apply them to other ideas; which would be to make them signs, and not signs, of his ideas at the same time; and so in effect to have no signification at all. Words being voluntary signs, they cannot be voluntary signs imposed by him on things he knows not. That would be to make them signs of nothing, sounds without signification. A man cannot make his words the signs either of qualities in things, or of conceptions in the mind of another, whereof he has none in his own. Till he has some ideas of his own, he cannot suppose them to correspond with the conceptions of another man; nor can he use any signs for them: For thus they would be the signs of he knows not what, which is in truth to be the signs of nothing. But when he represents to himself other men's ideas by some of his own, if he consent to give them the same names that other men do, it is still to his own ideas; to ideas that he has, and not to ideas that he has not.

3. This is so necessary in the use of language that in this respect the knowing and the ignorant, the learned and the unlearned, use the words they speak (with any meaning) all alike. They, in every man's mouth, stand for the ideas he has, and which he would express by them. A child having taken notice of nothing in the metal he hears called gold but the bright shining yellow colour, he applies the word *gold* only to his own idea of that colour, and nothing else; and therefore calls the same colour in a peacock's tail gold. Another that hath better observed adds to shining yellow great weight: And then the sound *gold* when he uses it stands for a complex idea of a shining yellow and very weighty substance. Another adds to those qualities fusibility; and then the word *gold* signifies to him a body, bright, yellow, fusible, and very heavy. Another adds malleability. Each of these uses equally the word *gold* when they have occasion to express the idea which they have applied it to: But it is evident that each can apply it only to his own idea; nor can he make it stand as a sign of such a complex idea as he has not.

4. But though words as they are used by men can properly and immediately signify nothing but the ideas that are in the mind of the speaker, yet they in their thoughts give them a secret reference to two other things.

First, They suppose their words to be marks of the ideas in the minds also of other men, with whom they communicate: For else they should talk in vain, and could not be understood, if the sounds they applied to one idea were such as by the hearer were applied to another: Which is to speak two languages. But in this, men stand not usually to examine whether the idea they and those they discourse with have in their minds be the same; but think it enough that they use the word, as they imagine, in the common acceptation of that language; in which they suppose that the idea they make it a sign of is precisely the same to which the understanding men of that country apply that name.

5. Secondly, Because men would not be thought to talk barely of their own imagination, but of things as really they are; therefore they often suppose the words to stand also for the reality of things. But this relating more particularly to substances, and their names, as perhaps the former does to simple ideas and modes, we shall speak of these two different ways of applying words more at large, when we come to treat of the names of fixed modes, and substances in particular: Though give me leave here to say that it is a perverting the use of words, and brings unavoidable obscurity and confusion into their signification, whenever we make them stand for anything but those ideas we have in our own minds.

6. Concerning words also it is farther to be considered: First, that they being immediately the signs of men's ideas, and by that means the instruments whereby men communicate their conceptions, and express to one another those thoughts and imaginations they have within their own breasts; there comes by constant use to be such a connexion between certain sounds and the ideas they stand for that the names heard almost as readily excite certain ideas as if the objects themselves, which are apt to produce them, did actually affect the senses. Which is manifestly so in all obvious sensible qualities;

and in all substances that frequently and familiarly occur to us.

7. Secondly, That though the proper and immediate signification of words are ideas in the mind of the speaker, yet because by familiar use from our cradles we come to learn certain articulate sounds very perfectly, and have them readily on our tongues, and always at hand in our memories, but yet are not always careful to examine, or settle their significations perfectly; it often happens that men, even when they would apply themselves to an attentive consideration, do set their thoughts more on words than things. Nay, because words are many of them learned before the ideas are known for which they stand; therefore some, not only children, but men, speak several words no otherwise than parrots do, only because they have learned them, and have been accustomed to those sounds. But so far as words are of use and signification, so far is there a constant connexion between the sound and the idea, and a designation that the one stands for the other; without which application of them, they are nothing but so much insignificant noise.

8. Words by long and familiar use, as has been said, come to excite in men certain ideas so constantly and readily that they are apt to suppose a natural connexion between them. But that they signify only men's peculiar ideas, and that by a perfect arbitrary imposition, is evident in that they often fail to excite in others (even that use the same language) the same ideas we take them to be signs of: And every man has so inviolable a liberty to make words stand for what ideas he pleases that no one hath the power to make others have the same ideas in their minds that he has, when they use the same words that he does. And therefore the great Augustus himself, in the possession of that power which ruled the world, acknowledged he could not make a new Latin word: Which was as much as to say that he could not arbitrarily appoint what idea any sound should be a sign of, in the mouths and common language of his subjects. It is true, common use by a tacit consent appropriates certain sounds to certain ideas in all languages, which so far limits the signification of that sound that unless a man applies it to the same idea, he does not speak properly: And let me add that unless a man's words excite the same ideas in the hearer which he makes them stand for in speaking, he does not speak intelligibly. But whatever be the consequence of any man's using of words differently, either from their general meaning or the particular sense of the person to whom he addresses them, this is certain, their signification, in his use of them, is limited to his ideas, and they can be signs of nothing else.

Chapter III. Of General Terms

1. All things that exist being particulars, it may perhaps be thought reasonable that words, which ought to be conformed to things, should be so too; I mean in their signification: But yet we find the quite contrary. The far greatest part of words, that make all languages, are general terms; which has not been the effect of neglect or chance, but of reason and necessity.

2. First, It is impossible that every particular thing should have a distinct peculiar name. For the signification and use of words, depending on that connexion which the mind makes between its ideas and the sounds it uses as signs of them, it is necessary, in the application of names to things, that the mind should have distinct ideas of the things, and retain also the particular name that belongs to every one, with its peculiar appropriation to that idea. But it is beyond the power of human capacity to frame and retain distinct ideas of all the particular things we meet with: Every bird and beast men saw, every tree and plant that affected the senses, could not find a place in the most capacious understanding. If it be looked on as an instance of a prodigious memory that some generals have been able to call every soldier in their army by his proper name, we may easily find a reason why men have never attempted to give names to each sheep in their flock, or crow that flies over their heads; much less to call every leaf of plants, or grain of sand that came in their way, by a peculiar name.

3. Secondly, If it were possible, it would yet be useless; because it would not serve to the chief end of language. Men would in vain heap up names of particular things, that would not serve them to communicate their thoughts. Men learn names, and use them in talk with others, only that they may be understood: Which is then only done when by use or consent the sound I make by the organs of speech

excites in another man's mind, who hears it, the idea I apply it to in mine, when I speak it. This cannot be done by names applied to particular things, whereof I alone having the ideas in my mind, the names of them could not be significant or intelligible to another, who was not acquainted with all those very particular things which had fallen under my notice.

4. Thirdly, But yet granting this also feasible (which I think is not), yet a distinct name for every particular thing would not be of any great use for the improvement of knowledge: Which, though founded in particular things, enlarges itself by general views: To which things reduced into sorts, under general names, are properly subservient. These, with the names belonging to them, come within some compass, and do not multiply every moment, beyond what either the mind can contain, or use requires: And therefore, in these, men have for the most part stopped; but yet not so as to hinder themselves from distinguishing particular things, by appropriated names, where convenience demands it. And therefore in their own species, which they have most to do with, and wherein they have often occasion to mention particular persons, they make use of proper names; and there distinct individuals have distinct denominations.

5. Besides persons, countries also, cities, rivers, mountains, and other the like distinctions of place have usually found peculiar names, and that for the same reason; they being such as men have often an occasion to mark particularly, and, as it were, set before others in their discourses with them. And I doubt not but if we had reason to mention particular horses as often as we have to mention particular men, we should have proper names for the one as familiar as for the other; and Bucephalus would be a word as much in use as Alexander. And therefore we see that, amongst jockeys, horses have their proper names to be known and distinguished by, as commonly as their servants; because, amongst them, there is often occasion to mention this or that particular horse, when he is out of sight.

6. The next thing to be considered is, how general words come to be made. For since all things that exist are only particulars, how come we by general terms, or where find we those general natures they are supposed to stand for? Words become general by being made the signs of general ideas; and ideas become general by separating from them the circumstances of time, and place, and any other ideas that may determine them to this or that particular existence. By this way of abstraction they are made capable of representing more individuals than one; each of which, having in it a conformity to that abstract idea, is (as we call it) of that sort.

7. But to deduce this a little more distinctly, it will not perhaps be amiss to trace our notions and names from their beginning, and observe by what degrees we proceed, and by what steps we enlarge our ideas from our first infancy. There is nothing more evident than that the ideas of the persons children converse with (to instance in them alone) are like the persons themselves, only particular. The ideas of the nurse, and the mother, are well framed in their minds; and, like pictures of them there, represent only those individuals. The names they first gave to them are confined to these individuals; and the names of *nurse* and *mamma* the child uses determine themselves to those persons. Afterwards, when time and a larger acquaintance have made them observe that there are a great many other things in the world that in some common agreements of shape, and several other qualities, resemble their father and mother, and those persons they have been used to, they frame an idea, which they find those many particulars do partake in; and to that they give, with others, the name *man,* for example. And thus they come to have a general name, and a general idea. Wherein they make nothing new, but only leave out of the complex idea they had of Peter and James, Mary and Jane, that which is peculiar to each, and retain only what is common to them all.

8. By the same way that they come by the general name and idea of man, they easily advance to more general names and notions. For observing that several things that differ from their idea of man, and cannot therefore be comprehended under that name, have yet certain qualities wherein they agree with man, by retaining only those qualities, and uniting them into one idea, they have again another and more general idea; to which having given a name, they make a term of a more comprehensive extension: Which new idea is made, not by any new

addition, but only, as before, by leaving out the shape and some other properties signified by the name *man,* and retaining only a body, with life, sense, and spontaneous motion, comprehended under the name *animal.*

9. That this is the way whereby men first formed general ideas, and general names to them, I think, is so evident that there needs no other proof of it but the considering of a man's self, or others, and the ordinary proceedings of their minds in knowledge: And he that thinks general natures or notions are anything else but such abstract and partial ideas of more complex ones, taken at first from particular existences, will, I fear, be at a loss where to find them. For let anyone reflect, and then tell me, wherein does his idea of man differ from that of Peter and Paul, or his idea of horse from that of Bucephalus, but in the leaving out something that is peculiar to each individual, and retaining so much of those particular complex ideas of several particular existences as they are found to agree in? Of the complex ideas signified by the names *man* and *horse,* leaving out but those particulars wherein they differ, and retaining only those wherein they agree, and of those making a new distinct complex idea, and giving the name *animal* to it; one has a more general term, that comprehends with man several other creatures. Leave out of the idea of animal sense and spontaneous motion; and the remaining complex idea, made up of the remaining simple ones of body, life, and nourishment, becomes a more general one, under the more comprehensive term *vivens.* And not to dwell longer upon this particular, so evident in itself, by the same way the mind proceeds to *body, substance,* and at last to *being, thing,* and such universal terms which stand for any of our ideas whatsoever. To conclude, this whole mystery of genera and species, which make such a noise in the schools, and are with justice so little regarded out of them, is nothing else but abstract ideas, more or less comprehensive, with names annexed to them. In all which this is constant and unvariable, that every more general term stands for such an idea, and is but a part of any of those contained under it.

10. This may show us the reason why, in the defining of words, which is nothing but declaring their significations, we make use of the genus, or

next general word that comprehends it. Which is not out of necessity, but only to save the labour of enumerating the several simple ideas which the next general word or genus stands for; or, perhaps, sometimes the shame of not being able to do it. But though defining by genus and differentia (I crave leave to use these terms of art, though originally Latin, since they most properly suit those notions they are applied to), I say, though defining by the genus be the shortest way, yet I think it may be doubted whether it be the best. This I am sure, it is not the only, and so not absolutely necessary. For definition being nothing but making another understand by words what idea the term defined stands for, a definition is best made by enumerating those simple ideas that are combined in the signification of the term defined; and if instead of such an enumeration, men have accustomed themselves to use the next general term, it has not been out of necessity, or for greater clearness, but for quickness and dispatch sake. For, I think, that to one who desired to know what idea the word *man* stood for, if it should be said that man was a solid extended substance, having life, sense, spontaneous motion, and the faculty of reasoning: I doubt not but the meaning of the term *man* would be as well understood, and the idea it stands for be at least as clearly made known, as when it is defined to be a rational animal; which by the several definitions of *animal, vivens,* and *corpus,* resolves itself into those enumerated ideas. I have, in explaining the term *man,* followed here the ordinary definition of the schools, which though perhaps not the most exact, yet serves well enough to my present purpose. And one may, in this instance, see what gave occasion to the rule, that a definition must consist of genus and differentia; and it suffices to show us the little necessity there is of such a rule, or advantage in the strict observing of it. For definitions, as has been said, being only the explaining of one word by several others, so that the meaning or idea it stands for may be certainly known; languages are not always so made according to the rules of logic, that every term can have its signification exactly and clearly expressed by two others. Experience sufficiently satisfies us to the contrary: Or else those who have made this rule have done ill, that they have given us so few definitions conformable to it. But of definitions more in the next chapter.

11. To return to general words, it is plain by what has been said that general and universal belong not to the real existence of things, but are the inventions and creatures of the understanding, made by it for its own use, and concern only signs, whether words or ideas. Words are general, as has been said, when used for signs of general ideas, and so are applicable indifferently to many particular things: And ideas are general when they are set up as the representatives of many particular things: But universality belongs not to things themselves, which are all of them particular in their existence; even those words and ideas which in their signification are general. When therefore we quit particulars, the generals that rest are only creatures of our own making, their general nature being nothing but the capacity they are put into by the understanding, of signifying or representing many particulars. For the signification they have is nothing but a relation that by the mind of man is added to them.

12. The next thing therefore to be considered is, what kind of signification it is that general words have. For as it is evident that they do not signify barely one particular thing, for then they would not be general terms, but proper names; so on the other side it is as evident they do not signify a plurality; for *man* and *men* would then signify the same, and the distinction of numbers (as the grammarians call them) would be superfluous and useless. That then which general words signify is a sort of things; and each of them does that, by being a sign of an abstract idea in the mind, to which idea, as things existing are found to agree, so they come to be ranked under that name; or, which is all one, be of that sort. Whereby it is evident that the essences of the sorts or (if the Latin word pleases better) species of things are nothing else but these abstract ideas. For the having the essence of any species, being that which makes anything to be of that species, and the conformity to the idea to which the name is annexed, being that which gives a right to that name; the having the essence, and the having that conformity, must needs be the same thing: Since to be of any species, and to have a right to the name of that species, is all one. As for example, to be a man, or of the species man, and to have right to the name *man,* is the same thing. Again, to be a man, or of the species man, and have the essence of a man, is the same thing. Now since nothing can be a man, or have a right to the name *man,* but what has a conformity to the abstract idea the name *man* stands for; nor anything be a man, or have a right to the species man, but what has the essence of that species; it follows that the abstract idea for which the name stands, and the essence of the species, is one and the same. From whence it is easy to observe that the essences of the sorts of things, and consequently the sorting of things, is the workmanship of the understanding, that abstracts and makes those general ideas.

13. I would not here be thought to forget, much less to deny, that nature in the production of things makes several of them alike: There is nothing more obvious, especially in the races of animals, and all things propagated by seed. But yet, I think, we may say the sorting of them under names is the workmanship of the understanding, taking occasion from the similitude it observes amongst them to make abstract general ideas, and set them up in the mind, with names annexed to them as patterns or forms (for in that sense the word *form* has a very proper signification) to which as particular things existing are found to agree, so they come to be of that species, have that denomination, or are put into that *classis.* For when we say, this is a man, that a horse; this justice, that cruelty; this a watch, that a jack; what do we else but rank things under different specific names, as agreeing to those abstract ideas of which we have made those names the signs? And what are the essences of those species set out and marked by names but those abstract ideas in the mind; which are, as it were, the bonds between particular things that exist and the names they are to be ranked under? And when general names have any connexion with particular beings, these abstract ideas are the medium that unites them: So that the essences of species, as distinguished and denominated by us, neither are nor can be anything but these precise abstract ideas we have in our minds. And therefore the supposed real essences of substances, if different from our abstract ideas, cannot be the essences of the species we rank things into. For two species may be one as rationally as two different essences be the essence of one species; and I demand what are the alterations which may or may not be made in a horse or lead, without making either of them to be of another species? In

determining the species of things by our abstract ideas, this is easy to resolve: But if anyone will regulate himself herein by supposed real essences, he will, I suppose, be at a loss; and he will never be able to know when anything precisely ceases to be of the species of a horse or lead.

14. Nor will anyone wonder that I say these essences, or abstract ideas (which are the measures of name, and the boundaries of species), are the workmanship of the understanding, who considers that at least the complex ones are often, in several men, different collections of simple ideas: And therefore that is covetousness to one man, which is not so to another. Nay, even in substances, where their abstract ideas seem to be taken from the things themselves, they are not constantly the same; no, not in that species which is most familiar to us, and with which we have the most intimate acquaintance: It having been more than once doubted whether the foetus born of a woman were a man; even so far as that it hath been debated whether it were or were not to be nourished and baptized: Which could not be, if the abstract idea or essence to which the name *man* belonged were of nature's making; and were not the uncertain and various collection of simple ideas, which the understanding put together, and then abstracting it, affixed a name to it. So that, in truth, every distinct abstract idea is a distinct essence: And the names that stand for such distinct ideas are the names of things essentially different. Thus a circle is as essentially different from an oval as a sheep from a goat: And rain is as essentially different from snow as water from earth; that abstract idea which is the essence of one being impossible to be communicated to the other. And thus any two abstract ideas, that in any part vary one from another, with two distinct names annexed to them, constitute two distinct sorts, or, if you please, species, as essentially different as any two of the most remote or opposite in the world.

15. But since the essences of things are thought, by some (and not without reason), to be wholly unknown, it may not be amiss to consider the several significations of the word *essence.*

First, essence may be taken for the very being of anything, whereby it is what it is. And thus the real internal, but generally in substances unknown, constitution of things, whereon their discoverable qualities depend, may be called their essence. This is the proper original signification of the word, as is evident from the formation of it; *essentia*, in its primary notation, signifying properly being. And in this sense it is still used when we speak of the essence of particular things without giving them any name.

Secondly, the learning and disputes of the schools having been much busied about *genus* and *species*, the word *essence* has almost lost its primary signification, and instead of the real constitution of things, has been almost wholly applied to the artificial constitution of genus and species. It is true, there is ordinarily supposed a real constitution of the sorts of things; and it is past doubt, there must be some real constitution, on which any collection of simple ideas co-existing must depend. But it being evident that things are ranked under names into sorts or species only as they agree to certain abstract ideas to which we have annexed those names, the essence of each genus, or sort, comes to be nothing but that abstract idea which the general, or *sortal* (if I may have leave so to call it from *sort*, as I do *general* from *genus*) name stands for. And this we shall find to be that which the word *essence* imports in its most familiar use. These two sorts of essences, I suppose, may not unfitly be termed, the one the *real*, the other the *nominal*, essence.

16. Between the nominal essence and the name, there is so near a connexion that the name of any sort of things cannot be attributed to any particular being but what has this essence, whereby it answers that abstract idea whereof that name is the sign.

17. Concerning the real essences of corporeal substances (to mention these only), there are, if I mistake not, two opinions. The one is of those who, using the word *essence* for they know not what, suppose a certain number of those essences, according to which all natural things are made, and wherein they do exactly every one of them partake, and so become of this or that species. The other and more rational opinion is of those who look on all natural things to have a real but unknown constitution of their insensible parts; from which flow those sensible qualities which serve us to distinguish them one from another, according as we have occasion to rank them into sorts under common de-

nominations. The former of these opinions, which supposes these essences as a certain number of forms or moulds, wherein all natural things that exist are cast, and do equally partake, has, I imagine, very much perplexed the knowledge of natural things. The frequent productions of monsters, in all the species of animals, and of changelings, and other strange issues of human birth, carry with them difficulties not possible to consist with this hypothesis: Since it is as impossible that two things partaking exactly of the same real essence should have different properties as that two figures partaking of the same real essence of a circle should have different properties. But were there no other reason against it, yet the supposition of essences that cannot be known, and the making of them nevertheless to be that which distinguishes the species of things, is so wholly useless, and unserviceable to any part of our knowledge, that that alone were sufficient to make us lay it by, and content ourselves with such essences of the sorts or species of things as come within the reach of our knowledge: Which, when seriously considered, will be found, as I have said, to be nothing else but those abstract complex ideas to which we have annexed distinct general names.

18. Essences being thus distinguished into nominal and real, we may farther observe that in the species of simple ideas and modes, they are always the same; but in substances always quite different. Thus a figure including a space between three lines is the real as well as nominal essence of a triangle; it being not only the abstract idea to which the general name is annexed, but the very *essentia* or being of the thing itself, that foundation from which all its properties flow, and to which they are all inseparably annexed. But it is far otherwise concerning that parcel of matter which makes the ring on my finger, wherein these two essences are apparently different. For it is the real constitution of its insensible parts, on which depend all those properties of colour, weight, fusibility, fixedness, &c. which are to be found in it, which constitution we know not, and so having no particular idea of, have no name that is the sign of it. But yet it is its colour, weight, fusibility, fixedness, &c. which makes it to be gold, or gives it a right to that name, which is therefore its nominal essence: Since nothing can be called gold but what has a conformity of qualities to that abstract complex idea to which that name is annexed. But this distinction of essences belonging particularly to substances, we shall, when we come to consider their names, have an occasion to treat of more fully.

19. That such abstract ideas, with names to them, as we have been speaking of, are essences may farther appear by what we are told concerning essences, viz. that they are all ingenerable and incorruptible. Which cannot be true of the real constitutions of things which begin and perish with them. All things that exist, besides their author, are all liable to change; especially those things we are acquainted with, and have ranked into bands under distinct names or ensigns. Thus that which was grass to-day is to-morrow the flesh of a sheep; and within a few days after becomes part of a man: In all which and the like changes, it is evident their real essence, i.e. that constitution, whereon the properties of these several things depended, is destroyed and perishes with them. But essences being taken for ideas, established in the mind, with names annexed to them, they are supposed to remain steadily the same, whatever mutations the particular substances are liable to. For whatever becomes of Alexander and Bucephalus, the ideas to which *man* and *horse* are annexed are supposed nevertheless to remain the same; and so the essences of those species are preserved whole and undestroyed, whatever changes happen to any or all of the individuals of those species. By this means the essence of a species rests safe and entire, without the existence of so much as one individual of that kind. For were there now no circle existing anywhere in the world (as perhaps that figure exists not anywhere exactly marked out), yet the idea annexed to that name would not cease to be what it is; nor cease to be as a pattern to determine which of the particular figures we meet with have or have not a right to the name *circle,* and so to show which of them by having that essence was of that species. And though there neither were nor had been in nature such a beast as an unicorn, or such a fish as a mermaid; yet supposing those names to stand for complex abstract ideas that contained no inconsistency in them, the essence of a mermaid is as intelligible as that of a man; and the idea of an unicorn as certain, steady, and permanent as that of a horse.

From what has been said it is evident that the doctrine of the immutability of essences proves them to be only abstract ideas; and is founded on the relation established between them, and certain sounds as signs of them; and will always be true as long as the same name can have the same signification.

20. To conclude, this is that which in short I would say, viz. that all the great business of genera and species, and their essences, amounts to no more but this, That men making abstract ideas, and settling them in their minds with names annexed to them, do thereby enable themselves to consider things and discourse of them, as it were, in bundles, for the easier and readier improvement and communication of their knowledge; which would advance but slowly were their words and thoughts confined only to particulars.

Chapter IV. Of the Names of Simple Ideas

1. Though all words, as I have shown, signify nothing immediately but the ideas in the mind of the speaker; yet upon a nearer survey we shall find the names of simple ideas, mixed modes (under which I comprise relations too), and natural substances have each of them something peculiar and different from the other. For example:

2. First, The names of simple ideas and substances, with the abstract ideas in the mind which they immediately signify, intimate also some real existence, from which was derived their original pattern. But the names of mixed modes terminate in the idea that is in the mind, and lead not the thoughts any farther, as we shall see more at large in the following chapter.

3. Secondly, The names of simple ideas and modes signify always the real as well as nominal essence of their species. But the names of natural substances signify rarely, if ever, anything but barely the nominal essences of those species; as we shall show in the chapter that treats of the names of substances in particular.

4. Thirdly, The names of simple ideas are not capable of any definition; the names of all complex ideas are. It has not, that I know, been yet observed by anybody what words are and what are not capable of being defined; the want whereof is (as I

am apt to think) not seldom the occasion of great wrangling and obscurity in men's discourses, whilst some demand definitions of terms that cannot be defined; and others think they ought not to rest satisfied in an explication made by a more general word, and its restriction (or to speak in terms of art, by a genus and difference), when even after such definition made according to rule, those who hear it have often no more a clear conception of the meaning of the word than they had before. This at least I think, that the showing what words are and what are not capable of definitions, and wherein consists a good definition, is not wholly besides our present purpose; and perhaps will afford so much light to the nature of these signs, and our ideas, as to deserve a more particular consideration.

5. I will not here trouble myself to prove that all terms are not definable from that progress *in infinitum,* which it will visibly lead us into, if we should allow that all names could be defined. For if the terms of one definition were still to be defined by another, where at last should we stop? But I shall from the nature of our ideas, and the signification of our words, show why some names can and others cannot be defined, and which they are.

6. I think it is agreed that a definition is nothing else but the showing the meaning of one word by several other not synonymous terms. The meaning of words being only the ideas they are made to stand for by him that uses them, the meaning of any term is then showed, or the word is defined, when by other words the idea it is made the sign of, and annexed to, in the mind of the speaker is, as it were, represented, or set before the view of another; and thus its signification ascertained: This is the only use and end of definitions; and therefore the only measure of what is or is not a good definition.

7. This being premised, I say, that the names of simple ideas and those only are incapable of being defined. The reason whereof is this, that the several terms of a definition, signifying several ideas, they can all together by no means represent an idea, which has no composition at all: And therefore definition, which is properly nothing but the showing the meaning of one word by several others not signifying each the same thing, can in the names of simple ideas have no place.

8. The not observing this difference in our ideas, and their names, has produced that eminent trifling in the schools, which is so easy to be observed in the definitions they give us of some few of these simple ideas. For as to the greatest part of them, even those masters of definitions were fain to leave them untouched, merely by the impossibility they found in it. What more exquisite jargon could the wit of man invent than this definition, "The act of a being in power, as far forth as in power"? Which would puzzle any rational man, to whom it was not already known by its famous absurdity, to guess what word it could ever be supposed to be the explication of. If Tully, asking a Dutchman what *beweeginge* was, should have received this explication in his own language, that it was "*actus entis in potentia quatenus in potentia*"; I ask whether anyone can imagine he could thereby have understood what the word *beweeginge* signified, or have guessed what idea a Dutchman ordinarily had in his mind, and would signify to another, when he used that sound.

9. Nor have the modern philosophers, who have endeavoured to throw off the jargon of the schools, and speak intelligibly, much better succeeded in defining simple ideas, whether by explaining their causes, or any otherwise. The atomists, who define *motion* to be a passage from one place to another, what do they more than put one synonymous word for another? For what is *passage* other than motion? And if they were asked what *passage* was, how would they better define it than by motion? For is it not at least as proper and significant to say, passage is a motion from one place to another, as to say, motion is a passage, &c.? This is to translate, and not to define, when we change two words of the same signification one for another; which, when one is better understood than the other, may serve to discover what idea the unknown stands for; but is very far from a definition, unless we will say every English word in the dictionary is the definition of the Latin word it answers, and that *motion* is a definition of *motus.* Nor will the successive application of the parts of the superficies of one body to those of another, which the Cartesians give us, prove a much better definition of motion, when well examined.

10. "The act of perspicuous, as far forth as perspicuous" is another peripatetic definition of a simple idea; which though not more absurd than the former of motion, yet betrays its uselessness and insignificancy more plainly, because experience will easily convince anyone that it cannot make the meaning of the word *light* (which it pretends to define) at all understood by a blind man; but the definition of *motion* appears not at first sight so useless, because it escapes this way of trial. For this simple idea, entering by the touch as well as sight, it is impossible to show an example of anyone who has no other way to get the idea of motion, but barely by the definition of that name. Those who tell us that light is a great number of little globules, striking briskly on the bottom of the eye, speak more intelligibly than the schools; but yet these words ever so well understood would make the idea the word *light* stands for no more known to a man that understands it not before than if one should tell him that light was nothing but a company of little tennis-balls, which fairies all day long struck with rackets against some men's foreheads, whilst they passed by others. For granting this explication of the thing to be true, yet the idea of the cause of light, if we had it ever so exact, would no more give us the idea of light itself, as it is such a particular perception in us, than the idea of the figure and motion of a sharp piece of steel would give us the idea of that pain which it is able to cause in us. For the cause of any sensation and the sensation itself, in all the simple ideas of one sense, are two ideas; and two ideas so different and distant one from another that no two can be more so. And therefore should Des Cartes's globules strike ever so long on the retina of a man who was blind by a *gutta serena,* he would thereby never have any idea of light, or anything approaching it, though he understood what little globules were, and what striking on another body was, ever so well. And therefore the Cartesians very well distinguish between that light which is the cause of that sensation in us, and the idea which is produced in us by it, and is that which is properly light.

11. Simple ideas, as has been shown, are only to be got by those impressions objects themselves make on our minds, by the proper inlets appointed to each sort. If they are not received this way, all the words in the world, made use of to explain or

define any of their names, will never be able to produce in us the idea it stands for. For words being sounds can produce in us no other simple ideas than of those very sounds; nor excite any in us but by that voluntary connexion which is known to be between them and those simple ideas which common use has made them signs of. He that thinks otherwise, let him try if any words can give him the taste of a pineapple, and make him have the true idea of the relish of that celebrated delicious fruit. So far as he is told it has a resemblance with any tastes whereof he has the ideas already in his memory, imprinted there by sensible objects not strangers to his palate, so far may he approach that resemblance in his mind. But this is not giving us that idea by a definition, but exciting in us other simple ideas by their known names; which will be still very different from the true taste of that fruit itself. In light and colours, and all other simple ideas, it is the same thing; for the signification of sounds is not natural, but only imposed and arbitrary. And no definition of *light,* or *redness,* is more fitted or able to produce either of those ideas in us than the sound *light* or *red* by itself. For to hope to produce an idea of light, or colour, by a sound, however formed, is to expect that sounds should be visible, or colours audible, and to make the ears do the office of all the other senses. Which is all one as to say that we might taste, smell, and see by the ears; a sort of philosophy worthy only of Sancho Panca, who had the faculty to see Dulcinea by hearsay. And therefore he that has not before received into his mind, by the proper inlet, the simple idea which any word stands for can never come to know the signification of that word by any other words or sounds whatsoever, put together according to any rules of definition. The only way is by applying to his senses the proper object, and so producing that idea in him for which he has learned the name already. A studious blind man, who had mightily beat his head about visible objects, and made use of the explication of his books and friends to understand those names of light and colours which often came in his way, bragged one day that he now understood what *scarlet* signified. Upon which his friend demanding, what scarlet was? the blind man answered, It was like the sound of a trumpet. Just such an understanding of the name of any other simple idea will he have who hopes to get it only from a definition, or other words made use of to explain it.

12. The case is quite otherwise in complex ideas; which consisting of several simple ones, it is in the power of words, standing for the several ideas that make that composition, to imprint complex ideas in the mind, which were never there before, and so make their names be understood. In such collections of ideas, passing under one name, definition, or the teaching the signification of one word by several others, has place, and may make us understand the names of things which never came within the reach of our senses; and frame ideas suitable to those in other men's minds, when they use those names: provided that none of the terms of the definition stand for any such simple ideas which he to whom the explication is made has never yet had in his thought. Thus the word *statue* may be explained to a blind man by other words, when picture cannot; his senses having given him the idea of figure, but not of colours, which therefore words cannot excite in him. This gained the prize to the painter against the statuary: Each of which contending for the excellency of his art, and the statuary bragging that his was to be preferred, because it reached farther, and even those who had lost their eyes could yet perceive the excellency of it, the painter agreed to refer himself to the judgment of a blind man; who being brought where there was a statue made by the one and a picture drawn by the other, he was first led to the statue, in which he traced with his hands all the lineaments of the face and body, and with great admiration applauded the skill of the workman. But being led to the picture, and having his hands laid upon it, was told that now he touched the head, and then the forehead, eyes, nose, &c., as his hand moved over the parts of the picture on the cloth, without finding any the least distinction: Whereupon he cried out that certainly that must needs be a very admirable and divine piece of workmanship which could represent to them all those parts, where he could neither feel nor perceive anything.

13. He that should use the word *rainbow* to one who knew all those colours but yet had never seen that phaenomenon would, by enumerating the figure, largeness, position and order of the colours, so well define that word that it might be perfectly understood. But yet that definition, how exact and perfect soever, would never make a blind man understand it; because several of the simple ideas that make that complex one, being such as he never received by sensation and experience, no words are able to excite them in his mind.

14. Simple ideas, as has been showed, can only be got by experience, from those objects which are proper to produce in us those perceptions. When by this means we have our minds stored with them, and know the names for them, then we are in a condition to define, and by definition to understand, the names of complex ideas that are made up of them. But when any term stands for a simple idea that a man has never yet had in his mind, it is impossible by any words to make known its meaning to him. When any term stands for an idea a man is acquainted with, but is ignorant that that term is the sign of it, there another name, of the same idea which he has been accustomed to, may make him understand its meaning. But in no case whatsoever is any name, of any simple idea, capable of a definition.

15. Fourthly, But though the names of simple ideas have not the help of definition to determine their signification, yet that hinders not but that they are generally less doubtful and uncertain than those of mixed modes and substances: Because they standing only for one simple perception, men, for the most part, easily and perfectly agree in their signification, and there is little room for mistake and wrangling about their meaning. He that knows once that *whiteness* is the name of that colour he has observed in snow or milk will not be apt to misapply that word, as long as he retains that idea; which when he has quite lost, he is not apt to mistake the meaning of it, but perceives he understands it not. There is neither a multiplicity of simple ideas to be put together, which makes the doubtfulness in the names of mixed modes; nor a supposed but an unknown real essence, with properties depending thereon, the precise number whereof is also unknown, which makes the difficulty in the names of substances. But on the contrary, in simple ideas the whole signification of the name is known at once, and consists not of parts, whereof more or less being

put in, the idea may be varied, and so the signification of name be obscure or uncertain.

16. Fifthly, This farther may be observed concerning simple ideas and their names, that they
have but few ascents *in linea praedicamentali* (as they
call it) from the lowest species to the *summum genus*.
The reason whereof is that the lowest species being but one simple idea, nothing can be left out
of it; that so the difference being taken away it
may agree with some other thing in one idea common to them both; which, having one name, is the
genus of the other two: v.g. there is nothing that
can be left out of the idea of white and red to make
them agree in one common appearance, and so
have one general name; as rationality being left
out of the complex idea of man, makes it agree
with brute, in the more general idea and name of
animal: And therefore when to avoid unpleasant
enumerations, men would comprehend both white
and red, and several other such simple ideas, under
one general name, they have been fain to do it by a
word which denotes only the way they get into the
mind. For when white, red, and yellow are all comprehended under the genus or name *colour,* it signifies no more but such ideas as are produced in the
mind only by the sight, and have entrance only
through the eyes. And when they would frame yet
a more general term, to comprehend both colours
and sounds, and the like simple ideas, they do it
by a word that signifies all such as come into the
mind only by one sense: And so the general term
quality, in its ordinary acceptation, comprehends
colours, sounds, tastes, smells, and tangible qualities, with distinction from extension, number, motion, pleasure, and pain, which make impressions
on the mind, and introduce their ideas by more
senses than one.

17. Sixthly, The names of simple ideas, substances, and mixed modes have also this difference:
that those of mixed modes stand for ideas perfectly
arbitrary; those of substances are not perfectly so,
but refer to a pattern, though with some latitude;
and those of simple ideas are perfectly taken from
the existence of things, and are not arbitrary at all.
Which, what difference it makes in the significations of their names, we shall see in the following
chapters.

The names of simple modes differ little from
those of simple ideas.

Chapter V. *Of the Names of Mixed Modes and Relations*

1. The names of mixed modes being general, they
stand, as has been shown, for sorts or species of
things, each of which has its peculiar essence. The
essences of these species also, as has been showed,
are nothing but the abstract ideas in the mind, to
which the name is annexed. Thus far the names and
essences of mixed modes have nothing but what is
common to them with other ideas: But if we take a
little nearer survey of them, we shall find that they
have something peculiar, which perhaps may deserve our attention.

2. The first particularity I shall observe in them
is that the abstract ideas or, if you please, the essences of the several species of mixed modes are
made by the understanding, wherein they differ
from those of simple ideas: In which sort the mind
has no power to make any one, but only receives
such as are presented to it, by the real existence of
things, operating upon it.

3. In the next place, these essences of the species of mixed modes are not only made by the mind,
but made very arbitrarily, made without patterns,
or reference to any real existence. Wherein they
differ from those of substances, which carry with
them the supposition of some real being, from
which they are taken, and to which they are conformable. But in its complex ideas of mixed modes,
the mind takes a liberty not to follow the existence
of things exactly. It unites and retains certain collections, as so many distinct specific ideas, whilst others, that as often occur in nature, and are as plainly
suggested by outward things, pass neglected, without particular names or specifications. Nor does the
mind, in these of mixed modes, as in the complex
idea of substances, examine them by the real existence of things; or verify them by patterns, containing such peculiar compositions in nature. To know
whether his idea of adultery or incest be right, will
a man seek it anywhere amongst things existing? Or
is it true, because anyone has been witness to such
an action? No: But it suffices here that men have put

together such a collection into one complex idea that makes the archetype and specific idea, whether ever any such action were committed *in rerum natura* or no.

4. To understand this right, we must consider wherein this making of these complex ideas consists; and that is not in the making any new idea, but putting together those which the mind had before. Wherein the mind does these three things: First, it chooses a certain number: Secondly, it gives them connexion, and makes them into one idea: Thirdly, it ties them together by a name. If we examine how the mind proceeds in these, and what liberty it takes in them, we shall easily observe how these essences of the species of mixed modes are the workmanship of the mind; and consequently, that the species themselves are of men's making.

5. Nobody can doubt but that these ideas of mixed modes are made by a voluntary collection of ideas put together in the mind, independent from any original patterns in nature, who will but reflect that this sort of complex ideas may be made, abstracted, and have names given them, and so a species be constituted, before any one individual of that species ever existed. Who can doubt but the ideas of sacrilege or adultery might be framed in the minds of men, and have names given them; and so these species of mixed modes be constituted, before either of them was ever committed; and might be as well discoursed of and reasoned about, and as certain truths discovered of them, whilst yet they had no being but in the understanding, as well as now, that they have but too frequently a real existence? Whereby it is plain how much the sorts of mixed modes are the creatures of the understanding, where they have a being as subservient to all the ends of real truth and knowledge as when they really exist: And we cannot doubt but lawmakers have often made laws about species of actions which were only the creatures of their own understandings; beings that had no other existence but in their own minds. And I think nobody can deny but that the resurrection was a species of mixed modes in the mind, before it really existed.

6. To see how arbitrarily these essences of mixed modes are made by the mind, we need but take a view of almost any of them. A little looking into them will satisfy us that it is the mind that combines several scattered independent ideas into one complex one, and, by the common name it gives them, makes them the essence of a certain species, without regulating itself by any connexion they have in nature. For what greater connexion in nature has the idea of a man than the idea of a sheep with killing; that this is made a particular species of action, signified by the word *murder,* and the other not? Or what union is there in nature between the idea of the relation of a father with killing than that of a son or neighbour; that those are combined into one complex idea, and thereby made the essence of the distinct species parricide, whilst the other makes no distinct species at all? But though they have made killing a man's father, or mother, a distinct species from killing his son, or daughter; yet in some other cases, son and daughter are taken in too, as well as father and mother: And they are all equally comprehended in the same species, as in that of incest. Thus the mind in mixed modes arbitrarily unites into complex ideas such as it finds convenient; whilst others that have altogether as much union in nature are left loose, and never combined into one idea, because they have no need of one name. It is evident, then, that the mind by its free choice gives a connexion to a certain number of ideas, which in nature have no more union with one another than others that it leaves out: Why else is the part of the weapon the beginning of the wound is made with taken notice of to make the distinct species called stabbing, and the figure and matter of the weapon left out? I do not say this is done without reason, as we shall see more by and by; but this I say, that it is done by the free choice of the mind, pursuing its own ends; and that therefore these species of mixed modes are the workmanship of the understanding: And there is nothing more evident than that, for the most part, in the framing these ideas the mind searches not its patterns in nature, nor refers the ideas it makes to the real existence of things; but puts such together as may best serve its own purposes, without tying itself to a precise imitation of anything that really exists.

7. But, though these complex ideas, or essences of mixed modes, depend on the mind, and are made by it with great liberty; yet they are not made at random, and jumbled together without any reason at all. Though these complex ideas be not always copied from nature, yet they are always suited to the end for which abstract ideas are made: And though they be combinations made of ideas that are loose enough, and have as little union in themselves as several other to which the mind never gives a connexion that combines them into one idea; yet they are always made for the convenience of communication, which is the chief end of language. The use of language is by short sounds to signify with ease and dispatch general conceptions: Wherein not only abundance of particulars may be contained, but also a great variety of independent ideas collected into one complex one. In the making therefore of the species of mixed modes, men have had regard only to such combinations as they had occasion to mention one to another. Those they have combined into distinct complex ideas, and given names to; whilst others, that in nature have as near a union, are left loose and unregarded. For to go no farther than human actions themselves, if they would make distinct abstract ideas of all the varieties which might be observed in them, the number must be infinite, and the memory confounded with the plenty, as well as overcharged to little purpose. It suffices that men make and name so many complex ideas of these mixed modes as they find they have occasion to have names for, in the ordinary occurrence of their affairs. If they join to the idea of killing the idea of father, or mother, and so make a distinct species from killing a man's son or neighbour, it is because of the different heinousness of the crime, and the distinct punishment is due to the murdering a man's father and mother, different from what ought to be inflicted on the murder of a son or neighbour; and therefore they find it necessary to mention it by a distinct name, which is the end of making that distinct combination. But though the ideas of mother and daughter are so differently treated, in reference to the idea of killing, that the one is joined with it to make a distinct abstract idea with a name, and so a distinct species, and the other not; yet in respect of carnal knowledge, they are both taken in under incest: And that still for the same convenience of expressing under one name, and reckoning of one species, such unclean mixtures as have a peculiar turpitude beyond others; and this to avoid circumlocutions and tedious descriptions.

8. A moderate skill in different languages will easily satisfy one of the truth of this, it being so obvious to observe great store of words in one language which have not any that answer them in another. Which plainly shows that those of one country, by their customs and manner of life, have found occasion to make several complex ideas, and given names to them, which others never collected into specific ideas. This could not have happened if these species were the steady workmanship of nature, and not collections made and abstracted by the mind, in order to naming, and for the convenience of communication. The terms of our law, which are not empty sounds, will hardly find words that answer them in the Spanish or Italian, no scanty languages; much less, I think, could anyone translate them into the Caribbee or Westoe tongues: And the *Versura* of the Romans, or *Corban* of the Jews, have no words in other languages to answer them, the reason whereof is plain, from what has been said. Nay, if we look a little more nearly into this matter, and exactly compare different languages, we shall find that though they have words which in translations and dictionaries are supposed to answer one another, yet there is scarce one of ten amongst the names of complex ideas, especially of mixed modes, that stands for the same precise idea which the word does that in dictionaries it is rendered by. There are no ideas more common, and less compounded, than the measures of time, extension, and weight, and the Latin names *hora, pes, libra* are without difficulty rendered by the English names *hour, foot,* and *pound:* But yet there is nothing more evident than that the ideas a Roman annexed to these Latin names were very far different from those which an Englishman expresses by those English ones. And if either of these should make use of the measures that those of the other language designed by their names, he would be quite out in his account. These are too sensible proofs to be doubted; and we shall find this much more so in the names of more abstract and compounded ideas, such as are the greatest part of those which make up moral discourses: Whose names, when men come curiously to compare with those they are translated into in

other languages, they will find very few of them exactly to correspond in the whole extent of their significations.

9. The reason why I take so particular notice of this is that we may not be mistaken about genera and species, and their essences, as if they were things regularly and constantly made by nature, and had a real existence in things: When they appear, upon a more wary survey, to be nothing else but an artifice of the understanding, for the easier signifying such collections of ideas as it should often have occasion to communicate by one general term; under which divers particulars, as far forth as they agreed to that abstract idea, might be comprehended. And if the doubtful signification of the word *species* may make it sound harsh to some that I say the species of mixed modes are made by the understanding; yet, I think, it can by nobody be denied that it is the mind makes those abstract complex ideas, to which specific names are given. And if it be true, as it is, that the mind makes the patterns for sorting and naming of things, I leave it to be considered who makes the boundaries of the sort or species; since with me species and sort have no other difference than that of a Latin and English idiom.

10. The near relation that there is between species, essences, and their general name, at least in mixed modes, will farther appear when we consider that it is the name that seems to preserve those essences, and give them their lasting duration. For the connexion between the loose parts of those complex ideas being made by the mind, this union, which has no particular foundation in nature, would cease again, were there not something that did, as it were, hold it together, and keep the parts from scattering. Though therefore it be the mind that makes the collection, it is the name which is, as it were, the knot that ties them fast together. What a vast variety of different ideas does the word *triumphus* hold together, and deliver to us as one species? Had this name been never made, or quite lost, we might, no doubt, have had descriptions of what passed in that solemnity: But yet, I think, that which holds those different parts together, in the unity of one complex idea, is that very word annexed to it; without which the several parts of that would no more be thought to make one thing than any other show,

which having never been made but once, had never been united into one complex idea, under one denomination. How much, therefore, in mixed modes, the unity necessary to any essence depends on the mind, and how much the continuation and fixing of that unity depends on the name in common use annexed to it, I leave to be considered by those who look upon essences and species as real established things in nature.

11. Suitable to this, we find that men speaking of mixed modes seldom imagine or take any other for species of them, but such as are set out by name: Because they being of man's making only, in order to naming, no such species are taken notice of, or supposed to be, unless a name be joined to it, as the sign of man's having combined into one idea several loose ones; and by that name giving a lasting union to the parts, which would otherwise cease to have any, as soon as the mind laid by that abstract idea, and ceased actually to think on it. But when a name is once annexed to it, wherein the parts of that complex idea have a settled and permanent union; then is the essence, as it were, established, and the species looked on as complete. For to what purpose should the memory charge itself with such compositions, unless it were by abstraction to make them general? And to what purpose make them general, unless it were that they might have general names for the convenience of discourse and communication? Thus we see that killing a man with a sword or a hatchet are looked on as no distinct species of action: But if the point of the sword first enter the body, it passes for a distinct species, where it has a distinct name; as in England, in whose language it is called stabbing: But in another country, where it has not happened to be specified under a peculiar name, it passes not for a distinct species. But in the species of corporeal substances, though it be the mind that makes the nominal essence; yet since those ideas which are combined in it are supposed to have an union in nature, whether the mind joins them or no, therefore those are looked on as distinct names, without any operation of the mind, either abstracting or giving a name to that complex idea.

12. Conformable also to what has been said concerning the essences of the species of mixed modes, that they are the creatures of the understanding, rather than the works of nature; conformable, I say, to this, we find that their names lead our thoughts to the mind, and no farther. When we speak of justice, or gratitude, we frame to ourselves no imagination of anything existing, which we would conceive; but our thoughts terminate in the abstract ideas of those virtues, and look no farther, as they do when we speak of a horse, or iron, whose specific ideas we consider not as barely in the mind, but as in things themselves, which afford the original patterns of those ideas. But in mixed modes, at least the most considerable parts of them, which are moral beings, we consider the original patterns as being in the mind; and to those we refer for the distinguishing of particular beings under names. And hence I think it is, that these essences of the species of mixed modes are by a more particular name called *notions,* as, by a peculiar right, appertaining to the understanding.

13. Hence likewise we may learn why the complex ideas of mixed modes are commonly more compounded and decompounded than those of natural substances. Because they being the workmanship of the understanding, pursuing only its own ends, and the conveniency of expressing in short those ideas it would make known to another, it does with great liberty unite often into one abstract idea things that in their nature have no coherence; and so, under one term, bundle together a great variety of compounded and decompounded ideas. Thus the name of *procession;* what a great mixture of independent ideas of persons, habits, tapers, orders, motions, sounds, does it contain in that complex one, which the mind of man has arbitrarily put together, to express by that one name? Whereas the complex ideas of the sorts of substances are usually made up of only a small number of simple ones; and in the species of animals, these two, viz. shape and voice, commonly make the whole nominal essence.

14. Another thing we may observe from what has been said is that the names of mixed modes always signify (when they have any determined signification) the real essences of their species. For these abstract ideas being the workmanship of the mind, and not referred to the real existence of things, there is no supposition of anything more signified by that name, but barely that complex idea the mind itself has formed, which is all it would have expressed by it: And is that on which all the

properties of the species depend, and from which alone they all flow: And so in these the real and nominal essence is the same; which of what concernment it is to the certain knowledge of general truth, we shall see hereafter.

15. This also may show us the reason why, for the most part, the names of mixed modes are got before the ideas they stand for are perfectly known. Because there being no species of these ordinarily taken notice of but what have names; and those species, or rather their essences, being abstract complex ideas made arbitrarily by the mind; it is convenient, if not necessary, to know the names before one endeavour to frame these complex ideas: Unless a man will fill his head with a company of abstract complex ideas, which others having no names for, he has nothing to do with but to lay by and forget again. I confess that in the beginning of languages it was necessary to have the idea before one gave it the name: And so it is still, where making a new complex idea, one also, by giving it a new name, makes a new word. But this concerns not languages made, which have generally pretty well provided for ideas, which men have frequent occasion to have and communicate: And in such, I ask, whether it be not the ordinary method, that children learn the names of mixed modes before they have their ideas? What one of a thousand ever frames the abstract ideas of glory and ambition before he has heard the names of them? In simple ideas and substances I grant it is otherwise; which being such ideas as have a real existence and union in nature, the ideas and names are got one before the other, as it happens.

16. What has been said here of mixed modes is with very little difference applicable also to relations; which, since every man himself may observe, I may spare myself the pains to enlarge on: Especially since what I have here said concerning words in this third book will possibly be thought by some to be much more than what so slight a subject required. I allow it might be brought into a narrower compass: But I was willing to stay my reader on an argument that appears to me new, and a little out of the way (I am sure it is one I thought not of when I began to write), that by searching it to the bottom, and turning it on every side, some part or other might meet with everyone's thoughts, and give occasion to the most averse or negligent to reflect on a general miscarriage; which, though of great consequence, is little taken notice of. When it is considered what a pudder is made about essences, and how much all sorts of knowledge, discourse, and conversation are pestered and disordered by the careless and confused use and application of words, it will perhaps be thought worth while thoroughly to lay it open. And I shall be pardoned if I have dwelt long on an argument which I think therefore needs to be inculcated; because the faults men are usually guilty of in this kind are not only the greatest hindrances of true knowledge, but are so well thought of as to pass for it. Men would often see what a small pittance of reason and truth, or possibly none at all, is mixed with those huffing opinions they are swelled with, if they would but look beyond fashionable sounds, and observe what ideas are or are not comprehended under those words with which they are so armed at all points, and with which they so confidently lay about them. I shall imagine I have done some service to truth, peace, and learning if, by any enlargement on this subject, I can make men reflect on their own use of language; and give them reason to suspect that, since it is frequent for others, it may also be possible for them to have sometimes very good and approved words in their mouths and writings, with very uncertain, little, or no signification. And therefore it is not unreasonable for them to be wary herein themselves, and not to be unwilling to have them examined by others. With this design therefore I shall go on with what I have farther to say concerning this matter.

Chapter VI. *Of the Names of Substances*

1. The common names of substances, as well as other general terms, stand for sorts; which is nothing else but the being made signs of such complex ideas, wherein several particular substances do or might agree, by virtue of which they are capable of being comprehended in one common conception, and signified by one name. I say, do or might agree: For though there be but one sun existing in the world, yet the idea of it being abstracted, so that more substances (if there were several) might each agree in it; it is as much a sort as if there were as many suns as there are stars. They want not their reasons who think there are, and that each fixed star

would answer the idea the name *sun* stands for, to one who was placed in a due distance; which, by the way, may show us how much the sorts, or, if you please, genera and species of things (for those Latin terms signify to me no more than the English word *sort*) depend on such collections of ideas as men have made, and not on the real nature of things; since it is not impossible but that, in propriety of speech, that might be a sun to one which is a star to another.

2. The measure and boundary of each sort, or species, whereby it is constituted that particular sort, and distinguished from others, is that we call its *essence,* which is nothing but that abstract idea to which the name is annexed; so that everything contained in that idea is essential to that sort. This, though it be all the essence of natural substances that we know, or by which we distinguish them into sorts; yet I call it by a peculiar name, the *nominal essence,* to distinguish it from the real constitution of substances, upon which depends this nominal essence, and all the properties of that sort; which therefore, as has been said, may be called the *real essence:* v.g. the nominal essence of gold is that complex idea the word *gold* stands for, let it be, for instance, a body yellow, of a certain weight, malleable, fusible, and fixed. But the real essence is the constitution of the insensible parts of that body, on which those qualities and all the other properties of gold depend. How far these two are different, though they are both called essence, is obvious at first sight to discover.

3. For though perhaps voluntary motion, with sense and reason, joined to a body of a certain shape, be the complex idea to which I, and others, annex the name *man,* and so be the nominal essence of the species so called; yet nobody will say that complex idea is the real essence and source of all those operations which are to be found in any individual of that sort. The foundation of all those qualities, which are the ingredients of our complex idea, is something quite different; and had we such a knowledge of that constitution of man, from which his faculties of moving, sensation, and reasoning, and other powers flow, and on which his so regular shape depends, as it is possible angels have, and it is certain his Maker has; we should have a quite other idea of his essence than what now is contained in our definition of that species, be it what it will: And our idea of any individual man would be as far different from what it is now as is his who knows all the springs and wheels, and other contrivances within, of the famous clock at Strasburgh, from that which a gazing countryman has of it, who barely sees the motion of the hand, and hears the clock strike, and observes only some of the outward appearances.

4. That essence, in the ordinary use of the word, relates to sorts; and that it is considered in particular beings no farther than as they are ranked into sorts; appears from hence: That take but away the abstract ideas, by which we sort individuals, and rank them under common names, and then the thought of anything essential to any of them instantly vanishes; we have no notion of the one without the other; which plainly shows their relation. It is necessary for me to be as I am; God and nature has made me so: But there is nothing I have is essential to me. An accident, or disease, may very much alter my colour, or shape; a fever or fall may take away my reason or memory, or both, and an apoplexy leave neither sense nor understanding, no, nor life. Other creatures of my shape may be made with more and better, or fewer and worse, faculties than I have; and others may have reason and sense in a shape and body very different from mine. None of these are essential to the one, or the other, or to any individual whatever, till the mind refers it to some sort or species of things; and then presently, according to the abstract idea of that sort, something is found essential. Let anyone examine his own thoughts, and he will find that as soon as he supposes or speaks of essential, the consideration of some species, or the complex idea, signified by some general name, comes into his mind; and it is in reference to that that this or that quality is said to be essential. So that if it be asked, whether it be essential to me or any other particular corporeal being to have reason? I say no; no more than it is essential to this white thing I write on to have words in it. But if that particular being be to be counted of the sort *man*, and to have the name *man* given it, then reason is essential to it, supposing reason to be a part of the complex idea the name *man* stands for: As it is essential to this thing I write on to contain words, if I will give it the name *treatise*, and rank it under that species. So that essential and not essential re-

late only to our abstract ideas, and the names annexed to them; which amounts to no more than this, that whatever particular thing has not in it those qualities which are contained in the abstract idea, which any general term stands for, cannot be ranked under that species, nor be called by that name, since that abstract idea is the very essence of that species.

5. Thus, if the idea of body, with some people, be bare extension or space, then solidity is not essential to body: If others make the idea to which they give the name *body* to be solidity and extension, then solidity is essential to body. That, therefore, and that alone, is considered as essential which makes a part of the complex idea the name of a sort stands for, without which no particular thing can be reckoned of that sort, nor be entitled to that name. Should there be found a parcel of matter that had all the other qualities that are in iron, but wanted obedience to the lodestone; and would neither be drawn by it, nor receive direction from it; would anyone question whether it wanted anything essential? It would be absurd to ask whether a thing really existing wanted anything essential to it. Or could it be demanded whether this made an essential or specific difference or no, since we have no other measure of essential or specific but our abstract ideas? And to talk of specific differences in nature, without reference to general ideas and names, is to talk unintelligibly. For I would ask anyone, What is sufficient to make an essential difference in nature, between any two particular beings, without any regard had to some abstract idea which is looked upon as the essence and standard of a species? All such patterns and standards being quite laid aside, particular beings, considered barely in themselves, will be found to have all their qualities equally essential; and everything, in each individual, will be essential to it, or, which is more, nothing at all. For though it may be reasonable to ask whether obeying the magnet be essential to iron, yet, I think, it is very improper and insignificant to ask whether it be essential to the particular parcel of matter I cut my pen with, without considering it under the name *iron*, or as being of a certain species. And if, as has been said, our abstract ideas, which have names annexed to them, are the boundaries of species, nothing can be essential but what is contained in those ideas.

6. It is true, I have often mentioned a real essence, distinct in substances from those abstract ideas of them, which I call their nominal essence. By this real essence I mean the real constitution of anything which is the foundation of all those properties that are combined in, and are constantly found to co-exist with, the nominal essence; that particular constitution which everything has within itself, without any relation to anything without it. But essence, even in this sense, relates to a sort, and supposes a species; for being that real constitution on which the properties depend, it necessarily supposes a sort of things, properties belonging only to species, and not to individuals; v.g. supposing the nominal essence of gold to be a body of such a peculiar colour and weight, with malleability and fusibility, the real essence is that constitution of the parts of matter on which these qualities and their union depend, and is also the foundation of its solubility in *aqua regia* and other properties accompanying that complex idea. Here are essences and properties, but all upon supposition of a sort, or general abstract idea, which is considered as immutable; but there is no individual parcel of matter to which any of these qualities are so annexed as to be essential to it, or inseparable from it. That which is essential belongs to it as a condition whereby it is of this or that sort; but take away the consideration of its being ranked under the name of some abstract idea, and then there is nothing necessary to it, nothing inseparable from it. Indeed, as to the real essences of substances, we only suppose their being, without precisely knowing what they are: But that which annexes them still to the species is the nominal essence, of which they are the supposed foundation and cause.

7. The next thing to be considered is, by which of those essences it is that substances are determined into sorts, or species; and that, it is evident, is by the nominal essence. For it is that alone that the name, which is the mark of the sort, signifies. It is impossible therefore that anything should determine the sorts of things, which we rank under general names, but that idea which that name is designed as a mark for; which is that, as has been shown, which we call nominal essence. Why do we say, this is a horse, that a mule; this is an animal, that an herb? How comes any particular thing to be of

this or that sort, but because it has that nominal essence, or, which is all one, agrees to that abstract idea that name is annexed to? And I desire anyone but to reflect on his own thoughts, when he hears or speaks any of those, or other names of substances, to know what sort of essences they stand for.

8. And that the species of things to us are nothing but the ranking them under distinct names according to the complex ideas in us, and not according to precise, distinct, real essences in them, is plain from hence, that we find many of the individuals that are ranked into one sort, called by one common name, and so received as being of one species, have yet qualities depending on their real constitutions as far different one from another as from others from which they are accounted to differ specifically. This, as it is easy to be observed by all who have to do with natural bodies; so chemists especially are often, by sad experience, convinced of it, when they, sometimes in vain, seek for the same qualities in one parcel of sulphur, antimony or vitriol, which they have found in others. For though they are bodies of the same species, having the same nominal essence, under the same name; yet do they often, upon severe ways of examination, betray qualities so different one from another as to frustrate the expectation and labour of very wary chemists. But if things were distinguished into species, according to their real essences, it would be as impossible to find different properties in any two individual substances of the same species as it is to find different properties in two circles, or two equilateral triangles. That is properly the essence to us, which determines every particular to this or that *classis;* or, which is the same thing, to this or that general name; and what can that be else but that abstract idea to which that name is annexed? and so has, in truth, a reference, not so much to the being of particular things, as to their general denominations.

9. Nor indeed can we rank and sort things, and consequently (which is the end of sorting) denominate them by their real essences, because we know them not. Our faculties carry us no farther towards the knowledge and distinction of substances than a collection of those sensible ideas which we observe in them; which, however made with the greatest diligence and exactness we are capable of, yet is more remote from the true internal constitution, from which those qualities flow, than, as I said, a countryman's idea is from the inward contrivance of that famous clock at Strasburgh, whereof he only sees the outward figure and motions. There is not so contemptible a plant or animal that does not confound the most enlarged understanding. Though the familiar use of things about us take off our onder; yet it cures not our ignorance. When we come to examine the stones we tread on, or the iron we daily handle, we presently find we know not their make, and can give no reason of the different qualities we find in them. It is evident the internal constitution, whereon their properties depend, is unknown to us. For to go no farther than the grossest and most obvious we can imagine amongst them, what is that texture of parts, that real essence, that makes lead and antimony fusible; wood and stones not? What makes lead and iron malleable, antimony and stones not? And yet how infinitely these come short of the fine contrivances and inconceivable real essences of plants or animals, everyone knows. The workmanship of the all-wise and powerful God, in the great fabric of the universe, and every part thereof, farther exceeds the capacity and comprehension of the most inquisitive and intelligent man than the best contrivance of the most ingenious man doth the conceptions of the most ignorant of rational creatures. Therefore we in vain pretend to range things into sorts, and dispose them into certain classes, under names, by their real essences, that are so far from our discovery or comprehension. A blind man may as soon sort things by their colours, and he that has lost his smell as well distinguish a lily and a rose by their odours, as by those internal constitutions which he knows not. He that thinks he can distinguish sheep and goats by their real essences, that are unknown to him, may be pleased to try his skill in those species, called cassiowary and querechinchio; and by their internal real essences determine the boundaries of those species, without knowing the complex idea of sensible qualities that each of those names stand for, in the countries where those animals are to be found.

10. Those therefore who have been taught that the several species of substances had their distinct internal substantial forms; and that it was those forms which made the distinction of substances into their true species and genera; were led yet farther out of the way by having their minds set upon fruitless inquiries after substantial forms, wholly unintelligible, and whereof we have scarce so much as any obscure or confused conception in general.

11. That our ranking and distinguishing natural substances into species consists in the nominal essences the mind makes, and not in the real essences to be found in the things themselves, is farther evident from our ideas of spirits. For the mind getting, only by reflecting on its own operations, those simple ideas which it attributes to spirits, it hath or can have no other notion of spirit but by attributing all those operations it finds in itself to a sort of beings, without consideration of matter. And even the most advanced notion we have of God is but attributing the same simple ideas which we have got from reflection on what we find in ourselves, and which we conceive to have more perfection in them than would be in their absence; attributing, I say, those simple ideas to him in an unlimited degree. Thus having got, from reflecting on ourselves, the idea of existence, knowledge, power, and pleasure, each of which we find it better to have than to want; and the more we have of each, the better: Joining all these together, with infinity to each of them, we have the complex idea of an eternal, omniscient, omnipotent, infinitely wise and happy Being. And though we are told that there are different species of angels, yet we know not how to frame distinct specific ideas of them; not out of any conceit that the existence of more species than one of spirits is impossible, but because having no more simple ideas (nor being able to frame more) applicable to such beings, but only those few taken from ourselves, and from the actions of our own minds in thinking, and being delighted, and moving several parts of our bodies, we can no otherwise distinguish in our conceptions the several species of spirits one from another but by attributing those operations and powers we find in ourselves to them in a higher or lower degree; and so have no very distinct specific ideas of spirits, except only of God, to whom we attribute both duration and all those other ideas with infinity; to the other spirits, with limitation. Nor as I humbly conceive do we, between God and them in our ideas, put any difference by any number of simple ideas, which we have of one, and not of the other, but only that of infinity. All the particular ideas of existence, knowledge, will, power, and motion, &c. being ideas derived from the operations of our minds, we attribute all of them to all sorts of spirits with the difference only of degrees, to the utmost we can imagine, even infinity, when we would frame, as well as we can, an idea of the first Being; who yet, it is certain, is infinitely more remote, in the real excellency of his nature, from the highest and perfectest of all created beings, than the greatest man, nay purest seraph, is from the most contemptible part of matter; and consequently must infinitely exceed what our narrow understandings can conceive of him.

12. It is not impossible to conceive, nor repugnant to reason, that there may be many species of spirits, as much separated and diversified one from another by distinct properties whereof we have no ideas, as the species of sensible things are distinguished one from another by qualities which we know and observe in them. That there should be more species of intelligent creatures above us than there are of sensible and material below us is probable to me from hence; that in all the visible corporeal world, we see no chasms or gaps. All quite down from us the descent is by easy steps, and a continued series of things that in each remove differ very little one from the other. There are fishes that have wings, and are not strangers to the airy region; and there are some birds that are inhabitants of the water, whose blood is cold as fishes, and their flesh so like in taste that the scrupulous are allowed them on fish-days. There are animals so near of kin both to birds and beasts that they are in the middle between both: Amphibious animals link the terrestrial and aquatic together; seals live at land and sea, and porpoises have the warm blood and entrails of a hog, not to mention what is confidently reported of mermaids or sea-men. There are some brutes that seem to have as much knowledge and reason as some that are called men; and the animal and vegetable kingdoms are so nearly joined that if you will take the lowest of one, and the highest of the other, there will scarce be perceived any great difference between them; and so on, till we come to the lowest and the most inorganical parts of matter, we shall find everywhere that the several species are linked

together, and differ but in almost insensible degrees. And when we consider the infinite power and wisdom of the Maker, we have reason to think that it is suitable to the magnificent harmony of the universe, and the great design and infinite goodness of the architect, that the species of creatures should also, by gentle degrees, ascend upward from us toward his infinite perfection, as we see they gradually descend from us downwards: Which if it be probable, we have reason then to be persuaded that there are far more species of creatures above us than there are beneath: We being, in degrees of perfection, much more remote from the infinite being of God than we are from the lowest state of being, and that which approaches nearest to nothing. And yet of all those distinct species, for the reasons above-said, we have no clear distinct ideas.

13. But to return to the species of corporeal substances. If I should ask anyone whether ice and water were two distinct species of things, I doubt not but I should be answered in the affirmative: And it cannot be denied but he that says they are two distinct species is in the right. But if an Englishman, bred in Jamaica, who perhaps had never seen nor heard of ice, coming into England in the winter, find the water he put in his bason at night in a great part frozen in the morning, and not knowing any peculiar name it had, should call it hardened water; I ask whether this would be a new species to him different from water? And, I think, it would be answered here, it would not be to him a new species, no more than congealed jelly, when it is cold, is a distinct species from the same jelly fluid and warm; or than liquid gold, in the furnace, is a distinct species from hard gold in the hands of a workman. And if this be so, it is plain that our distinct species are nothing but distinct complex ideas, with distinct names annexed to them. It is true, every substance that exists has its peculiar constitution, whereon depend those sensible qualities and powers we observe in it; but the ranking of things into species, which is nothing but sorting them under several titles, is done by us according to the ideas that we have of them: Which though sufficient to distinguish them by names, so that we may be able to discourse of them, when we have them not present before us; yet if we suppose it to be done by their real internal constitutions, and that things existing are distinguished by nature into species, by real essences, according as we distinguish them into species by names, we shall be liable to great mistakes.

14. To distinguish substantial beings into species, according to the usual supposition, that there are certain precise essences or forms of things, whereby all the individuals existing are by nature distinguished into species, these things are necessary.

15. First, To be assured that nature, in the production of things, always designs them to partake of certain regulated established essences, which are to be the models of all things to be produced. This, in that crude sense it is usually proposed, would need some better explication before it can fully be assented to.

16. Secondly, It would be necessary to know whether nature always attains that essence it designs in the production of things. The irregular and monstrous births that in divers sorts of animals have been observed will always give us reason to doubt of one or both of these.

17. Thirdly, It ought to be determined whether those we call monsters be really a distinct species, according to the scholastic notion of the word *species*; since it is certain that everything that exists has its particular constitution: And yet we find that some of these monstrous productions have few or none of those qualities which are supposed to result from and accompany the essence of that species from whence they derive their originals, and to which, by their descent, they seem to belong.

18. Fourthly, The real essences of those things which we distinguish into species, and as so distinguished we name, ought to be known; i.e. we ought to have ideas of them. But since we are ignorant in these four points, the supposed real essences of things stand us not in stead for the distinguishing substances into species.

19. Fifthly, The only imaginable help in this case would be that having framed perfect complex ideas of the properties of things, flowing from their different real essences, we should thereby distinguish them into species. But neither can this be done; for being ignorant of the real essence itself, it is impossible to know all those properties that flow from it, and are so annexed to it, that any one of them being away, we may certainly conclude that that essence is not there, and so the thing is not of that species. We can never know what is the precise number of properties depending on the real essence of gold, any one of which failing, the real essence of gold, and consequently gold, would not be there, unless we knew the real essence of gold itself, and by that determined that species. By the word *gold* here, I must be understood to design a particular piece of matter; v.g. the last guinea that was coined. For if it should stand here in its ordinary signification for that complex idea which I or anyone else calls gold; i.e. for the nominal essence of gold, it would be jargon: so hard is it to show the various meaning and imperfection of words when we have nothing else but words to do it by.

20. By all which it is clear that our distinguishing substances into species by names is not at all founded on their real essences; nor can we pretend to range and determine them exactly into species, according to internal essential differences.

21. But since, as has been remarked, we have need of general words, though we know not the real essences of things; all we can do is to collect such a number of simple ideas, as by examination we find to be united together in things existing, and therefore to make one complex idea. Which though it be not the real essence of any substance that exists, is yet the specific essence, to which our name belongs, and is convertible with it; by which we may at least try the truth of these nominal essences. For example, there be that say that the essence of body is extension: If it be so, we can never mistake in putting the essence of any thing for the thing itself. Let us then in discourse put extension for body; and when we would say that body moves, let us say that extension moves, and see how it will look. He that should say that one extension by impulse moves another extension would, by the bare expression, sufficiently show the absurdity of such a notion. The essence of any thing, in respect of us, is the whole complex idea comprehended and marked by that name; and in substances, besides the several distinct simple ideas that make them up, the confused one of substance, or of an unknown support and cause of their union, is always a part: And therefore the essence of body is not bare extension, but an extended solid thing: And so to say an extended solid thing moves, or impels another, is all one, and as intelligible as to say body moves or impels. Likewise to say that a rational animal is capable of conversation is all one as to say a man. But no one will say that rationality is capable of conversation, because it makes not the whole essence to which we give the name *man.*

22. There are creatures in the world that have shapes like ours, but are hairy, and want language and reason. There are naturals amongst us that have perfectly our shape, but want reason, and some of them language too. There are creatures, as it is said ("*sit fides penes authorem,*" but there appears no contradiction that there should be such), that, with language and reason, and a shape in other things agreeing with ours, have hairy tails; others where the males have no beards, and others where the females have. If it be asked whether these be all men or no, all of human species? It is plain, the question refers only to the nominal essence: For those of them to whom the definition of the word *man,* or the complex idea signified by that name, agrees, are men, and the other not. But if the inquiry be made concerning the supposed real essence, and whether the internal constitution and frame of these several creatures be specifically different, it is wholly impossible for us to answer, no part of that going into our specific idea, only we have reason to think that where the faculties or outward frame so much differs, the internal constitution is not exactly the same. But what difference in the internal real constitution makes a specific difference, it is in vain to inquire; whilst our measures of species be, as they are, only our abstract ideas, which we know; and not that internal constitution, which makes no part of them. Shall the difference of hair only on the skin be a mark of a different internal specific constitution between a changeling and a drill, when they agree in shape, and want of reason and speech? And shall not the want of reason and speech be a sign to us of different real constitutions and species between a changeling and a reasonable man? And so of the rest, if we pretend that distinction of species or sorts is fixedly established by the real frame and secret constitutions of things.

23. Nor let anyone say that the power of propagation in animals by the mixture of male and female, and in plants by seeds, keeps the supposed real species distinct and entire. For granting this to be true, it would help us in the distinction of the species of things no farther than the tribes of animals and vegetables. What must we do for the rest? But in those too it is not sufficient: For if history lie not, women have conceived by drills; and what real species, by that measure, such a production will be in nature, will be a new question: And we have reason to think this is not impossible, since mules and jumarts, the one from the mixture of an ass and a mare, the other from the mixture of a bull and a mare, are so frequent in the world. I once saw a creature that was the issue of a cat and a rat, and had the plain marks of both about it; wherein nature appeared to have followed the pattern of neither sort alone, but to have jumbled them both together. To which, he that shall add the monstrous productions that are so frequently to be met with in nature will find it hard, even in the race of animals, to determine by the pedigree of what species every animal's issue is; and be at a loss about the real essence, which he thinks certainly conveyed by generation, and has alone a right to the specific name. But farther, if the species of animals and plants are to be distinguished only by propagation, must I go to the Indies to see the sire and dam of the one, and the plant from which the seed was gathered that produced the other, to know whether this be a tiger or that tea?

24. Upon the whole matter, it is evident that it is their own collections of sensible qualities that men make the essences of their several sorts of substances; and that their real internal structures are not considered by the greatest part of men in the sorting them. Much less were any substantial forms ever thought on by any but those who have in this one part of the world learned the language of the schools: And yet those ignorant men who pretend not any insight into the real essences, nor trouble themselves about substantial forms, but are content with knowing things one from another by their sensible qualities, are often better acquainted with their differences, can more nicely distinguish them from their uses, and better know what they expect from each, than those learned quick-sighted men who look so deep into them, and talk so confidently of something more hidden and essential.

25. But supposing that the real essences of substances were discoverable by those that would severely apply themselves to that inquiry, yet we could not reasonably think that the ranking of things under general names was regulated by those internal real constitutions, or anything else but their obvious appearances, since languages, in all countries, have been established long before sciences. So that they have not been philosophers, or logicians, or such who have troubled themselves about forms and essences, that have made the general names that are in use amongst the several nations of men; but those more or less comprehensive terms have, for the most part, in all languages, received their birth and signification from ignorant and illiterate people, who sorted and denominated things by those sensible qualities they found in them; thereby to signify them, when absent, to others, whether they had an occasion to mention a sort or a particular thing.

26. Since then it is evident that we sort and name substances by their nominal and not by their real essences, the next thing to be considered is, how and by whom these essences come to be made. As to the latter, it is evident they are made by the mind, and not by nature: For were they nature's workmanship, they could not be so various and different in several men as experience tells us they are. For if we will examine it, we shall not find the nominal essence of any one species of substances in all men the same; no, not of that, which of all others we are the most intimately acquainted with. It could not possibly be that the abstract idea to which the name *man* is given should be different in several men, if it were of nature's making; and that to one it should be *"animal rationale,"* and to another, *"animal implume bipes latis unguibus."* He that annexes the name *man* to a complex idea made up of sense and spontaneous motion, joined to a body of such a shape, has thereby one essence of the species man; and he that, upon farther examination, adds rationality has another essence of the species he calls man: By which means, the same individual will be a true man to the one which is not so to the other. I think there is scarce anyone will allow this upright figure, so well known, to be the essential difference of the species man; and yet how far men determine of the sorts of animals rather by their shape than descent is very visible: Since it has been

more than once debated whether several human foetuses should be preserved or received to baptism or no, only because of the difference of their outward configuration from the ordinary make of children, without knowing whether they were not as capable of reason as infants cast in another mould: Some whereof, though of an approved shape, are never capable of as much appearance of reason all their lives as is to be found in an ape, or an elephant, and never give any signs of being acted by a rational soul. Whereby it is evident that the outward figure, which only was found wanting, and not the faculty of reason, which nobody could know would be wanting in its due season, was made essential to the human species. The learned divine and lawyer must, on such occasions, renounce his sacred definition of *"animal rationale,"* and substitute some other essence of the human species. Monsieur Menage furnishes us with an example worth the taking notice of on this occasion: "When the abbot of Saint Martin (says he) was born, he had so little of the figure of a man that it bespake him rather a monster. It was for some time under deliberation whether he should be baptized or no. However, he was baptized and declared a man provisionally [till time should show what he would prove]. Nature had moulded him so untowardly that he was called all his life the Abbot Malotru, i.e. ill-shaped. He was of Caen. Menagiana, 278/430." This child, we see, was very near being excluded out of the species of man, barely by his shape. He escaped very narrowly as he was, and it is certain a figure a little more oddly turned had cast him, and he had been executed as a thing not to be allowed to pass for a man. And yet there can be no reason given why if the lineaments of his face had been a little altered, a rational soul could not have been lodged in him: Why a visage somewhat longer, or a nose flatter, or a wider mouth, could not have consisted, as well as the rest of his ill figure, with such a soul, such parts as made him, disfigured as he was, capable to be a dignitary in the church.

27. Wherein then, would I gladly know, consist the precise and unmovable boundaries of that species? It is plain, if we examine, there is no such thing made by nature, and established by her amongst men. The real essence of that or any other sort of substances, it is evident we know not; and therefore are so undetermined in our nominal essences, which we make ourselves, that if several men were to be asked concerning some oddly shaped foetus, as soon as born, whether it were a man or no, it is past doubt one should meet with different answers. Which could not happen if the nominal essences, whereby we limit and distinguish the species of substances, were not made by man, with some liberty; but were exactly copied from precise boundaries set by nature, whereby it distinguished all substances into certain species. Who would undertake to resolve what species that monster was of, which is mentioned by Licetus, lib. i. c. 3., with a man's head and hog's body? Or those other, which to the bodies of men had the heads of beasts, as dogs, horses, &c. If any of these creatures had lived, and could have spoke, it would have increased the difficulty. Had the upper part to the middle been of human shape, and all below swine; had it been murder to destroy it? Or must the bishop have been consulted whether it were man enough to be admitted to the font or no? As I have been told, it happened in France some years since, in somewhat a like case. So uncertain are the boundaries of species of animals to us, who have no other measures than the complex ideas of our own collecting; and so far are we from certainly knowing what a man is; though, perhaps it will be judged great ignorance to make any doubt about it. And yet, I think, I may say that the certain boundaries of that species are so far from being determined, and the precise number of simple ideas, which make the nominal essence, so far from being settled and perfectly known, that very material doubts may still arise about it. And I imagine none of the definitions of the word *man* which we yet have, nor descriptions of that sort of animal, are so perfect and exact as to satisfy a considerate inquisitive person; much less to obtain a general consent, and to be that which men would everywhere stick by, in the decision of cases, and determining of life and death, baptism or no baptism, in productions that might happen.

28. But though these nominal essences of substances are made by the mind, they are not yet made so arbitrarily as those of mixed modes. To the making of any nominal essence, it is necessary, first, that the ideas whereof it consists have such a union as to make but one idea, how compounded soever. Secondly, that the particular idea so united be ex-

actly the same, neither more nor less. For if two abstract complex ideas differ either in number or sorts of their component parts, they make two different and not one and the same essence. In the first of these, the mind, in making its complex ideas of substances, only follows nature; and puts none together which are not supposed to have a union in nature. Nobody joins the voice of a sheep with the shape of a horse, nor the colour of lead with the weight and fixedness of gold, to be the complex ideas of any real substances, unless he has a mind to fill his head with chimeras, and his discourse with unintelligible words. Men observing certain qualities always joined and existing together therein copied nature; and of ideas so united, made their complex ones of substances. For though men may make what complex ideas they please, and give what names to them they will, yet if they will be understood when they speak of things really existing, they must in some degree conform their ideas to the things they would speak of: or else men's language will be like that of Babel; and every man's words being intelligible only to himself, would no longer serve to conversation, and the ordinary affairs of life, if the ideas they stand for be not some way answering the common appearances and agreement of substances, as they really exist.

29. Secondly, though the mind of man, in making its complex ideas of substances, never puts any together that do not really or are not supposed to co-exist; and so it truly borrows that union from nature; yet the number it combines depends upon the various care, industry, or fancy of him that makes it. Men generally content themselves with some few sensible obvious qualities; and often, if not always, leave out others as material, and as firmly united, as those that they take. Of sensible substances there are two sorts: one of organized bodies, which are propagated by seed; and in these, the shape is that which to us is the leading quality and most characteristical part that determines the species. And therefore in vegetables and animals, an extended solid substance of such a certain figure usually serves the turn. For however some men seem to prize their definition of *"animal rationale,"* yet should there a creature be found that had language and reason, but partaked not of the usual shape of a man, I believe it would hardly pass for a man, how much soever it were *"animal rationale."* And if Balaam's ass had, all his life, discoursed as rationally as he did once with his master, I doubt yet whether anyone would have thought him worthy the name *man*, or allowed him to be of the same species with himself. As in vegetables and animals it is the shape, so in most other bodies, not propagated by seed, it is the colour we most fix on, and are most led by. Thus where we find the colour of gold, we are apt to imagine all the other qualities comprehended in our complex idea to be there also; and we commonly take these two obvious qualities, viz. shape and colour, for so presumptive ideas of several species, that in a good picture we readily say this is a lion, and that a rose; this is a gold, and that a silver goblet, only by the different figures and colours represented to the eye by the pencil.

35. From what has been said, it is evident that men make sorts of things. For it being different essences alone that make different species, it is plain that they who make those abstract ideas, which are the nominal essences, do thereby make the species, or sort. Should there be a body found having all the other qualities of gold except malleableness, it would no doubt be made a question whether it were gold or no, i.e. whether it were of that species. This could be determined only by that abstract idea to which everyone annexed the name *gold*; so that it would be true gold to him, and belong to that species, who included not malleableness in his nominal essence, signified by the sound *gold*; and on the other side it would not be true gold, or of that species, to him who included malleableness in his specific idea. And who, I pray, is it that makes these divers species even under one and the same name, but men that make two different abstract ideas consisting not exactly of the same collection of qualities? Nor is it a mere supposition to imagine that a body may exist wherein the other obvious qualities of gold may be without malleableness; since it is certain that gold itself will be sometimes so eager (as artists call it) that it will as little endure the hammer as glass itself. What we have said of the putting in or leaving out of malleableness out of the complex idea the name *gold* is by anyone annexed to may be said of its peculiar weight, fixedness, and several other the like qualities; for whatever is left out, or put in, it is still the complex idea

to which that name is annexed that makes the species; and as any particular parcel of matter answers that idea, so the name of the sort belongs truly to it; and it is of that species. And thus anything is true gold, perfect metal. All which determination of the species, it is plain, depends on the understanding of man, making this or that complex idea.

36. This, then, in short, is the case: Nature makes many particular things which do agree one with another, in many sensible qualities, and probably too in their internal frame and constitution: But it is not this real essence that distinguishes them into species; it is men, who, taking occasion from the qualities they find united in them, and wherein they observe often several individuals to agree, range them into sorts, in order to their naming, for the convenience of comprehensive signs; under which individuals, according to their conformity to this or that abstract idea, come to be ranked as under ensigns; so that this is of the blue, that the red regiment; this is a man, that a drill: And in this, I think, consists the whole business of genus and species.

37. I do not deny but nature, in the constant production of particular beings, makes them not always new and various, but very much alike and of kin one to another: But I think it nevertheless true that the boundaries of the species whereby men sort them are made by men; since the essences of the species, distinguished by different names, are, as has been proved, of man's making, and seldom adequate to the internal nature of the things they are taken from. So that we may truly say such a manner of sorting of things is the workmanship of men.

38. One thing I doubt not but will seem very strange in this doctrine; which is, that from what has been said it will follow, that each abstract idea, with a name to it, makes a distinct species. But who can help it if truth will have it so? For so it must remain till somebody can show us the species of things limited and distinguished by something else; and let us see that general terms signify not our abstract ideas, but something different from them. I would fain know why a shock and a hound are not as distinct species as a spaniel and an elephant. We have no other idea of the different essence of an elephant and a spaniel than we have of the different

essence of a shock and a hound; all the essential difference, whereby we know and distinguish them one from another, consisting only in the different collection of simple ideas, to which we have given those different names.

39. How much the making of species and genera is in order to general names, and how much general names are necessary, if not to the being, yet at least to the completing of a species, and making it pass for such, will appear, besides what has been said above concerning ice and water, in a very familiar example. A silent and a striking watch are but one species to those who have but one name for them: But he that has the name *watch* for one and *clock* for the other, and distinct complex ideas to which those names belong, to him they are different species. It will be said perhaps that the inward contrivance and constitution is different between these two, which the watch-maker has a clear idea of. And yet, it is plain, they are but one species to him when he has but one name for them. For what is sufficient in the inward contrivance to make a new species? There are some watches that are made with four wheels, others with five: Is this a specific difference to the workman? Some have strings and physies, and others none; some have the balance loose, and others regulated by a spiral spring, and others by hog's bristles: Are any or all of these enough to make a specific difference to the workman that knows each of these and several other different contrivances in the internal constitutions of watches? It is certain each of these hath a real difference from the rest: But whether it be an essential, a specific difference or no relates only to the complex idea to which the name *watch* is given: As long as they all agree in the idea which that name stands for, and that name does not as a generical name comprehend different species under it, they are not essentially nor specifically different. But if anyone will make minuter divisions from differences that he knows in the internal frame of watches, and to such precise complex ideas give names that shall prevail, they will then be new species to them who have those ideas with names to them, and can, by those differences, distinguish watches into these several sorts, and then *watch* will be a generical name. But yet they would be no distinct species to men ignorant of clock-work and the inward contrivances of watches, who had no other idea but the

outward shape and bulk, with the marking of the hours by the hand. For to them all those other names would be but synonymous terms for the same idea, and signify no more nor no other thing but a watch. Just thus, I think, it is in natural things. Nobody will doubt that the wheels or springs (if I may so say) within are different in a rational man and a changeling, no more than that there is a difference in the frame between a drill and a changeling. But whether one or both these differences be essential or specifical is only to be known to us by their agreement or disagreement with the complex idea that the name *man* stands for: For by that alone can it be determined whether one, or both, or neither of those be a man or no.

44. Let us suppose Adam in the state of a grown man, with a good understanding, but in a strange country, with all things new and unknown about him; and no other faculties to attain the knowledge of them but what one of this age has now. He observes Lamech more melancholy than usual, and imagines it to be from a suspicion he has of his wife Adah (whom he most ardently loved), that she had too much kindness for another man. Adam discourses these his thoughts to Eve, and desires her to take care that Adah commit not folly: And in these discourses with Eve he makes use of these two new words, *kinneah* and *niouph*. In time Adam's mistake appears, for he finds Lamech's trouble proceeded from having killed a man; but yet the two names *kinneah* and *niouph* (the one standing for suspicion, in a husband, of his wife's disloyalty to him, and the other for the act of committing disloyalty) lost not their distinct significations. It is plain, then, that here were two distinct complex ideas of mixed modes with names to them, two distinct species of actions essentially different; I ask wherein consisted the essences of these two distinct species of actions? And it is plain it consisted in a precise combination of simple ideas, different in one from the other. I ask whether the complex idea in Adam's mind, which he called *kinneah*, were adequate or no? And it is plain it was; for it being a combination of simple ideas, which he, without any regard to any archetype, without respect to anything as a pattern, voluntarily put together, abstracted and gave the name *kinneah* to, to express in short to others, by that one sound, all the simple ideas contained and united in that complex one; it must necessarily follow that it

was an adequate idea. His own choice having made that combination, it had all in it he intended it should, and so could not but be perfect, could not but be adequate, it being referred to no other archetype which it was supposed to represent.

45. These words, *kinneah* and *niouph,* by degrees grew into common use; and then the case was somewhat altered. Adam's children had the same faculties, and thereby the same power that he had to make what complex ideas of mixed modes they pleased in their own minds; to abstract them, and make what sounds they pleased the signs of them: But the use of names being to make our ideas within us known to others, that cannot be done but when the same sign stands for the same idea in two who would communicate their thoughts and discourse together. Those therefore of Adam's children that found these two words, *kinneah* and *niouph,* in familiar use could not take them for insignificant sounds; but must needs conclude they stood for something, for certain ideas, abstract ideas, they being general names, which abstract ideas were the essences of the species distinguished by those names. If therefore they would use these words, as names of species already established and agreed on, they were obliged to conform the ideas in their minds, signified by these names, to the ideas that they stood for in other men's minds, as to their patterns and archetypes; and then indeed their ideas of these complex modes were liable to be inadequate, as being very apt (especially those that consisted of combinations of many simple ideas) not to be exactly conformable to the ideas in other men's minds, using the same names; though for this there be usually a remedy at hand, which is to ask the meaning of any word we understand not, of him that uses it: It being as impossible to know certainly what the words *jealousy* and *adultery* (which I think answer ⟨*hor'nk*⟩ and ⟨*fvor'n*⟩) stand for in another man's mind, with whom I would discourse about them, as it was impossible, in the beginning of language, to know what *kinneah* and *niouph* stood for in another man's mind, without explication, they being voluntary signs in everyone.

46. Let us now also consider, after the same manner, the names of substances in their first application. One of Adam's children, roving in the mountains, lights on a glittering substance which pleases his eye; home he carries it to Adam, who upon consideration of it finds it to be hard, to have a bright yellow colour, and an exceeding great weight. These perhaps, at first, are all the qualities he takes notice of in it; and abstracting this complex idea, consisting of a substance having that peculiar bright yellowness, and a weight very great in proportion to its bulk, he gives it the name *zahab,* to denominate and mark all substances that have these sensible qualities in them. It is evident now that, in this case, Adam acts quite differently from what he did before in forming those ideas of mixed modes, to which he gave the names *kinneah* and *niouph.* For there he put ideas together only by his own imagination, not taken from the existence of anything; and to them he gave names to denominate all things that should happen to agree to those his abstract ideas, without considering whether any such thing did exist or no; the standard there was of his own making. But in the forming his idea of this new substance, he takes the quite contrary course; here he has a standard made by nature; and therefore being to represent that to himself, by the idea he has of it, even when it is absent, he puts in no simple idea into his complex one but what he has the perception of from the thing itself. He takes care that his idea be conformable to this archetype, and intends the name should stand for an idea so conformable.

47. This piece of matter, thus denominated *zahab* by Adam, being quite different from any he had seen before, nobody, I think, will deny to be a distinct species, and to have its peculiar essence; and that the name *zahab* is the mark of the species, and a name belonging to all things partaking in that essence. But here it is plain the essence Adam made the name *zahab* stand for was nothing but a body hard, shining, yellow, and very heavy. But the inquisitive mind of man, not content with the knowledge of these, as I may say, superficial qualities, puts Adam upon farther examination of this matter. He therefore knocks and beats it with flints, to see what was discoverable in the inside: He finds it yield to blows, but not easily separate into pieces: He finds it will bend without breaking. Is not now ductility to be added to his former idea, and made part of the essence of the species that name *zahab* stands for? Farther trials discover fusibility and fixedness. Are not they also, by the same reason that any of the others were, to be put into the complex idea signified by the name *zahab?* If not, what reason will there be shown more for the one than the other? If these must, then all the other properties which any farther trials shall discover in this matter ought by the same reason to make a part of the ingredients of the complex idea which the name *zahab* stands for, and so be the essence of the species marked by that name. Which properties, because they are endless, it is plain that the idea made after this fashion, by this archetype, will be always inadequate.

48. But this is not all; it would also follow that the names of substances would not only have (as in truth they have) but would also be supposed to have different significations, as used by different men, which would very much cumber the use of language. For if every distinct quality that were discovered in any matter by anyone were supposed to make a necessary part of the complex idea, signified by the common name given it, it must follow that men must suppose the same word to signify different things in different men; since they cannot doubt but different men may have discovered several qualities in substances of the same denomination, which others know nothing of.

49. To avoid this, therefore, they have supposed a real essence belonging to every species from which these properties all flow, and would have their name of the species stand for that. But they not having any idea of that real essence in substances, and their words signifying nothing but the ideas they have, that which is done by this attempt is only to put the name or sound in the place and stead of the thing having that real essence, without knowing what the real essence is: And this is that which men do, when they speak of species of things, as supposing them made by nature, and distinguished by real essences.

50. For let us consider, when we affirm that all gold is fixed, either it means that fixedness is a part of the definition, part of the nominal essence the word *gold* stands for; and so this affirmation, all gold is fixed, contains nothing but the signification of the term *gold.* Or else it means that fixedness, not being a part of the definition of the gold, is a property of that substance itself: In which case, it is plain that the word *gold* stands in the place of a substance having the real essence of a species of things made

by nature. In which way of substitution it has so confused and uncertain a signification that though this proposition, gold is fixed, be in that sense an affirmation of something real, yet it is a truth will always fail us in its particular application, and so is of no real use nor certainty. For let it be ever so true that all gold, i.e. all that has the real essence of gold, is fixed, what serves this for, whilst we know not in this sense what is or is not gold? For if we know not the real essence of gold, it is impossible we should know what parcel of matter has that essence, and so whether it be true gold or no.

51. To conclude: What liberty Adam had at first to make any complex ideas of mixed modes by no other pattern but by his own thoughts, the same have all men ever since had. And the same necessity of conforming his ideas of substances to things without him, as to archetypes made by nature, that Adam was under, if he would not wilfully impose upon himself; the same are all men ever since under too. The same liberty also that Adam had of affixing any new name to any idea, the same has anyone still (especially the beginners of languages, if we can imagine any such), but only with this difference, that, in places where men in society have already established a language amongst them, the significations of words are very warily and sparingly to be altered. Because men being furnished already with names for their ideas, and common use having appropriated known names to certain ideas, an affected misapplication of them cannot but be very ridiculous. He that hath new notions will perhaps venture sometimes on the coining of new terms to express them; but men think it a boldness, and it is uncertain whether common use will ever make them pass for current. But in communication with others, it is necessary that we conform the ideas we make the vulgar words of any language stand for to their known proper significations (which I have explained at large already), or else to make known that new signification we apply them to.

Chapter VII. *Of Particles*

1. Besides words which are names of ideas in the mind, there are a great many others that are made use of to signify the connexion that the mind gives to ideas, or to propositions, one with another. The mind, in communicating its thoughts to others, does not only need signs of the ideas it has then before it, but others also, to show or intimate some particular action of its own, at that time, relating to those ideas. This it does several ways; as *is* and *is not* are the general marks of the mind, affirming or denying. But besides affirmation or negation, without which there is in words no truth or falsehood, the mind does, in declaring its sentiments to others, connect not only the parts of propositions, but whole sentences one to another, with their several relations and dependencies, to make a coherent discourse.

2. The words whereby it signifies what connexion it gives to the several affirmations and negations that it unites in one continued reasoning or narration are generally called particles; and it is in the right use of these that more particularly consists the clearness and beauty of a good style. To think well, it is not enough that a man has ideas clear and distinct in his thoughts, nor that he observes the agreement or disagreement of some of them; but he must think in train, and observe the dependence of his thoughts and reasonings upon one another. And to express well such methodical and rational thoughts, he must have words to show what connexion, restriction, distinction, opposition, emphasis, &c. he gives to each respective part of his discourse. To mistake in any of these is to puzzle instead of informing his hearer; and therefore it is that those words which are not truly by themselves the names of any ideas are of such constant and indispensable use in language, and do much contribute to men's well expressing themselves.

3. This part of grammar has been perhaps as much neglected as some others overdiligently cultivated. It is easy for men to write, one after another, of cases and genders, moods and tenses, gerunds and supines: In these, and the like, there has been great diligence used; and particles themselves, in some languages, have been, with great show of exactness, ranked into their several orders. But though prepositions and conjunctions, &c., are names well known in grammar, and the particles contained under them carefully ranked into their distinct subdivisions; yet he who would show the right use of particles, and what significancy and force they have, must take a little more pains, enter into his own thoughts, and observe nicely the several postures of his mind in discoursing.

4. Neither is it enough, for the explaining of these words, to render them, as is usual in dictionaries, by words of another tongue which come nearest to their signification; for what is meant by them is commonly as hard to be understood in one as another language. They are all marks of some action, or intimation of the mind; and therefore to understand them rightly, the several views, postures, stands, turns, limitations, and exceptions, and several other thoughts of the mind, for which we have either none or very deficient names, are diligently to be studied. Of these there is a great variety, much exceeding the number of particles that most languages have to express them by; and therefore it is not to be wondered that most of these particles have divers and sometimes almost opposite significations. In the Hebrew tongue there is a particle consisting of but one single letter, of which there are reckoned up, as I remember, seventy, I am sure above fifty, several significations.

5. *But* is a particle, none more familiar in our language; and he that says it is a discretive conjunction, and that it answers *sed* in Latin, or *mais* in French, thinks he has sufficiently explained it. But it seems to me to intimate several relations the mind gives to the several propositions or parts of them, which it joins by this monosyllable.

First, "but to say no more": Here it intimates a stop of the mind in the course it was going, before it came quite to the end of it.

Secondly, "I saw but two plants": Here it shows that the mind limits the sense to what is expressed, with a negation of all other.

Thirdly, "You pray; but it is not that God would bring you to the true religion."

Fourthly, "But that he would confirm you in your own." The first of these *Buts* intimates a supposition in the mind of something otherwise than it should be; the latter shows that the mind makes a direct opposition between *that* and what goes before it.

Fifthly, "All animals have sense; but a dog is an animal": Here it signifies little more but that the latter proposition is joined to the former, as the minor of a syllogism.

6. To these, I doubt not, might be added a great many other significations of this particle, if it were my business to examine it in its full latitude, and consider it in all the places it is to be found: Which if one should do, I doubt whether in all those manners it is made use of it would deserve the title of discretive which grammarians give to it. But I intend not here a full explication of this sort of signs. The instances I have given in this one may give occasion to reflect on their use and force in language, and lead us into the contemplation of several actions of our minds in discoursing, which it has found a way to intimate to others by these particles; some whereof constantly, and others in certain constructions, have the sense of a whole sentence contained in them.

Chapter VIII. Of Abstract and Concrete Terms

1. The ordinary words of language, and our common use of them, would have given us light into the nature of our ideas, if they had been but considered with attention. The mind, as has been shown, has a power to abstract its ideas, and so they become essences, general essences, whereby the sorts of things are distinguished. Now each abstract idea being distinct, so that of any two the one can never be the other, the mind will, by its intuitive knowledge, perceive their difference; and therefore in propositions no two whole ideas can ever be affirmed one of another. This we see in the common use of language, which permits not any two abstract words, or names of abstract ideas, to be affirmed one of another. For how near of kin soever they may seem to be, and how certain soever it is, that man is an animal, or rational, or white, yet everyone at first hearing perceives the falsehood of these propositions: Humanity is animality, or rationality, or whiteness: And this is as evident as any of the most allowed maxims. All our affirmations, then, are only in concrete, which is the affirming, not one abstract idea to be another, but one abstract idea to be joined to another; which abstract ideas, in substances, may be of any sort; in all the rest, are little else but of relations; and in substances, the most frequent are of powers; v.g. "a man is white" signifies that the thing that has the essence of a man has also in it the essence of whiteness, which is nothing but a power to produce the idea of whiteness in one whose eyes can discover ordinary objects: Or "a man is rational" signifies that the same thing that hath the essence of a man hath also in it the essence of rationality, i.e. a power of reasoning.

2. This distinction of names shows us also the difference of our ideas: For if we observe them, we shall find that our simple ideas have all abstract, as well as concrete, names; the one whereof is (to speak the language of grammarians) a substantive, the other an adjective; as *whiteness, white, sweetness, sweet*. The like also holds in our ideas of modes and relations; as *justice, just; equality, equal;* only with this difference, that some of the concrete names of relations, amongst men chiefly, are substantives; as *paternitas, pater;* whereof it were easy to render a reason. But as to our ideas of substances, we have very few or no abstract names at all. For though the schools have introduced *animalitas, humanitas, corporietas,* and some others; yet they hold no proportion with that infinite number of names of substances to which they never were ridiculous enough to attempt the coining of abstract ones: And those few that the schools forged, and put into the mouths of their scholars, could never yet get admittance into common use, or obtain the licence of public approbation. Which seems to me at least to intimate the confession of all mankind, that they have no ideas of the real essences of substances, since they have not names for such ideas: Which no doubt they would have had, had not their consciousness to themselves of their ignorance of them kept them from so idle an attempt. And therefore though they had ideas enough to distinguish gold from a stone, and metal from wood; yet they but timorously ventured on such terms as *aurietas* and *saxietas, metallietas* and *lignietas,* or the like names, which should pretend to signify the real essences of those substances, whereof they knew they had no ideas. And indeed it was only the doctrine of substantial forms, and the confidence of mistaken pretenders to a knowledge that they had not, which first coined and then introduced *animalitas,* and *humanitas,* and the like; which yet went very little farther than their own schools, and could never get to be current amongst understanding men. Indeed, *humanitas* was a word familiar amongst the Romans, but in a far different sense, and stood not for the abstract essence of any substance; but was the abstracted name of a mode, and its concrete *humanus*, not *homo*.

Book IV. Of Knowledge and Opinion

Chapter I. Of Knowledge in General

Chapter II. Of the Degrees of Our Knowledge

Chapter III. Of the Extent of Human Knowledge

Chapter IV. Of the Reality of Our Knowledge

. . .

Chapter IX. Of Our Knowledge of Existence

Sections

Chapter XI. Of Our Knowledge of the Existence of Other Things

Sections

Chapter XII. Of the Improvement of Our Knowledge

Sections

Chapter XIV. Of Judgment

Sections

Book IV. Of Knowledge and Opinion

Chapter I. Of Knowledge in General

1. Since the mind, in all its thoughts and reasonings, hath no other immediate object but its own ideas, which it alone does or can contemplate, it is evident that our knowledge is only conversant about them.

2. Knowledge then seems to me to be nothing but the perception of the connexion and agreement, or disagreement and repugnancy, of any of our ideas. In this alone it consists. Where this perception is, there is knowledge; and where it is not, there, though we may fancy, guess, or believe, yet we always come short of knowledge. For when we know that white is not black, what do we else but perceive that these two ideas do not agree? When we possess ourselves with the utmost security of the demonstration that the three angles of a triangle are equal to two right ones, what do we more but perceive that equality to two right ones does necessarily agree to, and is inseparable from, the three angles of a triangle?

3. But to understand a little more distinctly wherein this agreement or disagreement consists, I think we may reduce it all to these four sorts: (1) Identity, or diversity. (2) Relation. (3) Coexistence, or necessary connexion. (4) Real existence.

4. First, as to the first sort of agreement or disagreement, viz. identity or diversity. It is the first act of the mind, when it has any sentiments or ideas at all, to perceive its ideas; and so far as it perceives them, to know each what it is, and thereby also to perceive their difference, and that one is not another. This is so absolutely necessary that without it there could be no knowledge, no reasoning, no imagination, no distinct thoughts, at all. By this the mind clearly and infallibly perceives each idea to agree with itself, and to be what it is; and all distinct ideas to disagree, i.e. the one not to be the other: And this it does without pains, labour, or deduction; but at first view, by its natural power of perception and distinction. And though men of art have reduced this into those general rules, "What is, is"; and "It is impossible for the same thing to be and not to be," for ready application in all cases, wherein there may be occasion to reflect on it: Yet it is certain that the first exercise of this faculty is about particular ideas. A man infallibly knows, as soon as ever he has them in his mind, that the ideas he calls *white* and *round* are the very ideas they are, and that they are not other ideas which he calls *red* or *square*. Nor can any maxim or proposition in the world make him know it clearer or surer than he did before, and without any such general rule. This then is the first agreement or disagreement, which the mind perceives in its ideas; which it always perceives at first sight: And if there ever happen any doubt about it, it will always be found to be about the names, and not the ideas themselves, whose identity and diversity will always be perceived as soon and clearly as the ideas themselves are; nor can it possibly be otherwise.

5. Secondly, the next sort of agreement or disagreement the mind perceives in any of its ideas may, I think, be called relative, and is nothing but the perception of the relation between any two ideas, of what kind soever, whether substances, modes, or any other. For since all distinct ideas must eternally be known not to be the same, and so be universally and constantly denied one of another, there could be no room for any positive knowledge at all if we could not perceive any relation between our ideas, and find out the agreement or disagreement they have one with another, in several ways the mind takes of comparing them.

6. Thirdly, the third sort of agreement, or disagreement, to be found in our ideas, which the perception of the mind is employed about, is co-existence or non-co-existence in the same subject; and this belongs particularly to substances. Thus when we pronounce concerning gold that it is fixed, our knowledge of this truth amounts to no more but this, that fixedness, or a power to remain in the fire unconsumed, is an idea that always accompanies and is joined with that particular sort of yellowness,

weight, fusibility, malleableness, and solubility in *aq. regia,* which make our complex idea, signified by the word *gold.*

7. Fourthly, the fourth and last sort is that of actual real existence agreeing to any idea. Within these four sorts of agreement or disagreement is, I suppose, contained all the knowledge we have, or are capable of: For all the enquiries we can make concerning any of our ideas, all that we know or can affirm concerning any of them, is, that it is or is not the same with some other; that it does or does not always co-exist with some other idea in the same subject; that it has this or that relation with some other idea; or that it has a real existence without the mind. Thus "blue is not yellow" is of identity; "two triangles upon equal bases between two parallels are equal" is of relation; "iron is susceptible of magnetical impressions" is of co-existence; "God is" is of real existence. Though identity and co-existence are truly nothing but relations, yet they are such peculiar ways of agreement or disagreement of our ideas that they deserve well to be considered as distinct heads, and not under relation in general; since they are so different grounds of affirmation and negation, as will easily appear to anyone who will but reflect on what is said in several places of this essay. I should now proceed to examine the several degrees of our knowledge, but that it is necessary first to consider the different acceptations of the word *knowledge.*

8. There are several ways wherein the mind is possessed of truth, each of which is called knowledge.

1. There is actual knowledge, which is the present view the mind has of the agreement or disagreement of any of its ideas, or of the relation they have one to another.

2. A man is said to know any proposition which having been once laid before his thoughts, he evidently perceived the agreement or disagreement of the ideas whereof it consists; and so lodged it in his memory that whenever that proposition comes again to be reflected on, he, without doubt or hesitation, embraces the right side, assents to and is certain of the truth of it. This, I think, one may call *habitual knowledge:* And thus a man may be said to know all those truths which are lodged in his

memory by a foregoing, clear, and full perception, whereof the mind is assured past doubt, as often as it has occasion to reflect on them. For our finite understandings being able to think clearly and distinctly but on one thing at once, if men had no knowledge of any more than what they actually thought on, they would all be very ignorant; and he that knew most would know but one truth, that being all he was able to think on at one time.

9. Of habitual knowledge, there are also, vulgarly speaking, two degrees:

First, The one is of such truths laid up in the memory as, whenever they occur to the mind, it actually perceives the relation is between those ideas. And this is in all those truths whereof we have an intuitive knowledge; where the ideas themselves, by an immediate view, discover their agreement or disagreement one with another.

Secondly, The other is of such truths whereof the mind having been convinced, it retains the memory of the conviction, without the proofs. Thus a man that remembers certainly that he once perceived the demonstration that the three angles of a triangle are equal to two right ones is certain that he knows it, because he cannot doubt the truth of it. In his adherence to a truth, where the demonstration by which it was at first known is forgot, though a man may be thought rather to believe his memory than really to know, and this way of entertaining a truth seemed formerly to me like something between opinion and knowledge; a sort of assurance which exceeds bare belief, for that relies on the testimony of another: Yet upon a due examination I find it comes not short of perfect certainty, and is in effect true knowledge. That which is apt to mislead our first thoughts into a mistake in this matter is that the agreement or disagreement of the ideas in this case is not perceived, as it was at first, by an actual view of all the intermediate ideas, whereby the agreement or disagreement of those in the proposition was at first perceived; but by other intermediate ideas that show the agreement or disagreement of the ideas contained in the proposition whose certainty we remember. For example, in this proposition, that "the three angles of a triangle are equal to two right ones," one who has seen and clearly perceived the demonstration of this truth knows it to be true when that demonstration is gone out of his

mind, so that at present it is not actually in view, and possibly cannot be recollected: But he knows it in a different way from what he did before. The agreement of the two ideas joined in that proposition is perceived, but it is by the intervention of other ideas than those which at first produced that perception. He remembers, i.e. he knows (for remembrance is but the reviving of some past knowledge) that he was once certain of the truth of this proposition, that the three angles of a triangle are equal to two right ones. The immutability of the same relations between the same immutable things is now the idea that shows him that if the three angles of a triangle were once equal to two right ones, they will always be equal to two right ones. And hence he comes to be certain that what was once true in the case is always true; what ideas once agreed will always agree; and consequently what he once knew to be true, he will always know to be true; as long as he can remember that he once knew it. Upon this ground it is that particular demonstrations in mathematics afford general knowledge. If then the perception that the same ideas will eternally have the same habitudes and relations be not a sufficient ground of knowledge, there could be no knowledge of general propositions in mathematics; for no mathematical demonstration would be any other than particular: And when a man had demonstrated any proposition concerning one triangle or circle, his knowledge would not reach beyond that particular diagram. If he would extend it farther, he must renew his demonstration in another instance before he could know it to be true in another like triangle, and so on: By which means one could never come to the knowledge of any general propositions. Nobody, I think, can deny that Mr. Newton certainly knows any proposition that he now at any time reads in his book to be true; though he has not in actual view that admirable chain of intermediate ideas whereby he at first discovered it to be true. Such a memory as that, able to retain such a train of particulars, may be well thought beyond the reach of human faculties; when the very discovery, perception, and laying together that wonderful connexion of ideas is found to surpass most readers' comprehension. But yet it is evident, the author himself knows the proposition to be true, remembering he once saw the connexion of those ideas, as certainly as he knows such a man wounded another, remembering that he saw him run him through. But because the memory is not always so clear as actual perception, and does in all men more or less decay in length of time, this amongst other differences is one which shows that demonstrative knowledge is much more imperfect than intuitive, as we shall see in the following chapter.

Chapter II. Of the Degrees of Our Knowledge

1. All our knowledge consisting, as I have said, in the view the mind has of its own ideas, which is the utmost light and greatest certainty we, with our faculties, and in our way of knowledge, are capable of, it may not be amiss to consider a little the degrees of its evidence. The different clearness of our knowledge seems to me to lie in the different way of perception the mind has of the agreement or disagreement of any of its ideas. For if we will reflect on our own ways of thinking, we shall find, that sometimes the mind perceives the agreement or disagreement of two ideas immediately by themselves, without the intervention of any other: And this, I think, we may call *intuitive knowledge.* For in this the mind is at no pains of proving or examining, but perceives the truth, as the eye doth light, only by being directed towards it. Thus the mind perceives that white is not black, that a circle is not a triangle, that three are more than two, and equal to one and two. Such kinds of truths the mind perceives at the first sight of the ideas together, by bare intuition, without the intervention of any other idea; and this kind of knowledge is the clearest and most certain that human frailty is capable of. This part of knowledge is irresistible, and like bright sunshine forces itself immediately to be perceived, as soon as ever the mind turns its view that way; and leaves no room for hesitation, doubt, or examination, but the mind is presently filled with the clear light of it. It is on this intuition that depends all the certainty and evidence of all our knowledge; which certainty everyone finds to be so great that he cannot imagine, and therefore not require, a greater: For a man cannot conceive himself capable of a greater certainty than to know that any idea in his mind is such as he perceives it to be; and that two ideas wherein he perceives a difference are different and not pre-

cisely the same. He that demands a greater certainty than this demands he knows not what, and shows only that he has a mind to be a sceptic, without being able to be so. Certainty depends so wholly on this intuition that in the next degree of knowledge, which I call demonstrative, this intuition is necessary in all the connexions of the intermediate ideas, without which we cannot attain knowledge and certainty.

2. The next degree of knowledge is, where the mind perceives the agreement or disagreement of any ideas, but not immediately. Though wherever the mind perceives the agreement or disagreement of any of its ideas, there be certain knowledge: Yet it does not always happen that the mind sees that agreement or disagreement which there is between them, even where it is discoverable, and in that case remains in ignorance, and at most gets no farther than a probable conjecture. The reason why the mind cannot always perceive presently the agreement or disagreement of two ideas is because those ideas, concerning whose agreement or disagreement the inquiry is made, cannot by the mind be so put together as to show it. In this case, then, when the mind cannot so bring its ideas together, as by their immediate comparison, and as it were juxtaposition or application one to another, to perceive their agreement or disagreement, it is fain, by the intervention of other ideas (one or more, as it happens), to discover the agreement or disagreement which it searches; and this is that which we call *reasoning.* Thus the mind being willing to know the agreement or disagreement in bigness between the three angles of a triangle and two right ones cannot by an immediate view and comparing them do it: Because the three angles of a triangle cannot be brought at once, and be compared with any other one or two angles; and so of this the mind has no immediate, no intuitive knowledge. In this case the mind is fain to find out some other angles to which the three angles of a triangle have an equality; and, finding those equal to two right ones, comes to know their equality to two right ones.

3. Those intervening ideas which serve to show the agreement of any two others are called *proofs;* and where the agreement and disagreement is by this means plainly and clearly perceived, it is called *demonstration,* it being shown to the understanding, and the mind made to see that it is so. A quickness in the mind to find out these intermediate ideas (that shall discover the agreement or disagreement of any other) and to apply them right is, I suppose, that which is called *sagacity*.

4. This knowledge by intervening proofs, though it be certain, yet the evidence of it is not altogether so clear and bright, nor the assent so ready, as in intuitive knowledge. For though, in demonstration, the mind does at last perceive the agreement or disagreement of the ideas it considers, yet it is not without pains and attention: There must be more than one transient view to find it. A steady application and pursuit are required to this discovery: And there must be a progression by steps and degrees, before the mind can in this way arrive at certainty, and come to perceive the agreement or repugnancy between two ideas that need proofs and the use of reason to show it.

5. Another difference between intuitive and demonstrative knowledge is that though in the latter all doubt be removed, when by the intervention of the intermediate ideas the agreement or disagreement is perceived; yet before the demonstration there was a doubt, which in intuitive knowledge cannot happen to the mind that has its faculty of perception left to a degree capable of distinct ideas, no more than it can be a doubt to the eye (that can distinctly see white and black) whether this ink and this paper be all of a colour. If there be sight in the eyes, it will at first glimpse, without hesitation, perceive the words printed on this paper different from the colour of the paper: And so if the mind have the faculty of distinct perception, it will perceive the agreement or disagreement of those ideas that produce intuitive knowledge. If the eyes have lost the faculty of seeing, or the mind of perceiving, we in vain enquire after the quickness of sight in one, or clearness of perception in the other.

6. It is true the perception produced by demonstration is also very clear, yet it is often with a great abatement of that evident lustre and full assurance that always accompany that which I call intuitive; like a face reflected by several mirrors one to another, where as long as it retains the similitude and agreement with the object, it produces a knowledge; but it is still in every successive reflection with a lessening of that perfect clearness and distinctness which is in the first; till at last, after many removes, it has a great mixture of dimness, and is not at first sight so knowable, especially to weak eyes. Thus it is with knowledge made out by a long train of proof.

7. Now, in every step reason makes in demonstrative knowledge, there is an intuitive knowledge of that agreement or disagreement it seeks with the next intermediate idea, which it uses as a proof; for if it were not so, that yet would need a proof; since without the perception of such agreement or disagreement, there is no knowledge produced. If it be perceived by itself, it is intuitive knowledge: If it cannot be perceived by itself, there is need of some intervening idea, as a common measure to show their agreement or disagreement. By which it is plain that every step in reasoning that produces knowledge has intuitive certainty; which when the mind perceives, there is no more required, but to remember it to make the agreement or disagreement of the ideas, concerning which we enquire, visible and certain. So that to make anything a demonstration, it is necessary to perceive the immediate agreement of the intervening ideas, whereby the agreement or disagreement of the two ideas under examination (whereof the one is always the first, and the other the last in the account) is found. This intuitive perception of the agreement or disagreement of the intermediate ideas, in each step and progression of the demonstration, must also be carried exactly in the mind, and a man must be sure that no part is left out: Which because in long deductions, and the use of many proofs, the memory does not always so readily and exactly retain; therefore it comes to pass that this is more imperfect than intuitive knowledge, and men embrace often falsehood for demonstrations.

8. The necessity of this intuitive knowledge, in each step of scientifical or demonstrative reasoning, gave occasion, I imagine, to that mistaken axiom, that all reasoning was *"ex praecognitis & praeconcessis"*; which how far it is a mistake, I shall have occasion to show more at large, when I come to consider propositions, and particularly those propositions which are called maxims; and to show that it is by a mistake that they are supposed to be the foundations of all our knowledge and reasonings.

9. It has been generally taken for granted that mathematics alone are capable of demonstrative certainty; but to have such an agreement or disagreement, as may intuitively be perceived, being, as I imagine, not the privilege of the ideas of number, extension, and figure alone, it may possibly be the want of due method and application in us, and not of sufficient evidence in things, that demonstration has been thought to have so little to do in other parts of knowledge, and been scarce so much as aimed at by any but mathematicians. For whatever ideas we have, wherein the mind can perceive the immediate agreement or disagreement that is between them, there the mind is capable of intuitive knowledge; and where it can perceive the agreement or disagreement of any two ideas, by an intuitive perception of the agreement or disagreement they have with any intermediate ideas, there the mind is capable of demonstration, which is not limited to ideas of extension, figure, number, and their modes.

10. The reason why it has been generally sought for, and supposed to be only in those, I imagine has been not only the general usefulness of those sciences; but because, in comparing their equality or excess, the modes of numbers have every the least difference very clear and perceivable; and though in extension, every the least excess is not so perceptible, yet the mind has found out ways to examine and discover demonstratively the just equality of two angles, or extensions, or figures: And both these, i.e. numbers and figures, can be set down by visible and lasting marks, wherein the ideas under consideration are perfectly determined; which for the most part they are not, where they are marked only by names and words.

11. But in other simple ideas, whose modes and differences are made and counted by degrees, and not quantity, we have not so nice and accurate a distinction of their differences as to perceive or find ways to measure their just equality, or the least differences. For those other simple ideas, being appearances of sensations produced in us by the size, figure, number, and motion of minute corpuscles singly insensible; their different degrees also depend upon the variation of some or of all those causes: Which since it cannot be observed by us in particles of matter, whereof each is too subtle to be perceived, it is impossible for us to have any exact measures of the different degrees of these simple ideas. For supposing the sensation or idea we name whiteness be produced in us by a certain number of globules, which, having a verticity about their own centres, strike upon the retina of the eye with a certain degree of rotation, as well as progressive swiftness; it will hence easily follow, that the more the superficial parts of any body are so ordered as to reflect the greater number of globules of light, and to give them the proper rotation, which is fit to produce this sensation of white in us, the more white will that body appear, that from an equal space sends to the retina the greater number of such corpuscles, with that peculiar sort of motion. I do not say that the nature of light consists in very small round globules, nor of whiteness in such a texture of parts, as gives a certain rotation to these globules, when it reflects them; for I am not now treating physically of light or colours. But this, I think, I may say, that I cannot (and I would be glad anyone would make intelligible that he did) conceive how bodies without us can any ways affect our senses, but by the immediate contact of the sensible bodies themselves, as in tasting and feeling, or the impulse of some insensible particles coming from them, as in seeing, hearing, and smelling; by the different impulse of which parts, caused by their different size, figure, and motion, the variety of sensations is produced in us.

12. Whether then they be globules, or no; or whether they have a verticity about their own centres that produces the idea of whiteness in us: This is certain, that the more particles of light are reflected from a body, fitted to give them that peculiar motion, which produces the sensation of whiteness in us; and possibly too, the quicker that peculiar motion is; the whiter does the body appear, from which the greater number are reflected, as is evident in the same piece of paper put in the sunbeams, in the shade, and in a dark hole; in each of which it will produce in us the idea of whiteness in far different degrees.

13. Not knowing therefore what number of particles nor what motion of them is fit to produce any precise degree of whiteness, we cannot demonstrate the certain equality of any two degrees of whiteness; because we have no certain standard to measure them by, nor means to distinguish every the least real difference, the only help we have being from our senses, which in this point fail us. But where the difference is so great as to produce in the mind clearly distinct ideas, whose differences can be perfectly retained, there these ideas or colours, as we see in different kinds, as blue and red, are as capable of demonstration as ideas of number and extension. What I have here said of whiteness and colours, I think, holds true in all secondary qualities, and their modes.

14. These two, viz. intuition and demonstration, are the degrees of our knowledge; whatever comes short of one of these, with what assurance soever embraced, is but faith, or opinion, but not knowledge, at least in all general truths. There is, indeed, another perception of the mind, employed about the particular existence of finite beings without us; which going beyond bare probability, and yet not reaching perfectly to either of the foregoing degrees of certainty, passes under the name of knowledge. There can be nothing more certain than that the idea we receive from an external object is in our minds; this is intuitive knowledge. But whether there be anything more than barely that idea in our minds; whether we can thence certainly infer the existence of anything without us which corresponds to that idea is that whereof some men think there may be a question made; because men may have such ideas in their minds when no such thing exists, no such object affects their senses. But yet here, I think, we are provided with an evidence that puts us past doubting: For I ask anyone whether he be not invincibly conscious to himself of a different perception when he looks on the sun by day, and thinks on it by night; when he actually tastes wormwood, or smells a rose, or only thinks on that savour or odour? We as plainly find the difference there is between any idea revived in our minds by our own memory, and actually coming into our minds by our senses, as we do between any two distinct ideas. If anyone say a dream may do the same thing, and all these ideas may be produced in us without any external objects; he may please to dream that I make him this answer: (1) That it is no great matter whether I remove his scruple or no: Where all is but dream, reasoning and arguments are of no use, truth and knowledge nothing. (2) That I believe he will allow a very manifest difference between dreaming of being in the fire and being actually in it. But yet if he be resolved to appear so scep-

tical as to maintain that what I call being actually in the fire is nothing but a dream; and that we cannot thereby certainly know that any such thing as fire actually exists without us: I answer that we certainly finding that pleasure or pain follows upon the application of certain objects to us, whose existence we perceive, or dream that we perceive by our senses; this certainty is as great as our happiness or misery, beyond which we have no concernment to know or to be. So that, I think, we may add to the two former sorts of knowledge this also of the existence of particular external objects, by that perception and consciousness we have of the actual entrance of ideas from them, and allow these three degrees of knowledge, viz. intuitive, demonstrative, and sensitive: In each of which there are different degrees and ways of evidence and certainty.

15. But since our knowledge is founded on and employed about our ideas only, will it not follow from thence that it is conformable to our ideas; and that where our ideas are clear and distinct, or obscure and confused, our knowledge will be so too? To which I answer, no: For our knowledge consisting in the perception of the agreement or disagreement of any two ideas, its clearness or obscurity consists in the clearness or obscurity of that perception, and not in the clearness or obscurity of the ideas themselves; v.g. a man that has as clear ideas of the angles of a triangle, and of equality to two right ones, as any mathematician in the world may yet have but a very obscure perception of their agreement, and so have but a very obscure knowledge of it. But ideas, which by reason of their obscurity or otherwise, are confused, cannot produce any clear or distinct knowledge; because, as far as any ideas are confused, so far the mind cannot perceive clearly whether they agree or disagree. Or to express the same thing in a way less apt to be misunderstood: He that hath not determined ideas to the words he uses cannot make propositions of them, of whose truth he can be certain.

Chapter III. Of the Extent of Human Knowledge

1. Knowledge, as has been said, lying in the perception of the agreement or disagreement of any of our ideas, it follows from hence that,

First, we can have knowledge no farther than we have ideas.

2. Secondly, that we can have no knowledge farther than we can have perceptions of that agreement or disagreement. Which perception being (1) either by intuition, or the immediate comparing any two ideas; or (2) by reason, examining the agreement or disagreement of two ideas, by the intervention of some others; or (3) by sensation, perceiving the existence of particular things: Hence it also follows,

3. Thirdly, that we cannot have an intuitive knowledge that shall extend itself to all our ideas, and all that we would know about them; because we cannot examine and perceive all the relations they have one to another by juxta-position, or an immediate comparison one with another. Thus having the ideas of an obtuse and an acute angled triangle, both drawn from equal bases, and between parallels, I can, by intuitive knowledge, perceive the one not to be the other, but cannot that way know whether they be equal or no; because their agreement or disagreement in equality can never be perceived by an immediate comparing them: The difference of figure makes their parts incapable of an exact immediate application; and therefore there is need of some intervening qualities to measure them by, which is demonstration, or rational knowledge.

4. Fourthly, it follows also, from what is above observed, that our rational knowledge cannot reach to the whole extent of our ideas: Because between two different ideas we would examine, we cannot always find such mediums as we can connect one to another with an intuitive knowledge, in all the parts of the deduction; and wherever that fails, we come short of knowledge and demonstration.

5. Fifthly, sensitive knowledge, reaching no farther than the existence of things actually present to our senses, is yet much narrower than either of the former.

6. From all which it is evident that the extent of our knowledge comes not only short of the reality of things, but even of the extent of our own ideas. Though our knowledge be limited to our ideas, and cannot exceed them either in extent or perfection; and though these be very narrow bounds, in

respect of the extent of all being, and far short of what we may justly imagine to be in some even created understandings, not tied down to the dull and narrow information, is to be received from some few and not very acute ways of perception, such as are our senses; yet it would be well with us if our knowledge were but as large as our ideas, and there were not many doubts and enquiries concerning the ideas we have, whereof we are not, nor I believe ever shall be in this world, resolved. Nevertheless I do not question but that human knowledge, under the present circumstances of our beings and constitutions, may be carried much farther than it has hitherto been, if men would sincerely, and with freedom of mind, employ all that industry and labour of thought, in improving the means of discovering truth, which they do for the colouring or support of falsehood, to maintain a system, interest, or party they are once engaged in. But yet after all, I think I may, without injury to human perfection, be confident that our knowledge would never reach to all we might desire to know concerning those ideas we have: Nor be able to surmount all the difficulties, and resolve all the questions that might arise concerning any of them. We have the ideas of a square, a circle, and equality; and yet, perhaps, shall never be able to find a circle equal to a square, and certainly know that it is so. We have the ideas of matter and thinking, but possibly shall never be able to know whether any mere material being thinks, or no; it being impossible for us, by the contemplation of our own ideas, without revelation, to discover whether omnipotency has not given to some systems of matter fitly disposed a power to perceive and think, or else joined and fixed to matter so disposed a thinking immaterial substance: It being, in respect of our notions, not much more remote from our comprehension to conceive that God can, if he pleases, superadd to matter a faculty of thinking than that he should superadd to it another substance with a faculty of thinking; since we know not wherein thinking consists, nor to what sort of substances the Almighty has been pleased to give that power, which cannot be in any created being, but merely by the good pleasure and bounty of the Creator. For I see no contradiction in it, that the first eternal thinking Being or omnipotent Spirit should, if he pleased, give to certain systems of created senseless matter, put together as he thinks fit, some degrees of sense, perception, and thought: Though, as I think, I have proved, Book IV, Chapter X, sec. 14, &c., it is no less than a contradiction to suppose matter (which is evidently in its own nature void of sense and thought) should be that eternal first-thinking being. What certainty of knowledge can anyone have that some perceptions, such as, v.g. pleasure and pain, should not be in some bodies themselves, after a certain manner modified and moved, as well as that they should be in an immaterial substance, upon the motion of the parts of body? Body, as far as we can conceive, being able only to strike and affect body; and motion, according to the utmost reach of our ideas, being able to produce nothing but motion: So that when we allow it to produce pleasure or pain, or the idea of a colour or sound, we are fain to quit our reason, go beyond our ideas, and attribute it wholly to the good pleasure of our Maker. For since we must allow he has annexed effects to motion, which we can no way conceive motion able to produce, what reason have we to conclude that he could not order them as well to be produced in a subject we cannot conceive capable of them, as well as in a subject we cannot conceive the motion of matter can any way operate upon? I say not this, that I would any way lessen the belief of the soul's immateriality: I am not here speaking of probability, but knowledge; and I think not only that it becomes the modesty of philosophy not to pronounce magisterially, where we want that evidence that can produce knowledge; but also, that it is of use to us to discern how far our knowledge does reach; for the state we are at present in, not being that of vision, we must, in many things, content ourselves with faith and probability; and in the present question, about the immateriality of the soul, if our faculties cannot arrive at demonstrative certainty, we need not think it strange. All the great ends of morality and religion are well enough secured, without philosophical proofs of the soul's immateriality; since it is evident that he who made us at the beginning to subsist here, sensible intelligent beings, and for several years continued us in such a state, can and will restore us to the like state of sensibility in another world, and make us capable there to receive the retribution he has designed to men, according to their doings in this life. And therefore it is not of such mighty necessity to determine one way or the other, as some, over-

zealous for or against the immateriality of the soul, have been forward to make the world believe. Who, either on the one side, indulging too much their thoughts, immersed altogether in matter, can allow no existence to what is not material: Or who, on the other side, finding not cogitation within the natural powers of matter, examined over and over again by the utmost intention of mind, have the confidence to conclude that omnipotency itself cannot give perception and thought to a substance which has the modification of solidity. He that considers how hardly sensation is, in our thoughts, reconcilable to extended matter; or existence to anything that hath no extension at all; will confess that he is very far from certainly knowing what his soul is. It is a point which seems to me to be put out of the reach of our knowledge: And he who will give himself leave to consider freely, and look into the dark and intricate part of each hypothesis, will scarce find his reason able to determine him fixedly for or against the soul's materiality. Since on which side soever he views it, either as an unextended substance or as a thinking extended matter, the difficulty to conceive either will, whilst either alone is in his thoughts, still drive him to the contrary side. An unfair way which some men take with themselves; who, because of the inconceivableness of something they find in one, throw themselves violently into the contrary hypothesis, though altogether as unintelligible to an unbiassed understanding. This serves not only to show the weakness and the scantiness of our knowledge, but the insignificant triumph of such sort of arguments, which, drawn from our own views, may satisfy us that we can find no certainty on one side of the question; but do not at all thereby help us to truth by running into the opposite opinion, which, on examination, will be found clogged with equal difficulties. For what safety, what advantage to anyone is it, for the avoiding the seeming absurdities, and to him unsurmountable rubs he meets with in one opinion, to take refuge in the contrary, which is built on something altogether as inexplicable, and as far remote from his comprehension? It is past controversy that we have in us something that thinks; our very doubts about what it is confirm the certainty of its being, though we must content ourselves in the ignorance of what kind of being it is: And it is in vain to go about to be sceptical in this, as it is unreasonable in most other cases to be positive against the being of anything, because we cannot comprehend its nature. For I would fain know what substance exists that has not something in it which manifestly baffles our understandings. Other spirits, who see and know the nature and inward constitution of things, how much must they exceed us in knowledge? To which if we add larger comprehension, which enables them at one glance to see the connexion and agreement of very many ideas, and readily supplies to them the intermediate proofs, which we by single and slow steps, and long poring in the dark, hardly at last find out, and are often ready to forget one before we have hunted out another: We may guess at some part of the happiness of superior ranks of spirits, who have a quicker and more penetrating sight, as well as a larger field of knowledge. But to return to the argument in hand: Our knowledge, I say, is not only limited to the paucity and imperfections of the ideas we have, and which we employ it about, but even comes short of that too. But how far it reaches, let us now enquire.

7. The affirmations or negations we make concerning the ideas we have may, as I have before intimated in general, be reduced to these four sorts, viz. identity, co-existence, relation, and real existence. I shall examine how far our knowledge extends in each of these.

8. First, as to identity and diversity, in this way of agreement or disagreement of our ideas, our intuitive knowledge is as far extended as our ideas themselves; and there can be no idea in the mind which it does not presently, by an intuitive knowledge, perceive to be what it is, and to be different from any other.

9. Secondly, as to the second sort, which is the agreement or disagreement of our ideas in co-existence, in this our knowledge is very short, though in this consists the greatest and most material part of our knowledge concerning substances. For our ideas of the species of substances being, as I have showed, nothing but certain collections of simple ideas united in one subject, and so co-existing together; v.g. our idea of flame is a body hot, luminous, and moving upward; of gold, a body heavy to a certain degree, yellow, malleable, and fusible: These, or some such complex ideas as these

in men's minds, do these two names of the different substances, *flame* and *gold*, stand for. When we would know anything farther concerning these, or any other sort of substances, what do we enquire, but what other qualities or power these substances have or have not? Which is nothing else but to know what other simple ideas do or do not co-exist with those that make up that complex idea.

10. This, how weighty and considerable a part soever of human science, is yet very narrow, and scarce any at all. The reason whereof is that the simple ideas, whereof our complex ideas of substances are made up, are, for the most part, such as carry with them, in their own nature, no visible necessary connexion or inconsistency with any other simple ideas whose co-existence with them we would inform ourselves about.

11. The ideas that our complex ones of substances are made up of, and about which our knowledge concerning substances is most employed, are those of their secondary qualities: Which depending all (as has been shown) upon the primary qualities of their minute and insensible parts; or if not upon them, upon something yet more remote from our comprehension; it is impossible we should know which have a necessary union or inconsistency one with another: For not knowing the root they spring from, not knowing what size, figure, and texture of parts they are, on which depend, and from which result, those qualities which make our complex idea of gold, it is impossible we should know what other qualities result from, or are incompatible with, the same constitution of the insensible parts of gold; and so consequently must always co-exist with that complex idea we have of it, or else are inconsistent with it.

12. Besides this ignorance of the primary qualities of the insensible parts of bodies, on which depend all their secondary qualities, there is yet another and more incurable part of ignorance, which sets us more remote from a certain knowledge of the co-existence or in-co-existence (if I may so say) of different ideas in the same subject; and that is, that there is no discoverable connexion between any secondary quality and those primary qualities which it depends on.

13. That the size, figure, and motion of one body should cause a change in the size, figure, and motion of another body is not beyond our conception: The separation of the parts of one body upon the intrusion of another; and the change from rest to motion upon impulse; these and the like seem to have some connexion one with another. And if we knew these primary qualities of bodies, we might have reason to hope we might be able to know a great deal more of these operations of them one upon another: But our minds not being able to discover any connexion betwixt these primary qualities of bodies and the sensations that are produced in us by them, we can never be able to establish certain and undoubted rules of the consequence or co-existence of any secondary qualities, though we could discover the size, figure, or motion of those invisible parts which immediately produce them. We are so far from knowing what figure, size, or motion of parts produce a yellow colour, a sweet taste, or a sharp sound, that we can by no means conceive how any size, figure, or motion of any particles can possibly produce in us the idea of any colour, taste, or sound whatsoever; there is no conceivable connexion betwixt the one and the other.

14. In vain therefore shall we endeavour to discover by our ideas (the only true way of certain and universal knowledge) what other ideas are to be found constantly joined with that of our complex idea of any substance: Since we neither know the real constitution of the minute parts on which their qualities do depend, nor, did we know them, could we discover any necessary connexion between them and any of the secondary qualities; which is necessary to be done before we can certainly know their necessary co-existence. So that let our complex idea of any species of substances be what it will, we can hardly, from the simple ideas contained in it, certainly determine the necessary co-existence of any other quality whatsoever. Our knowledge in all these enquiries reaches very little farther than our experience. Indeed, some few of the primary qualities have a necessary dependence and visible connexion one with another, as figure necessarily supposes extension: Receiving or communicating motion by impulse supposes solidity. But though these and perhaps some others of our ideas have; yet there are so few of them that have a visible

connexion one with another that we can by intuition or demonstration discover the co-existence of very few of the qualities are to be found united in substances: And we are left only to the assistance of our senses, to make known to us what qualities they contain. For of all the qualities that are co-existent in any subject, without this dependence and evident connexion of their ideas one with another, we cannot know certainly any two to co-exist any farther than experience, by our senses, informs us. Thus though we see the yellow colour, and upon trial find the weight, malleableness, fusibility, and fixedness, that are united in a piece of gold; yet because no one of these ideas has any evident dependence or necessary connexion with the other, we cannot certainly know that where any four of these are, the fifth will be there also, how highly probable soever it may be; because the highest probability amounts not to certainty, without which there can be no true knowledge. For this co-existence can be no farther known than it is perceived; and it cannot be perceived but either in particular subjects, by the observation of our senses, or in general, by the necessary connexion of the ideas themselves.

15. As to the incompatibility or repugnancy to co-existence, we may know that any subject may have of each sort of primary qualities but one particular at once; v.g. each particular extension, figure, number of parts, motion, excludes all other of each kind. The like also is certain of all sensible ideas peculiar to each sense; for whatever of each kind is present in any subject excludes all other of that sort; v.g. no one subject can have two smells or two colours at the same time. To this perhaps will be said, Has not an opal, or the infusion of *lignum nephriticum*, two colours at the same time? To which I answer, that these bodies, to eyes differently placed, may at the same time afford different colours: But I take liberty also to say, that to eyes differently placed, it is different parts of the object that reflect the particles of light: And therefore it is not the same part of the object, and so not the very same subject, which at the same time appears both yellow and azure. For it is as impossible that the very same particle of any body should at the same time differently modify or reflect the rays of light as that it should have two different figures and textures at the same time.

16. But as to the powers of substances to change the sensible qualities of other bodies, which make a great part of our enquiries about them, and is no inconsiderable branch of our knowledge: I doubt, as to these, whether our knowledge reaches much farther than our experience; or whether we can come to the discovery of most of these powers, and be certain that they are in any subject, by the connexion with any of those ideas which to us make its essence. Because the active and passive powers of bodies, and their ways of operating, consisting in a texture and motion of parts, which we cannot by any means come to discover; it is but in very few cases we can be able to perceive their dependence on, or repugnance to, any of those ideas which make our complex one of that sort of things. I have here instanced in the corpuscularian hypothesis as that which is thought to go farthest in an intelligible explication of those qualities of bodies; and I fear the weakness of human understanding is scarce able to substitute another which will afford us a fuller and clearer discovery of the necessary connexion and co-existence of the powers which are to be observed united in several sorts of them. This at least is certain, that whichever hypothesis be clearest and truest (for of that it is not my business to determine), our knowledge concerning corporeal substances will be very little advanced by any of them, till we are made to see what qualities and powers of bodies have a necessary connexion or repugnancy one with another; which in the present state of philosophy, I think, we know but to a very small degree: And I doubt whether, with those faculties we have, we shall ever be able to carry our general knowledge (I say not particular experience) in this part much farther. Experience is that which in this part we must depend on. And it were to be wished that it were more improved. We find the advantages some men's generous pains have this way brought to the stock of natural knowledge. And if others, especially the philosophers by fire, who pretend to it had been so wary in their observations, and sincere in their reports, as those who call themselves philosophers ought to have been, our acquaintance with the bodies here about us, and our insight into their powers and operations, had been yet much greater.

17. If we are at a loss in respect of the powers and operations of bodies, I think it is easy to conclude, we are much more in the dark in reference to spirits; whereof we naturally have no ideas but what we draw from that of our own, by reflecting on the operations of our own souls within us, as far as they can come within our observation. But how inconsiderable a rank the spirits that inhabit our bodies hold amongst those various and possibly innumerable kinds of nobler beings; and how far short they come of the endowments and perfections of cherubims and seraphims, and infinite sorts of spirits above us; is what by a transient hint, in another place, I have offered to my reader's consideration.

18. As to the third sort of our knowledge, viz. the agreement or disagreement of any of our ideas in any other relation: This, as it is the largest field of our knowledge, so it is hard to determine how far it may extend: Because the advances that are made in this part of knowledge, depending on our sagacity in finding intermediate ideas, that may show the relations and habitudes of ideas, whose co-existence is not considered, it is a hard matter to tell when we are at an end of such discoveries; and when reason has all the helps it is capable of, for the finding of proofs, or examining the agreement or disagreement of remote ideas. They that are ignorant of algebra cannot imagine the wonders in this kind are to be done by it: And what farther improvements and helps, advantageous to other parts of knowledge, the sagacious mind of man may yet find out, it is not easy to determine. This at least I believe, that the ideas of quantity are not those alone that are capable of demonstration and knowledge; and that other, and perhaps more useful, parts of contemplation would afford us certainty, if vices, passions, and domineering interest did not oppose or menace such endeavours.

The idea of a supreme being, infinite in power, goodness, and wisdom, whose workmanship we are, and on whom we depend; and the idea of ourselves, as understanding rational creatures; being such as are clear in us, would, I suppose, if duly considered and pursued, afford such foundations of our duty and rules of action as might place morality amongst the sciences capable of demonstration; wherein I doubt not but from self-evident propositions, by necessary consequences, as incontestable as those in mathematics, the measures of right and wrong might be made out to anyone that will apply himself with the same indifferency and attention to the one as he does to the other of these sciences. The relation of other modes may certainly be perceived, as well as those of number and extension: And I cannot see why they should not also be capable of demonstration, if due methods were thought on to examine or pursue their agreement or disagreement. "Where there is no property, there is no injustice" is a proposition as certain as any demonstration in Euclid: For the idea of property being a right to any thing, and the idea to which the name *injustice* is given being the invasion or violation of that right; it is evident that these ideas, being thus established, and these names annexed to them, I can as certainly know this proposition to be true as that a triangle has three angles equal to two right ones. Again, "No government allows absolute liberty": The idea of government being the establishment of society upon certain rules or laws which require conformity to them; and the idea of absolute liberty being for anyone to do whatever he pleases; I am as capable of being certain of the truth of this proposition as of any in the mathematics.

19. That which in this respect has given the advantage to the ideas of quantity, and made them thought more capable of certainty and demonstration, is,

First, that they can be set down and represented by sensible marks, which have a greater and nearer correspondence with them than any words or sounds whatsoever. Diagrams drawn on paper are copies of the ideas in the mind, and not liable to the uncertainty that words carry in their signification. An angle, circle, or square, drawn in lines, lies open to the view, and cannot be mistaken: It remains unchangeable, and may at leisure be considered and examined, and the demonstration be revised, and all the parts of it may be gone over more than once without any danger of the least change in the ideas. This cannot be thus done in moral ideas; we have no sensible marks that resemble them, whereby we can set them down; we have nothing but words to express them by; which though, when written, they remain the same, yet the ideas they stand for may change in the same man; and it is very seldom that they are not different in different persons.

Secondly, another thing that makes the greater difficulty in ethics is that moral ideas are commonly more complex than those of the figures ordinarily considered in mathematics. From whence these two inconveniences follow: First, that their names are of more uncertain signification, the precise collection of simple ideas they stand for not being so easily agreed on, and so the sign that is used for them in communication always, and in thinking often, does not steadily carry with it the same idea. Upon which the same disorder, confusion, and error follow as would if a man, going to demonstrate something of an heptagon, should, in the diagram he took to do it, leave out one of the angles, or by oversight make the figure with one angle more than the name ordinarily imported, or he intended it should, when at first he thought of his demonstration. This often happens, and is hardly avoidable in very complex moral ideas, where the same name being retained, one angle, i.e. one simple idea, is left out or put in the complex one (still called by the same name) more at one time than another. Secondly, from the complexedness of these moral ideas, there follows another inconvenience, viz. that the mind cannot easily retain those precise combinations so exactly and perfectly as is necessary in the examination of the habitudes and correspondencies, agreements or disagreements, of several of them one with another; especially where it is to be judged of by long deductions, and the intervention of several other complex ideas, to show the agreement or disagreement of two remote ones.

The great help against this which mathematicians find in diagrams and figures, which remain unalterable in their draughts, is very apparent, and the memory would often have great difficulty otherwise to retain them so exactly, whilst the mind went over the parts of them step by step, to examine their several correspondencies. And though in casting up a long sum either in addition, multiplication, or division, every part be only a progression of the mind, taking a view of its own ideas, and considering their agreement or disagreement; and the resolution of the question be nothing but the result of the whole, made up of such particulars whereof the mind has a clear perception: Yet without setting down the several parts by marks whose precise significations are known, and by marks that last and remain in view when the memory had let them go, it would be almost impossible to carry so many different ideas in the mind, without confounding or letting slip some parts of the reckoning, and thereby making all our reasonings about it useless. In which case, the ciphers or marks help not the mind at all to perceive the agreement of any two or more numbers, their equalities or proportions: That the mind has only by intuition of its own ideas of the numbers themselves. But the numerical characters are helps to the memory, to record and retain the several ideas about which the demonstration is made, whereby a man may know how far his intuitive knowledge, in surveying several of the particulars, has proceeded; that so he may without confusion go on to what is yet unknown, and at last have in one view before him the result of all his perceptions and reasonings.

20. One part of these disadvantages in moral ideas, which has made them be thought not capable of demonstration, may in a good measure be remedied by definitions, setting down that collection of simple ideas which every term shall stand for, and then using the terms steadily and constantly for that precise collection. And what methods algebra, or something of that kind, may hereafter suggest to remove the other difficulties, it is not easy to foretell. Confident I am that if men would, in the same method, and with the same indifferency, search after moral as they do mathematical truths, they would find them have a stronger connexion one with another, and a more necessary consequence from our clear and distinct ideas, and to come nearer perfect demonstration than is commonly imagined. But much of this is not to be expected, whilst the desire of esteem, riches, or power makes men espouse the well-endowed opinions in fashion, and then seek arguments either to make good their beauty, or varnish over and cover their deformity: Nothing being so beautiful to the eye as truth is to the mind; nothing so deformed and irreconcilable to the understanding as a lie. For though many a man can with satisfaction enough own a no very handsome wife in his bosom; yet who is bold enough openly to avow that he has espoused a falsehood, and received into his breast so ugly a thing as a lie? Whilst the parties of men cram their tenets down all men's throats whom they can get into their power, without permitting them to examine their truth or falsehood, and will not let truth have fair play in the world, nor men the liberty to search after it; what improvements can be expected of this kind? What greater light can be hoped for in the moral sciences? The subject part of mankind in most places

might, instead thereof, with Egyptian bondage expect Egyptian darkness, were not the candle of the Lord set up by himself in men's minds, which it is impossible for the breath or power of man wholly to extinguish.

21. As to the fourth sort of our knowledge, viz. of the real actual existence of things, we have an intuitive knowledge of our own existence; and a demonstrative knowledge of the existence of a God; of the existence of anything else, we have no other but a sensitive knowledge, which extends not beyond the objects present to our senses.

22. Our knowledge being so narrow, as I have showed, it will perhaps give us some light into the present state of our minds if we look a little into the dark side, and take a view of our ignorance: Which, being infinitely larger than our knowledge, may serve much to the quieting of disputes and improvement of useful knowledge; if discovering how far we have clear and distinct ideas, we confine our thoughts within the contemplation of those things that are within the reach of our understandings, and launch not out into that abyss of darkness (where we have not eyes to see, nor faculties to perceive anything) out of a presumption that nothing is beyond our comprehension. But to be satisfied of the folly of such a conceit, we need not go far. He that knows anything knows this in the first place, that he need not seek long for instances of his ignorance. The meanest and most obvious things that come in our way, have dark sides, that the quickest sight cannot penetrate into. The clearest and most enlarged understandings of thinking men find themselves puzzled, and at a loss, in every particle of matter. We shall the less wonder to find it so when we consider the causes of our ignorance; which, from what has been said, I suppose, will be found to be these three:

First, want of ideas.

Secondly, want of a discoverable connexion between the ideas we have.

Thirdly, want of tracing and examining our ideas.

23. First, there are some things, and those not a few, that we are ignorant of, for want of ideas.

First, all the simple ideas we have are confined (as I have shown) to those we receive from corporeal objects by sensation, and from the operations of our own minds as the objects of reflection. But how much these few and narrow inlets are disproportionate to the vast whole extent of all beings will not be hard to persuade those who are not so foolish as to think their span the measure of all things. What other simple ideas it is possible the creatures in other parts of the universe may have, by the assistance of senses and faculties more, or perfecter, than we have, or different from ours, it is not for us to determine. But to say or think there are no such, because we conceive nothing of them, is no better an argument than if a blind man should be positive in it that there was no such thing as sight and colours because he had no manner of idea of any such thing, nor could by any means frame to himself any notions about seeing. The ignorance and darkness that is in us no more hinders nor confines the knowledge that is in others than the blindness of a mole is an argument against the quicksightedness of an eagle. He that will consider the infinite power, wisdom, and goodness of the Creator of all things will find reason to think it was not all laid out upon so inconsiderable, mean, and impotent a creature as he will find man to be; who, in all probability, is one of the lowest of all intellectual beings. What faculties therefore other species of creatures have, to penetrate into the nature and inmost constitutions of things; what ideas they may receive of them, far different from ours; we know not. This we know, and certainly find, that we want several other views of them, besides those we have, to make discoveries of them more perfect. And we may be convinced that the ideas we can attain to by our faculties are very disproportionate to things themselves, when a positive, clear, distinct one of substance itself, which is the foundation of all the rest, is concealed from us. But want of ideas of this kind, being a part as well as cause of our ignorance, cannot be described. Only this, I think, I may confidently say of it, that the intellectual and sensible world are in this perfectly alike; that that part which we see of either of them holds no proportion with what we see not; and whatsoever we can reach with our eyes or our thoughts of either of them is but a point, almost nothing, in comparison of the rest.

24. Secondly, another great cause of ignorance is the want of ideas we are capable of. As the want of ideas which our faculties are not able to give us shuts us wholly from those views of things which it is reasonable to think other beings, perfecter than we, have, of which we know nothing; so the want of ideas I now speak of keeps us in ignorance of things we conceive capable of being known to us. Bulk, figure, and motion we have ideas of. But though we are not without ideas of these primary qualities of bodies in general, yet not knowing what is the particular bulk, figure, and motion of the greatest part of the bodies of the universe, we are ignorant of the several powers, efficacies, and ways of operation whereby the effects which we daily see are produced. These are hid from us in some things by being too remote; and in others, by being too minute. When we consider the vast distance of the known and visible parts of the world, and the reasons we have to think that what lies within our ken is but a small part of the universe, we shall then discover an huge abyss of ignorance. What are the particular fabrics of the great masses of matter, which make up the whole stupendous frame of corporeal beings, how far they are extended, what is their motion, and how continued or communicated, and what influence they have one upon another, are contemplations that at first glimpse our thoughts lose themselves in. If we narrow our contemplations, and confine our thoughts to this little canton, I mean this system of our sun, and the grosser masses of matter that visibly move about it; what several sorts of vegetables, animals, and intellectual corporeal beings, infinitely different from those of our little spot of earth, may there probably be in the other planets, to the knowledge of which, even of their outward figures and parts, we can no way attain whilst we are confined to this earth; there being no natural means, either by sensation or reflection, to convey their certain ideas into our minds? They are out of the reach of those inlets of all our knowledge: And what sorts of furniture and inhabitants those mansions contain in them, we cannot so much as guess, much less have clear and distinct ideas of them.

25. If a great, nay, far the greatest part of the several ranks of bodies in the universe escape our notice by their remoteness, there are others that are no less concealed from us by their minuteness. These insensible corpuscles being the active parts of matter, and the great instruments of nature, on which depend not only all their secondary qualities, but also most of their natural operations, our want of precise distinct ideas of their primary qualities keeps us in an incurable ignorance of what we desire to know about them. I doubt not but if we could discover the figure, size, texture, and motion of the minute constituent parts of any two bodies, we should know without trial several of their operations one upon another, as we do now the properties of a square or a triangle. Did we know the mechanical affections of the particles of rhubarb, hemlock, opium, and a man, as a watch-maker does those of a watch, whereby it performs its operations, and of a file which by rubbing on them will alter the figure of any of the wheels; we should be able to tell before-hand that rhubarb will purge, hemlock kill, and opium make a man sleep; as well as a watch-maker can, that a little piece of paper laid on the balance will keep the watch from going, till it be removed; or that, some small part of it being rubbed by a file, the machine would quite lose its motion, and the watch go no more. The dissolving of silver in *aqua fortis,* and gold in *aqua regia,* and not vice versa, would be then perhaps no more difficult to know than it is to a smith to understand why the turning of one key will open a lock, and not the turning of another. But whilst we are destitute of senses acute enough to discover the minute particles of bodies, and to give us ideas of their mechanical affections, we must be content to be ignorant of their properties and ways of operation; nor can we be assured about them any farther than some few trials we make are able to reach. But whether they will succeed again another time, we cannot be certain. This hinders our certain knowledge of universal truths concerning natural bodies; and our reason carries us herein very little beyond particular matter of fact.

26. And therefore I am apt to doubt that how far soever human industry may advance useful and experimental philosophy in physical things, scientifical will still be out of our reach; because we want perfect and adequate ideas of those very bodies which are nearest to us, and most under our command. Those which we have ranked into classes under names, and we think ourselves best acquainted with, we have but very imperfect and incomplete ideas of. Distinct ideas of the several sorts of bodies that fall under the examination of our senses perhaps we may have: But adequate ideas, I suspect,

we have not of any one amongst them. And though the former of these will serve us for common use and discourse, yet whilst we want the latter, we are not capable of scientifical knowledge; nor shall ever be able to discover general, instructive, unquestionable truths concerning them. Certainty and demonstration are things we must not, in these matters, pretend to. By the colour, figure, taste, and smell, and other sensible qualities, we have as clear and distinct ideas of sage and hemlock as we have of a circle and a triangle: But having no ideas of the particular primary qualities of the minute parts of either of these plants, nor of other bodies which we would apply them to, we cannot tell what effects they will produce; nor when we see those effects can we so much as guess, much less know, their manner of production. Thus having no ideas of the particular mechanical affections of the minute parts of bodies that are within our view and reach, we are ignorant of their constitutions, powers, and operations: And of bodies more remote we are yet more ignorant, not knowing so much as their very outward shapes, or the sensible and grosser parts of their constitutions.

27. This, at first sight, will show us how disproportionate our knowledge is to the whole extent even of material beings; to which if we add the consideration of that infinite number of spirits that may be and probably are, which are yet more remote from our knowledge, whereof we have no cognizance, nor can frame to ourselves any distinct ideas of their several ranks and sorts, we shall find this cause of ignorance conceal from us, in an impenetrable obscurity, almost the whole intellectual world; a greater, certainly, and more beautiful world than the material. For bating some very few, and those, if I may so call them, superficial ideas of spirit, which by reflection we get of our own, and from thence the best we can collect of the father of all spirits, the eternal independent author of them and us and all things; we have no certain information, so much as of the existence of other spirits, but by revelation. Angels of all sorts are naturally beyond our discovery: And all those intelligences whereof it is likely there are more orders than of corporeal substances are things whereof our natural faculties give us no certain account at all. That there are minds and thinking beings in other men as well as himself, every man has a reason, from their words and actions, to be satisfied: And the knowledge of his own mind cannot suffer a man that considers to be ignorant that there is a God. But that there are degrees of spiritual beings between us and the great God, who is there that by his own search and ability can come to know? Much less have we distinct ideas of their different natures, conditions, states, powers, and several constitutions wherein they agree or differ from one another, and from us. And therefore in what concerns their different species and properties, we are under an absolute ignorance.

28. Secondly, what a small part of the substantial beings that are in the universe, the want of ideas leaves open to our knowledge, we have seen. In the next place, another cause of ignorance, of no less moment, is a want of a discoverable connexion between those ideas we have. For wherever we want that, we are utterly incapable of universal and certain knowledge; and are, in the former case, left only to observation and experiment: Which, how narrow and confined it is, how far from general knowledge, we need not be told. I shall give some few instances of this cause of our ignorance, and so leave it. It is evident that the bulk, figure, and motion of several bodies about us produce in us several sensations, as of colours, sounds, tastes, smells, pleasure and pain, &c. These mechanical affections of bodies having no affinity at all with those ideas they produce in us (there being no conceivable connexion between any impulse of any sort of body and any perception of a colour or smell, which we find in our minds), we can have no distinct knowledge of such operations beyond our experience; and can reason no otherwise about them than as effects produced by the appointment of an infinitely wise agent, which perfectly surpass our comprehensions. As the ideas of sensible secondary qualities which we have in our minds can by us be no way deduced from bodily causes, nor any correspondence or connexion be found between them and those primary qualities which (experience shows us) produce them in us; so on the other side, the operation of our minds upon our bodies is as inconceivable. How any thought should produce a motion in body is as remote from the nature of our ideas as how any body should produce any thought in the mind.

That it is so, if experience did not convince us, the consideration of the things themselves would never be able in the least to discover to us. These, and the like, though they have a constant and regular connexion, in the ordinary course of things; yet that connexion being not discoverable in the ideas themselves, which appearing to have no necessary dependence one on another, we can attribute their connexion to nothing else but the arbitrary determination of that all-wise agent who has made them to be, and to operate as they do, in a way wholly above our weak understandings to conceive.

29. In some of our ideas there are certain relations, habitudes, and connexions so visibly included in the nature of the ideas themselves that we cannot conceive them separable from them by any power whatsoever. And in these only we are capable of certain and universal knowledge. Thus the idea of a right-lined triangle necessarily carries with it an equality of its angles to two right ones. Nor can we conceive this relation, this connexion of these two ideas, to be possibly mutable, or to depend on any arbitrary power, which of choice made it thus, or could make it otherwise. But the coherence and continuity of the parts of matter; the production of sensation in us of colours and sounds, &c. by impulse and motion; nay, the original rules and communication of motion being such wherein we can discover no natural connexion with any ideas we have; we cannot but ascribe them to the arbitrary will and good pleasure of the wise architect. I need not, I think, here mention the resurrection of the dead, the future state of this globe of earth, and such other things which are by everyone acknowledged to depend wholly on the determination of a free agent. The things that, as far as our observation reaches, we constantly find to proceed regularly, we may conclude do act by a law set them; but yet by a law that we know not: Whereby, though causes work steadily, and effects constantly flow from them, yet their connexions and dependencies being not discoverable in our ideas, we can have but an experimental knowledge of them. From all which it is easy to perceive what a darkness we are involved in, how little it is of being, and the things that are, that we are capable to know. And therefore we shall do no injury to our knowledge when we modestly think with ourselves that we are so far from being able to

comprehend the whole nature of the universe, and all the things contained in it, that we are not capable of a philosophical knowledge of the bodies that are about us, and make a part of us: Concerning their secondary qualities, powers, and operations, we can have no universal certainty. Several effects come ery day within the notice of our senses, of which have so far sensitive knowledge; but the causes, manner, and certainty of their production, for the two foregoing reasons, we must be content to be very ignorant of. In these we can go no farther than particular experience informs us of matter of fact, and by analogy to guess what effects the like bodies are, upon other trials, like to produce. But as to a perfect science of natural bodies (not to mention spiritual beings) we are, I think, so far from being capable of any such thing that I conclude it lost labour to seek after it.

30. Thirdly, where we have adequate ideas, where there is a certain and discoverable connexion between them, yet we are often ignorant, for want of tracing those ideas which we have, or may have; and for want of finding out those intermediate ideas, which may show us what habitude of agreement or disagreement they have one with another. And thus many are ignorant of mathematical truths, not out of any imperfection of their faculties, or uncertainty in the things themselves, but for want of application in acquiring, examining, and by due ways comparing those ideas. That which has most contributed to hinder the due tracing of our ideas, and finding out their relations, and agreements or disagreements one with another, has been, I suppose, the ill use of words. It is impossible that men should ever truly seek or certainly discover the agreement or disagreement of ideas themselves whilst their thoughts flutter about, or stick only in sounds of doubtful and uncertain significations. Mathematicians abstracting their thoughts from names, and accustoming themselves to set before their minds the ideas themselves that they would consider, and not sounds instead of them, have avoided thereby a great part of that perplexity, puddering, and confusion which has so much hindered men's progress in other parts of knowledge. For whilst they stick in words of undetermined and uncertain signification, they are unable to distinguish true from false, certain from probable, consistent from inconsistent, in their own opinions. This having been the fate or misfortune of

a great part of men of letters, the increase brought into the stock of real knowledge has been very little, in proportion to the schools, disputes, and writings the world has been filled with; whilst students, being lost in the great wood of words, knew not whereabout they were, how far their discoveries were advanced, or what was wanting in their own or the general stock of knowledge. Had men, in the discoveries of the material, done as they have in those of the intellectual world, involved all in the obscurity of uncertain and doubtful ways of talking, volumes writ of navigation and voyages, theories and stories of zones and tides, multiplied and disputed; nay, ships built, and fleets sent out, would never have taught us the way beyond the line; and the Antipodes would be still as much unknown as when it was declared heresy to hold there were any. But having spoken sufficiently of words, and the ill or careless use that is commonly made of them, I shall not say anything more of it here.

31. Hitherto we have examined the extent of our knowledge, in respect of the several sorts of beings that are. There is another extent of it, in respect of universality, which will also deserve to be considered; and in this regard, our knowledge follows the nature of our ideas. If the ideas are abstract, whose agreement or disagreement we perceive, our knowledge is universal. For what is known of such general ideas will be true of every particular thing in whom that essence, i.e. that abstract idea, is to be found; and what is once known of such ideas will be perpetually and for ever true. So that as to all general knowledge, we must search and find it only in our minds, and it is only the examining of our own ideas that furnisheth us with that. Truths belonging to essences of things (that is, to abstract ideas) are eternal, and are to be found out by the contemplation only of those essences: As the existence of things is to be known only from experience. But having more to say of this in the chapters where I shall speak of general and real knowledge, this may here suffice as to the universality of our knowledge in general.

Chapter IV. Of the Reality of Our Knowledge

1. I doubt not but my reader by this time may be apt to think that I have been all this while only building a castle in the air; and be ready to say to me, "To what purpose all this stir? Knowledge, say you, is only the perception of the agreement or disagreement of our own ideas: But who knows what those ideas may be? Is there anything so extravagant as the imaginations of men's brains? Where is the head that has no chimeras in it? Or if there be a sober and a wise man, what difference will there be, by your rules, between his knowledge and that of the most extravagant fancy in the world? They both have their ideas, and perceive their agreement and disagreement one with another. If there be any difference between them, the advantage will be on the warm-headed man's side, as having the more ideas, and the more lively: And so, by your rules, he will be the more knowing. If it be true that all knowledge lies only in the perception of the agreement or disagreement of our own ideas, the visions of an enthusiast and the reasonings of a sober man will be equally certain. It is no matter how things are; so a man observe but the agreement of his own imaginations, and talk conformably, it is all truth, all certainty. Such castles in the air will be as strong-holds of truth as the demonstrations of Euclid. That an harpy is not a centaur is by this way as certain knowledge, and as much a truth, as that a square is not a circle.

"But of what use is all this fine knowledge of men's own imaginations to a man that enquires after the reality of things? It matters not what men's fancies are, it is the knowledge of things that is only to be prized: It is this alone gives a value to our reasonings, and preference to one man's knowledge over another's, that it is of things as they really are, and not of dreams and fancies."

2. To which I answer, that if our knowledge of our ideas terminate in them, and reach no farther, where there is something farther intended, our most serious thoughts will be of little more use than the reveries of a crazy brain; and the truths built thereon of no more weight than the discourses of a man who sees things clearly in a dream, and with great assurance utters them. But, I hope, before I have done, to make it evident that this way of certainty, by the knowledge of our own ideas, goes a little farther than bare imagination: And I believe it will appear that all the certainty of general truths a man has lies in nothing else.

3. It is evident the mind knows not things immediately, but only by the intervention of the ideas it has of them. Our knowledge therefore is real only so far as there is a conformity between our ideas and the reality of things. But what shall be here the criterion? How shall the mind, when it perceives nothing but its own ideas, know that they agree with things themselves? This, though it seems not to want difficulty, yet, I think, there be two sorts of ideas that, we may be assured, agree with things.

4. The first are simple ideas, which since the mind, as has been showed, can by no means make to itself, must necessarily be the product of things operating on the mind in a natural way, and producing therein those perceptions which by the wisdom and will of our maker they are ordained and adapted to. From whence it follows that simple ideas are not fictions of our fancies, but the natural and regular productions of things without us, really operating upon us, and so carry with them all the conformity which is intended, or which our state requires: For they represent to us things under those appearances which they are fitted to produce in us, whereby we are enabled to distinguish the sorts of particular substances, to discern the states they are in, and so to take them for our necessities, and apply them to our uses. Thus the idea of whiteness, or bitterness, as it is in the mind, exactly answering that power, which is in any body to produce it there, has all the real conformity it can or ought to have with things without us. And this conformity between our simple ideas and the existence of things is sufficient for real knowledge.

5. Secondly, all our complex ideas, except those of substances, being archetypes of the mind's own making, not intended to be the copies of anything, nor referred to the existence of anything as to their originals; cannot want any conformity necessary to real knowledge. For that which is not designed to represent anything but itself can never be capable of a wrong representation, nor mislead us from the true apprehension of anything, by its dislikeness to it; and such, excepting those of substances, are all our complex ideas: Which, as I have showed in another place, are combinations of ideas, which the mind, by its free choice, puts together, without considering any connexion they have in nature. And hence it is that in all these sorts the ideas themselves are considered as the archetypes, and things no otherwise regarded but as they are conformable to them. So that we cannot but be infallibly certain that all the knowledge we attain concerning these ideas is real, and reaches things themselves; because in all our thoughts, reasonings, and discourses of this kind, we intend things no farther than as they are conformable to our ideas. So that in these we cannot miss of a certain and undoubted reality.

6. I doubt not but it will be easily granted that the knowledge we have of mathematical truths is not only certain, but real knowledge; and not the bare empty vision of vain insignificant chimeras of the brain: And yet, if we will consider, we shall find that it is only of our own ideas. The mathematician considers the truth and properties belonging to a rectangle, or circle, only as they are in idea in his own mind. For it is possible he never found either of them existing mathematically, i.e. precisely true, in his life. But yet the knowledge he has of any truths or properties belonging to a circle, or any other mathematical figure, are nevertheless true and certain, even of real things existing; because real things are no farther concerned, nor intended to be meant by any such propositions than as things really agree to those archetypes in his mind. Is it true of the idea of a triangle that its three angles are equal to two right ones? It is true also of a triangle, wherever it really exists. Whatever other figure exists that is not exactly answerable to that idea of a triangle in his mind is not at all concerned in that proposition: And therefore he is certain all his knowledge concerning such ideas is real knowledge; because intending things no farther than they agree with those his ideas, he is sure what he knows concerning those figures when they have barely an ideal existence in his mind will hold true of them also when they have real existence in matter; his consideration being barely of those figures which are the same, wherever or however they exist.

7. And hence it follows that moral knowledge is as capable of real certainty as mathematics. For certainty being but the perception of the agreement or disagreement of our ideas; and demonstration nothing but the perception of such agreement, by the intervention of other ideas, or mediums; our moral ideas, as well as mathematical, being archetypes themselves, and so adequate and complete ideas; all the agreement or disagreement which we shall find in them will produce real knowledge, as well as in mathematical figures.

8. For the attaining of knowledge and certainty, it is requisite that we have determined ideas; and, to make our knowledge real, it is requisite that the ideas answer their archetypes. Nor let it be wondered that I place the certainty of our knowledge in the consideration of our ideas, with so little care and regard (as it may seem) to the real existence of things: Since most of those discourses which take up the thoughts, and engage the disputes of those who pretend to make it their business to enquire after truth and certainty, will, I presume, upon examination be found to be general propositions and notions in which existence is not at all concerned. All the discourses of the mathematicians about the squaring of a circle, conic sections, or any other part of mathematics concern not the existence of any of those figures; but their demonstrations, which depend on their ideas, are the same, whether there be any square or circle existing in the world, or no. In the same manner the truth and certainty of moral discourses abstracts from the lives of men, and the existence of those virtues in the world whereof they treat. Nor are Tully's offices less true because there is nobody in the world that exactly practises his rules, and lives up to that pattern of a virtuous man which he has given us, and which existed nowhere, when he writ, but in idea. If it be true in speculation, i.e. in idea, that murder deserves death, it will also be true in reality of any action that exists conformable to that idea of murder. As for other actions, the truth of that proposition concerns them not. And thus it is of all other species of things, which have no other essences but those ideas which are in the minds of men.

9. But it will here be said, that if moral knowledge be placed in the contemplation of our own moral ideas, and those, as other modes, be of our own making, what strange notions will there be of justice and temperance? What confusion of virtues and vices, if everyone may make what ideas of them he pleases? No confusion or disorder in the things themselves, nor the reasonings about them; no more than (in mathematics) there would be a disturbance in the demonstration, or a change in the properties of figures, and their relations one to another, if a man should make a triangle with four corners, or a trapezium with four right angles: That is, in plain English, change the names of the figures, and call that by one name which mathematicians call ordinarily by another. For let a man make to himself the idea of a figure with three angles, whereof one is a right one, and call it, if he please, equilaterum or trapezium, or anything else, the properties of and demonstrations about that idea will be the same, as if he called it a rectangular triangle. I confess the change of the name, by the impropriety of speech, will at first disturb him who knows not what idea it stands for; but as soon as the figure is drawn, the consequences and demonstration are plain and clear. Just the same is it in moral knowledge, let a man have the idea of taking from others, without their consent, what their honest industry has possessed them of, and call this justice, if he please. He that takes the name here without the idea put to it will be mistaken, by joining another idea of his own to that name; but strip the idea of that name, or take it such as it is in the speaker's mind, and the same things will agree to it, as if you called it injustice. Indeed wrong names in moral discourses breed usually more disorder, because they are not so easily rectified as in mathematics, where the figure, once drawn and seen, makes the name useless and of no force. For what need of a sign, when the thing signified is present and in view? But in moral names that cannot be so easily and shortly done, because of the many decompositions that go to the making up the complex ideas of those modes. But yet for all this, the miscalling of any of those ideas, contrary to the usual signification of the words of that language, hinders not but that we may have certain and demonstrative knowledge of their several agreements and disagreements, if we will carefully, as in mathematics, keep to the same precise ideas, and trace them in their several relations one to another, without being led away by their names. If we but separate the idea under consideration from the sign that stands for it, our knowledge goes equally on in the discovery of real truth and certainty, whatever sounds we make use of.

10. One thing more we are to take notice of, that where God, or any other law-maker, hath defined any moral names, there they have made the essence of that species to which that name belongs; and there it is not safe to apply or use them otherwise: But in other cases it is bare impropriety of speech to apply them contrary to the common usage of the country. But yet even this too disturbs not the certainty of that knowledge which is still to be had by a due contemplation and comparing of those even nick-named ideas.

11. Thirdly, there is another sort of complex ideas, which, being referred to archetypes without us, may differ from them, and so our knowledge about them may come short of being real. Such are our ideas of substances, which consisting of a collection of simple ideas, supposed taken from the works of nature, may yet vary from them, by having more or different ideas united in them, than are to be found united in the things themselves. From whence it comes to pass that they may, and often do, fail of being exactly conformable to things themselves.

12. I say, then, that to have ideas of substances, which, by being conformable to things, may afford us real knowledge, it is not enough, as in modes, to put together such ideas as have no inconsistence, though they did never before so exist; v.g. the ideas of sacrilege or perjury, &c. were as real and true ideas before as after the existence of any such fact. But our ideas of substances being supposed copies, and referred to archetypes without us, must still be taken from something that does or has existed; they must not consist of ideas put together at the pleasure of our thoughts, without any real pattern they were taken from, though we can perceive no inconsistence in such a combination. The reason whereof is, because we knowing not what real constitution it is of substances, whereon our simple ideas depend, and which really is the cause of the strict union of some of them one with another, and the exclusion of others; there are very few of them that we can be sure are, or are not, inconsistent in nature, any farther than experience and sensible observation reach. Herein therefore is founded the reality of our knowledge concerning substances, that all our complex ideas of them must be such, and such only, as are made up of such simple ones, as have been discovered to co-exist in nature. And our ideas being thus true: Though not, perhaps, very exact copies, are yet the subjects of real (as far as we have any) knowledge of them. Which (as has been already shown) will not be found to reach very far: But so far as it does, it will still be real knowledge. Whatever ideas we have, the agreement we find they have with others will still be knowledge. If those ideas be abstract, it will be general knowledge. But, to make it real concerning substances, the ideas must be taken from the real existence of things. Whatever simple ideas have been found to co-exist in any substance, these we may with confidence join together again, and so make abstract ideas of substances. For whatever have once had an union in nature may be united again.

13. This, if we rightly consider, and confine not our thoughts and abstract ideas to names, as if there were or could be no other sorts of things than what known names had already determined, and, as it were, set out; we should think of things with greater freedom and less confusion than perhaps we do. It would possibly be thought a bold paradox, if not a very dangerous falsehood, if I should say that some changelings, who have lived forty years together without any appearance of reason, are something between a man and a beast: Which prejudice is founded upon nothing else but a false supposition, that these two names, *man* and *beast,* stand for distinct species so set out by real essences that there can come no other species between them: Whereas if we will abstract from those names, and the supposition of such specific essences made by nature, wherein all things of the same denominations did exactly and equally partake; if we would not fancy that there were a certain number of these essences, wherein all things, as in moulds, were cast and formed; we should find that the idea of the shape, motion, and life of a man without reason is as much a distinct idea, and makes as much a distinct sort of things from man and beast, as the idea of the shape of an ass with reason would be different from either that of man or beast, and be a species of an animal between, or distinct from both.

14. Here everybody will be ready to ask, If changelings may be supposed something between man and beast, pray what are they? I answer, changelings; which is as good a word to signify something different from the signification of man or beast as the names *man* and *beast* are to have significations different one from the other. This, well considered, would resolve this matter, and show my meaning without any more ado. But I am not so unacquainted with the zeal of some men, which enables them to spin consequences, and to see religion

threatened whenever anyone ventures to quit their forms of speaking, as not to foresee what names such a proposition as this is like to be charged with: And without doubt it will be asked, If changelings are something between man and beast, what will become of them in the other world? To which I answer, (1) It concerns me not to know or enquire. To their own master they stand or fall. It will make their state neither better nor worse whether we determine anything of it or no. They are in the hands of a faithful Creator and a bountiful Father, who disposes not of his creatures according to our narrow thoughts or opinions, nor distinguishes them according to names and species of our contrivance. And we that know so little of this present world we are in may, I think, content ourselves without being peremptory in defining the different states which creatures shall come into when they go off this stage. It may suffice us that he hath made known to all those who are capable of instruction, discoursing, and reasoning that they shall come to an account, and receive according to what they have done in this body.

15. But, secondly, I answer, the force of these men's question (viz. will you deprive changelings of a future state?) is founded on one of these two suppositions, which are both false. The first is, that all things that have the outward shape and appearance of a man must necessarily be designed to an immortal future being after this life: Or, secondly, that whatever is of human birth must be so. Take away these imaginations, and such questions will be groundless and ridiculous. I desire then those who think there is no more but an accidental difference between themselves and changelings, the essence in both being exactly the same, to consider whether they can imagine immortality annexed to any outward shape of the body? The very proposing it, is, I suppose, enough to make them disown it. No one yet, that ever I heard of, how much soever immersed in matter, allowed that excellency to any figure of the gross sensible outward parts as to affirm eternal life due to it, or a necessary consequence of it; or that any mass of matter should, after its dissolution here, be again restored hereafter to an everlasting state of sense, perception, and knowledge, only because it was moulded into this or that figure, and had such a particular frame of its visible parts. Such an opinion as this, placing immortality in a certain superficial figure, turns out of doors all consideration of soul or spirit, upon whose account alone some corporeal beings have hitherto been concluded immortal, and others not. This is to attribute more to the outside than inside of things; and to place the excellency of a man more in the external shape of his body than internal perfections of his soul: Which is but little better than to annex the great and inestimable advantage of immortality and life everlasting, which he has above other material beings, to annex it, I say, to the cut of his beard, or the fashion of his coat. For this or that outward mark of our bodies no more carries with it the hope of an eternal duration, than the fashion of a man's suit gives him reasonable grounds to imagine it will never wear out, or that it will make him immortal. It will perhaps be said, that nobody thinks that the shape makes anything immortal, but it is the shape is the sign of a rational soul within, which is immortal. I wonder who made it the sign of any such thing: For barely saying it will not make it so. It would require some proofs to persuade one of it. No figure that I know speaks any such language. For it may as rationally be concluded that the dead body of a man, wherein there is to be found no more appearance or action of life than there is in a statue, has yet nevertheless a living soul in it because of its shape, as that there is a rational soul in a changeling, because he has the outside of a rational creature; when his actions carry far less marks of reason with them, in the whole course of his life, than what are to be found in many a beast.

16. But it is the issue of rational parents, and must therefore be concluded to have a rational soul. I know not by what logic you must so conclude. I am sure this is a conclusion that men nowhere allow of. For if they did, they would not make bold, as everywhere they do, to destroy ill-formed and misshaped productions. Ay, but these are monsters. Let them be so; what will your drivling, unintelligent, intractable changeling be? Shall a defect in the body make a monster; a defect in the mind (the far more noble, and in the common phrase, the far more essential part) not? Shall the want of a nose, or a neck, make a monster, and put such issue out of the rank of men; the want of reason and understanding, not? This is to bring all back again to what was exploded

just now: This is to place all in the shape, and to take the measure of a man only by his outside. To show that, according to the ordinary way of reasoning in this matter, people do lay the whole stress on the figure, and resolve the whole essence of the species of man (as they make it) into the outward shape, how unreasonable soever it be, and how much soever they disown it; we need but trace their thoughts and practice a little farther, and then it will plainly appear. The well-shaped changeling is a man, has a rational soul, though it appear not; this is past doubt, say you. Make the ears a little longer, and more pointed, and the nose a little flatter than ordinary, and then you begin to boggle: Make the face yet narrower, flatter, and longer, and then you are at a stand: Add still more and more of the likeness of a brute to it, and let the head be perfectly that of some other animal, then presently it is a monster; and it is demonstration with you that it hath no rational soul, and must be destroyed. Where now (I ask) shall be the just measure; which the utmost bounds of that shape, that carries with it a rational soul? For since there have been human foetuses produced, half beast, and half man; and others three parts one, and one part the other; and so it is possible they may be in all the variety of approaches to the one or the other shape, and may have several degrees of mixture of the likeness of a man or a brute; I would gladly know what are those precise lineaments which, according to this hypothesis, are or are not capable of a rational soul to be joined to them. What sort of outside is the certain sign that there is or is not such an inhabitant within? For till that be done, we talk at random of man: And shall always, I fear, do so, as long as we give ourselves up to certain sounds, and the imaginations of settled and fixed species in nature, we know not what. But after all, I desire it may be considered that those who think they have answered the difficulty by telling us that a mis-shaped foetus is a monster run into the same fault they are arguing against, by constituting a species between man and beast. For what else, I pray, is their monster in the case (if the word *monster* signifies anything at all) but something neither man nor beast, but partaking somewhat of either? And just so is the changeling before-mentioned. So necessary is it to quit the common notion of species and essences, if we will truly look into the nature of things, and examine them, by what our faculties can discover in them as they exist, and not by groundless fancies that have been taken up about them.

17. I have mentioned this here because I think we cannot be too cautious that words and species, in the ordinary notions which we have been used to of them, impose not on us. For I am apt to think, therein lies one great obstacle to our clear and distinct knowledge, especially in reference to substances; and from thence has rose a great part of the difficulties about truth and certainty. Would we accustom ourselves to separate our contemplations and reasonings from words, we might, in a great measure, remedy this inconvenience within our own thoughts; but yet it would still disturb us in our discourse with others, as long as we retained the opinion that species and their essences were anything else but our abstract ideas (such as they are) with names annexed to them, to be the signs of them.

18. Wherever we perceive the agreement or disagreement of any of our ideas, there is certain knowledge: And wherever we are sure those ideas agree with the reality of things, there is certain real knowledge. Of which agreement of our ideas, with the reality of things, having here given the marks, I think I have shown wherein it is, that certainty, real certainty, consists: Which, whatever it was to others, was, I confess, to me heretofore one of those desiderata which I found great want of.

. . .

Chapter IX. Of Our Knowledge of Existence

1. Hitherto we have only considered the essences of things, which being only abstract ideas, and thereby removed in our thoughts from particular existence (that being the proper operation of the mind, in abstraction, to consider an idea under no other existence but what it has in the understanding), gives us no knowledge of real existence at all. Where by the way we may take notice that universal propositions, of whose truth or falsehood we can have certain knowledge, concern not existence; and farther, that all particular affirmations or negations, that would not be certain if they were made general, are only concerning existence; they declaring only the accidental union or separation of ideas in things existing which, in their abstract natures, have no known necessary union or repugnancy.

2. But leaving the nature of propositions and different ways of predication to be considered more at large in another place, let us proceed now to enquire concerning our knowledge of the existence of things, and how we come by it. I say, then, that we have the knowledge of our own existence by intuition; of the existence of God by demonstration; and of other things by sensation.

3. As for our own existence, we perceive it so plainly and so certainly that it neither needs nor is capable of any proof. For nothing can be more evident to us than our own existence; I think, I reason, I feel pleasure and pain: Can any of these be more evident to me than my own existence? If I doubt of all other things, that very doubt makes me perceive my own existence, and will not suffer me to doubt of that. For if I know I feel pain, it is evident I have as certain perception of my own existence as of the existence of the pain I feel: Or if I know I doubt, I have as certain perception of the existence of the thing doubting as of that thought which I call doubt. Experience then convinces us that we have an intuitive knowledge of our own existence, and an internal infallible perception that we are. In every act of sensation, reasoning, or thinking, we are conscious to ourselves of our own being; and, in this matter, come not short of the highest degree of certainty.

Chapter XI. Of Our Knowledge of the Existence of Other Things

1. The knowledge of our own being we have by intuition. The existence of a God reason clearly makes known to us, as has been shown.

The knowledge of the existence of any other thing, we can have only by sensation: For there being no necessary connexion of real existence with any idea a man hath in his memory, nor of any other existence but that of God, with the existence of any particular man, no particular man can know the existence of any other being but only when by actual operating upon him, it makes itself perceived by him. For the having the idea of anything in our mind no more proves the existence of that thing than the picture of a man evidences his being in the world, or the visions of a dream make thereby a true history.

2. It is therefore the actual receiving of ideas from without that gives us notice of the existence of other things, and makes us know that something doth exist at that time without us, which causes that idea in us, though perhaps we neither know nor consider how it does it: For it takes not from the certainty of our senses, and the ideas we receive by them, that we know not the manner wherein they are produced: V.g. whilst I write this, I have, by the paper affecting my eyes, that idea produced in my mind which whatever object causes, I call white; by which I know that that quality or accident (i.e. whose appearance before my eyes always causes that idea) doth really exist, and hath a being without me. And of this, the greatest assurance I can possibly have, and to which my faculties can attain, is the testimony of my eyes, which are the proper and sole judges of this thing, whose testimony I have reason to rely on as so certain that I can no more doubt, whilst I write this, that I see white and black, and that something really exists that causes that sensation in me, than that I write or move my hand; which is a certainty as great as human nature is capable of, concerning the existence of anything, but a man's self alone, and of God.

3. The notice we have by our senses of the existing of things without us, though it be not altogether so certain as our intuitive knowledge, or the deductions of our reason employed about the clear abstract ideas of our own minds yet, it is an assurance that deserves the name of knowledge. If we persuade ourselves that our faculties act and inform us right, concerning the existence of those objects that affect them, it cannot pass for an ill-grounded confidence: For I think nobody can, in earnest, be so sceptical as to be uncertain of the existence of those things which he sees and feels. At least, he that can doubt so far (whatever he may have with his own thoughts) will never have any controversy with me; since he can never be sure I say anything contrary to his own opinion. As to myself, I think God has given me assurance enough of the existence of things without me; since by their different application I can produce in myself both pleasure and pain, which is one great concernment of my present state.

This is certain: The confidence that our faculties do not herein deceive us is the greatest assurance we are capable of, concerning the existence of material beings. For we cannot act anything but by our faculties; nor talk of knowledge itself but by the help of those faculties, which are fitted to apprehend even what knowledge is. But besides the assurance we have from our senses themselves, that they do not err in the information they give us, of the existence of things without us, when they are affected by them, we are farther confirmed in this assurance by other concurrent reasons.

4. First, it is plain those perceptions are produced in us by exterior causes affecting our senses, because those that want the organs of any sense never can have the ideas belonging to that sense produced in their minds. This is too evident to be doubted: And therefore we cannot but be assured that they come in by the organs of that sense, and no other way. The organs themselves, it is plain, do not produce them, for then the eyes of a man in the dark would produce colours, and his nose smell roses in the winter: But we see nobody gets the relish of a pineapple, till he goes to the Indies, where it is, and tastes it.

5. Secondly, because sometimes I find that I cannot avoid the having those ideas produced in my mind. For though when my eyes are shut, or windows fast, I can at pleasure recall to my mind the ideas of light, or the sun, which former sensations had lodged in my memory; so I can at pleasure lay by that idea, and take into my view that of the smell of a rose, or taste of sugar. But, if I turn my eyes at noon towards the sun, I cannot avoid the ideas which the light, or sun, then produces in me. So that there is a manifest difference between the ideas laid up in my memory (over which, if they were there only, I should have constantly the same power to dispose of them, and lay them by at pleasure) and those which force themselves upon me, and I cannot avoid having. And therefore it must needs be some exterior cause, and the brisk acting of some objects without me, whose efficacy I cannot resist, that produces those ideas in my mind, whether I will or no. Besides, there is nobody who doth not perceive the difference in himself between contemplating the sun, as he hath the idea of it in his memory, and actually looking upon it: Of which two, his perception

is so distinct that few of his ideas are more distinguishable one from another. And therefore he hath certain knowledge that they are not both memory, or the actions of his mind, and fancies only within him; but that actual seeing hath a cause without.

6. Thirdly, add to this, that many of those ideas are produced in us with pain, which afterwards we remember without the least offence. Thus the pain of heat or cold, when the idea of it is revived in our minds, gives us no disturbance; which, when felt, was very troublesome, and is again, when actually repeated; which is occasioned by the disorder the external object causes in our bodies when applied to it. And we remember the pains of hunger, thirst, or the head-ache, without any pain at all; which would either never disturb us, or else constantly do it, as often as we thought of it, were there nothing more but ideas floating in our minds, and appearances entertaining our fancies, without the real existence of things affecting us from abroad. The same may be said of pleasure, accompanying several actual sensations: And though mathematical demonstration depends not upon sense, yet the examining them by diagrams gives great credit to the evidence of our sight, and seems to give it a certainty approaching to that of demonstration itself. For it would be very strange that a man should allow it for an undeniable truth that two angles of a figure, which he measures by lines and angles of a diagram, should be bigger one than the other; and yet doubt of the existence of those lines and angles, which by looking on he makes use of to measure that by.

7. Fourthly, our senses in many cases bear witness to the truth of each other's report, concerning the existence of sensible things without us. He that sees a fire may, if he doubt whether it be anything more than a bare fancy, feel it too; and be convinced by putting his hand in it. Which certainly could never be put into such exquisite pain by a bare idea or phantom, unless that the pain be a fancy too: Which yet he cannot, when the burn is well, by raising the idea of it, bring upon himself again.

Thus I see, whilst I write this, I can change the appearance of the paper: And by designing the letters tell before-hand what new idea it shall exhibit the very next moment, by barely drawing my pen over it: Which will neither appear (let me fancy as much as I will) if my hands stand still; or though I move my pen, if my eyes be shut: Nor when those characters are once made on the paper, can I choose afterwards but see them as they are; that is, have the ideas of such letters as I have made. Whence it is manifest that they are not barely the sport and play of my own imagination, when I find that the characters, that were made at the pleasure of my own thoughts, do not obey them; nor yet cease to be, whenever I shall fancy it; but continue to affect my senses constantly and regularly, according to the figures I made them. To which if we will add that the sight of those shall, from another man, draw such sounds as I beforehand design they shall stand for, there will be little reason left to doubt, that those words I write do really exist without me, when they cause a long series of regular sounds to affect my ears, which could not be the effect of my imagination, nor could my memory retain them in that order.

8. But yet, if after all this anyone will be so sceptical as to distrust his senses, and to affirm that all we see and hear, feel and taste, think and do, during our whole being, is but the series and deluding appearances of a long dream, whereof there is no reality; and therefore will question the existence of all things, or our knowledge of anything; I must desire him to consider that if all be a dream, then he doth but dream that he makes the question; and so it is not much matter that a waking man should answer him. But yet, if he pleases, he may dream that I make him this answer, that the certainty of things existing *in rerum natura,* when we have the testimony of our senses for it, is not only as great as our frame can attain to, but as our condition needs. For our faculties being suited not to the full extent of being, nor to a perfect, clear, comprehensive knowledge of things free from all doubt and scruple, but to the preservation of us, in whom they are; and accommodated to the use of life; they serve to our purpose well enough, if they will but give us certain notice of those things which are convenient or inconvenient to us. For he that sees a candle burning, and hath experimented the force of its flame by putting his finger in it, will little doubt that this is something existing without him, which does him harm, and puts him to great pain: Which is assurance enough, when no man requires greater certainty to govern his actions by than what is as certain as his actions themselves. And if our dreamer pleases to try whether the glowing heat of a glass furnace be barely a wandering imagination in a drowsy man's fancy by putting his hand into it, he may perhaps be wakened into a certainty greater than he could wish, that it is something more than bare imagination. So that this evidence is as great as we can desire, being as certain to us as our pleasure or pain, i.e. happiness or misery; beyond which we have no concernment, either of knowing or being. Such an assurance of the existence of things without us is sufficient to direct us in the attaining the good, and avoiding the evil, which is caused by them; which is the important concernment we have of being made acquainted with them.

9. In fine, then, when our senses do actually convey into our understandings any idea, we cannot but be satisfied that there doth something at that time really exist without us, which doth affect our senses, and by them give notice of itself to our apprehensive faculties, and actually produce that idea which we then perceive: And we cannot so far distrust their testimony as to doubt that such collections of simple ideas as we have observed by our senses to be united together do really exist together. But this knowledge extends as far as the present testimony of our senses, employed about particular objects that do then affect them, and no farther. For if I saw such a collection of simple ideas, as is wont to be called *man,* existing together one minute since, and am now alone, I cannot be certain that the same man exists now, since there is no necessary connexion of his existence a minute since with his existence now: By a thousand ways he may cease to be, since I had the testimony of my senses for his existence. And if I cannot be certain that the man I saw last to-day is now in being, I can less be certain that he is so, who hath been longer removed from my senses, and I have not seen since yesterday, or since the last year; and much less can I be certain of the existence of men that I never saw. And therefore though it be highly probable that millions of men do now exist, yet, whilst I am alone writing this, I have not that certainty of it which we strictly call knowledge; though the great likelihood of it puts me past doubt, and it be reasonable for me to do

several things upon the confidence that there are men (and men also of my acquaintance, with whom I have to do) now in the world: But this is but probability, not knowledge.

10. Whereby yet we may observe how foolish and vain a thing it is for a man of a narrow knowledge, who having reason given him to judge of the different evidence and probability of things, and to be swayed accordingly; how vain, I say, it is to expect demonstration and certainty in things not capable of it; and refuse assent to very rational propositions, and act contrary to very plain and clear truths, because they cannot be made out so evident as to surmount every the least (I will not say reason, but) pretence of doubting. He that in the ordinary affairs of life would admit of nothing but direct plain demonstration would be sure of nothing in this world but of perishing quickly. The wholesomeness of his meat or drink would not give him reason to venture on it: And I would fain know what it is he could do upon such grounds as are capable of no doubt, no objection.

11. As when our senses are actually employed about any object, we do know that it does exist; so by our memory we may be assured that heretofore things that affected our senses have existed. And thus we have knowledge of the past existence of several things, whereof our senses having informed us, our memories still retain the ideas; and of this we are past all doubt, so long as we remember well. But this knowledge also reaches no farther than our senses have formerly assured us. Thus seeing water at this instant, it is an unquestionable truth to me that water doth exist: And remembering that I saw it yesterday, it will also be always true; and as long as my memory retains it, always an undoubted proposition to me, that water did exist the 10th of July, 1688, as it will also be equally true that a certain number of very fine colours did exist, which at the same time I saw upon a bubble of that water: But, being now quite out of sight both of the water and bubbles too, it is no more certainly known to me that the water doth now exist than that the bubbles or colours therein do so: It being no more necessary that water should exist to-day because it existed yesterday than that the colours or bubbles exist to-day because they existed yesterday, though

it be exceedingly much more probable, because water hath been observed to continue long in existence, but bubbles and the colours on them quickly cease to be.

12. What ideas we have of spirits, and how we come by them, I have already shown. But though we have those ideas in our minds, and know we have them there, the having the ideas of spirits does not make us know that any such things do exist without us, or that there are any finite spirits, or any other spiritual beings but the Eternal God. We have ground from revelation, and several other reasons, to believe with assurance that there are such creatures: But, our senses not being able to discover them, we want the means of knowing their particular existences. For we can no more know that there are finite spirits really existing by the idea we have of such beings in our minds than by the ideas anyone has of fairies, or centaurs, he can come to know that things answering those ideas do really exist.

And therefore concerning the existence of finite spirits, as well as several other things, we must content ourselves with the evidence of faith; but universal certain propositions concerning this matter are beyond our reach. For however true it may be, v.g. that all the intelligent spirits that God ever created do still exist; yet it can never make a part of our certain knowledge. These and the like propositions we may assent to as highly probable, but are not, I fear, in this state capable of knowing. We are not then to put others upon demonstrating, nor ourselves upon search of universal certainty in all those matters wherein we are not capable of any other knowledge but what our senses give us in this or that particular.

13. By which it appears that there are two sorts of propositions. (1) There is one sort of propositions concerning the existence of anything answerable to such an idea: As having the idea of an elephant, phoenix, motion, or an angel, in my mind, the first and natural enquiry is, Whether such a thing does anywhere exist? And this knowledge is only of particulars. No existence of anything without us, but only of God, can certainly be known farther than our senses inform us. (2) There is another sort of propositions, wherein is expressed the agreement or disagreement of our abstract ideas, and their

dependence on one another. Such propositions may be universal and certain. So having the idea of God and myself, of fear and obedience, I cannot but be sure that God is to be feared and obeyed by me; and this proposition will be certain, concerning man in general, if I have made an abstract idea of such a species, whereof I am one particular. But yet this proposition, how certain soever, that men ought to fear and obey God proves not to me the existence of men in the world, but will be true of all such creatures, whenever they do exist: Which certainty of such general propositions depends on the agreement or disagreement to be discovered in those abstract ideas.

14. In the former case, our knowledge is the consequence of the existence of things producing ideas in our minds by our senses: In the latter, knowledge is the consequence of the ideas (be they what they will) that are in our minds producing there general certain propositions. Many of these are called *aeternae veritates*, and all of them indeed are so; not from being written all or any of them in the minds of all men, or that they were any of them propositions in anyone's mind, till he, having got the abstract ideas, joined or separated them by affirmation or negation. But wheresoever we can suppose such a creature as man is, endowed with such faculties, and thereby furnished with such ideas as we have, we must conclude he must needs, when he applies his thoughts to the consideration of his ideas, know the truth of certain propositions that will arise from the agreement or disagreement which he will perceive in his own ideas. Such propositions are therefore called eternal truths, not because they are eternal propositions actually formed, and antecedent to the understanding that at any time makes them; nor because they are imprinted on the mind from any patterns that are anywhere out of the mind and existed before: But because being once made about abstract ideas so as to be true, they will, whenever they can be supposed to be made again at any time past or to come, by a mind having those ideas, always actually be true. For names being supposed to stand perpetually for the same ideas, and the same ideas having immutably the same habitudes one to another, propositions concerning any abstract ideas that are once true must needs be eternal verities.

Chapter XII. Of the Improvement of Our Knowledge

1. It having been the common received opinion amongst men of letters that maxims were the foundation of all knowledge; and that the sciences were each of them built upon certain *praecognita*, from whence the understanding was to take its rise, and by which it was to conduct itself in its enquiries into the matters belonging to that science; the beaten road of the schools has been to lay down in the beginning one or more general propositions, as foundations whereon to build the knowledge that was to be had of that subject. These doctrines, thus laid down for foundations of any science, were called *principles*, as the beginnings from which we must set out, and look no farther backwards in our enquiries, as we have already observed.

2. One thing which might probably give an occasion to this way of proceeding in other sciences was (as I suppose) the good success it seemed to have in mathematics, wherein men, being observed to attain a great certainty of knowledge, these sciences came by pre-eminence to be called ⟨*mathemata*⟩ and ⟨*mathesis*⟩, learning, or things learned, thoroughly learned, as having of all others the greatest certainty, clearness, and evidence in them.

3. But if anyone will consider, he will (I guess) find that the great advancement and certainty of real knowledge which men arrived to in these sciences was not owing to the influence of these principles, nor derived from any peculiar advantage they received from two or three general maxims, laid down in the beginning; but from the clear, distinct, complete ideas their thoughts were employed about, and the relation of equality and excess so clear between some of them that they had an intuitive knowledge, and by that a way to discover it in others, and this without the help of those maxims. For I ask, is it not possible for a young lad to know that his whole body is bigger than his little finger but by virtue of this axiom, that the whole is bigger than a part; nor be assured of it till he has learned that maxim? Or cannot a country wench know that having received a shilling from one that owes her three, and a shilling also from another that owes her three, the remaining debts in each of their hands are equal? Cannot she know this, I say, unless she fetch the certainty of it from this maxim, that if you take equals from equals, the remainder will be equals, a maxim which possibly she never heard or thought of? I desire anyone to consider, from what has been elsewhere said, which is known first and clearest by most people, the particular instance, or the general rule; and which it is that gives life and birth to the other. These general rules are but the comparing our more general and abstract ideas, which are the workmanship of the mind made, and names given to them, for the easier dispatch in its reasonings, and drawing into comprehensive terms, and short rules, its various and multiplied observations. But knowledge began in the mind, and was founded on particulars; though afterwards, perhaps, no notice be taken thereof: It being natural for the mind (forward still to enlarge its knowledge) most attentively to lay up those general notions, and make the proper use of them, which is to disburden the memory of the cumbersome load of particulars. For I desire it may be considered what more certainty there is to a child, or anyone, that his body, little finger and all, is bigger than his little finger alone, after you have given to his body the name *whole,* and to his little finger the name *part,* than he could have had before; or what new knowledge concerning his body can these two relative terms give him which he could not have without them? Could he not know that his body was bigger than his little finger if his language were yet so imperfect that he had no such relative terms as *whole* and *part*? I ask farther, when he has got these names, how is he more certain that his body is a whole, and his little finger a part, than he was or might be certain, before he learnt those terms, that his body was bigger than his little finger? Anyone may as reasonably doubt or deny that his little finger is a part of his body as that it is less than his body. And he that can doubt whether it be less will as certainly doubt whether it be a part. So that the maxim, the whole is bigger than a part, can never be made use of to prove the little finger less than the body but when it is useless, by being brought to convince one of a truth which he knows already. For he that does not certainly know that any parcel of matter with another parcel of matter joined to it is bigger than either of them alone will never be able to know it by the help of these two relative terms *whole* and *part,* make of them what maxim you please.

4. But be it in the mathematics as it will, whether it be clearer that taking an inch from a black line of two inches, and an inch from a red line of two inches, the remaining parts of the two lines will be equal, or that if you take equals from equals, the remainder will be equals: Which, I say, of these two is the clearer and first known, I leave to anyone to determine, it not being material to my present occasion. That which I have here to do is to enquire whether if it be the readiest way to knowledge to begin with general maxims, and build upon them, it be yet a safe way to take the principles, which are laid down in any other science as unquestionable truths; and so receive them without examination, and adhere to them without suffering them to be doubted of, because mathematicians have been so happy, or so fair, to use none but self-evident and undeniable. If this be so, I know not what may not pass for truth in morality, what may not be introduced and proved in natural philosophy.

Let that principle of some of the old philosophers, that all is matter, and that there is nothing else, be received for certain and indubitable, and it will be easy to be seen by the writings of some that have revived it again in our days, what consequences it will lead us into. Let anyone, with Polemo, take the world; or with the stoics, the aether, or the sun; or with Anaximenes, the air; to be God; and what a divinity, religion and worship must we needs have! Nothing can be so dangerous as principles thus taken up without questioning or examination; especially if they be such as concern morality, which influence men's lives, and give a bias to all their actions. Who might not justly expect another kind of life in Aristippus, who placed happiness in bodily pleasure; and in Antisthenes, who made virtue sufficient to felicity? And he who, with Plato, shall place beatitude in the knowledge of God will have his thoughts raised to other contemplations than those who look not beyond this spot of earth, and those perishing things which are to be had in it. He that, with Archelaus, shall lay it down as a principle that right and wrong, honest and dishonest, are defined only by laws and not by nature will have other measures of moral rectitude, and pravity, than those who take it for granted that we are under obligations antecedent to all human constitutions.

5. If therefore those that pass for principles are not certain (which we must have some way to know, that we may be able to distinguish them from those that are doubtful) but are only made so to us by our blind assent, we are liable to be misled by them; and instead of being guided into truth, we shall, by principles, be only confirmed in mistake and errour.

6. But since the knowledge of the certainty of principles, as well as of all other truths, depends only upon the perception we have of the agreement or disagreement of our ideas, the way to improve our knowledge is not, I am sure, blindly, and with an implicit faith, to receive and swallow principles; but is, I think, to get and fix in our minds clear, distinct, and complete ideas, as far as they are to be had, and annex to them proper and constant names. And thus, perhaps, without any other principles, but barely considering those perfect ideas, and by comparing them one with another, finding their agreement and disagreement, and their several relations and habitudes; we shall get more true and clear knowledge, by the conduct of this one rule, than by taking up principles, and thereby putting our minds into the disposal of others.

7. We must therefore, if we will proceed as reason advises, adapt our methods of enquiry to the nature of the ideas we examine, and the truth we search after. General and certain truths are only founded in the habitudes and relations of abstract ideas. A sagacious and methodical application of our thoughts, for the finding out these relations, is the only way to discover all that can be put with truth and certainty concerning them into general propositions. By what steps we are to proceed in these is to be learned in the schools of the mathematicians, who from very plain and easy beginnings, by gentle degrees, and a continued chain of reasonings, proceed to the discovery and demonstration of truths that appear at first sight beyond human capacity. The art of finding proofs, and the admirable methods they have invented for the singling out, and laying in order, those intermediate ideas that demonstratively show the equality or inequality of unapplicable quantities is that which has carried them so far, and produced such wonderful and unexpected discoveries: But whether something like this, in respect of other ideas, as well as those of magnitude, may not in time be found out, I will not determine. This, I think, I may say, that if other ideas that are the real as well as nominal essences of their species were pursued in the way familiar to mathematicians, they would carry our thoughts farther, and with greater evidence and clearness, than possibly we are apt to imagine.

8. This gave me the confidence to advance that conjecture, which I suggest, Chapter III, viz. that morality is capable of demonstration as well as mathematics. For the ideas that ethics are conversant about being all real essences, and such as I imagine have a discoverable connexion and agreement one with another; so far as we can find their habitudes and relations, so far we shall be possessed of certain, real, and general truths: And I doubt not but, if a right method were taken, a great part of morality might be made out with that clearness that could leave, to a considering man, no more reason to doubt than he could have to doubt of the truth of propositions in mathematics which have been demonstrated to him.

9. In our search after the knowledge of substances, our want of ideas that are suitable to such a way of proceeding obliges us to a quite different method. We advance not here, as in the other (where our abstract ideas are real as well as nominal essences), by contemplating our ideas, and considering their relations and correspondences; that helps us very little, for the reasons that in another place we have at large set down. By which I think it is evident that substances afford matter of very little general knowledge; and the bare contemplation of their abstract ideas will carry us but a very little way in the search of truth and certainty. What then are we to do for the improvement of our knowledge in substantial beings? Here we are to take a quite contrary course; the want of ideas of their real essences sends us from our own thoughts to the things themselves, as they exist. Experience here must teach me what reason cannot; and it is by trying alone that I can certainly know what other qualities co-exist with those of my complex idea, v.g. whether that yellow, heavy, fusible body I call gold be malleable, or no; which experience (which way ever it prove in that particular body I examine) makes me not certain that it is so in all or any other yellow, heavy,

fusible bodies but that which I have tried. Because it is no consequence one way or the other from my complex idea; the necessity or inconsistence of malleability hath no visible connexion with the combination of that colour, weight, and fusibility in any body. What I have said here of the nominal essence of gold, supposed to consist of a body of such a determinate colour, weight, and fusibility, will hold true, if malleableness, fixedness, and solubility in *aqua regia* be added to it. Our reasonings from these ideas will carry us but a little way in the certain discovery of the other properties in those masses of matter wherein all these are to be found. Because the other properties of such bodies, depending not on these but on that unknown real essence, on which these also depend, we cannot by them discover the rest; we can go no farther than the simple ideas of our nominal essence will carry us, which is very little beyond themselves; and so afford us but very sparingly any certain, universal, and useful truths. For upon trial having found that particular piece (and all others of that colour, weight, and fusibility that I ever tried) malleable, that also makes now perhaps a part of my complex idea, part of my nominal essence of gold: Whereby though I make my complex idea, to which I affix the name *gold*, to consist of more simple ideas than before; yet still it not containing the real essence of any species of bodies, it helps me not certainly to know (I say *to know*, perhaps it may be *to conjecture*) the other remaining properties of that body, farther than they have a visible connexion with some or all of the simple ideas that make up my nominal essence. For example, I cannot be certain from this complex idea whether gold be fixed, or no; because, as before, there is no necessary connexion or inconsistence to be discovered betwixt a complex idea of a body yellow, heavy, fusible, malleable; betwixt these, I say, and fixedness; so that I may certainly know that in whatsoever body these are found, there fixedness is sure to be. Here again for assurance, I must apply myself to experience; as far as that reaches, I may have certain knowledge, but no farther.

10. I deny not but a man accustomed to rational and regular experiments shall be able to see farther into the nature of bodies, and guess righter at their yet unknown properties, than one that is a stranger

to them: But yet, as I have said, this is but judgment and opinion, not knowledge and certainty. This way of getting and improving our knowledge in substances only by experience and history, which is all that the weakness of our faculties in this state of mediocrity, which we are in in this world, can attain to, makes me suspect that natural philosophy is not capable of being made a science. We are able, I imagine, to reach very little general knowledge concerning the species of bodies, and their several properties. Experiments and historical observations we may have, from which we may draw advantages of ease and health, and thereby increase our stock of conveniences for this life; but beyond this I fear our talents reach not, nor are our faculties, as I guess, able to advance.

11. From whence it is obvious to conclude that since our faculties are not fitted to penetrate into the internal fabric and real essences of bodies, but yet plainly discover to us the being of a God, and the knowledge of ourselves, enough to lead us into a full and clear discovery of our duty and great concernment, it will become us, as rational creatures, to employ those faculties we have about what they are most adapted to, and follow the direction of nature, where it seems to point us out the way. For it is rational to conclude that our proper employment lies in those enquiries and in that sort of knowledge which is most suited to our natural capacities, and carries in it our greatest interest, i.e. the condition of our eternal estate. Hence I think I may conclude that morality is the proper science and business of mankind in general (who are both concerned and fitted to search out their *summum bonum*), as several arts, conversant about several parts of nature, are the lot and private talent of particular men, for the common use of human life, and their own particular subsistence in this world. Of what consequence the discovery of one natural body, and its properties, may be to human life, the whole great continent of America is a convincing instance: Whose ignorance in useful arts, and want of the greatest part of the conveniences of life, in a country that abounded with all sorts of natural plenty, I think may be attributed to their ignorance of what was to be found in a very ordinary despicable stone, I mean the mineral of iron. And whatever we think of our parts or improvements in this part of the world, where

knowledge and plenty seem to vie with each other; yet to anyone, that will seriously reflect on it, I suppose it will appear past doubt that were the use of iron lost among us, we should in a few ages be unavoidably reduced to the wants and ignorance of the ancient savage Americans, whose natural endowments and provisions come no way short of those of the most flourishing and polite nations. So that he who first made known the use of that contemptible mineral may be truly styled the father of arts, and author of plenty.

12. I would not therefore be thought to disesteem or dissuade the study of nature. I readily agree the contemplation of his works gives us occasion to admire, revere, and glorify their Author: and, if rightly directed, may be of greater benefit to mankind than the monuments of exemplary charity that have at so great charge been raised by the founders of hospitals and almshouses. He that first invented printing, discovered the use of the compass, or made public the virtue and right use of quinine, did more for the propagation of knowledge, for the supply and increase of useful commodities, and saved more from the grave than those who built colleges, work-houses, and hospitals. All that I would say is that we should not be too forwardly possessed with the opinion or expectation of knowledge where it is not to be had; or by ways that will not attain to it: That we should not take doubtful systems for complete sciences, nor unintelligible notions for scientifical demonstrations. In the knowledge of bodies, we must be content to glean what we can from particular experiments: Since we cannot, from a discovery of their real essences, grasp at a time whole sheaves, and in bundles comprehend the nature and properties of whole species together. Where our enquiry is concerning co-existence, or repugnancy to co-exist, which by contemplation of our ideas we cannot discover, there experience, observation, and natural history must give us by our senses, and by retail, an insight into corporeal substances. The knowledge of bodies we must get by our senses, warily employed in taking notice of their qualities and operations on one another: And what we hope to know of separate spirits in this world, we must, I think, expect only from revelation. He that shall consider how little general maxims, precarious principles, and hypotheses laid down at pleasure have promoted true knowledge, or helped to satisfy the enquiries of rational men after real improvements; how little, I say, the setting out at that end has, for many ages together, advanced men's progress towards the knowledge of natural philosophy; will think we have reason to thank those who in this latter age have taken another course, and have trod out to us, though not an easier way to learned ignorance, yet a surer way to profitable knowledge.

13. Not that we may not, to explain any phenomena of nature, make use of any probable hypothesis whatsoever: Hypotheses, if they are well made, are at least great helps to the memory, and often direct us to new discoveries. But my meaning is that we should not take up any one too hastily (which the mind, that would always penetrate into the causes of things, and have principles to rest on, is very apt to do) till we have very well examined particulars, and made several experiments, in that thing which we would explain by our hypothesis, and see whether it will agree to them all; whether our principles will carry us quite through, and not be as inconsistent with one phenomenon of nature as they seem to accommodate and explain another. And at least that we take care that the name of principles deceive us not, nor impose on us, by making us receive that for an unquestionable truth which is really at best but a very doubtful conjecture, such as are most (I had almost said *all*) of the hypotheses in natural philosophy.

14. But whether natural philosophy be capable of certainty or no, the ways to enlarge our knowledge, as far as we are capable, seem to me, in short, to be these two:

The first is to get and settle in our minds determined ideas of those things whereof we have general or specific names; at least so many of them as we would consider and improve our knowledge in, or reason about. And if they be specific ideas of substances, we should endeavour also to make them as complete as we can, whereby I mean that we should put together as many simple ideas as, being constantly observed to co-exist, may perfectly determine the species: And each of those simple ideas, which are the ingredients of our complex ones, should be clear and distinct in our minds. For it be-

ing evident that our knowledge cannot exceed our ideas, as far as they are either imperfect, confused, or obscure, we cannot expect to have certain, perfect, or clear knowledge.

The other is the art of finding out those intermediate ideas which may show us the agreement or repugnancy of other ideas, which cannot be immediately compared.

15. That these two (and not the relying on maxims, and drawing consequences from some general propositions) are the right methods of improving our knowledge in the ideas of other modes besides those of quantity, the consideration of mathematical knowledge will easily inform us. Where first we shall find that he that has not a perfect and clear idea of those angles or figures of which he desires to know anything is utterly thereby incapable of any knowledge about them. Suppose but a man not to have a perfect exact idea of a right angle, a scalenum, or trapezium; and there is nothing more certain than that he will in vain seek any demonstration about them. Farther, it is evident that it was not the influence of those maxims, which are taken for principles in mathematics, that hath led the masters of that science into those wonderful discoveries they have made. Let a man of good parts know all the maxims generally made use of in mathematics ever so perfectly, and contemplate their extent and consequences as much as he pleases, he will by their assistance, I suppose, scarce ever come to know that the square of the hypothenuse in a rightangled triangle is equal to the squares of the two other sides. The knowledge, that "the whole is equal to all its parts," and "if you take equals from equals, the remainder will be equal," &c. helped him not, I presume, to this demonstration: And a man may, I think, pore long enough on those axioms without ever seeing one jot the more of mathematical truths. They have been discovered by the thoughts otherwise applied: The mind had other objects, other views before it, far different from those maxims, when it first got the knowledge of such truths in mathematics, which men well enough acquainted with those received axioms, but ignorant of their method who first made these demonstrations, can never sufficiently admire. And who knows what methods, to enlarge our knowledge in other parts of science, may hereafter be invented, answering that of algebra in mathematics, which so readily finds out the ideas of quantities to measure others by; whose equality or proportion we could otherwise very hardly, or, perhaps, never come to know?

Chapter XIV. Of Judgment

1. The understanding faculties being given to man not barely for speculation, but also for the conduct of his life, man would be at a great loss if he had nothing to direct him but what has the certainty of true knowledge. For that being very short and scanty, as we have seen, he would be often utterly in the dark, and in most of the actions of his life, perfectly at a stand, had he nothing to guide him in the absence of clear and certain knowledge. He that will not eat till he has demonstration that it will nourish him; he that will not stir till he infallibly knows the business he goes about will succeed; will have little else to do but to sit still and perish.

2. Therefore as God has set some things in broad day-light; as he has given us some certain knowledge, though limited to a few things in comparison, probably, as a taste of what intellectual creatures are capable of, to excite in us a desire and endeavour after a better state: So in the greatest part of our concernments he has afforded us only the twilight, as I may so say, of probability; suitable, I presume, to that state of mediocrity and probationership he has been pleased to place us in here; wherein, to check our over-confidence and presumption, we might by every day's experience be made sensible of our short-sightedness and liableness to errour; the sense whereof might be a constant admonition to us, to spend the days of this our pilgrimage with industry and care, in the search and following of that way which might lead us to a state of greater perfection: It being highly rational to think, even were revelation silent in the case, that as men employ those talents God has given them here, they shall accordingly receive their rewards at the close of the day, when their sun shall set, and night shall put an end to their labours.

3. The faculty which God has given man to supply the want of clear and certain knowledge, in cases where that cannot be had, is judgment: Whereby the mind takes its ideas to agree or disagree; or which is the same, any proposition to be

true or false, without perceiving a demonstrative evidence in the proofs. The mind sometimes exercises this judgment out of necessity, where demonstrative proofs and certain knowledge are not to be had; and sometimes out of laziness, unskilfulness, or haste, even where demonstrative and certain proofs are to be had. Men often stay not warily to examine the agreement or disagreement of two ideas, which they are desirous or concerned to know; but either incapable of such attention as is requisite in a long train of gradations, or impatient of delay, lightly cast their eyes on or wholly pass by the proofs; and so without making out the demonstration, determine of the agreement or disagreement of two ideas, as it were, by a view of them as they are at a distance, and take it to be the one or the other, as seems most likely to them upon such a loose survey. This faculty of the mind, when it is exercised immediately about things, is called *judgment:* When about truths delivered in words, is most commonly called *assent* or *dissent:* Which being the most usual way, wherein the mind has occasion to employ this faculty, I shall under these terms treat of it, as least liable in our language to equivocation.

4. Thus the mind has two faculties, conversant about truth and falsehood.

First, knowledge, whereby it certainly perceives, and is undoubtedly satisfied of, the agreement or disagreement of any ideas.

Secondly, judgment, which is the putting ideas together, or separating them from one another in the mind, when their certain agreement or disagreement is not perceived, but presumed to be so; which is, as the word imports, taken to be so before it certainly appears. And if it so unites or separates them, as in reality things are, it is right judgment.

Chapter XV. Of Probability

1. As demonstration is the showing the agreement or disagreement of two ideas by the intervention of one or more proofs, which have a constant, immutable, and visible connexion one with another; so probability is nothing but the appearance of such an agreement or disagreement by the intervention of proofs, whose connexion is not constant and immutable, or at least is not perceived to be so, but is, or appears for the most part to be so, and is enough to induce the mind to judge the proposition to be true or false, rather than the contrary. For example: In the demonstration of it a man perceives the certain immutable connexion there is of equality between the three angles of a triangle, and those intermediate ones which are made use of to show their equality to two right ones; and so by an intuitive knowledge of the agreement or disagreement of the intermediate ideas in each step of the progress, the whole series is continued with an evidence which clearly shows the agreement or disagreement of those three angles in equality to two right ones: And thus he has certain knowledge that it is so. But another man, who never took the pains to observe the demonstration, hearing a mathematician, a man of credit, affirm the three angles of a triangle to be equal to two right ones, assents to it, i.e. receives it for true. In which case the foundation of his assent is the probability of the thing, the proof being such as for the most part carries truth with it, the man, on whose testimony he receives it not being wont to affirm anything contrary to or besides his knowledge, especially in matters of this kind. So that that which causes his assent to this proposition, that the three angles of a triangle are equal to two right ones, that which makes him take these ideas to agree, without knowing them to do so, is the wonted veracity of the speaker in other cases, or his supposed veracity in this.

2. Our knowledge, as has been shown, being very narrow, and we not happy enough to find certain truth in everything which we have occasion to consider, most of the propositions we think, reason, discourse, nay, act upon are such as we cannot have undoubted knowledge of their truth; yet some of them border so near upon certainty that we make no doubt at all about them; but assent to them as firmly, and act, according to that assent, as resolutely, as if they were infallibly demonstrated, and that our knowledge of them was perfect and certain. But there being degrees herein from the very neighbourhood of certainty and demonstration, quite down to improbability and unlikeness, even to the confines of impossibility; and also degrees of assent from full assurance and confidence, quite down to conjecture, doubt, and distrust: I shall come now (having, as I think, found out the bounds of human knowledge and certainty) in the next place to consider the several degrees and grounds of probability, and assent or faith.

3. Probability is likeliness to be true, the very notation of the word signifying such a proposition for which there be arguments or proofs to make it pass or be received for true. The entertainment the mind gives this sort of propositions is called *belief*, *assent*, or *opinion*, which is the admitting or receiving any proposition for true, upon arguments or proofs that are found to persuade us to receive it as true, without certain knowledge that it is so. And herein lies the difference between probability and certainty, faith and knowledge, that in all the parts of knowledge there is intuition; each immediate idea, each step has its visible and certain connexion; in belief, not so. That which makes me believe is something extraneous to the thing I believe; something not evidently joined on both sides to, and so not manifestly showing the agreement or disagreement of, those ideas that are under consideration.

4. Probability then being to supply the defect of our knowledge, and to guide us where that fails, is always conversant about propositions whereof we have no certainty, but only some inducements to receive them for true. The grounds of it are, in short, these two following.

First, the conformity of anything with our own knowledge, observation, and experience.

Secondly, the testimony of others, vouching their observation and experience. In the testimony of others is to be considered: (1) The number. (2) The integrity. (3) The skill of the witnesses. (4) The design of the author, where it is a testimony out of a book cited. (5) The consistency of the parts, and circumstances of the relation. (6) Contrary testimonies.

5. Probability wanting that intuitive evidence which infallibly determines the understanding, and produces certain knowledge, the mind, if it will proceed rationally, ought to examine all the grounds of probability, and see how they make more or less for or against any proposition, before it assents to or dissents from it; and upon a due balancing the whole, reject or receive it with a more or less firm assent, proportionably to the preponderancy of the greater grounds of probability on one side or the other. For example:

If I myself see a man walk on the ice, it is past probability; it is knowledge; but if another tells me he saw a man in England, in the midst of a sharp winter, walk upon water hardened with cold, this has so great conformity with what is usually observed to happen that I am disposed by the nature of the thing itself to assent to it, unless some manifest suspicion attend the relation of that matter of fact. But if the same thing be told to one born between the tropics, who never saw nor heard of any such thing before, there the whole probability relies on testimony: And as the relators are more in number, and of more credit, and have no interest to speak contrary to the truth; so that matter of fact is like to find more or less belief. Though to a man whose experience has always been quite contrary, and who has never heard of anything like it, the most untainted credit of a witness will scarce be able to find belief. As it happened to a Dutch ambassador who, entertaining the King of Siam with the particularities of Holland, which he was inquisitive after, amongst other things told him that the water in his country would sometimes, in cold weather, be so hard that men walked upon it, and that it would bear an elephant if he were there. To which the king replied, "Hitherto I have believed the strange things you have told me, because I look upon you as a sober fair man, but now I am sure you lie."

6. Upon these grounds depends the probability of any proposition: And as the conformity of our knowledge, as the certainty of observations, as the frequency and constancy of experience, and the number and credibility of testimonies do more or less agree or disagree with it, so is any proposition in itself more or less probable. There is another, I confess, which though by itself it be no true ground of probability, yet is often made use of for one, by which men most commonly regulate their assent, and upon which they pin their faith more than anything else, and that is the opinion of others: Though there cannot be a more dangerous thing to rely on, nor more likely to mislead one; since there is much more falsehood and errour among men than truth and knowledge. And if the opinions and persuasions of others, whom we know and think well of, be a ground of assent, men have reason to be Heathens in Japan, Mahometans in Turkey, Papists in Spain, Protestants in England, and Lutherans in Sweden. But of this wrong ground of assent I shall have occasion to speak more at large in another place.

Chapter XVII. *Of Reason*

1. The word *reason* in the English language has different significations: Sometimes it is taken for true and clear principles; sometimes for clear and fair deductions from those principles; and sometimes for the cause, and particularly the final cause. But the consideration I shall have of it here is in a signification different from all these: And that is, as it stands for a faculty in man, that faculty whereby man is supposed to be distinguished from beasts, and wherein it is evident he much surpasses them.

2. If general knowledge, as has been shown, consists in a perception of the agreement or disagreement of our own ideas; and the knowledge of the existence of all things without us (except only of a God, whose existence every man may certainly know and demonstrate to himself from his own existence) be had only by our senses: What room is there for the exercise of any other faculty but outward sense and inward perception? What need is there of reason? Very much; both for the enlargement of our knowledge, and regulating our assent: For it hath to do both in knowledge and opinion, and is necessary and assisting to all our other intellectual faculties, and indeed contains two of them, viz. sagacity and illation. By the one, it finds out; and by the other, it so orders the intermediate ideas as to discover what connexion there is in each link of the chain, whereby the extremes are held together; and thereby, as it were, to draw into view the truth sought for, which is that which we call *illation* or *inference,* and consists in nothing but the perception of the connexion there is between the ideas, in each step of the deduction, whereby the mind comes to see either the certain agreement or disagreement of any two ideas, as in demonstration, in which it arrives at knowledge; or their probable connexion, on which it gives or withholds its assent, as in opinion. Sense and intuition reach but a very little way. The greatest part of our knowledge depends upon deductions and intermediate ideas: And in those cases where we are fain to substitute assent instead of knowledge, and take propositions for true without being certain they are so, we have need to find out, examine, and compare the grounds of their probability. In both these cases, the faculty which finds out the means, and rightly applies them to discover certainty in the one, and probability in the other, is that which we call reason. For as reason perceives the necessary and indubitable connexion of all the ideas or proofs one to another, in each step of any demonstration that produces knowledge: So it likewise perceives the probable connexion of all the ideas or proofs one to another, in every step of a discourse, to which it will think assent due. This is the lowest degree of that which can be truly called reason. For where the mind does not perceive this probable connexion, where it does not discern whether there be any such connexion or no, there men's opinions are not the product of judgment, or the consequence of reason, but the effects of chance and hazard, of a mind floating at all adventures, without choice and without direction.

3. So that we may in reason consider these four degrees: The first and highest is the discovering and finding out of truths; the second, the regular and methodical disposition of them, and laying them in a clear and fit order, to make their connexion and force be plainly and easily perceived; the third is the perceiving their connexion; and the fourth, a making a right conclusion. These several degrees may be observed in any mathematical demonstration; it being one thing to perceive the connexion of each part, as the demonstration is made by another; another, to perceive the dependence of the conclusion on all the parts; a third, to make out a demonstration clearly and neatly one's self; and something different from all these, to have first found out these intermediate ideas or proofs by which it is made.

5. But however it be in knowledge, I think I may truly say, it is of far less or no use at all in probabilities. For, the assent there being to be determined by the preponderancy, after due weighing of all the proofs, with all circumstances on both sides, nothing is so unfit to assist the mind in that as syllogism; which running away with one assumed probability, or one topical argument, pursues that till it has led the mind quite out of sight of the thing under consideration; and forcing it upon some remote difficulty, holds it fast there, intangled perhaps, and, as it were, manacled in the chain of syllogisms, without allowing it the liberty, much less affording it the helps, requisite to show on which side, all things considered, is the greater probability.

6. But let it help us (as perhaps may be said) in convincing men of their errours and mistakes (and yet I would fain see the man that was forced out of his opinion by dint of syllogism): Yet still it fails our reason in that part which, if not its highest perfection, is yet certainly its hardest task, and that which we most need its help in; and that is the finding out of proofs, and making new discoveries. The rules of syllogism serve not to furnish the mind with those intermediate ideas that may show the connexion of remote ones. This way of reasoning discovers no new proofs, but is the art of marshalling and ranging the old ones we have already. The forty-seventh proposition of the first book of Euclid is very true; but the discovery of it, I think, not owing to any rules of common logic. A man knows first, and then he is able to prove syllogistically. So that syllogism comes after knowledge, and then a man has little or no need of it. But it is chiefly by the finding out those ideas that show the connexion of distant ones that our stock of knowledge is increased, and that useful arts and sciences are advanced. Syllogism at best is but the art of fencing with the little knowledge we have, without making any addition to it. And if a man should employ his reason all this way, he will not do much otherwise than he who having got some iron out of the bowels of the earth, should have it beaten up all into swords, and put it into his servants' hands to fence with, and bang one another. Had the king of Spain employed the hands of his people, and his Spanish iron so, he had brought to light but little of that treasure that lay so long hid in the dark entrails of America. And I am apt to think that he who shall employ all the force of his reason only in brandishing of syllogisms will discover very little of that mass of knowledge which lies yet concealed in the secret recesses of nature; and which, I am apt to think, native rustic reason (as it formerly has done) is likelier to open a way to, and add to the common stock of mankind, rather than any scholastic proceeding by the strict rules of mode and figure.

7. I doubt not, nevertheless, but there are ways to be found to assist our reason in this most useful part; and this the judicious Hooker encourages me to say, who, in his *Eccl. Pol.* l. 1. sec. 6, speaks thus: "If there might be added the right helps of true art and learning (which helps, I must plainly confess, this age of the world carrying the name of a learned age, doth neither much know, nor generally regard) there would undoubtedly be almost as much difference in maturity of judgment between men therewith inured, and that which men now are, as between men that are now, and innocents." I do not pretend to have found or discovered here any of those right helps of art this great man of deep thought mentions; but this is plain, that syllogism, and the logic now in use, which were as well known in his days, can be none of those he means. It is sufficient for me, if by a discourse, perhaps something out of the way, I am sure as to me wholly new and unborrowed, I shall have given occasion to others to cast about for new discoveries, and to seek in their own thoughts for those right helps of art, which will scarce be found, I fear, by those who servilely confine themselves to the rules and dictates of others. For beaten tracks lead this sort of cattle (as an observing Roman calls them) whose thoughts reach only to imitation, *non quo eundum est, sed quo itur.* But I can be bold to say that this age is adorned with some men of that strength of judgment, and largeness of comprehension, that if they would employ their thoughts on this subject, could open new and undiscovered ways to the advancement of knowledge.

9. Reason, though it penetrates into the depths of the sea and earth, elevates our thoughts as high as the stars, and leads us through the vast spaces and large rooms of this mighty fabric, yet it comes far short of the real extent of even corporeal being: And there are many instances wherein it fails us: As,

First, it perfectly fails us where our ideas fail. It neither does nor can extend itself farther than they do. And therefore wherever we have no ideas, our reasoning stops, and we are at an end of our reckoning: And if at any time we reason about words which do not stand for any ideas, it is only about those sounds, and nothing else.

10. Secondly, our reason is often puzzled, and at a loss, because of the obscurity, confusion, or imperfection of the ideas it is employed about; and there we are involved in difficulties and contradictions. Thus, not having any perfect idea of the least extension of matter, nor of infinity, we are at a loss about the divisibility of matter; but having perfect,

clear, and distinct ideas of number, our reason meets with none of those inextricable difficulties in numbers, nor finds itself involved in any contradictions about them. Thus, we having but imperfect ideas of the operations of our minds, and of the beginning of motion, or thought, how the mind produces either of them in us, and much imperfecter yet of the operation of God; run into great difficulties about free created agents, which reason cannot well extricate itself out of.

11. Thirdly, our reason is often at a stand, because it perceives not those ideas which could serve to show the certain or probable agreement or disagreement of any other two ideas: And in this some men's faculties far outgo others. Till algebra, that great instrument and instance of human sagacity, was discovered, men, with amazement, looked on several of the demonstrations of ancient mathematicians, and could scarce forbear to think the finding several of those proofs to be something more than human.

12. Fourthly, the mind, by proceeding upon false principles, is often engaged in absurdities and difficulties, brought into straits and contradictions, without knowing how to free itself; and in that case it is in vain to implore the help of reason, unless it be to discover the falsehood and reject the influence of those wrong principles. Reason is so far from clearing the difficulties which the building upon false foundations brings a man into that if he will pursue it, it entangles him the more, and engages him deeper in perplexities.

13. Fifthly, as obscure and imperfect ideas often involve our reason, so, upon the same ground, do dubious words, and uncertain signs, often in discourses and arguings, when not warily attended to, puzzle men's reason, and bring them to a non-plus. But these two latter are our fault, and not the fault of reason. But yet the consequences of them are nevertheless obvious; and the perplexities or errors they fill men's minds with are everywhere observable.

14. Some of the ideas that are in the mind are so there that they can be by themselves immediately compared one with another: And in these the mind is able to perceive that they agree or disagree as clearly as that it has them. Thus the mind perceives that an arch of a circle is less than the whole circle as clearly as it does the idea of a circle: And this therefore, as has been said, I call intuitive knowledge; which is certain, beyond all doubt, and needs no probation, nor can have any; this being the highest of all human certainty. In this consists the evidence of all those maxims, which nobody has any doubt about, but every man (does not, as is said, only assent to, but) knows to be true, as soon as ever they are proposed to his understanding. In the discovery of and assent to these truths, there is no use of the discursive faculty, no need of reasoning, but they are known by a superior and higher degree of evidence. And such, if I may guess at things unknown, I am apt to think, that angels have now, and the spirits of just men made perfect shall have, in a future state, of thousands of things, which now either wholly escape our apprehensions, or which, our short-sighted reason having got some faint glimpse of, we, in the dark, grope after.

15. But though we have, here and there, a little of this clear light, some sparks of bright knowledge; yet the greatest part of our ideas are such that we cannot discern their agreement or disagreement by an immediate comparing them. And in all these we have need of reasoning, and must, by discourse and inference, make our discoveries. Now of these there are two sorts, which I shall take the liberty to mention here again.

First, those whose agreement or disagreement, though it cannot be seen by an immediate putting them together, yet may be examined by the intervention of other ideas which can be compared with them. In this case when the agreement or disagreement of the intermediate idea, on both sides with those which we would compare, is plainly discerned, there it amounts to demonstration, whereby knowledge is produced; which though it be certain, yet it is not so easy nor altogether so clear as intuitive knowledge. Because in that there is barely one simple intuition, wherein there is no room for any the least mistake or doubt; the truth is seen all perfectly at once. In demonstration, it is true, there is intuition too, but not altogether at once; for there must be a remembrance of the intuition of the agreement of the medium, or intermediate idea, with that we compared it with before, when we compare it with the other; and where there be many mediums,

there the danger of the mistake is the greater. For each agreement or disagreement of the ideas must be observed and seen in each step of the whole train, and retained in the memory, just as it is; and the mind must be sure that no part of what is necessary to make up the demonstration is omitted or overlooked. This makes some demonstrations long and perplexed, and too hard for those who have not strength of parts distinctly to perceive and exactly carry so many particulars orderly in their heads. And even those who are able to master such intricate speculations are fain sometimes to go over them again, and there is need of more than one review before they can arrive at certainty. But yet where the mind clearly retains the intuition it had of the agreement of any idea with another, and that with a third, and that with a fourth, &c. there the agreement of the first and the fourth is a demonstration, and produces certain knowledge, which may be called rational knowledge, as the other is intuitive.

16. Secondly, there are other ideas whose agreement or disagreement can no otherwise be judged of but by the intervention of others which have not a certain agreement with the extremes, but an usual or likely one: And in these it is that the judgment is properly exercised, which is the acquiescing of the mind, that any ideas do agree, by comparing them with such probable mediums. This, though it never amounts to knowledge, no, not to that which is the lowest degree of it: Yet sometimes the intermediate ideas tie the extremes so firmly together, and the probability is so clear and strong, that assent as necessarily follows it as knowledge does demonstration. The great excellency and use of the judgment is to observe right, and take a true estimate of the force and weight of each probability; and then casting them up all right together, choose that side which has the overbalance.

17. Intuitive knowledge is the perception of the certain agreement or disagreement of two ideas immediately compared together.

Rational knowledge is the perception of the certain agreement or disagreement of any two ideas, by the intervention of one or more other ideas.

Judgment is the thinking or taking two ideas to agree or disagree, by the intervention of one or more ideas, whose certain agreement or disagreement with them it does not perceive, but hath observed to be frequent and usual.

18. Though the deducing one proposition from another, or making inferences in words, be a great part of reason, and that which it is usually employed about; yet the principal act of ratiocination is the finding the agreement or disagreement of two ideas one with another, by the intervention of a third. As a man, by a yard, finds two houses to be of the same length, which could not be brought together to measure their equality by juxta-position. Words have their consequences, as the signs of such ideas: And things agree or disagree, as really they are; but we observe it only by our ideas.

Chapter XXI. Of the Division of the Sciences

1. All that can fall within the compass of human understanding being either, first, the nature of things as they are in themselves, their relations, and their manner of operation; or, secondly, that which man himself ought to do, as a rational and voluntary agent, for the attainment of any end, especially happiness; or, thirdly, the ways and means, whereby the knowledge of both the one and the other of these is attained and communicated: I think, science may be divided properly into these three sorts.

2. First, the knowledge of things as they are in their own proper beings, their constitution, properties, and operations; whereby I mean not only matter and body, but spirits also, which have their proper natures, constitutions, and operations, as well as bodies. This, in a little more enlarged sense of the word, I call ⟨*phusike*⟩, or natural philosophy. The end of this is bare speculative truth; and whatsoever can afford the mind of man any such falls under this branch, whether it be God himself, angels, spirits, bodies, or any of their affections, as number, and figure, &c.

3. Secondly, ⟨*praktike*⟩, the skill of right applying our own powers and actions, for the attainment of things good and useful. The most considerable under this head is ethics, which is the seeking out those rules and measures of human actions which lead to happiness, and the means to practise them. The end of this is not bare speculation, and the knowledge of truth; but right, and a conduct suitable to it.

4. Thirdly, the third branch may be called ⟨*semeiotike*⟩, or the doctrine of signs, the most usual whereof being words, it is aptly enough termed also ⟨*logike*⟩, logic; the business whereof is to consider the nature of signs, the mind makes use of for the understanding of things, or conveying its knowledge to others. For since the things the mind contemplates are none of them, besides itself, present to the understanding, it is necessary that something else, as a sign or representation of the thing it considers, should be present to it; and these are ideas. And because the scene of ideas that makes one man's thoughts cannot be laid open to the immediate view of another, nor laid up anywhere but in the memory, a no very sure repository; therefore to communicate our thoughts to one another, as well as record them for our own use, signs of our ideas are also necessary. Those which men have found most convenient, and therefore generally make use of, are articulate sounds. The consideration then of ideas and words, as the great instruments of knowledge, makes no despicable part of their contemplation, who would take a view of human knowledge in the whole extent of it. And perhaps if they were distinctly weighed, and duly considered, they would afford us another sort of logic and critic than what we have been hitherto acquainted with.

5. This seems to me the first and most general, as well as natural, division of the objects of our understanding. For a man can employ his thoughts about nothing but either the contemplation of things themselves, for the discovery of truth; or about the things in his own power, which are his own actions, for the attainment of his own ends; or the signs the mind makes use of both in the one and the other, and the right ordering of them for its clearer information. All which three, viz. things as they are in themselves knowable; actions as they depend on us, in order to happiness; and the right use of signs in order to knowledge, being *toto coelo* different, they seemed to me to be the three great provinces of the intellectual world, wholly separate and distinct one from another.

George Berkeley
(1685–1753)

Berkeley was born near Kilkenny in Ireland. Though his grandfather was English, he always regarded himself as Irish. His well-to-do family had no trouble providing him with a first-rate education. He left the distinguished Kilkenny College to go to Trinity College, Dublin, taking his B.A. in 1704 at the age of nineteen. At Trinity, Berkeley studied Latin, Greek, French, and Hebrew, as well as mathematics, including the works of Newton, and Locke's *Essay Concerning Human Understanding*. Encouraged by his success as a student, he stayed on in the college as a graduate waiting for a fellowship. In 1707 he was admitted as a fellow, taking religious orders at the same time, as required by the statutes.

As a graduate, Berkeley seems to have written three short works discussing mathematics, a subject in which he took great interest though he disapproved of most of the mathematicians of his time, considering their views to be full of absurdities. In 1707 shortly after becoming a fellow, he began to fill two notebooks with philosophical remarks, many of which contain the seeds of his later works. *An Essay Towards a New Theory of Vision* appeared in 1709, and *A Treatise Concerning the Principles of Human Knowledge* the next year. Three years later, in 1713, Berkeley published *Three Dialogues Between Hylas and Philonous*, largely as an attempt to clarify the central doctrines of the *Principles*. Thus, by the age of twenty-eight, Berkeley had completed the works that made him a major figure in modern philosophy. Though Berkeley claimed to speak for common sense against scholastic metaphysics and what he took to be Locke's too credulous attitude toward natural philosophy (that is, the atomism of Robert Boyle and the mathematical physics of Newton), he was immediately perceived by the public as a skeptic and revisionary metaphysician himself, for he denied the existence of everything but spirits and their ideas. Indeed, Berkeley thought he had made a profound discovery, one that would revolutionize all philosophy and science: To exist is to perceive or to be perceived. A prominent doctor responded by diagnosing insanity. Berkeley's readers never have been convinced that he was the defender of common sense he claimed to be.

In 1713 Berkeley set off for what was to be a short visit to London—his first visit to England—but he wound up staying away from Ireland for eight years. We know that he was intimate with the intellectual elite in London, and we know that he met Nicolas Malebranche in Paris in 1713. For four years, mostly spent on the Continent, Berkeley served as tutor to George Ashe, son of the Bishop of Clogher. In 1719 he returned to Trinity College, Dublin, as senior fellow, a position he resigned in 1724 to become Dean of Derry.

It was during this period that Berkeley conceived the idea of building a seminary or college in Bermuda. By 1728 expressing doubts about the Bermuda site, he left for Newport, Rhode Island, where he bought a hundred acres for the project, evidently anticipating that the funds from the Crown were on the way. After two and a half years of waiting, during which time he wrote *Alciphron*, he gave up and returned to London, realizing that the funds would never be forthcoming. There, waiting for preferment, he wrote *The Analyst*, which is mainly notable for its critique of infinitesimals, a critique that generated a good deal of controversy among mathematicians. In 1734 on being appointed Bishop of Cloyne, he returned to Ireland. There he remained until moving to Oxford in 1752 to supervise the education of his second son. (Three of Berkeley's seven children died in infancy, and his eldest son died at the age of fourteen.) *The Querist*, a sociopolitical work written entirely as questions, was completed by 1737, and *Siris*, an extraordinary tract on the medicinal virtues of tar-water, chemistry, cosmology, and religion, was published in 1744. Berkeley died in 1753 in Oxford.

Note on the text: There is no standard or obvious way to identify passages in Berkeley's *Dialogues*. We have remedied this (and hope to start a tradition) by numbering the speeches of Philonous, Berkeley's spokesman, starting with one at the beginning of each dialogue. Thus, "d2, 45" refers to Philonous's forty-fifth speech in the second dialogue.

The text is based on the third edition of the *Dialogues* of 1734.

A Treatise Concerning the Principles of Human Knowledge, Wherein the Chief Causes of Error and Difficulty in the Sciences, with the Grounds of Scepticism, Atheism, and Irreligion, Are Inquired Into

Of the Principles of Human Knowledge

Preface
Introduction

Excerpted with permission from the Past Masters Berkeley text base, InteLex Corp., 1989.

Part I

Preface

What I here make public has, after a long and scrupulous inquiry, seemed to me evidently true, and not unuseful to be known, particularly to those who are tainted with scepticism, or want a demonstration of the existence and immateriality of God, or the natural immortality of the soul. Whether it be so or no, I am content the reader should impartially examine. Since I do not think myself any further concerned for the success of what I have written than as it is agreeable to truth. But to the end this may not suffer, I make it my request that the reader suspend his judgment till he has once, at least, read the whole through with that degree of attention and thought which the subject matter shall seem to deserve. For as there are some passages that, taken by themselves, are very liable (nor could it be remedied) to gross misinterpretation, and to be charged with most absurd consequences, which, nevertheless, upon an entire perusal will appear not to follow from them: so likewise, though the whole should be read over, yet if this be done transiently, it is very probable my sense may be mistaken; but to a thinking reader, I flatter myself, it will be throughout clear and obvious. As for the characters of novelty and singularity, which some of the following notions may seem to bear, it is, I hope, needless to make any apology on that account. He must surely be either very weak, or very little acquainted with the sciences, who shall reject a truth that is capable of demonstration, for no other reason but because it is newly known and contrary to the prejudices of mankind. Thus much I thought fit to premise, in order to prevent, if possible, the hasty censures of a sort of men, who are too apt to condemn an opinion before they rightly comprehend it.

Introduction

1. Philosophy being nothing else but the study of wisdom and truth, it may with reason be expected that those who have spent most time and pains in it should enjoy a greater calm and serenity of mind, a greater clearness and evidence of knowledge, and be less disturbed with doubts and difficulties than other men. Yet so it is, we see the illiterate bulk of mankind, that walk the high road of plain, common sense, and are governed by the dictates of nature, for the most part easy and undisturbed. To them nothing that is familiar appears unaccountable or difficult to comprehend. They complain not of any want of evidence in their senses, and are out of all danger of becoming sceptics. But no sooner do we depart from sense and instinct to follow the light of a superior principle, to reason, meditate, and reflect on the nature of things, but a thousand scruples spring up in our minds, concerning those things which before we seemed fully to comprehend. Prejudices and errors of sense do from all parts discover themselves to our view; and endeavouring to correct these by reason, we are insensibly drawn into uncouth paradoxes, difficulties, and inconsistencies, which multiply and grow upon us as we advance in speculation; till at length, having wandered through many intricate mazes, we find ourselves just where we were, or, which is worse, sit down in a forlorn scepticism.

2. The cause of this is thought to be the obscurity of things, or the natural weakness and imperfection of our understandings. It is said the faculties we have are few, and those designed by nature for the support and comfort (pleasure) of life, and not to penetrate into the inward essence and constitution of things. Besides, the mind of man being finite, when it treats of things which partake of infinity, it is not to be wondered at if it run into absurdities and contradictions; out of which it is impossible it should ever extricate itself, it being of the nature of infinite not to be comprehended by that which is finite.

3. But perhaps we may be too partial to ourselves in placing the fault originally in our faculties, and not rather in the wrong use we make of them. It is a hard thing to suppose, that right deductions from true principles should ever end in consequences which cannot be maintained or made consistent. We should believe that God has dealt more bountifully with the sons of men, than to give them a strong desire for that knowledge which he had placed quite out of their reach. This were not agreeable to the wonted indulgent methods of Providence, which, whatever appetites it may have implanted in the creatures, doth usually furnish them with such means as, if rightly made use of, will not fail to satisfy them. Upon the whole I am inclined to think that the far greater part, if not all, of those difficulties which have hitherto amused philosophers, and blocked up the way to knowledge, are entirely owing to ourselves. That we have first raised a dust, and then complain we cannot see.

4. My purpose therefore is to try if I can discover what those principles are, which have introduced all that doubtfulness and uncertainty, those absurdities and contradictions into the several sects of philosophy; insomuch that the wisest men have thought our ignorance incurable, conceiving it to arise from the natural dullness and limitation of our faculties. And surely it is a work well deserving our pains, to make a strict inquiry concerning the first principles of human knowledge, to sift and examine them on all sides: especially since there may be some grounds to suspect that those lets and difficulties, which stay and embarrass the mind in its search after truth, do not spring from any darkness and intricacy in the objects, or natural defect in the understanding, so much as from false principles which have been insisted on, and might have been avoided.

5. How difficult and discouraging soever this attempt may seem, when I consider how many great and extraordinary men have gone before me in the same designs: yet I am not without some hopes, upon the consideration that the largest views are not always the clearest, and that he who is short-sighted will be obliged to draw the object nearer, and may, perhaps, by a close and narrow survey discern that which had escaped far better eyes.

6. In order to prepare the mind of the reader for the easier conceiving what follows, it is proper to premise somewhat, by way of introduction, concerning the nature and abuse of language. But the unravelling this matter leads me in some measure to anticipate my design, by taking notice of what seems to have had a chief part in rendering speculation intricate and perplexed, and to have occasioned innumerable errors and difficulties in almost all parts of knowledge. And that is the opinion that the mind hath a power of framing abstract ideas or notions of things. He who is not a perfect stranger to the writings and disputes of philosophers must needs acknowledge that no small part of them are spent about abstract ideas. These are, in a more especial manner, thought to be the object of those sciences which go by the name of logic and metaphysics, and of all that which passes under the notion of the most abstracted and sublime learning, in all which one shall scarce find any question handled in such a manner, as does not suppose their existence in the mind, and that it is well acquainted with them.

7. It is agreed, on all hands, that the qualities or modes of things do never really exist each of them apart by itself, and separated from all others, but are mixed, as it were, and blended together, several in the same object. But we are told, the mind being able to consider each quality singly, or abstracted from those other qualities with which it is united, does by that means frame to itself abstract ideas. For example, there is perceived by sight an object extended, coloured, and moved: this mixed or compound idea the mind resolving into its simple, constituent parts, and viewing each by itself, exclusive of the rest, does frame the abstract ideas of extension, colour, and motion. Not that it is possible for colour or motion to exist without extension: but only that the mind can frame to itself by abstraction

the idea of colour exclusive of extension, and of motion exclusive of both colour and extension.

8. Again, the mind having observed that in the particular extensions perceived by sense, there is something common and alike in all, and some other things peculiar, as this or that figure or magnitude, which distinguish them one from another; it considers apart or singles out by itself that which is common, making thereof a most abstract idea of extension, which is neither line, surface, nor solid, nor has any figure or magnitude, but is an idea entirely prescinded from all these. So likewise the mind, by leaving out of the particular colours perceived by sense that which distinguishes them one from another, and retaining that only which is common to all, makes an idea of colour in abstract, which is neither red, nor blue, nor white, nor any other determinate colour. And in like manner, by considering motion abstractedly not only from the body moved, but likewise from the figure it describes, and all particular directions and velocities, the abstract idea of motion is framed; which equally corresponds to all particular motions whatsoever that may be perceived by sense.

9. And as the mind frames to itself abstract ideas of qualities or modes, so does it, by the same precision or mental separation, attain abstract ideas of the more compounded beings, which include several coexistent qualities. For example, the mind having observed that Peter, James, and John resemble each other, in certain common agreements of shape and other qualities, leaves out of the complex or compounded idea it has of Peter, James, and any other particular man that which is peculiar to each, retaining only what is common to all; and so makes an abstract idea wherein all the particulars equally partake, abstracting entirely from and cutting off all those circumstances and differences, which might determine it to any particular existence. And after this manner it is said we come by the abstract idea of man, or, if you please, humanity or human nature; wherein it is true there is included colour, because there is no man but has some colour, but then it can be neither white, nor black, nor any particular colour; because there is no one particular colour wherein all men partake. So likewise there is included stature, but then it is nei-

ther tall stature nor low stature, nor yet middle stature, but something abstracted from all these. And so of the rest. Moreover, there being a great variety of other creatures that partake in some parts, but not all, of the complex idea of man, the mind leaving out those parts which are peculiar to men, and retaining those only which are common to all the living creatures, frameth the idea of animal, which abstracts not only from all particular men, but also all birds, beasts, fishes, and insects. The constituent parts of the abstract idea of animal are body, life, sense, and spontaneous motion. By body is meant body without any particular shape or figure, there being no one shape or figure common to all animals, without covering, either of hair or feathers, or scales, &c., nor yet naked: hair, feathers, scales, and nakedness being the distinguishing properties of particular animals, and for that reason left out of the abstract idea. Upon the same account the spontaneous motion must be neither walking, nor flying, nor creeping; it is nevertheless a motion, but what that motion is, it is not easy to conceive.

10. Whether others have this wonderful faculty of abstracting their ideas, they best can tell: for myself I find indeed I have a faculty of imagining, or representing to myself the ideas of those particular things I have perceived, and of variously compounding and dividing them. I can imagine a man with two heads, or the upper parts of a man joined to the body of a horse. I can consider the hand, the eye, the nose, each by itself abstracted or separated from the rest of the body. But then whatever hand or eye I imagine, it must have some particular shape and colour. Likewise the idea of man that I frame to myself must be either of a white, or a black, or a tawny, a straight, or a crooked, a tall, or a low, or a middle-sized man. I cannot by any effort of thought conceive the abstract idea above described. And it is equally impossible for me to form the abstract idea of motion distinct from the body moving, and which is neither swift nor slow, curvilinear nor rectilinear; and the like may be said of all other abstract general ideas whatsoever. To be plain, I own myself able to abstract in one sense, as when I consider some particular parts or qualities separated from others, with which though they are united in some object, yet it is possible they may really exist without them. But I deny that I can abstract one

from another, or conceive separately, those qualities which it is impossible should exist so separated; or that I can frame a general notion by abstracting from particulars in the manner aforesaid. Which two last are the proper acceptations of abstraction. And there are grounds to think most men will acknowledge themselves to be in my case. The generality of men which are simple and illiterate never pretend to abstract notions. It is said they are difficult, and not to be attained without pains and study. We may therefore reasonably conclude that, if such there be, they are confined only to the learned.

11. I proceed to examine what can be alleged in defence of the doctrine of abstraction, and try if I can discover what it is that inclines the men of speculation to embrace an opinion so remote from common sense as that seems to be. There has been a late deservedly esteemed philosopher, who, no doubt, has given it very much countenance by seeming to think the having abstract general ideas is what puts the widest difference in point of understanding betwixt man and beast. "The having of general ideas," saith he, "is that which puts a perfect distinction betwixt man and brutes, and is an excellency which the faculties of brutes do by no means attain unto. For it is evident we observe no footsteps in them of making use of general signs for universal ideas; from which we have reason to imagine that they have not the faculty of abstracting, or making general ideas, since they have no use of words or any other general signs." And a little after: "Therefore, I think, we may suppose that it is in this that the species of brutes are discriminated from men, and it is that proper difference wherein they are wholly separated, and which at last widens to so wide a distance. For if they have any ideas at all, and are not bare machines (as some would have them), we cannot deny them to have some reason. It seems as evident to me that they do some of them in certain instances reason as that they have sense, but it is only in particular ideas, just as they receive them from their senses. They are the best of them tied up within those narrow bounds, and have not (as I think) the faculty to enlarge them by any kind of abstraction." (*Essay on Hum. Underst.*, b. ii. ch. xi. sect. 10, 11.) I readily agree with this learned author, that the faculties of brutes can by no means attain to abstraction. But then if this be made the distinguish-

ing property of that sort of animals, I fear a great many of those that pass for men must be reckoned into their number. The reason that is here assigned why we have no grounds to think brutes have abstract general ideas, is that we observe in them no use of words or any other general signs; which is built on this supposition, to wit, that the making use of words implies the having general ideas. From which it follows that men who use language are able to abstract or generalize their ideas. That this is the sense and arguing of the author will further appear by his answering the question he in another place puts. "Since all things that exist are only particulars, how come we by general terms?" His answer is, "Words become general by being made the signs of general ideas." (*Essay on Hum. Underst.*, b. iii. ch. iii. sect. 6). But it seems that a word becomes general by being made the sign, not of an abstract general idea, but of several particular ideas, any one of which it indifferently suggests to the mind. For example, when it is said the change of motion is proportional to the impressed force, or that whatever has extension is divisible; these propositions are to be understood of motion and extension in general, and nevertheless it will not follow that they suggest to my thoughts an idea of motion without a body moved, or any determinate direction and velocity, or that I must conceive an abstract general idea of extension, which is neither line, surface, nor solid, neither great nor small, black, white, nor red, nor of any other determinate colour. It is only implied that whatever motion I consider, whether it be swift or slow, perpendicular, horizontal, or oblique, or in whatever object, the axiom concerning it holds equally true. As does the other of every particular extension, it matters not whether line, surface, or solid, whether of this or that magnitude or figure.

12. By observing how ideas become general, we may the better judge how words are made so. And here it is to be noted that I do not deny absolutely there are general ideas, but only that there are any abstract general ideas: for in the passages above quoted, wherein there is mention of general ideas, it is always supposed that they are formed by abstraction, after the manner set forth in Sect. 8 and 9. Now if we will annex a meaning to our words, and speak only of what we can conceive, I believe we shall acknowledge that an idea, which considered in itself is particular, becomes general, by being made to represent or stand for all other particular ideas of the same sort. To make this plain by an example, suppose a geometrician is demonstrating the method of cutting a line in two equal parts. He draws, for instance, a black line of an inch in length; this, which in itself is a particular line, is nevertheless with regard to its signification general, since, as it is there used, it represents all particular lines whatsoever; so that what is demonstrated of it is demonstrated of all lines, or, in other words, of a line in general. And as that particular line becomes general, by being made a sign, so the name *line,* which taken absolutely is particular, by being a sign is made general. And as the former owes its generality, not to its being the sign of an abstract or general line, but of all particular right lines that may possibly exist, so the latter must be thought to derive its generality from the same cause, namely, the various particular lines which it indifferently denotes.

13. To give the reader a yet clearer view of the nature of abstract ideas, and the uses they are thought necessary to, I shall add one more passage out of the *Essay on Human Understanding,* which is as follows. "Abstract ideas are not so obvious or easy to children or the yet unexercised mind as particular ones. If they seem so to grown men, it is only because by constant and familiar use they are made so. For when we nicely reflect upon them, we shall find that general ideas are fictions and contrivances of the mind, that carry difficulty with them, and do not so easily offer themselves as we are apt to imagine. For example, does it not require some pains and skill to form the general idea of a triangle? (which is yet none of the most abstract, comprehensive, and difficult) for it must be neither oblique nor rectangle, neither equilateral, equicrural, nor scalenon, but all and none of these at once. In effect, it is something imperfect that cannot exist, an idea wherein some parts of several different and inconsistent ideas are put together. It is true the mind in this imperfect state has need of such ideas, and makes all the haste to them it can, for the conveniency of communication and enlargement of knowledge, to both which it is naturally very much inclined. But yet one has reason to suspect such ideas are marks of our imperfection. At least this is enough to show that the most abstract and general ideas are not those

that the mind is first and most easily acquainted with, nor such as its earliest knowledge is conversant about." Book iv. ch. vii. sect. 9. If any man has the faculty of framing in his mind such an idea of a triangle as is here described, it is in vain to pretend to dispute him out of it, nor would I go about it. All I desire is, that the reader would fully and certainly inform himself whether he has such an idea or no. And this, methinks, can be no hard task for anyone to perform. What more easy than for anyone to look a little into his own thoughts, and there try whether he has, or can attain to have, an idea that shall correspond with the description that is here given of the general idea of a triangle, which is neither oblique, nor rectangle, equilateral, equicrural, nor scalenon, but all and none of these at once?

14. Much is here said of the difficulty that abstract ideas carry with them, and the pains and skill requisite to the forming them. And it is on all hands agreed that there is need of great toil and labour of the mind to emancipate our thoughts from particular objects, and raise them to those sublime speculations that are conversant about abstract ideas. From all which the natural consequence should seem to be, that so difficult a thing as the forming abstract ideas was not necessary for communication, which is so easy and familiar to all sorts of men. But we are told, if they seem obvious and easy to grown men, it is only because by constant and familiar use they are made so. Now I would fain know at what time it is men are employed in surmounting that difficulty, and furnishing themselves with those necessary helps for discourse. It cannot be when they are grown up, for then it seems they are not conscious of any such pains-taking; it remains therefore to be the business of their childhood. And surely, the great and multiplied labour of framing abstract notions will be found a hard task for that tender age. Is it not a hard thing to imagine, that a couple of children cannot prate together of their sugar-plums, and rattles, and the rest of their little trinkets, till they have first tacked together numberless inconsistencies, and so framed in their minds abstract general ideas, and annexed them to every common name they make use of?

15. Nor do I think them a whit more needful for the enlargement of knowledge than for communi-

cation. It is, I know, a point much insisted on, that all knowledge and demonstration are about universal notions, to which I fully agree: but then it doth not appear to me that those notions are formed by abstraction in the manner premised; universality, so far as I can comprehend, not consisting in the absolute, positive nature or conception of any thing, but in the relation it bears to the particulars signified or represented by it: by virtue whereof it is that things, names, or notions, being in their own nature particular, are rendered universal. Thus when I demonstrate any proposition concerning triangles, it is to be supposed that I have in view the universal idea of a triangle; which ought not to be understood as if I could frame an idea of a triangle which was neither equilateral, nor scalenon, nor equicrural. But only that the particular triangle I consider, whether of this or that sort it matters not, doth equally stand for and represent all rectilinear triangles whatsoever, and is, in that sense, universal. All which seems very plain, and not to include any difficulty in it.

16. But here it will be demanded, how we can know any proposition to be true of all particular triangles, except we have first seen it demonstrated of the abstract idea of a triangle which equally agrees to all? For because a property may be demonstrated to agree to some one particular triangle, it will not thence follow that it equally belongs to any other triangle, which in all respects is not the same with it. For example, having demonstrated that the three angles of an isosceles rectangular triangle are equal to two right ones, I cannot therefore conclude this affection agrees to all other triangles, which have neither a right angle, nor two equal sides. It seems therefore that, to be certain this proposition is universally true, we must either make a particular demonstration for every particular triangle, which is impossible, or once for all demonstrate it of the abstract idea of a triangle, in which all the particulars do indifferently partake, and by which they are all equally represented. To which I answer, that though the idea I have in view whilst I make the demonstration be, for instance, that of an isosceles rectangular triangle, whose sides are of a determinate length, I may nevertheless be certain it extends to all other rectilinear triangles, of what sort or bigness soever. And that, because neither the right

angle, nor the equality, nor determinate length of the sides, are at all concerned in the demonstration. It is true, the diagram I have in view includes all these particulars, but then there is not the least mention made of them in the proof of the proposition. It is not said, the three angles are equal to two right ones, because one of them is a right angle, or because the sides comprehending it are of the same length. Which sufficiently shows that the right angle might have been oblique, and the sides unequal, and for all that the demonstration have held good. And for this reason it is, that I conclude that to be true of any obliquangular or scalenon, which I had demonstrated of a particular right-angled, equicrural triangle; and not because I demonstrated the proposition of the abstract idea of a triangle. And here it must be acknowledged, that a man may consider a figure merely as triangular, without attending to the particular qualities of the angles, or relations of the sides. So far he may abstract: but this will never prove that he can frame an abstract general inconsistent idea of a triangle. In like manner we may consider Peter so far forth as man, or so far forth as animal, without framing the forementioned abstract idea, either of man or of animal, inasmuch as all that is perceived is not considered.

17. It were an endless, as well as a useless, thing, to trace the schoolmen, those great masters of abstraction, through all the manifold, inextricable labyrinths of error and dispute, which their doctrine of abstract natures and notions seems to have led them into. What bickerings and controversies, and what a learned dust have been raised about those matters, and what mighty advantage hath been from thence derived to mankind, are things at this day too clearly known to need being insisted on. And it had been well if the ill effects of that doctrine were confined to those only who make the most avowed profession of it. When men consider the great pains, industry, and parts that have, for so many ages, been laid out on the cultivation and advancement of the sciences, and that notwithstanding all this, the far greater part of them remain full of darkness and uncertainty, and disputes that are like never to have an end, and even those that are thought to be supported by the most clear and cogent demonstrations, contain in them paradoxes which are perfectly irreconcilable

to the understandings of men, and that, taking all together, a small portion of them doth supply any real benefit to mankind, otherwise than by being an innocent diversion and amusement: I say, the consideration of all this is apt to throw them into a despondency, and perfect contempt of all study. But this may perhaps cease, upon a view of the false principles that have obtained in the world, amongst all which there is none, methinks, hath a more wide influence over the thoughts of speculative men than this of abstract general ideas.

18. I come now to consider the source of this prevailing notion, and that seems to me to be language. And surely nothing of less extent than reason itself could have been the source of an opinion so universally received. The truth of this appears as from other reasons, so also from the plain confession of the ablest patrons of abstract ideas, who acknowledge that they are made in order to naming; from which it is a clear consequence, that if there had been no such thing as speech or universal signs, there never had been any thought of abstraction. See book iii. ch. vi. sect. 39, and elsewhere, of the *Essay on Human Understanding.* Let us therefore examine the manner wherein words have contributed to the origin of that mistake. First, then, it is thought that every name hath, or ought to have, one only precise and settled signification, which inclines men to think there are certain abstract, determinate ideas, which constitute the true and only immediate signification of each general name. And that it is by the mediation of these abstract ideas, that a general name comes to signify any particular thing. Whereas, in truth, there is no such thing as one precise and definite signification annexed to any general name, they all signifying indifferently a great number of particular ideas. All which doth evidently follow from what has been already said, and will clearly appear to anyone by a little reflection. To this it will be objected, that every name that has a definition is thereby restrained to one certain signification. For example, a triangle is defined to be a plain surface comprehended by three right lines; by which that name is limited to denote one certain idea and no other. To which I answer, that in the definition it is not said whether the surface be great or small, black or white, nor whether the sides are long or short, equal or unequal, nor with what angles they are inclined to each other; in all which there may be great variety, and consequently there is no one settled idea which limits the signification of the word *triangle.* It is one thing for to keep a name constantly to the same definition, and another to make it stand everywhere for the same idea: the one is necessary, the other useless and impracticable.

19. Secondly, But to give a further account how words came to produce the doctrine of abstract ideas, it must be observed that it is a received opinion, that language has no other end but the communicating our ideas, and that every significant name stands for an idea. This being so, and it being withal certain, that names, which yet are not thought altogether insignificant, do not always mark out particular conceivable ideas, it is straightway concluded that they stand for abstract notions. That there are many names in use amongst speculative men, which do not always suggest to others determinate particular ideas, is what nobody will deny. And a little attention will discover that it is not necessary (even in the strictest reasonings) significant names which stand for ideas should, every time they are used, excite in the understanding the ideas they are made to stand for: in reading and discoursing, names being, for the most part, used as letters are in algebra, in which, though a particular quantity be marked by each letter, yet to proceed right it is not requisite that in every step each letter suggest to your thoughts that particular quantity it was appointed to stand for.

20. Besides, the communicating of ideas marked by words is not the chief and only end of language, as is commonly supposed. There are other ends, as the raising of some passion, the exciting to, or deterring from, an action, the putting the mind in some particular disposition; to which the former is, in many cases, barely subservient, and sometimes entirely omitted, when these can be obtained without it, as I think doth not infrequently happen in the familiar use of language. I entreat the reader to reflect with himself, and see if it doth not often happen, either in hearing or reading a discourse, that the passions of fear, love, hatred, admiration, disdain, and the like, arise immediately in his mind upon the perception of certain words, without any ideas coming between. At first, indeed, the words might have

occasioned ideas that were fit to produce those emotions; but, if I mistake not, it will be found that when language is once grown familiar, the hearing of the sounds or sight of the characters is oft immediately attended with those passions, which at first were wont to be produced by the intervention of ideas, that are now quite omitted. May we not, for example, be affected with the promise of a good thing, though we have not an idea of what it is? Or is not the being threatened with danger sufficient to excite a dread, though we think not of any particular evil likely to befall us, nor yet frame to ourselves an idea of danger in abstract? If anyone shall join ever so little reflection of his own to what has been said, I believe it will evidently appear to him, that general names are often used in the propriety of language without the speaker's designing them for marks of ideas in his own, which he would have them raise in the mind of the hearer. Even proper names themselves do not seem always spoken with a design to bring into our view the ideas of those individuals that are supposed to be marked by them. For example, when a schoolman tells me "Aristotle hath said it," all I conceive he means by it is to dispose me to embrace his opinion with the deference and submission which custom has annexed to that name. And this effect may be so instantly produced in the minds of those who are accustomed to resign their judgment to the authority of that philosopher, as it is impossible any idea either of his person, writings, or reputation should go before. Innumerable examples of this kind may be given, but why should I insist on those things which everyone's experience will, I doubt not, plentifully suggest unto him?

21. We have, I think, shown the impossibility of abstract ideas. We have considered what has been said for them by their ablest patrons; and endeavoured to show they are of no use for those ends to which they are thought necessary. And lastly, we have traced them to the source from whence they flow, which appears to be language. It cannot be denied that words are of excellent use; in that, by their means, all that stock of knowledge, which has been purchased by the joint labours of inquisitive men in all ages and nations, may be drawn into the view and made the possession of one single person. But at the same time it must be owned that most parts of knowledge have been strangely perplexed and darkened by the abuse of words, and general ways of speech wherein they are delivered. Since, therefore, words are so apt to impose on the understanding, whatever ideas I consider, I shall endeavour to take them bare and naked into my view, keeping out of my thoughts, so far as I am able, those names which long and constant use hath so strictly united with them; from which I may expect to derive the following advantages:

22. First, I shall be sure to get clear of all controversies purely verbal; the springing up of which weeds in almost all the sciences has been a main hindrance to the growth of true and sound knowledge. Secondly, this seems to be a sure way to extricate myself out of that fine and subtle net of abstract ideas, which has so miserably perplexed and entangled the minds of men, and that with this peculiar circumstance, that by how much the finer and more curious was the wit of any man, by so much the deeper was he like to be ensnared, and faster held therein. Thirdly, so long as I confine my thoughts to my own ideas divested of words, I do not see how I can be easily mistaken. The objects, I consider, I clearly and adequately know. I cannot be deceived in thinking I have an idea which I have not. It is not possible for me to imagine that any of my own ideas are like or unlike, that are not truly so. To discern the agreements or disagreements that are between my ideas, to see what ideas are included in any compound idea, and what not, there is nothing more requisite than an attentive perception of what passes in my own understanding.

23. But the attainment of all these advantages doth presuppose an entire deliverance from the deception of words, which I dare hardly promise myself; so difficult a thing it is to dissolve a union so early begun, and confirmed by so long a habit as that betwixt words and ideas. Which difficulty seems to have been very much increased by the doctrine of abstraction. For so long as men thought abstract ideas were annexed to their words, it doth not seem strange that they should use words for ideas: it being found an impracticable thing to lay aside the word, and retain the abstract idea in the mind, which in itself was perfectly inconceivable. This seems to me the principal cause, why those men who have so emphatically recommended to others

the laying aside all use of words in their meditations, and contemplating their bare ideas, have yet failed to perform it themselves. Of late many have been very sensible of the absurd opinions and insignificant disputes which grow out of the abuse of words. And in order to remedy these evils they advise well, that we attend to the ideas signified, and draw off our attention from the words which signify them. But how good soever this advice may be they have given others, it is plain they could not have a due regard to it themselves, so long as they thought the only immediate use of words was to signify ideas, and that the immediate signification of every general name was a determinate, abstract idea.

24. But these being known to be mistakes, a man may with greater ease prevent his being imposed on by words. He that knows he has no other than particular ideas will not puzzle himself in vain to find out and conceive the abstract idea, annexed to any name. And he that knows names do not always stand for ideas will spare himself the labour of looking for ideas where there are none to be had. It were therefore to be wished that everyone would use his utmost endeavours to obtain a clear view of the ideas he would consider, separating from them all that dress and encumbrance of words which so much contribute to blind the judgment and divide the attention. In vain do we extend our view into the heavens, and pry into the entrails of the earth; in vain do we consult the writings of learned men, and trace the dark footsteps of antiquity; we need only draw the curtain of words, to behold the fairest tree of knowledge, whose fruit is excellent, and within the reach of our hand.

25. Unless we take care to clear the first principles of knowledge, from the embarras and delusion of words, we may make infinite reasonings upon them to no purpose: we may draw consequences from consequences, and be never the wiser. The further we go, we shall only lose ourselves the more irrecoverably, and be the deeper entangled in difficulties and mistakes. Whoever therefore designs to read the following sheets, I entreat him to make my words the occasion of his own thinking, and endeavour to attain the same train of thoughts in reading that I had in writing them. By this means it will be easy for him to discover the truth or falsity of what I say. He will be out of all danger of being deceived by my words, and I do not see how he can be led into an error by considering his own naked, undisguised ideas.

Of The *Principles* of Human Knowledge

Part I

1. It is evident to anyone who takes a survey of the objects of human knowledge that they are either ideas actually imprinted on the senses, or else such as are perceived by attending to the passions and operations of the mind, or lastly, ideas formed by help of memory and imagination, either compounding, dividing, or barely representing those originally perceived in the aforesaid ways. By sight I have the ideas of light and colours with their several degrees and variations. By touch I perceive, for example, hard and soft, heat and cold, motion and resistance, and of all these more and less either as to quantity or degree. Smelling furnishes me with odours; the palate with tastes; and hearing conveys sounds to the mind in all their variety of tone and composition. And as several of these are observed to accompany each other, they come to be marked by one name, and so to be reputed as one thing. Thus, for example, a certain colour, taste, smell, figure, and consistence having been observed to go together, are accounted one distinct thing, signified by the name *apple*. Other collections of ideas constitute a stone, a tree, a book, and the like sensible things; which, as they are pleasing or disagreeable, excite the passions of love, hatred, joy, grief, and so forth.

2. But besides all that endless variety of ideas or objects of knowledge, there is likewise something which knows or perceives them, and exercises divers operations, as willing, imagining, remembering about them. This perceiving, active being is what I call *mind, spirit, soul,* or *myself.* By which words I do not denote any one of my ideas, but a thing entirely distinct from them, wherein they exist, or, which is the same thing, whereby they are perceived; for the existence of an idea consists in being perceived.

3. That neither our thoughts, nor passions, nor ideas formed by the imagination, exist without the mind, is what everybody will allow. And (to me) it seems no less evident that the various sensations or ideas imprinted on the sense, however blended or combined together (that is, whatever objects they compose), cannot exist otherwise than in a mind perceiving them. I think an intuitive knowledge may be obtained of this, by anyone that shall attend to what is meant by the term *exist*, when applied to sensible things. The table I write on, I say, exists, that is, I see and feel it; and if I were out of my study I should say it existed, meaning thereby that if I was in my study I might perceive it, or that some other spirit actually does perceive it. There was an odour, that is, it was smelled; there was a sound, that is to say, it was heard; a colour or figure, and it was perceived by sight or touch. This is all that I can understand by these and the like expressions. For as to what is said of the absolute existence of unthinking things without any relation to their being perceived, that seems perfectly unintelligible. Their *esse* is *percipi*, nor is it possible they should have any existence out of the minds or thinking things which perceive them.

4. It is indeed an opinion strangely prevailing amongst men that houses, mountains, rivers, and in a word sensible objects have an existence natural or real, distinct from their being perceived by the understanding. But with how great an assurance and acquiescence soever this principle may be entertained in the world; yet whoever shall find in his heart to call it in question, may, if I mistake not, perceive it to involve a manifest contradiction. For what are the forementioned objects but the things we perceive by sense, and what do we perceive besides our own ideas or sensations; and is it not plainly repugnant that any one of these or any combination of them should exist unperceived?

5. If we thoroughly examine this tenet, it will, perhaps, be found at bottom to depend on the doctrine of abstract ideas. For can there be a nicer strain of abstraction than to distinguish the existence of sensible objects from their being perceived, so as to conceive them existing unperceived? Light and colours, heat and cold, extension and figures, in a word the things we see and feel, what are they but so many sensations, notions, ideas, or impressions on the sense; and is it possible to separate, even in

thought, any of these from perception? For my part I might as easily divide a thing from itself. I may indeed divide in my thoughts or conceive apart from each other those things which, perhaps, I never perceived by sense so divided. Thus I imagine the trunk of a human body without the limbs, or conceive the smell of a rose without thinking on the rose itself. So far I will not deny I can abstract, if that may properly be called abstraction, which extends only to the conceiving separately such objects as it is possible may really exist or be actually perceived asunder. But my conceiving or imagining power does not extend beyond the possibility of real existence or perception. Hence as it is impossible for me to see or feel anything without an actual sensation of that thing, so is it impossible for me to conceive in my thoughts any sensible thing or object distinct from the sensation or perception of it.

6. Some truths there are so near and obvious to the mind that a man need only open his eyes to see them. Such I take this important one to be, to wit, that all the choir of heaven and furniture of the earth, in a word all those bodies which compose the mighty frame of the world, have not any subsistence without a mind, that their being (*esse*) is to be perceived or known; that consequently so long as they are not actually perceived by me, or do not exist in my mind or that of any other created spirit, they must either have no existence at all, or else subsist in the mind of some eternal spirit: it being perfectly unintelligible and involving all the absurdity of abstraction, to attribute to any single part of them an existence independent of a spirit. To be convinced of which, the reader need only reflect and try to separate in his own thoughts the being of a sensible thing from its being perceived.

7. From what has been said, it follows, there is not any other substance than spirit, or that which perceives. But for the fuller proof of this point, let it be considered, the sensible qualities are colour, figure, motion, smell, taste, and such like, that is, the ideas perceived by sense. Now for an idea to exist in an unperceiving thing is a manifest contradiction; for to have an idea is all one as to perceive: that therefore wherein colour, figure, and the like qualities exist, must perceive them; hence it is clear there can be no unthinking substance or substratum of those ideas.

8. But say you, though the ideas themselves do not exist without the mind, yet there may be things like them whereof they are copies or resemblances, which things exist without the mind, in an unthinking substance. I answer, an idea can be like nothing but an idea; a colour or figure can be like nothing but another colour or figure. If we look but ever so little into our thoughts, we shall find it impossible for us to conceive a likeness except only between our ideas. Again, I ask whether those supposed originals or external things, of which our ideas are the pictures or representations, be themselves perceivable or no? If they are, then they are ideas, and we have gained our point; but if you say they are not, I appeal to anyone whether it be sense, to assert a colour is like something which is invisible; hard or soft, like something which is intangible; and so of the rest.

9. Some there are who make a distinction betwixt primary and secondary qualities: by the former, they mean extension, figure, motion, rest, solidity or impenetrability, and number: by the latter they denote all other sensible qualities, as colours, sounds, tastes, and so forth. The ideas we have of these they acknowledge not to be the resemblances of anything existing without the mind or unperceived; but they will have our ideas of the primary qualities to be patterns or images of things which exist without the mind, in an unthinking substance which they call *matter*. By matter therefore we are to understand an inert, senseless substance, in which extension, figure, and motion do actually subsist. But it is evident from what we have already shown that extension, figure, and motion are only ideas existing in the mind, and that an idea can be like nothing but another idea, and that consequently neither they nor their archetypes can exist in an unperceiving substance. Hence it is plain that the very notion of what is called *matter,* or *corporeal substance,* involves a contradiction in it.

10. They who assert that figure, motion, and the rest of the primary or original qualities do exist without the mind, in unthinking substances, do at the same time acknowledge that colours, sounds, heat, cold, and such like secondary qualities do not, which they tell us are sensations existing in the mind alone, that depend on and are occasioned by the different size, texture, and motion of the minute particles of matter. This they take for an undoubted truth, which they can demonstrate beyond all exception. Now if it be certain that those original qualities are inseparably united with the other sensible qualities, and not, even in thought, capable of being abstracted from them, it plainly follows that they exist only in the mind. But I desire anyone to reflect and try, whether he can, by any abstraction of thought, conceive the extension and motion of a body, without all other sensible qualities. For my own part, I see evidently that it is not in my power to frame an idea of a body extended and moved, but I must withal give it some colour or other sensible quality which is acknowledged to exist only in the mind. In short, extension, figure, and motion, abstracted from all other qualities, are inconceivable. Where therefore the other sensible qualities are, there must these be also, to wit, in the mind and nowhere else.

11. Again, *great* and *small, swift* and *slow,* are allowed to exist nowhere without the mind, being entirely relative, and changing as the frame or position of the organs of sense varies. The extension therefore which exists without the mind is neither great nor small, the motion neither swift nor slow, that is, they are nothing at all. But, say you, they are extension in general, and motion in general: thus we see how much the tenet of extended, moveable substances existing without the mind depends on that strange doctrine of abstract ideas. And here I cannot but remark, how nearly the vague and indeterminate description of matter or corporeal substance, which the modern philosophers are run into by their own principles, resembles that antiquated and so much ridiculed notion of *materia prima,* to be met with in Aristotle and his followers. Without extension solidity cannot be conceived; since therefore it has been shown that extension exists not in an unthinking substance, the same must also be true of solidity.

12. That number is entirely the creature of the mind, even though the other qualities be allowed to exist without, will be evident to whoever considers that the same thing bears a different denomination of number as the mind views it with different respects. Thus, the same extension is one, or three, or thirty-six, according as the mind considers it with reference to a yard, a foot, or an inch. Number is so visibly relative, and dependent on men's understanding, that it is strange to think how anyone should give it an absolute existence without the mind. We say, one book, one page, one line; all these are equally units, though some contain several of the others. And in each instance it is plain, the unit relates to some particular combination of ideas arbitrarily put together by the mind.

13. Unity, I know, some will have to be a simple or uncompounded idea, accompanying all other ideas into the mind. That I have any such idea, answering the word *unity,* I do not find; and if I had, methinks I could not miss finding it; on the contrary, it should be the most familiar to my understanding, since it is said to accompany all other ideas, and to be perceived by all the ways of sensation and reflection. To say no more, it is an abstract idea.

14. I shall further add, that after the same manner as modern philosophers prove certain sensible qualities to have no existence in matter, or without the mind, the same thing may be likewise proved of all other sensible qualities whatsoever. Thus, for instance, it is said that heat and cold are affections only of the mind, and not at all patterns of real beings, existing in the corporeal substances which excite them, for that the same body which appears cold to one hand, seems warm to another. Now why may we not as well argue that figure and extension are not patterns or resemblances of qualities existing in matter, because to the same eye at different stations, or eyes of a different texture at the same station, they appear various, and cannot therefore be the images of anything settled and determinate without the mind? Again, it is proved that sweetness is not really in the sapid thing, because, the thing remaining unaltered, the sweetness is changed into bitter, as in case of a fever or otherwise vitiated palate. Is it not as reasonable to say that motion is not without the mind, since if the succession of ideas in the mind become swifter, the motion, it is acknowledged, shall appear slower without any alteration in any external object.

15. In short, let anyone consider those arguments which are thought manifestly to prove that colours and tastes exist only in the mind, and he shall find they may with equal force be brought to prove the same thing of extension, figure, and motion. Though it must be confessed, this method of arguing doth not so much prove that there is no extension or colour in an outward object, as that we do not know by sense which is the true extension or colour of the object. But the arguments foregoing plainly show it to be impossible that any colour or extension at all, or other sensible quality whatsoever, should exist in an unthinking subject without the mind, or in truth, that there should be any such thing as an outward object.

16. But let us examine a little the received opinion. It is said extension is a mode or accident of matter, and that matter is the substratum that supports it. Now I desire that you would explain what is meant by matter's supporting extension: say you, I have no idea of matter, and therefore cannot explain it. I answer, though you have no positive, yet if you have any meaning at all, you must at least have a relative idea of matter; though you know not what it is, yet you must be supposed to know what relation it bears to accidents, and what is meant by its supporting them. It is evident support cannot here be taken in its usual or literal sense, as when we say that pillars support a building: in what sense therefore must it be taken?

17. If we inquire into what the most accurate philosophers declare themselves to mean by *material substance,* we shall find them acknowledge, they have no other meaning annexed to those sounds, but the idea of being in general, together with the relative notion of its supporting accidents. The general idea of being appeareth to me the most abstract and incomprehensible of all other; and as for its supporting accidents, this, as we have just now observed, cannot be understood in the common sense of those words; it must therefore be taken in some other sense, but what that is they do not explain. So that when I consider the two parts or branches which make the signification of the words *material substance,* I am convinced there is no distinct meaning annexed to them. But why should we trouble ourselves any further, in discussing this material substratum or support of figure and motion, and other sensible qualities? Does it not suppose they have an existence without the mind? And is not this a direct repugnancy, and altogether inconceivable?

18. But though it were possible that solid, figured, moveable substances may exist without the mind, corresponding to the ideas we have of bodies, yet how is it possible for us to know this? Either we must know it by sense, or by reason. As for our senses, by them we have the knowledge only of our sensations, ideas, or those things that are immediately perceived by sense, call them what you will: but they do not inform us that things exist without the mind, or unperceived, like to those which are perceived. This the materialists themselves acknowledge. It remains therefore that if we have any knowledge at all of external things, it must be by reason, inferring their existence from what is immediately perceived by sense. But (I do not see) what reason can induce us to believe the existence of bodies without the mind, from what we perceive, since the very patrons of matter themselves do not pretend there is any necessary connexion betwixt them and our ideas. I say, it is granted on all hands (and what happens in dreams, frenzies, and the like, puts it beyond dispute) that it is possible we might be affected with all the ideas we have now, though no bodies existed without, resembling them. Hence it is evident the supposition of external bodies is not necessary for the producing our ideas: since it is granted they are produced sometimes, and might possibly be produced always, in the same order we see them in at present, without their concurrence.

19. But though we might possibly have all our sensations without them, yet perhaps it may be thought easier to conceive and explain the manner of their production, by supposing external bodies in their likeness rather than otherwise; and so it might be at least probable there are such things as bodies that excite their ideas in our minds. But neither can this be said; for though we give the materialists their external bodies, they, by their own confession, are never the nearer knowing how our ideas are produced: since they own themselves unable to comprehend in what manner body can act upon spirit, or how it is possible it should imprint any idea in the mind. Hence it is evident, the production of ideas or sensations in our minds can be no reason why we should suppose matter or corporeal substances, since that is acknowledged to remain equally inexplicable with or without this supposition. If therefore it were possible for bodies to exist without the mind, yet to hold they do so must needs be a very precarious opinion; since it is to suppose, without any reason at all, that God has created innumerable beings that are entirely useless, and serve to no manner of purpose.

20. In short, if there were external bodies, it is impossible we should ever come to know it; and if there were not, we might have the very same reasons to think there were that we have now. Suppose, what no one can deny possible, an intelligence, without the help of external bodies, to be affected with the same train of sensations or ideas that you are, imprinted in the same order and with like vividness in his mind. I ask, whether that intelligence hath not all the reason to believe the existence of corporeal substances, represented by his ideas, and exciting them in his mind, that you can possibly have for believing the same thing? Of this there can be no question; which one consideration is enough to make any reasonable person suspect the strength of whatever arguments he may think himself to have for the existence of bodies without the mind.

21. Were it necessary to add any further proof against the existence of matter, after what has been said, I could instance several of those errors and difficulties (not to mention impieties) which have sprung from that tenet. It has occasioned numberless controversies and disputes in philosophy, and not a few of greater moment in religion. But I shall not enter into the detail of them in this place, as well because I think arguments *a posteriori* are unnecessary for confirming what has been, if I mistake not, sufficiently demonstrated a *priori,* as because I shall hereafter find occasion to say somewhat of them.

22. I am afraid I have given cause to think me needlessly prolix in handling this subject. For to what purpose is it to dilate on that which may be demonstrated with the utmost evidence in a line or two, to anyone that is capable of the least reflection? It is but looking into your own thoughts, and so trying whether you can conceive it possible for a sound, or figure, or motion, or colour, to exist without the mind, or unperceived. This easy trial may make you see that what you contend for is a downright contradiction. Insomuch that I am content to put the whole upon this issue; if you can but conceive it possible for one extended moveable substance, or in general, for any one idea, or anything like an idea, to exist otherwise than in a mind perceiving it, I shall readily give up the cause: and as for all that *compages* of external bodies which you contend for, I shall grant you its existence, though you cannot either give me any reason why you believe it exists, or assign any use to it when it is supposed to exist. I say, the bare possibility of your opinion's being true shall pass for an argument that it is so.

23. But say you, surely there is nothing easier than to imagine trees, for instance, in a park, or books existing in a closet, and nobody by to perceive them. I answer, you may so, there is no difficulty in it: but what is all this, I beseech you, more than framing in your mind certain ideas which you call *books* and *trees,* and at the same time omitting to frame the idea of anyone that may perceive them? But do not you yourself perceive or think of them all the while? This therefore is nothing to the purpose; it only shows you have the power of imagining or forming ideas in your mind; but it doth not show that you can conceive it possible the objects of your thought may exist without the mind: to make out this, it is necessary that you conceive them existing unconceived or unthought-of, which is a manifest repugnancy. When we do our utmost to conceive the existence of external bodies, we are all the while only contemplating our own ideas. But the mind, taking no notice of itself, is deluded to think it can and doth conceive bodies existing unthought-of or without the mind; though at the same time they are apprehended by or exist in itself. A little attention will discover to anyone the truth and evidence of what is here said, and make it unnecessary to insist on any other proofs against the existence of material substance.

24. It is very obvious, upon the least inquiry into our own thoughts, to know whether it be possible for us to understand what is meant by *the absolute existence of sensible objects in themselves or without the mind.* To me it is evident those words mark out either a direct contradiction, or else nothing at all. And to convince others of this, I know no readier or fairer way than to entreat they would calmly attend to their own thoughts: and if by this attention the emptiness or repugnancy of those expressions does appear, surely nothing more is requisite for their conviction. It is on this therefore that I insist, to wit, that the absolute existence of un-thinking things are words without a meaning, or which include a contradiction. This is what I repeat and inculcate, and earnestly recommend to the attentive thoughts of the reader.

25. All our ideas, sensations, or the things which we perceive, by whatsoever names they may be distinguished, are visibly inactive; there is nothing of power or agency included in them. So that one idea or object of thought cannot produce, or make any alteration in another. To be satisfied of the truth of this, there is nothing else requisite but a bare observation of our ideas. For since they and every part of them exist only in the mind, it follows that there is nothing in them but what is perceived. But whoever shall attend to his ideas, whether of sense or reflection, will not perceive in them any power or activity; there is therefore no such thing contained in them. A little attention will discover to us that the very being of an idea implies passiveness and inertness in it, insomuch that it is impossible for an idea to do anything, or, strictly speaking, to be the cause of anything: neither can it be the resemblance or pattern of any active being, as is evident from Sect. 8. Whence it plainly follows that extension, figure, and motion cannot be the cause of our sensations. To say, therefore, that these are the effects of powers resulting from the configuration, number, motion, and size of corpuscles must certainly be false.

26. We perceive a continual succession of ideas, some are anew excited, others are changed or totally disappear. There is therefore some cause of these ideas whereon they depend, and which produces and changes them. That this cause cannot be any quality or idea or combination of ideas is clear from the preceding section. It must therefore be a substance; but it has been shown that there is no corporeal or material substance: it remains therefore that the cause of ideas is an incorporeal active substance or spirit.

27. A spirit is one simple, undivided, active being: as it perceives ideas, it is called the *understanding,* and as it produces or otherwise operates about them, it is called the *will.* Hence there can be no idea formed of a soul or spirit: for all ideas whatever, being passive and inert (*vide* Sect. 25), they cannot represent unto us, by way of image or likeness, that which acts. A little attention will make it plain to

anyone, that to have an idea which shall be like that active principle of motion and change of ideas is absolutely impossible. Such is the nature of spirit, or that which acts, that it cannot be of itself perceived but only by the effects which it produceth. If any man shall doubt of the truth of what is here delivered, let him but reflect and try if he can frame the idea of any power or active being; and whether he hath ideas of two principal powers, marked by the names *will* and *understanding*, distinct from each other as well as from a third idea of substance or being in general, with a relative notion of its supporting or being the subject of the aforesaid powers, which is signified by the name *soul* or *spirit*. This is what some hold; but so far as I can see, the words *will, soul, spirit* do not stand for different ideas, or in truth, for any idea at all, but for something which is very different from ideas, and which being an agent cannot be like unto, or represented by, any idea whatsoever. Though it must be owned at the same time, that we have some notion of soul, spirit, and the operations of the mind, such as willing, loving, hating, inasmuch as we know or understand the meaning of those words.

28. I find I can excite ideas in my mind at pleasure, and vary and shift the scene as oft as I think fit. It is no more than willing, and straightway this or that idea arises in my fancy: and by the same power it is obliterated, and makes way for another. This making and unmaking of ideas doth very properly denominate the mind active. Thus much is certain, and grounded on experience: but when we talk of unthinking agents, or of exciting ideas exclusive of volition, we only amuse ourselves with words.

29. But whatever power I may have over my own thoughts, I find the ideas actually perceived by sense have not a like dependence on my will. When in broad day-light I open my eyes, it is not in my power to choose whether I shall see or no, or to determine what particular objects shall present themselves to my view; and so likewise as to the hearing and other senses, the ideas imprinted on them are not creatures of my will. There is therefore some other will or spirit that produces them.

30. The ideas of sense are more strong, lively, and distinct than those of the imagination; they have likewise a steadiness, order, and coherence, and are not excited at random, as those which are the effects of human wills often are, but in a regular train or series, the admirable connexion whereof sufficiently testifies the wisdom and benevolence of its author. Now the set rules or established methods, wherein the mind we depend on excites in us the ideas of sense, are called the *laws of nature:* and these we learn by experience, which teaches us that such and such ideas are attended with such and such other ideas, in the ordinary course of things.

31. This gives us a sort of foresight, which enables us to regulate our actions for the benefit of life. And without this we should be eternally at a loss: we could not know how to act anything that might procure us the least pleasure, or remove the least pain of sense. That food nourishes, sleep refreshes, and fire warms us; that to sow in the seed-time is the way to reap in the harvest, and, in general, that to obtain such or such ends, such or such means are conducive, all this we know, not by discovering any necessary connexion between our ideas, but only by the observation of the settled laws of nature, without which we should be all in uncertainty and confusion, and a grown man no more know how to manage himself in the affairs of life than an infant just born.

32. And yet this consistent, uniform working, which so evidently displays the goodness and wisdom of that governing Spirit whose will constitutes the laws of nature, is so far from leading our thoughts to him, that it rather sends them a wandering after second causes. For when we perceive certain ideas of sense constantly followed by other ideas, and we know this is not of our own doing, we forthwith attribute power and agency to the ideas themselves, and make one the cause of another, than which nothing can be more absurd and unintelligible. Thus, for example, having observed that when we perceive by sight a certain round luminous figure, we at the same time perceive by touch the idea or sensation called *heat,* we do from thence conclude the sun to be the cause of heat. And in like manner perceiving the motion and collision of bodies to be attended with sound, we are inclined to think the latter an effect of the former.

33. The ideas imprinted on the senses by the author of nature are called *real things:* and those excited in the imagination, being less regular, vivid, and constant, are more properly termed *ideas,* or *im-*

ages of things, which they copy and represent. But then our sensations, be they never so vivid and distinct, are nevertheless ideas, that is, they exist in the mind, or are perceived by it, as truly as the ideas of its own framing. The ideas of sense are allowed to have more reality in them, that is, to be more strong, orderly, and coherent than the creatures of the mind: but this is no argument that they exist without the mind. They are also less dependent on the spirit, or thinking substance which perceives them, in that they are excited by the will of another and more powerful spirit: yet still they are ideas, and certainly no idea, whether faint or strong, can exist otherwise than in a mind perceiving it.

34. Before we proceed any further, it is necessary to spend some time in answering objections which may probably be made against the principles hitherto laid down. In doing of which, if I seem too prolix to those of quick apprehensions, I hope it may be pardoned, since all men do not equally apprehend things of this nature; and I am willing to be understood by everyone. First then, it will be objected that by the foregoing principles, all that is real and substantial in nature is banished out of the world: and instead thereof a chimerical scheme of ideas takes place. All things that exist, exist only in the mind, that is, they are purely notional. What therefore becomes of the sun, moon, and stars? What must we think of houses, rivers, mountains, trees, stones; nay, even of our own bodies? Are all these but so many chimeras and illusions on the fancy? To all which, and whatever else of the same sort may be objected, I answer, that by the principles premised, we are not deprived of any one thing in nature. Whatever we see, feel, hear, or any wise conceive or understand, remains as secure as ever, and is as real as ever. There is a *rerum natura,* and the distinction between realities and chimeras retains its full force. This is evident from Sect. 29, 30, and 33, where we have shown what is meant by real things in opposition to chimeras, or ideas of our own framing; but then they both equally exist in the mind, and in that sense are alike ideas.

35. I do not argue against the existence of any one thing that we can apprehend, either by sense or reflection. That the things I see with mine eyes and touch with my hands do exist, really exist, I make not the least question. The only thing whose existence we deny is that which philosophers call matter or corporeal substance. And in doing of this, there is no damage done to the rest of mankind, who, I dare say will never miss it. The atheist indeed will want the colour of an empty name to support his impiety; and the philosophers may possibly find they have lost a great handle for trifling and disputation.

36. If any man thinks this detracts from the existence or reality of things, he is very far from understanding what hath been premised in the plainest terms I could think of. Take here an abstract of what has been said. There are spiritual substances, minds, or human souls, which will or excite ideas in themselves at pleasure: but these are faint, weak, and unsteady in respect of others they perceive by sense, which being impressed upon them according to certain rules or laws of nature, speak themselves the effects of a mind more powerful and wise than human spirits. These latter are said to have more *reality* in them than the former: by which is meant that they are affecting, orderly, and distinct, and that they are not fictions of the mind perceiving them. And in this sense, the sun that I see by day is the real sun, and that which I imagine by night is the idea of the former. In the sense here given of *reality,* it is evident that every vegetable, star, mineral, and in general each part of the mundane system, is as much a real being by our principles as by any other. Whether others mean anything by the term *reality* different from what I do, I entreat them to look into their own thoughts and see.

37. It will be urged that thus much at least is true, to wit, that we take away all corporeal substances. To this my answer is, that if the word *substance* be taken in the vulgar sense, for a combination of sensible qualities, such as extension, solidity, weight, and the like: this we cannot be accused of taking away. But if it be taken in a philosophic sense, for the support of accidents or qualities without the mind, then indeed I acknowledge that we take it away, if one may be said to take away that which never had any existence, not even in the imagination.

38. But, say you, it sounds very harsh to say we eat and drink ideas, and are clothed with ideas. I acknowledge it does so, the word *idea* not being used in common discourse to signify the several combinations of sensible qualities, which are called *things:* and it is certain that any expression which varies from the familiar use of language will seem harsh and ridiculous. But this doth not concern the truth of the proposition, which in other words is no more than to say, we are fed and clothed with those things which we perceive immediately by our senses. The hardness or softness, the colour, taste, warmth, figure, and such like qualities, which combined together constitute the several sorts of victuals and apparel, have been shown to exist only in the mind that perceives them; and this is all that is meant by calling them *ideas;* which word, if it was as ordinarily used as *thing,* would sound no harsher nor more ridiculous than it. I am not for disputing about the propriety, but the truth of the expression. If therefore you agree with me that we eat, and drink, and are clad with the immediate objects of sense, which cannot exist unperceived or without the mind; I shall readily grant it is more proper or conformable to custom, that they should be called things rather than ideas.

39. If it be demanded why I make use of the word *idea,* and do not rather in compliance with custom call them *things,* I answer, I do it for two reasons: first, because the term *thing,* in contradistinction to *idea,* is generally supposed to denote somewhat existing without the mind: secondly, because *thing* hath a more comprehensive signification than *idea,* including spirits, or thinking things, as well as ideas. Since therefore the objects of sense exist only in the mind, and are withal thoughtless and inactive, I chose to mark them by the word *idea,* which implies those properties.

40. But, say what we can, someone perhaps may be apt to reply, he will still believe his senses, and never suffer any arguments, how plausible soever, to prevail over the certainty of them. Be it so, assert the evidence of sense as high as you please, we are willing to do the same. That what I see, hear, and feel doth exist, that is to say, is perceived by me, I no more doubt than I do of my own being. But I do not see how the testimony of sense can be alleged as a proof for the existence of anything which is not perceived by sense. We are not for having any man turn sceptic, and disbelieve his senses; on the contrary, we give them all the stress and assurance imaginable; nor are there any principles more op-

posite to scepticism than those we have laid down, as shall be hereafter clearly shown.

41. Secondly, it will be objected that there is a great difference betwixt real fire, for instance, and the idea of fire, betwixt dreaming or imagining one's self burnt, and actually being so: this and the like may be urged in opposition to our tenets. To all which the answer is evident from what hath been already said, and I shall only add in this place, that if real fire be very different from the idea of fire, so also is the real pain that it occasions very different from the idea of the same pain: and yet nobody will pretend that real pain either is, or can possibly be, in an unperceiving thing or without the mind, any more than its idea.

42. Thirdly, it will be objected that we see things actually without or at a distance from us, and which consequently do not exist in the mind, it being absurd that those things which are seen at the distance of several miles should be as near to us as our own thoughts. In answer to this, I desire it may be considered, that in a dream we do oft perceive things as existing at a great distance off, and yet for all that, those things are acknowledged to have their existence only in the mind.

43. But for the fuller clearing of this point, it may be worth while to consider, how it is that we perceive distance and things placed at a distance by sight. For that we should in truth see external space, and bodies actually existing in it, some nearer, others further off, seems to carry with it some opposition to what hath been said, of their existing nowhere without the mind. The consideration of this difficulty it was that gave birth to my *Essay towards a new Theory of Vision,* which was published not long since. Wherein it is shown that distance or outness is neither immediately of itself perceived by sight, nor yet apprehended or judged of by lines and angles, or anything that hath a necessary connexion with it: but that it is only suggested to our thoughts, by certain visible ideas and sensations attending vision, which in their own nature have no manner of similitude or relation, either with distance, or things placed at a distance. But by a connexion taught us by experience, they come to signify and suggest them to us, after the same manner that words of any language suggest the ideas they are made to stand for. Insomuch that a man born blind, and afterwards made to see, would not, at first sight, think the things he saw to be without his mind, or at any distance from him. See Sect. 41 of the forementioned treatise.

44. The ideas of sight and touch make two species, entirely distinct and heterogeneous. The former are marks and prognostics of the latter. That the proper objects of sight neither exist without the mind, nor are the images of external things, was shown even in that treatise. Though throughout the same, the contrary be supposed true of tangible objects: not that to suppose that vulgar error was necessary for establishing the notions therein laid down, but because it was beside my purpose to examine and refute it in a discourse concerning vision. So that in strict truth the ideas of sight, when we apprehend by them, distance and things placed at a distance, do not suggest or mark out to us things actually existing at a distance, but only admonish us what ideas of touch will be imprinted in our minds at such and such distances of time, and in consequence of such or such actions. It is, I say, evident from what has been said in the foregoing parts of this treatise, and in Sect. 147, and elsewhere of the essay concerning vision, that visible ideas are the language whereby the governing Spirit, on whom we depend, informs us what tangible ideas he is about to imprint upon us, in case we excite this or that motion in our own bodies. But for a fuller information in this point, I refer to the essay itself.

45. Fourthly, it will be objected, that from the foregoing principles it follows, things are every moment annihilated and created anew. The objects of sense exist only when they are perceived: the trees therefore are in the garden, or the chairs in the parlour, no longer than while there is somebody by to perceive them. Upon shutting my eyes, all the furniture in the room is reduced to nothing, and barely upon opening them it is again created. In answer to all which, I refer the reader to what has been said in Sect. 3, 4, &c., and desire he will consider whether he means anything by the actual existence of an idea, distinct from its being perceived. For my part, after the nicest inquiry I could make, I am not able to discover that anything else is meant by those words. And I once more entreat the reader to sound his own thoughts, and not suffer himself to be imposed on by words. If he can conceive it possible

either for his ideas or their archetypes to exist without being perceived, then I give up the cause: but if he cannot, he will acknowledge it is unreasonable for him to stand up in defence of he knows not what, and pretend to charge on me as an absurdity the not assenting to those propositions which at bottom have no meaning in them.

46. It will not be amiss to observe, how far the received principles of philosophy are themselves chargeable with those pretended absurdities. It is thought strangely absurd that upon closing my eyelids all the visible objects round me should be reduced to nothing; and yet is not this what philosophers commonly acknowledge when they agree on all hands that light and colours, which alone are the proper and immediate objects of sight, are mere sensations, that exist no longer than they are perceived? Again, it may to some perhaps seem very incredible that things should be every moment creating; yet this very notion is commonly taught in the schools. For the schoolmen, though they acknowledge the existence of matter, and that the whole mundane fabric is framed out of it, are nevertheless of opinion that it cannot subsist without the divine conservation, which by them is expounded to be a continual creation.

47. Further, a little thought will discover to us that though we allow the existence of matter or corporeal substance, yet it will unavoidably follow from the principles which are now generally admitted, that the particular bodies, of what kind soever, do none of them exist whilst they are not perceived. For it is evident from Sect. 11 and the following sections, that the matter philosophers contend for is an incomprehensible somewhat, which hath none of those particular qualities whereby the bodies falling under our senses are distinguished one from another. But to make this more plain, it must be remarked that the infinite divisibility of matter is now universally allowed, at least by the most approved and considerable philosophers, who, on the received principles, demonstrate it beyond all exception. Hence it follows that there is an infinite number of parts in each particle of matter, which are not perceived by sense. The reason, therefore, that any particular body seems to be of a finite magnitude, or exhibits only a finite number of parts to sense, is, not because it contains no more, since in

itself it contains an infinite number of parts, but because the sense is not acute enough to discern them. In proportion, therefore, as the sense is rendered more acute, it perceives a greater number of parts in the object; that is, the object appears greater, and its figure varies, those parts in its extremities which were before unperceivable, appearing now to bound it in very different lines and angles from those perceived by an obtuser sense. And, at length, after various changes of size and shape, when the sense becomes infinitely acute, the body shall seem infinite. During all which, there is no alteration in the body, but only in the sense. Each body, therefore, considered in itself, is infinitely extended, and consequently void of all shape or figure. From which it follows that though we should grant the existence of matter to be ever so certain, yet it is withal as certain, the materialists themselves are by their own principles forced to acknowledge, that neither the particular bodies perceived by sense, nor anything like them, exist without the mind. Matter, I say, and each particle thereof, is according to them infinite and shapeless, and it is the mind that frames all that variety of bodies which compose the visible world, any one whereof does not exist longer than it is perceived.

48. If we consider it, the objection proposed in Sect. 45 will not be found reasonably charged on the principles we have premised, so as in truth to make any objection at all against our notions. For though we hold, indeed, the objects of sense to be nothing else but ideas which cannot exist unperceived, yet we may not hence conclude they have no existence, except only while they are perceived by us, since there may be some other spirit that perceives them, though we do not. Wherever bodies are said to have no existence without the mind, I would not be understood to mean this or that particular mind, but all minds whatsoever. It does not therefore follow from the foregoing principles that bodies are annihilated and created every moment, or exist not at all during the intervals between our perception in them.

49. Fifthly, it may perhaps be objected that if extension and figure exist only in the mind, it follows that the mind is extended and figured; since extension is a mode or attribute, which (to speak with the schools) is predicated of the subject in which it exists. I answer, Those qualities are in the mind only as they are perceived by it, that is, not by way of mode or attribute, but only by way of idea; and it no more follows that the soul or mind is extended because extension exists in it alone, than it does that it is red or blue, because those colours are on all hands acknowledged to exist in it, and nowhere else. As to what philosophers say of subject and mode, that seems very groundless and unintelligible. For instance, in this proposition, a die is hard, extended, and square; they will have it that the word *die* denotes a subject or substance, distinct from the hardness, extension, and figure, which are predicated of it, and in which they exist. This I cannot comprehend: to me a die seems to be nothing distinct from those things which are termed its modes or accidents. And to say a die is hard, extended, and square is not to attribute those qualities to a subject distinct from and supporting them, but only an explication of the meaning of the word *die*.

50. Sixthly, you will say there have been a great many things explained by matter and motion: take away these, and you destroy the whole corpuscular philosophy, and undermine those mechanical principles which have been applied with so much success to account for the phenomena. In short, whatever advances have been made, either by ancient or modern philosophers, in the study of nature, do all proceed on the supposition that corporeal substance or matter doth really exist. To this I answer, that there is not any one phenomenon explained on that supposition, which may not as well be explained without it, as might easily be made appear by an induction of particulars. To explain the phenomena is all one as to show, why upon such and such occasions we are affected with such and such ideas. But how matter should operate on a spirit, or produce any idea in it, is what no philosopher will pretend to explain. It is therefore evident, there can be no use of matter in natural philosophy. Besides, they who attempt to account for things do it not by corporeal substance, but by figure, motion, and other qualities, which are in truth no more than mere ideas, and therefore cannot be the cause of anything, as hath been already shown. See Sect. 25.

51. Seventhly, it will upon this be demanded whether it does not seem absurd to take away natural causes, and ascribe everything to the immediate operation of spirits? We must no longer say upon these principles that fire heats, or water cools, but

that a spirit heats, and so forth. Would not a man be deservedly laughed at, who should talk after this manner? I answer, he would so; in such things we ought to think with the learned, and speak with the vulgar. They who to demonstration are convinced of the truth of the Copernican system, do nevertheless say the sun rises, the sun sets, or comes to the meridian: and if they affected a contrary style in common talk, it would without doubt appear very ridiculous. A little reflection on what is here said will make it manifest, that the common use of language would receive no manner of alteration or disturbance from the admission of our tenets.

52. In the ordinary affairs of life, any phrases may be retained, so long as they excite in us proper sentiments, or dispositions to act in such a manner as is necessary for our well-being, how false soever they may be, if taken in a strict and speculative sense. Nay this is unavoidable, since propriety being regulated by custom, language is suited to the received opinions, which are not always the truest. Hence it is impossible, even in the most rigid philosophic reasonings, so far to alter the bent and genius of the tongue we speak, as never to give a handle for cavillers to pretend difficulties and inconsistencies. But a fair and ingenuous reader will collect the sense from the scope and tenor and connexion of a discourse, making allowances for those inaccurate modes of speech which use has made inevitable.

53. As to the opinion that there are no corporeal causes, this has been heretofore maintained by some of the schoolmen, as it is of late by others among the modern philosophers, who though they allow matter to exist, yet will have God alone to be the immediate efficient cause of all things. These men saw that amongst all the objects of sense, there was none which had any power or activity included in it, and that by consequence this was likewise true of whatever bodies they supposed to exist without the mind, like unto the immediate objects of sense. But then, that they should suppose an innumerable multitude of created beings, which they acknowledge are not capable of producing any one effect in nature, and which therefore are made to no manner of purpose, since God might have done everything as well without them; this I say, though we should allow it possible, must yet be a very unaccountable and extravagant supposition.

Three Dialogues between Hylas and Philonous

The First Dialogue

1. *Philonous.* Good morrow, Hylas. I did not expect to find you abroad so early.

Hylas. It is indeed something unusual; but my thoughts were so taken up with a subject I was discoursing of last night that finding I could not sleep, I resolved to rise and take a turn in the garden.

2. *Phil.* It happened well, to let you see what innocent and agreeable pleasures you lose every morning. Can there be a pleasanter time of the day or a more delightful season of the year? That purple sky, these wild but sweet notes of birds, the fragrant bloom upon the trees and flowers, the gentle influence of the rising sun—these and a thousand nameless beauties of nature inspire the soul with secret transports; its faculties, too, being at this time fresh and lively, are fit for those meditations which the solitude of a garden and tranquility of the morning naturally dispose us to. But I am afraid I interrupt your thoughts, for you seemed very intent on something.

Hyl. It is true, I was, and shall be obliged to you if you will permit me to go on in the same vein; not that I would by any means deprive myself of your

Reprinted from *Reason and Responsibility,* 6th ed., ed. Joel Feinberg (Belmont, Calif.: Wadsworth, 1985), pp. 144–87.

company, for my thoughts always flow more easily in conversation with a friend than when I am alone; but my request is that you would suffer me to impart my reflections to you.

3. *Phil.* With all my heart, it is what I should have requested myself if you had not prevented me.

Hyl. I was considering the odd fate of those men who have in all ages, through an affectation of being distinguished from the vulgar, or some unaccountable turn of thought, pretended either to believe nothing at all or to believe the most extravagant things in the world. This, however, might be borne if their paradoxes and skepticism did not draw after them some consequences of general disadvantage to mankind. But the mischief lies here: that when men of less leisure see them who are supposed to have spent their whole time in the pursuits of knowledge professing an entire ignorance of all things or advancing such notions as are repugnant to plain and commonly received principles, they will be tempted to entertain suspicions concerning the most important truths, which they had hitherto held sacred and unquestionable.

4. *Phil.* I entirely agree with you as to the ill tendency of the affected doubts of some philosophers and fantastical conceits of others. I am even so far gone of late in this way of thinking that I have quitted several of the sublime notions I had got in their schools for vulgar opinions. And I give it you on my word, since this revolt from metaphysical notions to the plain dictates of nature and common sense, I find my understanding strangely enlightened, so that I can now easily comprehend a great many things which before were all mystery and riddle.

Hyl. I am glad to find there was nothing in the accounts I heard of you.

5. *Phil.* Pray, what were those?

Hyl. You were represented in last night's conversation as one who maintained the most extravagant opinion that ever entered into the mind of man, to wit, that there is no such thing as "material substance" in the world.

6. *Phil.* That there is no such thing as what philosophers call "material substance," I am seriously persuaded; but if I were made to see anything absurd or skeptical in this, I should then have the same reason to renounce this that I imagine I have now to reject the contrary opinion.

Hyl. What! Can anything be more fantastical, more repugnant to common sense or a more mani-

fest piece of skepticism than to believe there is no such thing as matter?

7. *Phil.* Softly, good Hylas. What if it should prove that you, who hold there is, are, by virtue of that opinion, a greater skeptic and maintain more paradoxes and repugnances to common sense than I who believe no such thing?

Hyl. You may as soon persuade me the part is greater than the whole, as that, in order to avoid absurdity and skepticism, I should ever be obliged to give up my opinion in this point.

8. *Phil.* Well then, are you content to admit that opinion for true which, upon examination, shall appear most agreeable to common sense and remote from skepticism?

Hyl. With all my heart. Since you are for raising disputes about the plainest things in nature, I am content for once to hear what you have to say.

9. *Phil.* Pray, Hylas, what do you mean by a "skeptic"?

Hyl. I mean what all men mean, one that doubts of everything.

10. *Phil.* He then who entertains no doubt concerning some particular point, with regard to that point cannot be thought a skeptic.

Hyl. I agree with you.

11. *Phil.* Whether does doubting consist in embracing the affirmative or negative side of a question?

Hyl. In neither; for whoever understands English cannot but know that *doubting* signifies a suspense between both.

12. *Phil.* He then that denies any point can no more be said to doubt of it than he who affirms it with the same degree of assurance.

Hyl. True.

13. *Phil.* And, consequently, for such his denial is no more to be esteemed a skeptic than the other.

Hyl. I acknowledge it.

14. *Phil.* How comes it to pass then, Hylas, that you pronounce me a skeptic because I deny what you affirm, to wit, the existence of matter? Since, for aught you can tell, I am as peremptory in my denial as you in your affirmation.

Hyl. Hold, Philonous, I have been a little out in my definition; but every false step a man makes in discourse is not to be insisted on. I said indeed that a "skeptic" was one who doubted of everything, but I should have added: or who denies the reality and truth of things.

15. *Phil.* What things? Do you mean the principles and theorems of sciences? But these you know are universal intellectual notions, and consequently independent of matter; the denial therefore of this does not imply the denying them.

Hyl. I grant it. But are there no other things? What think you of distrusting the senses, of denying the real existence of sensible things, or pretending to know nothing of them. Is not this sufficient to denominate a man a skeptic?

16. *Phil.* Shall we therefore examine which of us it is that denies the reality of sensible things or professes the greatest ignorance of them, since, if I take you rightly, he is to be esteemed the greatest skeptic?

Hyl. That is what I desire.

17. *Phil.* What mean you by "sensible things"?

Hyl. Those things which are perceived by the senses. Can you imagine that I mean anything else?

18. *Phil.* Pardon me, Hylas, if I am desirous clearly to apprehend your notions, since this may much shorten our inquiry. Suffer me then to ask you this further question. Are those things only perceived by the senses which are perceived immediately? Or may those things properly be said to be "sensible" which are perceived immediately, or not without the intervention of others?

Hyl. I do not sufficiently understand you.

19. *Phil.* In reading a book, what I immediately perceive are the letters, but mediately, or by means of these, are suggested to my mind the notions of God, virtue, truth, etc. Now, that the letters are truly sensible things, or perceived by sense, there is no doubt; but I would know whether you take the things suggested by them to be so too.

Hyl. No, certainly; it were absurd to think God or virtue sensible things, though they may be signified and suggested to the mind by sensible marks with which they have an arbitrary connection.

20. *Phil.* It seems, then, that by "sensible things" you mean those only which can be perceived immediately by sense.

Hyl. Right.

21. *Phil.* Does it not follow from this that, though I see one part of the sky red, and another blue, and that my reason does thence evidently conclude there must be some cause of that diversity of colors, yet that cause cannot be said to be a sensible thing or perceived by the sense of seeing?

Hyl. It does.

22. *Phil.* In like manner, though I hear variety of sounds, yet I cannot be said to hear the causes of those sounds.

Hyl. You cannot.

23. *Phil.* And when by my touch I perceive a thing to be hot and heavy, I cannot say, with any truth or propriety, that I feel the cause of its heat or weight.

Hyl. To prevent any more questions of this kind, I tell you once for all that by "sensible things" I mean those only which are perceived by sense, and that in truth the senses perceive nothing which they do not perceive immediately, for they make no inferences. The deducing therefore of causes or occasions from effects and appearances, which alone are perceived by sense, entirely relates to reason.

24. *Phil.* This point then is agreed between us— that *sensible things are those only which are immediately perceived by sense.* You will further inform me whether we immediately perceive by sight anything besides light and colors and figures; or by hearing, anything but sounds; by the palate, anything besides tastes; by the smell, besides odors; or by the touch, more than tangible qualities.

Hyl. We do not.

25. *Phil.* It seems, therefore, that if you take away all sensible qualities, there remains nothing sensible?

Hyl. I grant it.

26. *Phil.* Sensible things therefore are nothing else but so many sensible qualities or combinations of sensible qualities?

Hyl. Nothing else.

27. *Phil.* Heat is then a sensible thing?

Hyl. Certainly.

28. *Phil.* Does the reality of sensible things consist in being perceived, or is it something distinct from their being perceived, and that bears no relation to the mind?

Hyl. To *exist* is one thing, and to be *perceived* is another.

29. *Phil.* I speak with regard to sensible things only; and of these I ask, whether by their real existence you mean a subsistence exterior to the mind and distinct from their being perceived?

Hyl. I mean a real absolute being, distinct from and without any relation to their being perceived.

30. *Phil.* Heat therefore, if it be allowed a real being, must exist without the mind?

Hyl. It must.

31. *Phil.* Tell me, Hylas, is this real existence equally compatible to all degrees of heat, which we perceive, or is there any reason why we should attribute it to some and deny it to others? And if there be, pray, let me know that reason.

Hyl. Whatever degree of heat we perceive by sense, we may be sure the same exists in the object that occasions it.

32. *Phil.* What! the greatest as well as the least?

Hyl. I tell you, the reason is plainly the same in respect of both: they are both perceived by sense; nay, the greater degree of heat is more sensibly perceived; and consequently, if there is any difference, we are more certain of its real existence than we can be of the reality of a lesser degree.

33. *Phil.* But is not the most vehement and intense degree of heat a very great pain?

Hyl. No one can deny it.

34. *Phil.* And is any unperceiving thing capable of pain or pleasure?

Hyl. No, certainly.

35. *Phil.* Is your material substance a senseless being or a being endowed with sense and perception?

Hyl. It is senseless, without doubt.

36. *Phil.* It cannot, therefore, be the subject of pain?

Hyl. By no means.

37. *Phil.* Nor, consequently, of the greatest heat perceived by sense, since you acknowledge this to be no small pain?

Hyl. I grant it.

38. *Phil.* What shall we say then of your external object: is it a material substance, or no?

Hyl. It is a material substance with the sensible qualities inhering in it.

39. *Phil.* How then can a great heat exist in it, since you own it cannot in a material substance? I desire you would clear this point.

Hyl. Hold, Philonous, I fear I was out in yielding intense heat to be a pain. It should seem rather that pain is something distinct from heat, and the consequence or effect of it.

40. *Phil.* Upon putting your hand near the fire, do you perceive one simple uniform sensation or two distinct sensations?

Hyl. But one simple sensation.

41. *Phil.* Is not the heat immediately perceived?
Hyl. It is.

42. *Phil.* And the pain?
Hyl. True.

43. *Phil.* Seeing therefore they are both immediately perceived at the same time, and the fire affects you only with one simple or uncompounded idea, it follows that this same simple idea is both the intense heat immediately perceived and the pain; and, consequently, that the intense heat immediately perceived is nothing distinct from a particular sort of pain.

Hyl. It seems so.

44. *Phil.* Again, try in your thoughts, Hylas, if you can conceive a vehement sensation to be without pain or pleasure.

Hyl. I cannot.

45. *Phil.* Or can you frame to yourself an idea of sensible pain or pleasure, in general, abstracted from every particular idea of heat, cold, tastes, smells, etc.?

Hyl. I do not find that I can.

46. *Phil.* Does it not therefore follow that sensible pain is nothing distinct from those sensations or ideas—in an intense degree?

Hyl. It is undeniable; and, to speak the truth, I begin to suspect a very great heat cannot exist but in a mind perceiving it.

47. *Phil.* What! are you then in that *skeptical* state of suspense, between affirming and denying?

Hyl. I think I may be positive in the point. A very violent and painful heat cannot exist without the mind.

48. *Phil.* It has not therefore, according to you, any real being?

Hyl. I own it.

49. *Phil.* Is it therefore certain that there is no body in nature really hot?

Hyl. I have not denied there is any real heat in bodies. I only say there is no such thing as an intense real heat.

50. *Phil.* But did you not say before that all degrees of heat were equally real, or, if there was any difference, that the greater were more undoubtedly real than the lesser?

Hyl. True; but it was because I did not then consider the ground there is for distinguishing between them, which I now plainly see. And it is this: because intense heat is nothing else but a particular kind of painful sensation, and pain cannot exist but in a perceiving being, it follows that no intense heat can really exist in an unperceiving corporeal substance. But this is no reason why we should deny heat in an inferior degree to exist in such a substance.

51. *Phil.* But how shall we be able to discern those degrees of heat which exist only in the mind from those which exist without it?

Hyl. That is no difficult matter. You know the least pain cannot exist unperceived; whatever, therefore, degree of heat is a pain exists only in the mind. But as for all other degrees of heat nothing obliges us to think the same of them.

52. *Phil.* I think you granted before that no unperceiving being was capable of pleasure any more than of pain.

Hyl. I did.

53. *Phil.* And is not warmth, or a more gentle degree of heat than what causes uneasiness, a pleasure?

Hyl. What then?

54. *Phil.* Consequently, it cannot exist without the mind in an unperceiving substance, or body.

Hyl. So it seems.

55. *Phil.* Since, therefore, as well those degrees of heat that are not painful, as those that are, can exist only in a thinking substance, may we not conclude that external bodies are absolutely incapable of any degree of heat whatsoever?

Hyl. On second thoughts, I do not think it is so evident that warmth is a pleasure as that a great degree of heat is pain.

56. *Phil.* I do not pretend that warmth is as great a pleasure as heat is a pain. But if you grant it to be even a small pleasure, it serves to make good my conclusion.

Hyl. I could rather call it an "indolence." It seems to be nothing more than a privation of both pain and pleasure. And that such a quality or state as this may agree to an unthinking substance, I hope you will not deny.

57. *Phil.* If you are resolved to maintain that warmth, or a gentle degree of heat, is no pleasure, I know not how to convince you otherwise than by appealing to your own sense. But what think you of cold?

Hyl. The same that I do of heat. An intense degree of cold is a pain; for to feel a very great cold is to perceive a great uneasiness; it cannot therefore exist without the mind; but a lesser degree of cold may, as well as a lesser degree of heat.

58. *Phil.* Those bodies, therefore, upon whose application to our own we perceive a moderate degree of heat must be concluded to have a moderate degree of heat or warmth in them; and those upon whose application we feel a like degree of cold must be thought to have cold in them.

Hyl. They must.

59. *Phil.* Can any doctrine be true that necessarily leads a man into an absurdity?

Hyl. Without doubt it cannot.

60. *Phil.* Is it not an absurdity to think that the same thing should be at the same time both cold and warm?

Hyl. It is.

61. *Phil.* Suppose now one of your hands is hot, and the other cold, and that they are both at once put into the same vessel of water, in an intermediate state, will not the water seem cold to one hand, and warm to the other?

Hyl. It will.

62. *Phil.* Ought we not therefore, by your principles, to conclude it is really both cold and warm at the same time, that is, according to your own concession, to believe an absurdity?

Hyl. I confess it seems so.

63. *Phil.* Consequently, the principles themselves are false, since you have granted that no true principle leads to an absurdity.

Hyl. But, after all, can anything be more absurd than to say, *there is no heat in the fire?*

64. *Phil.* To make the point still clearer: tell me whether, in two cases exactly alike, we ought not to make the same judgment?

Hyl. We ought.

65. *Phil.* When a pin pricks your finger, does it not rend and divide the fibers of your flesh?

Hyl. It does.

66. *Phil.* And when a coal burns your finger, does it any more?

Hyl. It does not.

67. *Phil.* Since, therefore, you neither judge the sensation itself occasioned by the pin, nor anything like it to be in the pin, you should not, conformably to what you have now granted, judge the sensation occasioned by the fire, or anything like it, to be in the fire.

Hyl. Well, since it must be so, I am content to yield this point and acknowledge that heat and cold are only sensations existing in our minds. But there still remain qualities enough to secure the reality of external things.

68. *Phil.* But what will you say, Hylas, if it shall appear that the case is the same with regard to all other sensible qualities, and that they can no more be supposed to exist without the mind than heat and cold?

Hyl. Then, indeed, you will have done something to the purpose; but that is what I despair of seeing proved.

69. *Phil.* Let us examine them in order. What think you of tastes—do they exist without the mind, or no?

Hyl. Can any man in his senses doubt whether sugar is sweet or wormwood bitter?

70. *Phil.* Inform me, Hylas. Is a sweet taste a particular kind of pleasure or pleasant sensation, or is it not?

Hyl. It is.

71. *Phil.* And is not bitterness some kind of uneasiness or pain?

Hyl. I grant it.

72. *Phil.* If therefore, sugar and wormwood are unthinking corporeal substances existing without the mind, how can sweetness and bitterness, that is, pleasure and pain, agree to them?

Hyl. Hold, Philonous. I now see what it was [that] deluded me all this time. You asked whether heat and cold, sweetness and bitterness, were not particular sorts of pleasure and pain; to which I answered simply that they were. Whereas I should have thus distinguished: those qualities as perceived by us are pleasures or pains, but not as existing in the external objects. We must not therefore conclude absolutely that there is no heat in the fire or sweetness in the sugar, but only that heat or sweetness, as perceived by us, are not in the fire or sugar. What say you to this?

73. *Phil.* I say it is nothing to the purpose. Our discourse proceeded altogether concerning sensible things, which you defined to be "the things we immediately perceive by our senses." Whatever other qualities, therefore, you speak of, as distinct from these, I know nothing of them, neither do they at all belong to the point in dispute. You may, indeed, pretend to have discovered certain qualities which you do not perceive and assert those insensible qualities exist in fire and sugar. But what use can be made of this to your present purpose, I am at a loss

to conceive. Tell me then once more, do you acknowledge that heat and cold, sweetness and bitterness (meaning those qualities which are perceived by the senses), do not exist without the mind?

Hyl. I see it is to no purpose to hold out, so I give up the cause as to those mentioned qualities, though I profess it sounds oddly to say that sugar is not sweet.

74. *Phil.* But, for your further satisfaction, take this along with you: that which at other times seems sweet shall, to a distempered palate, appear bitter, and nothing can be plainer than that divers persons perceive different tastes in the same food, since that which one man delights in, another abhors. And how could this be if the taste was something really inherent in the food?

Hyl. I acknowledge I know not how.

75. *Phil.* In the next place, odors are to be considered. And with regard to these I would fain know whether what has been said of tastes does not exactly agree to them? Are they not so many pleasing or displeasing sensations?

Hyl. They are.

76. *Phil.* Can you then conceive it possible that they should exist in an unperceiving thing?

Hyl. I cannot.

77. *Phil.* Or can you imagine that filth and ordure affect those brute animals that feed on them out of choice with the same smells which we perceive in them?

Hyl. By no means.

78. *Phil.* May we not therefore conclude of smells, as of the other forementioned qualities, that they cannot exist in any but a perceiving substance or mind?

Hyl. I think so.

79. *Phil.* Then as to sounds, what must we think of them, are they accidents really inherent in external bodies or not?

Hyl. That they inhere not in the sonorous bodies is plain from hence; because a bell struck in the exhausted receiver of an air-pump sends forth no sound. The air, therefore, must be thought the subject of sound.

80. *Phil.* What reason is there for that, Hylas?

Hyl. Because, when any motion is raised in the air, we perceive a sound greater or less, in proportion to the air's motion; but without some motion in the air we never hear any sound at all.

81. *Phil.* And granting that we never hear a sound but when some motion is produced in the air, yet I do not see how you can infer from thence that the sound itself is in the air.

Hyl. It is this very motion in the external air that produces in the mind the sensation of sound. For, striking on the drum of the ear, it causes a vibration which by the auditory nerves being communicated to the brain, the soul is thereupon affected with the sensation called "sound."

82. *Phil.* What! is sound then a sensation?

Hyl. I tell you, as perceived by us it is a particular sensation in the mind.

83. *Phil.* And can any sensation exist without the mind?

Hyl. No, certainly.

84. *Phil.* How then can sound, being a sensation, exist in the air if by the "air" you mean a senseless substance existing without the mind?

Hyl. You must distinguish, Philonous, between sound as it is perceived by us, and as it is in itself; or (which is the same thing) between the sound we immediately perceive and that which exists without us. The former, indeed, is a particular kind of sensation, but the latter is merely a vibrative or undulatory motion in the air.

85. *Phil.* I thought I had already obviated that distinction by the answer I gave when you were applying it in a like case before. But, to say no more of that, are you sure then that sound is really nothing but motion?

Hyl. I am.

86. *Phil.* Whatever, therefore, agrees to real sound may with truth be attributed to motion?

Hyl. It may.

87. *Phil.* It is then good sense to speak of "motion" as of a thing that is *loud, sweet, acute,* or *grave.*

Hyl. I see you are resolved not to understand me. Is it not evident those accidents or modes belong only to sensible sound, or sound in the common acceptation of the word, but not to sound in the real and philosophic sense, which, as I just now told you, is nothing but a certain motion of the air?

88. *Phil.* It seems then there are two sorts of sound—the one vulgar, or that which is heard, the other philosophical and real?

Hyl. Even so.

89. *Phil.* And the latter consists in motion?

Hyl. I told you so before.

90. *Phil.* Tell me, Hylas, to which of the senses, think you, the idea of motion belongs? To the hearing?

Hyl. No, certainly; but to the sight and touch.

91. *Phil.* It should follow then that, according to you, real sounds may possibly be *seen* or *felt,* but never *heard.*

Hyl. Look you, Philonous, you may, if you please, make a jest of my opinion, but that will not alter the truth of things. I own, indeed, the inferences you draw me into sound something oddly, but common language, you know, is framed by, and for the use of, the vulgar. We must not therefore wonder if expressions adapted to exact philosophic notions seem uncouth and out of the way.

92. *Phil.* Is it come to that? I assure you I imagine myself to have gained no small point since you make so light of departing from common phrases and opinions, it being a main part of our inquiry to examine whose notions are widest of the common road and most repugnant to the general sense of the world. But can you think it no more than a philosophical paradox to say that "real sounds are never heard," and that the idea of them is obtained by some other sense? And is there nothing in this contrary to nature and the truth of things?

Hyl. To deal ingenuously, I do not like it. And, after the concessions already made, I had as well grant that sounds, too, have no real being without the mind.

93. *Phil.* And I hope you will make no difficulty to acknowledge the same of colors.

Hyl. Pardon me; the case of colors is very different. Can anything be plainer than that we see them on the objects?

94. *Phil.* The objects you speak of are, I suppose, corporeal substances existing without the mind?

Hyl. They are.

95. *Phil.* And have true and real colors inhering in them?

Hyl. Each visible object has that color which we see in it.

96. *Phil.* How! is there anything visible but what we perceive by sight?

Hyl. There is not.

97. *Phil.* And do we perceive anything by sense which we do not perceive immediately?

Hyl. How often must I be obliged to repeat the same thing? I tell you, we do not.

98. *Phil.* Have patience, good Hylas, and tell me once more whether there is anything immediately perceived by the senses except sensible qualities. I know you asserted there was not; but I would now be informed whether you still persist in the same opinion.

Hyl. I do.

99. *Phil.* Pray, is your corporeal substance either a sensible quality or made up of sensible qualities?

Hyl. What a question that is! Who ever thought it was?

100. *Phil.* My reason for asking was, because in saying "each visible object has that color which we see in it," you make visible objects to be corporeal substances, which implies either that corporeal substances are sensible qualities or else that there is something besides sensible qualities perceived by sight; but as this point was formerly agreed between us, and is still maintained by you, it is a clear consequence that your corporeal substance is nothing distinct from sensible qualities.

Hyl. You may draw as many absurd consequences as you please and endeavor to perplex the plainest things, but you shall never persuade me out of my senses. I clearly understand my own meaning.

101. *Phil.* I wish you would make me understand it, too. But, since you are unwilling to have your notion of corporeal substance examined, I shall urge that point no further. Only be pleased to let me know whether the same colors which we see exist in external bodies or some other.

Hyl. The very same.

102. *Phil.* What! are then the beautiful red and purple we see on yonder clouds really in them? Or do you imagine they have in themselves any other form than that of a dark mist of vapor?

Hyl. I must own, Philonous, those colors are not really in the clouds as they seem to be at this distance. They are only apparent colors.

103. *Phil.* "Apparent" call you them? How shall we distinguish these apparent colors from real?

Hyl. Very easily. Those are to be thought apparent which, appearing only at a distance, vanish upon a nearer approach.

104. *Phil.* And those, I suppose, are to be thought real which are discovered by the most near and exact survey.

Hyl. Right.

105. *Phil.* Is the nearest and exactest survey made by the help of a microscope or by the naked eye?

Hyl. By a microscope, doubtless.

106. *Phil.* But a microscope often discovers colors in an object different from those perceived by the unassisted sight. And, in case we had microscopes magnifying to any assigned degree, it is certain that no object whatsoever, viewed through them, would appear in the same color which it exhibits to the naked eye.

Hyl. And what will you conclude from all this? You cannot argue that there are really and naturally no colors on objects because by artificial managements they may be altered or made to vanish.

107. *Phil.* I think it may evidently be concluded from your own concessions that all the colors we see with our naked eyes are only apparent as those on the clouds, since they vanish upon a more close and accurate inspection which is afforded us by a microscope. Then, as to what you say by way of prevention: I ask you whether the real and natural state of an object is better discovered by a very sharp and piercing sight or by one which is less sharp?

Hyl. By the former without doubt.

108. *Phil.* Is it not plain from dioptrics that microscopes make the sight more penetrating and represent objects as they would appear to the eye in case it were naturally endowed with a most exquisite sharpness?

Hyl. It is.

109. *Phil.* Consequently, the microscopical representation is to be thought that which best sets forth the real nature of the thing, or what it is in itself. The colors, therefore, by it perceived are more genuine and real than those perceived otherwise.

Hyl. I confess there is something in what you say.

110. *Phil.* Besides, it is not only possible but manifest that there actually are animals whose eyes are by nature framed to perceive those things which by reason of their minuteness escape our sight. What think you of those inconceivably small animals perceived by glasses? Must we suppose they are all stark blind? Or, in case they see, can it be imagined their sight has not the same use in preserving their bodies from injuries which appears in that of all other animals? And if it has, is it not evident they must see particles less than their own

bodies, which will present them with a far different view in each object from that which strikes our senses? Even our own eyes do not always represent objects to us after the same manner. In the jaundice everyone knows that all things seem yellow. Is it not therefore highly probable those animals in whose eyes we discern a very different texture from that of ours, and whose bodies abound with different humors, do not see the same colors in every object that we do? From all which should it not seem to follow that all colors are equally apparent, and that none of those which we perceive are really inherent in any outward object?

Hyl. It should.

111. *Phil.* The point will be past all doubt if you consider that, in case colors were real properties or affections inherent in external bodies, they could admit of no alteration without some change wrought in the very bodies themselves; but is it not evident from what has been said that, upon the use of microscopes, upon a change happening in the humors of the eye, or a variation of distance, without any manner of real alteration in the thing itself, the colors of any object are either changed or totally disappear? Nay, all other circumstances remaining the same, change but the situation of some objects and they shall present different colors to the eye. The same thing happens upon viewing an object in various degrees of light. And what is more known than that the same bodies appear differently colored by candlelight from what they do in the open day? Add to these the experiment of a prism which, separating the heterogeneous rays of light alters the color of any object and will cause the whitest to appear of a deep blue or red to the naked eye. And now tell me whether you are still of opinion that every body has its true real color inhering in it; and if you think it has, I would fain know further from you what certain distance and position of the object, what peculiar texture and formation of the eye, what degree or kind of light is necessary for ascertaining that true color and distinguishing it from apparent ones.

Hyl. I own myself entirely satisfied that they are all equally apparent and that there is no such thing as color really inhering in external bodies, but that it is altogether in the light. And what confirms me in this opinion is that in proportion to the light colors are still more or less vivid; and if there be no light, then are there no colors perceived. Besides, allowing there are colors on external objects, yet, how is it possible for us to perceive them? For no external body affects the mind unless it acts first on our organs of sense. But the only action of bodies is motion, and motion cannot be communicated otherwise than by impulse. A distant object, therefore, cannot act on the eye, nor consequently make itself or its properties perceivable to the soul. Whence it plainly follows that it is immediately some contiguous substance which, operating on the eye, occasions a perception of colors; and such is light.

112. *Phil.* How! is light then a substance?

Hyl. I tell you, Philonous, external light is nothing but a thin fluid substance whose minute particles, being agitated with a brisk motion and in various manners reflected from the different surfaces of outward objects to the eyes, communicate different motions to the optic nerves; which, being propagated to the brain, cause therein various impressions, and these are attended with the sensations of red, blue, yellow, etc.

113. *Phil.* It seems, then, the light does no more than shake the optic nerves.

Hyl. Nothing else.

114. *Phil.* And, consequent to each particular motion of the nerves, the mind is affected with a sensation which is some particular color.

Hyl. Right.

115. *Phil.* And these sensations have no existence without the mind.

Hyl. They have not.

116. *Phil.* How then do you affirm that colors are in the light, since by "light" you understand a corporeal substance external to the mind?

Hyl. Light and colors, as immediately perceived by us, I grant cannot exist without the mind. But in themselves they are only the motions and configurations of certain insensible particles of matter.

117. *Phil.* Colors, then, in the vulgar sense, or taken for the immediate objects of sight, cannot agree to any but a perceiving substance.

Hyl. That is what I say.

118. *Phil.* Well then, since you give up the point as to those sensible qualities which are alone thought colors by all mankind besides, you may hold what you please with regard to those invisible ones of the philosophers. It is not my business to dispute them; only I would advise you to bethink

yourself whether, considering the inquiry we are upon, it be prudent for you to affirm—*the red and blue which we see are not real colors, but certain unknown motions and figures which no man ever did or can see are truly so.* Are not these shocking notions, and are not they subject to as many ridiculous inferences as those you were obliged to renounce before in the case of sounds?

Hyl. I frankly own, Philonous, that it is in vain to stand out any longer. Colors, sounds, tastes, in a word, all those termed "secondary qualities," have certainly no existence without the mind. But by this acknowledgment I must not be supposed to derogate anything from the reality of matter or external objects; seeing it is no more than several philosophers maintain, who nevertheless are the farthest imaginable from denying matter. For the clearer understanding of this you must know sensible qualities are by philosophers divided into "primary" and "secondary." The former are extension, figure, solidity, gravity, motion, and rest. And these they hold exist really in bodies. The latter are those above enumerated, or, briefly, all sensible qualities besides the primary, which they assert are only so many sensations or ideas existing nowhere but in the mind. But all this, I doubt not, you are already apprised of. For my part I have been a long time sensible there was such an opinion current among philosophers, but was never thoroughly convinced of its truth till now.

119. *Phil.* You are still then of opinion that *extension* and *figures* are inherent in external unthinking substances?

Hyl. I am.

120. *Phil.* But what if the same arguments which are brought against secondary qualities will hold good against these also?

Hyl. Why then I shall be obliged to think they too exist only in the mind.

121. *Phil.* Is it your opinion the very figure and extension which you perceive by sense exist in the outward object or material substance?

Hyl. It is.

122. *Phil.* Have all other animals as good grounds to think the same of the figure and extension which they see and feel?

Hyl. Without doubt, if they have any thought at all.

123. *Phil.* Answer me, Hylas. Think you the senses were bestowed upon all animals for their preservation and well-being in life? Or were they given to men alone for this end?

Hyl. I make no question but they have the same use in all other animals.

124. *Phil.* If so, is it not necessary they should be enabled by them to perceive their own limbs and those bodies which are capable of harming them?

Hyl. Certainly.

125. *Phil.* A mite therefore must be supposed to see his own foot, and things equal or even less than it, as bodies of some considerable dimension, though at the same time they appear to you scarce discernible or at best at so many visible points?

Hyl. I cannot deny it.

126. *Phil.* And to creatures less than the mite they will seem yet larger?

Hyl. They will.

127. *Phil.* Insomuch that what you can hardly discern will to another extremely minute animal appear as some huge mountain?

Hyl. All this I grant.

128. *Phil.* Can one and the same thing be at the same time in itself of different dimensions?

Hyl. That were absurd to imagine.

129. *Phil.* But from what you have laid down it follows that both the extension by you perceived and that perceived by the mite itself, as likewise all those perceived by lesser animals, are each of them the true extension of the mite's foot; that is to say, by your own principles you are led into an absurdity.

Hyl. There seems to be some difficulty in the point.

130. *Phil.* Again, have you not acknowledged that no real inherent property of any object can be changed without some change in the thing itself?

Hyl. I have.

131. *Phil.* But, as we approach to or recede from an object, the visible extension varies, being at one distance ten or a hundred times greater than at another. Does it not therefore follow from hence likewise that it is not really inherent in the object?

Hyl. I own I am at a loss what to think.

132. *Phil.* Your judgment will soon be determined if you will venture to think as freely concerning this quality as you have done concerning the rest. Was it not admitted as a good argument that neither heat nor cold was in the water because it seemed warm to one hand and cold to the other?

Hyl. It was.

133. *Phil.* Is it not the very same reasoning to conclude there is no extension or figure in an object because to one eye it shall seem little, smooth, and round, when at the same time it appears to the other great, uneven, and angular?

Hyl. The very same. But does this latter fact ever happen?

134. *Phil.* You may at any time make the experiment by looking with one eye bare and with the other through a microscope.

Hyl. I know not how to maintain it, and yet I am loath to give up *extension;* I see so many odd consequences following upon such a concession.

135. *Phil.* Odd, say you? After the concessions already made, I hope you will stick at nothing for its oddness. But, on the other hand, should it not seem very odd if the general reasoning which includes all other sensible qualities did not also include extension? If it be allowed that no idea nor anything like an idea can exist in an unperceiving substance, then surely it follows that no figure or mode of extension, which we can either perceive or imagine, or have any idea of, can be really inherent in matter, not to mention the peculiar difficulty there must be in conceiving a material substance, prior to and distinct from extension, to be the substratum of extension. Be the sensible quality what it will—figure or sound or color—it seems alike impossible it should subsist in that which does not perceive it.

Hyl. I give up the point for the present, reserving still a right to retract my opinion in case I shall hereafter discover any false step in my progress to it.

136. *Phil.* That is a right you cannot be denied. Figures and extension being dispatched, we proceed next to *motion.* Can a real motion in any external body be at the same time both very swift and very slow?

Hyl. It cannot.

137. *Phil.* Is not the motion of a body swift in a reciprocal proportion to the time it takes up in describing any given space? Thus a body that describes a mile in an hour moves three times faster than it would in case it described only a mile in three hours.

Hyl. I agree with you.

138. *Phil.* And is not time measured by the succession of ideas in our minds?

Hyl. It is.

139. *Phil.* And is it not possible ideas should succeed one another twice as fast in your mind as they do in mine, or in that of some spirit of another kind?

Hyl. I own it.

140. *Phil.* Consequently, the same body may to another seem to perform its motion over any space in half the time that it does to you. And the same reasoning will hold as to any other proportion; that is to say, according to your principles (since the motions perceived are both really in the object) it is possible one and the same body shall be really moved the same way at once, both very swift and very slow. How is this consistent with common sense or with what you just now granted?

Hyl. I have nothing to say to it.

141. *Phil.* Then as for *solidity;* either you do not mean any sensible quality by that word, and so it is beside our inquiry; or if you do, it must be either hardness or resistance. But both the one and the other are plainly relative to our senses: it being evident that what seems hard to one animal may appear soft to another who has greater force and firmness of limbs. Nor is it less plain that the resistance I feel is not in the body.

Hyl. I own the very sensation of resistance, which is all you immediately perceive, is not in the *body,* but the cause of that sensation is.

142. *Phil.* But the causes of our sensations are not things immediately perceived, and therefore not sensible. This point I thought had been already determined.

Hyl. I own it was; but you will pardon me if I seem a little embarrassed; I know not how to quit my old notions.

143. *Phil.* To help you out, do but consider that if *extension* be once acknowledged to have no existence without the mind, the same must necessarily be granted of motion, solidity, and gravity, since they all evidently suppose extension. It is therefore superfluous to inquire particularly concerning each of them. In denying extension, you have denied them all to have any real existence.

Hyl. I wonder, Philonous, if what you say be true, why those philosophers who deny the secondary qualities any real existence should yet attribute it to the primary. If there is no difference between them, how can this be accounted for?

144. *Phil.* It is not my business to account for every opinion of the philosophers. But, among other reasons which may be assigned for this, it seems probable that pleasure and pain being rather annexed to the former than the latter may be one. Heat and cold, tastes and smells have something more vividly pleasing or disagreeable than the ideas of extension, figure, and motion affect us with. And, it being too visibly absurd to hold that pain or pleasure can be in an unperceiving substance, men are more easily weaned from believing the external existence of the secondary than the primary qualities. You will be satisfied there is something in this if you recollect the difference you made between an intense and more moderate degree of heat, allowing the one a real existence while you denied it to the other. But, after all, there is no rational ground for that distinction, for surely an indifferent sensation is as truly a *sensation* as one more pleasing or painful, and consequently should not any more than they be supposed to exist in an unthinking subject.

Hyl. It is just come into my head, Philonous, that I have somewhere heard of a distinction between *absolute* and *sensible* extension. Now though it be acknowledged that *great* and *small*, consisting merely in the relation which other extended beings have to the parts of our own bodies, do not really inhere in the substances themselves, yet nothing obliges us to hold the same with regard to *absolute* extension, which is something abstracted from *great* and *small*, from this or that particular magnitude or figure. So likewise as to motion: *swift* and *slow* are altogether relative to the succession of ideas in our own minds. But it does not follow, because those modifications of motion exist not without the mind, that therefore absolute motion abstracted from them does not.

145. *Phil.* Pray what is it that distinguishes one motion, or one part of extension, from another? Is it not something sensible, as some degree of swiftness or slowness, some certain magnitude or figure peculiar to each?

Hyl. I think so.

146. *Phil.* These qualities, therefore, stripped of all sensible properties, are without all specific and numerical differences, as the schools call them.

Hyl. They are.

147. *Phil.* That is to say, they are extension in general, and motion in general.

Hyl. Let it be so.

148. *Phil.* But it is a universally received maxim that *everything which exists is particular*. How then can motion in general, or extension in general, exist in any corporeal substance?

Hyl. I will take time to solve your difficulty.

149. *Phil.* But I think the point may be speedily decided. Without doubt you can tell whether you are able to frame this or that idea. Now I am content to put our dispute on this issue. If you can frame in your thoughts a distinct abstract idea of motion or extension divested of all those sensible modes as swift and slow, great and small, round and square, and the like, which are acknowledged to exist only in the mind, I will then yield the point you contend for. But if you cannot, it will be unreasonable on your side to insist any longer upon what you have no notion of.

Hyl. To confess ingenuously, I cannot.

150. *Phil.* Can you even separate the ideas of extension and motion from the ideas of all those qualities which they who make the distinction term "secondary"?

Hyl. What! is it not an easy matter to consider extension and motion by themselves, abstracted from all other sensible qualities? Pray how do the mathematicians treat of them?

151. *Phil.* I acknowledge, Hylas, it is not difficult to form general propositions and reasonings about those qualities without mentioning any other, and, in this sense, to consider or treat of them abstractedly. But how does it follow that, because I can pronounce the word "motion" by itself, I can form the idea of it in my mind exclusive of body? Or because theorems may be made of extension and figures, without any mention of *great* or *small*, or any other sensible mode or quality, that therefore it is possible such an abstract idea of extension, without any particular size or figure or sensible quality, should be distinctly formed and apprehended by the mind? Mathematicians treat of quantity without regarding what other sensible qualities it is attended with, as being altogether indifferent to their demonstrations. But when, laying aside the words, they contemplate the bare ideas, I believe you will find they are not the pure abstracted ideas of extension.

Hyl. But what say you to *pure intellect?* May not abstracted ideas be framed by that faculty?

152. *Phil.* Since I cannot frame abstract ideas at all, it is plain I cannot frame them by the help of

pure intellect, whatsoever faculty you understand by those words. Besides, not to inquire into the nature of pure intellect and its spiritual objects, as *virtue, reason, God,* or the like, thus much seems manifest that sensible things are only to be perceived by sense or represented by the imagination. Figures, therefore, and extension, being originally perceived by sense, do not belong to pure intellect; but, for your further satisfaction, try if you can frame the idea of any figure abstracted from all particularities of size or even from other sensible qualities.

Hyl. Let me think a little—I do not find that I can.

153. *Phil.* And can you think it possible that [an idea] should really exist in nature which implies a repugnancy in its conception?

Hyl. By no means.

154. *Phil.* Since therefore it is impossible even for the mind to disunite the ideas of extension and motion from all other sensible qualities, does it not follow that where the one exist there necessarily the other exist likewise?

Hyl. It should seem so.

155. *Phil.* Consequently the very same arguments which you admitted as conclusive against the secondary qualities are, without any further application of force, against the primary, too. Besides, if you will trust your senses, is it not plain all sensible qualities coexist, or to them appear as being in the same place? Do they ever represent a motion or figure as being divested of all other visible and tangible qualities?

Hyl. You need say no more on this head. I am free to own, if there be no secret error or oversight in our proceedings hitherto, that all sensible qualities are alike to be denied existence without the mind. But my fear is that I have been too liberal in my former concessions, or overlooked some fallacy or other. In short, I did not take time to think.

156. *Phil.* For that matter, Hylas, you may take what time you please in reviewing the progress of our inquiry. You are at liberty to recover any slips you might have made, or offer whatever you have omitted which makes for your first opinion.

Hyl. One great oversight I take to be this—that I did not sufficiently distinguish the *object* from the *sensation.* Now, though this latter may not exist without the mind, yet it will not thence follow that the former cannot.

157. *Phil.* What object do you mean? The object of the senses?

Hyl. The same.

158. *Phil.* It is then immediately perceived?

Hyl. Right.

159. *Phil.* Make me to understand the difference between what is immediately perceived and a sensation.

Hyl. The sensation I take to be an act of the mind perceiving; besides which there is something perceived, and this I call the "object." For example, there is red and yellow on that tulip. But then the act of perceiving those colors is in me only, and not in the tulip.

160. *Phil.* What tulip do you speak of? Is it that which you see?

Hyl. The same.

161. *Phil.* And what do you see besides color, figure, and extension?

Hyl. Nothing.

162. *Phil.* What you would say then is that the red and yellow are coexistent with the extension: is it not?

Hyl. That is not all; I would say they have a real existence without the mind, in some unthinking substance.

163. *Phil.* That the colors are really in the tulip which I see is manifest. Neither can it be denied that this tulip may exist independent of your mind or mine; but that any immediate object of the senses—that is, any idea, or combination of ideas—should exist in an unthinking substance, or exterior to all minds, is in itself an evident contradiction. Nor can I imagine how this follows from what you said just now, to wit, that the red and yellow were on the tulip *you saw,* since you do not pretend to *see* that unthinking substance.

Hyl. You have an artful way, Philonous, of diverting our inquiry from the subject.

164. *Phil.* I see you have no mind to be pressed that way. To return then to your distinction between *sensation* and *object*; if I take you right, you distinguish in every perception two things, the one an action of the mind, the other not.

Hyl. True.

165. *Phil.* And this action cannot exist in, or belong to, any unthinking thing, but whatever besides is implied in a perception may?

Hyl. That is my meaning.

166. *Phil.* So that if there was a perception without any act of the mind, it were possible such a perception should exist in an unthinking substance?

Hyl. I grant it. But it is impossible there should be such a perception.

167. *Phil.* When is the mind said to be active?

Hyl. When it produces, puts an end to, or changes anything.

168. *Phil.* Can the mind produce, discontinue, or change anything but by an act of the will?

Hyl. It cannot.

169. *Phil.* The mind therefore is to be accounted *active* in its perceptions so far forth as *volition* is included in them?

Hyl. It is.

170. *Phil.* In plucking this flower I am active, because I do it by the motion of my hand, which was consequent upon my volition; so likewise in applying it to my nose. But is either of these smelling?

Hyl. No.

171. *Phil.* I act, too, in drawing the air through my nose, because my breathing so rather than otherwise is the effect of my volition. But neither can this be called "smelling," for if it were I should smell every time I breathed in that manner?

Hyl. True.

172. *Phil.* Smelling then is somewhat consequent to all this?

Hyl. It is.

173. *Phil.* But I do not find my will concerned any further. Whatever more there is—as that I perceive such a particular smell, or any smell at all—this is independent of my will, and therein I am altogether passive. Do you find it otherwise with you, Hylas?

Hyl. No, the very same.

174. *Phil.* Then, as to seeing, is it not in your power to open your eyes or keep them shut, to turn them this or that way?

Hyl. Without doubt.

175. *Phil.* But does it in like manner depend on your will that in looking on this flower you perceive *white* rather than any other color? Or, directing your open eyes toward yonder part of the heaven, can you avoid seeing the sun? Or is light or darkness the effect of your volition?

Hyl. No, certainly.

176. *Phil.* You are then in these respects altogether passive?

Hyl. I am.

177. *Phil.* Tell me now whether *seeing* consists in perceiving light and colors or in opening and turning the eyes?

Hyl. Without doubt, in the former.

178. *Phil.* Since, therefore, you are in the very perception of light and colors altogether passive, what is become of that action you were speaking of as an ingredient in every sensation? And does it not follow from your own concessions that the perception of light and colors, including no action in it, may exist in an unperceiving substance? And is not this a plain contradiction?

Hyl. I know not what to think of it.

179. *Phil.* Besides, since you distinguish the *active* and *passive* in every perception, you must do it in that of pain. But how is it possible that pain, be it as little active as you please, should exist in an unperceiving substance? In short, do but consider the point and then confess ingenuously whether light and colors, tastes, sounds, etc., are not all equally passions or sensations in the soul. You may indeed call them "external objects" and give them in words what subsistence you please. But examine your own thoughts and then tell me whether it be not as I say?

Hyl. I acknowledge, Philonous, that, upon a fair observation of what passes in my mind, I can discover nothing else but that I am a thinking being affected with variety of sensations; neither is it possible to conceive how a sensation should exist in an unperceiving substance. But then, on the other hand, when I look on sensible things in a different view, considering them as so many modes and qualities, I find it necessary to suppose a material substratum, without which they cannot be conceived to exist.

180. *Phil.* "Material substratum" call you it? Pray, by which of your senses came you acquainted with that being?

Hyl. It is not itself sensible; its modes and qualities only being perceived by the senses.

181. *Phil.* I presume then it was by reflection and reason you obtained the idea of it?

Hyl. I do not pretend to any proper positive idea of it. However, I conclude it exists because qualities cannot be conceived to exist without a support.

182. *Phil.* It seems then you have only a relative notion of it, or that you conceive it not otherwise than by conceiving the relation it bears to sensible qualities?

Hyl. Right.

183. *Phil.* Be pleased, therefore, to let me know wherein that relation consists.

Hyl. Is it not sufficiently expressed in the term "substratum" or "substance"?

184. *Phil.* If so, the word "substratum" should import that it is spread under the sensible qualities or accidents?

Hyl. True.

185. *Phil.* And consequently under extension?

Hyl. I own it.

186. *Phil.* It is therefore somewhat in its own nature distinct from extension?

Hyl. I tell you extension is only a mode, and matter is something that supports modes. And is it not evident the thing supported is different from the thing supporting?

187. *Phil.* So that something distinct from, and exclusive of, extension is supposed to be the substratum of extension?

Hyl. Just so.

188. *Phil.* Answer me, Hylas, can a thing be spread without extension, or is not the idea of extension necessarily included in *spreading?*

Hyl. It is.

189. *Phil.* Whatsoever therefore you suppose spread under anything must have in itself an extension distinct from the extension of that thing under which it is spread?

Hyl. It must.

190. *Phil.* Consequently, every corporeal substance being the substratum of extension must have in itself another extension by which it is qualified to be a substratum, and so on to infinity? And I ask whether this be not absurd in itself and repugnant to what you granted just now, to wit, that the substratum was something distinct from and exclusive of extension?

Hyl. Aye, but, Philonous, you take me wrong. I do not mean that matter is *spread* in a gross literal sense under extension. The word "substratum" is used only to express in general the same thing with "substance."

191. *Phil.* Well then, let us examine the relation implied in the term "substance." Is it not that it stands under accidents?

Hyl. The very same.

192. *Phil.* But that one thing may stand under or support another, must it not be extended?

Hyl. It must.

193. *Phil.* Is not therefore this supposition liable to the same absurdity with the former?

Hyl. You still take things in a strict literal sense; that is not fair, Philonous.

194. *Phil.* I am not for imposing any sense on your words; you are at liberty to explain them as you please. Only, I beseech you, make me understand something by them. You tell me matter supports or stands under accidents. How! is it as your legs support your body?

Hyl. No; that is the literal sense.

195. *Phil.* Pray let me know any sense, literal or not literal, that you understand it in.—How long must I wait for an answer, Hylas?

Hyl. I declare I know not what to say. I once thought I understood well enough what was meant by matter's supporting accidents. But now, the more I think on it, the less can I comprehend it; in short, I find that I know nothing of it.

196. *Phil.* It seems then you have no idea at all, neither relative nor positive, of matter? you know neither what it is in itself nor what relation it bears to accidents?

Hyl. I acknowledge it.

197. *Phil.* And yet you asserted that you could not conceive how qualities or accidents should really exist without conceiving at the same time a material support of them?

Hyl. I did.

198. *Phil.* That is to say, when you conceive the real existence of qualities, you do withal conceive something which you cannot conceive?

Hyl. It was wrong I own. But still I fear there is some fallacy or other. Pray, what think you of this? It is just come into my head that the ground of all our mistake lies in your treating of each quality by itself. Now I grant that each quality cannot singly subsist without the mind. Color cannot without extension, neither can figure without some other sensible quality. But, as the several qualities united or blended together form entire sensible things, nothing hinders why such things may not be supposed to exist without the mind.

199. *Phil.* Either, Hylas, you are jesting or have a very bad memory. Though, indeed, we went through all the qualities by name one after another, yet my arguments, or rather your concessions, nowhere tended to prove that the secondary qualities

did not subsist each alone by itself, but that they were not *at all* without the mind. Indeed, in treating of figure and motion we concluded they could not exist without the mind, because it was impossible even in thought to separate them from all secondary qualities, so as to conceive them existing by themselves. But then this was not the only argument made use of upon that occasion. But (to pass by all that has been hitherto said and reckon it for nothing, if you will have it so) I am content to put the whole upon this issue. If you can conceive it possible for any mixture or combination of qualities, or any sensible object whatever, to exist without the mind, then I will grant it actually to be so.

Hyl. If it comes to that the point will soon be decided. What more easy than to conceive a tree or house existing by itself, independent of, and unperceived by, any mind whatsoever? I do at this present time conceive them existing after that manner.

200. *Phil.* How say you, Hylas, can you see a thing which is at the same time unseen?

Hyl. No, that were a contradiction.

201. *Phil.* Is it not as great a contradiction to talk of *conceiving* a thing which is *unconceived?*

Hyl. It is.

202. *Phil.* The tree or house, therefore, which you think of is conceived by you?

Hyl. How should it be otherwise?

203. *Phil.* And what is conceived is surely in the mind?

Hyl. Without question, that which is conceived is in the mind.

204. *Phil.* How then came you to say you conceived a house or tree existing independent and out of all minds whatsoever?

Hyl. That was I own an oversight, but stay, let me consider what let me into it.—It is a pleasant mistake enough. As I was thinking of a tree in a solitary place where no one was present to see it, methought that was to conceive a tree as existing unperceived or unthought of, not considering that I myself conceived it all the while. But now I plainly see that all I can do is to frame ideas in my own mind. I may indeed conceive in my own thoughts the idea of a tree, or a house, or a mountain, but that is all. And this is far from proving that I can conceive them *existing out of the minds of all spirits.*

205. *Phil.* You acknowledge then that you cannot possibly conceive how any one corporeal sensible thing should exist otherwise than in a mind?

Hyl. I do.

206. *Phil.* And yet you will earnestly contend for the truth of that which you cannot so much as conceive?

Hyl. I profess I know not what to think; but still there are some scruples remain with me. Is it not certain I see things at a distance? Do we not perceive the stars and moon, for example, to be a great way off? Is not this, I say, manifest to the senses?

207. *Phil.* Do you not in a dream, too, perceive those or the like objects?

Hyl. I do.

208. *Phil.* And have they not then the same appearance of being distant?

Hyl. They have.

209. *Phil.* But you do not thence conclude the apparitions in a dream to be without the mind?

Hyl. By no means.

210. *Phil.* You ought not therefore to conclude that sensible objects are without the mind, from their appearance or manner wherein they are perceived.

Hyl. I acknowledge it. But does not my sense deceive me in those cases?

211. *Phil.* By no means. The idea or thing which you immediately perceive, neither sense nor reason informs you that it actually exists without the mind. By sense you only know that you are affected with such certain sensations of light and colors, etc. And these you will not say are without the mind.

Hyl. True, but, besides all that, do you not think the sight suggests something of *outness* or *distance?*

212. *Phil.* Upon approaching a distant object, do the visible size and figure change perpetually or do they appear the same at all distances?

Hyl. They are in a continual change.

213. *Phil.* Sight, therefore, does not suggest or any way inform you that the visible object you immediately perceive exists at a distance, or will be perceived when you advance farther onward, there being a continued series of visible objects succeeding each other during the whole time of your approach.

Hyl. It does not; but still I know, upon seeing an object, what object I shall perceive after having passed over a certain distance? no matter whether it be exactly the same or no, there is still something of distance suggested in the case.

214. *Phil.* Good Hylas, do but reflect a little on the point, and then tell me whether there be any

more on it than this. From the ideas you actually perceive by sight, you have by experience learned to collect what other ideas you will (according to the standing order of nature) be affected with, after such a certain succession of time and motion.

Hyl. Upon the whole, I take it to be nothing else.

215. *Phil.* Now is it not plain that if we suppose a man born blind was on a sudden made to see, he could at first have no experience of what may be suggested by sight?

Hyl. It is.

216. *Phil.* He would not then, according to you, have any notion of distance annexed to the things he saw, but would take them for a new set of sensations existing only in his mind?

Hyl. It is undeniable.

217. *Phil.* But to make it more plain: is not *distance* a line turned endwise to the eye?

Hyl. It is.

218. *Phil.* And can a line so situated be perceived by sight?

Hyl. It cannot.

219. *Phil.* Does it not therefore follow that distance is not properly and immediately perceived by sight?

Hyl. It should seem so.

220. *Phil.* Again, is it your opinion that colors are at a distance?

Hyl. It must be acknowledged they are only in the mind.

221. *Phil.* But do not colors appear to the eye as coexisting in the same place with extension and figures?

Hyl. They do.

222. *Phil.* How can you then conclude from sight that figures exist without, when you acknowledge colors do not; the sensible appearances being the very same with regard to both?

Hyl. I know not what to answer.

223. *Phil.* But allowing that distance was truly and immediately perceived by the mind, yet it would not thence follow it existed out of the mind. For whatever is immediately perceived is an idea; and can any *idea* exist out of the mind?

Hyl. To suppose that were absurd; but, inform me, Philonous, can we perceive or know nothing besides our ideas?

224. *Phil.* As for the rational deducing of causes from effects, that is beside our inquiry. And by the senses you can best tell whether you perceive any-

thing which is not immediately perceived. And I ask you whether the things immediately perceived are other than your own sensations or ideas? You have indeed more than once, in the course of this conversation, declared yourself on those points, but you seem, by this last question, to have departed from what you then thought.

Hyl. To speak the truth, Philonous, I think there are two kinds of objects: the one perceived immediately, which are likewise called "ideas"; the other are real things or external objects, perceived by the mediation of ideas which are their images and representations. Now I own ideas do not exist without the mind, but the latter sort of objects do. I am sorry I did not think of this distinction sooner; it would probably have cut short your discourse.

225. *Phil.* Are those external objects perceived by sense or by some other faculty?

Hyl. They are perceived by sense.

226. *Phil.* How! is there anything perceived by sense which is not immediately perceived?

Hyl. Yes, Philonous, in some sort there is. For example, when I look on a picture or statue of Julius Caesar, I may be said, after a manner, to perceive him (though not immediately) by my senses.

227. *Phil.* It seems then you will have our ideas, which alone are immediately perceived, to be pictures of external things: and that these also are perceived by sense inasmuch as they have a conformity or resemblance to our ideas?

Hyl. That is my meaning.

228. *Phil.* And in the same way that Julius Caesar, in himself invisible, is nevertheless perceived by sight, real things, in themselves imperceptible, are perceived by sense.

Hyl. In the very same.

229. *Phil.* Tell me, Hylas, when you behold the picture of Julius Caesar, do you see with your eyes any more than some colors and figures, with a certain symmetry and composition of the whole?

Hyl. Nothing else.

230. *Phil.* And would not a man who had never known anything of Julius Caesar see as much?

Hyl. He would.

231. *Phil.* Consequently, he has his sight and the use of it in as perfect a degree as you?

Hyl. I agree with you.

232. *Phil.* Whence comes it then that your thoughts are directed to the Roman emperor, and his are not? This cannot proceed from the sensations

or ideas of sense by you then perceived, since you acknowledge you have no advantage over him in that respect. It should seem therefore to proceed from reason and memory, should it not?

Hyl. It should.

233. *Phil.* Consequently, it will not follow from that instance that anything is perceived by sense which is not immediately perceived. Though I grant we may, in one acceptation, be said to perceive sensible things mediately by sense—that is, when, from a frequently perceived connection, the immediate perception of ideas by one sense suggest to the mind others, perhaps belonging to another sense, which are wont to be connected with them. For instance, when I hear a coach drive along the streets, immediately I perceive only the sound; but from the experience I have had that such a sound is connected with a coach, I am said to hear the coach. It is nevertheless evident that, in truth and strictness, nothing can be *heard* but *sound;* and the coach is not then properly perceived by sense, but suggested from experience. So likewise when we are said to see a red-hot bar of iron; the solidity and heat of the iron are not the objects of sight, but suggested to the imagination by the color and figure which are properly perceived by that sense. In short, those things alone are actually and strictly perceived by any sense which would have been perceived in case that same sense had then been first conferred on us. As for other things, it is plain they are only suggested to the mind by experience grounded on former perceptions. But, to return to your comparison of Ceasar's picture, it is plain, if you keep to that, you must hold the real things or archetypes of our ideas are not perceived by sense, but by some internal faculty of the soul, as reason or memory. I would, therefore, fain know what arguments you can draw from reason for the existence of what you call "real things" or "material objects," or whether you remember to have seen them formerly as they are in themselves, or if you have heard or read of anyone that did.

Hyl. Philonous, you are disposed to raillery; but that will never convince me.

234. *Phil.* My aim is only to learn from you the way to come at the knowledge of "material beings." Whatever we perceive is perceived either immediately or mediately—by sense, or by reason and reflection. But, as you have excluded sense, pray show me what reason you have to believe their existence, or what *medium* you can possibly make use of to prove it, either to mine or your own understanding.

Hyl. To deal ingenuously, Philonous, now [that] I consider the point, I do not find I can give you any good reason for it. But this much seems pretty plain, that it is at least possible such things may really exist. And as long as there is no absurdity in supposing them, I am resolved to believe as I did, till you bring good reasons to the contrary.

235. *Phil.* What! is it come to this, that you only believe the existence of material objects, and that your belief is founded barely on the possibility of its being true? Then you will have me bring reasons against it, though another would think it reasonable the proof should lie on him who holds the affirmative. And, after all, this very point which you are now resolved to maintain, without any reason, is in effect what you have more than once during this discourse seen good reason to give up. But to pass over all this—if I understand you rightly, you say our ideas do not exist without the mind, but that they are copies, images, or representations of certain originals that do?

Hyl. You take me right.

236. *Phil.* They are then like external things?

Hyl. They are.

237. *Phil.* Have those things a stable and permanent nature, independent of our senses, or are they in a perpetual change, upon our producing any motions in our bodies, suspending, exerting, or altering our faculties or organs of sense?

Hyl. Real things, it is plain, have a fixed and real nature, which remains the same notwithstanding any change in our senses or in the posture and motion of our bodies; which indeed may affect the ideas in our minds, but it were absurd to think they had the same effect on things existing without the mind.

238. *Phil.* How then is it possible that things perpetually fleeting and variable as our ideas should be copies or images of anything fixed and constant? Or, in other words, since all sensible qualities, as size, figure, color, etc., that is, our ideas, are continually changing upon every alteration in the distance, medium, or instruments of sensation—how can any determinate material objects be properly represented or painted forth by several distinct things each of which is so different from

and unlike the rest? Or, if you say it resembles some one only of our ideas, how shall we be able to distinguish the true copy from all the false ones?

Hyl. I profess, Philonous, I am at a loss. I know not what to say to this.

239. *Phil.* But neither is this all. Which are material objects in themselves—perceptible or imperceptible?

Hyl. Properly and immediately nothing can be perceived but ideas. All material things, therefore, are in themselves insensible and to be perceived only by their ideas.

240. *Phil.* Ideas then are sensible, and their archetypes or originals insensible?

Hyl. Right.

241. *Phil.* But how can that which is sensible be like that which is insensible? Can a real thing, in itself *invisible,* be like a *color,* or a real thing which is not *audible* be like a *sound?* In a word, can anything be like a sensation or idea, but another sensation or idea?

Hyl. I must own, I think not.

242. *Phil.* Is it possible there should be any doubt on the point? Do you not perfectly know your own ideas?

Hyl. I know them perfectly, since what I do not perceive or know can be no part of my idea.

243. *Phil.* Consider, therefore, and examine them, and then tell me if there be anything in them which can exist without the mind, or if you can conceive anything like them existing without the mind?

Hyl. Upon inquiry I find it impossible for me to conceive or understand how anything but an idea can be like an idea. And it is most evident that *no idea can exist without the mind.*

244. *Phil.* You are, therefore, by your principles forced to deny the reality of sensible things, since you made it to consist in an absolute existence exterior to the mind. That is to say, you are a downright skeptic. So I have gained my point, which was to show your principles led to skepticism.

Hyl. For the present I am, if not entirely convinced, at least silenced.

245. *Phil.* I would fain know what more you would require in order to [achieve] a perfect conviction. Have you not had the liberty of explaining yourself all manner of ways? Were any little slips in discourse laid hold and insisted on? Or were you not allowed to retract or reinforce anything you had

offered, as best served your purpose? Has not everything you could say been heard and examined with all the fairness imaginable? In a word, have you not in every point been convinced out of your own mouth? And, if you can at present discover any flaw in any of your former concessions, or think of any remaining subterfuge, any new distinction, color, or comment whatsoever, why do you not produce it?

Hyl. A little patience, Philonous. I am at present so amazed to see myself ensnared, and as it were imprisoned in the labyrinths you have drawn me into, that on the sudden it cannot be expected I should find my way out. You must give me time to look about me and recollect myself.

246. *Phil.* Hark; is not this the college bell?

Hyl. It rings for prayers.

247. *Phil.* We will go in then, if you please, and meet here again tomorrow morning. In the meantime, you may employ your thoughts on this morning's discourse and try if you can find any fallacy in it, or invent any new means to extricate yourself.

Hyl. Agreed.

The Second Dialogue

Hylas. I beg your pardon, Philonous, for not meeting you sooner. All this morning my head was so filled with our late conversation that I had not leisure to think of the time of the day, or indeed of anything else.

1. *Philonous.* I am glad you were so intent upon it, in hopes if there were any mistakes in your concessions, or fallacies in my reasonings from them, you will now discover them to me.

Hyl. I assure you I have done nothing ever since I saw you but search after mistakes and fallacies, and, with that [in] view, have minutely examined the whole series of yesterday's discourse; but all in vain, for the notions it led me into, upon review, appear still more clear and evident; and the more I consider them, the more irresistibly do they force my assent.

2. *Phil.* And is not this, think you, a sign that they are genuine, that they proceed from nature and are conformable to right reason? Truth and beauty

are in this alike, that the strictest survey sets them both off to advantage, while the false luster of error and disguise cannot endure being reviewed or too nearly inspected.

Hyl. I own there is a great deal in what you say. Nor can anyone be more entirely satisfied of the truth of those odd consequences so long as I have in view the reasonings that lead to them. But when these are out of my thoughts, there seems, on the other hand, something so satisfactory, so natural and intelligible in the modern way of explaining things that I profess I know not how to reject it.

3. *Phil.* I know not what you mean.

Hyl. I mean the way of accounting for our sensations or ideas.

4. *Phil.* How is that?

Hyl. It is supposed the soul makes her residence in some part of the brain, from which the nerves take their rise, and are thence extended to all parts of the body; and that outward objects, by the different impressions they make on the organs of sense, communicate certain vibrative motions to the nerves, and these, being filled with spirits, propagate them to the brain or seat of the soul, which, according to the various impressions or traces thereby made in the brain, is variously affected with ideas.

5. *Phil.* And call you this an explication of the manner whereby we are affected with ideas?

Hyl. Why not, Philonous; have you anything to object against it?

6. *Phil.* I would first know whether I rightly understand your hypothesis. You make certain traces in the brain to be the causes or occasions of our ideas. Pray tell me whether by the "brain" you mean any sensible thing.

Hyl. What else think you I could mean?

7. *Phil.* Sensible things are all immediately perceivable; and those things which are immediately perceivable are ideas, and these exist only in the mind. This much you have, if I mistake not, long since agreed to.

Hyl. I do not deny it.

8. *Phil.* The brain therefore you speak of, being a sensible thing, exists only in the mind. Now I would fain know whether you think it reasonable to suppose that one idea or thing existing in the mind occasions all other ideas. And if you think so, pray how do you account for the origin of that primary idea or brain itself?

Hyl. I do not explain the origin of our ideas by that brain which is perceivable to sense, this being itself only a combination of sensible ideas, but by another which I imagine.

9. *Phil.* But are not things imagined as truly *in the mind* as things perceived?

Hyl. I must confess they are.

10. *Phil.* It comes, therefore, to the same thing; and you have been all this while accounting for ideas by certain motions or impressions of the brain, that is, by some alteration in an idea, whether sensible or imaginable it matters not.

Hyl. I begin to suspect my hypothesis.

11. *Phil.* Besides spirits, all that we know or conceive are our own ideas. When, therefore, you say all ideas are occasioned by impressions in the brain, do you conceive this brain or no? If you do, then you talk of ideas imprinted in an idea causing that same idea, which is absurd. If you do not conceive it, you talk unintelligibly, instead of forming a reasonable hypothesis.

Hyl. I now clearly see it was a mere dream. There is nothing in it.

12. *Phil.* You need not be much concerned at it, for, after all, this way of explaining things, as you called it, could never have satisfied any reasonable man. What connection is there between a motion in the nerves and the sensations of sound or color in the mind? Or how is it possible these should be the effect of that?

Hyl. But I could never think it had so little in it as now it seems to have.

13. *Phil.* Well then, are you at length satisfied that no sensible things have a real existence, and that you are in truth an arrant *skeptic?*

Hyl. It is too plain to be denied.

14. *Phil.* Look! are not the fields covered with a delightful verdure? Is there not something in the woods and groves, in the rivers and clear springs, that soothes, that delights, that transports the soul? At the prospect of the wide and deep ocean, or some huge mountain whose top is lost in the clouds, or of an old gloomy forest, are not our minds filled with a pleasing horror? Even in rocks and deserts is there not an agreeable wildness? How sincere a pleasure is it to behold the natural beauties of the earth! To preserve and renew our relish for them, is not the veil of night alternately drawn over her face, and does she not change her dress with the seasons?

How aptly are the elements disposed! What variety and use in the meanest productions of nature! What delicacy, what beauty, what contrivance in animal and vegetable bodies! How exquisitely are all things suited, as well to their particular ends as to constitute apposite parts of the whole! And while they mutually aid and support, do they not also set off and illustrate each other? Raise now your thoughts from this ball of earth to all those glorious luminaries that adorn the high arch of heaven. The motion and situation of the planets, are they not admirable for use and order? Were those (miscalled "erratic") globes ever known to stray in their repeated journeys through the pathless void? Do they not measure areas round the sun ever proportioned to the times? So fixed, so immutable are the laws by which the unseen Author of nature actuates the universe. How vivid and radiant is the luster of the fixed stars! How magnificent and rich that negligent profusion with which they appear to be scattered throughout the whole azure vault! Yet, if you take the telescope, it brings into your sight a new host of stars that escape the naked eye. Here they seem contiguous and minute, but to a nearer view, immense orbs of light at various distances, far sunk in the abyss of space. Now you must call imagination to your aid. The feeble narrow sense cannot descry innumerable worlds revolving round the central fires, and in those worlds the energy of an all-perfect Mind displayed in endless forms. But neither sense nor imagination [is] big enough to comprehend the boundless extent with all its glittering furniture. Though the laboring mind exert and strain each power to its utmost reach, there still stands out ungrasped a surplusage immeasurable. Yet all the vast bodies that compose this mighty frame, how distant and remote soever, are by some secret mechanism, some divine art and force, linked in a mutual dependence and intercourse with each other, even with this earth, which was almost slipt from my thoughts and lost in the crowd of worlds. Is not the whole system immense, beautiful, glorious beyond expression and beyond thought! What treatment, then, do those philosophers deserve who would deprive these noble and delightful scenes of all reality? How should those principles be entertained that lead us to think all the visible beauty of the creation a false imaginary glare? To be plain, can you expect this skepticism of yours will not be thought extravagantly absurd by all men of sense?

Hyl. Other men may think as they please, but for your part you have nothing to reproach me with. My comfort is you are as much a skeptic as I am.

15. *Phil.* There, Hylas, I must beg leave to differ from you.

Hyl. What! have you all along agreed to the premises, and do you now deny the conclusion and leave me to maintain those paradoxes by myself which you led me into? This surely is not fair.

16. *Phil.* I deny that I agreed with you in those notions that led to skepticism. You indeed said the *reality* of sensible things consisted in an *absolute existence* out of the minds of spirits, or distinct from their being perceived. And, pursuant to this notion of reality, you are obliged to deny sensible things any real existence; that is, according to your own definition, you profess yourself a skeptic. But I neither said nor thought the reality of sensible things was to be defined after that manner. To me it is evident, for the reasons you allow of, that sensible things cannot exist otherwise than in a mind or spirit. Whence I conclude, not that they have no real existence, but that, seeing they depend not on my thought and have an existence distinct from being perceived by me, *there must be some other mind wherein they exist.* As sure, therefore, as the sensible world really exists, so sure is there an infinite omnipresent Spirit, who contains and supports it.

Hyl. What! this is no more than I and all Christians hold; nay, and all others, too, who believe there is a God and that He knows and comprehends all things.

17. *Phil.* Aye, but here lies the difference. Men commonly believe that all things are known or perceived by God, because they believe the being of a God; whereas I, on the other side, immediately and necessarily conclude the being of a God, because all sensible things must be perceived by him.

Hyl. But so long as we all believe the same thing, what matter is it how we come by that belief?

18. *Phil.* But neither do we agree in the same opinion. For philosophers, though they acknowledge all corporeal beings to be perceived by God, yet they attribute to them an absolute subsistence distinct from their being perceived by any mind whatever, which I do not. Besides, is there no difference between saying, *there is a God, therefore He*

perceives all things, and saying, *sensible things do really exist; and if they really exist, they are necessarily perceived by an infinite mind: therefore there is an infinite mind, or God?* This furnishes you with a direct and immediate demonstration, from a most evident principle, of the *being of a God.* Divines and philosophers had proved beyond all controversy, from the beauty and usefulness of the several parts of the creation, that it was the workmanship of God. But that—setting aside all help of astronomy and natural philosophy, all contemplation of the contrivance, order, and adjustment of things—an infinite mind should be necessarily inferred from the bare *existence* of the sensible world is an advantage peculiar to them only who have made this easy reflection, that the sensible world is that which we perceive by our several senses; and that nothing is perceived by the senses besides ideas; and that no idea or archetype of an idea can exist otherwise than in a mind. You may now, without any laborious search into the sciences, without any subtlety of reason or tedious length of discourse, oppose and baffle the most strenuous advocate for atheism, those miserable refuges, whether in an eternal succession of unthinking causes and effects or in a fortuitous concourse of atoms; those wild imaginations of Vanini, Hobbes, and Spinoza: in a word, the whole system of atheism, is it not entirely overthrown by this single reflection on the repugnancy included in supposing the whole or any part, even the most rude and shapeless, of the visible world to exist without a mind? Let any one of those abettors of impiety but look into his own thoughts, and there try if he can conceive how so much as a rock, a desert, a chaos, or confused jumble of atoms, how anything at all, either sensible or imaginable, can exist independent of a mind, and he need go no further to be convinced of his folly. Can anything be fairer than to put a dispute on such an issue and leave it to a man himself to see if he can conceive, even in thought, what he holds to be true in fact, and from a notional to allow it a real existence?

Hyl. It cannot be denied there is something highly serviceable to religion in what you advance. But do you not think it looks very like a notion entertained by some eminent moderns, of *seeing all things in God?*

19. *Phil.* I would gladly know that opinion; pray explain it to me.

Hyl. They conceive that the soul, being immaterial, is incapable of being united with material things so as to perceive them in themselves, but that she perceives them by her union with the substance of God, which, being spiritual, is therefore purely intelligible, or capable of being the immediate object of a spirit's thought. Besides, the divine essence contains in it perfections correspondent to each created being, and which are, for that reason, proper to exhibit or represent them to the mind.

20. *Phil.* I do not understand how our ideas, which are things altogether passive and inert, can be the essence or any part (or like any part) of the essence or substance of God, who is an impassive, indivisible, purely active being. Many more difficulties and objections there are which occur at first view against this hypothesis; but I shall only add that it is liable to all the absurdities of the common hypothesis, in making a created world exist otherwise than in the mind of a Spirit. Beside all which it has this peculiar to itself that it makes that material world serve to no purpose. And if it pass for a good argument against other hypotheses in the sciences that they suppose nature or the divine wisdom to make something in vain, or do that by tedious roundabout methods which might have been performed in a much more easy and compendious way, what shall we think of that hypothesis which supposes the whole world made in vain?

Hyl. But what say you, are not you too of opinion that we see all things in God? If I mistake not, what you advance comes near it.

21. *Phil.* Few men think, yet all have opinions. Hence men's opinions are superficial and confused. It is nothing strange that tenets which in themselves are ever so different should nevertheless be confounded with each other by those who do not consider them attentively. I shall not therefore be surprised if some men imagine that I run into the enthusiasm of Malebranche, though in truth I am very remote from it. He builds on the most abstract general ideas, which I entirely disclaim. He asserts an absolute external world, which I deny. He maintains that we are deceived by our senses and know not the real natures or the true forms and figures of extended beings; of all which I hold the direct contrary. So that upon the whole there are no principles more fundamentally opposite than his and mine. It must be owned. I entirely agree with what the holy

Scripture says, "That in God we live and move and have our being." But that we see things in His essence, after the manner above set forth, I am far from believing. Take here in brief my meaning: It is evident that the things I perceive are my own ideas, and that no idea can exist unless it be in a mind. Nor is it less plain that these ideas or things by me perceived, either themselves or their archetypes, exist independently of my mind; since I know myself not to be their author, it being out of my power to determine at pleasure what particular ideas I shall be affected with upon opening my eyes or ears. They must therefore exist in some other mind, whose will it is they should be exhibited to me. The things, I say, immediately perceived are ideas or sensations, call them which you will. But how can any idea or sensation exist in, or be produced by, anything but a mind or spirit? This indeed is inconceivable; and to assert that which is inconceivable is to talk nonsense, is it not?

Hyl. Without doubt.

22. *Phil.* But, on the other hand, it is very conceivable that they should exist in and be produced by a spirit, since this is no more than I daily experience in myself, inasmuch as I perceive numberless ideas, and, by an act of my will, can form a great variety of them and raise them up in my imagination; though, it must be confessed, these creatures of the fancy are not altogether so distinct, so strong, vivid, and permanent as those perceived by my senses, which latter are called "real things." From all which I conclude, *there is a Mind which affects me every moment with all the sensible impressions I perceive.* And from the variety, order, and manner of these I conclude the Author of them to be *wise, powerful, and good beyond comprehension.* Mark it well; I do not say I see things by perceiving that which represents them in the intelligible Substance of God. This I do not understand; but I say the things by me perceived are known by the understanding and produced by the will of an infinite Spirit. And is not all this most plain and evident? Is there any more in it than what a little observation of our own minds, and that which passes in them, not only enables us to conceive but also obliges us to acknowledge?

Hyl. I think I understand you very clearly and own the proof you give of a Deity seems no less evident than it is surprising. But allowing that God is the supreme and universal cause of all things, yet may there not be still a third nature besides spirits and ideas? May we not admit a subordinate and limited cause of our ideas? In a word, may there not for all that be *matter?*

23. *Phil.* How often must I inculcate the same thing? You allow the things immediately perceived by sense to exist nowhere without the mind; but there is nothing perceived by sense which is not perceived immediately: therefore there is nothing sensible that exists without the mind. The matter, therefore, which you still insist on is something intelligible, I suppose something that may be discovered by reason, and not by sense.

Hyl. You are in the right.

24. *Phil.* Pray let me know what reasoning your belief of matter is grounded on, and what this matter is in your present sense of it.

Hyl. I find myself affected with various ideas whereof I know I am not the cause; neither are they the cause of themselves or of one another, or capable of subsisting by themselves, as being altogether inactive, fleeting, dependent beings. They have therefore some cause distinct from me and them, of which I pretend to know no more than that it is *the cause of my ideas.* And this thing, whatever it be, I call "matter."

25. *Phil.* Tell me, Hylas, has everyone a liberty to change the current proper signification annexed to a common name in any language? For example, suppose a traveler should tell you that in a certain country men pass unhurt through the fire; and, upon explaining himself, you found he meant by the word "fire" that which others call "water"; or, if he should assert that there are trees that walk upon two legs, meaning men by the term "trees." Would you think this reasonable?

Hyl. No, I should think it very absurd. Common custom is the standard of propriety in language. And for any man to affect speaking improperly is to pervert the use of speech, and can never serve to a better purpose than to protract and multiply disputes where there is no difference in opinion.

26. *Phil.* And does not "matter," in the common current acceptation of the word, signify an extended, solid, movable, unthinking, inactive substance?

Hyl. It does.

27. *Phil.* And has it not been made evident that no such substance can possibly exist? And though it

should be allowed to exist, yet how can that which is *inactive* be a *cause,* or that which is *unthinking* be a *cause of thought?* You may, indeed, if you please, annex to the word "matter" a contrary meaning to what is vulgarly received, and tell me you understand by it an unextended, thinking, active being which is the cause of our ideas. But what else is this than to play with words and run into that very fault you just now condemned with so much reason? I do by no means find fault with your reasoning, in that you collect a cause from the phenomena; but I deny that the cause deducible by reason can properly be termed "matter."

Hyl. There is indeed something in what you say. But I am afraid you do not thoroughly comprehend my meaning. I would by no means be thought to deny that God, or an infinite Spirit, is the Supreme Cause of all things. All I contend for is that, subordinate to the Supreme Agent, there is a cause of a limited and inferior nature which concurs in the production of our ideas, not by any act of will or spiritual efficiency, but by that kind of action which belongs to matter, *viz.,* motion.

28. *Phil.* I find you are at every turn relapsing into your old exploded conceit, of a movable and consequently an extended substance existing without the mind. What! have you already forgotten you were convinced, or are you willing I should repeat what has been said on that head? In truth, this is not fair dealing in you still to suppose the being of that which you have so often acknowledged to have no being. But, not to insist further on what has been so largely handled, I ask whether all your ideas are not perfectly passive and inert, including nothing of action in them.

Hyl. They are.

29. *Phil.* And are sensible qualities anything else but ideas?

Hyl. How often have I acknowledged that they are not.

30. *Phil.* But is not motion a sensible quality?

Hyl. It is.

31. *Phil.* Consequently, it is no action?

Hyl. I agree with you. And indeed it is very plain that when I stir my finger it remains passive, but my will which produced the motion is active.

32. *Phil.* Now I desire to know, in the first place, whether, motion being allowed to be no action, you can conceive any action besides volition; and, in the second place, whether to say something and conceive nothing be not to talk nonsense; and, lastly, whether, having considered the premises, you do not perceive that to suppose any efficient or active cause of our ideas other than *spirit* is highly absurd and unreasonable?

Hyl. I give up the point entirely. But, though matter may not be a cause, yet what hinders its being an *instrument* subservient to the Supreme Agent in the production of our ideas.

33. *Phil.* An instrument say you; pray what may be the figure, springs, wheels, and motions of that instrument?

Hyl. Those I pretend to determine nothing of, both the substance and its qualities being entirely unknown to me.

34. *Phil.* What! You are then of opinion it is made up of unknown parts, that it has unknown motions and an unknown shape?

Hyl. I do not believe that it has any figure or motion at all, being already convinced that no sensible qualities can exist in an unperceiving substance.

35. *Phil.* But what notion is it possible to frame of an instrument void of all sensible qualities, even extension itself?

Hyl. I do not pretend to have any notion of it.

36. *Phil.* And what reason have you to think this unknown, this inconceivable somewhat does exist? Is it that you imagine God cannot act as well without it, or that you find by experience the use of some such thing when you form ideas in your own mind?

Hyl. You are always teasing me for reasons of my belief. Pray what reasons have you not to believe it?

37. *Phil.* It is to me a sufficient reason not to believe the existence of anything if I see no reason for believing it. But, not to insist on reasons for believing, you will not so much as let me know what it is you would have me believe, since you say you have no manner of notion of it. After all, let me entreat you to consider whether it be like a philosopher, or even like a man of common sense, to pretend to believe you know not what, and you know not why.

Hyl. Hold, Philonous. When I tell you matter is an *instrument,* I do not mean altogether nothing. It is true I know not the particular kind of instrument, but, however, I have some notion of *instrument in general,* which I apply to it.

38. *Phil.* But what if it should prove that there is something, even in the most general notion of *instrument,* as taken in a distinct sense from *cause,* which makes the use of it inconsistent with the divine attributes?

Hyl. Make that appear and I shall give up the point.

39. *Phil.* What mean you by the general nature or notion of instrument?

Hyl. That which is common to all particular instruments composes the general notion.

40. *Phil.* Is it not common to all instruments that they are applied to the doing those things only which cannot be performed by the mere act of our wills? Thus, for instance, I never use an instrument to move my finger, because it is done by a volition. But I should use one if I were to remove part of a rock or tear up a tree by the roots. Are you of the same mind? Or can you show any example where an instrument is made use of in producing an effect immediately depending on the will of the agent?

Hyl. I own I cannot.

41. *Phil.* How, therefore, can you suppose that an all-perfect Spirit, on whose will all things have an absolute and immediate dependence, should need an instrument in his operations or, not needing it, make use of it? Thus it seems to me that you are obliged to own the use of a lifeless inactive instrument to be incompatible with the infinite perfection of God, that is, by your own confession, to give up the point.

Hyl. It does not readily occur what I can answer you.

42. *Phil.* But methinks you should be ready to own the truth when it has been fairly proved to you. We, indeed, who are beings of finite powers, are forced to make use of instruments. And the use of an instrument shows the agent to be limited by rules of another's prescription, and that he cannot obtain his end but in such a way and by such conditions. Whence it seems a clear consequence that the Supreme Unlimited Agent uses no tool or instrument at all. The will of an Omnipotent Spirit is no sooner exerted than executed, without the application of means, which, if they are employed by inferior agents, it is not upon account of any real efficacy that is in them, or necessary aptitude to produce any effect, but merely in compliance with the laws of nature or those conditions prescribed to them by the First Cause, who is Himself above all limitation or prescription whatsoever.

Hyl. I will no longer maintain that matter is an instrument. However, I would not be understood to give up its existence neither, since, notwithstanding what has been said, it may still be an *occasion.*

43. *Phil.* How many shapes is your matter to take? Or how often must it be proved not to exist before you are content to part with it? But to say no more of this (though by all the laws of disputation I may justly blame you for so frequently changing the signification of the principal term), I would fain know what you mean by affirming that matter is an "occasion," having already denied it to be a cause. And when you have shown in what sense you understand occasion, pray, in the next place, be pleased to show me what reason induces you to believe there is such an occasion of our ideas?

Hyl. As to the first point: by "occasion" I mean an inactive unthinking being, at the presence whereof God excites ideas in our minds.

44. *Phil.* And what may be the nature of that inactive unthinking being?

Hyl. I know nothing of its nature.

45. *Phil.* Proceed then to the second point and assign some reason why we should allow an existence to this inactive, unthinking, unknown thing.

Hyl. When we see ideas produced in our minds after an orderly and constant manner, it is natural to think they have some fixed and regular occasions at the presence of which they are excited.

46. *Phil.* You acknowledge then God alone to be the cause of our ideas, and that He causes them at the presence of those occasions.

Hyl. That is my opinion.

47. *Phil.* Those things which you say are present to God, without doubt He perceives.

Hyl. Certainly; otherwise they could not be to Him an occasion of acting.

48. *Phil.* Not to insist now on your making sense of this hypothesis, or answering all the puzzling questions and difficulties it is liable to: I only ask whether the order and regularity observable in the series of our ideas, or the course of nature, be not sufficiently accounted for by the wisdom and power of God; and whether it does not derogate from those attributes to suppose He is influenced, directed, or put in mind, when and what He is to act, by an unthinking substance? And,

lastly, whether, in case I granted all you contend for, it would make anything to your purpose, it not being easy to conceive how the external or absolute existence of an unthinking substance, distinct from its being perceived, can be inferred from my allowing that there are certain things perceived by the mind of God which are to Him the occasion of producing ideas in us?

Hyl. I am perfectly at a loss what to think, this notion of occasion seeming now altogether as groundless as the rest.

49. *Phil.* Do you not at length perceive that in all these different acceptations of matter you have been only supposing you know not what, for no manner of reason and to no kind of use?

Hyl. I freely own myself less fond of my notions since they have been so accurately examined. But still, methinks, I have some confused perception that there is such a thing as matter.

50. *Phil.* Either you perceive the being of matter immediately or mediately. If immediately, pray inform me by which of the senses you perceive it. If mediately, let me know by what reasoning it is inferred from those things which you perceive immediately. So much for the perception. Then for the matter itself, I ask whether it is object, substratum, cause, instrument, or occasion? You have already pleaded for each of these, shifting your notions and making matter to appear sometimes in one shape, then in another. And what you have offered has been disapproved and rejected by yourself. If you have anything new to advance I would gladly hear it.

Hyl. I think I have already offered all I had to say on those heads. I am at a loss what more to urge.

51. *Phil.* And yet you are loath to part with your old prejudice. But to make you quit it more easily, I desire that, besides what has been hitherto suggested, you will further consider whether, upon supposition that matter exists, you can possibly conceive how you should be affected by it? Or, supposing it did not exist, whether it be not evident you might for all that be affected with the same ideas you now are, and consequently have the very same reason to believe its existence that you now can have?

Hyl. I acknowledge it is possible we might perceive all things just as we do now, though there was no matter in the world; neither can I conceive, if there be matter, how it should produce any idea in

our minds. And I do further grant you have entirely satisfied me that it is impossible there should be such a thing as matter in any of the foregoing acceptations. But still I cannot help supposing that there is *matter* in some sense or other. What that is I do not indeed pretend to determine.

52. *Phil.* I do not expect you should define exactly the nature of that unknown being. Only be pleased to tell me whether it is a substance—and if so, whether you can suppose a substance without accidents; or in case you suppose it to have accidents or qualities, I desire you will let me know what those qualities are, at least what is meant by "matter's supporting them"?

Hyl. We have already argued on those points. I have no more to say to them. But, to prevent any further questions, let me tell you I at present understand by "matter" neither substance nor accident, thinking nor extended being, neither cause, instrument, nor occasion, but something entirely unknown, distinct from all these.

53. *Phil.* It seems then you include in your present notion of matter nothing but the general abstract idea of *entity*.

Hyl. Nothing else, save only that I superadd to this general idea the negation of all those particular things, qualities, or ideas that I perceive, imagine, or in anywise apprehend.

54. *Phil.* Pray where do you suppose this unknown matter to exist?

Hyl. Oh Philonous! now you think you have entangled me; for if I say it exists in place, then you will infer that it exists in the mind, since it is agreed that place or extension exists only in the mind; but I am not ashamed to own my ignorance. I know not where it exists; only I am sure it exists not in place. There is a negative answer for you. And you must expect no other to all the questions you put for the future about matter.

55. *Phil.* Since you will not tell me where it exists, be pleased to inform me after what manner you suppose it to exist, or what you mean by its "existence"?

Hyl. It neither thinks nor acts, neither perceives nor is perceived.

56. *Phil.* But what is there positive in your abstracted notion of its existence?

Hyl. Upon a nice observation, I do not find I have any positive notion or meaning at all. I tell you again, I am not ashamed to own my ignorance. I know not what is meant by its existence or how it exists.

57. *Phil.* Continue, good Hylas, to act the same ingenuous part and tell me sincerely whether you can frame a distinct idea of entity in general, prescinded from and exclusive of all thinking and corporeal beings, all particular things whatsoever.

Hyl. Hold, let me think a little—I profess, Philonous, I do not find that I can. At first glance methought I had some dilute and airy notion of pure entity in abstract, but, upon closer attention, it has quite vanished out of sight. The more I think on it, the more am I confirmed in my prudent resolution of giving none but negative answers and not pretending to the least degree of any positive knowledge or conception of matter, its *where*, its *how*, its *entity*, or anything belonging to it.

58. *Phil.* When, therefore, you speak of the existence of matter, you have not any notion in your mind?

Hyl. None at all.

59. *Phil.* Pray tell me if the case stands not thus: at first, from a belief of material substance, you would have it that the immediate objects existed without the mind; then, that they are archetypes; then, causes; next, instruments; then, occasions: lastly, *something in general*, which being interpreted proves *nothing*. So matter comes to nothing. What think you, Hylas, is not this a fair summary of your whole proceeding?

Hyl. Be that as it will, yet I still insist upon it, that our not being able to conceive a thing is no argument against its existence.

60. *Phil.* That from a cause, effect, operation, sign, or other circumstance there may reasonably be inferred the existence of a thing not immediately perceived; and that it were absurd for any man to argue against the existence of that thing, from his having no direct and positive notion of it, I freely own. But where there is nothing of all this, where neither reason nor revelation induces us to believe the existence of a thing, where we have not even a relative notion of it, where an abstraction is made from perceiving and being perceived, from spirit and idea, lastly, where there is not so much as the most inadequate or faint idea pretended to, I will not, indeed, thence conclude against the reality of any notion or existence of anything; but my infer-

ence shall be that you mean nothing at all, that you employ words to no manner of purpose, without any design or signification whatsoever. And I leave it to you to consider how mere jargon should be treated.

Hyl. To deal frankly with you, Philonous, your arguments seem in themselves unanswerable, but they have not so great an effect on me as to produce that entire conviction, that hearty acquiescence, which attends demonstration. I find myself still relapsing into an obscure surmise of I know not what—*matter*.

61. *Phil.* But are you not sensible, Hylas, that two things must concur to take away all scruple and work a plenary assent in the mind? Let a visible object be set in never so clear a light, yet, if there is any imperfection in the sight, or if the eye is not directed toward it, it will not be distinctly seen. And though a demonstration be never so well grounded and fairly proposed, yet, if there is withal a stain of prejudice or a wrong bias on the understanding, can it be expected on a sudden to perceive clearly and adhere firmly to the truth? No, there is need of time and pains: the attention must be awakened and detained by a frequent repetition of the same thing placed oft in the same, oft in different lights. I have said it already, and find I must still repeat and inculcate, that it is an unaccountable license you take in pretending to maintain you know not what, for you know not what reason, to you know not what purpose. Can this be paralleled in any art or science, any sect or profession of men? Or is there anything so barefacedly groundless and unreasonable to be met with even in the lowest of common conversation? But, perhaps, you will still say, matter may exist, though at the same time you neither know what is meant by "matter" or by its "existence." This indeed is surprising, and the more so because it is altogether voluntary, you not being led to it by any one reason, for I challenge you to show me that thing in nature which needs matter to explain or account for it.

Hyl. The reality of things cannot be maintained without supposing the existence of matter. And is not this, think you, a good reason why I should be earnest in its defense?

62. *Phil.* The reality of things! What things, sensible or intelligible?

Hyl. Sensible things.

63. *Phil.* My glove, for example?

Hyl. That or any other thing perceived by the senses.

64. *Phil.* But to fix on some particular thing, is it not a sufficient evidence to me of the existence of this *glove* that I see it and feel it and wear it? Or, if this will not do, how is it possible I should be assured of the reality of this thing which I actually see in this place by supposing that some unknown thing, which I never did or can see, exists after an unknown manner, in an unknown place, or in no place at all? How can the supposed reality of that which is intangible be a proof that anything tangible really exists? Or of that which is invisible, that any visible thing or, in general, of anything which is imperceptible, that a perceptible exists? Do but explain this and I shall think nothing too hard for you.

Hyl. Upon the whole, I am content to own the existence of matter is highly improbable; but the direct and absolute impossibility of it does not appear to me.

65. *Phil.* But granting matter to be possible, yet, upon that account merely, it can have no more claim to existence than a golden mountain or a centaur.

Hyl. I acknowledge it, but still you do not deny it is possible; and that which is possible, for aught you know, may actually exist.

66. *Phil.* I deny it to be possible; and have, if I mistake not, evidently proved, from your own concessions, that it is not. In the common sense of the word "matter," is there any more implied than an extended, solid, figured, movable substance existing without the mind? And have not you acknowledged, over and over, that you have seen evident reason for denying the possibility of such a substance?

Hyl. True, but that is only one sense of the term "matter."

67. *Phil.* But is it not the only proper genuine received sense? And if matter in such a sense be proved impossible, may it not be thought with good grounds absolutely impossible? Else how could anything be proved impossible? Or, indeed, how could there be any proof at all one way or other to a man who takes the liberty to unsettle and change the common signification of words?

Hyl. I thought philosophers might be allowed to speak more accurately than the vulgar, and were not always confined to the common acceptation of a term.

68. *Phil.* But this now mentioned is the common received sense among philosophers themselves. But, not to insist on that, have you not been allowed to take matter in what sense you pleased? And have you not used this privilege in the utmost extent, sometimes entirely changing, at others leaving out or putting into the definition of it whatever, for the present, best served your design, contrary to all the known rules of reason and logic? And has not this shifting, unfair method of yours spun out our dispute to an unnecessary length, matter having been particularly examined and by your own confession refuted in each of those senses? And can any more be required to prove the absolute impossibility of a thing than the proving it impossible in every particular sense that either you or anyone else understands it in?

Hyl. But I am not so thoroughly satisfied that you have proved the impossibility of matter in the last most obscure abstracted and indefinite sense.

69. *Phil.* When is a thing shown to be impossible?

Hyl. When a repugnancy is demonstrated between the ideas comprehended in its definition.

70. *Phil.* But where there are no ideas, there no repugnancy can be demonstrated between ideas?

Hyl. I agree with you.

71. *Phil.* Now, in that which you call the obscure indefinite sense of the word "matter," it is plain, by your own confession, there was included no idea at all, no sense except an unknown sense, which is the same thing as none. You are not, therefore, to expect I should prove a repugnancy between ideas where there are no ideas, or the impossibility of matter taken in an *unknown* sense, that is, no sense at all. My business was only to show you meant *nothing;* and this you were brought to own. So that, in all your various senses, you have been shown either to mean nothing at all or, if anything, an absurdity. And if this be not sufficient to prove the impossibility of a thing, I desire you will let me know what is.

Hyl. I acknowledge you have proved that matter is impossible, nor do I see what more can be said in defense of it. But, at the same time that I give up this, I suspect all my other notions. For surely none could be more seemingly evident than this once was; and yet it now seems as false and absurd as ever it did true before. But I think we have discussed the point sufficiently for the present. The remaining part of the day I would willingly spend in running over in my thoughts the several heads of this morning's conversation, and tomorrow shall be glad to meet you here again about the same time.

72. *Phil.* I will not fail to attend you.

The Third Dialogue

1. *Philonous.* Tell me, Hylas, what are the fruits of yesterday's meditation? Has it confirmed you in the same mind you were in at parting, or have you since seen cause to change your opinion?

Hylas. Truly my opinion is that all our opinions are alike vain and uncertain. What we approve today, we condemn tomorrow. We keep a stir about knowledge and spend our lives in pursuit of it, when, alas! we know nothing all the while; nor do I think it possible for us ever to know anything in this life. Our faculties are too narrow and too few. Nature certainly never intended us for speculation.

2. *Phil.* What! say you we can know nothing, Hylas?

Hyl. There is not that single thing in the world whereof we can know the real nature, or what it is in itself.

3. *Phil.* Will you tell me I do not really know what fire or water is?

Hyl. You may indeed know that fire appears hot, and water fluid; but this is no more than knowing what sensations are produced in your own mind upon the application of fire and water to your organs of sense. Their internal constitution, their true and real nature, you are utterly in the dark as to *that*.

4. *Phil.* Do I not know this to be a real stone that I stand on, and that which I see before my eyes to be a real tree?

Hyl. Know? No, it is impossible you or any man alive should know it. All you know is that you have such a certain idea or appearance in your own mind. But what is this to the real tree or stone? I tell you that color, figure, and hardness, which you perceive, are not the real natures of those things, or in the least like them. The same may be said of all other real things or corporeal substances which compose the world. They have, none of them, anything in themselves, like those sensible qualities by us perceived. We should not, therefore, pretend to affirm or know anything of them, as they are in their own nature.

5. *Phil.* But surely, Hylas, I can distinguish gold, for example, from iron; and how could this be if I knew not what either truly was?

Hyl. Believe me, Philonous, you can only distinguish between your own ideas. That yellowness, that weight, and other sensible qualities, think you they are really in the gold? They are only relative to the senses and have no absolute existence in nature. And in pretending to distinguish the species of real things by the appearances in your mind, you may perhaps act as wisely as he that should conclude two men were of a different species because their clothes were not of the same color.

6. *Phil.* It seems, then, we are altogether put off with the appearances of things, and those false ones, too. The very meat I eat, and the cloth I wear, have nothing in them like what I see and feel.

Hyl. Even so.

7. *Phil.* But is it not strange the whole world should be thus imposed on and so foolish as to believe their senses? And yet I know not how it is, but men eat, and drink, and sleep, and perform all the offices of life as comfortably and conveniently as if they really knew the things they are conversant about.

Hyl. They do so; but you know ordinary practice does not require a nicety of speculative knowledge. Hence the vulgar retain their mistakes, and for all that make a shift to bustle through the affairs of life. But philosophers know better things.

8. *Phil.* You mean they know that they *know nothing*.

Hyl. That is the very top and perfection of human knowledge.

9. *Phil.* But are you all this while in earnest, Hylas; and are you seriously persuaded that you know nothing real in the world? Suppose you are going to write, would you not call for pen, ink, and paper, like another man; and do you not know what it is you call for?

Hyl. How often must I tell you that I know not the real nature of any one thing in the universe? I may indeed upon occasion make use of pen, ink, and paper. But what any one of them is in its own true nature, I declare positively I know not. And the same is true with regard to every other corporeal thing. And what is more, we are not only ignorant of the true and real nature of things, but even of their existence. It cannot be denied that we perceive such certain appearances or ideas, but it cannot be concluded from thence that bodies really exist. Nay, now I think on it, I must, agreeably to my former concessions, further declare that it is impossible any real corporeal thing should exist in nature.

10. *Phil.* You amaze me. Was ever anything more wild and extravagant than the notions you now maintain? And is it not evident you are led into all these extravagances by the belief of *material substance?* This makes you dream of those unknown natures in everything. It is this occasions your distinguishing between the reality and sensible appearances of things. It is to this you are indebted for being ignorant of what everybody else knows perfectly well. Nor is this all: you are not only ignorant of the true nature of everything, but you know not whether any thing really exists or whether there are any true natures at all, forasmuch as you attribute to your material beings an absolute or external existence wherein you suppose their reality consists. And as you are forced in the end to acknowledge such an existence means either a direct repugnancy or nothing at all, it follows that you are obliged to pull down your own hypothesis of material substance and positively to deny the real existence of any part of the universe. And so you are plunged into the deepest and most deplorable skepticism that ever man was. Tell me, Hylas, is it not as I say?

Hyl. I agree with you. "Material substance" was no more than a hypothesis, and a false and groundless one, too. I will no longer spend my breath in defense of it. But whatever hypothesis you advance or whatsoever scheme of things you introduce in its stead, I doubt not it will appear every whit as false; let me but be allowed to question you upon it. That is, suffer me to serve you in your own kind, and I warrant it shall conduct you through as many perplexities and contradictions to the very same state of skepticism that I myself am in at present.

11. *Phil.* I assure you, Hylas, I do not pretend to frame any hypothesis at all. I am of a vulgar cast, simple enough to believe my senses and leave things as I find them. To be plain, it is my opinion that the real things are those very things I see and feel, and perceive by my senses. These I know and, finding they answer all the necessities and purposes of life, have no reason to be solicitous about any

other unknown beings. A piece of sensible bread, for instance, would stay my stomach better than ten thousand times as much of that insensible, unintelligible real bread you speak of. It is likewise my opinion that colors and other sensible qualities are on the objects. I cannot for my life help thinking that snow is white, and fire hot. You, indeed, who by "snow" and "fire" mean certain external, unperceived, unperceiving substances are in the right to deny whiteness or heat to be affections inherent in them. But I who understand by those words the things I see and feel am obliged to think like other folks. And as I am no skeptic with regard to the nature of things, so neither am I as to their existence. That a thing should be really perceived by my senses and at the same time not really exist is to me a plain contradiction, since I cannot prescind or abstract, even in thought, the existence of a sensible thing from its being perceived. Wood, stones, fire, water, flesh, iron, and the like things which I name and discourse of are things that I know. And I should not have known them but that I perceived them by my senses; and things perceived by the senses are immediately perceived; and things immediately perceived are ideas; and ideas cannot exist without the mind; their existence therefore consists in being perceived; when, therefore, they are actually perceived, there can be no doubt of their existence. Away then with all that skepticism, all those ridiculous philosophical doubts. What a jest is it for a philosopher to question the existence of sensible things till he has it proved to him from the veracity of God, or to pretend our knowledge in this point falls short of intuition or demonstration! I might as well doubt of my own being as of the being of those things I actually see and feel.

Hyl. Not so fast, Philonous: You say you cannot conceive how sensible things should exist without the mind. Do you not?

12. *Phil.* I do.

Hyl. Supposing you were annihilated, cannot you conceive it possible that things perceivable by sense may still exist?

13. *Phil.* I can, but then it must be in another mind. When I deny sensible things an existence out of the mind, I do not mean my mind in particular, but all minds. Now it is plain they have an existence exterior to my mind, since I find them by experience to be independent of it. There is therefore some

other mind wherein they exist during the intervals between the times of my perceiving them, as likewise they did before my birth, and would do after my supposed annihilation. And as the same is true with regard to all other finite created spirits, it necessarily follows there is an *omnipresent external Mind* which knows and comprehends all things, and exhibits them to our view in such a manner and according to such rules as He Himself has ordained and are by us termed the "laws of nature."

Hyl. Answer me, Philonous. Are all our ideas perfectly inert beings? Or have they any agency included in them?

14. *Phil.* They are altogether passive and inert.

Hyl. And is not God an agent, a being purely active?

15. *Phil.* I acknowledge it.

Hyl. No idea, therefore, can be like unto or represent the nature of God.

16. *Phil.* It cannot.

Hyl. Since, therefore, you have no idea of the mind of God, how can you conceive it possible that things should exist in His mind? Or, if you can conceive the mind of God without having an idea of it, why may not I be allowed to conceive the existence of matter, notwithstanding I have no idea of it?

17. *Phil.* As to your first question: I own I have properly no *idea* either of God or any other spirit; for these, being active, cannot be represented by things perfectly inert as our ideas are. I do nevertheless know that I, who am a spirit or thinking substance, exist as certainly as I know my ideas exist. Further, I know what I mean by the terms "I" and "myself"; and I know this immediately or intuitively, though I do not perceive it as I perceive a triangle, a color, or a sound. The mind, spirit, or soul is that indivisible unextended thing which thinks, acts, and perceives. I say "indivisible," because unextended; and "unextended," because extended, figured, movable things are ideas; and that which perceives ideas, which thinks and wills, is plainly itself no idea, nor like an idea. Ideas are things inactive and perceived. And spirits a sort of beings altogether different from them. I do not therefore say my soul is an idea, or like an idea. However, taking the word "idea" in a large sense, my soul may be said to furnish me with an idea, that is, an image or likeness of God, though indeed extremely inadequate. For all the notion I have of God is ob-

tained by reflecting on my own soul, heightening its powers, and removing its imperfections. I have, therefore, though not an inactive idea, yet in *myself* some sort of an active thinking image of the Deity. And though I perceive Him not by sense, yet I have a notion of Him, or know Him by reflection and reasoning. My own mind and my own ideas I have an immediate knowledge of; and, by the help of these, do mediately apprehend the possibility of the existence of other spirits and ideas. Further, from my own being, and from the dependency I find in myself and my ideas, I do, by an act of reason, necessarily infer the existence of a God and of all created things in the mind of God. So much for your first question. For the second: I suppose by this time you can answer it yourself. For you neither perceive matter objectively, as you do an inactive being or idea, nor know it, as you do yourself by a reflex act; neither do you mediately apprehend it by similitude of the one or the other, nor yet collect it by reasoning from that which you know immediately. All which makes the case of *matter* widely different from that of the *Deity*.

Hyl. You say your own soul supplies you with some sort of an idea or image of God. But, at the same time, you acknowledge you have, properly speaking, no idea of your own soul. You even affirm that spirits are a sort of beings altogether different from ideas. Consequently, that no idea can be like a spirit. We have, therefore, no idea of any spirit. You admit nevertheless that there is spiritual substance, although you have no idea of it, while you deny there can be such a thing as material substance, because you have no notion or idea of it. Is this fair dealing? To act consistently, you must either admit matter or reject spirit. What say you to this?

18. *Phil.* I say, in the first place, that I do not deny the existence of material substance merely because I have no notion of it, but because the notion of it is inconsistent, or, in other words, because it is repugnant that there should be a notion of it. Many things, for aught I know, may exist whereof neither I nor any other man has or can have any idea or notion whatsoever. But then those things must be possible, that is, nothing inconsistent must be included in their definition. I say, secondly, that, although we believe things to exist which we do not perceive, yet we may not believe that any particular thing exists without some reason for such belief; but I have no

reason for believing the existence of matter. I have no immediate intuition thereof, neither can I immediately from my sensations, ideas, notions, actions, or passions infer an unthinking, unperceiving, inactive substance, either by probable deduction or necessary consequence. Whereas the being of my self, that is, my own soul, mind, or thinking principle, I evidently know by reflection. You will forgive me if I repeat the same things in answer to the same objections. In the very notion or definition of "material substance" there is included a manifest repugnance and inconsistency. But this cannot be said of the notion of spirit. That ideas should exist in what does not perceive, or be produced by what does not act, is repugnant. But it is no repugnancy to say that a perceiving thing should be the subject of ideas, or an active thing the cause of them. It is granted we have neither an immediate evidence nor a demonstrative knowledge of the existence of other finite spirits, but it will not thence follow that such spirits are on a foot with material substances, if to suppose the one be inconsistent, and it be not inconsistent to suppose the other; if the one can be inferred by no argument, and there is a probability for the other; if we see signs and effects indicating distinct finite agents like ourselves, and see no sign or symptom whatever that leads to a rational belief of matter. I say, lastly, that I have a notion of spirit, though I have not, strictly speaking, an idea of it. I do not perceive it as an idea, or by means of an idea, but know it by reflection.

Hyl. Notwithstanding all you have said, to me it seems that, according to your own way of thinking, and in consequence of your own principles, it should follow that you are only a system of floating ideas without any substance to support them. Words are not to be used without a meaning. And, as there is no more meaning in *spiritual* substance than in *material* substance, the one is to be exploded as well as the other.

19. *Phil.* How often must I repeat that I know or am conscious of my own being, and that I *myself* am not my ideas, but somewhat else, a thinking, active principle that perceives, knows, wills, and operates about ideas. I know that I, one and the same self, perceive both colors and sounds, that a color cannot perceive a sound, nor a sound a color, that I am therefore one individual principle distinct from color and sound, and, for the same reason, from all

other sensible things and inert ideas. But I am not in like manner conscious either of the existence or essence of matter. On the contrary, I know that nothing inconsistent can exist, and that the existence of matter implies an inconsistency. Further, I know what I mean when I affirm that there is a spiritual substance or support of ideas, that is, that a spirit knows and perceives ideas. But I do not know what is meant when it is said that an unperceiving substance has inherent in it and supports either ideas or the archetypes of ideas. There is, therefore, upon the whole no parity of case between spirit and matter.

Hyl. I own myself satisfied in this point. But do you in earnest think the real existence of sensible things consists in their being actually perceived? If so, how comes it that all mankind distinguish between them? Ask the first man you meet, and he shall tell you, "to be perceived" is one thing, and "to exist" is another.

20. *Phil.* I am content, Hylas, to appeal to the common sense of the world for the truth of my notion. Ask the gardener why he thinks yonder cherry tree exists in the garden, and he shall tell you, because he sees and feels it; in a word, because he perceives it by his senses. Ask him why he thinks an orange tree not to be there, and he shall tell you, because he does not perceive it. What he perceives by sense, that he terms a real being and says it "is" or "exists"; but that which is not perceivable, the same, he says, has no being.

Hyl. Yes, Philonous, I grant the existence of a sensible thing consists in being perceivable, but not in being actually perceived.

21. *Phil.* And what is perceivable but an idea? And can an idea exist without being actually perceived? These are points long since agreed between us.

Hyl. But be your opinion never so true, yet surely you will not deny it is shocking and contrary to the common sense of men. Ask the fellow whether yonder tree has an existence out of his mind; what answer think you he would make?

22. *Phil.* The same that I should myself, to wit, that it does exist out of his mind. But then to a Christian it cannot surely be shocking to say, the real tree, existing without his mind, is truly known and comprehended by (that is, *exists in*) the infinite mind of God. Probably he may not at first glance be aware of the direct and immediate proof there is of this, in-

asmuch as the very being of a tree, or any other sensible thing, implies a mind wherein it is. But the point itself he cannot deny. The question between the materialists and me is not whether things have a *real* existence out of the mind of this or that person, but, whether they have an *absolute* existence, distinct from being perceived by God, and exterior to all minds. This, indeed, some heathens and philosophers have affirmed, but whoever entertains notions of the Deity suitable to the Holy Scriptures will be of another opinion.

Hyl. But, according to your notions, what difference is there between real things and chimeras formed by the imagination or the visions of a dream, since they are all equally in the mind?

23. *Phil.* The ideas formed by the imagination are faint and indistinct; they have, besides, an entire dependence on the will. But the ideas perceived by sense, that is, real things, are more vivid and clear, and, being imprinted on the mind by a spirit distinct from us, have not the like dependence on our will. There is, therefore, no danger of confounding these with the foregoing, and there is as little of confounding them with the visions of a dream, which are dim, irregular, and confused. And though they should happen to be never so lively and natural, yet, by their not being connected and of a piece with the preceding and subsequent transaction of our lives, they might easily be distinguished from realities. In short, by whatever method you distinguish *things* from *chimeras* on your own scheme, the same, it is evident, will hold also upon mind. For it must be, I presume, by some perceived difference, and I am not for depriving you of any one thing that you perceive.

Hyl. But still, Philonous, you hold there is nothing in the world but spirits and ideas. And this you must needs acknowledge sounds very oddly.

24. *Phil.* I own the word "idea," not being commonly used for "thing," sounds something out of the way. My reason for using it was because a necessary relation to the mind is understood to be implied by the term; and it is now commonly used by philosophers to denote the immediate objects of the understanding. But however oddly the proposition may sound in words, yet it includes nothing so very strange or shocking in its sense, which in effect amounts to no more than this, to wit, that there are only things perceiving and things perceived, or

that every unthinking being is necessarily, and from the very nature of its existence, perceived by some mind, if not by any finite created mind, yet certainly by the infinite mind of God, in whom "we live, and move, and have our being." Is this as strange as to say the sensible qualities are not on the object or that we cannot be sure of the existence of things, or know anything of their real natures, though we both see and feel them and perceive them by all our senses?

Hyl. And, in consequence of this, must we not think there are no such things as physical or corporeal causes, but that a spirit is the immediate cause of all the *phenomena* in nature? Can there be anything more extravagant than this?

25. *Phil.* Yes, it is infinitely more extravagant to say a thing which is inert operates on the mind, and which is unperceiving is the cause of our perceptions. Besides, that which to you I know not for what reason seems so extravagant is no more than the Holy Scriptures assert in a hundred places. In them God is represented as the sole and immediate Author of all those effects which some heathens and philosophers are wont to ascribe to Nature, Matter, Fate, or the like unthinking principle. This is so much the constant language of Scripture that it were needless to confirm it by citations.

Hyl. You are not aware, Philonous, that, in making God the immediate Author of all the motions in nature, you make Him the Author of murder, sacrilege, adultery, and the like heinous sins.

26. *Phil.* In answer to that I observe, first, that the imputation of guilt is the same whether a person commits an action with or without an instrument. In case, therefore, you suppose God to act by the mediation of an instrument or occasion called "matter," you as truly make Him the Author of sin as I, who think Him the immediate agent in all those operations vulgarly ascribed to Nature. I further observe that sin or moral turpitude does not consist in the outward physical action or motion, but in the internal deviation of the will from the laws of reason and religion. This is plain, in that the killing an enemy in the battle or putting a criminal legally to death is not thought sinful, though the outward act be the very same with that in the case of murder. Since, therefore, sin does not consist in the physical action, the making God an immediate cause of all such actions is not making Him the Author of sin.

Lastly, I have nowhere said that God is the only agent who produces all the motions in bodies. It is true I have denied there are any other agents besides spirits, but this is very consistent with allowing to thinking rational beings, in the production of motions, the use of limited powers, ultimately, indeed, derived from God but immediately under the direction of their own wills, which is sufficient to entitle them to all the guilt of their actions.

Hyl. But the denying matter, Philonous, or corporeal substance, there is the point. You can never persuade me that this is not repugnant to the universal sense of mankind. Were our dispute to be determined by most voices, I am confident you would give up the point without gathering the votes.

27. *Phil.* I wish both our opinions were fairly stated and submitted to the judgment of men who had plain common sense, without the prejudices of a learned education. Let me be represented as one who trusts his senses, who thinks he knows the things he sees and feels, and entertains no doubts of their existence; and you fairly set forth with all your doubts, your paradoxes, and your skepticism about you, and I shall willingly acquiesce in the determination of any indifferent person. That there is no substance wherein ideas can exist besides spirit is to me evident, and that the objects immediately perceived are ideas is on all hands agreed. And that sensible qualities are objects immediately perceived no one can deny. It is therefore evident there can be no substratum of those qualities but spirit, in which they exist, not by way of mode or property, but as a thing perceived in that which perceives it. I deny, therefore, that there is any unthinking substratum of the objects of sense, and in that acceptation that there is any material substance. But if by "material substance" is meant only sensible body, that which is seen and felt (and the unphilosophical part of the world, I dare say, mean no more), then I am more certain of matter's existence than you or any other philosopher pretend to be. If there be anything which makes the generality of mankind averse from the notions I espouse, it is a misapprehension that I deny the reality of sensible things; but as it is you who are guilty of that and not I, it follows that in truth their aversion is against your notions and not mine. I do therefore assert that I am as certain as of my own being that there are bodies or corporeal substances (meaning the things I perceive by my senses), and that, granting this, the bulk of mankind will take no thought about, nor think themselves at all concerned in the fate of, those unknown natures and philosophical quiddities which some men are so fond of.

Hyl. What say you to this? Since, according to you, men judge of the reality of things by their senses, how can a man be mistaken in thinking the moon a plain lucid surface, about a foot in diameter, or a square tower, seen at a distance, round, or an oar, with one end in the water, crooked?

28. *Phil.* He is not mistaken with regard to the ideas he actually perceives, but in the inferences he makes from his present perceptions. Thus, in the case of the oar, what he immediately perceives by sight is certainly crooked, and so far he is in the right. But if he thence conclude that upon taking the oar out of the water he shall perceive the same crookedness, or that it would affect his touch as crooked things are wont to do, in that he is mistaken. In like manner, if he shall conclude, from what he perceives in one station, that, in case he advances toward the moon or tower, he should still be affected with the like ideas, he is mistaken. But his mistake lies not in what he perceives immediately and at present (it being a manifest contradiction to suppose he should err in respect of that), but in the wrong judgment he makes concerning the ideas he apprehends to be connected with those immediately perceived, or, concerning the ideas, that from what he perceives at present he imagines would be perceived in other circumstances. The case is the same with regard to the Copernican system. We do not here perceive any motion of the earth, but it were erroneous thence to conclude that, in case we were placed at as great a distance from that as we are now from the other planets, we should not then perceive its motion.

Hyl. I understand you and must needs own you say things plausible enough, but give me leave to put you in mind of one thing. Pray, Philonous, were you not formerly as positive that matter existed as you are now that it does not?

29. *Phil.* I was. But here lies the difference. Before, my positiveness was founded, without examination, upon prejudice, but now, after inquiry, upon evidence.

Hyl. After all, it seems our dispute is rather about words than things. We agree in the thing, but differ in the name. That we are affected with ideas from without is evident; and it is no less evident that there must be (I will not say archetypes, but) powers without the mind corresponding to those ideas. And as these powers cannot subsist by themselves, there is some subject of them necessarily to be admitted, which I call "matter," and you call "spirit." This is all the difference.

30. *Phil.* Pray, Hylas, is that powerful being, or subject of powers, extended?

Hyl. It has not extension, but it has the power to raise in you the idea of extension.

31. *Phil.* It is therefore itself unextended?

Hyl. I grant it.

32. *Phil.* Is it not also active?

Hyl. Without doubt; otherwise, how could we attribute powers to it?

33. *Phil.* Now let me ask you two questions: *First,* whether it be agreeable to the usage either of philosophers or others to give the name "matter" to an unextended active being? And, secondly, whether it be not ridiculously absurd to misapply names contrary to the common use of language?

Hyl. Well then, let it not be called "matter," since you will have it so, but some "third nature," distinct from matter and spirit. For what reason is there why you should call it spirit? Does not the notion of spirit imply that it is thinking as well as active and unextended?

34. *Phil.* My reason is this: because I have a mind to have some notion or meaning in what I say, but I have no notion of any action distinct from volition, neither can I conceive volition to be anywhere but in a spirit; therefore, when I speak of an active being I am obliged to mean a spirit. Besides, what can be plainer than that a thing which has no ideas in itself cannot impart them to me; and, if it has ideas, surely it must be a spirit. To make you comprehend the point still more clearly, if it be possible: I assert as well as you that, since we are affected from without, we must allow powers to be without, in a being distinct from ourselves. So far we are agreed. But then we differ as to the kind of this powerful being. I will have it to be spirit, you matter or I know not what (I may add, too, you know not what) third nature. Thus I prove it to be spirit. From the effects I see produced I conclude there are actions; and because actions, volitions; and because there are volitions, there must be a will. Again, the things

I perceive must have an existence, they or their archetypes, out of my mind; but, being ideas, neither they nor their archetypes can exist otherwise than in an understanding, there is therefore an understanding. But will and understanding constitute in the strictest sense a mind or spirit. The powerful cause, therefore, of my ideas is in strict propriety of speech a *spirit*.

Hyl. And now I warrant you think you have made the point very clear, little suspecting that what you advance leads directly to a contradiction. Is it not an absurdity to imagine any imperfection in God?

35. *Phil.* Without a doubt.

Hyl. To suffer pain is an imperfection?

36. *Phil.* It is.

Hyl. Are we not sometimes affected with pain and uneasiness by some other being?

37. *Phil.* We are.

Hyl. And have you not said that being is a spirit, and is not that spirit God?

38. *Phil.* I grant it.

Hyl. But you have asserted that whatever ideas we perceive from without are in the mind which affects us. The ideas, therefore, of pain and uneasiness are in God, or, in other words, God suffers pain; that is to say, there is an imperfection in the divine nature, which, you acknowledge, was absurd. So you are caught in a plain contradiction.

39. *Phil.* That God knows or understands all things, and that He knows, among other things, what pain is, even every sort of painful sensation, and what it is for His creatures to suffer pain, I make no question. But that God, though He knows and sometimes causes painful sensations in us, can Himself suffer pain I positively deny. We, who are limited and dependent spirits, are liable to impressions of sense, the effects of an external agent, which, being produced against our wills, are sometimes painful and uneasy. But God, whom no external being can affect, who perceives nothing by sense as we do, whose will is absolute and independent, causing all things, and liable to be thwarted or resisted by nothing, it is evident such a Being as this can suffer nothing, nor be affected with any painful sensation or, indeed, any sensation at all. We are chained to a body; that is to say, our perceptions are connected with corporeal motions. By the law of our nature we are affected upon every alteration in

the nervous parts of our sensible body; which sensible body, rightly considered, is nothing but a complexion of such qualities or ideas as have no existence distinct from being perceived by a mind; so that this connection of sensations with corporeal motions means no more than a correspondence in the order of nature between two sets of ideas, or things immediately perceivable. But God is a pure spirit, disengaged from all such sympathy or natural ties. No corporeal motions are attended with the sensations of pain or pleasure in His mind. To know everything knowable is certainly a perfection, but to endure or suffer or feel anything by sense is an imperfection. The former, I say, agrees to God, but not the latter. God knows or has ideas, but His ideas are not conveyed to Him by sense, as ours are. Your not distinguishing where there is so manifest a difference makes you fancy you see an absurdity where there is none.

Hyl. But all this while you have not considered that the quantity of matter has been demonstrated to be proportional to the gravity of bodies. And what can withstand demonstration?

40. *Phil.* Let me see how you demonstrate that point.

Hyl. I lay it down for a principle that the moments or quantities of motion in bodies are in a direct compounded reason of the velocities and quantities of matter contained in them. Hence, where the velocities are equal, it follows the moments are directly as the quantity of matter in each. But it is found by experience that all bodies (bating the small inequalities arising from the resistance of the air) descend with an equal velocity; the motion therefore of descending bodies, and consequently their gravity, which is the cause or principle of that motion, is proportional to the quantity of matter, which was to be demonstrated.

41. *Phil.* You lay it down as a self-evident principle that the quantity of motion in any body is proportional to the velocity and matter taken together; and this is made use of to prove a proposition from whence the existence of matter is inferred. Pray is not this arguing in a circle?

Hyl. In the premise I only mean that the motion is proportional to the velocity, jointly with the extension and solidity.

42. *Phil.* But allowing this to be true, yet it will not thence follow that gravity is proportional to

matter in your philosophic sense of the word, except you take it for granted that unknown substratum, or whatever else you call it, is proportional to those sensible qualities which to suppose is plainly begging the question. That there is magnitude and solidity or resistance perceived by sense I readily grant, as likewise, that gravity may be proportional to those qualities I will not dispute. But that either these qualities as perceived by us, or the powers producing them, do exist in a *material substratum*— this is what I deny, and you, indeed, affirm but, notwithstanding your demonstration, have not yet proved.

Hyl. I shall insist no longer on that point. Do you think, however, you shall persuade me the natural philosophers have been dreaming all this while? Pray what becomes of all their hypotheses and explications of the phenomena which suppose the existence of matter?

43. *Phil.* What mean you, Hylas, by the "phenomena"?

Hyl. I mean the appearances which I perceive by my senses.

44. *Phil.* And the appearances perceived by sense, are they not ideas?

Hyl. I have told you so a hundred times.

45. *Phil.* Therefore, to explain the phenomena is to show how we come to be affected with ideas in that manner and order wherein they are imprinted on our senses. Is it not?

Hyl. It is.

46. *Phil.* Now, if you can prove that any philosopher has explained the production of any one idea in our minds by the help of *matter*, I shall forever acquiesce and look on all that has been said against it as nothing; but if you cannot, it is vain to urge the explication of phenomena. That a being endowed with knowledge and will should produce or exhibit ideas is easily understood. But that a being which is utterly destitute of these faculties should be able to produce ideas, or in any sort to affect an intelligence, this I can never understand. This I say, though we had some positive conception of matter, though we knew its qualities and could comprehend its existence, would yet be so far from explaining things that it is itself the most inexplicable thing in the world. And yet, for all this, it will not follow that philosophers have been doing nothing; for by observing and reasoning upon the connection of

ideas, they discover the laws and methods of nature, which is a part of knowledge both useful and entertaining.

Hyl. After all, can it be supposed God would deceive all mankind? Do you imagine He would have induced the whole world to believe the being of matter if there was no such thing?

47. *Phil.* That every epidemical opinion arising from prejudice, or passion, or thoughtlessness may be imputed to God, as the Author of it, I believe you will not affirm. Whatsoever opinion we father on Him, it must be either because He has discovered it to us by supernatural revelation or because it is so evident to our natural faculties, which were framed and given us by God, that it is impossible we should withhold our assent from it. But where is the revelation? Or where is the evidence that extorts the belief of matter? Nay, how does it appear that matter, taken for something distinct from what we perceive by our senses is thought to exist by all mankind, or, indeed, by any except a few philosophers who do not know what they would be at? Your question supposes these points are clear; and, when you have cleared them, I shall think myself obliged to give you another answer. In the meantime let it suffice that I tell you I do not suppose God has deceived mankind at all.

Hyl. But the novelty, Philonous, the novelty! There lies the danger. New notions should always be discountenanced; they unsettle men's minds, and nobody knows where they will end.

48. *Phil.* Why the rejecting a notion that has no foundation, either in sense or in reason or in Divine authority, should be thought to unsettle the belief of such opinions as are grounded on all or any of these, I cannot imagine. That innovations in government and religion are dangerous and ought to be discountenanced, I freely own. But is there the like reason why they should be discouraged in philosophy? The making anything known which was unknown before is an innovation in knowledge; and if all such innovations had been forbidden, men would [not] have made a notable progress in the arts and sciences. But it is none of my business to plead for novelties and paradoxes. That the qualities we perceive are not on the objects, that we must not believe our senses, that we know nothing of the real nature of things and can never be assured even of their existence, that real colors and sounds are

nothing but certain unknown figures and motions, that motions are in themselves neither swift nor slow, that there are in bodies absolute extensions without any particular magnitude or figure, that a thing stupid, thoughtless, and inactive operates on a spirit, that the least particle of a body contains innumerable extended parts these are the novelties, these are the strange notions which shock the genuine uncorrupted judgment of all mankind, and, being once admitted, embarrass the mind with endless doubts and difficulties. And it is against these and the like innovations I endeavor to vindicate Common Sense. It is true, in doing this I may, perhaps, be obliged to use some ambages and ways of speech not common. But if my notions are once thoroughly understood, that which is most singular in them will, in effect, be found to amount to no more than this—that it is absolutely impossible and a plain contradiction to suppose any unthinking being should exist without being perceived by a mind. And if this notion be singular, it is a shame it should be so at this time of day and in a Christian country.

Hyl. As for the difficulties other opinions may be liable to, those are out of the question. It is your business to defend your own opinion. Can anything be plainer than that you are for changing all things into ideas? You, I say, who are not ashamed to charge me with skepticism. This is so plain, there is no denying it.

49. *Phil.* You mistake me. I am not for changing things into ideas but rather ideas into things, since those immediate objects of perception, which, according to you, are only appearances of things, I take to be the real things themselves.

Hyl. Things! you may pretend what you please; but it is certain you leave us nothing but the empty forms of things, the outside only which strikes the senses.

50. *Phil.* What you call the empty forms and outside of things seem to me the very things themselves. Nor are they empty or incomplete otherwise than upon your supposition that matter is an essential part of all corporeal things. We both, therefore, agree in this, that we perceive only sensible forms; but herein we differ: you will have them to be empty appearances, I real beings. In short, you do not trust your senses, I do.

Hyl. You say you believe your senses, and seem to applaud yourself that in this you agree with the vulgar. According to you, therefore, the true nature of a thing is discovered by the senses. If so, whence comes that disagreement? Why, is not the same figure, and other sensible qualities, perceived all manner of ways? And why should we use a microscope the better to discover the true nature of a body, if it were discoverable to the naked eye?

51. *Phil.* Strictly speaking, Hylas, we do not see the same object that we feel; neither is the same object perceived by the microscope which was by the naked eye. But in case every variation was thought sufficient to constitute a new kind of individual, the endless number or confusion of names would render language impracticable. Therefore, to avoid this as well as other inconveniences which are obvious upon a little thought, men combine together several ideas, apprehended by divers senses, or by the same sense at different times or in different circumstances, but observed, however, to have some connection in nature, either with respect to coexistence or succession; all which they refer to one name and consider as one thing. Hence it follows that when I examine by my other senses a thing I have seen, it is not in order to understand better the same object which I had perceived by sight, the object of one sense not being perceived by the other senses. And when I look through a microscope, it is not that I may perceive more clearly what I perceived already with my bare eyes, the object perceived by the glass being quite different from the former. But in both cases my aim is only to know what ideas are connected together; and the more a man knows of the connection of ideas, the more he is said to know of the nature of things. What, therefore, if our ideas are variable, what if our senses are not in all circumstances affected with the same appearances? It will not thence follow they are not to be trusted or that they are inconsistent either with themselves or anything else, except it be with your preconceived notion of (I know not what) one single, unchanged, unperceivable, real nature, marked by each name; which prejudice seems to have taken its rise from not rightly understanding the common language of men speaking of several distinct ideas as united into one thing by the mind. And, indeed, there is cause to suspect several erroneous conceits of the philosophers are owing to the same original: while they began to build their schemes not so much on notions as words which were framed by the vulgar merely for convenience and dispatch in the common actions of life, without any regard to speculation.

Hyl. Methinks I apprehend your meaning.

52. *Phil.* It is your opinion the ideas we perceive by our senses are not real things, but images or copies of them. Our knowledge, therefore, is no further real than as our ideas are the true representations of those originals. But as these supposed originals are in themselves unknown, it is impossible to know how far our ideas resemble them, or whether they resemble them at all. We cannot, therefore, be sure we have any real knowledge. Further, as our ideas are perpetually varied, without any change in the supposed real things, it necessarily follows they cannot all be true copies of them, if some are and others are not, it is impossible to distinguish the former from the latter. And this plunges us yet deeper in uncertainty. Again, when we consider the point, we cannot conceive how any idea, or anything like an idea, should have an absolute existence out of a mind, nor consequently, according to you, how there should be any real thing in nature. The result of all which is that we are thrown into the most hopeless and abandoned skepticism. Now give me leave to ask you, *first*, whether your referring ideas to certain absolutely existing unperceived substances, as their originals, be not the source of all this skepticism? *Secondly*, whether you are informed, either by sense or reason, of the existence of those unknown originals? And in case you are not, whether it be not absurd to suppose them? *Thirdly*, whether, upon inquiry, you find there is anything distinctly conceived or meant by the "absolute or external existence of unperceiving substances"; *Lastly*, whether, the premises considered, it be not the wisest way to follow nature, trust your senses, and, laying aside all anxious thought about unknown natures or substances, admit with the vulgar those for real things which are perceived by the senses?

Hyl. For the present I have no inclination to the answering part. I would much rather see how you can get over what follows. Pray, are not the objects perceived by the senses of one likewise perceivable to others present? If there were a hundred more here, they would all see the garden, the trees and flowers, as I see them. But they are not in the same manner affected with the ideas I frame in my imagination. Does not this make a difference between the former sort of objects and the latter?

53. *Phil.* I grant it does. Nor have I ever denied a difference between the objects of sense and those of imagination. But what would you infer from thence? You cannot say that sensible objects exist unperceived because they are perceived by many.

Hyl. I own I can make nothing of that objection, but it has led me into another. Is it not your opinion that by our senses we perceive only the ideas existing in our minds?

54. *Phil.* It is.

Hyl. But the same idea which is in my mind cannot be in yours or in any other mind. Does it not, therefore, follow from your principles that no two can see the same thing? And is not this highly absurd?

55. *Phil.* If the term "same" be taken in the vulgar acceptation, it is certain (and not at all repugnant to the principles I maintain) that different persons may perceive the same thing, or the same thing or idea exist in different minds. Words are of arbitrary imposition; and since men are used to apply the word "same" where no distinction or variety is perceived, and I do not pretend to alter their perceptions, it follows that, as men have said before, *several saw the same thing*, so they may, upon like occasions, still continue to use the same phrase without any deviation either from propriety of language or the truth of things. But if the term "same" be used in the acceptation of philosophers who pretend to an abstracted notion of identity, then, according to their sundry definitions of this notion (for it is not yet agreed wherein that philosophic identity consists), it may or may not be possible for divers persons to perceive the same thing. But whether philosophers shall think fit to call a thing the "same" or no is, I conceive, of small importance. Let us suppose several men together, all endued with the same faculties, and consequently affected in like sort by their senses, and who had yet never known the use of language; they would without question agree in their perceptions. Though perhaps, when they came to the use of speech, some regarding the uniformness of what was perceived might call it the "same" thing; others, especially regarding the diversity of persons who perceived, might choose the denomi-

nation of "different" things. But who sees not that all the dispute is about a word, to wit, whether what is perceived by different persons may yet have the term "same" applied to it? Or suppose a house whose walls or outward shell remaining unaltered, the chambers are all pulled down, and new ones built in their place, and that you should call this the "same," and I should say it was not the "same," house—would we not, for all this, perfectly agree in our thoughts of the house considered in itself? And would not all the difference consist in a sound? If you should say we differed in our notions, for that you superadded to your idea of the house the simple abstracted idea of identity, whereas I did not, I would tell you I know not what you mean by that "abstracted idea of identity," and should desire you to look into your own thoughts and be sure you understood yourself.—Why so silent, Hylas? Are you not yet satisfied men may dispute about identity and diversity without any real difference in their thoughts and opinions abstracted from names? Take this further reflection with you—that, whether matter be allowed to exist or no, the case is exactly the same as to the point in hand. For the materialists themselves acknowledge what we immediately perceive by our senses to be our own ideas. Your difficulty, therefore, that no two see the same thing makes equally against the materialists and me.

Hyl. But they suppose an external archetype to which referring their several ideas they may truly be said to perceive the same thing.

56. *Phil.* And (not to mention your having discarded those archetypes) so may you suppose an external archetype on my principles; *external*, I mean, to your own mind, though, indeed, it must be supposed to exist in that mind which comprehends all things; but then, this serves all the ends of *identity*, as well as if it existed out of a mind. And I am sure you yourself will not say it is less intelligible.

Hyl. You have indeed clearly satisfied me either that there is no difficulty at the bottom in this point or, if there be, that it makes equally against both opinions.

57. *Phil.* But that which makes equally against two contradictory opinions can be a proof against neither.

Hyl. I acknowledge it. But, after all, Philonous, when I consider the substance of what you advance against skepticism, it amounts to no more than this: we are sure that we really see, hear, feel, in a word, that we are affected with sensible impressions.

58. *Phil.* And how are we concerned any further? I see this cherry, I feel it, I taste it, and I am sure *nothing* cannot be seen or felt or tasted; it is therefore *real.* Take away the sensations of softness, moisture, redness, tartness, and you take away the cherry. Since it is not a being distinct from sensations, a cherry, I say, is nothing but a congeries of sensible impressions, or ideas perceived by various senses, which ideas are united into one thing (or have one name given them) by the mind because they are observed to attend each other. Thus, when the palate is affected with such a particular taste, the sight is affected with a red color, the touch with roundness, softness, etc. Hence, when I see and feel and taste in sundry certain manners, I am sure the cherry exists or is real, its reality being in my opinion nothing abstracted from those sensations. But if by the word "cherry" you mean an unknown nature distinct from all those sensible qualities, and by its "existence" something distinct from its being perceived, then, indeed, I own neither you nor I, nor anyone else, can be sure it exists.

Hyl. But what would you say, Philonous, if I should bring the very same reasons against the existence of sensible things in a mind which you have offered against their existing in a material substratum?

59. *Phil.* When I see your reasons, you shall hear what I have to say to them.

Hyl. Is the mind extended or unextended?

60. *Phil.* Unextended, without doubt.

Hyl. Do you say the things you perceive are in your mind?

61. *Phil.* They are.

Hyl. Again, have I not heard you speak of sensible impressions?

62. *Phil.* I believe you may.

Hyl. Explain to me now, O Philonous! how is it possible there should be room for all those trees and houses to exist in your mind. Can extended things be contained in that which is unextended? Or are we to imagine impressions made on a thing void of all solidity? You cannot say objects are in your mind, as books in your study, or that things are imprinted on it, as the figure of a seal upon wax. In what sense, therefore, are we to understand those

expressions? Explain me this if you can, and I shall then be able to answer all those queries you formerly put to me about my substratum.

63. *Phil.* Look you, Hylas, when I speak of objects as existing in the mind or imprinted on the senses, I would not be understood in the gross literal sense—as when bodies are said to exist in a place or a seal to make an impression upon wax. My meaning is only that the mind comprehends or perceives them, and that it is affected from without or by some being distinct from itself. This is my explication of your difficulty; and how it can serve to make your tenet of an unperceiving material substratum intelligible, I would fain know.

Hyl. Nay, if that be all, I confess I do not see what use can be made of it. But are you not guilty of some abuse of language in this?

64. *Phil.* None at all. It is no more than common custom, which you know is the rule of language, has authorized, nothing being more usual than for philosophers to speak of the immediate objects of the understanding as things existing in the mind. Nor is there anything in this but what is conformable to the general analogy of language; most part of the mental operations being signified by words borrowed from sensible things, as is plain in the terms "comprehend," "reflect," "discourse," etc., which, being applied to the mind, must not be taken in their gross original sense.

Hyl. You have, I own, satisfied me in this point. But there still remains one great difficulty which I know not how you will get over. And, indeed, it is of such importance that if you could solve all others without being able to find a solution for this, you must never expect to make me a proselyte to your principles.

65. *Phil.* Let me know this mighty difficulty.

Hyl. The Scripture account of the creation is what appears to me utterly irreconcilable with your notions. Moses tells us of a creation—a creation of what? of ideas? No, certainly, but of things, of real things, solid corporeal substances. Bring your principles to agree with this and I shall perhaps agree with you.

66. *Phil.* Moses mentions the sun, moon, and stars, earth and sea, plants and animals. That all these do really exist and were in the beginning created by God, I make no question. If by "ideas" you mean fictions and fancies of the mind, then these are

no ideas. If by "ideas" you mean immediate objects of the understanding, or sensible things which cannot exist unperceived, or out of a mind, then these things are ideas. But whether you do or do not call them "ideas," it matters little. The difference is only about a name. And whether that name be retained or rejected, the sense, the truth, and reality of things continues the same. In common talk, the objects of our senses are not termed "ideas" but "things." Call them so still, provided you do not attribute to them any absolute external existence, and I shall never quarrel with you for a word. The creation, therefore, I allow to have been a creation of things, of *real* things. Neither is this in the least inconsistent with my principles, as is evident from what I have now said; and would have been evident to you without this if you had not forgotten what had been so often said before. But as for solid corporeal substances, I desire you to show where Moses makes any mention of them; and if they should be mentioned by him or any other inspired writer, it would still be incumbent on you to show those words were not taken in the vulgar acceptation for things falling under our senses, but in the philosophic acceptation for matter or an unknown quiddity with an absolute existence. When you have proved these points, then (and not till then) may you bring the authority of Moses into our dispute.

Hyl. It is in vain to dispute about a point so clear. I am content to refer it to your own conscience. Are you not satisfied there is some peculiar repugnancy between the Mosaic account of the creation and your notions?

67. *Phil.* If all possible sense which can be put on the first chapter of Genesis may be conceived as consistently with my principles as any other, then it has no peculiar repugnancy with them. But there is no sense you may not as well conceive, believing as I do. Since, besides spirits, all you conceive are ideas, and the existence of these I do not deny. Neither do you pretend they exist without the mind.

Hyl. Pray let me see any sense you can understand it in.

68. *Phil.* Why, I imagine that if I had been present at the creation, I should have seen things produced into being—that is become perceptible—in the order prescribed by the sacred historian. I ever before believed the Mosaic account of the creation, and now find no alteration in my manner of believ-

ing it. When things are said to begin or end their existence, we do not mean this with regard to God, but His creatures. All objects are eternally known by God, or, which is the same thing, have an eternal existence in His mind; but when things, before imperceptible to creatures, are, by a decree of God, made perceptible to them, then are they said to begin a relative existence with respect to created minds. Upon reading therefore the Mosaic account of the creation, I understand that the several parts of the world became gradually perceivable to finite spirits endowed with proper faculties, so that, whoever such were present, they were in truth perceived by them. This is the literal obvious sense suggested to me by the words of the Holy Scripture, in which is included no mention or thought either of substratum, instrument, occasion, or absolute existence. And, upon inquiry, I doubt not it will be found that most plain honest men who believe the creation never think of those things any more than I. What metaphysical sense you may understand it in, you only can tell.

Hyl. But, Philonous, you do not seem to be aware that you allow created things in the beginning only a relative and consequently hypothetical being; that is to say, upon supposition there were men to perceive them, without which they have no actuality of absolute existence wherein creation might terminate. Is it not, therefore, according to you, plainly impossible the creation of any inanimate creatures should precede that of man? And is not this directly contrary to the Mosaic account?

69. *Phil.* In answer to that, I say, *first,* created beings might begin to exist in the mind of other created intelligences besides men. You will not, therefore, be able to prove any contradiction between Moses and my notions unless you first show there was no other order of finite created spirits in being before man. I say further, in case we conceive the creation as we should at this time a parcel of plants or vegetables of all sorts produced by an invisible power in a desert where nobody was present—that this way of explaining or conceiving it is consistent with my principles, since they deprive you of nothing, either sensible or imaginable; that it exactly suits with the common, natural, and undebauched notions of mankind; that it manifests the dependence of all things on God, and consequently has all the good effect or influence, which it is possible that

important article of our faith should have in making men humble, thankful, and resigned to their Creator. I say, moreover, that, in this naked conception of things, divested of words, there will not be found any notion of what you call the "actuality of absolute existence." You may indeed raise a dust with those terms and so lengthen our dispute to no purpose. But I entreat you calmly to look into your own thoughts and then tell me if they are not a useless and unintelligible jargon.

Hyl. I own I have no very clear notion annexed to them. But what say you to this? Do you not make the existence of sensible things consist in their being in a mind? And were not all things externally in the mind of God? Did they not therefore exist from all eternity, according to you? And how could that which was eternal be created in time? Can anything be clearer or better connected than this?

70. *Phil.* And are not you too of opinion that God knew all things from eternity?

Hyl. I am.

71. *Phil.* Consequently, they always had a being in the Divine intellect.

Hyl. This I acknowledge.

72. *Phil.* By your own confession, therefore, nothing is new, or begins to be, in respect of the mind of God. So we are agreed in that point.

Hyl. What shall we make then of the creation?

73. *Phil.* May we not understand it to have been entirely in respect of finite spirits, so that things, with regard to us, may properly be said to begin their existence, or be created, when God decreed they should become perceptible to intelligent creatures in that order and manner which He then established and we now call the laws of nature? You may call this a "relative," or "hypothetical existence," if you please. But so long as it supplies us with the most natural, obvious, and literal sense of the Mosaic history of the creation, so long as it answers all the religious ends of that great article, in a word, so long as you can assign no other sense or meaning in its stead, why should we reject this? Is it to comply with a ridiculous skeptical humor of making everything nonsense and unintelligible? I am sure you cannot say it is for the glory of God. For allowing it to be a thing possible and conceivable that the corporeal world should have an absolute existence extrinsical to the mind of God, as well as the minds of all created spirits, yet how could this set forth either the immensity or omniscience of the Deity or the necessary and immediate dependence of all things on Him? Nay, would it not rather seem to derogate from those attributes?

Hyl. Well, but as to this decree of God's for making things perceptible, what say you, Philonous, is it not plain God did either execute that decree from all eternity or at some certain time began to will what He had not actually willed before, but only designed to will? If the former, then there could be no creation or beginning of existence in finite things. If the latter, then we must acknowledge something new to befall the Deity, which implies a sort of change; and all change argues imperfection.

74. *Phil.* Pray consider what you are doing. Is it not evident this objection concludes equally against a creation in any sense, nay, against every other act of the Deity discoverable by the light of nature? None of which can we conceive otherwise than as performed in time and having a beginning. God is a Being of transcendent and unlimited perfections; His Nature, therefore, is incomprehensible to finite spirits. It is not, therefore, to be expected that any man, whether *materialist* or *immaterialist,* should have exactly just notions of the Deity, His attributes, and ways of operation. If then you would infer anything against me, your difficulty must not be drawn from the inadequateness of our conceptions of the Divine nature, which is unavoidable on any scheme, but from the denial of matter, of which there is not one word, directly or indirectly, in what you have now objected.

Hyl. I must acknowledge the difficulties you are concerned to clear are such only as arise from the nonexistence of matter and are peculiar to that notion. So far you are in the right. But I cannot by any means bring myself to think there is no such peculiar repugnancy between the creation and your opinion, though, indeed, where to fix it I do not distinctly know.

75. *Phil.* What would you have? Do I not acknowledge a two-fold state of things, the one ectypal or nature, the other archetypal and eternal? The former was created in time, the latter existed from everlasting in the mind of God. Is not this agreeable to the common notions of divines? Or is any more than this necessary in order to conceive the cre-

ation? But you suspect some peculiar repugnancy, though you know not where it lies. To take away all possibility of scruple in the case, do but consider this one point: either you are not able to conceive the creation on any hypothesis whatsoever, and if so, there is no ground for dislike or complaint against my particular opinion on that score; or you are able to conceive it, and if so, why not on my principles, since thereby nothing conceivable is taken away? You have all along been allowed the full scope of sense, imagination, and reason. Whatever, therefore, you could before apprehend, either immediately or mediately by your senses, or by ratiocination from your senses, whatever you could perceive, imagine, or understand, remains still with you. If, therefore, the notion you have of the creation by other principles be intelligible, you have it still upon mine; if it be not intelligible, I conceive it to be no notion at all, and so there is no loss of it. And, indeed, it seems to me very plain that the supposition of matter, that is, a thing perfectly unknown and inconceivable, cannot serve to make us conceive anything. And I hope it need not be proved to you that if the existence of matter does not make the creation conceivable, the creation's being without it inconceivable can be no objection against its nonexistence.

Hyl. I confess, Philonous, you have almost satisfied me in this point of the creation.

76. *Phil.* I would fain know why you are not quite satisfied. You tell me indeed of a repugnancy between the Mosaic history and immaterialism, but you know not where it lies. Is this reasonable, Hylas? Can you expect I should solve a difficulty without knowing what it is? But, to pass by all that, would not a man think you were assured there is no repugnancy between the received notions of materialists and the inspired writings?

Hyl. And so I am.

77. *Phil.* Ought the historical part of Scripture to be understood in a plain obvious sense or in a sense which is metaphysical and out of the way?

Hyl. In the plain sense, doubtless.

78. *Phil.* When Moses speaks of herbs, earth, water, etc., as having been created by God, think you not the sensible things commonly signified by those words are suggested to every unphilosophical reader?

Hyl. I cannot help thinking so.

79. *Phil.* And are not all ideas, or things perceived by sense, to be denied a real existence by the doctrine of the materialists?

Hyl. This I have already acknowledged.

80. *Phil.* The creation, therefore, according to them, was not the creation of things sensible, which have only a relative being, but of certain unknown natures which have an absolute being wherein creation might terminate?

Hyl. True.

81. *Phil.* Is it not, therefore, evident the assertors of matter destroy the plain obvious sense of Moses, with which their notions are utterly inconsistent, and instead of it obtrude on us I know not what, something equally unintelligible to themselves and me?

Hyl. I cannot contradict you.

82. *Phil.* Moses tells us of a creation. A creation of what? of unknown quiddities, of occasions, or substratum? No, certainly, but of things obvious to the senses. You must first reconcile this with your notions if you expect I should be reconciled to them.

Hyl. I see you can assault me with my own weapons.

83. *Phil.* Then as to *absolute existence*, was there ever known a more jejune notion than that? Something it is so abstracted and unintelligible that you have frankly owned you could not conceive it, much less explain anything by it. But allowing matter to exist and the notion of absolute existence to be as clear as light, yet, was this ever known to make the creation more credible? Nay, has it not furnished the atheists and infidels of all ages with the most plausible arguments against a creation? That a corporeal substance which has an absolute existence without the minds of spirits should be produced out of nothing, by the mere will of a spirit, has been looked upon as a thing so contrary to all reason, so impossible and absurd, that not only the most celebrated among the ancients, but even divers modern and Christian philosophers have thought matter coeternal with the Deity. Lay these things together and then judge you whether materialism disposes men to believe the creation of things.

Hyl. I own, Philonous, I think it does not. This of the creation is the last objection I can think of: and I must needs own it has been sufficiently answered as well as the rest. Nothing now remains to be overcome but a sort of unaccountable backwardness that I find in myself toward your notions.

84. *Phil.* When a man is swayed, he knows not why, to one side of a question, can this, think you, be anything else but the effect of prejudice, which never fails to attend old and rooted notions? And, indeed, in this respect I cannot deny the belief of matter to have very much the advantage over the contrary opinion with men of a learned education.

Hyl. I confess it seems to be as you say.

85. *Phil.* As a balance, therefore, to this weight of prejudice, let us throw into the scale the great advantages that arise from the belief of immaterialism, both in regard to religion and human learning. The being of a God and incorruptibility of the soul, those great articles of religion, are they not proved with the clearest and most immediate evidence? When I say the being of a *God,* I do not mean an obscure general cause of things whereof we have no conception, but *God* in the strict and proper sense of the word, a Being whose spirituality, omnipresence, providence, omniscience, infinite power, and goodness are as conspicuous as the existence of sensible things, of which (notwithstanding the fallacious pretenses and affected scruples of skeptics) there is no more reason to doubt than of our own being. Then, with relation to human sciences: in Natural Philosophy, what intricacies, what obscurities, what contradictions has the belief of matter led men into! To say nothing of the numberless disputes about its extent, continuity, homogeneity, gravity, divisibility, etc.—do they not pretend to explain all things by bodies operating on bodies, according to the laws of motion? And yet, are they able to comprehend how any one body should move another? Nay, admitting there was no difficulty in reconciling the notion of an inert being with a cause, or in conceiving how an accident might pass from one body to another, yet, by all their strained thoughts and extravagant suppositions, have they been able to reach the mechanical production of any one animal or vegetable body? Can they account, by the laws of motion, for sounds, tastes, smells, or colors, or for the regular course of things? Have they accounted, by physical principles, for the aptitude and contrivance even of the most inconsiderable parts of the universe? But laying aside matter and corporeal causes and admitting only the efficiency of an All-

perfect Mind, are not all the effects of nature easy and intelligible? If the *phenomena* are nothing else but *ideas,* God is a *spirit,* but matter an unintelligent, unperceiving being. If they demonstrate an unlimited power in their cause, God is active and omnipotent, but matter an inert mass. If the order, regularity, and usefulness of them can never be sufficiently admired, God is infinitely wise and provident, but matter destitute of all contrivance and design. These surely are great advantages in physics. Not to mention that the apprehension of a distant Deity naturally disposes men to a negligence of their moral actions, which they would be more cautious of, in case they thought him immediately present and acting on their minds without the interposition of matter or unthinking second causes. Then in metaphysics: what difficulties concerning entity in abstract, substantial forms, hylarchic principles, plastic natures, substance and accident, principle of individuation, possibility of matter's thinking, origin of ideas, the manner how two independent substances so widely different as *spirit* and *matter* should mutually operate on each other? What difficulties, I say, and endless disquisitions concerning these and innumerable other the like points do we escape by supposing only spirits and ideas? Even the mathematics themselves, if we take away the absolute existence of extended things, become much more clear and easy, the most shocking paradoxes and intricate speculations in those sciences depending on the infinite divisibility of finite extension, which depends on that supposition. But what need is there to insist on the particular sciences? Is not that opposition to all science whatsoever, that frenzy of the ancient and modern skeptics, built on the same foundation? Or can you produce so much as one argument against the reality of corporeal things or in behalf of that avowed utter ignorance of their natures which does not suppose their reality to consist in an external absolute existence? Upon this supposition, indeed, the objections from the change of colors in a pigeon's neck, or the appearance of the broken oar in the water, must be allowed to have weight. But these and the like objections vanish if we do not maintain the being of absolute external originals, but place the reality of things in ideas, fleeting, indeed, and changeable; however, not changed at random, but according to the fixed order of nature. For herein consists that constancy and truth of things which secures all the concerns of life, and distinguishes that which is real from the irregular visions of the fancy.

Hyl. I agree to all you have now said and must own that nothing can incline me to embrace your opinion more than the advantages I see it is attended with. I am by nature lazy, and this would be a mighty abridgment in knowledge. What doubts, what hypotheses, what labyrinths of amusement, what fields of disputation, what an ocean of false learning may be avoided by that single notion of *immaterialism!*

86. *Phil.* After all, is there anything further remaining to be done? You may remember you promised to embrace that opinion which upon examination should appear most agreeable to common sense and remote from skepticism. This, by your own confession, is that which denies matter or the absolute existence of corporeal things. Nor is this all; the same notion has been proved several ways, viewed in different lights, pursued in its consequences, and all objections against it cleared. Can there be a greater evidence of its truth? Or is it possible it should have all the marks of a true opinion and yet be false?

Hyl. I own myself entirely satisfied for the present in all respects. But what security can I have that I shall still continue the same full assent to your opinion and that no unthought-of objection or difficulty will occur hereafter?

87. *Phil.* Pray, Hylas, do you in other cases, when a point is once evidently proved, withhold your assent on account of objections or difficulties it may be liable to? Are the difficulties that attend the doctrine of incommensurable quantities, of the angle of contact, of the asymptotes to curves, or the like, sufficient to make you hold out against mathematical demonstration? Or will you disbelieve the Providence of God because there may be some particular things which you know not how to reconcile with it? If there are difficulties attending immaterialism, there are at the same time direct and evident proofs of it. But for the existence of matter there is not one proof, and far more numerous and insurmountable objections lie against it. But where are those mighty difficulties you insist on? Alas! you know not where or what they are; something which may possibly occur hereafter. If this be a sufficient pretense for withholding your full assent, you should never yield it to any proposition, how free soever from exceptions, how clearly and solidly soever demonstrated.

Hyl. You have satisfied me, Philonous.

David Hume
(1711–1776)

Hume was born in Edinburgh and attended the university there. Destined for a career in law, he discovered that he had, in his own words, "an insurmountable aversion to everything but the pursuits of philosophy and general learning." After a few years of self-study, he retreated to France, where at La Flèche (Descartes's old college), he completed the *Treatise of Human Nature* at the age of twenty-six. Published in England, the work "fell dead-born from the press, without reaching such distinction as even to excite a murmur among the zealots." After a few years in service to various political and military figures, Hume returned to his studies. Convinced that his "want of success in publishing the *Treatise* had proceeded more from the manner than the matter," Hume rewrote the first book of that work and published it eventually under the name *An Enquiry Concerning Human Understanding*. It was not the success he had hoped for, either.

In the end, Hume achieved literary fame as an essayist and historian, and was lionized in France. He never achieved success in Britain during his lifetime, and was turned down for chairs of philosophy in Edinburgh and Glasgow, probably owing to charges of atheism. With the exception of Thomas Reid, who merely disagreed with him profoundly, he was ridiculed by the philosophers of the Scottish school of Common Sense, including "that bigoted, silly fellow, Beattie." Hume's genius was recognized by Immanuel Kant, who credited Hume with awakening him from his "dogmatic slumber." Hume's critics, Kant thought, utterly misunderstood him, "taking for granted that which he doubted, and demonstrating with zeal and often impudence that which he never thought of doubting."

The *Enquiry* encompasses the main thread of argument from Book I of the *Treatise,* while adding chapters on free will, miracles, and the argument from design. Like Locke, Hume started with the thought that all knowledge is concerned with our ideas, and that all our ideas come from experience. His distinction between ideas and impressions provides him with a new and more precise way of expressing this thought, while sidestepping the innateness controversy entirely. He aimed to provide a precise account of how our ideas become connected with each other, and so issue into things we know and believe. Like Locke, he thought that what we could know was rather circumscribed, and that in most matters we had to settle for belief. He was largely concerned not just with what we immediately perceive or remember, but with how we reason from those to things that we have not experienced. Locke seemed to take such probable reasoning for granted; Hume offered a sustained critique introducing what has come to be called "the problem of induction." Hume provided his own solution to the problem, which offers a naturalistic account of the process, including the attribution of such reasoning to animals.

The chapter on miracles had originally been intended to be part of Hume's overall account of probable reasoning in the *Treatise,* but was excised for prudential reasons. In the *Enquiry,* it resumes its rightful place, immediately following the chapter "Of the Reasons of Animals." Hume argues that any proper application of the rules of probable evidence would make it irrational ever to believe testimony reporting the occurrence of a miracle. And in the next chapter, Hume provides a foretaste of the sustained critique of the argument from design that eventually appeared in the *Dialogues Concerning Natural Religion,* published posthumously.

Note on the text: The text contains some important footnotes and variants in square brackets.

An Enquiry Concerning Human Understanding

Author's Advertisement

Most of the principles, and reasonings, contained in this volume were published in a work in three volumes, called *A Treatise of Human Nature:* a work which the Author had projected before he left College, and which he wrote and published not long after. But not finding it successful, he was sensible of his error in going to the press too early, and he cast the whole anew in the following pieces, where some negligences in his former reasoning and more in the expression are, he hopes, corrected. Yet several writers who have honored the Author's Philosophy with answers have taken care to direct all their batteries against that juvenile work, which the author never acknowledged, and have affected to triumph in any advantages which, they imagined, they had obtained over it: a practice very contrary to all rules of candour and fairdealing, and a strong instance of those polemical artifices which a bigotted zeal thinks itself authorised to employ. Henceforth, the Author desires that the following Pieces may alone be regarded as containing his philosophical sentiments and principles.

Section I. Of the Different Species of Philosophy

Moral philosophy, or the science of human nature, may be treated after two different manners; each of which has its peculiar merit, and may contribute to the entertainment, instruction, and reformation of mankind. The one considers man chiefly as born for action; and as influenced in his measures by taste

Excerpted with permission from the Past Masters Hume text base, InteLex Corp., 1989.

and sentiment; pursuing one object, and avoiding another, according to the value which these objects seem to possess, and according to the light in which they present themselves. As virtue, of all objects, is allowed to be the most valuable, this species of philosophers paint her in the most amiable colours; borrowing all helps from poetry and eloquence, and treating their subject in an easy and obvious manner, and such as is best fitted to please the imagination, and engage the affections. They select the most striking observations and instances from common life; place opposite characters in a proper contrast; and alluring us into the paths of virtue by the views of glory and happiness, direct our steps in these paths by the soundest precepts and most illustrious examples. They make us feel the difference between vice and virtue; they excite and regulate our sentiments; and so they can but bend our hearts to the love of probity and true honour, they think that they have fully attained the end of all their labours.

The other species of philosophers consider man in the light of a reasonable rather than an active being, and endeavour to form his understanding more than cultivate his manners. They regard human nature as a subject of speculation; and with a narrow scrutiny examine it, in order to find those principles which regulate our understanding, excite our sentiments, and make us to approve or blame any particular object, action, or behaviour. They think it a reproach to all literature that philosophy should not yet have fixed, beyond controversy, the foundation of morals, reasoning, and criticism; and should forever talk of truth and falsehood, vice and virtue, beauty and deformity, without being able to determine the source of these distinctions. While they attempt this arduous task, they are deterred by no difficulties; but proceeding from particular instances to general principles, they still push on their enquiries to principles more general, and rest not satisfied till they arrive at those original principles, by which, in every science, all human curiosity must be bounded. Though their speculations seem abstract, and even unintelligible to common readers, they aim at the approbation of the learned and the wise; and think themselves sufficiently compensated for the labour of their whole lives, if they can discover some hidden truths, which may contribute to the instruction of posterity.

It is certain that the easy and obvious philosophy will always, with the generality of mankind, have the preference above the accurate and abstruse; and by many will be recommended, not only as more agreeable, but more useful than the other. It enters more into common life; moulds the heart and affections; and, by touching those principles which actuate men, reforms their conduct, and brings them nearer to that model of perfection which it describes. On the contrary, the abstruse philosophy, being founded on a turn of mind which cannot enter into business and action, vanishes when the philosopher leaves the shade, and comes into open day; nor can its principles easily retain any influence over our conduct and behaviour. The feelings of our heart, the agitation of our passions, the vehemence of our affections, dissipate all its conclusions, and reduce the profound philosopher to a mere plebeian.

This also must be confessed, that the most durable, as well as justest, fame has been acquired by the easy philosophy, and that abstract reasoners seem hitherto to have enjoyed only a momentary reputation, from the caprice or ignorance of their own age, but have not been able to support their renown with more equitable posterity. It is easy for a profound philosopher to commit a mistake in his subtle reasonings; and one mistake is the necessary parent of another, while he pushes on his consequences, and is not deterred from embracing any conclusion by its unusual appearance, or its contradiction to popular opinion. But a philosopher, who purposes only to represent the common sense of mankind in more beautiful and more engaging colours, if by accident he falls into error, goes no farther; but renewing his appeal to common sense, and the natural sentiments of the mind, returns into the right path, and secures himself from any dangerous illusions. The fame of Cicero flourishes at present; but that of Aristotle is utterly decayed. La Bruyere passes the seas, and still maintains his reputation: But the glory of Malebranche is confined to his own nation, and to his own age. And Addison, perhaps, will be read with pleasure, when Locke shall be entirely forgotten.

The mere philosopher is a character which is commonly but little acceptable in the world, as being supposed to contribute nothing either to the advantage or pleasure of society; while he lives remote from communication with mankind, and is wrapped up in principles and notions equally remote from their comprehension. On the other hand, the mere ignorant is still more despised; nor is anything deemed a surer sign of an illiberal genius in an age and nation where the sciences flourish, than to be entirely destitute of all relish for those noble entertainments. The most perfect character is supposed to lie between those extremes; retaining an equal ability and taste for books, company, and business; preserving in conversation that discernment and delicacy which arise from polite letters; and in business, that probity and accuracy which are the natural result of a just philosophy. In order to diffuse and cultivate so accomplished a character, nothing can be more useful than compositions of the easy style and manner, which draw not too much from life, require no deep application or retreat to be comprehended, and send back the student among mankind full of noble sentiments and wise precepts, applicable to every exigence of human life. By means of such compositions, virtue becomes amiable, science agreeable, company instructive, and retirement entertaining.

Man is a reasonable being; and as such, receives from science his proper food and nourishment: But so narrow are the bounds of human understanding that little satisfaction can be hoped for in this particular, either from the extent or security of his acquisitions. Man is a sociable, no less than a reasonable, being: But neither can he always enjoy company agreeable and amusing, or preserve the proper relish for them. Man is also an active being; and from that disposition, as well as from the various necessities of human life, must submit to business and occupation: But the mind requires some relaxation, and cannot always support its bent to care and industry. It seems, then, that nature has pointed out a mixed kind of life as most suitable to human race, and secretly admonished them to allow none of these biasses to draw too much, so as to incapacitate them for other occupations and entertainments. Indulge your passion for science, says she, but let your science be human, and such as may have a direct reference to action and society. Abstruse thought and profound researches I prohibit, and will severely punish, by the pensive melancholy which they introduce, by the endless uncertainty in which they involve you, and by the cold reception which your pretended discoveries shall meet with, when communicated. Be a philosopher; but, amidst all your philosophy, be still a man.

Were the generality of mankind contented to prefer the easy philosophy to the abstract and profound, without throwing any blame or contempt on the latter, it might not be improper, perhaps, to comply with this general opinion, and allow every man to enjoy, without opposition, his own taste and sentiment. But as the matter is often carried farther, even to the absolute rejecting of all profound reasonings, or what is commonly called metaphysics, we shall now proceed to consider what can reasonably be pleaded in their behalf.

We may begin with observing that one considerable advantage which results from the accurate and abstract philosophy is its subserviency to the easy and humane; which, without the former, can never attain a sufficient degree of exactness in its sentiments, precepts, or reasonings. All polite letters are nothing but pictures of human life in various attitudes and situations; and inspire us with different sentiments, of praise or blame, admiration or ridicule, according to the qualities of the object, which they set before us. An artist must be better qualified to succeed in this undertaking, who, besides a delicate taste and a quick apprehension, possesses an accurate knowledge of the internal fabric, the operations of the understanding, the workings of the passions, and the various species of sentiment which discriminate vice and virtue. How painful soever this inward search or enquiry may appear, it becomes, in some measure, requisite to those who would describe with success the obvious and outward appearances of life and manners. The anatomist presents to the eye the most hideous and disagreeable objects; but his science is useful to the painter in delineating even a Venus or an Helen. While the latter employs all the richest colours of his art, and gives his figures the most graceful and engaging airs; he must still carry his attention to the inward structure of the human body, the position of the muscles, the fabric of the bones, and the use and figure of every part or organ. Accuracy is, in every case, advantageous to beauty, and just reasoning to delicate sentiment. In vain would we exalt the one by depreciating the other.

Besides, we may observe, in every art or profession, even those which most concern life or action, that a spirit of accuracy, however acquired, carries all of them nearer their perfection, and renders them more subservient to the interests of society. And though a philosopher may live remote from business, the genius of philosophy, if carefully cultivated by several, must gradually diffuse itself throughout the whole society, and bestow a similar correctness on every art and callling. The politician will acquire greater foresight and subtlety, in the subdividing and balancing of power; the lawyer more method and finer principles in his reasonings; and the general more regularity in his discipline, and more caution in his plans and operations. The stability of modern governments above the ancient, and the accuracy of modern philosophy, have improved, and probably will still improve, by similar gradations.

Were there no advantage to be reaped from these studies, beyond the gratification of an innocent curiosity, yet ought not even this to be despised; as being one accession to those few safe and harmless pleasures which are bestowed on the human race. The sweetest and most inoffensive path of life leads through the avenues of science and learning; and whoever can either remove any obstructions in this way, or open up any new prospect, ought so far to be esteemed a benefactor to mankind. And though these researches may appear painful and fatiguing, it is with some minds as with some bodies, which being endowed with vigorous and florid health, require severe exercise, and reap a pleasure from what, to the generality of mankind, may seem burdensome and laborious. Obscurity, indeed, is painful to the mind as well as to the eye; but to bring light from obscurity, by whatever labour, must needs be delightful and rejoicing.

But this obscurity in the profound and abstract philosophy is objected to, not only as painful and fatiguing, but as the inevitable source of uncertainty and error. Here indeed lies the justest and most plausible objection against a considerable part of metaphysics, that they are not properly a science; but arise either from the fruitless efforts of human vanity, which would penetrate into subjects utterly inaccessible to the understanding, or from the craft of popular superstitions, which, being unable to defend themselves on fair ground, raise these entangling brambles to cover and protect their weakness. Chased from the open country, these robbers fly into the forest, and lie in wait to break in upon every unguarded avenue of the mind, and overwhelm it with religious fears and prejudices. The stoutest antagonist, if he remit his watch a moment, is oppressed. And many, through cowardice and folly, open the gates to the enemies, and willingly receive them with reverence and submission, as their legal sovereigns.

But is this a sufficient reason why philosophers should desist from such researches, and leave superstition still in possession of her retreat? Is it not proper to draw an opposite conclusion, and perceive the necessity of carrying the war into the most secret recesses of the enemy? In vain do we hope that men, from frequent disappointment, will at last abandon such airy sciences, and discover the proper province of human reason. For, besides, that many persons find too sensible an interest in perpetually recalling such topics; besides this, I say, the motive of blind despair can never reasonably have place in the sciences; since, however unsuccessful former attempts may have proved, there is still room to hope that the industry, good fortune, or improved sagacity of succeeding generations may reach discoveries unknown to former ages. Each adventurous genius will still leap at the arduous prize, and find himself stimulated, rather than discouraged, by the failures of his predecessors; while he hopes that the glory of achieving so hard an adventure is reserved for him alone. The only method of freeing learning, at once, from these abstruse questions is to enquire seriously into the nature of human understanding, and show, from an exact analysis of its powers and capacity, that it is by no means fitted for such remote and abstruse subjects. We must submit to this fatigue, in order to live at ease ever after: and must cultivate true metaphysics with some care, in order to destroy the false and adulterate. Indolence, which, to some persons, affords a safeguard against this deceitful philosophy is, with others, overbalanced by curiosity; and despair, which, at some moments, prevails, may give place afterwards to sanguine hopes and expectations. Accurate and just reasoning is the only catholic remedy, fitted for all persons and all dispositions; and is alone able to subvert that abstruse philosophy and metaphysical jargon, which, being mixed up with popular superstition, renders it in a manner impenetrable to careless reasoners, and gives it the air of science and wisdom.

Besides this advantage of rejecting, after deliberate enquiry, the most uncertain and disagreeable part of learning, there are many positive advantages which result from an accurate scrutiny into the powers and faculties of human nature. It is remarkable concerning the operations of the mind that, though most intimately present to us, yet, whenever they become the object of reflection, they seem involved in obscurity; nor can the eye readily find those lines and boundaries which discriminate and distinguish them. The objects are too fine to remain long in the same aspect or situation; and must be apprehended in an instant, by a superior penetration, derived from nature, and improved by habit and reflection. It becomes, therefore, no inconsiderable part of science barely to know the different operations of the mind, to separate them from each other, to class them under their proper heads, and to correct all that seeming disorder in which they lie involved, when made the object of reflection and enquiry. This task of ordering and distinguishing, which has no merit when performed with regard to external bodies, the objects of our senses, rises in its value when directed towards the operations of the mind, in proportion to the difficulty and labour which we meet with in performing it. And if we can go no farther than this mental geography, or delineation of the distinct parts and powers of the mind, it is at least a satisfaction to go so far; and the more obvious this science may appear (and it is by no means obvious) the more contemptible still must the ignorance of it be esteemed, in all pretenders to learning and philosophy.

Nor can there remain any suspicion that this science is uncertain and chimerical; unless we should entertain such a scepticism as is entirely subversive of all speculation, and even action. It cannot be doubted that the mind is endowed with several powers and faculties, that these powers are distinct from each other, that what is really distinct to the immediate perception may be distinguished by reflection; and consequently, that there is a truth and falsehood in all propositions on this subject, and a truth and falsehood which lie not beyond the compass of human understanding. There are many obvious distinctions of this kind, such as those between the will and understanding, the imagination and passions, which fall within the comprehension of every human creature; and the finer and more philosophical distinctions are no less real and certain, though more difficult to be comprehended. Some instances, especially late ones, of success in these enquiries may give us a juster notion of the certainty and solidity of this branch of learning. And shall we esteem it worthy the labour of a philosopher to give us a true system of the planets, and adjust the position and order of those remote bodies; while we affect to overlook those who, with so much success, delineate the parts of the mind, in which we are so intimately concerned?

[That Faculty by which we discern Truth and Falshood and that by which we perceive Vice and Virtue had long been confounded with each other, and all Morality was suppos'd to be built on eternal and immutable Relations, which, to every intelligent Mind, were equally invariable as any Proposition concerning Quantity or Number. But a late Philosopher has taught us, by the most convincing Arguments, that Morality is nothing in the abstract Nature of Things, but is entirely relative to the Sentiment or mental Taste of each particular Being; in the same Manner as the Distinctions of sweet and bitter, hot and cold, arise from the particular feeling of each Sense or Organ. Moral Perceptions, therefore, ought not to be class'd with the Operations of the Understanding, but with the Tastes or Sentiments.

It had been usual with Philosophers to divide all the Passions of the Mind into two Classes, the selfish and benevolent, which were suppos'd to stand in constant Opposition and Contrariety; nor was it thought that the latter could ever attain their proper Object but at the Expense of the former. Among the selfish Passions were rank'd Avarice, Ambition, Revenge: Among the benevolent, natural Affection, Friendship, Public spirit. Philosophers may now perceive the Impropriety of this Division. It has been prov'd, beyond all Controversy, that even the Passions, commonly esteem'd selfish, carry the Mind beyond Self, directly to the Object; that tho' the Satisfaction of these Passions gives us Enjoyment, yet the Prospect of this Enjoyment is not the Cause of the Passion, but on the contrary the Passion is antecedent to the Enjoyment, and without the former, the latter could never possibly exist; that the Case is precisely the same with the Passions, denominated benevolent, and consequently that a Man is no more interested when he seeks his own Glory than when the Happiness of his Friend is the Object of his Wishes; nor is he any more disinterested when he sacrifices his Ease and Quiet to public Good than when he labours for the Gratification of Avarice or Ambition. Here therefore is a considerable Adjustment in the Boundaries of the Passions, which had been confounded by the Negligence or Inaccuracy of former Philosophers. These two Instances may suffice to show us the Nature and Importance of this Species of Philosophy.]

But may we not hope that philosophy, if cultivated with care, and encouraged by the attention of the public, may carry its researches still farther, and discover, at least in some degree, the secret springs and principles by which the human mind is actuated in its operations? Astronomers had long contented themselves with proving, from the phenomena, the true motions, order, and magnitude of the heavenly bodies: Till a philosopher, at last, arose, who seems, from the happiest reasoning, to have also determined the laws and forces by which the revolutions of the planets are governed and directed. The like has been performed with regard to other parts of nature. And there is no reason to despair of equal success in our enquiries concerning the mental powers and economy, if prosecuted with equal capacity and caution. It is probable that one operation and principle of the mind depends on another; which, again, may be resolved into one more general and universal: And how far these researches may possibly be carried, it will be difficult for us before, or even after, a careful trial exactly to determine. This is certain, that attempts of this kind are every day made even by those who philosophize the most negligently: And nothing can be more requisite than to enter upon the enterprise with thorough care and attention; that, if it lie within the compass of human understanding, it may at last be happily achieved; if not, it may, however, be rejected with some confidence and security. This last conclusion, surely, is not desirable; nor ought it to be embraced too rashly. For how much must we diminish from the beauty and value of this species of philosophy, upon such a supposition? Moralists have hitherto been accustomed, when they considered the vast multitude and diversity of those actions that excite our approbation or dislike, to search for some common principle on which this variety of sentiments might depend. And though they have sometimes carried the matter too far, by their passion for some one general principle, it must, however, be confessed that they are excusable in expecting to find some general principles, into which all the vices and virtues were justly to be resolved. The like has been the endeavour of critics, logicians, and even politicians: Nor have their attempts been wholly unsuccessful; though perhaps longer time, greater accuracy, and more ardent application may bring these sciences still nearer their perfection. To throw up at once all pretensions of this kind may justly be deemed more rash, precipitate, and dogmatical than even the boldest and most affirmative philosophy that has ever attempted to impose its crude dictates and principles on mankind.

What though these reasonings concerning human nature seem abstract, and of difficult comprehension? This affords no presumption of their falsehood. On the contrary, it seems impossible that what has hitherto escaped so many wise and profound philosophers can be very obvious and easy. And whatever pains these researches may cost us, we may think ourselves sufficiently rewarded, not only in point of profit but of pleasure, if, by that means, we can make any addition to our stock of knowledge, in subjects of such unspeakable importance.

But as, after all, the abstractedness of these speculations is no recommendation, but rather a disadvantage to them, and as this difficulty may perhaps be surmounted by care and art, and the avoiding of all unnecessary detail, we have, in the following enquiry, attempted to throw some light upon subjects from which uncertainty has hitherto deterred the wise, and obscurity the ignorant. Happy, if we can unite the boundaries of the different species of philosophy, by reconciling profound enquiry with clearness, and truth with novelty! And still more happy, if, reasoning in this easy manner, we can undermine the foundations of an abstruse philosophy, which seems to have hitherto served only as a shelter to superstition, and a cover to absurdity and error!

Section II. *Of the Origin of Ideas*

Everyone will readily allow that there is a considerable difference between the perceptions of the mind, when a man feels the pain of excessive heat, or the pleasure of moderate warmth, and when he afterwards recalls to his memory this sensation, or anticipates it by his imagination. These faculties may mimic or copy the perceptions of the senses; but they never can entirely reach the force and vivacity of the original sentiment. The utmost we say of them, even when they operate with greatest vigour, is that they represent their object in so lively a manner that we could almost say we feel or see it: But, except the mind be disordered by disease or madness, they never can arrive at such a pitch of vivacity as to render these perceptions altogether undistinguishable. All the colours of poetry, however splendid, can never paint natural objects in such a manner as to make the description be taken for a real landscape. The most lively thought is still inferior to the dullest sensation.

We may observe a like distinction to run through all the other perceptions of the mind. A man in a fit of anger is actuated in a very different manner from one who only thinks of that emotion. If you tell me that any person is in love, I easily understand your meaning, and form a just conception of his situation; but never can mistake that conception for the real disorders and agitations of the passion. When we reflect on our past sentiments and affections, our thought is a faithful mirror, and copies its objects truly; but the colours which it employs are faint and dull in comparison of those in which our original perceptions were clothed. It requires no nice discernment or metaphysical head to mark the distinction between them.

Here therefore we may divide all the perceptions of the mind into two classes or species, which are distinguished by their different degrees of force and vivacity. The less forcible and lively are commonly denominated Thoughts or Ideas. The other species want a name in our language, and in most others; I suppose, because it was not requisite for any, but philosophical purposes, to rank them under a general term or appellation. Let us, therefore, use a little freedom, and call them Impressions; employing that word in a sense somewhat different from the usual. By the term *impression,* then, I mean all our more lively perceptions, when we hear, or see, or feel, or love, or hate, or desire, or will. And impressions are distinguished from ideas, which are the less lively perceptions of which we are conscious, when we reflect on any of those sensations or movements above mentioned.

Nothing, at first view, may seem more unbounded than the thought of man, which not only escapes all human power and authority, but is not even restrained within the limits of nature and reality. To form monsters, and join incongruous shapes and appearances, costs the imagination no more trouble than to conceive the most natural and familiar objects. And while the body is confined to one planet, along which it creeps with pain and difficulty, the thought can in an instant transport us into the most distant regions of the universe; or even beyond the universe, into the unbounded chaos, where nature is supposed to lie in total confusion. What never was seen, or heard of, may yet be conceived; nor is anything beyond the power of thought, except what implies an absolute contradiction.

But though our thought seems to possess this unbounded liberty, we shall find, upon a nearer examination, that it is really confined within very narrow limits, and that all this creative power of the mind amounts to no more than the faculty of compounding, transposing, augmenting, or diminishing the materials afforded us by the senses and experience. When we think of a golden mountain, we only join two consistent ideas, gold, and mountain, with which we were formerly acquainted. A virtuous horse we can conceive; because, from our own feeling, we can conceive virtue; and this we may unite to the figure and shape of a horse, which is an animal familiar to us. In short, all the materials of thinking are derived either from our outward or inward sentiment: The mixture and composition

of these belongs alone to the mind and will. Or, to express myself in philosophical language, all our ideas or more feeble perceptions are copies of our impressions or more lively ones.

To prove this, the two following arguments will, I hope, be sufficient. First, when we analyse our thoughts or ideas, however compounded or sublime, we always find that they resolve themselves into such simple ideas as were copied from a precedent feeling or sentiment. Even those ideas which, at first view, seem the most wide of this origin are found, upon a nearer scrutiny, to be derived from it. The idea of God, as meaning an infinitely intelligent, wise, and good Being, arises from reflecting on the operations of our own mind, and augmenting, without limit, those qualities of goodness and wisdom. We may prosecute this enquiry to what length we please; where we shall always find that every idea which we examine is copied from a similar impression. Those who would assert that this position is not universally true nor without exception have only one, and that an easy method of refuting it; by producing that idea which, in their opinion, is not derived from this source. It will then be incumbent on us, if we would maintain our doctrine, to produce the impression or lively perception which corresponds to it.

Secondly, If it happen, from a defect of the organ, that a man is not susceptible of any species of sensation, we always find that he is as little susceptible of the correspondent ideas. A blind man can form no notion of colours; a deaf man of sounds. Restore either of them that sense in which he is deficient; by opening this new inlet for his sensations, you also open an inlet for the ideas; and he finds no difficulty in conceiving these objects. The case is the same if the object proper for exciting any sensation has never been applied to the organ. A Laplander or Negro has no notion of the relish of wine. And though there are few or no instances of a like deficiency in the mind, where a person has never felt or is wholly incapable of a sentiment or passion that belongs to his species; yet we find the same observation to take place in a less degree. A man of mild manners can form no idea of inveterate revenge or cruelty; nor can a selfish heart easily conceive the heights of friendship and generosity. It is readily allowed that other beings may possess many senses of which we can have no conception; because the ideas of them have never been introduced to us, in the only manner by which an idea can have access to the mind, to wit, by the actual feeling and sensation.

There is, however, one contradictory phenomenon, which may prove that it is not absolutely impossible for ideas to arise independent of their correspondent impressions. I believe it will readily be allowed that the several distinct ideas of colour, which enter by the eye, or those of sound, which are conveyed by the ear, are really different from each other; though, at the same time, resembling. Now if this be true of different colours, it must be no less so of the different shades of the same colour; and each shade produces a distinct idea, independent of the rest. For if this should be denied, it is possible, by the continual gradation of shades, to run a colour insensibly into what is most remote from it; and if you will not allow any of the means to be different, you cannot, without absurdity, deny the extremes to be the same. Suppose, therefore, a person to have enjoyed his sight for thirty years, and to have become perfectly acquainted with colours of all kinds, except one particular shade of blue, for instance, which it never has been his fortune to meet with. Let all the different shades of that colour, except that single one, be placed before him, descending gradually from the deepest to the lightest; it is plain that he will perceive a blank where that shade is wanting, and will be sensible that there is a greater distance in that place between the contiguous colours than in any other. Now I ask, whether it be possible for him, from his own imagination, to supply this deficiency, and raise up to himself the idea of that particular shade, though it had never been conveyed to him by his senses? I believe there are few but will be of opinion that he can: And this may serve as a proof that the simple ideas are not always, in every instance, derived from the correspondent impressions; though this instance is so singular that it is scarcely worth our observing, and does not merit that for it alone we should alter our general maxim.

Here, therefore, is a proposition which not only seems, in itself, simple and intelligible but, if a proper use were made of it, might render every dispute equally intelligible, and banish all that jargon which has so long taken possession of metaphysical reasonings, and drawn disgrace upon them. All ideas, especially abstract ones, are naturally faint and obscure: The mind has but a slender hold of them: they are apt to be confounded with other resembling ideas; and when we have often employed any term, though without a distinct meaning, we are apt to imagine it has a determinate idea, annexed to it. On the contrary, all impressions, that is, all sensations, either outward or inward, are strong and vivid: The limits between them are more exactly determined: Nor is it easy to fall into any error or mistake with regard to them. When we entertain, therefore, any suspicion that a philosophical term is employed without any meaning or idea (as is but too frequent), we need but enquire, from what impression is that supposed idea derived? And if it be impossible to assign any, this will serve to confirm our suspicion. By bringing ideas into so clear a light, we may reasonably hope to remove all dispute which may arise, concerning their nature and reality.

[It is probable that no more was meant by those who denied innate ideas than that all ideas were copies of our impressions; though it must be confessed that the terms, which they employed were not chosen with such caution, nor so exactly defined, as to prevent all mistakes about their doctrine. For what is meant by *innate*? If *innate* be equivalent to *natural*, then all the perceptions and ideas of the mind must be allowed to be innate or natural, in whatever sense we take the latter word, whether in opposition to what is uncommon, artificial, or miraculous. If by *innate* be meant contemporary to our birth, the dispute seems to be frivolous; nor is it worth while to enquire at what time thinking begins, whether before, at, or after our birth. Again, the word *idea* seems to be commonly taken in a very loose sense, by Locke and others, as standing for any of our perceptions, our sensations and passions, as well as thoughts. Now in this sense, I should desire to know, what can be meant by asserting that self-love, or resentment of injuries, or the passion between the sexes is not innate?

But admitting these terms, *impressions* and *ideas*, in the sense above explained, and understanding by *innate*, what is original or copied from no precedent perception, then may we assert that all our impressions are innate and our ideas not innate.

To be ingenuous, I must own it to be my opinion that Mr. Locke was betrayed into this question by the schoolmen, who, making use of undefined terms, draw out their disputes to a tedious length, without ever touching the point in question. A like ambiguity and circumlocution seem to run through all that great philosopher's reasonings on this as well as most other subjects.]

Section III. Of the Association of Ideas

It is evident that there is a principle of connexion between the different thoughts or ideas of the mind, and that, in their appearance to the memory or imagination, they introduce each other with a certain degree of method and regularity. In our more serious thinking or discourse, this is so observable that any particular thought which breaks in upon the regular tract or chain of ideas is immediately remarked and rejected. And even in our wildest and most wandering reveries, nay in our very dreams, we shall find, if we reflect, that the imagination ran not altogether at adventures, but that there was still a connexion upheld among the different ideas which succeeded each other. Were the loosest and freest conversation to be transcribed, there would immediately be observed something which connected it in all its transitions. Or where this is wanting, the person who broke the thread of discourse might still inform you that there had secretly revolved in his mind a succession of thought, which had gradually led him from the subject of conversation. Among different languages, even where we cannot suspect the least connexion or communication, it is found that the words, expressive of ideas, the most compounded, do yet nearly correspond to each other: A certain proof that the simple ideas, comprehended in the compound ones, were bound together by some universal principle, which had an equal influence on all mankind.

Though it be too obvious to escape observation, that different ideas are connected together, I do not find that any philosopher has attempted to enumerate or class all the principles of association; a subject, however, that seems worthy of curiosity. To me, there appear to be only three principles of connexion among ideas, namely, Resemblance, Contiguity in time or place, and Cause or Effect.

That these principles serve to connect ideas will not, I believe, be much doubted. A picture naturally leads our thoughts to the original [resemblance]: The mention of one apartment in a building naturally introduces an enquiry or discourse concerning the others [contiguity]: and if we think of a wound, we can scarcely forbear reflecting on the pain which follows it [cause and effect]. But that this enumeration is complete, and that there are no other principles of association, except these, may be difficult to prove to the satisfaction of the reader, or even to a man's own satisfaction. All we can do, in such cases, is to run over several instances, and examine carefully the principle which binds the different thoughts to each other, never stopping till we render the principle as general as possible. [For instance, Contrast or Contrariety is also a connexion among Ideas: But it may, perhaps, be considered as a mixture of Causation and Resemblance. Where two objects are contrary, the one destroys the other; that is, the cause of its annihilation, and the idea of the annihilation of an object, implies the idea of its former existence.] The more instances we examine, and the more care we employ, the more assurance shall we acquire that the enumeration, which we form from the whole, is complete and entire.

Section IV. Sceptical Doubts Concerning the Operations of the Understanding

Part I

All the objects of human reason or enquiry may naturally be divided into two kinds, to wit, Relations of Ideas, and Matters of Fact. Of the first kind are the sciences of Geometry, Algebra, and Arithmetic; and in short, every affirmation which is either intuitively or demonstratively certain. That the square of the hypothenuse is equal to the squares of the two sides is a proposition which expresses a relation between these figures. That three times five is equal to the half of thirty expresses a relation between these numbers. Propositions of this kind are discoverable by the mere operation of thought, without dependence on what is anywhere existent in the universe. Though there never were a circle or triangle in nature, the truths, demonstrated by Euclid, would forever retain their certainty and evidence.

Matters of fact, which are the second objects of human reason, are not ascertained in the same manner; nor is our evidence of their truth, however great, of a like nature with the foregoing. The contrary of every matter of fact is still possible; because it can never imply a contradiction, and is conceived by the mind with the same facility and distinctness, as if ever so conformable to reality. That the sun will not rise tomorrow is no less intelligible a proposition, and implies no more contradiction, than the affirmation that it will rise. We should in vain, therefore, attempt to demonstrate its falsehood. Were it demonstratively false, it would imply a contradiction, and could never be distinctly conceived by the mind.

It may, therefore, be a subject worthy of curiosity, to enquire what is the nature of that evidence which assures us of any real existence and matter of fact, beyond the present testimony of our senses, or the records of our memory. This part of philosophy, it is observable, has been little cultivated, either by the ancients or moderns; and therefore our doubts and errors, in the prosecution of so important an enquiry, may be the more excusable; while we march through such difficult paths, without any guide or direction. They may even prove useful, by exciting curiosity, and destroying that implicit faith and security which is the bane of all reasoning and free enquiry. The discovery of defects in the common philosophy, if any such there be, will not, I presume, be a discouragement, but rather an incitement, as is usual, to attempt something more full and satisfactory than has yet been proposed to the public.

All reasonings concerning matter of fact seem to be founded on the relation of Cause and Effect. By means of that relation alone we can go beyond the evidence of our memory and senses. If you were to ask a man why he believes any matter of fact, which is absent; for instance, that his friend is in the country, or in France; he would give you a reason; and this reason would be some other fact; as a letter received from him, or the knowledge of his former resolutions and promises. A man, finding a watch or any other machine in a desert island, would con-

clude that there had once been men in that island. All our reasonings concerning fact are of the same nature. And here it is constantly supposed that there is a connexion between the present fact and that which is inferred from it. Were there nothing to bind them together, the inference would be entirely precarious. The hearing of an articulate voice and rational discourse in the dark assures us of the presence of some person: Why? because these are the effects of the human make and fabric, and closely connected with it. If we anatomize all the other reasonings of this nature, we shall find that they are founded on the relation of cause and effect, and that this relation is either near or remote, direct or collateral. Heat and light are collateral effects of fire, and the one effect may justly be inferred from the other.

If we would satisfy ourselves, therefore, concerning the nature of that evidence, which assures us of matters of fact, we must enquire how we arrive at the knowledge of cause and effect.

I shall venture to affirm, as a general proposition, which admits of no exception, that the knowledge of this relation is not, in any instance, attained by reasonings *a priori*; but arises entirely from experience, when we find that any particular objects are constantly conjoined with each other. Let an object be presented to a man of ever so strong natural reason and abilities; if that object be entirely new to him, he will not be able, by the most accurate examination of its sensible qualities, to discover any of its causes or effects. Adam, though his rational faculties be supposed, at the very first, entirely perfect, could not have inferred from the fluidity and transparency of water that it would suffocate him, or from the light and warmth of fire that it would consume him. No object ever discovers, by the qualities which appear to the senses, either the causes which produced it, or the effects which will arise from it; nor can our reason, unassisted by experience, ever draw any inference concerning real existence and matter of fact.

This proposition, that causes and effects are discoverable, not by reason but by experience, will readily be admitted with regard to such objects as we remember to have once been altogether unknown to us; since we must be conscious of the utter inability, which we then lay under, of foretelling what would arise from them. Present two smooth pieces of marble to a man who has no tincture of natural philosophy; he will never discover that they will adhere together in such a manner as to require great force to separate them in a direct line, while they make so small a resistance to a lateral pressure. Such events, as bear little analogy to the common course of nature, are also readily confessed to be known only by experience; nor does any man imagine that the explosion of gunpowder, or the attraction of a lodestone, could ever be discovered by arguments *a priori*. In like manner, when an effect is supposed to depend upon an intricate machinery or secret structure of parts, we make no difficulty in attributing all our knowledge of it to experience. Who will assert that he can give the ultimate reason why milk or bread is proper nourishment for a man, not for a lion or a tiger?

But the same truth may not appear, at first sight, to have the same evidence with regard to events which have become familiar to us from our first appearance in the world, which bear a close analogy to the whole course of nature, and which are supposed to depend on the simple qualities of objects, without any secret structure of parts. We are apt to imagine that we could discover these effects by the mere operation of our reason, without experience. We fancy that were we brought, on a sudden, into this world, we could at first have inferred that one billiard-ball would communicate motion to another upon impulse; and that we needed not to have waited for the event in order to pronounce with certainty concerning it. Such is the influence of custom that, where it is strongest, it not only covers our natural ignorance, but even conceals itself, and seems not to take place, merely because it is found in the highest degree.

But to convince us that all the laws of nature, and all the operations of bodies without exception, are known only by experience, the following reflections may, perhaps, suffice. Were any object presented to us, and were we required to pronounce concerning the effect, which will result from it, without consulting past observation; after what manner, I beseech you, must the mind proceed in this operation? It must invent or imagine some event, which it ascribes to the object as its effect; and it is plain that this invention must be entirely arbitrary. The mind can never possibly find the effect in the supposed cause, by the most accurate scrutiny and examination. For the effect is totally different from the cause, and consequently can never be discovered in it. Motion in the second billiard-ball is a quite distinct event from motion in the first; nor is there anything in the one to suggest the smallest hint of the other. A stone or piece of metal raised into the air, and left without any support, immediately falls: But to consider the matter *a priori*, is there anything we discover in this situation which can beget the idea of a downward, rather than an upward, or any other, motion, in the stone or metal?

And as the first imagination or invention of a particular effect, in all natural operations, is arbitrary, where we consult not experience; so must we also esteem the supposed tie or connexion between the cause and effect, which binds them together, and renders it impossible that any other effect could result from the operation of that cause. When I see, for instance, a billiard-ball moving in a straight line towards another; even suppose motion in the second ball should by accident be suggested to me, as the result of their contact or impulse; may I not conceive that a hundred different events might as well follow from that cause? May not both these balls remain at absolute rest? May not the first ball return in a straight line, or leap off from the second in any line or direction? All the suppositions are consistent and conceivable. Why then should we give the preference to one, which is no more consistent or conceivable than the rest? All our reasonings *a priori* will never be able to show us any foundation for this preference.

In a word, then, every effect is a distinct event from its cause. It could not, therefore, be discovered in the cause, and the first invention or conception of it, *a priori*, must be entirely arbitrary. And even after it is suggested, the conjunction of it with the cause must appear equally arbitrary; since there are always many other effects which, to reason, must seem fully as consistent and natural. In vain, therefore, should we pretend to determine any single event, or infer any cause or effect, without the assistance of observation and experience.

Hence we may discover the reason why no philosopher who is rational and modest has ever pretended to assign the ultimate cause of any natural operation, or to show distinctly the action of that power which produces any single effect in the universe. It is confessed that the utmost effort of human reason is to reduce the principles, productive of natural phenomena, to a greater simplicity, and to resolve the many particular effects into a few general causes, by means of reasonings from analogy, experience, and observation. But as to the causes of these general causes, we should in vain attempt their discovery; nor shall we ever be able to satisfy ourselves by any particular explication of them. These ultimate springs and principles are totally shut up from human curiosity and enquiry. Elasticity, gravity, cohesion of parts, communication of motion by impulse; these are probably the ultimate causes and principles which we shall ever discover in nature; and we may esteem ourselves sufficiently happy, if, by accurate enquiry and reasoning, we can trace up the particular phenomena to, or near to, these general principles. The most perfect philosophy of the natural kind only staves off our ignorance a little longer: As perhaps the most perfect philosophy of the moral or metaphysical kind serves only to discover larger portions of it. Thus the observation of human blindness and weakness is the result of all philosophy, and meets us, at every turn, in spite of our endeavours to elude or avoid it.

Nor is geometry, when taken into the assistance of natural philosophy, ever able to remedy this defect, or lead us into the knowledge of ultimate causes, by all that accuracy of reasoning, for which it is so justly celebrated. Every part of mixed mathematics proceeds upon the supposition that certain laws are established by nature in her operations; and abstract reasonings are employed, either to assist experience in the discovery of these laws, or to determine their influence in particular instances, where it depends upon any precise degree of distance and quantity. Thus, it is a law of motion, discovered by experience, that the moment or force of any body in motion is in the compound ratio or proportion of its solid contents and its velocity; and consequently, that a small force may remove the greatest obstacle or raise the greatest weight, if, by any contrivance or machinery, we can increase the velocity of that force, so as to make it an overmatch for its antagonist. Geometry assists us in the application of this law, by giving us the just dimensions of all the parts and figures which can enter into any species of machine; but still the discovery of the law itself is owing merely to experience, and all the abstract reasonings in the world could never lead us one step towards the knowledge of it. When we reason *a priori*, and consider merely any object or cause, as it appears to the mind, independent of all observation, it never could suggest to us the notion of any distinct object, such as its effect; much less, show us the inseparable and inviolable connexion between them. A man must be very sagacious who could discover by reasoning that crystal is the effect of heat, and ice of cold, without being previously acquainted with the operation of these qualities.

Part II

But we have not, yet, attained any tolerable satisfaction with regard to the question first proposed. Each solution still gives rise to a new question as difficult as the foregoing, and leads us on to farther enquiries. When it is asked, What is the nature of all our reasonings concerning matter of fact? the proper answer seems to be, that they are founded on the relation of cause and effect. When again it is asked, What is the foundation of all our reasonings and conclusions concerning that relation? it may be replied in one word, Experience. But if we still carry on our sifting humour, and ask, What is the foundation of all conclusions from experience? this implies a new question, which may be of more difficult solution and explication. Philosophers, that give themselves airs of superior wisdom and sufficiency, have a hard task, when they encounter persons of inquisitive dispositions, who push them from every corner, to which they retreat, and who are sure at last to bring them to some dangerous dilemma. The best expedient to prevent this confusion is to be modest in our pretensions; and even to discover the difficulty ourselves before it is objected to us. By this means, we may make a kind of merit of our very ignorance.

I shall content myself, in this section, with an easy task, and shall pretend only to give a negative answer to the question here proposed. I say then, that, even after we have experience of the operations of cause and effect, our conclusions from that experience are not founded on reasoning, or any process of the understanding. This answer we must endeavour both to explain and to defend.

It must certainly be allowed that nature has kept us at a great distance from all her secrets, and has afforded us only the knowledge of a few superficial qualities of objects; while she conceals from us those powers and principles on which the influence of these objects entirely depends. Our senses inform us of the colour, weight, and consistence of bread; but neither sense nor reason can ever inform us of those qualities which fit it for the nourishment and support of a human body. Sight or feeling conveys an idea of the actual motion of bodies; but as to that wonderful force or power which would carry on a moving body forever in a continued change of place, and which bodies never lose but by communicating it to others; of this we cannot form the most distant conception. But notwithstanding this ignorance of natural powers [The word *power* is here used in a loose and popular sense. The more accurate explication of it would give additional evidence to this argument. See Sec. 7.] and principles, we always presume, when we see like sensible qualities, that they have like secret powers, and expect that effects similar to those which we have experienced will follow from them. If a body of like colour and consistence with that bread, which we have formerly eaten, be presented to us, we make no scruple of repeating the experiment, and foresee, with certainty, like nourishment and support. Now this is a process of the mind or thought of which I would willingly know the foundation. It is allowed on all hands that there is no known connexion between the sensible qualities and the secret powers; and consequently, that the mind is not led to form such a conclusion concerning their constant and regular conjunction, by anything which it knows of their nature. As to past Experience, it can be allowed to give direct and certain information of those precise objects only, and that precise period of time, which fell under its cognizance: But why this experience should be extended to future times, and to other objects, which for aught we know may be only in appearance similar; this is the main question on which I would insist. The bread, which I formerly ate, nourished me; that is, a body of such sensible qualities was, at that time, endued with such secret powers: But does it follow that other bread must also nourish me at another time, and that like sensible qualities must always be attended with like secret powers? The consequence seems nowise necessary. At least, it must be acknowledged that there is here a consequence drawn by the mind; that there is a certain step taken; a process of thought, and an inference, which wants to be explained. These two

propositions are far from being the same, I have found that such an object has always been attended with such an effect, and I foresee that other objects, which are, in appearance, similar, will be attended with similar effects. I shall allow, if you please, that the one proposition may justly be inferred from the other: I know, in fact, that it always is inferred. But if you insist that the inference is made by a chain of reasoning, I desire you to produce that reasoning. The connexion between these propositions is not intuitive. There is required a medium, which may enable the mind to draw such an inference, if indeed it be drawn by reasoning and argument. What that medium is, I must confess, passes my comprehension; and it is incumbent on those to produce it who assert that it really exists, and is the origin of all our conclusions concerning matter of fact.

This negative argument must certainly, in process of time, become altogether convincing, if many penetrating and able philosophers shall turn their enquiries this way; and no one be ever able to discover any connecting proposition or intermediate step, which supports the understanding in this conclusion. But as the question is yet new, every reader may not trust so far to his own penetration as to conclude, because an argument escapes his enquiry, that therefore it does not really exist. For this reason it may be requisite to venture upon a more difficult task; and enumerating all the branches of human knowledge, endeavour to show that none of them can afford such an argument.

All reasonings may be divided into two kinds, namely demonstrative reasoning, or that concerning relations of ideas, and moral [or probable] reasoning, or that concerning matter of fact and existence. That there are no demonstrative arguments in the case seems evident; since it implies no contradiction that the course of nature may change, and that an object, seemingly like those which we have experienced, may be attended with different or contrary effects. May I not clearly and distinctly conceive that a body, falling from the clouds, and which, in all other respects, resembles snow, has yet the taste of salt or feeling of fire? Is there any more intelligible proposition than to affirm that all the trees will flourish in December and January, and decay in May and June? Now whatever is intelligible, and can be distinctly conceived, implies no contradiction, and can never be proved false by any demonstrative argument or abstract reasoning *a priori*.

If we be, therefore, engaged by arguments to put trust in past experience, and make it the standard of our future judgment, these arguments must be probable only, or such as regard matter of fact and real existence, according to the division above mentioned. But that there is no argument of this kind must appear, if our explication of that species of reasoning be admitted as solid and satisfactory. We have said that all arguments concerning existence are founded on the relation of cause and effect; that our knowledge of that relation is derived entirely from experience; and that all our experimental conclusions proceed upon the supposition that the future will be conformable to the past. To endeavour, therefore, the proof of this last supposition by probable arguments, or arguments regarding existence, must be evidently going in a circle, and taking that for granted which is the very point in question.

In reality, all arguments from experience are founded on the similarity which we discover among natural objects, and by which we are induced to expect effects similar to those which we have found to follow from such objects. And though none but a fool or madman will ever pretend to dispute the authority of experience, or to reject that great guide of human life; it may surely be allowed a philosopher to have so much curiosity, at least, as to examine the principle of human nature which gives this mighty authority to experience, and makes us draw advantage from that similarity which nature has placed among different objects. From causes which appear similar, we expect similar effects. This is the sum of all our experimental conclusions. Now it seems evident that, if this conclusion were formed by reason, it would be as perfect at first, and upon one instance, as after ever so long a course of experience. But the case is far otherwise. Nothing so like as eggs; yet no one on account of this appearing similarity expects the same taste and relish in all of them. It is only after a long course of uniform experiments in any kind that we attain a firm reliance and security with regard to a particular event. Now where is that process of reasoning which, from one instance, draws a conclusion so different from that which it infers from a hundred instances, that are nowise different from that single one? This ques-

tion I propose as much for the sake of information, as with an intention of raising difficulties. I cannot find, I cannot imagine any such reasoning. But I keep my mind still open to instruction, if anyone will vouchsafe to bestow it on me.

Should it be said that, from a number of uniform experiments, we infer a connexion between the sensible qualities and the secret powers; this, I must confess, seems the same difficulty, couched in different terms. The question still recurs, on what process of argument this inference is founded? Where is the medium, the interposing ideas, which join propositions so very wide of each other? It is confessed that the colour, consistence, and other sensible qualities of bread appear not, of themselves, to have any connexion with the secret powers of nourishment and support. For otherwise we could infer these secret powers from the first appearance of these sensible qualities, without the aid of experience; contrary to the sentiment of all philosophers, and contrary to plain matter of fact. Here then is our natural state of ignorance with regard to the powers and influence of all objects. How is this remedied by experience? It only shows us a number of uniform effects, resulting from certain objects, and teaches us that those particular objects, at that particular time, were endowed with such powers and forces. When a new object, endowed with similar sensible qualities, is produced, we expect similar powers and forces, and look for a like effect. From a body of like colour and consistence with bread, we expect like nourishment and support. But this surely is a step or progress of the mind, which wants to be explained. When a man says, I have found, in all past instances, such sensible qualities conjoined with such secret powers: And when he says, Similar sensible qualities will always be conjoined with similar secret powers; he is not guilty of a tautology, nor are these propositions in any respect the same. You say that the one proposition is an inference from the other. But you must confess that the inference is not intuitive; neither is it demonstrative: Of what nature is it then? To say it is experimental, is begging the question. For all inferences from experience suppose, as their foundation, that the future will resemble the past, and that similar powers will be conjoined with similar sensible qualities. If there be any suspicion that the course of nature may change, and that the past may be no rule for the future, all experience becomes useless, and can give rise to no inference or conclusion. It is impossible, therefore, that any arguments from experience can prove this resemblance of the past to the future; since all these arguments are founded on the supposition of that resemblance. Let the course of things be allowed hitherto ever so regular; that alone, without some new argument or inference, proves not that, for the future, it will continue so. In vain do you pretend to have learned the nature of bodies from your past experience. Their secret nature, and consequently, all their effects and influence, may change, without any change in their sensible qualities. This happens sometimes, and with regard to some objects: Why may it not happen always, and with regard to all objects? What logic, what process of argument secures you against this supposition? My practice, you say, refutes my doubts. But you mistake the purport of my question. As an agent, I am quite satisfied in the point; but as a philosopher, who has some share of curiosity, I will not say scepticism, I want to learn the foundation of this inference. No reading, no enquiry has yet been able to remove my difficulty, or give me satisfaction in a matter of such importance. Can I do better than propose the difficulty to the public, even though, perhaps, I have small hopes of obtaining a solution? We shall at least, by this means, be sensible of our ignorance, if we do not augment our knowledge.

I must confess, that a man is guilty of unpardonable arrogance who concludes, because an argument has escaped his own investigation, that therefore it does not really exist. I must also confess, that, though all the learned, for several ages, should have employed themselves in fruitless search upon any subject, it may still, perhaps, be rash to conclude positively that the subject must, therefore, pass all human comprehension. Even though we examine all the sources of our knowledge, and conclude them unfit for such a subject, there may still remain a suspicion that the enumeration is not complete, or the examination not accurate. But with regard to the present subject, there are some considerations which seem to remove all this accusation of arrogance or suspicion of mistake.

It is certain that the most ignorant and stupid peasants, nay infants, nay even brute beasts, improve by experience, and learn the qualities of natural objects by observing the effects which result from them. When a child has felt the sensation of pain from touching the flame of a candle, he will be careful not to put his hand near any candle; but will expect a similar effect from a cause which is similar in its sensible qualities and appearance. If you assert, therefore, that the understanding of the child is led into this conclusion by any process of argument or ratiocination, I may justly require you to produce that argument; nor have you any pretence to refuse so equitable a demand. You cannot say that the argument is abstruse, and may possibly escape your enquiry; since you confess that it is obvious to the capacity of a mere infant. If you hesitate, therefore, a moment, or if, after reflection, you produce any intricate or profound argument, you, in a manner, give up the question, and confess that it is not reasoning which engages us to suppose the past resembling the future, and to expect similar effects from causes, which are, to appearance, similar. This is the proposition which I intended to enforce in the present section. If I be right, I pretend not to have made any mighty discovery. And if I be wrong, I must acknowledge myself to be indeed a very backward scholar; since I cannot now discover an argument which, it seems, was perfectly familiar to me, long before I was out of my cradle.

Section V. Sceptical Solution of These Doubts

Part I

The passion for philosophy, like that for religion, seems liable to this inconvenience, that, though it aims at the correction of our manners, and extirpation of our vices, it may only serve, by imprudent management, to foster a predominant inclination, and push the mind, with more determined resolution, towards that side, which already draws too much, by the bias and propensity of the natural temper. It is certain that, while we aspire to the magnanimous firmness of the philosophic sage, and endeavour to confine our pleasures altogether within our own minds, we may, at last, render our philosophy like that of Epictetus, and other Stoics, only a

more refined system of selfishness, and reason ourselves out of all virtue, as well as social enjoyment.
While we study with attention the vanity of human
life, and turn all our thoughts towards the empty
and transitory nature of riches and honours, we are,
perhaps, all the while, flattering our natural indolence, which, hating the bustle of the world, and
drudgery of business, seeks a pretence of reason to
give itself a full and uncontrolled indulgence. There
is, however, one species of philosophy which seems
little liable to this inconvenience, and that because
it strikes in with no disorderly passion of the human mind, nor can mingle itself with any natural
affection or propensity; and that is the Academic or
Sceptical philosophy. The academics always talk of
doubt and suspense of judgment, of danger in hasty
determinations, of confining to very narrow bounds
the enquiries of the understanding, and of renounc-
ing all speculations which lie not within the limits
of common life and practice. Nothing, therefore,
can be more contrary than such a philosophy to the
supine indolence of the mind, its rash arrogance,
its lofty pretensions, and its superstitious credulity.
Every passion is mortified by it, except the love of
truth; and that passion never is, nor can be, carried
to too high a degree. It is surprising, therefore, that
this philosophy, which, in almost every instance,
must be harmless and innocent, should be the subject of so much groundless reproach and obloquy.
But, perhaps, the very circumstance which renders
it so innocent is what chiefly exposes it to the public hatred and resentment. By flattering no irregular passion, it gains few partisans: By opposing so
many vices and follies, it raises to itself abundance
of enemies, who stigmatize it as libertine, profane,
and irreligious.

Nor need we fear that this philosophy, while it
endeavours to limit our enquiries to common life,
should ever undermine the reasonings of common
life, and carry its doubts so far as to destroy all action, as well as speculation. Nature will always
maintain her rights, and prevail in the end over any
abstract reasoning whatsoever. Though we should
conclude, for instance, as in the foregoing section,
that, in all reasonings from experience, there is a
step taken by the mind which is not supported
by any argument or process of the understanding,
there is no danger that these reasonings, on which
almost all knowledge depends, will ever be affected

by such a discovery. If the mind be not engaged by
argument to make this step, it must be induced by
some other principle of equal weight and authority;
and that principle will preserve its influence as long
as human nature remains the same. What that principle is may well be worth the pains of enquiry.

Suppose a person, though endowed with the
strongest faculties of reason and reflection, to be
brought on a sudden into this world; he would, indeed, immediately observe a continual succession
of objects, and one event following another; but he
would not be able to discover anything farther. He
would not, at first, by any reasoning, be able to
reach the idea of cause and effect; since the particular powers by which all natural operations are performed never appear to the senses; nor is it reasonable to conclude, merely because one event, in one
instance, precedes another, that therefore the one is
the cause, the other the effect. Their conjunction
may be arbitrary and casual. There may be no reason to infer the existence of one from the appearance of the other. And in a word, such a person,
without more experience, could never employ his
conjecture or reasoning concerning any matter of
fact, or be assured of anything beyond what was immediately present to his memory and senses.

Suppose again, that he has acquired more experience, and has lived so long in the world as to
have observed similar objects or events to be constantly conjoined together; what is the consequence
of this experience? He immediately infers the existence of one object from the appearance of the other.
Yet he has not, by all his experience, acquired any
idea or knowledge of the secret power by which
the one object produces the other; nor is it, by any
process of reasoning, he is engaged to draw this
inference. But still he finds himself determined to
draw it: And though he should be convinced that
his understanding has no part in the operation, he
would nevertheless continue in the same course of
thinking. There is some other principle which determines him to form such a conclusion.

This principle is Custom or Habit. For wherever the repetition of any particular act or operation
produces a propensity to renew the same act or operation, without being impelled by any reasoning or
process of the understanding; we always say, that
this propensity is the effect of Custom. By employing that word, we pretend not to have given the ul-

timate reason of such a propensity. We only point out a principle of human nature, which is universally acknowledged, and which is well known by its effects. Perhaps, we can push our enquiries no farther, or pretend to give the cause of this cause; but must rest contented with it as the ultimate principle, which we can assign, of all our conclusions from experience. It is sufficient satisfaction that we can go so far; without repining at the narrowness of our faculties, because they will carry us no farther. And it is certain we here advance a very intelligible proposition at least, if not a true one, when we assert that, after the constant conjunction of two objects, heat and flame, for instance, weight and solidity, we are determined by custom alone to expect the one from the appearance of the other. This hypothesis seems even the only one which explains the difficulty, why we draw, from a thousand instances, an inference, which we are not able to draw from one instance, that is, in no respect, different from them. Reason is incapable of any such variation. The conclusions, which it draws from considering one circle, are the same which it would form upon surveying all the circles in the universe. But no man, having seen only one body move after being impelled by another, could infer that every other body will move after a like impulse. All inferences from experience, therefore, are effects of custom, not of reasoning.

[Nothing is more usual than for writers, even on moral, political, or physical subjects, to distinguish between reason and experience, and to suppose that these species of argumentation are entirely different from each other. The former are taken for the mere result of our intellectual faculties, which, by considering *a priori* the nature of things, and examining the effects that must follow from their operation, establish particular principles of science and philosophy. The latter are supposed to be derived entirely from sense and observation, by which we learn what has actually resulted from the operation of particular objects, and are thence able to infer what will, for the future, result from them. Thus, for instance, the limitations and restraints of civil government, and a legal constitution, may be defended, either from reason, which, reflecting on the great frailty and corruption of human nature, teaches that no man can safely be trusted with unlimited authority; or from experience and history,

which inform us of the enormous abuses that ambition, in every age and country, has been found to make of so imprudent a confidence.

The same distinction between reason and experience is maintained in all our deliberations concerning the conduct of life; while the experienced statesman, general, physician, or merchant is trusted and followed; and the unpractised novice, with whatever natural talents endowed, neglected and despised. Though it be allowed that reason may form very plausible conjectures with regard to the consequences of such a particular conduct in such particular circumstances; it is still supposed imperfect, without the assistance of experience, which is alone able to give stability and certainty to the maxims, derived from study and reflection.

But notwithstanding that this distinction be thus universally received, both in the active speculative scenes of life, I shall not scruple to pronounce that it is, at bottom, erroneous, at least, superficial.

If we examine those arguments which, in any of the sciences above-mentioned, are supposed to be the mere effects of reasoning and reflection, they will be found to terminate, at last, in some general principle or conclusion, for which we can assign no reason but observation and experience. The only difference between them and those maxims which are vulgarly esteemed the result of pure experience is that the former cannot be established without some process of thought, and some reflection on what we have observed, in order to distinguish its circumstances, and trace its consequences: Whereas in the latter, the experienced event is exactly and fully similar to that which we infer as the result of any particular situation. The history of a Tiberius or a Nero makes us dread a like tyranny, were our monarchs freed from the restraints of laws and senates: But the observation of any fraud or cruelty in private life is sufficient, with the aid of a little thought, to give us the same apprehension; while it serves as an instance of the general corruption of human nature, and shows us the danger which we must incur by reposing an entire confidence in mankind. In both cases, it is experience which is ultimately the foundation of our inference and conclusion.

There is no man so young and unexperienced as not to have formed, from observation, many general and just maxims concerning human affairs and the conduct of life; but it must be confessed that, when a man comes to put these in practice, he will be extremely liable to error, till time and farther experience both enlarge these maxims, and teach him their proper use and application. In every situation or incident, there are many particular and seemingly minute circumstances which the man of greatest talents is, at first, apt to overlook, though on them the justness of his conclusions, and consequently the prudence of his conduct, entirely depend. Not to mention that, to a young beginner, the general observations and maxims occur not always on the proper occasions, nor can be immediately applied with due calmness and distinction. The truth is, an unexperienced reasoner could be no reasoner at all, were he absolutely unexperienced; and when we assign that character to anyone, we mean it only in a comparative sense, and suppose him possessed of experience, in a smaller and more imperfect degree.]

Custom, then, is the great guide of human life. It is that principle alone which renders our experience useful to us, and makes us expect, for the future, a similar train of events with those which have appeared in the past. Without the influence of custom, we should be entirely ignorant of every matter of fact, beyond what is immediately present to the memory and senses. We should never know how to adjust means to ends, or to employ our natural powers in the production of any effect. There would be an end at once of all action, as well as of the chief part of speculation.

But here it may be proper to remark that though our conclusions from experience carry us beyond our memory and senses, and assure us of matters of fact, which happened in the most distant places and most remote ages; yet some fact must always be present to the senses or memory, from which we may first proceed in drawing these conclusions. A man who should find in a desert country the remains of pompous buildings would conclude that the country had, in ancient times, been cultivated by civilized inhabitants; but did nothing of this nature occur to him, he could never form such an inference. We learn the events of former ages from history; but then we must peruse the volumes in which this instruction is contained, and thence carry up our inferences from one testimony to another, till we arrive at the eye-witnesses and spec-

tators of these distant events. In a word, if we proceed not upon some fact, present to the memory or senses, our reasonings would be merely hypothetical; and however the particular links might be connected with each other, the whole chain of inferences would have nothing to support it, nor could we ever, by its means, arrive at the knowledge of any real existence. If I ask why you believe any particular matter of fact which you relate, you must tell me some reason; and this reason will be some other fact, connected with it. But as you cannot proceed after this manner, *in infinitum,* you must at last terminate in some fact, which is present to your memory or senses; or must allow that your belief is entirely without foundation.

What then is the conclusion of the whole matter? A simple one; though, it must be confessed, pretty remote from the common theories of philosophy. All belief of matter of fact or real existence is derived merely from some object, present to the memory or senses, and a customary conjunction between that and some other object. Or in other words; having found, in many instances, that any two kinds of objects, flame and heat, snow and cold, have always been conjoined together; if flame or snow be presented anew to the senses, the mind is carried by custom to expect heat or cold, and to believe that such a quality does exist, and will discover itself upon a nearer approach. This belief is the necessary result of placing the mind in such circumstances. It is an operation of the soul, when we are so situated, as unavoidable as to feel the passion of love, when we receive benefits: or hatred, when we meet with injuries. All these operations are a species of natural instincts, which no reasoning or process of the thought and understanding is able either to produce, or to prevent.

At this point, it would be very allowable for us to stop our philosophical researches. In most questions, we can never make a single step farther; and in all questions, we must terminate here at last, after our most restless and curious enquiries. But still our curiosity will be pardonable, perhaps commendable, if it carry us on to still farther researches, and make us examine more accurately the nature of this belief, and of the customary conjunction, whence it is derived. By this means we may meet with some explications and analogies that will give satisfaction; at least to such as love the abstract sciences, and can be entertained with speculations which, however accurate, may still retain a degree of doubt and uncertainty. As to readers of a different taste: the remaining part of this section is not calculated for them, and the following enquiries may well be understood, though it be neglected.

Part II

Nothing is more free than the imagination of man; and though it cannot exceed that original stock of ideas, furnished by the internal and external senses, it has unlimited power of mixing, compounding, separating, and dividing these ideas, in all the varieties of fiction and vision. It can feign a train of events, with all the appearance of reality, ascribe to them a particular time and place, conceive them as existent, and paint them out to itself with every circumstance that belongs to any historical fact, which it believes with the greatest certainty. Wherein, therefore, consists the difference between such a fiction and belief? It lies not merely in any peculiar idea, which is annexed to such a conception as commands our assent, and which is wanting to every known fiction. For as the mind has authority over all its ideas, it could voluntarily annex this particular idea to any fiction, and consequently be able to believe whatever it pleases, contrary to what we find by daily experience. We can, in our conception, join the head of a man to the body of a horse; but it is not in our power to believe that such an animal has ever really existed.

It follows, therefore, that the difference between fiction and belief lies in some sentiment or feeling which is annexed to the latter, not to the former, and which depends not on the will, nor can be commanded at pleasure. It must be excited by nature, like all other sentiments; and must arise from the particular situation in which the mind is placed at any particular juncture. Whenever any object is presented to the memory or senses, it immediately, by the force of custom, carries the imagination to conceive that object which is usually conjoined to it; and this conception is attended with a feeling or sentiment different from the loose reveries of the fancy. In this consists the whole nature of belief. For as there is no matter of fact which we believe so firmly that we cannot conceive the contrary, there would be no difference between the conception as-

sented to, and that which is rejected, were it not for some sentiment which distinguishes the one from the other. If I see a billiard-ball moving towards another, on a smooth table, I can easily conceive it to stop upon contact. This conception implies no contradiction; but still it feels very differently from that conception by which I represent to myself the impulse and the communication of motion from one ball to another.

Were we to attempt a definition of this sentiment, we should, perhaps, find it a very difficult, if not an impossible, task; in the same manner as if we should endeavour to define the feeling of cold or passion of anger to a creature who never had any experience of these sentiments. Belief is the true and proper name of this feeling; and no one is ever at a loss to know the meaning of that term; because every man is every moment conscious of the sentiment represented by it. It may not, however, be improper to attempt a description of this sentiment; in hopes we may, by that means, arrive at some analogies, which may afford a more perfect explication of it. I say, then, that belief is nothing but a more vivid, lively, forcible, firm, steady conception of an object than what the imagination alone is ever able to attain. This variety of terms, which may seem so unphilosophical, is intended only to express that act of the mind, which renders realities, or what is taken for such, more present to us than fictions, causes them to weigh more in the thought, and gives them a superior influence on the passions and imagination. Provided we agree about the thing, it is needless to dispute about the terms. The imagination has the command over all its ideas, and can join and mix and vary them, in all the ways possible. It may conceive fictitious objects with all the circumstances of place and time. It may set them, in a manner, before our eyes, in their true colours, just as they might have existed. But as it is impossible that this faculty of imagination can ever, of itself, reach belief, it is evident that belief consists not in the peculiar nature or order of ideas, but in the manner of their conception, and in their feeling to the mind. I confess that it is impossible perfectly to explain this feeling or manner of conception. We may make use of words, which express something near it. But its true and proper name, as we observed before, is *belief*; which is a term that everyone sufficiently understands in common life. And in philosophy, we can go no farther than assert that *belief* is something felt by the mind, which distinguishes the ideas of the judgment from the fictions of the imagination. It gives them more weight and influence; makes them appear of greater importance; inforces them in the mind; and renders them the governing principle of our actions. I hear at present, for instance, a person's voice, with whom I am acquainted; and the sound comes as from the next room. This impression of my senses immediately conveys my thought to the person, together with all the surrounding objects. I paint them out to myself as existing at present, with the same qualities and relations, of which I formerly knew them possessed. These ideas take faster hold of my mind than ideas of an enchanted castle. They are very different to the feeling, and have a much greater influence of every kind, either to give pleasure or pain, joy or sorrow.

Let us, then, take in the whole compass of this doctrine, and allow that the sentiment of belief is nothing but a conception more intense and steady than what attends the mere fictions of the imagination, and that this manner of conception arises from a customary conjunction of the object with something present to the memory or senses: I believe that it will not be difficult, upon these suppositions, to find other operations of the mind analogous to it, and to trace up these phenomena to principles still more general.

We have already observed that nature has established connexions among particular ideas, and that no sooner one idea occurs to our thoughts than it introduces its correlative, and carries our attention towards it, by a gentle and insensible movement. These principles of connexion or association we have reduced to three, namely, Resemblance, Contiguity, and Causation; which are the only bonds that unite our thoughts together, and beget that regular train of reflection or discourse which, in a greater or less degree, takes place among mankind. Now here arises a question, on which the solution of the present difficulty will depend. Does it happen, in all these relations, that, when one of the objects is presented to the senses or memory, the mind is not only carried to the conception of the correlative, but reaches a steadier and stronger conception of it than what otherwise it would have been able to attain? This seems to be the case with that

belief which arises from the relation of cause and effect. And if the case be the same with the other relations or principles of associations, this may be established as a general law, which takes place in all the operations of the mind.

We may, therefore, observe, as the first experiment to our present purpose, that, upon the appearance of the picture of an absent friend, our idea of him is evidently enlivened by the resemblance, and that every passion which that idea occasions, whether of joy or sorrow, acquires new force and vigour. In producing this effect, there concur both a relation and a present impression. Where the picture bears him no resemblance, at least was not intended for him, it never so much as conveys our thought to him: And where it is absent, as well as the person; though the mind may pass from the thought of the one to that of the other; it feels its idea to be rather weakened than enlivened by that transition. We take a pleasure in viewing the picture of a friend, when it is set before us; but when it is removed, rather choose to consider him directly than by reflection in an image, which is equally distant and obscure.

The ceremonies of the Roman Catholic religion may be considered as instances of the same nature. The devotees of that [strange] superstition usually plead in excuse for the mummeries, with which they are upbraided, that they feel the good effect of those external motions, and postures, and actions, in enlivening their devotion and quickening their fervour, which otherwise would decay, if directed entirely to distant and immaterial objects. We shadow out the objects of our faith, say they, in sensible types and images, and render them more present to us by the immediate presence of these types than it is possible for us to do merely by an intellectual view and contemplation. Sensible objects have always a greater influence on the fancy than any other; and this influence they readily convey to those ideas to which they are related, and which they resemble. I shall only infer from these practices, and this reasoning, that the effect of resemblance in enlivening the ideas is very common; and as in every case a resemblance and a present impression must concur, we are abundantly supplied with experiments to prove the reality of the foregoing principle.

We may add force to these experiments by others of a different kind, in considering the effects of contiguity as well as of resemblance. It is certain that distance diminishes the force of every idea, and that, upon our approach to any object; though it does not discover itself to our senses; it operates upon the mind with an influence, which imitates an immediate impression. The thinking on any object readily transports the mind to what is contiguous; but it is only the actual presence of an object that transports it with a superior vivacity. When I am a few miles from home, whatever relates to it touches me more nearly than when I am two hundred leagues distant; though even at that distance the reflecting on anything in the neighbourhood of my friends or family naturally produces an idea of them. But as in this latter case, both the objects of the mind are ideas; notwithstanding there is an easy transition between them; that transition alone is not able to give a superior vivacity to any of the ideas, for want of some immediate impression.

["Naturane nobis, inquit, datum dicam, an errore quodam, ut, cum ea loca videamus, in quibus memoria dignos viros acceperimus multum esse versatos, magis moveamur, quam siquando eorum ipsorum aut facta audiamus aut scriptum aliquod legamus? Velut ego nunc moveor. Venit enim mihi Platonis in mentem, quem accepimus primum hic disputare solitum: Cujus etiam illi hortuli propinqui non memoriam solum mihi afferunt, sed ipsum videntur in conspectu meo hic ponere. Hic Speusippus, hic Xenocrates, hic ejus auditor Polemo; cujus ipsa illa sessio fuit, quam videamus. Equidem etiam curiam nostram Hostiliam dico, non hanc novam, quae mihi minor esse videtur postquam est major, solebam intuens, Scipionem, Catonem, Laelium, nostrum vero in primis avum cogitare. Tanta vis admonitionis est in locis; ut non sine causa ex his memoriae deducta sit disciplina." Cicero de Finibus. Lib. v. 2.]

No one can doubt but causation has the same influence as the other two relations of resemblance and contiguity. Superstitious people are fond of the reliques of saints and holy men, for the same reason that they seek after types or images, in order to enliven their devotion, and give them a more intimate and strong conception of those exemplary lives, which they desire to imitate. Now it is evident that one of the best reliques which a devotee could procure would be the handywork of a saint; and if his clothes and furniture are ever to be considered in this light, it is because they were once at his disposal, and were moved and affected by him; in which respect they are to be considered as imperfect effects, and as connected with him by a shorter chain of consequences than any of those by which we learn the reality of his existence.

Suppose that the son of a friend, who had been long dead or absent, were presented to us; it is evident that this object would instantly revive its correlative idea, and recall to our thoughts all past intimacies and familiarities, in more lively colours than they would otherwise have appeared to us. This is another phenomenon which seems to prove the principle above-mentioned.

We may observe that, in these phenomena, the belief of the correlative object is always presupposed; without which the relation could have no effect. The influence of the picture supposes that we believe our friend to have once existed. Contiguity to home can never excite our ideas of home, unless we believe that it really exists. Now I assert that this belief, where it reaches beyond the memory or senses, is of a similar nature, and arises from similar causes, with the transition of thought and vivacity of conception here explained. When I throw a piece of dry wood into a fire, my mind is immediately carried to conceive that it augments, not extinguishes, the flame. This transition of thought from the cause to the effect proceeds not from reason. It derives its origin altogether from custom and experience. And as it first begins from an object, present to the senses, it renders the idea or conception of flame more strong and lively than any loose, floating reverie of the imagination. That idea arises immediately. The thought moves instantly towards it, and conveys to it all that force of conception, which is derived from the impression present to the senses. When a sword is levelled at my breast, does not the idea of wound and pain strike me more strongly than when a glass of wine is presented to me, even though by accident this idea should occur after the appearance of the latter object? But what is there in this whole matter to cause such a strong conception, except only a present object and a customary transition to the idea of another object, which we have been accustomed to conjoin with the former? This is the whole operation of the mind, in all our conclusions concerning matter of fact and existence; and it is a satisfaction to find some analogies by which it may be explained. The transition from a present object does in all cases give strength and solidity to the related idea.

Here, then, is a kind of pre-established harmony between the course of nature and the succession of our ideas; and though the powers and forces by which the former is governed be wholly unknown to us; yet our thoughts and conceptions have still, we find, gone on in the same train with the other works of nature. Custom is that principle by which this correspondence has been effected; so necessary to the subsistence of our species, and the regulation of our conduct, in every circumstance and occurrence of human life. Had not the presence of an object instantly excited the idea of those objects, commonly conjoined with it, all our knowledge must have been limited to the narrow sphere of our memory and senses; and we should never have been able to adjust means to ends, or employ our natural powers, either to the producing of good, or avoiding of evil. Those who delight in the discovery and contemplation of final causes have here ample subject to employ their wonder and admiration.

I shall add, for a further confirmation of the foregoing theory, that, as this operation of the mind, by which we infer like effects from like causes, and vice versa, is so essential to the subsistence of all human creatures, it is not probable that it could be trusted to the fallacious deductions of our reason, which is slow in its operations; appears not, in any degree, during the first years of infancy; and at best is, in every age and period of human life, extremely liable to error and mistake. It is more conformable to the ordinary wisdom of nature to secure so necessary an act of the mind, by some instinct or mechanical tendency, which may be infallible in its operations, may discover itself at the first appearance of life and thought, and may be independent of all the laboured deductions of the understanding. As nature has taught us the use of our limbs, without giving us the knowledge of the muscles and nerves by which they are actuated; so has she implanted in us an instinct, which carries forward the thought in a correspondent course to that which she has established among external objects: though we are ignorant of those powers and forces on which this regular course and succession of objects totally depends.

Section VI. Of Probability

[Mr. Locke divides all arguments into demonstrative and probable. In this view, we must say that it is only probable all men must die, or that the sun will rise tomorrow. But to conform our language more to common use, we ought to divide arguments into demonstrations, proofs, and probabilities. By proofs meaning such arguments from experience as leave no room for doubt or opposition.]

Though there be no such thing as Chance in the world, our ignorance of the real cause of any event has the same influence on the understanding, and begets a like species of belief or opinion.

There is certainly a probability, which arises from a superiority of chances on any side; and according as this superiority increases, and surpasses the opposite chances, the probability receives a proportionable increase, and begets still a higher degree of belief or assent to that side in which we discover the superiority. If a die were marked with one figure or number of spots on four sides, and with another figure or number of spots on the two remaining sides, it would be more probable that the former would turn up than the latter; though, if it had a thousand sides marked in the same manner, and only one side different, the probability would be much higher, and our belief or expectation of the event more steady and secure. This process of the thought or reasoning may seem trivial and obvious; but to those who consider it more narrowly, it may, perhaps, afford matter for curious speculation.

It seems evident that, when the mind looks forward to discover the event which may result from the throw of such a die, it considers the turning up of each particular side as alike probable; and this is the very nature of chance, to render all the particular events comprehended in it entirely equal. But finding a greater number of sides concur in the one event than in the other, the mind is carried more frequently to that event, and meets it oftener, in revolving the various possibilities or chances on which the ultimate result depends. This concurrence of several views in one particular event begets immediately, by an inexplicable contrivance of nature, the sentiment of belief, and gives that event the advantage over its antagonist, which is supported by a smaller number of views, and recurs less frequently to the mind. If we allow that belief is nothing but a firmer and stronger conception of an object than what attends the mere fictions of the imagination, this operation may, perhaps, in some measure be accounted for. The concurrence of these several views or glimpses imprints the idea more strongly on the imagination; gives it superior force and vigour; renders its influence on the passions and affections more sensible; and in a word, begets that reliance or security which constitutes the nature of belief and opinion.

The case is the same with the probability of causes as with that of chance. There are some causes which are entirely uniform and constant in producing a particular effect; and no instance has ever yet been found of any failure or irregularity in their operation. Fire has always burned, and water suffocated every human creature: The production of motion by impulse and gravity is a universal law, which has hitherto admitted of no exception. But there are other causes which have been found more irregular and uncertain; nor has rhubarb always proved a purge, or opium a soporific to everyone who has taken these medicines. It is true, when any cause fails of producing its usual effect, philosophers ascribe not this to any irregularity in nature, but suppose that some secret causes, in the particular structure of parts, have prevented the operation. Our reasonings, however, and conclusions concerning the event are the same as if this principle had no place. Being determined by custom to transfer the past to the future, in all our inferences; where the past has been entirely regular and uniform, we expect the event with the greatest assurance, and leave no room for any contrary supposition. But where different effects have been found to follow from causes, which are to appearance exactly similar, all these various effects must occur to the mind in transferring the past to the future, and enter into our consideration, when we determine the probability of the event. Though we give the preference to that which has been found most usual, and believe that this effect will exist, we must not overlook the other effects, but must assign to each of them a particular weight and authority, in proportion as we have found it to be more or less frequent. It is more probable, in almost every country of Europe, that there will be frost sometime in January than that the weather will continue open throughout that whole month; though this probability varies according to the different climates, and approaches to a certainty in the more northern kingdoms. Here then it seems evident that, when we transfer the past to the future, in order to determine the effect which will result from any cause, we transfer all the different events, in the same proportion as they have appeared in the past, and conceive one to have existed a hundred times, for instance, another ten times, and another once. As a great number of views do here concur in one event, they fortify and confirm it to the imagination, beget that sentiment which we call belief, and give its object the preference above the contrary event, which is not supported by an equal number of experiments, and recurs not so frequently to the thought in transferring the past to the future. Let anyone try to account for this operation of the mind upon any of the received systems of philosophy, and he will be sensible of the difficulty. For my part, I shall think it sufficient if the present hints excite the curiosity of philosophers, and make them sensible how defective all common theories are in treating of such curious and such sublime subjects.

Section VII. Of the Idea of Necessary Connexion

Part I

The great advantage of the mathematical sciences above the moral consists in this, that the ideas of the former, being sensible, are always clear and determinate, the smallest distinction between them is immediately perceptible, and the same terms are still expressive of the same ideas, without ambiguity or variation. An oval is never mistaken for a circle, nor an hyperbola for an ellipsis. The isosceles and scalenum are distinguished by boundaries more exact than vice and virtue, right and wrong. If any term be defined in geometry, the mind readily, of itself, substitutes, on all occasions, the definition for the term defined: Or even when no definition is employed, the object itself may be presented to the senses, and by that means be steadily and clearly apprehended. But the finer sentiments of the mind, the operations of the understanding, the various agitations of the passions, though really in themselves distinct, easily escape us, when surveyed by reflection; nor is it in our power to recall the original object, as often as we have occasion to contemplate it. Ambiguity, by this means, is gradually introduced into our reasonings: Similar objects are readily taken to be the same: And the conclusion becomes at last very wide of the premises.

One may safely, however, affirm that, if we consider these sciences in a proper light, their advantages and disadvantages nearly compensate each other, and reduce both of them to a state of equality. If the mind, with greater facility, retains the ideas of geometry clear and determinate, it must carry on a much longer and more intricate chain of reasoning, and compare ideas much wider of each other, in order to reach the abstruser truths of that science. And if moral ideas are apt, without extreme care, to fall into obscurity and confusion, the inferences are always much shorter in these disquisitions, and the intermediate steps, which lead to the conclusion, much fewer than in the sciences which treat of quantity and number. In reality, there is scarcely a proposition in Euclid so simple as not to consist of more parts than are to be found in any moral reasoning which runs not into chimera and conceit. Where we trace the principles of the human mind through a few steps, we may be very well satisfied with our progress, considering how soon nature throws a bar to all our enquiries concerning causes, and reduces us to an acknowledgment of our ignorance. The chief obstacle, therefore, to our improvement in the moral or metaphysical sciences is the obscurity of the ideas, and ambiguity of the terms. The principal difficulty in the mathematics is the length of inferences and compass of thought requisite to the forming of any conclusion. And, perhaps, our progress in natural philosophy is chiefly retarded by the want of proper experiments and phenomena, which are often discovered by chance, and cannot always be found, when requisite, even by the most diligent and prudent enquiry. As moral philosophy seems hitherto to have received less improvement than either geometry or physics, we may conclude that, if there be any difference in this respect among these sciences, the difficulties which obstruct the progress of the former require superior care and capacity to be surmounted.

There are no ideas which occur in metaphysics more obscure and uncertain than those of power, force, energy, or necessary connexion, of which it is every moment necessary for us to treat in all our disquisitions. We shall, therefore, endeavour, in this section, to fix, if possible, the precise meaning of these terms, and thereby remove some part of that obscurity which is so much complained of in this species of philosophy.

It seems a proposition which will not admit of much dispute that all our ideas are nothing but copies of our impressions, or, in other words, that it is impossible for us to think of anything which we have not antecedently felt, either by our external or internal senses. I have endeavoured [Section II. Of the Origin of Ideas.] to explain and prove this proposition, and have expressed my hopes that, by a proper application of it, men may reach a greater clearness and precision in philosophical reasonings than what they have hitherto been able to attain. Complex ideas may, perhaps, be well known by definition, which is nothing but an enumeration of those parts or simple ideas that compose them. But when we have pushed up definitions to the most simple ideas, and find still some ambiguity and obscurity; what resource are we then possessed of? By what invention can we throw light upon these ideas, and render them altogether precise and determinate to our intellectual view? Produce the impressions or original sentiments, from which the ideas are copied. These impressions are all strong and sensible. They admit not of ambiguity. They are not only placed in a full light themselves, but may throw light on their correspondent ideas, which lie in obscurity. And by this means, we may, perhaps, attain a new microscope or species of optics, by which, in the moral sciences, the most minute, and most simple, ideas may be so enlarged as to fall readily under our apprehension, and be equally known with the grossest and most sensible ideas that can be the object of our enquiry.

To be fully acquainted, therefore, with the idea of power or necessary connexion, let us examine its impression; and in order to find the impression with greater certainty, let us search for it in all the sources from which it may possibly be derived.

When we look about us towards external objects, and consider the operation of causes, we are never able, in a single instance, to discover any power or necessary connexion; any quality which binds the effect to the cause, and renders the one an infallible consequence of the other. We only find that the one does actually, in fact, follow the other. The impulse of one billiard-ball is attended with motion in the second. This is the whole that appears to the outward senses. The mind feels no sentiment or inward impression from this succession of objects: Consequently, there is not, in any single, particular instance of cause and effect, anything which can suggest the idea of power or necessary connexion.

From the first appearance of an object, we never can conjecture what effect will result from it. But were the power or energy of any cause discoverable by the mind, we could foresee the effect, even without experience; and might, at first, pronounce with certainty concerning it, by the mere dint of thought and reasoning.

In reality, there is no part of matter that does ever, by its sensible qualities, discover any power or energy, or give us ground to imagine, that it could produce anything, or be followed by any other object, which we could denominate its effect. Solidity, extension, motion; these qualities are all complete in themselves, and never point out any other event which may result from them. The scenes of the universe are continually shifting, and one object follows another in an uninterrupted succession; but the power or force, which actuates the whole machine, is entirely concealed from us, and never discovers itself in any of the sensible qualities of body. We know that, in fact, heat is a constant attendant of flame; but what is the connexion between them, we have no room so much as to conjecture or imagine. It is impossible, therefore, that the idea of power can be derived from the contemplation of bodies, in single instances of their operation; because no bodies ever discover any power, which can be the original of this idea. [Mr. Locke, in his chapter of power says that, finding from experience, there are several new productions in matter, and concluding that there must somewhere be a power capable of pro-

ducing them, we arrive at last by this reasoning at the idea of power. But no reasoning can ever give us a new, original simple idea, as this philosopher himself confesses. This, therefore, can never be the origin of that idea.]

Since, therefore, external objects as they appear to the senses give us no idea of power or necessary connexion by their operation in particular instances, let us see whether this idea be derived from reflection on the operations of our own minds, and be copied from any internal impression. It may be said that we are every moment conscious of internal power; while we feel that, by the simple command of our will, we can move the organs of our body, or direct the faculties of our mind. An act of volition produces motion in our limbs, or raises a new idea in our Imagination. This influence of the will we know by consciousness. Hence we acquire the idea of power or energy; and are certain that we ourselves and all other intelligent beings are possessed of power. This idea, then, is an idea of reflection, since it arises from reflecting on the operations of our own mind, and on the command which is exercised by will, both over the organs of the body and faculties of the soul.

We shall proceed to examine this pretension; and first with regard to the influence of volition over the organs of the body. This influence, we may observe, is a fact, which, like all other natural events, can be known only by experience, and can never be foreseen from any apparent energy or power in the cause, which connects it with the effect, and renders the one an infallible consequence of the other. The motion of our body follows upon the command of our will. Of this we are every moment conscious. But the means by which this is effected; the energy by which the will performs so extraordinary an operation; of this we are so far from being immediately conscious, that it must forever escape our most diligent enquiry.

For first: Is there any principle in all nature more mysterious than the union of soul with body; by which a supposed spiritual substance acquires such an influence over a material one that the most refined thought is able to actuate the grossest matter? Were we empowered, by a secret wish, to remove mountains, or control the planets in their orbit, this extensive authority would not be more extraordinary, nor more beyond our comprehension. But if by consciousness we perceived any power or energy in the will, we must know this power; we must know its connexion with the effect; we must know the secret union of soul and body, and the nature of both these substances; by which the one is able to operate, in so many instances, upon the other.

Secondly, We are not able to move all the organs of the body with a like authority; though we cannot assign any reason besides experience for so remarkable a difference between one and the other. Why has the will an influence over the tongue and fingers, not over the heart and liver? This question would never embarrass us, were we conscious of a power in the former case, not in the latter. We should then perceive, independent of experience, why the authority of will over the organs of the body is circumscribed within such particular limits. Being in that case fully acquainted with the power or force by which it operates, we should also know why its influence reaches precisely to such boundaries, and no farther.

A man suddenly struck with palsy in the leg or arm, or who had newly lost those members, frequently endeavours at first to move them, and employ them in their usual offices. Here he is as much conscious of power to command such limbs as a man in perfect health is conscious of power to actuate any member which remains in its natural state and condition. But consciousness never deceives. Consequently, neither in the one case nor in the other are we ever conscious of any power. We learn the influence of our will from experience alone. And experience only teaches us how one event constantly follows another, without instructing us in the secret connexion which binds them together, and renders them inseparable.

Thirdly, We learn from anatomy that the immediate object of power in voluntary motion is not the member itself which is moved, but certain muscles, and nerves, and animal spirits and, perhaps, something still more minute and more unknown, through which the motion is successively propagated, ere it reach the member itself whose motion is the immediate object of volition. Can there be a more certain proof that the power by which this whole operation is performed, so far from being directly and fully known by an inward sentiment or consciousness, is, to the last degree, mysterious and unintelligible? Here the mind wills a certain event: Immediately another event, un-known to ourselves, and totally different from the one intended, is produced: This event produces another, equally unknown: Till at last, through a long succession, the desired event is produced. But if the original power were felt, it must be known: Were it known, its effect also must be known, since all power is relative to its effect. And vice versa, if the effect be not known, the power cannot be known nor felt. How indeed can we be conscious of a power to move our limbs, when we have no such power; but only that to move certain animal spirits, which, though they produce at last the motion of our limbs, yet operate in such a manner as is wholly beyond our comprehension?

We may, therefore, conclude from the whole, I hope, without any temerity, though with assurance, that our idea of power is not copied from any sentiment or consciousness of power within ourselves, when we give rise to animal motion, or apply our limbs to their proper use and office. That their motion follows the command of the will is a matter of common experience, like other natural events: But the power or energy by which this is effected, like that in other natural events, is unknown and inconceivable. [It may be pretended that the resistance which we meet with in bodies, obliging us frequently to exert our force, and call up all our power, this gives us the idea of force and power. It is this *nisus*, or strong endeavour, of which we are conscious, that is the original impression from which this idea is copied. But, first, we attribute power to a vast number of objects, where we never can suppose this resistance or exertion of force to take place; to the Supreme Being, who never meets with any resistance; to the mind in its command over its ideas and limbs, in common thinking and motion, where the effect follows immediately upon the will, without any exertion or summoning up of force; to inanimate matter, which is not capable of this sentiment. Secondly, This sentiment of an endeavour to overcome resistance has no known connexion with any event: What follows it, we know by experience; but could not know it *a priori*. It must, however, be confessed, that the animal *nisus*, which we experience, though it can afford no accurate precise idea of power, enters very much into that vulgar, inaccurate idea which is formed of it.]

Shall we then assert that we are conscious of a power or energy in our own minds, when, by an act or command of our will, we raise up a new idea, fix the mind to the contemplation of it, turn it on all sides, and at last dismiss it for some other idea, when we think that we have surveyed it with sufficient accuracy? I believe the same arguments will prove that even this command of the will gives us no real idea of force or energy.

First, It must be allowed that, when we know a power, we know that very circumstance in the cause by which it is enabled to produce the effect: For these are supposed to be synonymous. We must, therefore, know both the cause and effect, and the relation between them. But do we pretend to be acquainted with the nature of the human soul and the nature of an idea, or the aptitude of the one to produce the other? This is a real creation; a production of something out of nothing: Which implies a power so great that it may seem, at first sight, beyond the reach of any being less than infinite. At least it must be owned that such a power is not felt, nor known, nor even conceivable by the mind. We only feel the event, namely, the existence of an idea, consequent to a command of the will: But the manner in which this operation is performed, the power by which it is produced, is entirely beyond our comprehension.

Secondly, The command of the mind over itself is limited, as well as its command over the body; and these limits are not known by reason, or any acquaintance with the nature of cause and effect, but only by experience and observation, as in all other natural events and in the operation of external objects. Our authority over our sentiments and passions is much weaker than that over our ideas; and even the latter authority is circumscribed within very narrow boundaries. Will anyone pretend to assign the ultimate reason of these boundaries, or show why the power is deficient in one case, not in another?

Thirdly, This self-command is very different at different times. A man in health possesses more of it than one languishing with sickness. We are more master of our thoughts in the morning than in the evening: Fasting, than after a full meal. Can we give any reason for these variations, except experience? Where then is the power, of which we pretend to be conscious? Is there not here, either in a spiritual or material substance, or both, some secret mechanism or structure of parts, upon which the effect depends, and which, being entirely unknown to us, renders the power or energy of the will equally unknown and incomprehensible?

Volition is surely an act of the mind with which we are sufficiently acquainted. Reflect upon it. Consider it on all sides. Do you find anything in it like this creative power, by which it raises from nothing a new idea, and with a kind of Fiat, imitates the omnipotence of its Maker, if I may be allowed so to speak, who called forth into existence all the various scenes of nature? So far from being conscious of this energy in the will, it requires as certain experience, as that of which we are possessed, to convince us that such extraordinary effects do ever result from a simple act of volition.

The generality of mankind never find any difficulty in accounting for the more common and familiar operations of nature, such as the descent of heavy bodies, the growth of plants, the generation of animals, or the nourishment of bodies by food: But suppose that, in all these cases, they perceive the very force or energy of the cause, by which it is connected with its effect, and is forever infallible in its operation. They acquire, by long habit, such a turn of mind that, upon the appearance of the cause, they immediately expect with assurance its usual attendant, and hardly conceive it possible that any other event could result from it. It is only on the discovery of extraordinary phenomena, such as earthquakes, pestilence, and prodigies of any kind, that they find themselves at a loss to assign a proper cause, and to explain the manner in which the effect is produced by it. It is usual for men, in such difficulties, to have recourse to some invisible intelligent principle [*Quasi Deus ex machina. Cic. de Nat. Deorum.*] as the immediate cause of that event which surprises them, and which, they think, cannot be accounted for from the common powers of nature. But philosophers, who carry their scrutiny a little farther, immediately perceive that, even in the most familiar events, the energy of the cause is as unintelligible as in the most unusual, and that we only learn by experience the frequent Conjunction of objects, without being ever able to comprehend anything like Connexion between them. Here, then, many philosophers think themselves obliged by reason to have recourse, on all occasions, to the same principle, which the vulgar never appeal to but in cases that appear miraculous and supernatural. They acknowledge mind and intelligence to be, not only the ultimate and original cause of all things, but the immediate and sole cause of every event which appears in nature. They pretend that those objects which are commonly denominated causes are in reality nothing but occasions; and that the true and direct principle of every effect is not any power or force in nature, but a volition of the Supreme Being, who wills that such particular objects should, forever, be conjoined with each other. Instead of saying that one billiard-ball moves another by a force, which it has derived from the author of nature; it is the Deity himself, they say, who, by a particular volition, moves the second ball, being determined to this operation by the impulse of the first ball: in consequence of those general laws which he has laid down to himself in the government of the universe. But philosophers advancing still in their enquiries discover that, as we are totally ignorant of the power on which depends the mutual operation of bodies, we are no less ignorant of that power on which depends the operation of mind on body, or of body on mind; nor are we able, either from our senses or consciousness, to assign the ultimate principle in one case, more than in the other. The same ignorance, therefore, reduces them to the same conclusion. They assert that the Deity is the immediate cause of the union between soul and body; and that they are not the organs of sense, which, being agitated by external objects, produce sensations in the mind; but that it is a particular volition of our omnipotent Maker which excites such a sensation, in consequence of such a motion in the organ. In like manner, it is not any energy in the will that produces local motion in our members: It is God himself, who is pleased to second our will, in itself impotent, and to command that motion which we erroneously attribute to our own power and efficacy. Nor do philosophers stop at this conclusion. They sometimes extend the same inference to the mind itself, in its internal operations. Our mental vision or conception of ideas is nothing but a revelation made to us by our Maker. When we voluntarily turn our thoughts to any object, and raise up its image in the fancy, it is not the will which creates that idea: It is the universal Creator, who discovers it to the mind, and renders it present to us.

Thus, according to these philosophers, everything is full of God. Not content with the principle that nothing exists but by his will, that nothing possesses any power but by his concession: They rob nature, and all created beings, of every power, in order to render their dependence on the Deity still more sensible and immediate. They consider not that, by this theory, they diminish, instead of magnifying, the grandeur of those attributes which they affect so much to celebrate. It argues surely more power in the Deity to delegate a certain degree of power to inferior creatures than to produce everything by his own immediate volition. It argues more wisdom to contrive at first the fabric of the world with such perfect foresight that, of itself, and by its proper operation, it may serve all the purposes of providence, than if the great Creator were obliged every moment to adjust its parts, and animate by his breath all the wheels of that stupendous machine.

But if we would have a more philosophical confutation of this theory, perhaps the two following reflections may suffice.

First, It seems to me that this theory of the universal energy and operation of the Supreme Being is too bold ever to carry conviction with it to a man sufficiently apprized of the weakness of human reason, and the narrow limits to which it is confined in all its operations. Though the chain of arguments which conduct to it were ever so logical, there must arise a strong suspicion, if not an absolute assurance, that it has carried us quite beyond the reach of our faculties, when it leads to conclusions so extraordinary, and so remote from common life and experience. We are got into fairy land, long ere we have reached the last steps of our theory; and there we have no reason to trust our common methods of argument, or to think that our usual analogies and probabilities have any authority. Our line is too short to fathom such immense abysses. And however we may flatter ourselves that we are guided, in every step which we take, by a kind of verisimilitude and experience, we may be assured that this fancied experience has no authority when we thus apply it to subjects that lie entirely out of the sphere of experience. But on this we shall have occasion to touch afterwards [Section XII].

Secondly, I cannot perceive any force in the arguments on which this theory is founded. We are ignorant, it is true, of the manner in which bodies operate on each other: Their force or energy is entirely incomprehensible: But are we not equally ignorant of the manner or force by which a mind, even the supreme mind, operates either on itself or on body? Whence, I beseech you, do we acquire any idea of it? We have no sentiment or consciousness of this power in ourselves. We have no idea of the Supreme Being but what we learn from reflection on our own faculties. Were our ignorance, therefore, a good reason for rejecting anything, we should be led into that principle of denying all energy in the Supreme Being as much as in the grossest matter. We surely comprehend as little the operations of one as of the other. Is it more difficult to conceive that motion may arise from impulse than that it may arise from volition? All we know is our profound ignorance in both cases. [I need not examine at length the *vis inertiae* which is so much talked of in the new philosophy, and which is ascribed to matter. We find by experience that a body at rest or in motion continues forever in its present state, till put from it by some new cause: And that a body impelled takes as much motion from the impelling body as it acquires itself. These are facts. When we call this a *vis inertiae*, we only mark these facts, without pretending to have any idea of the inert power; in the same manner as, when we talk of gravity, we mean certain effects without comprehending that active power. It was never the meaning of Sir Isaac Newton to rob second causes of all force or energy; though some of his followers have endeavoured to establish that theory upon his authority. On the contrary, that great philosopher had recourse to an ethereal active fluid to explain his universal attraction; though he was so cautious and modest as to allow that it was a mere hypothesis, not to be insisted on without more experiments. I must confess that there is something in the fate of opinions a little extraordinary. Descartes insinuated that doctrine of the universal and sole efficacy of the Deity, without insisting on it. Malebranche and other Cartesians made it the foundation of all their philosophy. It had, however, no authority in England. Locke, Clarke, and Cudworth never so much as take notice of it, but suppose all along that matter has a real, though subordinate and derived, power. By what means has it become so prevalent among our modern metaphysicians?]

Part II

But to hasten to a conclusion of this argument, which is already drawn out to too great a length: We have sought in vain for an idea of power or necessary connexion, in all the sources from which we could suppose it to be derived. It appears that, in single instances of the operation of bodies, we never can, by our utmost scrutiny, discover anything but one event following another, without being able to comprehend any force or power by which the cause operates, or any connexion between it and its supposed effect. The same difficulty occurs in contemplating the operations of mind on body, where we observe the motion of the latter to follow upon the volition of the former, but are not able to observe or conceive the tie which binds together the motion and volition, or the energy by which the mind produces this effect. The authority of the will over its own faculties and ideas is not a whit more comprehensible: So that, upon the whole, there appears not, throughout all nature, any one instance of connexion which is conceivable by us. All events seem entirely loose and separate. One event follows another; but we never can observe any tie between them. They seem conjoined, but never connected. And as we can have no idea of anything which never appeared to our outward sense or inward sentiment, the necessary conclusion seems to be that we have no idea of connexion or power at all, and that these words are absolutely without any meaning, when employed either in philosophical reasonings or common life.

But there still remains one method of avoiding this conclusion, and one source which we have not yet examined. When any natural object or event is presented, it is impossible for us, by any sagacity or penetration, to discover, or even conjecture, without experience, what event will result from it, or to carry our foresight beyond that object which is immediately present to the memory and senses. Even after one instance or experiment, where we have observed a particular event to follow upon another, we are not entitled to form a general rule, or foretell what will happen in like cases; it being justly esteemed an unpardonable temerity to judge of the whole course of nature from one single experiment, however accurate or certain. But when one particular species of event has always, in all instances, been conjoined with another, we make no longer any scruple of foretelling one upon the appearance of the other, and of employing that reasoning which can alone assure us of any matter of fact or existence. We then call the one object Cause; the other, Effect. We suppose that there is some connexion between them; some power in the one, by which it infallibly produces the other, and operates with the greatest certainty and strongest necessity.

It appears, then, that this idea of a necessary connexion among events arises from a number of similar instances, which occur of the constant conjunction of these events; nor can that idea ever be suggested by any one of these instances, surveyed in all possible lights and positions. But there is nothing in a number of instances, different from every single instance, which is supposed to be exactly similar; except only that after a repetition of similar instances, the mind is carried by habit, upon the appearance of one event, to expect its usual attendant, and to believe that it will exist. This connexion, therefore, which we feel in the mind, this customary transition of the imagination from one object to its usual attendant, is the sentiment or impression from which we form the idea of power or necessary connexion. Nothing farther is in the case. Contemplate the subject on all sides; you will never find any other origin of that idea. This is the sole difference between one instance, from which we can never receive the idea of connexion, and a number of similar instances, by which it is suggested. The first time a man saw the communication of motion by impulse, as by the shock of two billiard-balls, he could not pronounce that the one event was connected: but only that it was conjoined with the other. After he has observed several instances of this nature, he then pronounces them to be connected. What alteration has happened to give rise to this new idea of connexion? Nothing but that he now feels these events to be connected in his imagination, and can readily foretell the existence of one from the appearance of the other. When we say, therefore, that one object is connected with another, we mean only that they have acquired a connexion in our thought, and give rise to this inference, by which they become proofs of each other's existence: a conclusion, which is somewhat extraordinary, but which seems founded on sufficient evidence. Nor will its evidence be weakened by any general diffidence of the understanding, or sceptical suspicion concerning every conclusion which is new and extraordinary. No conclusions can be more agreeable to scepticism than such as make discoveries concerning the weakness and narrow limits of human reason and capacity.

And what stronger instance can be produced of the surprising ignorance and weakness of the understanding than the present? For surely, if there be any relation among objects which it imports to us to know perfectly, it is that of cause and effect. On this are founded all our reasonings concerning matter of fact or existence. By means of it alone we attain any assurance concerning objects which are removed from the present testimony of our memory and senses. The only immediate utility of all sciences is to teach us how to control and regulate future events by their causes. Our thoughts and enquiries are, therefore, every moment employed about this relation: Yet so imperfect are the ideas which we form concerning it, that it is impossible to give any just definition of cause, except what is drawn from something extraneous and foreign to it. Similar objects are always conjoined with similar. Of this we have experience. Suitably to this experience, therefore, we may define a cause to be an object, followed by another, and where all the objects similar to the first are followed by objects similar to the second. Or, in other words, where, if the first object had not been, the second never had existed. The appearance of a cause always conveys the mind, by a customary transition, to the idea of the effect. Of this also we have experience. We may, therefore, suitably to this experience, form another definition of cause, and call it an object followed by another, and whose appearance always conveys the thought to that other. But though both these definitions be drawn from circumstances foreign to the cause, we cannot remedy this inconvenience, or attain any more perfect definition, which may point out that circumstance in the cause which gives it a connexion with its effect. We have no idea of this connexion; nor even any distinct notion what it is we desire to know, when we endeavour at a conception of it. We say, for instance, that the vibration of this string is the cause of this particular sound. But what do we mean by that affirmation? We either mean that this vibration is followed by this sound, and that all similar vibrations have been followed by similar sounds: or that this vibration is followed by this sound, and that upon the appearance of one, the mind anticipates the senses, and forms immediately an idea of the other. We may consider the relation of cause and effect in either of these two lights; but beyond these, we have no idea of it.

[According to these explications and definitions, the idea of power is relative as much as that of cause; and both have a reference to an effect, or some other event constantly conjoined with the former. When we consider the unknown circumstance of an object by which the degree or quantity of its effect is fixed and determined, we call that its power: And accordingly, it is allowed by all philosophers, that the effect is the measure of the power. But if they had any idea of power, as it is in itself, why could not they measure it in itself? The dispute whether the force of a body in motion be as its velocity, or the square of its velocity; this dispute, I say, needed not be decided by comparing its effects in equal or unequal times, but by a direct mensuration and comparison.

As to the frequent use of the words Force, Power, Energy, &c. which everywhere occur in common conversation, as well as in philosophy: That is no proof that we are acquainted, in any instance, with the connecting principle between cause and effect, or can account ultimately for the production of one thing to another. These words, as commonly used, have very loose meanings annexed to them; and their ideas are very uncertain and confused. No animal can put external bodies in motion without the sentiment of a *nisus* or endeavour; and every animal has a sentiment or feeling from the stroke or blow of an external object that is in motion. These sensations, which are merely animal, and from which we can *a priori* draw no inference, we are apt to transfer to inanimate objects, and to suppose that they have some such feelings, whenever they transfer or receive motion. With regard to energies, which are exerted without our annexing to them any idea of communicated motion, we consider only the constant experienced conjunction of the events; and as we feel a customary connexion between the ideas, we transfer that feeling to the objects, as nothing is more usual than to apply to external bodies every internal sensation which they occasion.]

To recapitulate, therefore, the reasonings of this section: Every idea is copied from some preceding impression or sentiment; and where we cannot find any impression, we may be certain that there is no idea. In all single instances of the operation of bodies or minds, there is nothing that produces any impression, nor consequently can suggest any idea of power or necessary connexion. But when many uniform instances appear, and the same object is always followed by the same event, we then begin to entertain the notion of cause and connexion. We then feel a new sentiment or impression, to wit, a customary connexion in the thought or imagination between one object and its usual attendant; and this sentiment is the original of that idea which we seek for. For as this idea arises from a number of similar instances, and not from any single instance, it must arise from that circumstance in which the number of instances differ from every individual instance. But this customary connexion or transition of the imagination is the only circumstance in which they differ. In every other particular they are alike. The first instance which we saw of motion, communicated by the shock of two billiard-balls (to return to this obvious illustration), is exactly similar to any instance that may, at present, occur to us; except only, that we could not, at first, infer one event from the other; which we are enabled to do at present, after so long a course of uniform experience. I know not whether the reader will readily apprehend this reasoning. I am afraid that, should I multiply words about it, or throw it into a greater variety of lights, it would only become more obscure and intricate. In all abstract reasonings, there is one point of view, which, if we can happily hit, we shall go farther towards illustrating the subject than by all the eloquence and copious expression in the world. This point of view we should endeavour to reach, and reserve the flowers of rhetoric for subjects which are more adapted to them.

Section VIII. *Of Liberty and Necessity*

Part I

It might reasonably be expected, in questions which have been canvassed and disputed with great eagerness since the first origin of science and philosophy, that the meaning of all the terms, at least, should have been agreed upon among the disputants; and our enquiries, in the course of two thousand years, been able to pass from words to the true and real subject of the controversy. For how easy may it seem to give exact definitions of the terms employed in reasoning, and make these definitions, not the mere sound of words, the object of future scrutiny and examination? But if we consider the matter more narrowly, we shall be apt to draw a quite opposite conclusion. From this circumstance alone, that a controversy has been long kept on foot, and remains still undecided, we may presume that there is some ambiguity in the expression, and that the disputants affix different ideas to the terms employed in the controversy. For as the faculties of the mind are supposed to be naturally alike in every individual; otherwise nothing could be more fruitless than to reason or dispute together; it were impossible, if men affix the same ideas to their terms, that they could so long form different opinions of the same subject; especially when they communicate their views, and each party turn themselves on all sides, in search of arguments which may give them the victory over their antagonists. It is true; if men attempt the discussion of questions which lie entirely beyond the reach of human capacity, such as those concerning the origin of worlds, or the economy of the intellectual system or region of spirits, they may long beat the air in their fruitless contests, and never arrive at any determinate conclusion. But if the question regard any subject of common life and experience, nothing, one would think, could preserve the dispute so long undecided, but some ambiguous expressions, which keep the antagonists still at a distance, and hinder them from grappling with each other.

This has been the case in the long disputed question concerning liberty and necessity; and to so remarkable a degree, that, if I be not much mistaken, we shall find that all mankind, both learned and ignorant, have always been of the same opinion with regard to this subject, and that a few intelligible definitions would immediately have put an end to the whole controversy. I own that this dispute has been so much canvassed on all hands, and has led philosophers into such a labyrinth of obscure sophistry, that it is no wonder if a sensible reader indulge his ease so far as to turn a deaf ear to the proposal of such a question, from which he can expect neither instruction nor entertainment. But the state of the argument here proposed may, perhaps, serve to renew his attention, as it has more novelty, promises at least some decision of the controversy, and will not much disturb his ease by any intricate or obscure reasoning.

I hope, therefore, to make it appear that all men have ever agreed in the doctrine both of necessity and of liberty, according to any reasonable sense which can be put on these terms; and that the whole controversy has hitherto turned merely upon words. We shall begin with examining the doctrine of necessity.

It is universally allowed that matter, in all its operations, is actuated by a necessary force, and that every natural effect is so precisely determined by the energy of its cause, no other effect, in such particular circumstances, could possibly have resulted from it. The degree and direction of every motion is, by the laws of nature, prescribed with such exactness that a living creature may as soon arise from the shock of two bodies as motion, in any other degree or direction than what is actually produced by it. Would we, therefore, form a just and precise idea of necessity, we must consider whence that idea arises, when we apply it to the operation of bodies.

It seems evident that, if all the scenes of nature were continually shifted in such a manner that no two events bore any resemblance to each other, but every object was entirely new, without any similitude to whatever had been seen before, we should never, in that case, have attained the least idea of necessity, or of a connexion among these objects. We might say, upon such a supposition, that one object or event has followed another; not that one was produced by the other. The relation of cause and effect must be utterly unknown to mankind. Inference and reasoning concerning the operations of nature would, from that moment, be at an end; and the memory and senses remain the only canals by which the knowledge of any real existence could possibly have access to the mind. Our idea, therefore, of necessity and causation arises entirely from the uniformity observable in the operations of nature, where similar objects are constantly conjoined together, and the mind is determined by custom to infer the one from the appearance of the other. These two circumstances form the whole of that necessity which we ascribe to matter. Beyond the constant conjunction of similar objects, and the consequent inference from one to the other, we have no notion of any necessity, or connexion.

If it appear, therefore, that all mankind have ever allowed, without any doubt or hesitation, that these two circumstances take place in the voluntary actions of men, and in the operations of mind; it must follow that all mankind have ever agreed in the doctrine of necessity, and that they have hitherto disputed merely for not understanding each other.

As to the first circumstance, the constant and regular conjunction of similar events: We may possibly satisfy ourselves by the following considerations. It is universally acknowledged that there is a great uniformity among the actions of men, in all nations and ages, and that human nature remains still the same, in its principles and operations. The same motives always produce the same actions: The same events follow from the same causes. Ambition, avarice, self-love, vanity, friendship, generosity, public spirit; these passions, mixed in various degrees, and distributed through society, have been, from the beginning of the world, and still are, the source of all the actions and enterprises which have ever been observed among mankind. Would you know the sentiments, inclinations, and course of life of the Greeks and Romans? Study well the temper and actions of the French and English: You cannot be much mistaken in transferring to the former most of the observations which you have made with regard to the latter. Mankind are so much the same, in all times and places, that history informs us of nothing new or strange in this particular. Its chief use is only to discover the constant and universal principles of human nature, by showing men in all varieties of circumstances and situations, and furnishing us with materials from which we may form our observations, and become acquainted with the regular springs of human action and behaviour. These records of wars, intrigues, factions, and revolutions are so many collections of experiments, by which the politician or moral philosopher fixes the principles of his science; in the same manner as the physician or natural philosopher becomes acquainted with the nature of plants, minerals, and other external objects by the experiments which he forms concerning them. Nor are the earth, water, and other elements, examined by Aristotle, and Hippocrates, more like to those which at present lie under our observation than the men, described by Polybius and Tacitus, are to those who now govern the world.

Should a traveller, returning from a far country, bring us an account of men wholly different from any with whom we were ever acquainted; men who were entirely divested of avarice, ambition, or revenge; who knew no pleasure but friendship, generosity, and public spirit; we should immediately, from these circumstances, detect the falsehood, and prove him a liar, with the same certainty as if he had stuffed his narration with stories of centaurs and dragons, miracles and prodigies. And if we would explode any forgery in history, we cannot make use of a more convincing argument than to prove that the actions ascribed to any person are directly contrary to the course of nature, and that no human motives, in such circumstances, could ever induce him to such a conduct. The veracity of Quintus Curtius is as much to be suspected, when he describes the supernatural courage of Alexander, by which he was hurried on singly to attack multitudes, as when he describes his supernatural force and activity, by which he was able to resist them. So readily and universally do we acknowledge a uniformity in human motives and actions as well as in the operations of body.

Hence likewise the benefit of that experience, acquired by long life and a variety of business and company, in order to instruct us in the principles of human nature, and regulate our future conduct, as well as speculation. By means of this guide, we mount up to the knowledge of men's inclinations and motives, from their actions, expressions, and even gestures; and again, descend to the interpretation of their actions from our knowledge of their motives and inclinations. The general observations, treasured up by a course of experience, give us the clue of human nature, and teach us to unravel all its intricacies. Pretexts and appearances no longer deceive us. Public declarations pass for the specious colouring of a cause. And though virtue and honour be allowed their proper weight and authority, that perfect disinterestedness, so often pretended to, is never expected in multitudes and parties; seldom in their leaders; and scarcely even in individuals of any rank or station. But were there no uniformity in human actions, and were every experiment which we could form of this kind irregular and anomalous, it were impossible to collect any general observations concerning mankind; and no experience, however accurately digested by reflection, would ever serve to any purpose. Why is the aged husbandman more skilful in his calling than the young beginner, but because there is a certain uniformity in the operation of the sun, rain, and earth towards the production of vegetables; and experience teaches the old practitioner the rules by which this operation is governed and directed?

We must not, however, expect that this uniformity of human actions should be carried to such a length as that all men, in the same circumstances, will always act precisely in the same manner, without making any allowance for the diversity of characters, prejudices, and opinions. Such a uniformity in every particular is found in no part of nature. On the contrary, from observing the variety of conduct in different men, we are enabled to form a greater variety of maxims, which still suppose a degree of uniformity and regularity.

Are the manners of men different in different ages and countries? We learn thence the great force of custom and education, which mould the human mind from its infancy, and form it into a fixed and established character. Is the behaviour and conduct of the one sex very unlike that of the other? Is it thence we become acquainted with the different characters, which nature has impressed upon the sexes, and which she preserves with constancy and regularity? Are the actions of the same person much diversified in the different periods of his life, from infancy to old age? This affords room for many general observations concerning the gradual change of our sentiments and inclinations, and the different maxims which prevail in the different ages of human creatures. Even the characters which are peculiar to each individual have a uniformity in their influence; otherwise our acquaintance with the persons and our observation of their conduct could never teach us their dispositions, or serve to direct our behaviour with regard to them.

I grant it possible to find some actions which seem to have no regular connexion with any known motives, and are exceptions to all the measures of conduct, which have ever been established for the government of men. But if we would willingly know what judgment should be formed of such irregular and extraordinary actions, we may consider the sentiments, commonly entertained with regard to those irregular events, which appear in the course of nature, and the operations of external objects. All causes are not conjoined to their usual effects with like uniformity. An artificer, who handles only dead matter, may be disappointed of his aim, as well as the politician, who directs the conduct of sensible and intelligent agents.

The vulgar, who take things according to their first appearance, attribute the uncertainty of events to such an uncertainty in the causes as makes the latter often fail of their usual influence; though they meet with no impediment in their operation. But philosophers, observing that, almost in every part of nature, there is contained a vast variety of springs and principles, which are hid, by reason of their minuteness or remoteness, find that it is at least possible the contrariety of events may not proceed from any contingency in the cause, but from the secret operation of contrary causes. This possibility is converted into certainty by farther observation: when they remark that, upon an exact scrutiny, a contrariety of effects always betrays a contrariety of causes, and proceeds from their mutual opposition. A peasant can give no better reason for the stopping of any clock or watch than to say that it does not commonly go right: But an artist easily perceives that the same force in the spring or pendulum has always the same influence on the wheels, but fails of its usual effect perhaps by reason of a grain of dust, which puts a stop to the whole movement. From the observation of several parallel instances, philosophers form a maxim that the connexion between all causes and effects is equally necessary, and that its seeming uncertainty in some instances proceeds from the secret opposition of contrary causes.

Thus for instance, in the human body, when the usual symptoms of health or sickness disappoint our expectation; when medicines operate not with their wonted powers; when irregular events follow from any particular cause; the philosopher and physician are not surprised at the matter, nor are ever tempted to deny, in general, the necessity and uniformity of those principles by which the animal economy is conducted. They know that a human body is a mighty complicated machine: That many secret powers lurk in it, which are altogether beyond our comprehension: That to us it must often appear very uncertain in its operations: And that therefore the irregular events, which outwardly discover themselves, can be no proof that the laws of nature are not observed with the greatest regularity in its internal operations and government.

The philosopher, if he be consistent, must apply the same reasoning to the actions and volitions of intelligent agents. The most irregular and unexpected resolutions of men may frequently be accounted for by those who know every particular circumstance of their character and situation. A person of an obliging disposition gives a peevish answer: But he has the toothache, or has not dined. A stupid fellow discovers an uncommon alacrity in his carriage: But he has met with a sudden piece of good fortune. Or even when an action, as sometimes happens, cannot be particularly accounted for, either by the person himself or by others; we know, in general, that the characters of men are, to a certain degree, inconstant and irregular. This is, in a manner, the constant character of human nature; though it be applicable, in a more particular manner, to some persons, who have no fixed rule for their conduct, but proceed in a continued course of caprice and inconstancy. The internal principles and motives may operate in a uniform manner, notwithstanding these seeming irregularities; in the same manner as the winds, rain, clouds, and other variations of the weather are supposed to be governed by steady principles, though not easily discoverable by human sagacity and enquiry. Thus it appears, not only that the conjunction between motives and voluntary actions is as regular and uniform as that between the cause and effect in any part of nature; but also that this regular conjunction has been universally acknowledged among mankind, and has never been the subject of dispute, either in philosophy or common life. Now, as it is from past experience that we draw all inferences concerning the future, and as we conclude that objects will always be conjoined together which we find to have always been conjoined; it may seem superfluous to prove that this experienced uniformity in human actions is a source whence we draw inferences concerning them. But in order to throw the argument into a greater variety of lights, we shall also insist, though briefly, on this latter topic.

The mutual dependence of men is so great, in all societies, that scarce any human action is entirely complete in itself, or is performed without some reference to the actions of others, which are requisite to make it answer fully the intention of the agent.

The poorest artificer, who labours alone, expects at least the protection of the magistrate, to ensure him the enjoyment of the fruits of his labour. He also expects that, when he carries his goods to market, and offers them at a reasonable price, he shall find purchasers; and shall be able, by the money he acquires, to engage others to supply him with those commodities which are requisite for his subsistence. In proportion as men extend their dealings, and render their intercourse with others more complicated, they always comprehend, in their schemes of life, a greater variety of voluntary actions, which they expect, from the proper motives, to co-operate with their own. In all these conclusions, they take their measures from past experience, in the same manner as in their reasonings concerning external objects; and firmly believe that men, as well as all the elements, are to continue in their operations the same that they have ever found them. A manufacturer reckons upon the labour of his servants for the execution of any work, as much as upon the tools which he employs, and would be equally surprised, were his expectations disappointed. In short, this experimental inference and reasoning concerning the actions of others enters so much into human life that no man, while awake, is ever a moment without employing it. Have we not reason, therefore, to affirm that all mankind have always agreed in the doctrine of necessity, according to the foregoing definition and explication of it?

Nor have philosophers ever entertained a different opinion from the people in this particular. For not to mention that almost every action of their life supposes that opinion; there are even few of the speculative parts of learning to which it is not essential. What would become of history, had we not a dependence on the veracity of the historian, according to the experience which we have had of mankind? How could politics be a science, if laws and forms of government had not a uniform influence upon society? Where would be the foundation of morals, if particular characters had no certain or determinate power to produce particular sentiments, and if these sentiments had no constant operation on actions? And with what pretence could we employ our criticism upon any poet or polite author, if we could not pronounce the conduct and sentiments of his actors either natural or unnatural, to such characters, and in such circumstances? It seems almost impossible, therefore, to engage either in science or action of any kind, without acknowledging the doctrine of necessity, and this inference from motives to voluntary actions; from characters to conduct.

And indeed, when we consider how aptly natural and moral evidence link together, and form only one chain of argument, we shall make no scruple to allow that they are of the same nature, and derived from the same principles. A prisoner, who has neither money nor interest, discovers the impossibility of his escape as well when he considers the obstinacy of the gaoler as the walls and bars with which he is surrounded; and, in all attempts for his freedom, chooses rather to work upon the stone and iron of the one than upon the inflexible nature of the other. The same prisoner, when conducted to the scaffold, foresees his death as certainly from the constancy and fidelity of his guards as from the operation of the ax or wheel. His mind runs along a certain train of ideas: the refusal of the soldiers to consent to his escape; the action of the executioner; the separation of the head and body; bleeding, convulsive motions, and death. Here is a connected chain of natural causes and voluntary actions; but the mind feels no difference between them, in passing from one link to another: Nor is it less certain of the future event than if it were connected with the objects present to the memory or senses by a train of causes, cemented together by what we are pleased to call a physical necessity. The same experienced union has the same effect on the mind, whether the united objects be motives, volition, and actions; or figure and motion. We may change the name of things; but their nature and their operation on the understanding never change.

Were a man whom I know to be honest and opulent, and with whom I live in intimate friendship, to come into my house, where I am surrounded with my servants, I rest assured that he is not to stab me before he leaves it, in order to rob me of my silver standish; and I no more suspect this event than the falling of the house itself which is new, and solidly built and founded.—But he may have been seized with a sudden and unknown frenzy.—So may a sudden earthquake arise, and shake and tumble my house about my ears. I shall therefore change the suppositions. I shall say that I know with certainty that he is not to put his hand into the fire, and hold it there, till it be consumed: And this event I think I can foretell with the same assurance as that if he throw himself out at the window, and meet with no obstruction, he will not remain a moment suspended in the air. No suspicion of an unknown frenzy can give the least possibility to the former event, which is so contrary to all the known principles of human nature. A man who at noon leaves his purse full of gold on the pavement at Charing-Cross may as well expect that it will fly away like a feather as that he will find it untouched an hour after. Above one half of human reasonings contain inferences of a similar nature, attended with more or less degrees of certainty, proportioned to our experience of the usual conduct of mankind in such particular situations.

I have frequently considered what could possibly be the reason why all mankind, though they have ever, without hesitation, acknowledged the doctrine of necessity in their whole practice and reasoning, have yet discovered such a reluctance to acknowledge it in words, and have rather shown a propensity, in all ages, to profess the contrary opinion. The matter, I think, may be accounted for after the following manner. If we examine the operations of body, and the production of effects from their causes, we shall find that all our faculties can never carry us farther in our knowledge of this relation than barely to observe that particular objects are constantly conjoined together, and that the mind is carried, by a customary transition, from the appearance of one to the belief of the other. But though this conclusion concerning human ignorance be the result of the strictest scrutiny of this subject, men still entertain a strong propensity to believe that they penetrate farther into the powers of nature, and perceive something like a necessary connexion between the cause and the effect. When again they turn their reflections towards the operations of their own minds, and feel no such connexion of the motive and the action, they are thence apt to suppose that there is a difference between the effects which result from material force and those which arise from thought and intelligence. But being once convinced that we know nothing farther of causation of any kind than merely the constant conjunction of objects, and the consequent inference of the mind from one to another and finding that these two circumstances are universally allowed to have place in voluntary actions; we may be more easily led to own the same necessity common to all causes. And though this reasoning may contradict the systems of many philosophers, in ascribing necessity to the determinations of the will, we shall find, upon reflection, that they dissent from it in words only, not in their real sentiment. Necessity, according to the sense, in which it is here taken, has never yet been rejected, nor can ever, I think, be rejected by any philosopher. It may only, perhaps, be pretended that the mind can perceive, in the operations of matter, some farther connexion between the cause and effect; and a connexion that has not place in the voluntary actions of intelligent beings. Now whether it be so or not can only appear upon examination; and it is incumbent on these philosophers to make good their assertion, by defining or describing that necessity, and pointing it out to us in the operations of material causes.

It would seem, indeed, that men begin at the wrong end of this question concerning liberty and necessity when they enter upon it by examining the faculties of the soul, the influence of the understanding, and the operations of the will. Let them first discuss a more simple question, namely, the operations of body and of brute unintelligent matter; and try whether they can there form any idea of causation and necessity except that of a constant conjunction of objects, and subsequent inference of the mind from one to another. If these circumstances form, in reality, the whole of that necessity which we conceive in matter, and if these circumstances be also universally acknowledged to take place in the operations of the mind, the dispute is at an end; at least, must be owned to be thenceforth merely verbal. But as long as we will rashly suppose that we have some farther idea of necessity and causation in the operations of external objects; at the same time, that we can find nothing farther in the voluntary actions of the mind; there is no possibility of bringing the question to any determinate issue, while we proceed upon so erroneous a supposition. The only method of undeceiving us is to mount up higher; to examine the narrow extent of science when applied to material causes; and to convince ourselves that all we know of them is the constant conjunction and inference above mentioned. We may, perhaps, find that it is with difficulty we are induced to fix such narrow limits to human understanding: But we can afterwards find no difficulty when we come to apply this doctrine to the actions of the will. For as it is evident that these have a regular conjunction with motives and circumstances and characters, and as we always draw inferences from one to the other, we must be obliged to acknowledge in words that necessity, which we have already avowed, in every deliberation of our lives, and in every step of our conduct and behaviour.

The prevalence of the doctrine of liberty may be accounted for, from another cause, *viz.* a false sensation or seeming experience which we have, or may have, of liberty or indifference, in many of our actions. The necessity of any action, whether of matter or of mind, is not, properly speaking, a quality in the agent, but in any thinking or intelligent being who may consider the action; and it consists chiefly in the determination of his thoughts to infer the existence of that action from some preceding objects; as liberty, when opposed to necessity, is nothing but the want of that determination, and a certain looseness or indifference, which we feel, in passing, or not passing, from the idea of one object to that of any succeeding one. Now we may observe that, though in reflecting on human actions, we seldom feel such a looseness or indifference, but are commonly able to infer them with considerable certainty from their motives, and from the dispositions of the agent; yet it frequently happens that, in performing the actions themselves, we are sensible of something like it: And as all resembling objects are readily taken for each other, this has been employed as a demonstrative and even intuitive proof of human liberty. We feel that our actions are subject to our will, on most occasions; and imagine we feel that the will itself is subject to nothing, because, when by a denial of it we are provoked to try, we feel that it moves easily every way, and produces an image of itself (or a Velleity, as it is called in the schools) even on that side on which it did not settle. This image, or faint motion, we persuade ourselves, could, at that time, have been completed into the thing itself; because, should that be denied, we find, upon a second trial, that, at present, it can. We consider not that the fantastical desire of showing liberty is here the motive of our actions. And it seems certain that, however we may imagine we feel a liberty within ourselves, a spectator can commonly infer our actions from our motives and character; and even where he cannot, he concludes in general that he might, were he perfectly acquainted with every circumstance of our situation and temper, and the most secret springs of our complexion and disposition. Now this is the very essence of necessity, according to the foregoing doctrine.

But to proceed in this reconciling project with regard to the question of liberty and necessity, the most contentious question of metaphysics, the most contentious science: It will not require many words to prove that all mankind have ever agreed in the doctrine of liberty as well as in that of necessity, and that the whole dispute, in this respect also, has been hitherto merely verbal. For what is meant by liberty, when applied to voluntary actions? We cannot surely mean that actions have so little connexion with motives, inclinations, and circumstances that one does not follow with a certain degree of uniformity from the other, and that one affords no inference by which we can conclude the existence of the other. For these are plain and acknowledged matters of fact. By liberty, then, we can only mean a power of acting or not acting, according to the determinations of the will; that is, if we choose to remain at rest, we may; if we choose to move, we also may. Now this hypothetical liberty is universally allowed to belong to everyone who is not a prisoner and in chains. Here then is no subject of dispute.

Whatever definition we may give of liberty, we should be careful to observe two requisite circumstances: first, that it be consistent with plain matter of fact; secondly, that it be consistent with itself. If we observe these circumstances, and render our definition intelligible, I am persuaded that all mankind will be found of one opinion with regard to it.

It is universally allowed that nothing exists without a cause of its existence, and that chance, when strictly examined, is a mere negative word, and means not any real power which has anywhere a being in nature. But it is pretended that some causes are necessary, some not necessary. Here then is the advantage of definitions. Let anyone define a cause, without comprehending, as a part of the definition, a necessary connexion with its effect; and let him show distinctly the origin of the idea, expressed by the definition; and I shall readily give up the whole controversy. But if the foregoing explication of the matter be received, this must be absolutely impracticable. Had not objects a regular conjunc-

tion with each other, we should never have entertained any notion of cause and effect; and this regular conjunction produces that inference of the understanding, which is the only connexion that we can have any comprehension of. Whoever attempts a definition of cause, exclusive of these circumstances, will be obliged either to employ unintelligible terms, or such as are synonymous to the term which he endeavours to define. [Thus, if a cause be defined *that which produces anything,* it is easy to observe that *producing* is synonymous to *causing.* In like manner, if a cause be defined *that by which anything exists,* this is liable to the same objection. For what is meant by these words, *by which?* Had it been said that a cause is *that* after which *anything constantly exists,* we should have understood the terms. For this is, indeed, all we know of the matter. And this constancy forms the very essence of necessity, nor have we any other idea of it.] And if the definition above mentioned be admitted; liberty, when opposed to necessity, not to constraint, is the same thing with chance; which is universally allowed to have no existence.

Part II

There is no method of reasoning more common, and yet none more blameable, than, in philosophical disputes, to endeavour the refutation of any hypothesis by a pretence of its dangerous consequences to religion and morality. When any opinion leads to absurdities, it is certainly false; but it is not certain that an opinion is false because it is of dangerous consequence. Such topics, therefore, ought entirely to be forborne, as serving nothing to the discovery of truth, but only to make the person of an antagonist odious. This I observe in general, without pretending to draw any advantage from it. I frankly submit to an examination of this kind, and shall venture to affirm that the doctrines both of necessity and of liberty, as above explained, are not only consistent with morality, but are absolutely essential to its support.

Necessity may be defined two ways, conformably to the two definitions of cause, of which it makes an essential part. It consists either in the constant conjunction of like objects, or in the inference of the understanding from one object to another. Now necessity, in both these senses (which, indeed, are, at bottom, the same), has universally, though tacitly, in the schools, in the pulpit, and in common life, been allowed to belong to the will of man; and no one has ever pretended to deny that we can draw inferences concerning human actions, and that those inferences are founded on the experienced union of like actions, with like motives, inclinations, and circumstances. The only particular in which anyone can differ is that either, perhaps, he will refuse to give the name of necessity to this property of human actions: But as long as the meaning is understood, I hope the word can do no harm: Or that he will maintain it possible to discover something farther in the operations of matter. But this, it must be acknowledged, can be of no consequence to morality or religion, whatever it may be to natural philosophy or metaphysics. We may here be mistaken in asserting that there is no idea of any other necessity or connexion in the actions of body: But surely we ascribe nothing to the actions of the mind but what everyone does, and must readily allow of. We change no circumstance in the received orthodox system with regard to the will, but only in that with regard to material objects and causes. Nothing therefore can be more innocent, at least, than this doctrine.

All laws being founded on rewards and punishments, it is supposed as a fundamental principle that these motives have a regular and uniform influence on the mind, and both produce the good and prevent the evil actions. We may give to this influence what name we please; but, as it is usually conjoined with the action, it must be esteemed a cause, and be looked upon as an instance of that necessity, which we would here establish.

The only proper object of hatred or vengeance is a person or creature endowed with thought and consciousness; and when any criminal or injurious actions excite that passion, it is only by their relation to the person, or connexion with him. Actions are, by their very nature, temporary and perishing; and where they proceed not from some cause in the character and disposition of the person who performed them, they can neither redound to his honour, if good; nor infamy, if evil. The actions themselves may be blameable; they may be contrary to all the rules of morality and religion: But the person is not answerable for them; and as they proceeded from nothing in him that is durable and constant,

and leave nothing of that nature behind them, it is impossible he can, upon their account, become the object of punishment or vengeance. According to the principle, therefore, which denies necessity, and consequently causes, a man is as pure and untainted after having committed the most horrid crime as at the first moment of his birth, nor is his character any wise concerned in his actions, since they are not derived from it, and the wickedness of the one can never be used as a proof of the depravity of the other.

Men are not blamed for such actions as they perform ignorantly and casually, whatever may be the consequences. Why? But because the principles of these actions are only momentary, and terminate in them alone. Men are less blamed for such actions as they perform hastily and unpremeditatedly than for such as proceed from deliberation. For what reason? But because a hasty temper, though a constant cause or principle in the mind, operates only by intervals, and infects not the whole character. Again, repentance wipes off every crime, if attended with a reformation of life and manners. How is this to be accounted for? But by asserting that actions render a person criminal, merely as they are proofs of criminal principles in the mind; and when, by an alteration of these principles, they cease to be just proofs, they likewise cease to be criminal. But, except upon the doctrine of necessity, they never were just proofs, and consequently never were criminal.

It will be equally easy to prove, and from the same arguments, that liberty, according to that definition above mentioned, in which all men agree, is also essential to morality, and that no human actions where it is wanting are susceptible of any moral qualities, or can be the objects either of approbation or dislike. For as actions are objects of our moral sentiment, so far only as they are indications of the internal character, passions, and affections, it is impossible that they can give rise either to praise or blame, where they proceed not from these principles, but are derived altogether from external violence.

I pretend not to have obviated or removed all objections to this theory with regard to necessity and liberty. I can foresee other objections, derived from topics which have not here been treated of. It may be said, for instance, that if voluntary actions be subjected to the same laws of necessity with the operations of matter, there is a continued chain of necessary causes, pre-ordained and pre-determined, reaching from the original cause of all, to every single volition of every human creature. No contingency anywhere in the universe; no indifference; no liberty. While we act, we are, at the same time, acted upon. The ultimate Author of all our volitions is the Creator of the world, who first bestowed motion on this immense machine, and placed all beings in that particular position whence every subsequent event, by an inevitable necessity, must result. Human actions, therefore, either can have no moral turpitude at all, as proceeding from so good a cause; or if they have any turpitude, they must involve our Creator in the same guilt, while he is acknowledged to be their ultimate cause and author. For as a man who fired a mine is answerable for all the consequences, whether the train he employed be long or short; so wherever a continued chain of necessary causes is fixed, that Being, either finite or infinite, who produces the first is likewise the author of all the rest, and must both bear the blame and acquire the praise which belong to them. Our clear and unalterable ideas of morality establish this rule, upon unquestionable reasons, when we examine the consequences of any human action; and these reasons must still have greater force when applied to the volitions and intentions of a Being infinitely wise and powerful. Ignorance or impotence may be pleaded for so limited a creature as man; but those imperfections have no place in our Creator. He foresaw, he ordained, he intended all those actions of men which we so rashly pronounce criminal. And we must therefore conclude either that they are not criminal, or that the Deity, not man, is accountable for them. But as either of these positions is absurd and impious, it follows that the doctrine from which they are deduced cannot possibly be true, as being liable to all the same objections. An absurd consequence, if necessary, proves the original doctrine to be absurd; in the same manner as criminal actions render criminal the original cause, if the connexion between them be necessary and inevitable.

This objection consists of two parts, which we shall examine separately: First, that, if human actions can be traced up, by a necessary chain, to the Deity, they can never be criminal, on account of the infinite perfection of that Being from whom they are derived, and who can intend nothing but what is altogether good and laudable. Or, Secondly, if they be criminal, we must retract the attribute of perfection which we ascribe to the Deity, and must acknowledge him to be the ultimate author of guilt and moral turpitude in all his creatures.

The answer to the first objection seems obvious and convincing. There are many philosophers who, after an exact scrutiny of all the phenomena of nature, conclude that the WHOLE, considered as one system, is, in every period of its existence, ordered with perfect benevolence; and that the utmost possible happiness will, in the end, result to all created beings, without any mixture of positive or absolute ill and misery. Every physical ill, say they, makes an essential part of this benevolent system, and could not possibly be removed, even by the Deity himself, considered as a wise agent, without giving entrance to greater ill, or excluding greater good, which will result from it. From this theory, some philosophers, and the ancient Stoics among the rest, derived a topic of consolation under all afflictions, while they taught their pupils that those ills under which they laboured were, in reality, goods to the universe; and that to an enlarged view, which could comprehend the whole system of nature, every event became an object of joy and exultation. But though this topic be specious and sublime, it was soon found in practice weak and ineffectual. You would surely more irritate than appease a man, lying under the racking pains of the gout, by preaching up to him the rectitude of those general laws which produced the malignant humours in his body, and led them through the proper canals, to the sinews and nerves, where they now excite such acute torments. These enlarged views may, for a moment, please the imagination of a speculative man who is placed in ease and security; but neither can they dwell with constancy on his mind, even though undisturbed by the emotions of pain or passion; much less can they maintain their ground when attacked by such powerful antagonists. The affections take a narrower and more natural survey of their object; and by an economy more suitable to the infirmity of human minds regard alone the beings around us, and are actuated by such events as appear good or ill to the private system.

The case is the same with moral as with physical ill. It cannot reasonably be supposed that those remote considerations, which are found of so little efficacy with regard to one, will have a more powerful influence with regard to the other. The mind of man is so formed by nature that, upon the appearance of certain characters, dispositions, and actions, it immediately feels the sentiment of approbation or blame; nor are there any emotions more essential to its frame and constitution. The characters which engage our approbation are chiefly such as contribute to the peace and security of human society; as the characters which excite blame are chiefly such as tend to public detriment and disturbance: Whence it may reasonably be presumed that the moral sentiments arise, either mediately or immediately, from a reflection of these opposite interests. What though philosophical meditations establish a different opinion or conjecture; that everything is right with regard to the WHOLE, and that the qualities, which disturb society, are, in the main, as beneficial, and are as suitable to the primary intention of nature, as those which more directly promote its happiness and welfare? Are such remote and uncertain speculations able to counterbalance the sentiments which arise from the natural and immediate view of the objects? A man who is robbed of a considerable sum; does he find his vexation for the loss any wise diminished by these sublime reflections? Why then should his moral resentment against the crime be supposed incompatible with them? Or why should not the acknowledgment of a real distinction between vice and virtue be reconcileable to all speculative systems of philosophy, as well as that of a real distinction between personal beauty and deformity? Both these distinctions are founded in the natural sentiments of the human mind: And these sentiments are not to be controlled or altered by any philosophical theory or speculation whatsoever.

The second objection admits not of so easy and satisfactory an answer; nor is it possible to explain distinctly how the Deity can be the mediate cause of all the actions of men, without being the author of sin and moral turpitude. These are mysteries, which mere natural and unassisted reason is very unfit to handle; and whatever system she embraces, she must find herself involved in inextricable difficulties, and even contradictions, at every step which she takes with regard to such subjects. To reconcile the indifference and contingency of human actions with prescience; or to defend absolute decrees, and yet free the Deity from being the author of sin, has been found hitherto to exceed all the power of philosophy. Happy, if she be thence sensible of her temerity, when she pries into these sublime mysteries; and leaving a scene so full of obscurities and perplexities, return, with suitable modesty, to her true and proper province, the examination of common life; where she will find difficulties enow to employ her enquiries, without launching into so boundless an ocean of doubt, uncertainty, and contradiction!

Section IX. *Of the Reason of Animals*

All our reasonings concerning matter of fact are founded on a species of Analogy, which leads us to expect from any cause the same events which we have observed to result from similar causes. Where the causes are entirely similar, the analogy is perfect, and the inference drawn from it is regarded as certain and conclusive: Nor does any man ever entertain a doubt, where he sees a piece of iron, that it will have weight and cohesion of parts; as in all other instances which have ever fallen under his observation. But where the objects have not so exact a similarity, the analogy is less perfect, and the inference is less conclusive; though still it has some force, in proportion to the degree of similarity and resemblance. The anatomical observations formed upon one animal are, by this species of reasoning, extended to all animals; and it is certain that when the circulation of the blood, for instance, is clearly proved to have place in one creature, as a frog, or fish, it forms a strong presumption that the same principle has place in all. These analogical observations may be carried farther, even to this science of which we are now treating; and any theory by which we explain the operations of the understanding, or the origin and connexion of the passions in man, will acquire additional authority if we find that the same theory is requisite to explain the same phenomena in all other animals. We shall make trial of this, with regard to the hypothesis by which we have, in the foregoing discourse, endeavoured to account for all experimental reasonings; and it is hoped, that this new point of view will serve to confirm all our former observations.

First, It seems evident that animals, as well as men, learn many things from experience, and infer that the same events will always follow from the same causes. By this principle they become acquainted with the more obvious properties of external objects, and gradually, from their birth, treasure up a knowledge of the nature of fire, water, earth, stones, heights, depths, &c., and of the effects which result from their operation. The ignorance and inexperience of the young are here plainly distinguishable from the cunning and sagacity of the old, who have learned, by long observation, to avoid what hurt them, and to pursue what gave ease or pleasure. A horse that has been accustomed to the field becomes acquainted with the proper height which he can leap, and will never attempt what exceeds his force and ability. An old greyhound will trust the more fatiguing part of the chase to the younger, and will place himself so as to meet the hare in her doubles; nor are the conjectures which he forms on this occasion founded in anything but his observation and experience.

This is still more evident from the effects of discipline and education on animals, who, by the proper application of rewards and punishments, may be taught any course of action, the most contrary to their natural instincts and propensities. Is it not experience which renders a dog apprehensive of pain when you menace him, or lift up the whip to beat him? Is it not even experience which makes him answer to his name, and infer, from such an arbitrary sound, that you mean him rather than any of his fellows, and intend to call him, when you pronounce it in a certain manner, and with a certain tone and accent?

In all these cases, we may observe that the animal infers some fact beyond what immediately strikes his senses; and that this inference is altogether founded on past experience, while the creature expects from the present object the same consequences which it has always found in its observation to result from similar objects.

Secondly, It is impossible that this inference of the animal can be founded on any process of argument or reasoning by which he concludes that like events must follow like objects, and that the course of nature will always be regular in its operations. For if there be in reality any arguments of this nature, they surely lie too abstruse for the observation of such imperfect understandings; since it may well employ the utmost care and attention of a philosophic genius to discover and observe them. Animals, therefore, are not guided in these inferences by reasoning: Neither are children: Neither are the generality of mankind, in their ordinary actions and conclusions: Neither are philosophers themselves, who, in all the active parts of life, are, in the main, the same with the vulgar, and are governed by the same maxims. Nature must have provided some other principle, of more ready and more general use and application; nor can an operation of such immense consequence in life as that of inferring effects from causes be trusted to the uncertain process of reasoning and argumentation. Were this doubtful with regard to men, it seems to admit of no question with regard to the brute creation; and the conclusion being once firmly established in the one, we have a strong presumption, from all the rules of analogy, that it ought to be universally admitted, without any exception or reserve. It is custom alone which engages animals, from every object that strikes their senses, to infer its usual attendant, and carries their imagination from the appearance of the one to conceive the other, in that particular manner which we denominate belief. No other explication can be given of this operation, in all the higher, as well as lower, classes of sensitive beings which fall under our notice and observation.

[Since all reasonings concerning facts or causes are derived merely from custom, it may be asked how it happens that men so much surpass animals in reasoning, and one man so much surpasses another? Has not the same custom the same influence on all?

We shall here endeavour briefly to explain the great difference in human understandings, after which the reason of the difference between men and animals will easily be comprehended.

1. When we have lived any time, and have been accustomed to the uniformity of nature, we acquire a general habit by which we always transfer the known to the unknown, and conceive the latter to resemble the former. By means of this general habitual principle, we regard even one experiment as the foundation of reasoning, and expect a similar event with some degree of certainty, where the experiment has been made accurately, and free from all foreign circumstances. It is therefore considered as a matter of great importance to observe the consequences of things; and as one man may very much surpass another in attention and memory and observation, this will make a very great difference in their reasoning.

2. Where there is a complication of causes to produce any effect, one mind may be much larger than another, and better able to comprehend the whole system of objects, and to infer justly their consequences.

3. One man is able to carry on a chain of consequences to a greater length than another.

4. Few men can think long without running into a confusion of ideas, and mistaking one for another; and there are various degrees of this infirmity.

5. The circumstance on which the effect depends is frequently involved in other circumstances which are foreign and extrinsic. The separation of it often requires great attention, accuracy, and subtlety.

6. The forming of general maxims from particular observation is a very nice operation; and nothing is more usual, from haste or a narrowness of mind, which sees not on all sides, than to commit mistakes in this particular.

7. When we reason from analogies, the man who has the greater experience or the greater promptitude of suggesting analogies will be the better reasoner.

8. Biasses from prejudice, education, passion, party, &c. hang more upon one mind than another.

9. After we have acquired a confidence in human testimony, books and conversation enlarge much more the sphere of one man's experience and thought than those of another.

It would be easy to discover many other circumstances that make a difference in the understandings of men.]

But though animals learn many parts of their knowledge from observation, there are also many parts of it which they derive from the original hand of nature; which much exceed the share of capacity they possess on ordinary occasions; and in which they improve, little or nothing, by the longest practice and experience. These we denominate Instincts, and are so apt to admire as something very extraordinary, and inexplicable by all the disquisitions of human understanding. But our wonder will, perhaps, cease or diminish when we consider that the experimental reasoning itself, which we possess in common with beasts, and on which the whole conduct of life depends, is nothing but a species of instinct or mechanical power that acts in us unknown to ourselves; and in its chief operations is not directed by any such relations or comparisons of ideas as are the proper objects of our intellectual faculties. Though the instinct be different, yet still it is an instinct which teaches a man to avoid the fire; as much as that which teaches a bird, with such exactness, the art of incubation, and the whole economy and order of its nursery.

Section X.   Of Miracles

Part I

There is, in Dr. Tillotson's writings, an argument against the real presence, which is as concise, and elegant, and strong as any argument can possibly be supposed against a doctrine so little worthy of a serious refutation. It is acknowledged on all hands, says that learned prelate, that the authority, either of the scripture or of tradition, is founded merely in the testimony of the apostles, who were eyewitnesses to those miracles of our Saviour, by which he proved his divine mission. Our evidence, then, for the truth of the Christian religion is less than the evidence for the truth of our senses; because, even in the first authors of our religion, it was no greater; and it is evident it must diminish in passing from them to their disciples; nor can anyone rest such confidence in their testimony as in the immediate object of his senses. But a weaker evidence can never destroy a stronger; and therefore, were the doctrine of the real presence ever so clearly revealed in scripture, it were directly contrary to the rules of just reasoning to give our assent to it. It contradicts sense, though both the scripture and tradition, on which it is supposed to be built, carry not such evidence with them as sense; when they are considered merely as external evidences, and are not brought home to everyone's breast by the immediate operation of the Holy Spirit.

Nothing is so convenient as a decisive argument of this kind, which must at least silence the most arrogant bigotry and superstition, and free us from their impertinent solicitations. I flatter myself that I have discovered an argument of a like nature, which, if just, will, with the wise and learned, be an everlasting check to all kinds of superstitious delusion, and consequently, will be useful as long as the world endures. For so long, I presume, will the accounts of miracles and prodigies be found in all history, sacred and profane.

Though experience be our only guide in reasoning concerning matters of fact, it must be acknowledged that this guide is not altogether infallible, but in some cases is apt to lead us into errors. One who in our climate should expect better weather in any week of June than in one of December would reason justly, and conformably to experience; but it is certain that he may happen, in the event, to find himself mistaken. However, we may observe that, in such a case, he would have no cause to complain of experience; because it commonly informs us beforehand of the uncertainty, by that contrariety of events which we may learn from a diligent observation. All effects follow not with like certainty from their supposed causes. Some events are found, in all countries and all ages, to have been constantly conjoined together: Others are found to have been more variable, and sometimes to disappoint our expectations; so that, in our reasonings concerning matter of fact, there are all imaginable degrees of assurance, from the highest certainty to the lowest species of moral evidence.

A wise man, therefore, proportions his belief to the evidence. In such conclusions as are founded on an infallible experience, he expects the event with the last degree of assurance, and regards his past experience as a full proof of the future existence of that event. In other cases, he proceeds with more caution: He weighs the opposite experiments: He considers which side is supported by the greater number of experiments: To that side he inclines, with doubt and hesitation; and when at last he fixes his judgment, the evidence exceeds not what we

properly call probability. All probability, then, supposes an opposition of experiments and observations, where the one side is found to overbalance the other, and to produce a degree of evidence proportioned to the superiority. A hundred instances or experiments on one side, and fifty on another, afford a doubtful expectation of any event; though a hundred uniform experiments, with only one that is contradictory, reasonably beget a pretty strong degree of assurance. In all cases, we must balance the opposite experiments, where they are opposite, and deduct the smaller number from the greater, in order to know the exact force of the superior evidence.

To apply these principles to a particular instance: We may observe that there is no species of reasoning more common, more useful, and even necessary to human life, than that which is derived from the testimony of men, and the reports of eyewitnesses and spectators. This species of reasoning, perhaps, one may deny to be founded on the relation of cause and effect. I shall not dispute about a word. It will be sufficient to observe that our assurance in any argument of this kind is derived from no other principle than our observation of the veracity of human testimony, and of the usual conformity of facts to the reports of witnesses. It being a general maxim that no objects have any discoverable connexion together, and that all the inferences which we can draw from one to another are founded merely on our experience of their constant and regular conjunction; it is evident that we ought not to make an exception to this maxim in favour of human testimony, whose connexion with any event seems, in itself, as little necessary as any other. Were not the memory tenacious to a certain degree; had not men commonly an inclination to truth and a principle of probity; were they not sensible to shame, when detected in a falsehood: Were not these, I say, discovered by experience to be qualities inherent in human nature, we should never repose the least confidence in human testimony. A man delirious, or noted for falsehood and villainy, has no manner of authority with us.

And as the evidence, derived from witnesses and human testimony, is founded on past experience, so it varies with the experience, and is regarded either as a proof or a probability, according as the conjunction between any particular kind of report and any kind of object has been found to be constant or variable. There are a number of circumstances to be taken into consideration in all judgments of this kind; and the ultimate standard, by which we determine all disputes that may arise concerning them, is always derived from experience and observation. Where this experience is not entirely uniform on any side, it is attended with an unavoidable contrariety in our judgments, and with the same opposition and mutual destruction of argument as in every other kind of evidence. We frequently hesitate concerning the reports of others. We balance the opposite circumstances which cause any doubt or uncertainty; and when we discover a superiority on any side, we incline to it; but still with a diminution of assurance, in proportion to the force of its antagonist.

This contrariety of evidence, in the present case, may be derived from several different causes: from the opposition of contrary testimony; from the character or number of the witnesses; from the manner of their delivering their testimony; or from the union of all these circumstances. We entertain a suspicion concerning any matter of fact when the witnesses contradict each other; when they are but few, or of a doubtful character; when they have an interest in what they affirm; when they deliver their testimony with hesitation, or on the contrary, with too violent asseverations. There are many other particulars of the same kind which may diminish or destroy the force of any argument derived from human testimony.

Suppose, for instance, that the fact which the testimony endeavours to establish, partakes of the extraordinary and the marvellous; in that case, the evidence resulting from the testimony admits of a diminution, greater or less, in proportion as the fact is more or less unusual. The reason why we place any credit in witnesses and historians is not derived from any connexion, which we perceive *a priori*, between testimony and reality, but because we are accustomed to find a conformity between them. But when the fact attested is such a one as has seldom fallen under our observation, here is a contest of two opposite experiences; of which the one destroys the other, as far as its force goes, and the superior can only operate on the mind by the force which remains. The very same principle of experience which gives us a certain degree of assurance in the testimony of witnesses gives us also, in this case,

another degree of assurance against the fact which they endeavour to establish; from which contradiction there necessarily arises a counterpoise, and mutual destruction of belief and authority. "I should not believe such a story were it told me by Cato" was a proverbial saying in Rome, even during the lifetime of that philosophical patriot [Plutarch, in vita Catonis Min. 19.]. The incredibility of a fact, it was allowed, might invalidate so great an authority.

The Indian prince, who refused to believe the first relations concerning the effects of frost, reasoned justly; and it naturally required very strong testimony to engage his assent to facts that arose from a state of nature with which he was unacquainted, and which bore so little analogy to those events of which he had had constant and uniform experience. Though they were not contrary to his experience, they were not conformable to it. [No Indian, it is evident, could have experience that water did not freeze in cold climates. This is placing nature in a situation quite unknown to him; and it is impossible for him to tell *a priori* what will result from it. It is making a new experiment, the consequence of which is always uncertain. One may sometimes conjecture from analogy what will follow; but still this is but conjecture. And it must be confessed that, in the present case of freezing, the event follows contrary to the rules of analogy, and is such as a rational Indian would not look for. The operations of cold upon water are not gradual, according to the degrees of cold; but whenever it comes to the freezing point, the water passes in a moment from the utmost liquidity to perfect hardness. Such an event, therefore, may be denominated extraordinary, and requires a pretty strong testimony to render it credible to people in a warm climate: But still it is not miraculous, nor contrary to uniform experience of the course of nature in cases where all the circumstances are the same. The inhabitants of Sumatra have always seen water fluid in their own climate, and the freezing of their rivers ought to be deemed a prodigy: But they never saw water in Muscovy during the winter; and therefore they cannot reasonably be positive what would there be the consequence.]

But in order to increase the probability against the testimony of witnesses, let us suppose that the fact which they affirm, instead of being only marvellous, is really miraculous; and suppose also that the testimony, considered apart and in itself, amounts to an entire proof; in that case, there is proof against proof, of which the strongest must prevail, but still with a diminution of its force, in proportion to that of its antagonist.

A miracle is a violation of the laws of nature; and as a firm and unalterable experience has established these laws, the proof against a miracle, from the very nature of the fact, is as entire as any argument from experience can possibly be imagined. Why is it more than probable that all men must die; that lead cannot, of itself, remain suspended in the air; that fire consumes wood, and is extinguished by water; unless it be that these events are found agreeable to the laws of nature, and there is required a violation of these laws, or in other words, a miracle to prevent them? Nothing is esteemed a miracle if it ever happen in the common course of nature. It is no miracle that a man, seemingly in good health, should die on a sudden: because such a kind of death, though more unusual than any other, has yet been frequently observed to happen. But it is a miracle that a dead man should come to life; because that has never been observed, in any age or country. There must, therefore, be a uniform experience against every miraculous event, otherwise the event would not merit that appellation. And as a uniform experience amounts to a proof, there is here a direct and full proof, from the nature of the fact, against the existence of any miracle; nor can such a proof be destroyed, or the miracle rendered credible, but by an opposite proof, which is superior.

[Sometimes an event may not, in itself, seem to be contrary to the laws of nature, and yet, if it were real, it might, by reason of some circumstances, be denominated a miracle; because, in fact, it is contrary to these laws. Thus if a person, claiming a divine authority, should command a sick person to be well, a healthful man to fall down dead, the clouds to pour rain, the winds to blow, in short, should order many natural events, which immediately follow upon his command; these might justly be esteemed miracles, because they are really, in this case, contrary to the laws of nature. For if any suspicion remain that the event and command concurred by accident, there is no miracle and no transgression of the laws of nature. If this suspicion be removed, there is evidently a miracle, and a transgression of these laws; because nothing can be more contrary to nature than that the voice or command of a man

should have such an influence. A miracle may be accurately defined *a transgression of a law of nature by a particular volition of the Deity, or by the interposition of some invisible agent.* A miracle may either be discoverable by men or not. This alters not its nature and essence. The raising of a house or ship into the air is a visible miracle. The raising of a feather, when the wind wants ever so little of a force requisite for that purpose, is as real a miracle, though not so sensible with regard to us.]

The plain consequence is (and it is a general maxim worthy of our attention), "That no testimony is sufficient to establish a miracle, unless the testimony be of such a kind that its falsehood would be more miraculous than the fact which it endeavours to establish: And even in that case there is a mutual destruction of arguments, and the superior only gives us an assurance suitable to that degree of force which remains after deducting the inferior." When anyone tells me that he saw a dead man restored to life, I immediately consider with myself whether it be more probable, that this person should either deceive or be deceived, or that the fact which he relates should really have happened. I weigh the one miracle against the other; and according to the superiority which I discover, I pronounce my decision, and always reject the greater miracle. If the falsehood of his testimony would be more miraculous than the event which he relates, then, and not till then, can he pretend to command my belief or opinion.

Part II

In the foregoing reasoning we have supposed that the testimony upon which a miracle is founded may possibly amount to an entire proof, and that the falsehood of that testimony would be a real prodigy: But it is easy to show that we have been a great deal too liberal in our concession, and that there never was a miraculous event established on so full an evidence.

For first, there is not to be found in all history any miracle attested by a sufficient number of men of such unquestioned good-sense, education, and learning as to secure us against all delusion in themselves; of such undoubted integrity as to place them beyond all suspicion of any design to deceive others; of such credit and reputation in the eyes of mankind as to have a great deal to lose in case of their being detected in any falsehood; and at the same time, attesting facts performed in such a public manner, and in so celebrated a part of the world, as to render the detection unavoidable: All which circumstances are requisite to give us a full assurance in the testimony of men.

Secondly. We may observe in human nature a principle which, if strictly examined, will be found to diminish extremely the assurance which we might, from human testimony, have, in any kind of prodigy. The maxim, by which we commonly conduct ourselves in our reasonings, is that the objects of which we have no experience resemble those of which we have; that what we have found to be most usual is always most probable; and that where there is an opposition of arguments, we ought to give the preference to such as are founded on the greatest number of past observations. But though, in proceeding by this rule, we readily reject any fact which is unusual and incredible in an ordinary degree; yet in advancing farther, the mind observes not always the same rule; but when anything is affirmed utterly absurd and miraculous, it rather the more readily admits of such a fact, upon account of that very circumstance which ought to destroy all its authority. The passion of surprise and wonder, arising from miracles, being an agreeable emotion, gives a sensible tendency towards the belief of those events from which it is derived. And this goes so far, that even those who cannot enjoy this pleasure immediately, nor can believe those miraculous events of which they are informed, yet love to partake of the satisfaction at second-hand or by rebound, and place a pride and delight in exciting the admiration of others.

With what greediness are the miraculous accounts of travellers received, their descriptions of sea and land monsters, their relations of wonderful adventures, strange men, and uncouth manners? But if the spirit of religion join itself to the love of wonder, there is an end of common sense; and human testimony, in these circumstances, loses all pretensions to authority. A religionist may be an enthusiast, and imagine he sees what has no reality: He may know his narrative to be false, and yet persevere in it, with the best intentions in the world, for the sake of promoting so holy a cause: Or even where this delusion has not place, vanity, excited by so strong a temptation, operates on him more powerfully than on the rest of mankind in any other cir-

cumstances; and self-interest with equal force. His auditors may not have, and commonly have not, sufficient judgment to canvass his evidence: What judgment they have, they renounce by principle, in these sublime and mysterious subjects: Or if they were ever so willing to employ it, passion and a heated imagination disturb the regularity of its operations. Their credulity increases his impudence: And his impudence overpowers their credulity.

Eloquence, when at its highest pitch, leaves little room for reason or reflection, but addressing itself entirely to the fancy or the affections, captivates the willing hearers, and subdues their understanding. Happily, this pitch it seldom attains. But what a Tully or a Demosthenes could scarcely effect over a Roman or Athenian audience, every Capuchin, every itinerant or stationary teacher can perform over the generality of mankind, and in a higher degree, by touching such gross and vulgar passions.

The many instances of forged miracles, and prophecies, and supernatural events, which, in all ages, have either been detected by contrary evidence, or which detect themselves by their absurdity, prove sufficiently the strong propensity of mankind to the extraordinary and the marvellous, and ought reasonably to beget a suspicion against all relations of this kind. This is our natural way of thinking, even with regard to the most common and most credible events. For instance: There is no kind of report which rises so easily, and spreads so quickly, especially in country places and provincial towns, as those concerning marriages; insomuch that two young persons of equal condition never see each other twice, but the whole neighbourhood immediately join them together. The pleasure of telling a piece of news so interesting, of propagating it, and of being the first reporters of it, spreads the intelligence. And this is so well known that no man of sense gives attention to these reports till he find them confirmed by some greater evidence. Do not the same passions, and others still stronger, incline the generality of mankind to believe and report, with the greatest vehemence and assurance, all religious miracles?

Thirdly. It forms a strong presumption against all supernatural and miraculous relations, that they are observed chiefly to abound among ignorant and barbarous nations; or if a civilized people has ever given admission to any of them, that people will be found to have received them from ignorant and barbarous ancestors, who transmitted them with that inviolable sanction and authority which always attend received opinions. When we peruse the first histories of all nations, we are apt to imagine ourselves transported into some new world, where the whole frame of nature is disjointed, and every element performs its operations in a different manner from what it does at present. Battles, revolutions, pestilence, famine, and death are never the effect of those natural causes which we experience. Prodigies, omens, oracles, judgments quite obscure the few natural events that are intermingled with them. But as the former grow thinner every page, in proportion as we advance nearer the enlightened ages, we soon learn that there is nothing mysterious or supernatural in the case, but that all proceeds from the usual propensity of mankind towards the marvellous, and that, though this inclination may at intervals receive a check from sense and learning, it can never be thoroughly extirpated from human nature.

It is strange, a judicious reader is apt to say upon the perusal of these wonderful historians, that such prodigious events never happen in our days. But it is nothing strange, I hope, that men should lie in all ages. You must surely have seen instances enough of that frailty. You have yourself heard many such marvellous relations started, which, being treated with scorn by all the wise and judicious, have at last been abandoned even by the vulgar. Be assured that those renowned lies, which have spread and flourished to such a monstrous height, arose from like beginnings; but being sown in a more proper soil, shot up at last into prodigies almost equal to those which they relate.

It was a wise policy in that false prophet, Alexander, who, though now forgotten, was once so famous, to lay the first scene of his impostures in Paphlagonia, where, as Lucian tells us, the people were extremely ignorant and stupid, and ready to swallow even the grossest delusion. People at a distance, who are weak enough to think the matter at all worth enquiry, have no opportunity of receiving better information. The stories come magnified to them by a hundred circumstances. Fools are industrious in propagating the imposture; while the wise and learned are contented, in general, to deride its absurdity, without informing themselves of the particular facts, by which it may be distinctly refuted. And thus the impostor above-mentioned was enabled to proceed, from his ignorant Paphlagonians, to the enlisting of votaries, even among the Grecian philosophers, and men of the most eminent rank and distinction in Rome: Nay, could engage the attention of that sage emperor Marcus Aurelius; so far as to make him trust the success of a military expedition to his delusive prophecies.

The advantages are so great of starting an imposture among an ignorant people that, even though the delusion should be too gross to impose on the generality of them (which, though seldom, is sometimes the case), it has a much better chance for succeeding in remote countries than if the first scene had been laid in a city renowned for arts and knowledge. The most ignorant and barbarous of these barbarians carry the report abroad. None of their countrymen have a large correspondence, or sufficient credit and authority to contradict and beat down the delusion. Men's inclination to the marvellous has full opportunity to display itself. And thus a story which is universally exploded in the place where it was first started shall pass for certain at a thousand miles distance. But had Alexander fixed his residence at Athens, the philosophers of that renowned mart of learning had immediately spread, throughout the whole Roman empire, their sense of the matter; which, being supported by so great authority, and displayed by all the force of reason and eloquence, had entirely opened the eyes of mankind. It is true; Lucian, passing by chance through Paphlagonia, had an opportunity of performing this good office. But, though much to be wished, it does not always happen that every Alexander meets with a Lucian, ready to expose and detect his impostures.

I may add as a fourth reason which diminishes the authority of prodigies that there is no testimony for any, even those which have not been expressly detected, that is not opposed by an infinite number of witnesses; so that not only the miracle destroys the credit of testimony, but the testimony destroys itself. To make this the better understood, let us consider that, in matters of religion, whatever is different is contrary; and that it is impossible the religions of ancient Rome, of Turkey, of Siam, and of China should, all of them, be established on any solid foundation. Every miracle, therefore, pretended to have been wrought in any of these religions (and all of them abound in miracles), as its direct scope is to establish the particular system to which it is attributed; so has it the same force, though more indirectly, to overthrow every other system. In destroying a rival system, it likewise destroys the credit of those miracles on which that system was established; so that all the prodigies of different religions are to be regarded as contrary facts, and the evidences of these prodigies, whether weak or strong, as opposite to each other. According to this method of reasoning, when we believe any miracle of Mahomet or his successors, we have for our warrant the testimony of a few barbarous Arabians: And on the other hand, we are to regard the authority of Titus Livius, Plutarch, Tacitus, and, in short, of all the authors and witnesses, Grecian, Chinese, and Roman Catholic, who have related any miracle in their particular religion; I say, we are to regard their testimony in the same light as if they had mentioned that Mahometan miracle, and had in express terms contradicted it, with the same certainty as they have for the miracle they relate. This argument may appear over-subtle and refined; but is not in reality different from the reasoning of a judge who supposes that the credit of two witnesses, maintaining a crime against anyone, is destroyed by the testimony of two others, who affirm him to have been two hundred leagues distant at the same instant when the crime is said to have been committed.

One of the best attested miracles in all profane history is that which Tacitus reports of Vespasian, who cured a blind man in Alexandria by means of his spittle, and a lame man by the mere touch of his foot; in obedience to a vision of the god Serapis, who had enjoined them to have recourse to the Emperor for these miraculous cures. The story may be seen in that fine historian [Hist. lib. v. cap. 8. Suetonius gives nearly the same account *in vita* Vesp. 7.]; where every circumstance seems to add weight to the testimony, and might be displayed at large with all the force of argument and eloquence, if anyone were now concerned to enforce the evidence of that exploded and idolatrous superstition. The gravity, solidity, age, and probity of so great an emperor, who, through the whole course of his life, conversed in a familiar manner with his friends and courtiers, and never affected those extraordinary airs of divinity assumed by Alexander and Demetrius. The historian, a cotemporary writer, noted for candour

and veracity, and withal, the greatest and most penetrating genius, perhaps, of all antiquity; and so free from any tendency to credulity, that he even lies under the contrary imputation, of atheism and profaneness: The persons from whose authority he related the miracle, of established character for judgment and veracity, as we may well presume; eye-witnesses of the fact, and confirming their testimony, after the Flavian family was despoiled of the empire, and could no longer give any reward, as the price of a lie. *Utrumque, qui interfuere, nunc quoque memorant, postquam nullum mendacio pretium.* To which if we add the public nature of the facts, as related, it will appear that no evidence can well be supposed stronger for so gross and so palpable a falsehood.

There is also a memorable story related by Cardinal de Retz, which may well deserve our consideration. When that intriguing politician fled into Spain, to avoid the persecution of his enemies, he passed through Saragossa, the capital of Arragon, where he was shown, in the cathedral, a man who had served seven years as a door-keeper, and was well known to everybody in town that had ever paid his devotions at that church. He had been seen, for so long a time, wanting a leg; but recovered that limb by the rubbing of holy oil upon the stump; and the cardinal assures us that he saw him with two legs. This miracle was vouched by all the canons of the church; and the whole company in town were appealed to for a confirmation of the fact; whom the cardinal found, by their zealous devotion, to be thorough believers of the miracle. Here the relater was also cotemporary to the supposed prodigy, of an incredulous and libertine character, as well as of great genius; the miracle of so singular a nature as could scarcely admit of a counterfeit, and the witnesses very numerous, and all of them, in a manner, spectators of the fact to which they gave their testimony. And what adds mightily to the force of the evidence, and may double our surprise on this occasion, is that the cardinal himself, who relates the story, seems not to give any credit to it, and consequently cannot be suspected of any concurrence in the holy fraud. He considered justly that it was not requisite, in order to reject a fact of this nature, to be able accurately to disprove the testimony, and to trace its falsehood, through all the circumstances of knavery and credulity which produced it. He knew that, as this was commonly altogether impossible at any small distance of time and place; so was it extremely difficult, even where one was immediately present, by reason of the bigotry, ignorance, cunning, and roguery of a great part of mankind. He therefore concluded, like a just reasoner, that such an evidence carried falsehood upon the very face of it, and that a miracle supported by any human testimony was more properly a subject of derision than of argument.

There surely never was a greater number of miracles ascribed to one person than those which were lately said to have been wrought in France upon the tomb of Abbé Paris, the famous Jansenist, with whose sanctity the people were so long deluded. The curing of the sick, giving hearing to the deaf, and sight to the blind, were everywhere talked of as the usual effects of that holy sepulchre. But what is more extraordinary: Many of the miracles were immediately proved upon the spot, before judges of unquestioned integrity, attested by witnesses of credit and distinction, in a learned age, and on the most eminent theatre that is now in the world. Nor is this all: A relation of them was published and dispersed everywhere; nor were the Jesuits, though a learned body, supported by the civil magistrate, and determined enemies to those opinions in whose favour the miracles were said to have been wrought, ever able distinctly to refute or detect them. Where shall we find such a number of circumstances agreeing to the corroboration of one fact? And what have we to oppose to such a cloud of witnesses, but the absolute impossibility or miraculous nature of the events which they relate? And this surely, in the eyes of all reasonable people, will alone be regarded as a sufficient refutation.

Is the consequence just, because some human testimony has the utmost force and authority in some cases, when it relates the battle of Philippi or Pharsalia, for instance; that therefore all kinds of testimony must, in all cases, have equal force and authority? Suppose that the Caesarean and Pompeian factions had, each of them, claimed the victory in these battles, and that the historians of each party had uniformly ascribed the advantage to their own side; how could mankind, at this distance, have been able to determine between them? The contrariety is equally strong between the miracles related

by Herodotus or Plutarch and those delivered by Mariana, Bede, or any monkish historian.

The wise lend a very academic faith to every report which favours the passion of the reporter; whether it magnifies his country, his family, or himself, or in any other way strikes in with his natural inclinations and propensities. But what greater temptation than to appear a missionary, a prophet, an ambassador from heaven? Who would not encounter many dangers and difficulties, in order to attain so sublime a character? Or if, by the help of vanity and a heated imagination, a man has first made a convert of himself, and entered seriously into the delusion; who ever scruples to make use of pious frauds, in support of so holy and meritorious a cause?

The smallest spark may here kindle into the greatest flame, because the materials are always prepared for it. The *avidum genus auricularum* [Lucret. iv. 594.], the gazing populace, receive greedily, without examination, whatever sooths superstition, and promotes wonder.

How many stories of this nature have, in all ages, been detected and exploded in their infancy? How many more have been celebrated for a time, and have afterwards sunk into neglect and oblivion? Where such reports, therefore, fly about, the solution of the phenomenon is obvious; and we judge in conformity to regular experience and observation when we account for it by the known and natural principles of credulity and delusion. And shall we, rather than have a recourse to so natural a solution, allow of a miraculous violation of the most established laws of nature?

I need not mention the difficulty of detecting a falsehood in any private or even public history at the place where it is said to happen; much more when the scene is removed to ever so small a distance. Even a court of judicature, with all the authority, accuracy, and judgment which they can employ, find themselves often at a loss to distinguish between truth and falsehood in the most recent actions. But the matter never comes to any issue, if trusted to the common method of altercation and debate and flying rumours; especially when men's passions have taken part on either side.

In the infancy of new religions, the wise and learned commonly esteem the matter too inconsiderable to deserve their attention or regard. And when afterwards they would willingly detect the cheat, in order to undeceive the deluded multitude, the season is now past, and the records and witnesses which might clear up the matter have perished beyond recovery.

No means of detection remain but those which must be drawn from the very testimony itself of the reporters: And these, though always sufficient with the judicious and knowing, are commonly too fine to fall under the comprehension of the vulgar.

Upon the whole, then, it appears that no testimony for any kind of miracle has ever amounted to a probability, much less to a proof; and that, even supposing it amounted to a proof, it would be opposed by another proof, derived from the very nature of the fact which it would endeavour to establish. It is experience only which gives authority to human testimony; and it is the same experience which assures us of the laws of nature. When, therefore, these two kinds of experience are contrary, we have nothing to do but subtract the one from the other, and embrace an opinion, either on one side or the other, with that assurance which arises from the remainder. But according to the principle here explained, this subtraction, with regard to all popular religions, amounts to an entire annihilation; and therefore we may establish it as a maxim that no human testimony can have such force as to prove a miracle, and make it a just foundation for any such system of religion.

I beg the limitations here made may be remarked when I say that a miracle can never be proved so as to be the foundation of a system of religion. For I own that otherwise, there may possibly be miracles, or violations of the usual course of nature, of such a kind as to admit of proof from human testimony; though, perhaps, it will be impossible to find any such in all the records of history. Thus, suppose all authors, in all languages, agree that, from the first of January 1600, there was a total darkness over the whole earth for eight days: Suppose that the tradition of this extraordinary event is still strong and lively among the people: That all travellers, who return from foreign countries, bring us accounts of the same tradition, without the least variation or contradiction: It is evident that our present philosophers, instead of doubting the fact, ought to receive it as certain, and ought to search for the causes whence it might be derived. The decay, corruption, and dissolution of nature is an event rendered probable by so many analogies that any phenomenon which seems to have a tendency towards that catastrophe comes within the reach of human testimony, if that testimony be very extensive and uniform.

But suppose that all the historians who treat of England should agree that, on the first of January 1600, Queen Elizabeth died; that both before and after her death she was seen by her physicians and the whole court, as is usual with persons of her rank; that her successor was acknowledged and proclaimed by the parliament; and that, after being interred a month, she again appeared, resumed the throne, and governed England for three years: I must confess that I should be surprised at the concurrence of so many odd circumstances, but should not have the least inclination to believe so miraculous an event. I should not doubt of her pretended death, and of those other public circumstances that followed it: I should only assert it to have been pretended, and that it neither was, nor possibly could be, real. You would in vain object to me the difficulty, and almost impossibility, of deceiving the world in an affair of such consequence; the wisdom and solid judgment of that renowned queen; with the little or no advantage which she could reap from so poor an artifice: All this might astonish me; but I would still reply that the knavery and folly of men are such common phenomena that I should rather believe the most extraordinary events to arise from their concurrence than admit of so signal a violation of the laws of nature.

But should this miracle be ascribed to any new system of religion, men, in all ages, have been so much imposed on by ridiculous stories of that kind that this very circumstance would be a full proof of a cheat, and sufficient, with all men of sense, not only to make them reject the fact, but even reject it without farther examination. Though the Being to whom the miracle is ascribed be, in this case, Almighty, it does not, upon that account, become a whit more probable; since it is impossible for us to know the attributes or actions of such a Being, otherwise than from the experience which we have of his productions, in the usual course of nature. This still reduces us to past observation, and obliges us to compare the instances of the violation of truth in the testimony of men, with those of the violation of the laws of nature by miracles, in order to judge which of them is most likely and probable. As the violations of truth are more common in the testimony concerning religious miracles than in that concerning any other matter of fact, this must diminish very much the authority of the former testimony, and make us form a general resolution never to lend any attention to it, with whatever specious pretence it may be covered.

Lord Bacon seems to have embraced the same principles of reasoning. "We ought," says he, "to make a collection or particular history of all monsters and prodigious births or productions, and in a word of everything new, rare, and extraordinary in nature. But this must be done with the most severe scrutiny, lest we depart from truth. Above all, every relation must be considered as suspicious which depends in any degree upon religion, as the prodigies of Livy: And no less so, everything that is to be found in the writers of natural magic or alchimy, or such authors who seem, all of them, to have an unconquerable appetite for falsehood and fable." [*Nov. Org.* lib. ii. aph. 29.]

I am the better pleased with the method of reasoning here delivered, as I think it may serve to confound those dangerous friends or disguised enemies to the Christian Religion, who have undertaken to defend it by the principles of human reason. Our most holy religion is founded on Faith, not on reason; and it is a sure method of exposing it to put it to such a trial as it is, by no means, fitted to endure. To make this more evident, let us examine those miracles related in scripture; and not to lose ourselves in too wide a field, let us confine ourselves to such as we find in the Pentateuch, which we shall examine, according to the principles of those pretended Christians, not as the word or testimony of God himself, but as the production of a mere human writer and historian. Here then we are first to consider a book, presented to us by a barbarous and ignorant people, written in an age when they were still more barbarous, and in all probability long after the facts which it relates, corroborated by no concurring testimony, and resembling those fabulous accounts which every nation gives of its origin. Upon reading this book, we find it full of prodigies

and miracles. It gives an account of a state of the world and of human nature entirely different from the present: Of our fall from that state: Of the age of man, extended to near a thousand years: Of the destruction of the world by a deluge: Of the arbitrary choice of one people as the favourites of heaven; and that people the countrymen of the author: Of their deliverance from bondage by prodigies the most astonishing imaginable: I desire anyone to lay his hand upon his heart, and after a serious consideration declare whether he thinks that the falsehood of such a book, supported by such a testimony, would be more extraordinary and miraculous than all the miracles it relates; which is, however, necessary to make it be received, according to the measures of probability above established.

What we have said of miracles may be applied, without any variation, to prophecies; and indeed, all prophecies are real miracles, and as such only can be admitted as proofs of any revelation. If it did not exceed the capacity of human nature to foretell future events, it would be absurd to employ any prophecy as an argument for a divine mission or authority from heaven. So that, upon the whole, we may conclude that the Christian Religion not only was at first attended with miracles, but even at this day cannot be believed by any reasonable person without one. Mere reason is insufficient to convince us of its veracity: And whoever is moved by Faith to assent to it is conscious of a continued miracle in his own person, which subverts all the principles of his understanding, and gives him a determination to believe what is most contrary to custom and experience.

Section XI. *Of a Particular Providence and of a Future State*

I was lately engaged in conversation with a friend who loves sceptical paradoxes; where, though he advanced many principles, of which I can by no means approve, yet as they seem to be curious, and to bear some relation to the chain of reasoning carried on throughout this enquiry, I shall here copy them from my memory as accurately as I can, in order to submit them to the judgment of the reader.

Our conversation began with my admiring the singular good fortune of philosophy, which, as it requires entire liberty above all other privileges, and chiefly flourishes from the free opposition of sentiments and argumentation, received its first birth in an age and country of freedom and toleration, and was never cramped, even in its most extravagant principles, by any creeds, confessions, or penal statutes. For, except the banishment of Protagoras, and the death of Socrates, which last event proceeded partly from other motives, there are scarcely any instances to be met with, in ancient history, of this bigotted jealousy, with which the present age is so much infested. Epicurus lived at Athens to an advanced age, in peace and tranquillity: Epicureans were even admitted to receive the sacerdotal character, and to officiate at the altar, in the most sacred rites of the established religion: And the public encouragement of pensions and salaries was afforded equally, by the wisest of all the Roman emperors, to the professors of every sect of philosophy. How requisite such kind of treatment was to philosophy, in her early youth, will easily be conceived if we reflect that, even at present, when she may be supposed more hardy and robust, she bears with much difficulty the inclemency of the seasons, and those harsh winds of calumny and persecution which blow upon her.

You admire, says my friend, as the singular good fortune of philosophy, what seems to result from the natural course of things, and to be unavoidable in every age and nation. This pertinacious bigotry, of which you complain as so fatal to philosophy is really her offspring, who, after allying with superstition, separates himself entirely from the interest of his parent, and becomes her most inveterate enemy and persecutor. Speculative dogmas of religion, the present occasions of such furious dispute, could not possibly be conceived or admitted in the early ages of the world; when mankind, being wholly illiterate, formed an idea of religion more suitable to their weak apprehension, and composed their sacred tenets of such tales chiefly as were the objects of traditional belief, more than of argument or disputation. After the first alarm, therefore, was over, which arose from the new paradoxes and principles of the philosophers; these teachers seem ever after, during the ages of antiquity, to have lived in great harmony with the established superstition, and to have made a fair partition of mankind between them; the former claiming all the learned and wise, the latter possessing all the vulgar and illiterate.

It seems, then say I, that you leave politics entirely out of the question, and never suppose that a wise magistrate can justly be jealous of certain tenets of philosophy, such as those of Epicurus, which, denying a divine existence, and consequently a providence and a future state, seem to loosen, in a great measure, the ties of morality, and may be supposed, for that reason, pernicious to the peace of civil society.

I know, replied he, that in fact these persecutions never, in any age, proceeded from calm reason, or from experience of the pernicious consequences of philosophy; but arose entirely from passion and prejudice. But what if I should advance farther, and assert that, if Epicurus had been accused before the people, by any of the sycophants or informers of those days, he could easily have defended his cause, and proved his principles of philosophy to be as salutary as those of his adversaries, who endeavoured, with such zeal, to expose him to the public hatred and jealousy?

I wish, said I, you would try your eloquence upon so extraordinary a topic, and make a speech for Epicurus which might satisfy, not the mob of Athens, if you will allow that ancient and polite city to have contained any mob, but the more philosophical part of his audience, such as might be supposed capable of comprehending his arguments.

The matter would not be difficult, upon such conditions, replied he: And if you please, I shall suppose myself Epicurus for a moment, and make you stand for the Athenian people, and shall deliver you such an harangue as will fill all the urn with white beans, and leave not a black one to gratify the malice of my adversaries.

Very well: Pray proceed upon these suppositions.

I come hither, O ye Athenians, to justify in your assembly what I maintained in my school, and I find myself impeached by furious antagonists, instead of reasoning with calm and dispassionate enquirers. Your deliberations, which of right should be directed to questions of public good, and the interest of the commonwealth, are diverted to the disquisitions of speculative philosophy; and these magnificent, but perhaps fruitless, enquiries take place of your more familiar but more useful occupations. But so far as in me lies, I will prevent this abuse. We shall not here dispute concerning the origin and government of worlds. We shall only enquire how far such questions concern the public interest. And if I can persuade you that they are entirely indifferent to the peace of society and security of government, I hope that you will presently send us back to our schools, there to examine, at leisure, the question, the most sublime, but, at the same time, the most speculative of all philosophy.

The religious philosophers, not satisfied with the tradition of your forefathers, and doctrine of your priests (in which I willingly acquiesce), indulge a rash curiosity in trying how far they can establish religion upon the principles of reason; and they thereby excite, instead of satisfying, the doubts which naturally arise from a diligent and scrutinous enquiry. They paint, in the most magnificent colours, the order, beauty, and wise arrangement of the universe; and then ask if such a glorious display of intelligence could proceed from the fortuitous concourse of atoms, or if chance could produce what the greatest genius can never sufficiently admire. I shall not examine the justness of this argument. I shall allow it to be as solid as my antagonists and accusers can desire. It is sufficient, if I can prove, from this very reasoning, that the question is entirely speculative, and that when, in my philosophical disquisitions, I deny a providence and a future state, I undermine not the foundations of society, but advance principles which they themselves, upon their own topics, if they argue consistently, must allow to be solid and satisfactory.

You then, who are my accusers, have acknowledged that the chief or sole argument for a divine existence (which I never questioned) is derived from the order of nature; where there appear such marks of intelligence and design that you think it extravagant to assign for its cause either chance, or the blind and unguided force of matter. You allow that this is an argument drawn from effects to causes. From the order of the work, you infer that there must have been project and forethought in the workman. If you cannot make out this point, you allow that your conclusion fails; and you pretend not to establish the conclusion in a greater latitude than the phenomena of nature will justify. These are your concessions. I desire you to mark the consequences.

When we infer any particular cause from an effect, we must proportion the one to the other, and can never be allowed to ascribe to the cause any qualities but what are exactly sufficient to produce the effect. A body of ten ounces raised in any scale may serve as a proof that the counterbalancing weight exceeds ten ounces, but can never afford a reason that it exceeds a hundred. If the cause assigned for any effect be not sufficient to produce it, we must either reject that cause, or add to it such qualities as will give it a just proportion to the effect. But if we ascribe to it farther qualities, or affirm it capable of producing other effects, we can only indulge the licence of conjecture, and arbitrarily suppose the existence of qualities and energies, without reason or authority.

The same rule holds whether the cause assigned be brute unconscious matter, or a rational intelligent being. If the cause be known only by the effect, we never ought to ascribe to it any qualities beyond what are precisely requisite to produce the effect: Nor can we, by any rules of just reasoning, return back from the cause, and infer other effects from it beyond those by which alone it is known to us. No one, merely from the sight of one of Zeuxis's pictures, could know that he was also a statuary or architect, and was an artist no less skilful in stone and marble than in colours. The talents and taste displayed in the particular work before us; these we may safely conclude the workman to be possessed of. The cause must be proportioned to the effect; and if we exactly and precisely proportion it, we shall never find in it any qualities that point farther, or afford an inference concerning any other design or performance. Such qualities must be somewhat beyond what is merely requisite for producing the effect which we examine.

Allowing, therefore, the gods to be the authors of the existence or order of the universe, it follows that they possess that precise degree of power, intelligence, and benevolence which appears in their workmanship; but nothing farther can ever be proved, except we call in the assistance of exaggeration and flattery to supply the defects of argument and reasoning. So far as the traces of any attributes, at present, appear, so far may we conclude these attributes to exist. The supposition of farther attributes is mere hypothesis; much more the supposition that, in distant regions of space or periods of time, there has been, or will be, a more magnificent display of these attributes, and a scheme of administration more suitable to such imaginary virtues. We can never be allowed to mount up from the universe, the effect, to Jupiter, the cause; and then descend downwards, to infer any new effect from that cause; as if the present effects alone were not entirely worthy of the glorious attributes which we ascribe to that deity. The knowledge of the cause being derived solely from the effect, they must be exactly adjusted to each other; and the one can never refer to any thing farther, or be the foundation of any new inference and conclusion.

You find certain phenomena in nature. You seek a cause or author. You imagine that you have found him. You afterwards become so enamoured of this offspring of your brain that you imagine it impossible but he must produce something greater and more perfect than the present scene of things, which is so full of ill and disorder. You forget that this superlative intelligence and benevolence are entirely imaginary, or, at least, without any foundation in reason; and that you have no ground to ascribe to him any qualities but what you see he has actually exerted and displayed in his productions. Let your gods, therefore, O philosophers, be suited to the present appearances of nature: And presume not to alter these appearances by arbitrary suppositions, in order to suit them to the attributes which you so fondly ascribe to your deities.

When priests and poets, supported by your authority, O Athenians, talk of a golden or silver age, which preceded the present state of vice and misery, I hear them with attention and with reverence. But when philosophers, who pretend to neglect authority, and to cultivate reason, hold the same discourse, I pay them not, I own, the same obsequious submission and pious deference. I ask: Who carried them into the celestial regions, who admitted them into the councils of the gods, who opened to them the book of fate, that they thus rashly affirm that their deities have executed, or will execute, any purpose beyond what has actually appeared? If they tell me that they have mounted on the steps or by the gradual ascent of reason, and by drawing inferences from effects to causes, I still insist that they have aided the ascent of reason by the wings of imagina-

tion; otherwise they could not thus change their manner of inference, and argue from causes to effects; presuming that a more perfect production than the present world would be more suitable to such perfect beings as the gods, and forgetting that they have no reason to ascribe to these celestial beings any perfection or any attribute but what can be found in the present world.

Hence all the fruitless industry to account for the ill appearances of nature, and save the honour of the gods; while we must acknowledge the reality of that evil and disorder with which the world so much abounds. The obstinate and intractable qualities of matter, we are told, or the observance of general laws, or some such reason, is the sole cause which controlled the power and benevolence of Jupiter, and obliged him to create mankind and every sensible creature so imperfect and so unhappy. These attributes, then, are, it seems, beforehand, taken for granted, in their greatest latitude. And upon that supposition, I own that such conjectures may, perhaps, be admitted as plausible solutions of the ill phenomena. But still I ask: Why take these attributes for granted, or why ascribe to the cause any qualities but what actually appear in the effect? Why torture your brain to justify the course of nature upon suppositions which, for aught you know, may be entirely imaginary, and of which there are to be found no traces in the course of nature?

The religious hypothesis, therefore, must be considered only as a particular method of accounting for the visible phenomena of the universe: But no just reasoner will ever presume to infer from it any single fact, and alter or add to the phenomena, in any single particular. If you think that the appearances of things prove such causes, it is allowable for you to draw an inference concerning the existence of these causes. In such complicated and sublime subjects, everyone should be indulged in the liberty of conjecture and argument. But here you ought to rest. If you come backward, and arguing from your inferred causes, conclude that any other fact has existed, or will exist, in the course of nature, which may serve as a fuller display of particular attributes; I must admonish you that you have departed from the method of reasoning attached to the present subject, and have certainly added something to the attributes of the cause beyond what appears in the effect; otherwise you could never, with tolerable sense or propriety, add anything to the effect, in order to render it more worthy of the cause.

Where, then, is the odiousness of that doctrine which I teach in my school, or rather, which I examine in my gardens? Or what do you find in this whole question, wherein the security of good morals, or the peace and order of society, is in the least concerned?

I deny a providence, you say, and supreme governor of the world, who guides the course of events, and punishes the vicious with infamy and disappointment, and rewards the virtuous with honour and success, in all their undertakings. But surely, I deny not the course itself of events, which lies open to everyone's enquiry and examination. I acknowledge that, in the present order of things, virtue is attended with more peace of mind than vice, and meets with a more favourable reception from the world. I am sensible that, according to the past experience of mankind, friendship is the chief joy of human life, and moderation the only source of tranquillity and happiness. I never balance between the virtuous and the vicious course of life; but am sensible, that, to a well-disposed mind, every advantage is on the side of the former. And what can you say more, allowing all your suppositions and reasonings? You tell me, indeed, that this disposition of things proceeds from intelligence and design. But whatever it proceeds from, the disposition itself, on which depends our happiness or misery, and consequently our conduct and deportment in life, is still the same. It is still open for me, as well as you, to regulate my behaviour by my experience of past events. And if you affirm that, while a divine providence is allowed, and a supreme distributive justice in the universe, I ought to expect some more particular reward of the good, and punishment of the bad, beyond the ordinary course of events; I here find the same fallacy which I have before endeavoured to detect. You persist in imagining that, if we grant that divine existence, for which you so earnestly contend, you may safely infer consequences from it, and add something to the experienced order of nature, by arguing from the attributes which you ascribe to your gods. You seem not to remember that all your reasonings on this subject can only be drawn from effects to causes; and that every argument, deduced from causes to effects, must of necessity be a gross sophism; since it is impossible for

you to know anything of the cause but what you have antecedently not inferred, but discovered to the full, in the effect.

But what must a philosopher think of those vain reasoners who, instead of regarding the present scene of things as the sole object of their contemplation, so far reverse the whole course of nature as to render this life merely a passage to something farther: a porch, which leads to a greater, and vastly different building; a prologue, which serves only to introduce the piece, and give it more grace and propriety? Whence, do you think, can such philosophers derive their idea of the gods? From their own conceit and imagination surely. For if they derived it from the present phenomena, it would never point to anything farther, but must be exactly adjusted to them. That the divinity may possibly be endowed with attributes which we have never seen exerted; may be governed by principles of action which we cannot discover to be satisfied: All this will freely be allowed. But still this is mere possibility and hypothesis. We never can have reason to infer any attributes, or any principles of action, in him but so far as we know them to have been exerted and satisfied.

Are there any marks of a distributive justice in the world? If you answer in the affirmative, I conclude that, since justice here exerts itself, it is satisfied. If you reply in the negative, I conclude that you have then no reason to ascribe justice, in our sense of it, to the gods. If you hold a medium between affirmation and negation, by saying that the justice of the gods, at present, exerts itself in part, but not in its full extent; I answer that you have no reason to give it any particular extent, but only so far as you see it, at present, exert itself.

Thus I bring the dispute, O Athenians, to a short issue with my antagonists. The course of nature lies open to my contemplation as well as to theirs. The experienced train of events is the great standard by which we all regulate our conduct. Nothing else can be appealed to in the field, or in the senate. Nothing else ought ever to be heard of in the school, or in the closet. In vain would our limited understanding break through these boundaries, which are too narrow for our fond imagination. While we argue from the course of nature, and infer a particular intelligent cause, which first bestowed, and still preserves, order in the universe, we embrace a principle which is both uncertain and useless. It is uncertain because the subject lies entirely beyond the reach of human experience. It is useless because our knowledge of this cause being derived entirely from the course of nature, we can never, according to the rules of just reasoning, return back from the cause with any new inference, or making additions to the common and experienced course of nature, establish any new principles of conduct and behaviour.

I observe (said I, finding he had finished his harangue) that you neglect not the artifice of the demagogues of old; and as you were pleased to make me stand for the people, you insinuate yourself into my favour by embracing those principles to which, you know, I have always expressed a particular attachment. But allowing you to make experience (as indeed I think you ought) the only standard of our judgment concerning this, and all other questions of fact; I doubt not but, from the very same experience to which you appeal, it may be possible to refute this reasoning, which you have put into the mouth of Epicurus. If you saw, for instance, a half-finished building, surrounded with heaps of brick and stone and mortar, and all the instruments of masonry, could you not infer from the effect that it was a work of design and contrivance? And could you not return again, from this inferred cause, to infer new additions to the effect, and conclude that the building would soon be finished, and receive all the further improvements which art could bestow upon it? If you saw upon the sea-shore the print of one human foot, you would conclude that a man had passed that way, and that he had also left the traces of the other foot, though effaced by the rolling of the sands or inundation of the waters. Why then do you refuse to admit the same method of reasoning with regard to the order of nature? Consider the world and the present life only as an imperfect building, from which you can infer a superior intelligence; and arguing from that superior intelligence, which can leave nothing imperfect; why may you not infer a more finished scheme or plan, which will receive its completion in some distant point of space or time? Are not these methods of reasoning exactly similar? And under what pretence can you embrace the one, while you reject the other?

The infinite difference of the subjects, replied he, is a sufficient foundation for this difference in my conclusions. In works of human art and contrivance, it is allowable to advance from the effect to the cause, and returning back from the cause, to form new inferences concerning the effect, and examine the alterations which it has probably undergone, or may still undergo. But what is the foundation of this method of reasoning? Plainly this: that man is a being whom we know by experience, whose motives and designs we are acquainted with, and whose projects and inclinations have a certain connexion and coherence, according to the laws which nature has established for the government of such a creature. When, therefore, we find that any work has proceeded from the skill and industry of man, as we are otherwise acquainted with the nature of the animal, we can draw a hundred inferences concerning what may be expected from him; and these inferences will all be founded in experience and observation. But did we know man only from the single work or production which we examine, it were impossible for us to argue in this manner, because our knowledge of all the qualities which we ascribe to him, being in that case derived from the production, it is impossible they could point to anything farther, or be the foundation of any new inference. The print of a foot in the sand can only prove, when considered alone, that there was some figure adapted to it, by which it was produced: But the print of a human foot proves likewise, from our other experience, that there was probably another foot which also left its impression, though effaced by time or other accidents. Here we mount from the effect to the cause; and descending again from the cause, infer alterations in the effect; but this is not a continuation of the same simple chain of reasoning. We comprehend in this case a hundred other experiences and observations, concerning the usual figure and members of that species of animal, without which this method of argument must be considered as fallacious and sophistical.

The case is not the same with our reasonings from the works of nature. The Deity is known to us only by his productions, and is a single being in the universe, not comprehended under any species or genus, from whose experienced attributes or qualities we can, by analogy, infer any attribute or quality in him. As the universe shows wisdom and goodness, we infer wisdom and goodness. As it shows a particular degree of these perfections, we infer a particular degree of them, precisely adapted to the effect which we examine. But farther attributes or farther degrees of the same attributes we can never be authorised to infer or suppose, by any rules of just reasoning. Now, without some such licence of supposition, it is impossible for us to argue from the cause, or infer any alteration in the effect, beyond what has immediately fallen under our observation. Greater good produced by this Being must still prove a greater degree of goodness: A more impartial distribution of rewards and punishments must proceed from a greater regard to justice and equity. Every supposed addition to the works of nature makes an addition to the attributes of the Author of nature; and consequently, being entirely unsupported by any reason or argument, can never be admitted but as mere conjecture and hypothesis.

[In general, it may, I think, be established as a maxim that where any cause is known only by its particular effects, it must be impossible to infer any new effects from that cause; since the qualities which are requisite to produce these new effects along with the former must either be different, or superior, or of more extensive operation, than those which simply produced the effect, whence alone the cause is supposed to be known to us. We can never, therefore, have any reason to suppose the existence of these qualities. To say that the new effects proceed only from a continuation of the same energy which is already known from the first effects will not remove the difficulty. For even granting this to be the case (which can seldom be supposed), the very continuation and exertion of a like energy (for it is impossible it can be absolutely the same), I say, this exertion of a like energy, in a different period of space and time, is a very arbitrary supposition, and what there cannot possibly be any traces of in the effects, from which all our knowledge of the cause is originally derived. Let the inferred cause be exactly proportioned (as it should be) to the known effect; and it is impossible that it can possess any qualities from which new or different effects can be inferred.]

The great source of our mistake in this subject, and of the unbounded licence of conjecture which we indulge is that we tacitly consider ourselves as in the place of the Supreme Being, and conclude that he will, on every occasion, observe the same conduct which we ourselves, in his situation, would have embraced as reasonable and eligible. But, besides that the ordinary course of nature may convince us that almost everything is regulated by principles and maxims very different from ours; besides this, I say, it must evidently appear contrary to all rules of analogy to reason, from the intentions and projects of men, to those of a Being so different, and so much superior. In human nature, there is a certain experienced coherence of designs and inclinations, so that when, from any fact, we have discovered one intention of any man, it may often be reasonable, from experience, to infer another, and draw a long chain of conclusions concerning his past or future conduct. But this method of reasoning can never have place with regard to a Being so remote and incomprehensible, who bears much less analogy to any other being in the universe than the sun to a waxen taper, and who discovers himself only by some faint traces or outlines, beyond which we have no authority to ascribe to him any attribute or perfection. What we imagine to be a superior perfection may really be a defect. Or were it ever so much a perfection, the ascribing of it to the Supreme Being, where it appears not to have been really exerted, to the full, in his works, savours more of flattery and panegyric than of just reasoning and sound philosophy. All the philosophy, therefore, in the world, and all the religion, which is nothing but a species of philosophy, will never be able to carry us beyond the usual course of experience, or give us measures of conduct and behaviour different from those which are furnished by reflections on common life. No new fact can ever be inferred from the religious hypothesis; no event foreseen or foretold; no reward or punishment expected or dreaded, beyond what is already known by practice and observation. So that my apology for Epicurus will still appear solid and satisfactory; nor have the political interests of society any connexion with the philosophical disputes concerning metaphysics and religion.

There is still one circumstance, replied I, which you seem to have overlooked. Though I should allow your premises, I must deny your conclusion. You conclude that religious doctrines and reasonings can have no influence on life, because they ought to have no influence, never considering that men reason not in the same manner you do, but draw many consequences from the belief of a divine

Existence, and suppose that the Deity will inflict punishments on vice, and bestow rewards on virtue, beyond what appear in the ordinary course of nature. Whether this reasoning of theirs be just or not is no matter. Its influence on their life and conduct must still be the same. And those who attempt to disabuse them of such prejudices may, for aught I know, be good reasoners, but I cannot allow them to be good citizens and politicians, since they free men from one restraint upon their passions, and make the infringement of the laws of society, in one respect, more easy and secure.

After all, I may, perhaps, agree to your general conclusion in favour of liberty, though upon different premises from those on which you endeavour to found it. I think that the state ought to tolerate every principle of philosophy; nor is there an instance that any government has suffered in its political interests by such indulgence. There is no enthusiasm among philosophers; their doctrines are not very alluring to the people; and no restraint can be put upon their reasonings but what must be of dangerous consequence to the sciences, and even to the state, by paving the way for persecution and oppression in points where the generality of mankind are more deeply interested and concerned.

But there occurs to me (continued I), with regard to your main topic, a difficulty, which I shall just propose to you, without insisting on it, lest it lead into reasonings of too nice and delicate a nature. In a word, I much doubt whether it be possible for a cause to be known only by its effect (as you have all along supposed) or to be of so singular and particular a nature as to have no parallel and no similarity with any other cause or object that has ever fallen under our observation. It is only when two species of objects are found to be constantly conjoined that we can infer the one from the other; and were an effect presented which was entirely singular, and could not be comprehended under any known species, I do not see that we could form any conjecture or inference at all concerning its cause. If experience and observation and analogy be, indeed, the only guides which we can reasonably follow in inferences of this nature, both the effect and cause must bear a similarity and resemblance to other effects and causes which we know, and which we have found, in many instances, to be conjoined with each other. I leave it to your own reflection to pursue the consequences of this principle. I shall just observe that, as the antagonists of Epicurus always suppose the universe, an effect quite singular and unparalleled, to be the proof of a Deity, a cause no less singular and unparalleled; your reasonings, upon that supposition, seem, at least, to merit our attention. There is, I own, some difficulty, how we can ever return from the cause to the effect, and, reasoning from our ideas of the former, infer any alteration on the latter, or any addition to it.

Section XII. Of the Academical or Sceptical Philosophy

Part I

There is not a greater number of philosophical reasonings displayed upon any subject than those which prove the existence of a Deity, and refute the fallacies of Atheists; and yet the most religious philosophers still dispute whether any man can be so blinded as to be a speculative atheist. How shall we reconcile these contradictions? The knights-errant, who wandered about to clear the world of dragons and giants, never entertained the least doubt with regard to the existence of these monsters.

The Sceptic is another enemy of religion, who naturally provokes the indignation of all divines and graver philosophers, though it is certain that no man ever met with any such absurd creature, or conversed with a man who had no opinion or principle concerning any subject, either of action or speculation. This begets a very natural question: What is meant by a sceptic? And how far is it possible to push these philosophical principles of doubt and uncertainty?

There is a species of scepticism, antecedent to all study and philosophy, which is much inculcated by Descartes and others, as a sovereign preservative against error and precipitate judgment. It recommends a universal doubt, not only of all our former opinions and principles, but also of our very faculties; of whose veracity, say they, we must assure ourselves by a chain of reasoning deduced from some original principle, which cannot possibly be fallacious or deceitful. But neither is there any such original principle, which has a prerogative above others, that are self-evident and convincing: Or if there were, could we advance a step beyond it but by the use of those very faculties of which we are supposed to be already diffident. The Cartesian doubt, therefore, were it ever possible to be attained by any human creature (as it plainly is not), would be entirely incurable; and no reasoning could ever bring us to a state of assurance and conviction upon any subject.

It must, however, be confessed that this species of scepticism, when more moderate, may be understood in a very reasonable sense, and is a necessary preparative to the study of philosophy, by preserving a proper impartiality in our judgments, and weaning our mind from all those prejudices which we may have imbibed from education or rash opinion. To begin with clear and self-evident principles, to advance by timorous and sure steps, to review frequently our conclusions, and examine accurately all their consequences; though by these means we shall make both a slow and a short progress in our systems, are the only methods by which we can ever hope to reach truth, and attain a proper stability and certainty in our determinations.

There is another species of scepticism, consequent to science and enquiry, when men are supposed to have discovered either the absolute fallaciousness of their mental faculties, or their unfitness to reach any fixed determination in all those curious subjects of speculation about which they are commonly employed. Even our very senses are brought into dispute by a certain species of philosophers; and the maxims of common life are subjected to the same doubt as the most profound principles or conclusions of metaphysics and theology. As these paradoxical tenets (if they may be called tenets) are to be met with in some philosophers, and the refutation of them in several, they naturally excite our curiosity, and make us enquire into the arguments on which they may be founded.

I need not insist upon the more trite topics, employed by the sceptics in all ages, against the evidence of sense, such as those which are derived from the imperfection and fallaciousness of our organs, on numberless occasions; the crooked appearance of an oar in water; the various aspects of objects, according to their different distances; the double images which arise from the pressing one eye; with many other appearances of a like nature. These sceptical topics, indeed, are only sufficient to prove that the senses alone are not implicitly to be depended on; but that we must correct their evidence by reason, and by considerations derived from the nature of the medium, the distance of the object, and the disposition of the organ, in order to render them, within their sphere, the proper criteria of truth and falsehood. There are other more profound arguments against the senses, which admit not of so easy a solution.

It seems evident that men are carried, by a natural instinct or prepossession, to repose faith in their senses; and that, without any reasoning, or even almost before the use of reason, we always suppose an external universe, which depends not on our perception, but would exist, though we and every sensible creature were absent or annihilated. Even the animal creation are governed by a like opinion, and preserve this belief of external objects, in all their thoughts, designs, and actions.

It seems also evident that, when men follow this blind and powerful instinct of nature, they always suppose the very images presented by the senses to be the external objects, and never entertain any suspicion that the one are nothing but representations of the other. This very table, which we see white, and which we feel hard, is believed to exist, independent of our perception, and to be something external to our mind which perceives it. Our presence bestows not being on it: Our absence does not annihilate it. It preserves its existence uniform and entire, independent of the situation of intelligent beings who perceive or contemplate it.

But this universal and primary opinion of all men is soon destroyed by the slightest philosophy, which teaches us that nothing can ever be present to the mind but an image or perception, and that the senses are only the inlets through which these images are conveyed, without being able to produce any immediate intercourse between the mind and the object. The table, which we see, seems to diminish as we remove farther from it: But the real table, which exists independent of us, suffers no alteration: It was, therefore, nothing but its image, which was present to the mind. These are the obvious dictates of reason; and no man who reflects ever doubted that the existences which we consider when we say *this house* and *that tree* are nothing but perceptions in the mind, and fleeting copies or representations of other existences which remain uniform and independent.

So far, then, are we necessitated by reasoning to contradict or depart from the primary instincts of nature, and to embrace a new system with regard to the evidence of our senses. But here philosophy finds herself extremely embarrassed, when she would justify this new system, and obviate the cavils and objections of the sceptics. She can no longer plead the infallible and irresistible instinct of nature: For that led us to a quite different system, which is acknowledged fallible and even erroneous. And to justify this pretended philosophical system by a chain of clear and convincing argument, or even any appearance of argument, exceeds the power of all human capacity.

By what argument can it be proved that the perceptions of the mind must be caused by external objects, entirely different from them, though resembling them (if that be possible), and could not arise either from the energy of the mind itself, or from the suggestion of some invisible and unknown spirit, or from some other cause still more unknown to us? It is acknowledged that, in fact, many of these perceptions arise not from anything external, as in dreams, madness, and other diseases. And nothing can be more inexplicable than the manner in which body should so operate upon mind as ever to convey an image of itself to a substance, supposed of so different, and even contrary, a nature.

It is a question of fact whether the perceptions of the senses be produced by external objects resembling them: How shall this question be determined? By experience surely; as all other questions of a like nature. But here experience is, and must be, entirely silent. The mind has never anything present to it but the perceptions, and cannot possibly reach any experience of their connexion with objects. The supposition of such a connexion is, therefore, without any foundation in reasoning.

To have recourse to the veracity of the supreme Being, in order to prove the veracity of our senses, is surely making a very unexpected circuit. If his veracity were at all concerned in this matter, our senses would be entirely infallible, because it is not possible that he can ever deceive. Not to mention that, if the external world be once called in question,

we shall be at a loss to find arguments by which we may prove the existence of that Being or any of his attributes.

This is a topic, therefore, in which the profounder and more philosophical sceptics will always triumph, when they endeavour to introduce a universal doubt into all subjects of human knowledge and enquiry. Do you follow the instincts and propensities of nature, may they say, in assenting to the veracity of sense? But these lead you to believe that the very perception or sensible image is the external object. Do you disclaim this principle, in order to embrace a more rational opinion, that the perceptions are only representations of something external? You here depart from your natural propensities and more obvious sentiments; and yet are not able to satisfy your reason, which can never find any convincing argument from experience to prove that the perceptions are connected with any external objects.

There is another sceptical topic of a like nature, derived from the most profound philosophy, which might merit our attention, were it requisite to dive so deep, in order to discover arguments and reasonings which can so little serve to any serious purpose. It is universally allowed by modern enquirers that all the sensible qualities of objects, such as hard, soft, hot, cold, white, black, &c. are merely secondary, and exist not in the objects themselves, but are perceptions of the mind, without any external archetype or model, which they represent. If this be allowed, with regard to secondary qualities, it must also follow, with regard to the supposed primary qualities of extension and solidity; nor can the latter be any more entitled to that denomination than the former. The idea of extension is entirely acquired from the senses of sight and feeling; and if all the qualities perceived by the senses be in the mind, not in the object, the same conclusion must reach the idea of extension, which is wholly dependent on the sensible ideas or the ideas of secondary qualities. Nothing can save us from this conclusion but the asserting that the ideas of those primary qualities are attained by Abstraction, an opinion which, if we examine it accurately, we shall find to be unintelligible, and even absurd. An extension that is neither tangible nor visible cannot possibly be conceived: And a tangible or visible extension which is neither hard nor soft, black nor white, is equally beyond the reach of human conception. Let any man try to conceive a triangle in general, which is neither Isosceles nor Scalenum, nor has any particular length or proportion of sides; and he will soon perceive the absurdity of all the scholastic notions with regard to abstraction and general ideas. [This argument is drawn from Dr. Berkeley; and indeed most of the writings of that very ingenious author form the best lessons of scepticism, which are to be found either among the ancient or modern philosophers, Bayle not excepted. He professes, however, in his title-page (and undoubtedly with great truth) to have composed his book against the sceptics as well as against the atheists and free-thinkers. But that all his arguments, though otherwise intended, are, in reality, merely sceptical appears from this, that they admit of no answer and produce no conviction. Their only effect is to cause that momentary amazement and irresolution and confusion which is the result of scepticism.]

Thus the first philosophical objection to the evidence of sense or to the opinion of external existence consists in this, that such an opinion, if rested on natural instinct, is contrary to reason, and if referred to reason, is contrary to natural instinct, and at the same time carries no rational evidence with it to convince an impartial enquirer. The second objection goes farther, and represents this opinion as contrary to reason: at least, if it be a principle of reason, that all sensible qualities are in the mind, not in the object. Bereave matter of all its intelligible qualities, both primary and secondary, you in a manner annihilate it, and leave only a certain unknown, inexplicable something, as the cause of our perceptions; a notion so imperfect that no sceptic will think it worth while to contend against it.

Part II

It may seem a very extravagant attempt of the sceptics to destroy reason by argument and ratiocination; yet is this the grand scope of all their enquiries and disputes. They endeavour to find objections, both to our abstract reasonings and to those which regard matter of fact and existence.

The chief objection against all abstract reasonings is derived from the ideas of space and time; ideas which, in common life and to a careless view, are very clear and intelligible, but when they pass through the scrutiny of the profound sciences (and they are the chief object of these sciences) afford principles which seem full of absurdity and contradiction. No priestly dogmas, invented on purpose to tame and subdue the rebellious reason of mankind, ever shocked common sense more than the doctrine of the infinite divisibility of extension, with its consequences, as they are pompously displayed by all geometricians and metaphysicians, with a kind of triumph and exultation. A real quantity, infinitely less than any finite quantity, containing quantities infinitely less than itself, and so on *in infinitum;* this is an edifice so bold and prodigious that it is too weighty for any pretended demonstration to support, because it shocks the clearest and most natural principles of human reason. [Whatever disputes there may be about mathematical points, we must allow that there are physical points; that is, parts of extension, which cannot be divided or lessened, either by the eye or imagination. These images, then, which are present to the fancy or senses, are absolutely indivisible, and consequently must be allowed by mathematicians to be infinitely less than any real part of extension; and yet nothing appears more certain to reason than that an infinite number of them composes an infinite extension. How much more an infinite number of those infinitely small parts of extension, which are still supposed infinitely divisible?] But what renders the matter more extraordinary is that these seemingly absurd opinions are supported by a chain of reasoning, the clearest and most natural; nor is it possible for us to allow the premises without admitting the consequences. Nothing can be more convincing and satisfactory than all the conclusions concerning the properties of circles and triangles; and yet, when these are once received, how can we deny that the angle of contact between a circle and its tangent is infinitely less than any rectilineal angle, that as you may increase the diameter of the circle *in infinitum,* this angle of contact becomes still less, even *in infinitum,* and that the angle of contact between other curves and their tangents may be infinitely less than those between any circle and its tangent, and so on, *in infinitum?* The demonstration of these principles seems as unexceptionable as that which proves the three angles of a triangle to be equal to two right ones, though the latter opinion be natural and easy, and the former big with contradiction and absurdity. Reason here seems to be thrown into a kind of amazement and suspence, which, without the suggestions of any sceptic, gives her a diffidence of herself, and of the ground on which she treads. She sees a full light, which illuminates certain places; but that light borders upon the most profound darkness. And between these she is so dazzled and confounded that she scarcely can pronounce with certainty and assurance concerning any one object.

The absurdity of these bold determinations of the abstract sciences seems to become, if possible, still more palpable with regard to time than extension. An infinite number of real parts of time, passing in succession, and exhausted one after another, appears so evident a contradiction that no man, one should think, whose judgment is not corrupted, instead of being improved, by the sciences would ever be able to admit of it.

Yet still reason must remain restless, and unquiet, even with regard to that scepticism to which she is driven by these seeming absurdities and contradictions. How any clear, distinct idea can contain circumstances contradictory to itself, or to any other clear, distinct idea, is absolutely incomprehensible; and is, perhaps, as absurd as any proposition which can be formed. So that nothing can be more sceptical, or more full of doubt and hesitation, than this scepticism itself, which arises from some of the paradoxical conclusions of geometry or the science of quantity.

[It seems to me not impossible to avoid these absurdities and contradictions, if it be admitted that there is no such thing as abstract or general ideas, properly speaking; but that all general ideas are, in reality, particular ones attached to a general term, which recalls, upon occasion, other particular ones that resemble, in certain circumstances, the idea, present to the mind. Thus when the term *Horse* is pronounced, we immediately figure to ourselves the idea of a black or a white animal, of a particular size or figure: But as that term is also usually applied to animals of other colours, figures, and sizes, these ideas, though not actually present to the imagination, are easily recalled; and our reasoning and conclusion proceed in the same way as if they were actually present. If this be admitted (as seems reasonable) it follows that all the ideas of quantity, upon which mathematicians reason, are nothing but particular, and such as are suggested by the senses and imagination, and consequently, cannot be infinitely divisible. It is sufficient to have dropped this hint at present, without prosecuting it any farther. It certainly concerns all lovers of science not to expose themselves to the ridicule and contempt of the ignorant by their conclusions; and this seems the readiest solution of these difficulties.]

The sceptical objections to moral evidence, or to the reasonings concerning matter of fact, are either popular or philosophical. The popular objections are derived from the natural weakness of human understanding; the contradictory opinions which have been entertained in different ages and nations; the variations of our judgment in sickness and health, youth and old age, prosperity and adversity; the perpetual contradiction of each particular man's opinions and sentiments; with many other topics of that kind. It is needless to insist farther on this head. These objections are but weak. For as, in common life, we reason every moment concerning fact and existence, and cannot possibly subsist without continually employing this species of argument, any popular objections, derived from thence, must be insufficient to destroy that evidence. The great subverter of Pyrrhonism or the excessive principles of scepticism is action, and employment, and the occupations of common life. These principles may flourish and triumph in the schools; where it is, indeed, difficult, if not impossible, to refute them. But as soon as they leave the shade, and by the presence of the real objects which actuate our passions and sentiments are put in opposition to the more powerful principles of our nature, they vanish like smoke, and leave the most determined sceptic in the same condition as other mortals.

The sceptic, therefore, had better keep within his proper sphere, and display those philosophical objections which arise from more profound researches. Here he seems to have ample matter of triumph; while he justly insists that all our evidence for any matter of fact, which lies beyond the testimony of sense or memory, is derived entirely from the relation of cause and effect; that we have no other idea of this relation than that of two objects which have been frequently conjoined together; that we have no argument to convince us that objects which have, in our experience, been frequently conjoined will likewise, in other instances, be conjoined in the same manner; and that nothing leads us to this inference but custom or a certain instinct of our nature; which it is indeed difficult to resist, but which, like other instincts, may be fallacious and deceitful. While the sceptic insists upon these topics, he shows his force, or rather, indeed, his own and our weakness; and seems, for the time at least, to destroy all assurance and conviction. These arguments might be displayed at greater length, if any durable good or benefit to society could ever be expected to result from them.

For here is the chief and most confounding objection to excessive scepticism, that no durable good can ever result from it, while it remains in its full force and vigour. We need only ask such a sceptic, What his meaning is? And what he proposes by all these curious researches? He is immediately at a loss, and knows not what to answer. A Copernican or Ptolemaic, who supports each his different system of astronomy, may hope to produce a conviction which will remain constant and durable with his audience. A Stoic or Epicurean displays principles which may not only be durable, but which have an effect on conduct and behaviour. But a Pyrrhonian cannot expect that his philosophy will have any constant influence on the mind: or if it had, that its influence would be beneficial to society. On the contrary, he must acknowledge, if he will acknowledge anything, that all human life must perish, were his principles universally and steadily to prevail. All discourse, all action would immediately cease; and men remain in a total lethargy, till the necessities of nature, unsatisfied, put an end to their miserable existence. It is true; so fatal an event is very little to be dreaded. Nature is always too strong for principle. And though a Pyrrhonian may throw himself or others into a momentary amazement and confusion by his profound reasonings, the first and most trivial event in life will put to flight all his doubts and scruples, and leave him the same, in every point of action and speculation, with the philosophers of every other sect, or with those who never concerned themselves in any philosophical researches. When he awakes from his dream, he will be the first to join in the laugh against himself, and to confess that all his objections are mere amusement, and can have no other tendency than to show the whimsical condition of mankind, who must act and reason and believe; though they are not able, by their most diligent enquiry, to satisfy themselves concerning the foundation of these operations, or to remove the objections which may be raised against them.

Part III

There is, indeed, a more mitigated scepticism or academical philosophy, which may be both durable and useful, and which may, in part, be the result of this Pyrrhonism, or excessive scepticism, when its undistinguished doubts are, in some measure, corrected by common sense and reflection. The greater part of mankind are naturally apt to be affirmative and dogmatical in their opinions; and while they see objects only on one side, and have no idea of any counterpoising argument, they throw themselves precipitately into the principles to which they are inclined; nor have they any indulgence for those who entertain opposite sentiments. To hesitate or balance perplexes their understanding, checks their passion, and suspends their action. They are, therefore, impatient till they escape from a state which to them is so uneasy; and they think that they can never remove themselves far enough from it, by the violence of their affirmations and obstinacy of their belief. But could such dogmatical reasoners become sensible of the strange infirmities of human understanding, even in its most perfect state, and when most accurate and cautious in its determinations, such a reflection would naturally inspire them with more modesty and reserve, and diminish their fond opinion of themselves, and their prejudice against antagonists. The illiterate may reflect on the disposition of the learned, who, amidst all the advantages of study and reflection, are commonly still diffident in their determinations: And if any of the learned be inclined, from their natural temper, to haughtiness and obstinacy, a small tincture of Pyrrhonism might abate their pride, by showing them that the few advantages which they may have attained over their fellows are but inconsiderable if compared with the universal perplexity and confusion which is inherent in human nature. In general, there is a degree of doubt, and caution, and modesty, which, in all kinds of scrutiny and decision, ought forever to accompany a just reasoner.

Another species of mitigated scepticism, which may be of advantage to mankind, and which may be the natural result of the Pyrrhonian doubts and scruples, is the limitation of our enquiries to such subjects as are best adapted to the narrow capacity of human understanding. The imagination of man is naturally sublime, delighted with whatever is remote and extraordinary, and running, without control, into the most distant parts of space and time in order to avoid the objects which custom has rendered too familiar to it. A correct Judgment observes a contrary method, and avoiding all distant and high enquiries, confines itself to common life, and to such subjects as fall under daily practice and experience, leaving the more sublime topics to the embellishment of poets and orators, or to the arts of priests and politicians. To bring us to so salutary a determination, nothing can be more serviceable than to be once thoroughly convinced of the force of the Pyrrhonian doubt, and of the impossibility that anything but the strong power of natural instinct could free us from it. Those who have a propensity to philosophy will still continue their researches, because they reflect that, besides the immediate pleasure attending such an occupation, philosophical decisions are nothing but the reflections of common life, methodized and corrected. But they will never be tempted to go beyond common life, so long as they consider the imperfection of those faculties which they employ, their narrow reach, and their inaccurate operations. While we cannot give a satisfactory reason why we believe, after a thousand experiments, that a stone will fall, or fire burn; can we ever satisfy ourselves concerning any determination which we may form with regard to the origin of worlds, and the situation of nature, from, and to, eternity?

This narrow limitation, indeed, of our enquiries is, in every respect, so reasonable that it suffices to make the slightest examination into the natural powers of the human mind and to compare them with their objects, in order to recommend it to us. We shall then find what are the proper subjects of science and enquiry.

It seems to me that the only objects of the abstract science or of demonstration are quantity and number, and that all attempts to extend this more perfect species of knowledge beyond these bounds are mere sophistry and illusion. As the component parts of quantity and number are entirely similar, their relations become intricate and involved; and nothing can be more curious, as well

as useful, than to trace, by a variety of mediums, their equality or inequality, through their different appearances. But as all other ideas are clearly distinct and different from each other, we can never advance farther, by our utmost scrutiny, than to observe this diversity, and, by an obvious reflection, pronounce one thing not to be another. Or if there be any difficulty in these decisions, it proceeds entirely from the undeterminate meaning of words, which is corrected by juster definitions. That the square of the hypothenuse is equal to the square of the other two sides cannot be known, let the terms be ever so exactly defined, without a train of reasoning and enquiry. But to convince us of this proposition, that where there is no property, there can be no injustice, it is only necessary to define the terms, and explain injustice to be a violation of property. This proposition is, indeed, nothing but a more imperfect definition. It is the same case with all those pretended syllogistical reasonings, which may be found in every other branch of learning, except the sciences of quantity and number; and these may safely, I think, be pronounced the only proper objects of knowledge and demonstration.

All other enquiries of men regard only matter of fact and existence; and these are evidently incapable of demonstration. Whatever is may not be. No negation of a fact can involve a contradiction. The nonexistence of any being, without exception, is as clear and distinct an idea as its existence. The proposition which affirms it not to be, however false, is no less conceivable and intelligible than that which affirms it to be. The case is different with the sciences, properly so called. Every proposition which is not true is there confused and unintelligible. That the cube root of 64 is equal to the half of 10 is a false proposition, and can never be distinctly conceived. But that Caesar, or the angel Gabriel, or any being never existed may be a false proposition, but still is perfectly conceivable, and implies no contradiction.

The existence, therefore, of any being can only be proved by arguments from its cause or its effect; and these arguments are founded entirely on experience. If we reason *a priori*, anything may appear able to produce anything. The falling of a pebble may, for aught we know, extinguish the sun; or the wish of a man control the planets in their orbits. It is only experience which teaches us the nature and bounds of cause and effect, and enables us to infer the existence of one object from that of another. [That impious maxim of the ancient philosophy, *Ex nihilo, nihil fit,* by which the creation of matter was excluded, ceases to be a maxim, according to this philosophy. Not only the will of the supreme Being may create matter; but, for aught we know *a priori,* the will of any other being might create it, or any other cause, that the most whimsical imagination can assign.] Such is the foundation of moral reasoning, which forms the greater part of human knowledge, and is the source of all human action and behaviour.

Moral reasonings are either concerning particular or general facts. All deliberations in life regard the former; as also all disquisitions in history, chronology, geography, and astronomy.

The sciences which treat of general facts are politics, natural philosophy, physic, chemistry, &c. where the qualities, causes, and effects of a whole species of objects are enquired into.

Divinity or Theology, as it proves the existence of a Deity, and the immortality of souls, is composed partly of reasonings concerning particular, partly concerning general, facts. It has a foundation in reason, so far as it is supported by experience. But its best and most solid foundation is faith and divine revelation.

Morals and criticism are not so properly objects of the understanding as of taste and sentiment. Beauty, whether moral or natural, is felt more properly than perceived. Or if we reason concerning it, and endeavour to fix its standard, we regard a new fact, to wit, the general tastes of mankind, or some such fact, which may be the object of reasoning and enquiry.

When we run over libraries, persuaded of these principles, what havoc must we make? If we take in our hand any volume; of divinity or school metaphysics, for instance; let us ask, Does it contain any abstract reasoning concerning quantity or number? No. Does it contain any experimental reasoning concerning matter of fact and existence? No. Commit it then to the flames: For it can contain nothing but sophistry and illusion.

Immanuel Kant
(1724–1804)

Kant led what can only be described as a boring life as compared to the other authors represented in this volume. Born in Königsberg in East Prussia, son of a saddler and grandson of a Scottish emigrant, he was educated at the local high school and university. After leaving the university in 1746, he was employed for a few years as a private tutor. Continuing his studies, he was able to take his master's degree in 1755 and began teaching at the university as a *privatdozent,* teaching mathematics, physics, geography, and philosophy. He re-

mained quite poor until appointed in 1770 to the chair of logic and metaphysics.

Kant published his first book, *Thoughts on the True Estimation of Living Forces,* in 1747, and produced a steady stream of articles, mainly on natural science, between 1754 and his appointment to the chair. He thus had a substantial reputation when he assumed his professorship, but his public had to wait ten years for his next work, *Critique of Pure Reason,* the first and most famous of a three-part project which included the *Critique of Practical*

Reason and the *Critique of Judgment,* both in print by 1790.

The *Critique* was eagerly anticipated by Kant's colleagues, but when it at last appeared in 1781, the general reaction to this difficult work was bewilderment, prompting a second revised edition in 1787. This second edition, generally called the B edition, is the one reprinted here. Nevertheless, by the 1790s Kant enjoyed a tremendous reputation in Germany, and was beginning to be read abroad. In his final years, however, he was horrified to find young German philosophers such as Fichte and Schelling revamping his system on the grounds that Kant had not properly understood his own philosophical insights.

Kant's only brush with "the real world" came in 1794 when, in response to *Religion within the Bounds of Mere Reason,* the Prussian king asked him to desist writing on a topic on which his theories were causing alarm to the orthodox. But Kant obeyed, and that was the end of it. Kant admired Rousseau and the French Revolution from afar, but never traveled himself, though he is said to have conversed eagerly with travelers who came to Königsberg from abroad.

Note on the text. To understand the material reprinted here, it is useful to look at the structure of the *Critique of Pure Reason.*

Besides the introduction, the *Critique* has two parts, the Transcendental Doctrine of the Elements, and the Transcendental Doctrine of Method. The Elements is supposed to be about the elements that enter into reasoning, namely judgments and their elements, concepts. The Method is then supposed to be about reasoning proper, the relation between judgments. The Elements is in turn divided into two parts, the Transcendental Aesthetic and the Transcendental Logic. The first concerns sensory or imagistic representation, the later concerns conceptual representation. The Logic

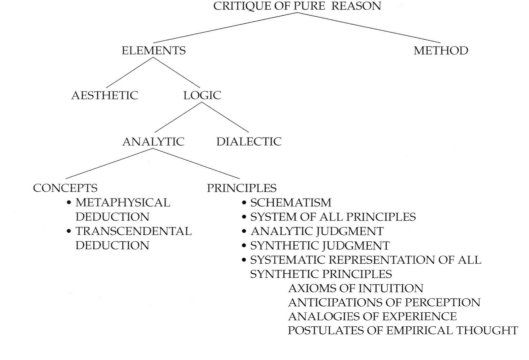

has two divisions, the Transcendental Analytic and the Transcendental Dialectic. The first has to do with the nature of conceptual representation and judgment, while the later contains a discussion of the difficulties that are alleged to arise from an improper application of concepts to things outside experience. The Analytic itself divides into the Analytic of Concepts and the Analytic of Principles. The second concerns various principles that Kant thinks can be known *a priori.* There are three Analogies of Experience. The second analogy contains Kant's famous discussion of the principle of causation, and is the culmination of his response to Hume, who, Kant tells us, first "awakened him from his dogmatic slumbers." The Postulates of Empirical Thought contains the Refutation of Idealism, plainly inserted into the manuscript after it was finished. We have put it before the Second Analogy to preserve a more or less continuous line of argumentation and development aimed at Hume, beginning with the Preface and passing through a refutation of Berkelian Idealism to a discussion of causal judgment.

The central argument. There are many themes in the *Critique.* We have chosen to emphasize one that relates more or less directly to the issue of our knowledge of an objective world that begins in Descartes and moves through Locke, Berkeley and Hume to Kant. Descartes set the problem by arguing that all knowledge is based on subjective knowledge, i.e., on what we know about the contents of our own consciousness. The problem of objective knowledge then became the problem of how knowledge of objective matters of fact could be inferred from the subjective knowledge that is available to us noninferentially. Locke argued that perception could give us knowledge of particular objective matters of fact,

but that we could only have probable opinions about such things as history and the laws of nature that do not fall under the current testimony of the senses. Berkeley argued that the inference from subjective knowledge—our ideas—to claims about things that are supposed to exist independently of the mind is fallacious: how, after all, are we supposed to compare our ideas with something external to the mind to determine if we are making the inference correctly? He concluded that all knowledge is knowledge of ideas. What we call objective knowledge is just knowledge of patterns and regularities in our ideas, as opposed to subjective knowledge which is knowledge of individual ideas. Hume accepted Berkeley's critique of realism, but challenged idealism as well by arguing that inductive inference generally, and causal inference in particular, cannot be rationally justified, the implication for idealism being that even the genuine (as opposed to coincidental) patterns and regularities in our ideas are beyond our knowledge.

Kant saw all of this in terms of the analysis of judgment summarized in the following table.

	SYNTHETIC	ANALYTIC
A PRIORI	MATHEMATICS PURE SCIENCE	TRUTHS OF LOGIC
A POSTERIORI	EMPIRICAL SCIENCE COMMON SENSE PERCEPTION	

The *a priori/a posteriori* distinction concerns how a judgment is known to be true or false: *a priori* judgments are made independently of experience, while *a posteriori* judgments are based on experience. The analytic/synthetic distinction concerns the structure of a judgment: analytic judgments are those whose denials are explicit contradictions, or whose denials can be turned into explicit contradictions by substitutions of definitions for the concepts they define. (Analytic judgments are so called because they emerge from a mere analysis of the concepts involved in the judgment.) Synthetic judgments are those that are not analytic.

Kant thought the tradition, culminating in Hume, had shown that the possibility of objective knowledge had been shown to be impossible on the basis of what is merely analytic (right column) or *a posteriori* (second row). But, he thought, the tradition had ignored synthetic *a priori* judgment (what's left when you cross out the analytic column and the *a posteriori* row). So: the possibility of objective knowledge reduces to the possibility of synthetic *a priori* knowledge. Kant's idea was to begin with objective judgments and subtract what is analytic and *a posteriori*. The "residue" must be a synthetic *a priori* judgment that grounds the objective nature of the judgment as a whole. Here's an example. Hume analyzed causal judgments into four components: x causes y = $_{df}$ (i) x is prior to y, (ii) x and y are spatially contiguous, (iii) events like x are constantly conjoined with events like y, and (iv) x and y are necessarily connected. Hume argued that (i)–(iii) could be known *a posteriori*, but that (iv) could not, nor was it analytic.

Kant agreed, but held that (iv) was synthetic *a priori*.

Kant was convinced that there is such knowledge and that mathematics and pure physics were examples (as he argues in the Introduction). But how is it possible? How can we know something independently of experience that yet goes beyond the mere analysis of our concepts involved in analytic judgment? Answering that question is Kant's concern in the text reprinted here. It is an unabridged version of the second edition of the *Critique of Pure Reason* up through the end of Analytic of Concepts. Here, Kant argued that Descartes and his followers were wrong to suppose that subjective knowledge without objective concepts is possible. Being capable of subjective knowledge presupposes the capacity for objective knowledge. Our text then skips to the Refutation of Idealism, where Kant attempted to show what is wrong with Berkeley's position, and finally to the Second Analogy where the whole doctrine is applied to undo Hume's critique of causal judgment. A long footnote from the Preface restating the argument of the Refutation is printed with the Refutation rather than in its original place in the Preface.

In this, the second edition, we have added a section from the Dialectic, Chapter II, The Antinomy of Pure Reason, of Book II (The Dialectical Inferences of Pure Reason).

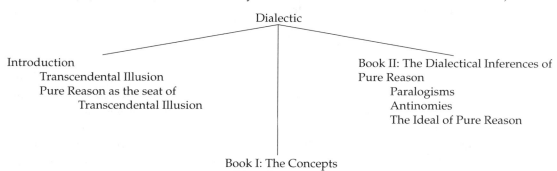

A central theme of the Aesthetic and Analytic is that concepts that are not grounded in intuition (experience) are defective. The Dialectic, recall, is a discussion of the pitfalls of the deployment of concepts in cases in which experience cannot function to keep us honest. Kant called dialectic the logic of illusion, the idea being that intellectual illusions are created when the judgment employs concepts in the absence of any possible experiential correction. These illusions are inevitable, Kant thought, being direct consequences of the structure of reason (the faculty of inferring) itself. Understanding these illusions does not make them go away, anymore than understanding an optical illusion makes it go away. But, in both cases, understanding the source of the illusion protects us from accepting the illusions at face value. Failure to identify the illusions of reason is, Kant thought, the origin of bad metaphysics: dogmas about such issues as whether the universe has a beginning in time (first antinomy) or whether there is a necessary being (fourth antinomy). We include this material not only because of the intrinsic interest of the topics discussed, but because it helps to bring home the signficance of Kant's theory about the relation of concepts to experience.

The illusions of reason that are Kant's target in the Dialectic are of three sorts: Paralogism, Antinomy and the Ideal of pure reason. These are supposed to correspond to the three types of syllogism: categorical, hypothetical and disjunctive. The logic is outdated, but the general idea is that by looking at the forms that valid inference can take, we can get some clue as to the presuppositions, if any, about the nature of reality that are involved in reasoning. When reason reflects on itself in this way, Kant thought, illusions inevitably arise, for it seems to us as if we can discover metaphysical truths that are the presuppositions of the very use of

reason. Here, Kant followed the same pattern he followed in the Analytic, where the central idea is that, by looking at the forms judgment can take, we can discover concepts that are the presupposition of having any experience whatever. That move, of course, Kant endorsed, because the resulting concepts, while *a priori*, nevertheless applied to experience. The *a priori* presuppositions of judgment are valid, but the analogous *a priori* presuppositions of reason are not.

The Paralogisms are arguments designed to establish "Rational Psychology," by which Kant means purely *a priori* presuppositions about the self or soul to the effect that it is a simple, immaterial and indestructible substance. Kant tried to show, in the Paralogisms chapter, that arguments for these propositions, put forward by Descartes and his rationalist followers, are intellectual illusions, mistakes to which Reason is inevitably subject. The proper conclusion, Kant emphasizes, is not the conclusions of Rational Psychology are false, but that they are unknowable.

"The Antimony of Pure Reason" is a long chapter, running just over 100 pages in the Kemp Smith translation of the *Critique*. We have included only the Thesis–Antithesis presentation, together with two other brief passages: (i) the first three paragraphs of the immediately following section ("The Interest of Reason in these Conflicts") and (ii) the "Concluding Note" at the end of the Antonomies chapter. This text is relatively self-contained and admirably illustrates the sort of problem the Dialectic is supposed to address. Still, a little stage setting will be helpful.

Kant's target in the Antinomy chapter is "Rational Cosmology," by which Kant means the attempt to answer *a priori* various questions about the nature of the universe: Does it have a beginning in time? Is it spatially limited? Is everything made up of simple parts? Do the laws of nature preclude freedom? When it comes to questions like these, Kant thought, reason can construct equally compelling arguments on both sides, and so is subject "to the temptation either of abandoning itself to a skeptical despair, or of assuming an obstinate attitude, dogmatically committing itself to certain assertions and refusing to grant a fair hearing to the arguments of the counterposition. Either attitude is the death of sound philosophy, although the former might perhaps be entitled the *euthanasia* of pure reason." (B434) The questions at issue in the Antimony chapter, Kant wrote, are ones that reason must inevitably confront, and just as inevitably result in paradox.". . . both it and its opposite must involve no mere artificial illusion such as at once vanishes upon detection, but a natural and unavoidable illusion, which even after it has ceased to beguile still continues to delude though not to deceive us, and which though thus capable of being rendered harmless can never be eradicated." (B450)

Kant thought these questions must inevitably arise when, as we must, we come to reflect on the *series of conditions* implicit in certain fundamental concepts. Each moment in time depends on the previous moment, and that again on the previous moment, and so on. Each region of space is limited by some neighboring region, and so on. Each event is dependent on some previous event as its cause, and that cause is itself an effect of some previous cause, and so on. Each substance is dependent on its parts, and those on their parts, and so on. The thought is, that in each of these cases, we cannot think of anything actually existing unless everything on which it depends exists also. But does this require that time or the series of causes have a beginning? Does it require that space have an end? Does it require that there be ultimately simple consitutents of things? In the reading presented here, Kant presents both sides of the arguments, and attempts to uncover the error in each in such a way that, while still deluded, we are no longer deceived.

The Antonomies chapter is followed by a chapter called "The Ideal of Pure Reason." Here, Kant discusses proofs for the existence of God, concluding, once again, that they rest on a misuse of reason. Readers interested in the Philosophy of Religion are encouraged to pursue this chapter after having studied the material reprinted here, which introduces the necessary background.

The page headers follow the universal practice (initiated by Kant) of identifying Chapter 1 of the Analytic of Concepts as the "Metaphysical Deduction." The numbers in the margin of the text, e.g., "B 25" refer to the original pagination of the B (i.e., second) edition of the *Critique*. They provide the standard way to refer to passages in Kant's text.

Critique of Pure Reason

B vii Preface to Second Edition

Whether the treatment of such knowledge as lies within the province of reason does or does not follow the secure path of a science, is easily to be determined from the outcome. For if after elaborate preparations, frequently renewed, it is brought to a stop immediately it nears its goal; if often it is compelled to retrace its steps and strike into some new line of approach; or again, if the various participants are unable to agree in any common plan of procedure, then we may rest assured that it is very far from having entered upon the secure path of a science, and is indeed a merely random groping. In these circumstances, we shall be rendering a service to reason should we succeed in discovering the path upon which it can securely travel, even if, as a result of so doing, much that is comprised in our original aims, adopted without reflection, may have to be abandoned as fruitless.

B viii   That logic has already, from the earliest times, proceeded upon this sure path is evidenced by the fact that since Aristotle it has not required to retrace a single step, unless, indeed, we care to count as improvements the removal of certain needless subtleties or the clearer exposition of its recognized teaching, features which concern the elegance rather than the certainty of the science. It is remarkable also that to the present day this logic has not been able to advance a single step, and is thus to all appearance a closed and completed body of doctrine. If some of the moderns have thought to enlarge it by introducing *psychological* chapters on the different faculties of knowledge (imagination, wit, etc.), *metaphysical* chapters on the origin of knowledge or on the different kinds of certainty according to differ-

Excerpted from *Critique of Pure Reason*, Norman Kemp Smith, trans. (New York: St. Martin's Press, 1965), pp. 17–247, 396–423, 483–84.

ence in the objects (idealism, scepticism, etc.), or *anthropological* chapters on prejudices, their causes and remedies, this could only arise from their ignorance of the peculiar nature of logical science. We do not enlarge but disfigure sciences, if we allow them to trespass upon one another's territory. The sphere of B ix logic is quite precisely delimited; its sole concern is to give an exhaustive exposition and a strict proof of the formal rules of all thought, whether it be *a priori* or empirical, whatever be its origin or its object, and whatever hindrances, accidental or natural, it may encounter in our minds.

That logic should have been thus successful is an advantage which it owes entirely to its limitations, whereby it is justified in abstracting—indeed, it is under obligation to do so—from all objects of knowledge and their differences, leaving the understanding nothing to deal with save itself and its form. But for reason to enter on the sure path of science is, of course, much more difficult, since it has to deal not with itself alone but also with objects. Logic, therefore, as a propaedeutic, forms, as it were, only the vestibule of the sciences; and when we are concerned with specific modes of knowledge, while logic is indeed presupposed in any critical estimate of them, yet for the actual acquiring of them we have to look to the sciences properly and objectively so called.

Now if reason is to be a factor in these sciences, something in them must be known *a priori*, and this knowledge may be related to its object in one or other of two ways, either as merely *determining* it and its concept (which must be supplied from elsewhere) or as also *making it actual*. The for- B x mer is *theoretical*, the latter *practical* knowledge of reason. In both, that part in which reason determines its object completely *a priori*, namely, the *pure* part—however much or little this part may contain—must be first and separately dealt with, in case it be confounded with what comes from other sources. For it is bad management if we blindly pay out what comes in, and are not able, when the income falls into arrears, to distinguish which part of it can justify expenditure, and in which line we must make reductions.

Mathematics and physics, the two sciences in which reason yields theoretical knowledge, have to determine their objects *a priori,* the former doing so quite purely, the latter having to reckon, at least partially, with sources of knowledge other than reason.

In the earliest times to which the history of human reason extends, *mathematics,* among that wonderful people, the Greeks, had already entered upon the sure path of science. But it must not be supposed that it was as easy for mathematics as it was for logic—in which reason has to deal with itself alone—to light upon, or rather to construct for

B xi itself, that royal road. On the contrary, I believe that it long remained, especially among the Egyptians, in the groping stage, and that the transformation must have been due to a *revolution* brought about by the happy thought of a single man, the experiment which he devised marking out the path upon which the science must enter, and by following which, secure progress throughout all time and in endless expansion is infallibly secured. The history of this intellectual revolution—far more important than the discovery of the passage round the celebrated Cape of Good Hope—and of its fortunate author, has not been preserved. But the fact that Diogenes Laertius, in handing down an account of these matters, names the reputed author of even the least important among the geometrical demonstrations, even of those which, for ordinary consciousness, stand in need of no such proof, does at least show that the memory of the revolution, brought about by the first glimpse of this new path, must have seemed to mathematicians of such outstanding importance as to cause it to survive the tide of oblivion. A new light flashed upon the mind of the first man (be he Thales or some other) who demonstrated the properties of the isosceles triangle. The true method, so he found, was not to

B xii inspect what he discerned either in the figure, or in the bare concept of it, and from this, as it were, to read off its properties; but to bring out what was necessarily implied in the concepts that he had himself formed *a priori,* and had put into the figure in the construction by which he presented it to himself. If he is to know anything with *a priori* certainty he must not ascribe to the figure anything save what necessarily follows from what he has himself set into it in accordance with his concept.

Natural science was very much longer in entering upon the highway of science. It is, indeed, only about a century and a half since Bacon, by his ingenious proposals, partly initiated this discovery, partly inspired fresh vigour in those who were already on the way to it. In this case also the discovery can be explained as being the sudden outcome of an intellectual revolution. In my present remarks I am referring to natural science only in so far as it is founded on *empirical* principles.

When Galileo caused balls, the weights of which he had himself previously determined, to roll down an inclined plane; when Torricelli made the air carry a weight which he had calculated beforehand to be equal to that of a definite volume of water; or in more recent times, when Stahl changed metals into oxides, and oxides back into B xiii metal, by withdrawing something and then restoring it, a light broke upon all students of nature. They learned that reason has insight only into that which it produces after a plan of its own, and that it must not allow itself to be kept, as it were, in nature's leading-strings, but must itself show the way with principles of judgment based upon fixed laws, constraining nature to give answer to questions of reason's own determining. Accidental observations, made in obedience to no previously thought-out plan, can never be made to yield a necessary law, which alone reason is concerned to discover. Reason, holding in one hand its principles, according to which alone concordant appearances can be admitted as equivalent to laws, and in the other hand the experiment which it has devised in conformity with these principles, must approach nature in order to be taught by it. It must not, however, do so in the character of a pupil who listens to everything that the teacher chooses to say, but of an appointed judge who compels the witnesses to answer questions which he has himself formulated. Even physics, therefore, owes the beneficent revolution in its point of view entirely to the happy thought, that B xiv while reason must seek in nature, not fictitiously ascribe to it, whatever as not being knowable through reason's own resources has to be learnt, if learnt at all, only from nature, it must adopt as its guide, in so seeking, that which it has itself put into nature. It is thus that the study of nature has entered on the secure path of a science, after having for so many centuries been nothing but a process of merely random groping.

Metaphysics is a completely isolated speculative science of reason, which soars far above the teachings of experience, and in which reason is indeed meant to be its own pupil. Metaphysics rests on concepts alone—not, like mathematics, on their application to intuition. But though it is older than all other sciences, and would survive even if all the rest were swallowed up in the abyss of an all-destroying barbarism, it has not yet had the good fortune to enter upon the secure path of a science. For in it reason is perpetually being brought to a stand, even when the laws into which it is seeking to have, as it professes, an *a priori* insight are those that are confirmed by our most common experiences. Ever and again we have to retrace our steps, as not leading us in the direction in which we desire to go. So far, too, are the students of metaphysics from exhibiting any kind of unanimity in their contentions, that metaphysics has rather to be regarded as a battle-ground quite peculiarly suited for those who desire to exercise themselves in mock combats, and in which no participant has ever yet succeeded in gaining even so much as an inch of territory, not at least in such manner as to secure him in its permanent possession. This shows, beyond all questioning, that the procedure of metaphysics has hitherto been a merely random groping, and, what is worst of all, a groping among mere concepts.

B xv

What, then, is the reason why, in this field, the sure road to science has not hitherto been found? Is it, perhaps, impossible of discovery? Why, in that case, should nature have visited our reason with the restless endeavour whereby it is ever searching for such a path, as if this were one of its most important concerns? Nay, more, how little cause have we to place trust in our reason, if, in one of the most important domains of which we would fain have knowledge, it does not merely fail us, but lures us on by deceitful promises, and in the end betrays us! Or if it be only that we have thus far failed to find the true path, are there any indications to justify the hope that by renewed efforts we may have better fortune than has fallen to our predecessors?

The examples of mathematics and natural science, which by a single and sudden revolution have become what they now are, seem to me sufficiently remarkable to suggest our considering what may have been the essential features in the changed point of view by which they have so

B xvi

greatly benefited. Their success should incline us, at least by way of experiment, to imitate their procedure, so far as the analogy which, as species of rational knowledge, they bear to metaphysics may permit. Hitherto it has been assumed that all our knowledge must conform to objects. But all attempts to extend our knowledge of objects by establishing something in regard to them *a priori*, by means of concepts, have, on this assumption, ended in failure. We must therefore make trial whether we may not have more success in the tasks of metaphysics, if we suppose that objects must conform to our knowledge. This would agree better with what is desired, namely, that it should be possible to have knowledge of objects *a priori*, determining something in regard to them prior to their being given. We should then be proceeding precisely on the lines of Copernicus' primary hypothesis. Failing of satisfactory progress in explaining the movements of the heavenly bodies on the supposition that they all revolved round the spectator, he tried whether he might not have better success if he made the spectator to revolve and the stars to remain at rest. A similar experiment can be tried in metaphysics, as regards the *intuition* of objects. If intuition must conform to the constitution of the objects, I do not see how we could know anything of the latter *a priori*; but if the object (as object of the senses) must conform to the constitution of our faculty of intuition, I have no difficulty in conceiving such a possibility. Since I cannot rest in these intuitions if they are to become known, but must relate them as representations to something as their object, and determine this latter through them, either I must assume that the *concepts*, by means of which I obtain this determination, conform to the object, or else I assume that the objects, or what is the same thing, that the *experience* in which alone, as given objects, they can be known, conform to the concepts. In the former case, I am again in the same perplexity as to how I can know anything *a priori* in regard to the objects. In the latter case the outlook is more hopeful. For experience is itself a species of knowledge which involves understanding; and understanding has rules which I must presuppose as being in me prior to objects being given to me, and therefore as being *a priori*. They find expression in *a priori* concepts to which all objects of experience necessarily conform, and with which they must

B xvii

B xviii

agree. As regards objects which are thought solely through reason, and indeed as necessary, but which can never—at least not in the manner in which reason thinks them—be given in experience, the attempts at thinking them (for they must admit of being thought) will furnish an excellent touchstone of what we are adopting as our new method of thought, namely, that we can know *a priori* of things only what we ourselves put into them.*

This experiment succeeds as well as could be desired, and promises to metaphysics, in its first part—the part that is occupied with those concepts *a priori* to which the corresponding objects, commensurate with them, can be given in experience— B xix the secure path of a science. For the new point of view enables us to explain how there can be knowledge *a priori*; and, in addition, to furnish satisfactory proofs of the laws which form the *a priori* basis of nature, regarded as the sum of the objects of experience—neither achievement being possible on the procedure hitherto followed. But this deduction of our power of knowing *a priori*, in the first part of metaphysics, has a consequence which is startling, and which has the appearance of being highly prejudicial to the whole purpose of metaphysics, as dealt with in the second part. For we are brought to the conclusion that we can never transcend the limits of possible experience, though

that is precisely what this science is concerned, B xx above all else, to achieve. This situation yields, however, just the very experiment by which, indirectly, we are enabled to prove the truth of this first estimate of our *a priori* knowledge of reason, namely, that such knowledge has to do only with appearances, and must leave the thing in itself as indeed real *per se,* but as not known by us. For what necessarily forces us to transcend the limits of experience and of all appearances is the *unconditioned,* which reason, by necessity and by right, demands in things in themselves, as required to complete the series of conditions. If, then, on the supposition that our empirical knowledge conforms to objects as things in themselves, we find that the unconditioned *cannot be thought without contradiction,* and that when, on the other hand, we suppose that our representation of things, as they are given to us, does not conform to these things as they are in themselves, but that these objects, as appearances, conform to our mode of representation, *the contradiction vanishes;* and if, therefore, we thus find that the unconditioned is not to be met with in things, so far as we know them, that is, so far as they are given to us, but only so far as we do not know them, that is, so far as they are things in themselves, we are justified in concluding that what we at first assumed for the purposes of experiment is now definitely confirmed.* But when all progress in the field of the B xxi supersensible has thus been denied to speculative reason, it is still open to us to enquire whether, in the practical knowledge of reason, data may not be found sufficient to determine reason's transcendent concept of the unconditioned, and so to enable us, in accordance with the wish of metaphysics, and by means of knowledge that is possible *a priori,* though only from a practical point of view, to pass

---

*This method, modelled on that of the student of nature, consists in looking for the elements of pure reason in *what admits of confirmation or refutation by experiment.* Now the propositions of pure reason, especially if they venture out beyond all limits of possible experience, cannot be brought to the test through any experiment with their *objects,* as in natural science. In dealing with those *concepts* and *principles* which we adopt *a priori,* all that we can do is to contrive that they be used for viewing objects from two different points of view—on the one hand, in connection with experience, as objects of the senses and of the understanding, and on the other hand, for the isolated reason that strives to transcend all limits of experience, as objects which are thought merely. If, when things are viewed from this twofold standpoint, we find that there is agreement with the principle of pure reason, but that when we regard them only from a single point of view reason is involved in unavoidable self-conflict, the experiment decides in favour of the correctness of this distinction.

---

*This experiment of pure reason bears a great similarity to what in chemistry is sometimes entitled the experiment of *reduction,* or more usually the *synthetic* process. The *analysis of the metaphysician* separates pure *a priori* knowledge into two very heterogeneous elements, namely, the knowledge of things as appearances, and the knowledge of things in themselves; his *dialectic* combines these two again, in *harmony* with the necessary idea of the *unconditioned* demanded by reason, and finds that this harmony can never be obtained except through the above distinction, which must therefore be accepted.

beyond the limits of all possible experience. Speculative reason has thus at least made room for such an extension; and if it must at the same time leave it empty, yet none the less we are at liberty, indeed we are summoned, to take occupation of it, if we can, by practical data of reason.*

B xxii

This attempt to alter the procedure which has hitherto prevailed in metaphysics, by completely revolutionising it in accordance with the example set by the geometers and physicists, forms indeed the main purpose of this critique of pure speculative reason. It is a treatise on the method, not a system of the science itself. But at the same time it marks out the whole plan of the science, both as regards its limits and as regards its entire internal structure. For pure speculative reason has this peculiarity, that it can measure its powers according to the different ways in which it chooses the objects of its thinking, and can also give an exhaustive enumeration of the various ways in which it propounds its problems, and so is able, nay bound, to trace the complete outline of a system of metaphysics. As regards the first point, nothing in *a priori* knowledge can be ascribed to objects save what the thinking subject derives from itself; as regards the second point, pure reason, so far as the principles of its knowledge are concerned, is a quite separate self-subsistent unity, in which, as in an organised body, every member exists for every other, and all for the sake of each, so that no principle can safely be taken

B xxiii

---

*Similarly, the fundamental laws of the motions of the heavenly bodies gave established certainty to what Copernicus had at first assumed only as an hypothesis, and at the same time yielded proof of the invisible force (the Newtonian attraction) which holds the universe together. The latter would have remained for ever undiscovered if Copernicus had not dared, in a manner contradictory of the senses, but yet true, to seek the observed movements, not in the heavenly bodies, but in the spectator. The change in point of view, analogous to this hypothesis, which is expounded in the *Critique*, I put forward in this preface as an hypothesis only, in order to draw attention to the character of these first attempts at such a change, which are always hypothetical. But in the *Critique* itself it will be proved, apodeictically not hypothetically, from the nature of our representations of space and time and from the elementary concepts of the understanding.

in *any one* relation, unless it has been investigated in the *entirety* of its relations to the whole employment of pure reason. Consequently, metaphysics has also this singular advantage, such as falls to the lot of no other science which deals with objects (for *logic* is concerned only with the form of thought in general), that should it, through this critique, be set upon the secure path of a science, it is capable of acquiring exhaustive knowledge of its entire field. Metaphysics has to deal only with principles, and with the limits of their employment as determined by these principles themselves, and it can therefore finish its work and bequeath it to posterity as a capital to which no addition can be made. Since it is a fundamental science, it is under obligation to achieve this completeness. We must be able to say of it: *nil actum reputans, si quid superesset agendum.*

B xxiv

But, it will be asked, what sort of a treasure is this that we propose to bequeath to posterity? What is the value of the metaphysics that is alleged to be thus purified by criticism and established once for all? On a cursory view of the present work it may seem that its results are merely *negative*, warning us that we must never venture with speculative reason beyond the limits of experience. Such is in fact its primary use. But such teaching at once acquires a *positive* value when we recognise that the principles with which speculative reason ventures out beyond its proper limits do not in effect *extend* the employment of reason, but, as we find on closer scrutiny, inevitably *narrow* it. These principles properly belong [not to reason but] to sensibility, and when thus employed they threaten to make the bounds of sensibility coextensive with the real, and so to supplant reason in its pure (practical) employment. So far, therefore, as our Critique limits speculative reason, it is indeed *negative*; but since it thereby removes an obstacle which stands in the way of the employment of practical reason, nay threatens to destroy it, it has in reality a *positive* and very important use. At least this is so, immediately we are convinced that there is an absolutely necessary *practical* employment of pure reason—the *moral*—in which it inevitably goes beyond the limits of sensibility. Though [practical] reason, in thus proceeding, requires no assistance from speculative reason, it must yet be assured against its opposition, that reason may not be brought into conflict with itself. To deny that the

B xxv

service which the Critique renders is *positive* in character, would thus be like saying that the police are of no positive benefit, inasmuch as their main business is merely to prevent the violence of which citizens stand in mutual fear, in order that each may pursue his vocation in peace and security. That space and time are only forms of sensible intuition, and so only conditions of the existence of things as appearances; that, moreover, we have no concepts of understanding, and consequently no elements for the knowledge of things, save in so far as intuition can be given corresponding to these concepts; and that we can therefore have no knowledge of any object as thing in itself, but only in so far as it is an object of sensible intuition, that is, an appearance—all this is proved in the analytical part of the Critique. Thus it does indeed follow that all possible speculative knowledge of reason is limited to mere objects of *experience*. But our further contention must also be duly borne in mind, namely, that though we cannot *know* these objects as things in themselves, we must yet be in position at least to *think* them as things in themselves;* otherwise we should be landed in the absurd conclusion that there can be appearance without anything that appears. Now let us suppose that the distinction, which our Critique has shown to be necessary, between things as objects of experience and those same things as things in themselves, had not been made. In that case all things in general, as far as they are efficient causes, would be determined by the principle of causality, and consequently by the mechanism of nature. I could not, therefore, without palpable contradiction, say of one and the same being, for instance the human soul, that its will is free and yet is subject to natural necessity, that is, is not

B xxvi

B xxvii

---

*To *know* an object I must be able to prove its possibility, either from its actuality as attested by experience, or *a priori* by means of reason. But I can *think* whatever I please, provided only that I do not contradict myself, that is, provided my concept is a possible thought. This suffices for the possibility of the concept, even though I may not be able to answer for there being, in the sum of all possibilities, an object corresponding to it. But something more is required before I can ascribe to such a concept objective validity, that is, real possibility; the former possibility is merely logical. This something more need not, however, be sought in the theoretical sources of knowledge; it may lie in those that are practical.

free. For I have taken the soul in both propositions *in one and the same sense,* namely as a thing in general, that is, as a thing in itself; and save by means of a preceding critique, could not have done otherwise. But if our Critique is not in error in teaching that the object is to be taken *in a twofold sense,* namely as appearance and as thing in itself; if the deduction of the concepts of understanding is valid, and the principle of causality therefore applies only to things taken in the former sense, namely, in so far as they are objects of experience—these same objects, taken in the other sense, not being subject to the principle—then there is no contradiction in supposing that one and the same will is, in the appearance, that is, in its visible acts, necessarily subject to the law of nature, and so far *not free,* while yet, as belonging to a thing in itself, it is not subject to that law, and is therefore *free.* My soul, viewed from the latter standpoint, cannot indeed be known by means of speculative reason (and still less through empirical observation); and freedom as a property of a being to which I attribute effects in the world, is therefore also not knowable in any such fashion. For I should then have to know such a being as determined in its existence, and yet as not determined in time—which is impossible, since I cannot support my concept by any intuition. But though I cannot *know,* I can yet *think* freedom; that is to say, the representation of it is at least not self-contradictory, provided due account be taken of our critical distinction between the two modes of representation, the sensible and the intellectual, and of the resulting limitation of the pure concepts of understanding and of the principles which flow from them.

B xxviii

If we grant that morality necessarily presupposes freedom (in the strictest sense) as a property of our will; if, that is to say, we grant that it yields practical principles—original principles, proper to our reason—as *a priori data* of reason, and that this would be absolutely impossible save on the assumption of freedom; and if at the same time we grant that speculative reason has proved that such freedom does not allow of being thought, then the former supposition—that made on behalf of morality—would have to give way to this other contention, the opposite of which involves a palpable contradiction. For since it is only on the assumption of freedom that the negation of morality contains any contradiction, freedom, and with it morality, would have to yield to the mechanism of nature.

B xxix

Morality does not, indeed, require that freedom should be understood, but only that it should not contradict itself, and so should at least allow of being thought, and that as thus thought it should place no obstacle in the way of a free act (viewed in another relation) likewise conforming to the mechanism of nature. The doctrine of morality and the doctrine of nature may each, therefore, make good its position. This, however, is only possible in so far as criticism has previously established our unavoidable ignorance of things in themselves, and has limited all that we can theoretically *know* to mere appearances.

This discussion as to the positive advantage of critical principles of pure reason can be similarly developed in regard to the concept of *God* and of the *simple nature* of our *soul;* but for the sake of brevity such further discussion may be omitted. [From what has already been said, it is evident that] even the *assumption*—as made on behalf of B xxx the necessary practical employment of my reason—of *God, freedom,* and *immortality* is not permissible unless at the same time speculative reason be deprived of its pretensions to transcendent insight. For in order to arrive at such insight it must make use of principles which, in fact, extend only to objects of possible experience, and which, if also applied to what cannot be an object of experience, always really change this into an appearance, thus rendering all *practical extension* of pure reason impossible. I have therefore found it necessary to deny *knowledge,* in order to make room for *faith.* The dogmatism of metaphysics, that is, the preconception that it is possible to make headway in metaphysics without a previous criticism of pure reason, is the source of all that unbelief, always very dogmatic, which wars against morality.

Though it may not, then, be very difficult to leave to posterity the bequest of a systematic metaphysic, constructed in conformity with a critique of pure reason, yet such a gift is not to be valued lightly. For not only will reason be enabled to follow the secure path of a science, instead of, as B xxxi hitherto, groping at random, without circumspection or self-criticism; our enquiring youth will also be in a position to spend their time more profitably than in the ordinary dogmatism by which they are so early and so greatly encouraged to indulge in easy speculation about things of which they understand nothing, and into which neither they nor any-

one else will ever have any insight—encouraged, indeed, to invent new ideas and opinions, while neglecting the study of the better-established sciences. But, above all, there is the inestimable benefit, that all objections to morality and religion will be for ever silenced, and this in Socratic fashion, namely, by the clearest proof of the ignorance of the objectors. There has always existed in the world, and there will always continue to exist, some kind of metaphysics, and with it the dialectic that is natural to pure reason. It is therefore the first and most important task of philosophy to deprive metaphysics, once and for all, of its injurious influence, by attacking its errors at their very source.

Notwithstanding this important change in the field of the sciences, and the *loss* of its fancied possessions which speculative reason must suffer, B xxxii general human interests remain in the same privileged position as hitherto, and the advantages which the world has hitherto derived from the teachings of pure reason are in no way diminished. The loss affects only the *monopoly of the schools,* in no respect the *interests of humanity.* I appeal to the most rigid dogmatist, whether the proof of the continued existence of our soul after death, derived from the simplicity of substance, or of the freedom of the will as opposed to a universal mechanism, arrived at through the subtle but ineffectual distinctions between subjective and objective practical necessity, or of the existence of God as deduced from the concept of an *ens realissimum* (of the contingency of the changeable and of the necessity of a prime mover), have ever, upon passing out from the schools, succeeded in reaching the public mind or in exercising the slightest influence on its convictions? That has never been found to occur, and in view of the unfitness of the common human understanding for such subtle speculation, ought never to have been expected. Such widely held convictions, so far as they rest on rational grounds, are due to quite other considerations. The hope of a *future life* has its source in that notable characteristic of our nature, never to be capable of being satisfied by what is temporal (as insufficient for the capacities of its whole destination); the consciousness of *freedom* rests exclusively on the clear exhibition of duties, in opposition B xxxiii to all claims of the inclinations; the belief in a wise and great *Author of the world* is generated solely by the glorious order, beauty, and providential care everywhere displayed in nature. When the Schools have been brought to recognise that they can lay no claim to higher and fuller insight in a matter of universal human concern than that which is equally within the reach of the great mass of men (ever to be held by us in the highest esteem), and that, as Schools of philosophy, they should limit themselves to the study of those universally comprehensible, and, for moral purposes, sufficient grounds of proof, then not only do these latter possessions remain undisturbed, but through this very fact they acquire yet greater authority. The change affects only the arrogant pretensions of the Schools, which would fain be counted the sole authors and possessors of such truths (as, indeed, they can justly claim to be in many other branches of knowledge), reserving the key to themselves, and communicating to the public their use only—*quod mecum nescit, solus vult scire videri.* At the same time due regard is paid to the more moderate claims of the speculative B xxxiv philosopher. He still remains the sole authority in regard to a science which benefits the public without their knowing it, namely, the critique of reason. That critique can never become popular, and indeed there is no need that it should. For just as fine-spun arguments in favour of useful truths make no appeal to the general mind, so neither do the subtle objections that can be raised against them. On the other hand, both inevitably present themselves to everyone who rises to the height of speculation; and it is therefore the duty of the Schools, by means of a thorough investigation of the rights of speculative reason, once for all to prevent the scandal which, sooner or later, is sure to break out even among the masses, as the result of the disputes in which metaphysicians (and, as such, finally also the clergy) inevitably become involved to the consequent perversion of their teaching. Criticism alone can sever the root of *materialism, fatalism, atheism, free-thinking, fanaticism,* and *superstition,* which can be injurious universally; as well as of *idealism* and *scepticism,* which are dangerous chiefly to the Schools, and hardly allow of being handed on to B xxxv the public. If governments think proper to interfere with the affairs of the learned, it would be more consistent with a wise regard for science as well as for mankind, to favour the freedom of such criticism, by which alone the labours of reason can be established on a firm basis, than to support the ridiculous despotism of the Schools, which raise a loud cry of public danger over the destruction of cobwebs to which the public has never paid any attention, and the loss of which it can therefore never feel.

This critique is not opposed to the *dogmatic procedure* of reason in its pure knowledge, as science, for that must always be dogmatic, that is, yield strict proof from sure principles *a priori.* It is opposed only to *dogmatism,* that is, to the presumption that it is possible to make progress with pure knowledge, according to principles, from concepts alone (those that are philosophical), as reason has long been in the habit of doing; and that it is possible to do this without having first investigated in what way and by what right reason has come into possession of these concepts. Dogmatism is thus the dogmatic procedure of pure reason, *without previous criticism of its own powers.* In withstanding dogmatism we must not allow ourselves to give free rein to that loquacious shallowness, which assumes for itself the B xxxvi name of popularity, nor yet to scepticism, which makes short work with all metaphysics. On the contrary, such criticism is the necessary preparation for a thoroughly grounded metaphysics, which, as science, must necessarily be developed dogmatically, according to the strictest demands of system, in such manner as to satisfy not the general public but the requirements of the Schools. For that is a demand to which it stands pledged, and which it may not neglect, namely, that it carry out its work entirely *a priori,* to the complete satisfaction of speculative reason. In the execution of the plan prescribed by the critique, that is, in the future system of metaphysics, we have therefore to follow the strict method of the celebrated Wolff, the greatest of all the dogmatic philosophers. He was the first to show by example (and by his example he awakened the spirit of thoroughness which is not extinct in Germany) how the secure progress of a science is to be attained only through orderly establishment of principles, clear determination of concepts, insistence upon strictness of proof, and avoidance of venturesome, non-consecutive steps in our inferences. He was thus peculiarly well fitted to raise metaphysics to the dignity of a science, if only it had occurred to him to prepare the ground beforehand by a critique of the organ, that is, of pure reason itself. The blame for his having failed to do so lies not so much with himself as with the B xxxvii dogmatic way of thinking prevalent in his day, and with which the philosophers of his time, and of all previous times, have no right to reproach one another. Those who reject both the method of Wolff and the procedure of a critique of pure reason can have no other aim than to shake off the fetters of *science* altogether, and thus to change work into play, certainty into opinion, philosophy into philodoxy.

Now, *as regards this second edition,* I have, as is fitting, endeavoured to profit by the opportunity, in order to remove, wherever possible, difficulties and obscurity which, not perhaps without my fault, may have given rise to the many misunderstandings into which even acute thinkers have fallen in passing judgment upon my book. In the propositions themselves and their proofs, and also in the form and completeness of the [architectonic] plan, I have found nothing to alter. This is due partly to the long examination to which I have subjected them, before offering them to the public, partly to the nature of the subject-matter with which we are dealing. For pure speculative reason has a structure wherein everything is an *organ,* the whole being for the sake of every part, and every part for the sake of all the

B xxxviii others, so that even the smallest imperfection, be it a fault (error) or a deficiency, must inevitably betray itself in use. This system will, as I hope, maintain, throughout the future, this unchangeableness. It is not self-conceit which justifies me in this confidence, but the evidence experimentally obtained through the parity of the result, whether we proceed from the smallest elements to the whole of pure reason or reversewise from the whole (for this also is presented to reason through its final end in the sphere of the practical) to each part. Any attempt to change even the smallest part at once gives rise to contradictions, not merely in the system, but in human reason in general. As to the mode of *exposition,* on the other hand, much still remains to be done; and in this edition I have sought to make improvements which should help in removing, first, the misunderstanding in regard to the Aesthetic, especially concerning the concept of time; secondly, the obscurity of the deduction of the concepts of understanding; thirdly, a supposed want of sufficient evidence in the proofs of the principles of pure understanding; and finally, the false interpretation placed upon the paralogisms charged against rational psychology. Beyond this point, that is, beyond

B xxxix the end of the first chapter of the Transcendental
B xl Dialectic, I have made no changes in the mode of

exposition.* Time was too short to allow of further changes; and besides, I have not found among competent and impartial critics any misapprehension in B xli regard to the remaining sections. Though I shall not venture to name these critics with the praise that is their due, the attention which I have paid to their B xlii comments will easily be recognised in the [new] passages [above mentioned]. These improvements involve, however, a small loss, not to be prevented save by making the book too voluminous, namely, that I have had to omit or abridge certain passages, which, though not indeed essential to the completeness of the whole, may yet be missed by many readers as otherwise helpful. Only so could I obtain space for what, as I hope, is now a more intelligible exposition, which, though altering absolutely nothing in the fundamentals of the propositions put forward or even in their proofs, yet here and there departs so far from the previous method of treatment, that mere interpolations could not be made to suffice. This loss, which is small and can be remedied by consulting the first edition, will, I hope, be compensated by the greater clearness of the new text. I have observed, with pleasure and thankfulness, in various published works—alike in critical reviews and in independent treatises—that the spirit of thoroughness is not extinct in Germany, but has only been temporarily overshadowed by the B xliii prevalence of a pretentiously free manner of thinking; and that the thorny paths of the Critique have not discouraged courageous and clear heads from setting themselves to master my book—a work which leads to a methodical, and as such alone enduring, and therefore most necessary, science of pure reason. To these worthy men, who so happily combine thoroughness of insight with a talent for lucid exposition—which I cannot regard myself as possessing—I leave the task of perfecting what, here and there, in its exposition, is still somewhat defective; for in this regard the danger is not that of being refuted, but of not being understood. From now on, though I cannot allow myself to enter into controversy, I shall take careful note of all suggestions, be they from friends or from opponents, for use, in accordance with this propaedeutic, in the further elaboration of the system. In the course of

---

*[Editor's note: The long footnote Kant placed here is reprinted with the Refutation of Idealism.]

these labours I have advanced somewhat far in years (this month I reach my sixty-fourth year), and I must be careful with my time if I am to succeed in my proposed scheme of providing a metaphysic of nature and of morals which will confirm the truth of my Critique in the two fields, of speculative and of practical reason. The clearing up of the ob-

B xliv scurities in the present work—they are hardly to be avoided in a new enterprise—and the defence of it as a whole, I must therefore leave to those worthy men who have made my teaching their own. A philosophical work cannot be armed at all points, like a mathematical treatise, and may therefore be open to objection in this or that respect, while yet the structure of the system, taken in its unity, is not in the least endangered. Few have the versatility of mind to familiarise themselves with a new system; and owing to the general distaste for all innovation, still fewer have the inclination to do so. If we take single passages, torn from their contexts, and compare them with one another, apparent contradictions are not likely to be lacking, especially in a work that is written with any freedom of expression. In the eyes of those who rely on the judgment of others, such contradictions have the effect of placing the work in an unfavourable light; but they are easily resolved by those who have mastered the idea of the whole. If a theory has in itself stability, the stresses and strains which may at first have seemed very threatening to it serve only, in the course of time, to smooth away its inequalities; and if men of impartiality, insight, and true popularity devote themselves to its exposition, it may also, in a short time, secure for itself the necessary elegance of statement.

Königsberg, *April* 1787.

B 1 # Introduction

I. The Distinction between Pure and Empirical Knowledge

There can be no doubt that all our knowledge begins with experience. For how should our faculty of knowledge be awakened into action did not objects affecting our senses partly of themselves produce representations, partly arouse the activity of our understanding to compare these representations, and, by combining or separating them, work up the raw material of the sensible impressions into that knowledge of objects which is entitled experience? In the order of time, therefore, we have no knowledge antecedent to experience, and with experience all our knowledge begins.

But though all our knowledge begins with experience, it does not follow that it all arises out of experience. For it may well be that even our empirical knowledge is made up of what we receive through impressions and of what our own faculty of knowledge (sensible impressions serving merely as the occasion) supplies from itself. If our faculty of knowledge makes any such addi-

B 2 tion, it may be that we are not in a position to distinguish it from the raw material, until with long practice of attention we have become skilled in separating it.

This, then, is a question which at least calls for closer examination, and does not allow of any off-hand answer:—whether there is any knowledge that is thus independent of experience and even of all impressions of the senses. Such knowledge is entitled *a priori*, and distinguished from the *empirical*, which has its sources *a posteriori*, that is, in experience.

The expression "*a priori*" does not, however, indicate with sufficient precision the full meaning of our question. For it has been customary to say, even of much knowledge that is derived from empirical sources, that we have it or are capable of having it *a priori*, meaning thereby that we do not derive it immediately from experience, but from a universal rule—a rule which is itself, however, borrowed by us from experience. Thus we would say of a man who undermined the foundations of his house, that he might have known *a priori* that it would fall, that is, that he need not have waited for the experience of its actual falling. But still he could not know this completely *a priori*. For he had first to learn through experience that bodies are heavy, and therefore fall when their supports are withdrawn.

In what follows, therefore, we shall understand by *a priori* knowledge, not knowledge independent of this or that experience, but knowledge absolutely independent of all experience. Opposed B 3 to it is empirical knowledge, which is knowledge possible only *a posteriori,* that is, through experience. *A priori* modes of knowledge are entitled pure when there is no admixture of anything empirical. Thus, for instance, the proposition "every alteration has its cause," while an *a priori* proposition, is not a pure proposition, because alteration is a concept which can be derived only from experience.

II. We Are in Possession of Certain Modes of A Priori *Knowledge, and Even the Common Understanding Is Never Without Them*

What we here require is a criterion by which to distinguish with certainty between pure and empirical knowledge. Experience teaches us that a thing is so and so, but not that it cannot be otherwise. First, then, if we have a proposition which in being thought is thought as *necessary,* it is an *a priori* judgment; and if, besides, is not derived from any proposition except one which also has the validity of a necessary judgment, it is an absolutely *a priori* judgment. Secondly, experience never confers on its judgments true or strict, but only assumed and comparative *universality,* through induction. We can properly only say, therefore, that, B4 so far as we have hitherto observed, there is no exception to this or that rule. If, then, a judgment is thought with strict universality, that is, in such manner that no exception is allowed as possible, it is not derived from experience, but is valid absolutely *a priori.* Empirical universality is only an arbitrary extension of a validity holding in most cases to one which holds in all, for instance, in the proposition, "all bodies are heavy." When, on the other hand, strict universality is essential to a judgment, this indicates a special source of knowledge, namely, a faculty of *a priori* knowledge. Necessity and strict universality are thus sure criteria of *a priori* knowledge, and are inseparable from one another. But since in the employment of these criteria the contingency of judgments is sometimes more easily shown than their empirical limitation, or, as sometimes also happens, their unlimited universality can be more convincingly proved than their necessity, it is advisable to use the two criteria separately, each by itself being infallible.

Now it is easy to show that there actually are in human knowledge judgments which are necessary and in the strictest sense universal, and which are therefore pure *a priori* judgments. If an example from the sciences be desired, we have only to look to any of the propositions of mathematics; if we seek an example from the understanding in its quite ordinary employment, the proposition, "every al- B5 teration must have a cause," will serve our purpose. In the latter case, indeed, the very concept of a cause so manifestly contains the concept of a necessity of connection with an effect and of the strict universality of the rule, that the concept would be altogether lost if we attempted to derive it, as Hume has done, from a repeated association of that which happens with that which precedes, and from a custom of connecting representations, a custom originating in this repeated association, and constituting therefore a merely subjective necessity. Even without appealing to such examples, it is possible to show that pure *a priori* principles are indispensable for the possibility of experience, and so to prove their existence *a priori.* For whence could experience derive its certainty, if all the rules, according to which it proceeds, were always themselves empirical, and therefore contingent? Such rules could hardly be regarded as first principles. At present, however, we may be content to have established the fact that our faculty of knowledge does have a pure employment, and to have shown what are the criteria of such an employment.

Such *a priori* origin is manifest in certain concepts, no less than in judgments. If we remove from our empirical concept of a body, one by one, every feature in it which is [merely] empirical, the colour, the hardness or softness, the weight, even the impenetrability, there still remains the space which the body (now entirely vanished) occupied, and this cannot be removed. Again, if we remove from our empirical concept of any object, corporeal B6 or incorporeal, all properties which experience has taught us, we yet cannot take away that property through which the object is thought as substance or as inhering in a substance (although this concept of substance is more determinate than that of an object in general). Owing, therefore, to the necessity with which this concept of substance forces itself upon us, we have no option save to admit that it has its seat in our faculty of *a priori* knowledge.

III. *Philosophy Stands in Need of a Science Which Shall Determine the Possibility, the Principles, and the Extent of All* A Priori *Knowledge*

But what is still more extraordinary than all the preceding is this, that certain modes of knowledge leave the field of all possible experiences and have the appearance of extending the scope of our judgments beyond all limits of experience, and this by means of concepts to which no corresponding object can ever be given in experience.

It is precisely by means of the latter modes of knowledge, in a realm beyond the world of the senses, where experience can yield neither guidance nor correction, that our reason carries on those enquiries which owing to their importance we consider to be far more excellent, and in their purpose far more lofty, than all that the understanding can learn in the field of appearances. Indeed we prefer to run every risk of error rather than desist from such urgent enquiries, on the ground of their dubious character, or from disdain and indifference. These unavoidable problems set by pure reason itself are *God, freedom,* and *immortality.* The science which, with all its preparations, is in its final intention directed solely to their solution is metaphysics; and its procedure is at first dogmatic, that is, it confidently sets itself to this task without any previous examination of the capacity or incapacity of reason for so great an undertaking.

Now it does indeed seem natural that, as soon as we have left the ground of experience, we should, through careful enquiries, assure ourselves as to the foundations of any building that we propose to erect, not making use of any knowledge that we possess without first determining whence it has come, and not trusting to principles without knowing their origin. It is natural, that is to say, that the question should first be considered, how the understanding can arrive at all this knowledge *a priori,* and what extent, validity, and worth it may have. Nothing, indeed, could be more natural, if by the term "natural" we signify what fittingly and reasonably ought to happen. But if we mean by "natural" what ordinarily happens, then on the contrary nothing is more natural and more intelligible than the fact that this enquiry has been so long ne-

glected. For one part of this knowledge, the mathematical, has long been of established reliability, and so gives rise to a favourable presumption as regards the other part, which may yet be of quite different nature. Besides, once we are outside the circle of experience, we can be sure of not being *contradicted* by experience. The charm of extending our knowledge is so great that nothing short of encountering a direct contradiction can suffice to arrest us in our course; and this can be avoided, if we are careful in our fabrications—which none the less will still remain fabrications. Mathematics gives us a shining example of how far, independently of experience, we can progress in *a priori* knowledge. It does, indeed, occupy itself with objects and with knowledge solely in so far as they allow of being exhibited in intuition. But this circumstance is easily overlooked, since this intuition can itself be given *a priori,* and is therefore hardly to be distinguished from a bare and pure concept. Misled by such a proof of the power of reason, the demand for the extension of knowledge recognises no limits. The light dove, cleaving the air in her free flight, and feeling its resistance, might imagine that its flight would be still easier in empty space. It was thus that Plato left the world of the senses, as setting too narrow limits to the understanding, and ventured out beyond it on the wings of the ideas, in the empty space of the pure understanding. He did not observe that with all his efforts he made no advance—meeting no resistance that might, as it were, serve as a support upon which he could take a stand, to which he could apply his powers, and so set his understanding in motion. It is, indeed, the common fate of human reason to complete its speculative structures as speedily as may be, and only afterwards to enquire whether the foundations are reliable. All sorts of excuses will then be appealed to, in order to reassure us of their solidity, or rather indeed to enable us to dispense altogether with so late and so dangerous an enquiry. But what keeps us, during the actual building, free from all apprehension and suspicion, and flatters us with a seeming thoroughness, is this other circumstance, namely, that a great, perhaps the greatest, part of the business of our reason consists in analysis of the concepts which we already have of objects. This analysis supplies us with a considerable body of knowledge, which, while nothing but explanation or elucidation of what has already been thought in our concepts, though in a confused manner, is yet prized as being, at least as regards its form, new insight. But so far as the matter or content is concerned, there has been no extension of our previously possessed concepts, but only an analysis of them. Since this procedure yields real knowledge *a priori,* which progresses in an assured and useful fashion, reason is so far misled as surreptitiously to introduce, without itself being aware of so doing, assertions of an entirely different order, in which it attaches to given concepts others completely foreign to them, and moreover attaches them *a priori.* And yet it is not known how reason can be in position to do this. Such a question is never so much as thought of. I shall therefore at once proceed to deal with the difference between these two kinds of knowledge.

B 10

IV. The Distinction between Analytic and Synthetic Judgments

In all judgments in which the relation of a subject to the predicate is thought (I take into consideration affirmative judgments only, the subsequent application to negative judgments being easily made), this relation is possible in two different ways. Either the predicate B belongs to the subject A, as something which is (covertly) contained in this concept A; or B lies outside the concept A, although it does indeed stand in connection with it. In the one case I entitle the judgment analytic, in the other synthetic. Analytic judgments (affirmative) are therefore those in which the connection of the predicate with the subject is thought through identity; those in which this connection is thought without identity should be entitled synthetic. The former, as adding nothing through the predicate to the concept of the subject, but merely breaking it up into those constituent concepts that have all along been thought in it, although confusedly, can also be entitled explicative. The latter, on the other hand, add to the concept of the subject a predicate which has not been in any wise thought in it, and which no analysis could possibly extract from it; and they may therefore be entitled ampliative. If I say, for instance, "All bodies are extended," this is an analytic judgment. For I do not require to go beyond the concept which I connect with "body" in order to find extension as

B 11

bound up with it. To meet with this predicate, I have merely to analyse the concept, that is, to become conscious to myself of the manifold which I always think in that concept. The judgment is therefore analytic. But when I say, "All bodies are heavy," the predicate is something quite different from anything that I think in the mere concept of body in general; and the addition of such a predicate therefore yields a synthetic judgment.

Judgments of experience, as such, are one and all synthetic. For it would be absurd to found an analytic judgment on experience. Since, in framing the judgment, I must not go outside my concept, there is no need to appeal to the testimony of experience in its support. That a body is extended is a proposition that holds *a priori* and is not empirical. For, before appealing to experience, I have already in the concept of body all the conditions required for my judgment. I have only to extract from it, in accordance with the principle of contradiction, the required predicate, and in so doing can at the same time become conscious of the necessity of the judgment—and that is what experience could never have taught me. On the other hand, though I do not include in the concept of a body in general the predicate "weight," none the less this concept indicates an object of experience through one of its parts, and I can add to that part other parts of this same experience, as in this way belonging together with the concept. From the start I can apprehend the concept of body analytically through the characters of extension, impenetrability, figure, etc., all of which are thought in the concept. Now, however, looking back on the experience from which I have derived this concept of body, and finding weight to be invariably connected with the above characters, I attach it as a predicate to the concept; and in doing so I attach it synthetically, and am therefore extending my knowledge. The possibility of the synthesis of the predicate "weight" with the concept of "body" thus rests upon experience. While the one concept is not contained in the other, they yet belong to one another, though only contingently, as parts of a whole, namely, of an experience which is itself a synthetic combination of intuitions.

B 12

But in *a priori* synthetic judgments this help is entirely lacking: I do not here have the advantage of looking around in the field of experience. Upon what, then, am I to rely, when I seek to go beyond

B 13

the concept A, and to know that another concept B is connected with it? Through what is the synthesis made possible? Let us take the proposition, "Everything which happens has its cause." In the concept of "something which happens," I do indeed think an existence which is preceded by a time, etc., and from this concept analytic judgments may be obtained. But the concept of a "cause" lies entirely outside the other concept, and signifies something different from "that which happens," and is not therefore in any way contained in this latter representation. How come I then to predicate of that which happens something quite different, and to apprehend that the concept of cause, though not contained in it, yet belongs, and indeed necessarily belongs, to it? What is here the unknown = X which gives support to the understanding when it believes that it can discover outside the concept A a predicate B foreign to this concept, which it yet at the same time considers to be connected with it? It cannot be experience, because the suggested principle has connected the second representation with the first, not only with greater universality, but also with the character of necessity, and therefore completely *a priori* and on the basis of mere concepts. Upon such synthetic, that is, ampliative principles, all our *a priori* speculative knowledge must ultimately rest; analytic judgments are very important, and indeed necessary, but only for obtaining that clearness in the concepts which is requisite for such a sure and wide synthesis as will lead to a genuinely new addition to all previous knowledge.

B 14

V. In All Theoretical Sciences of Reason Synthetic A Priori Judgments Are Contained as Principles

1. *All mathematical judgments, without exception, are synthetic*. This fact, though incontestably certain and in its consequences very important, has hitherto escaped the notice of those who are engaged in the analysis of human reason, and is, indeed, directly opposed to all their conjectures. For as it was found that all mathematical inferences proceed in accordance with the principle of contradiction (which the nature of all apodeictic certainty requires), it was supposed that the fundamental propositions of the science can themselves be known to be true through that principle. This is an erroneous view.

For though a synthetic proposition can indeed be discerned in accordance with the principle of contradiction, this can only be if another synthetic proposition is presupposed, and if it can then be apprehended as following from this other proposition; it can never be so discerned in and by itself.

First of all, it has to be noted that mathematical propositions, strictly so called, are always judgments *a priori*, not empirical; because they carry with them necessity, which cannot be derived from experience. If this be demurred to, I am willing to limit my statement to *pure* mathematics, the very concept of which implies that it does not contain empirical, but only pure *a priori* knowledge.

B 15

We might, indeed, at first suppose that the proposition 7 + 5 = 12 is a merely analytic proposition, and follows by the principle of contradiction from the concept of a sum of 7 and 5. But if we look more closely we find that the concept of the sum of 7 and 5 contains nothing save the union of the two numbers into one, and in this no thought is being taken as to what that single number may be which combines both. The concept of 12 is by no means already thought in merely thinking this union of 7 and 5; and I may analyse my concept of such a possible sum as long as I please, still I shall never find the 12 in it. We have to go outside these concepts, and call in the aid of the intuition which corresponds to one of them, our five fingers, for instance, or, as Segner does in his *Arithmetic,* five points, adding to the concept of 7, unit by unit, the five given in intuition. For starting with the number 7, and for the concept of 5 calling in the aid of the fingers of my hand as intuition, I now add one by one to the number 7 the units which I previously took together to form the number 5, and with the aid of that figure [the hand] see the number 12 come into being. That 5 should be added to 7, I have indeed already thought in the concept of a sum = 7 + 5, but not that this sum is equivalent to the number 12. Arithmetical propositions are therefore always synthetic. This is still more evident if we take larger numbers. For it is then obvious that, however we might turn and twist our concepts, we could never, by the mere analysis of them, and without the aid of intuition, discover what [the number is that] is the sum.

B 16

Just as little is any fundamental proposition of pure geometry analytic. That the straight line between two points is the shortest, is a synthetic proposition. For my concept of *straight* contains nothing of quantity, but only of quality. The concept of the shortest is wholly an addition, and cannot be derived, through any process of analysis, from the concept of the straight line. Intuition, therefore, must here be called in; only by its aid

B 17 is the synthesis possible. What here causes us commonly to believe that the predicate of such apodeictic judgments is already contained in our concept, and that the judgment is therefore analytic, is merely the ambiguous character of the terms used. We are required to join in thought a certain predicate to a given concept, and this necessity is inherent in the concepts themselves. But the question is not what we *ought* to join in thought to the given concept, but what we *actually* think in it, even if only obscurely; and it is then manifest that, while the predicate is indeed attached necessarily to the concept, it is so in virtue of an intuition which must be added to the concept, not as thought in the concept itself.

Some few fundamental propositions, presupposed by the geometrician, are, indeed, really analytic, and rest on the principle of contradiction. But, as identical propositions, they serve only as links in the chain of method and not as principles; for instance *a = a*; the whole is equal to itself; or *(a + b) > a*, that is, the whole is greater than its part. And even these propositions, though they are valid according to pure concepts, are only admitted in mathematics because they can be exhibited in intuition.

2. *Natural science (physics) contains* a priori *synthetic judgments as principles.* I need cite only two such judgments: that in all changes of the material world the quantity of matter remains unchanged; and that in all communication of motion, action and reaction must always be equal. Both propositions, it is evident, are not only necessary, and therefore in

B 18 their origin *a priori*, but also synthetic. For in the concept of matter I do not think its permanence, but only its presence in the space which it occupies. I go outside and beyond the concept of matter, joining to it *a priori* in thought something which I have not thought *in* it. The proposition is not, therefore, analytic, but synthetic, and yet is thought *a priori*; and so likewise are the other propositions of the pure part of natural science.

3. *Metaphysics*, even if we look upon it as having hitherto failed in all its endeavours, is yet, owing to the nature of human reason, a quite indispensable science, and *ought to contain* a priori *synthetic knowledge.* For its business is not merely to analyse concepts which we make for ourselves *a priori* of things, and thereby to clarify them analytically, but to extend our *a priori* knowledge. And for this purpose we must employ principles which add to the given concept something that was not contained in it, and through *a priori* synthetic judgments venture out so far that experience is quite unable to follow us, as, for instance, in the proposition, that the world must have a first beginning, and such like. Thus metaphysics consists, at least *in intention*, entirely of *a priori* synthetic propositions.

VI. The General Problem of Pure Reason   B 19

Much is already gained if we can bring a number of investigations under the formula of a single problem. For we not only lighten our own task, by defining it accurately, but make it easier for others, who would test our results, to judge whether or not we have succeeded in what we set out to do. Now the proper problem of pure reason is contained in the question: How are *a priori* synthetic judgments possible?

That metaphysics has hitherto remained in so vacillating a state of uncertainty and contradiction, is entirely due to the fact that this problem, and perhaps even the distinction between analytic and synthetic judgments, has never previously been considered. Upon the solution of this problem, or upon a sufficient proof that the possibility which it desires to have explained does in fact not exist at all, depends the success or failure of metaphysics. Among philosophers, David Hume came nearest to envisaging this problem, but still was very far from conceiving it with sufficient definiteness and universality. He occupied himself exclusively with the synthetic proposition regarding the connection of an effect with its cause (*principium causalitatis*), and he believed himself to have shown that such an B 20 *a priori* proposition is entirely impossible. If we accept his conclusions, then all that we call metaphysics is a mere delusion whereby we fancy ourselves to have rational insight into what, in actual fact, is borrowed solely from experience, and under the influence of custom has taken the illusory semblance of necessity. If he had envisaged our problem in all its universality, he would never have been guilty of this statement, so destructive of all pure philosophy. For he would then have recognised that, according to his own argument, pure mathematics, as certainly containing *a priori* synthetic propositions, would also not be possible; and from such an assertion his good sense would have saved him.

In the solution of the above problem, we are at the same time deciding as to the possibility of the employment of pure reason in establishing and developing all those sciences which contain a theoretical *a priori* knowledge of objects, and have therefore to answer the questions:

> *How is pure mathematics possible?*
> *How is pure science of nature possible?*

B 21　Since these sciences actually exist, it is quite proper to ask *how* they are possible; for that they must be possible is proved by the fact that they exist.* But the poor progress which has hitherto been made in metaphysics, and the fact that no system yet propounded can, in view of the essential purpose of metaphysics, be said really to exist, leaves everyone sufficient ground for doubting as to its possibility.

Yet, in a certain sense, this *kind of knowledge* is to be looked upon as a given; that is to say, metaphysics actually exists, if not as a science, yet still as a natural disposition (*metaphysica naturalis*). For human reason, without being moved merely by the idle desire for extent and variety of knowledge, proceeds impetuously, driven on by an inward need, to questions such as cannot be answered by any empirical employment of reason, or by principles thence derived. Thus in all men, as soon as their reason has become ripe for speculation, there has always existed and will always continue to exist some kind of metaphysics. And so we have the question:

---

*Many may still have doubts as regards pure natural science. We have only, however, to consider the various propositions that are to be found at the beginning of (empirical) physics, properly so called, those, for instance, relating to the permanence in the quantity of matter, to inertia, to the equality of action and reaction, etc., in order to be soon convinced that they constitute a *physica pura,* or *rationalis,* which well deserves, as an independent science, to be separately dealt with in its whole extent, be that narrow or wide.

How is metaphysics, as natural disposition, possible?　　　　　　　　　　　　　　　　　B 22

That is, how from the nature of universal human reason do those questions arise which pure reason propounds to itself, and which it is impelled by its own need to answer as best it can?

But since all attempts which have hitherto been made to answer these natural questions—for instance, whether the world has a beginning or is from eternity—have always met with unavoidable contradictions, we cannot rest satisfied with the mere natural disposition to metaphysics, that is, with the pure faculty of reason itself, from which, indeed, some sort of metaphysics (be it what it may) always arises. It must be possible for reason to attain to certainty whether we know or do not know the objects of metaphysics, that is, to come to a decision either in regard to the objects of its enquiries or in regard to the capacity or incapacity of reason to pass any judgment upon them, so that we may either with confidence extend our pure reason or set to it sure and determinate limits. This last question, which arises out of the previous general problem, may, rightly stated, take the form:

How is metaphysics, as science, possible?

Thus the critique of reason, in the end, necessarily leads to scientific knowledge; while its dogmatic employment, on the other hand, lands us in dogmatic assertions to which other assertions,　B 23 equally specious, can always be opposed—that is, in *scepticism.*

This science cannot be of any very formidable prolixity, since it has to deal not with the objects of reason, the variety of which is inexhaustible, but only with itself and the problems which arise entirely from within itself, and which are imposed upon it by its own nature, not by the nature of things which are distinct from it. When once reason has learnt completely to understand its own power in respect of objects which can be presented to it in experience, it should easily be able to determine, with completeness and certainty, the extent and the limits of its attempted employment beyond the bounds of all experience.

We may, then, and indeed we must, regard as abortive all attempts, hitherto made, to establish a metaphysic *dogmatically.* For the analytic part in any such attempted system, namely, the mere analysis of the concepts that inhere in our reason *a priori* is by no means the aim of, but only a preparation for, metaphysics proper, that is, the extension of its *a priori* synthetic knowledge. For such a purpose, the analysis of concepts is useless, since it merely shows what is contained in these concepts, not how we arrive at them *a priori*. A solution of this latter problem is required, that we may be able to determine the valid employment of such concepts in regard to the objects of all knowledge in general. Nor is much self-denial needed to give up these claims, seeing that the undeniable, and in the dogmatic procedure of reason also unavoidable, contradictions of reason within itself have long since undermined the authority of every metaphysical system yet propounded. Greater firmness will be required if we are not to be deterred by inward difficulties and outward opposition from endeavouring, through application of a method entirely different from any hitherto employed, at last to bring to a prosperous and fruitful growth a science indispensable to human reason—a science whose every branch may be cut away but whose root cannot be destroyed.

VII. The Idea and Division of a Special Science, under the Title "Critique of Pure Reason"

In view of all these considerations, we arrive at the idea of a special science which can be entitled the Critique of Pure Reason. For reason is the faculty which supplies the principles of *a priori* knowledge. Pure reason is, therefore, that which contains the principles whereby we know anything absolutely *a priori*. An organon of pure reason would be the sum-total of those principles according to which all modes of pure *a priori* knowledge can be acquired and actually brought into being. The exhaustive application of such an organon would give rise to a system of pure reason. But as this would be asking rather much, and as it is still doubtful whether, and in what cases, any extension of our knowledge be here possible, we can regard a science of the mere examination of pure reason, of its sources and limits, as the *propaedeutic* to the system of pure reason. As such, it should be called a critique, not a doctrine, of pure reason. Its utility, in speculation, ought properly to be only negative, not to extend,

but only to clarify our reason, and keep it free from errors—which is already a very great gain. I entitle *transcendental* all knowledge which is occupied not so much with objects as with the mode of our knowledge of objects in so far as this mode of knowledge is to be possible *a priori*. A system of such concepts might be entitled transcendental philosophy. But that is still, at this stage, too large an undertaking. For since such a science must contain, with completeness, both kinds of *a priori* knowledge, the analytic no less than the synthetic, it is, so far as our present purpose is concerned, much too comprehensive. We have to carry the analysis so far only as is indispensably necessary in order to comprehend, in their whole extent, the principles of *a priori* synthesis, with which alone we are called upon to deal. It is upon this enquiry, which should be entitled not a doctrine, but only a transcendental critique, that we are now engaged. Its purpose is not to extend knowledge, but only to correct it, and to supply a touchstone of the value, or lack of value, of all *a priori* knowledge. Such a critique is therefore a preparation, so far as may be possible, for an organon; and should this turn out not to be possible, then at least for a canon, according to which, in due course, the complete system of the philosophy of pure reason—be it in extension or merely in limitation of its knowledge—may be carried into execution, analytically as well as synthetically. That such a system is possible, and indeed that it may not be of such great extent as to cut us off from the hope of entirely completing it, may already be gathered from the fact that what here constitutes our subject-matter is not the nature of things, which is inexhaustible, but the understanding which passes judgment upon the nature of things; and this understanding, again, only in respect of its *a priori* knowledge. These *a priori* possessions of the understanding, since they have not to be sought for without, cannot remain hidden from us, and in all probability are sufficiently small in extent to allow of our apprehending them in their completeness, of judging as to their value or lack of value, and so of rightly appraising them. Still less may the reader here expect a critique of books and systems of pure reason; we are concerned only with the critique of the faculty of pure reason itself. Only in so far as we build upon this foundation do we have a reliable touchstone for estimating the philosophical value of old and new works in this field. Otherwise the unqualified historian or critic is passing judgments upon the groundless assertions of others by means of his own, which are equally groundless.

Transcendental philosophy is only the idea of a science, for which the critique of pure reason has to lay down the complete architectonic plan. That is to say, it has to guarantee, as following from principles, the completeness and certainty of the structure in all its parts. It is the system of all principles of pure reason. And if this critique is not itself to be entitled a transcendental philosophy, it is solely because, to be a complete system, it would also have to contain an exhaustive analysis of the whole of *a priori* human knowledge. Our critique must, indeed, supply a complete enumeration of all the fundamental concepts that go to constitute such pure knowledge. But it is not required to give an exhaustive analysis of these concepts, nor a complete review of those that can be derived from them. Such a demand would be unreasonable, partly because this analysis would not be appropriate to our main purpose, inasmuch as there is no such uncertainty in regard to analysis as we encounter in the case of synthesis, for the sake of which alone our whole critique is undertaken; and partly because it would be inconsistent with the unity of our plan to assume responsibility for the completeness of such an analysis and derivation, when in view of our purpose we can be excused from doing so. The analysis of these *a priori* concepts, which later we shall have to enumerate, and the derivation of other concepts from them, can easily, however, be made complete when once they have been established as exhausting the principles of synthesis, and if in this essential respect nothing be lacking in them.

B 28

The critique of pure reason therefore will contain all that is essential in transcendental philosophy. While it is the complete idea of transcendental philosophy, it is not equivalent to that latter science; for it carries the analysis only so far as is requisite for the complete examination of knowledge which is *a priori* and synthetic.

What has chiefly to be kept in view in the division of such a science, is that no concepts be allowed to enter which contain in themselves anything empirical, or, in other words, that it consist in knowledge wholly *a priori*. Accordingly, although the highest principles and fundamental concepts of morality are *a priori* knowledge, they have no place in transcendental philosophy, because, al-

B 29

though they do not lay at the foundation of their precepts the concepts of pleasure and pain, of the desires and inclinations, etc., all of which are of empirical origin, yet in the construction of a system of pure morality these empirical concepts must necessarily be brought into the concept of duty, as representing either a hindrance, which we have to overcome, or an allurement, which must not be made into a motive. Transcendental philosophy is therefore a philosophy of pure and merely speculative reason. All that is practical, so far as it contains motives, relates to feelings, and these belong to the empirical sources of knowledge.

If we are to make a systematic division of the science which we are engaged in presenting, it must have first a *doctrine of the elements,* and secondly, a *doctrine of the method of pure reason.* Each of these chief divisions will have its subdivisions, but the grounds of these we are not yet in a position to explain. By way of introduction or anticipation we need only say that there are two stems of human knowledge, namely, *sensibility* and *understanding,* which perhaps spring from a common, but to us unknown, root. Through the former, objects are given to us; through the latter, they are thought. Now in so far as sensibility may be found to contain *a priori* representations constituting the condition under which objects are given to us, it will belong to transcendental philosophy. And since the conditions under which alone the objects of human knowledge are given must precede those under which they are thought, the transcendental doctrine of sensibility will constitute the first part of the science of the elements.

B 30

Transcendental Doctrine of Elements

First Part: Transcendental Aesthetic

§ I In whatever manner and by whatever means a mode of knowledge may relate to objects, *intuition* is that through which it is in immediate relation to them, and to which all thought as a means is directed. But intuition takes place only in so far as the object is given to us. This again is only possible, to man at least, in so far as the mind is affected in a certain way. The capacity (receptivity)

for receiving representations through the mode in which we are affected by objects, is entitled *sensibility*. Objects are *given* to us by means of sensibility, and it alone yields us *intuitions;* they are *thought* through the understanding, and from the understanding arise *concepts*. But all thought must, directly or indirectly, by way of certain characters, relate ultimately to intuitions, and therefore, with us, to sensibility, because in no other way can an object be given to us.

B 34   The effect of an object upon the faculty of representation, so far as we are affected by it, is *sensation*. That intuition which is in relation to the object through sensation, is entitled *empirical*. The undetermined object of an empirical intuition is entitled *appearance*.

That in the appearance which corresponds to sensation I term its *matter;* but that which so determines the manifold of appearance that it allows of being ordered in certain relations, I term the *form* of appearance. That in which alone the sensations can be posited and ordered in a certain form cannot itself be sensation; and therefore; while the matter of all appearance is given to us *a posteriori* only, its form must lie ready for the sensations *a priori* in the mind, and so must allow of being considered apart from all sensation.

I term all representations *pure* (in the transcendental sense) in which there is nothing that belongs to sensation. The pure form of sensible intuition in general, in which all the manifold of intuition is intuited in certain relations, must be found in the mind *a priori*. This pure form of sensibility may

B 35   also itself be called *pure intuition*. Thus, if I take away from the representation of a body that which the understanding thinks in regard to it, substance, force, divisibility, etc., and likewise what belongs to sensation, impenetrability, hardness, colour, etc., something still remains over from this empirical intuition, namely, extension and figure. These belong to pure intuition, which, even without any actual object of the senses or of sensation, exists in the mind *a priori* as a mere form of sensibility.

The science of all principles of *a priori* sensibility I call *transcendental aesthetic*. There must be such a science, forming the first part of the

B 36   transcendental doctrine of elements, in distinction from that part which deals with the principles of pure thought, and which is called transcendental logic.

In the transcendental aesthetic we shall, therefore, first *isolate* sensibility, by taking away from it everything which the understanding thinks through its concepts, so that nothing may be left save empirical intuition. Secondly, we shall also separate off from it everything which belongs to sensation, so that nothing may remain save pure intuition and the mere form of appearances, which is all that sensibility can supply *a priori*. In the course of this investigation it will be found that there are two pure forms of sensible intuition, serving as principles of *a priori* knowledge, namely, space and time. To the consideration of these we shall now proceed.

Section I. Space   B 37

§ 2 Metaphysical Exposition of This Concept By means of outer sense, a property of our mind, we represent to ourselves objects as outside us, and all without exception in space. In space their shape, magnitude, and relation to one another are determined or determinable. Inner sense, by means of which the mind intuits itself or its inner state, yields indeed no intuition of the soul itself as an object; but there is nevertheless a determinate form [namely, time] in which alone the intuition of inner states is possible, and everything which belongs to inner determinations is therefore represented in relations of time. Time cannot be outwardly intuited, any more than space can be intuited as something in us. What, then, are space and time? Are they real existences? Are they only determinations or relations of things, yet such as would belong to things even if they were not intuited? Or are space and time such that they belong only to the form of intuition, and therefore to the subjective consti- B 38 tution of our mind, apart from which they could not be ascribed to anything whatsoever? In order to obtain light upon these questions, let us first give an exposition of the concept of space. By *exposition* (*expositio*) I mean the clear, though not necessarily exhaustive, representation of that which belongs to a concept: the exposition is *metaphysical* when it contains that which exhibits the concept *as given a priori*.

1. Space is not an empirical concept which has been derived from outer experiences. For in order

that certain sensations be referred to something outside me (that is, to something in another region of space from that in which I find myself), and similarly in order that I may be able to represent them as outside and alongside one another, and accordingly as not only different but as in different places, the representation of space must be presupposed. The representation of space cannot, therefore, be empirically obtained from the relations of outer appearance. On the contrary, this outer experience is itself possible at all only through that representation.

2. Space is a necessary *a priori* representation, which underlies all outer intuitions. We can never represent to ourselves the absence of space, though B 39 we can quite well think it as empty of objects. It must therefore be regarded as the condition of the possibility of appearances, and not as a determination dependent upon them. It is an *a priori* representation, which necessarily underlies outer appearances.

3. Space is not a discursive or, as we say, general concept of relations of things in general, but a pure intuition. For, in the first place, we can represent to ourselves only one space; and if we speak of diverse spaces, we mean thereby only parts of one and the same unique space. Secondly, these parts cannot precede the one all-embracing space, as being, as it were, constituents out of which it can be composed; on the contrary, they can be thought only as *in* it. Space is essentially one; the manifold in it, and therefore the general concept of spaces, depends solely on [the introduction of] limitations. Hence it follows that an *a priori*, and not an empirical, intuition underlies all concepts of space. For kindred reasons, geometrical propositions, that, for instance, in a triangle two sides together are greater than the third, can never be derived from the general concepts of line and triangle, but only from intuition, and this indeed *a priori*, with apodeictic certainty.

4. Space is represented as an infinite *given* B 40 magnitude. Now every concept must be thought as a representation which is contained in an infinite number of different possible representations (as their common character), and which therefore contains these *under* itself; but no concept, as such, can be thought as containing an infinite number of representations *within* itself. It is in this latter way, however, that space is thought; for all the parts of

space coexist *ad infinitum*. Consequently, the original representation of space is an *a priori* intuition, not a concept.

§ 3 *The Transcendental Exposition of the Concept of Space* I understand by a transcendental exposition the explanation of a concept, as a principle from which the possibility of other *a priori* synthetic knowledge can be understood. For this purpose it is required (1) that such knowledge does really flow from the given concept, (2) that this knowledge is possible only on the assumption of a given mode of explaining the concept.

Geometry is a science which determines the properties of space synthetically, and yet *a priori*. What, then, must be our representation of space, in order that such knowledge of it may be possible? It must in its origin be intuition; for from a mere B 41 concept no propositions can be obtained which go beyond the concept—as happens in geometry (Introduction, V). Further, this intuition must be *a priori*, that is, it must be found in us prior to any perception of an object, and must therefore be pure, not empirical, intuition. For geometrical propositions are one and all apodeictic, that is, are bound up with the consciousness of their necessity; for instance, that space has only three dimensions. Such propositions cannot be empirical or, in other words, judgments of experience, nor can they be derived from any such judgments (Introduction, II).

How, then, can there exist in the mind an outer intuition which precedes the objects themselves, and in which the concept of these objects can be determined *a priori*? Manifestly, not otherwise than in so far as the intuition has its seat in the subject only, as the formal character of the subject, in virtue of which, in being affected by objects, it obtains *immediate representation*, that is, *intuition*, of them; and only in so far, therefore, as it is merely the form of outer *sense* in general.

Our explanation is thus the only explanation that makes intelligible the *possibility* of geometry, as a body of *a priori* synthetic knowledge. Any mode of explanation which fails to do this, although it may otherwise seem to be somewhat similar, can by this criterion be distinguished from it with the greatest certainty.

Conclusions from the Above Concepts (a) Space does not represent any property of things in themselves, B 42 nor does it represent them in their relation to one another. That is to say, space does not represent any determination that attaches to the objects themselves, and which remains even when abstraction has been made of all the subjective conditions of intuition. For no determinations, whether absolute or relative, can be intuited prior to the existence of the things to which they belong, and none, therefore, can be intuited *a priori*.

(*b*) Space is nothing but the form of all appearances of outer sense. It is the subjective condition of sensibility, under which alone outer intuition is possible for us. Since, then, the receptivity of the subject, its capacity to be affected by objects, must necessarily precede all intuitions of these objects, it can readily be understood how the form of all appearances can be given prior to all actual perceptions, and so exist in the mind *a priori*, and how, as a pure intuition, in which all objects must be determined, it can contain, prior to all experience, principles which determine the relations of these objects.

It is, therefore, solely from the human standpoint that we can speak of space, of extended things, etc. If we depart from the subjective condition under which alone we can have outer intuition, namely, liability to be affected by objects, the representation of space stands for nothing whatsoever. This predicate can be ascribed to things only in so far as they appear to us, that is, only to objects of sensibility. The constant form of this receptivity, which we term sensibility, is a necessary condition of all the relations in which objects can be intuited as outside us; and if we abstract from these objects, it is a pure intuition, and bears the name of space. Since we cannot treat the special conditions of sensibility as conditions of the possibility of things, but only of their appearances, we can indeed say that space comprehends all things that appear to us as external, but not all things in themselves, by whatever subject they are intuited, or whether they be intuited or not. For we cannot judge in regard to the intuitions of other thinking beings, whether they are bound by the same conditions as those which limit our intuition and which for us are universally valid. If we add to the concept of the subject of a judgment the limitation under which the judgment is made, the judgment is then unconditionally valid. The proposition, that all things are side by side in space, is valid under the limitation that these things are viewed as objects of our sensible intuition. If, now, I add the condition to the concept, and say that all things, as outer appearances, are side by side in space, the rule is valid universally and without limitation. Our exposition therefore establishes the *reality*, that is, the objective validity, of space in respect of whatever can be presented to us outwardly as object, but also at the same time the *ideality* of space in respect of things when they are considered in themselves through reason, that is, without regard to the constitution of our sensibility. We assert, then, the *empirical reality* of space, as regards all possible outer experience; and yet at the same time we assert its *transcendental ideality*—in other words, that it is nothing at all, immediately we withdraw the above condition, namely, its limitation to possible experience, and so look upon it as something that underlies things in themselves.

With the sole exception of space there is no subjective representation, referring to something *outer*, which could be entitled [at once] objective [and] *a priori*. For there is no other subjective representation from which we can derive *a priori* synthetic propositions, as we can from intuition in space (§ 3). Strictly speaking, therefore, these other representations have no ideality, although they agree with the representation of space in this respect, that they belong merely to the subjective constitution of our manner of sensibility, for instance, of sight, hearing, touch, as in the case of the sensations of colours, sounds, and heat, which, since they are mere sensations and not intuitions, do not of themselves yield knowledge of any object, least of all any *a priori* knowledge.

The above remark is intended only to guard anyone from supposing that the ideality of space as here asserted can be illustrated by examples so altogether insufficient as colours, taste, etc. For these cannot rightly be regarded as properties of things, but only as changes in the subject, changes which may, indeed, be different for different men. In such examples as these, that which originally is itself only appearance, for instance, a rose, is being treated by the empirical understanding as a thing in itself, which, nevertheless, in respect of its colour, can appear differently to every observer. The transcendental concept of appearances in space, on the other hand, is a critical reminder that nothing intuited in space is a thing in itself, that space is not a form inhering in things in themselves as their intrinsic property, that objects in themselves are quite unknown to us, and that what we call outer objects are nothing but mere representations of our sensibility, the form of which is space. The true correlate of sensibility, the thing in itself, is not known, and cannot be known, through these representations; and in experience no question is ever asked in regard to it.

B 46 ## Section II. Time

§ 4 *Metaphysical Exposition of the Concept of Time*
1. Time is not an empirical concept that has been derived from any experience. For neither coexistence nor succession would ever come within our perception, if the representation of time were not presupposed as underlying them *a priori*. Only on the presupposition of time can we represent to ourselves a number of things as existing at one and the same time (simultaneously) or at different times (successively).

2. Time is a necessary representation that underlies all intuitions. We cannot, in respect of appearances in general, remove time itself, though we can quite well think time as void of appearances. Time is, therefore, given *a priori*. In it alone is actuality of appearances possible at all. Appearances may, one and all, vanish; but time (as the universal condition of their possibility) cannot itself be removed.

B 47 3. The possibility of apodeictic principles concerning the relations of time, or of axioms of time in general, is also grounded upon this *a priori* necessity. Time has only one dimension; different times are not simultaneous but successive (just as different spaces are not successive but simultaneous). These principles cannot be derived from experience, for experience would give neither strict universality nor apodeictic certainty. We should only be able to say that common experience teaches us that it is so; not that it must be so. These principles are valid as rules under which alone experiences are possible; and they instruct us in regard to the experiences, not by means of them.

4. Time is not a discursive, or what is called a general concept, but a pure form of sensible intuition. Different times are but parts of one and the same time; and the representation which can be

given only through a single object is intuition. Moreover, the proposition that different times cannot be simultaneous is not to be derived from a general concept. The proposition is synthetic, and cannot have its origin in concepts alone. It is immediately contained in the intuition and representation of time.

5. The infinitude of time signifies nothing more than that every determinate magnitude of time is possible only through limitations of one B 48 single time that underlies it. The original representation, *time*, must therefore be given as unlimited. But when an object is so given that its parts, and every quantity of it, can be determinately represented only through limitation, the whole representation cannot be given through concepts, since they contain only partial representations; on the contrary, such concepts must themselves rest on immediate intuition.

§ 5 *The Transcendental Exposition of the Concept of Time* I may here refer to No. 3, where, for the sake of brevity, I have placed under the title of metaphysical exposition what is properly transcendental. Here I may add that the concept of alteration, and with it the concept of motion, as alteration of place, is possible only through and in the representation of time; and that if this representation were not an *a priori* (inner) intuition, no concept, no matter what it might be, could render comprehensible the possibility of an alteration, that is, of a combination of contradictorily opposed predicates in one and the same object, for instance, the being and the not-being of one and the same thing in one and the same place. Only in time can two contradictorily B 49 opposed predicates meet in one and the same object, namely, *one after the other*. Thus our concept of time explains the possibility of that body of *a priori* synthetic knowledge which is exhibited in the general doctrine of motion, and which is by no means unfruitful.

§ 6 *Conclusions from These Concepts* (*a*) Time is not something which exists of itself, or which inheres in things as an objective determination, and it does not, therefore, remain when abstraction is made of all subjective conditions of its intuition. Were it self-subsistent, it would be something which would be actual and yet not an actual object. Were it a determination or order inhering in things themselves, it could not precede the objects as their condition, and be known and intuited *a priori* by means of synthetic propositions. But this last is quite possible if time is nothing but the subjective condition under which alone intuition can take place in us. For that being so, this form of inner intuition can be represented prior to the objects, and therefore *a priori.*

(b) Time is nothing but the form of inner sense, that is, of the intuition of ourselves and of our inner state. It cannot be a determination of outer appearances; it has to do neither with shape nor position, but with the relation of representations in our inner state. And just because this inner intuition yields no shape, we endeavour to make up for this want by analogies. We represent the time-sequence by a line progressing to infinity, in which the manifold constitutes a series of one dimension only; and we reason from the properties of this line to all the properties of time, with this one exception, that while the parts of the line are simultaneous the parts of time are always successive. From this fact also, that all the relations of time allow of being expressed in an outer intuition, it is evident that the representation is itself an intuition.

(c) Time is the formal *a priori* condition of all appearances whatsoever. Space, as the pure form of all *outer* intuition, is so far limited; it serves as the *a priori* condition only of outer appearances. But since all representations, whether they have for their objects outer things or not, belong, in themselves, as determinations of the mind, to our inner state; and since this inner state stands under the formal condition of inner intuition, and so belongs to time, time is an *a priori* condition of all appearance whatsoever. It is the immediate condition of inner appearances (of our souls), and thereby the mediate condition of outer appearances. Just as I can say *a priori* that all outer appearances are in space, and are determined *a priori* in conformity with the relations of space, I can also say, from the principle of inner sense, that all appearances whatsoever, that is, all objects of the senses, are in time, and necessarily stand in time-relations.

If we abstract from *our* mode of inwardly intuiting ourselves—the mode of intuition in terms of which we likewise take up into our faculty of representation all outer intuitions—and so take objects as they may be in themselves, then time is nothing.

B 50

B 51

It has objective validity only in respect of appearances, these being things which we take *as objects of our senses.* It is no longer objective, if we abstract from the sensibility of our intuition, that is, from that mode of representation which is peculiar to us, and speak of *things in general.* Time is therefore a purely subjective condition of our (human) intuition (which is always sensible, that is, so far as we are affected by objects), and in itself, apart from the subject, is nothing. Nevertheless, in respect of all appearances, and therefore of all the things which can enter into our experience, it is necessarily objective. We cannot say that all things are in time, because in this concept of things in general we are abstracting from every mode of their intuition and therefore from that condition under which alone objects can be represented as being in time. If, however, the condition be added to the concept, and we say that all things as appearances, that is, as objects of sensible intuition, are in time, then the proposition has legitimate objective validity and universality *a priori.*

What we are maintaining is, therefore, the *empirical reality* of time, that is, its objective validity in respect of all objects which allow of ever being given to our senses. And since our intuition is always sensible, no object can ever be given to us in experience which does not conform to the condition of time. On the other hand, we deny to time all claim to absolute reality; that is to say, we deny that it belongs to things absolutely, as their condition or property, independently of any reference to the form of our sensible intuition; properties that belong to things in themselves can never be given to us through the senses. This, then, is what constitutes the *transcendental ideality* of time. What we mean by this phrase is that if we abstract from the subjective conditions of sensible intuition, time is nothing, and cannot be ascribed to the objects in themselves (apart from their relation to our intuition) in the way either of subsistence or of inherence. This ideality, like that of space, must not, however, be illustrated by false analogies with sensation, because it is then assumed that the appearance, in which the sensible predicates inhere, itself has objective reality. In the case of time, such objective reality falls entirely away, save in so far as it is merely empirical, that is, save in so far as we regard the object itself merely as appearance. On

B 52

B 53

this subject, the reader may refer to what has been said at the close of the preceding section.

§ 7 *Elucidation* Against this theory, which admits the empirical reality of time, but denies its absolute and transcendental reality, I have heard men of intelligence so unanimously voicing an objection, that I must suppose it to occur spontaneously to every reader to whom this way of thinking is unfamiliar. The objection is this. Alterations are real, this being proved by change of our own representations— even if all outer appearances, together with their alterations, be denied. Now alterations are possible only in time, and time is therefore something real. There is no difficulty in meeting this objection. I grant the whole argument. Certainly time is something real, namely, the real form of inner intuition. It has therefore subjective reality in respect of inner experience; that is, I really have the representation
B 54 of time and of my determinations in it. Time is therefore to be regarded as real, not indeed as object but as the mode of representation of myself as object. If without this condition of sensibility I could intuit myself, or be intuited by another being, the very same determinations which we now represent to ourselves as alterations would yield knowledge into which the representation of time, and therefore also of alteration, would in no way enter. Thus empirical reality has to be allowed to time, as the condition of all our experiences; on our theory, it is only its absolute reality that has to be denied. It is nothing but the form of our inner intuition.* If we take away from our inner intuition the peculiar condition of our sensibility, the concept of time likewise vanishes; it does not inhere in the objects, but merely in the subject which intuits them.

But the reason why this objection is so unani-
B 55 mously urged, and that too by those who have nothing very convincing to say against the doctrine of the ideality of space, is this. They have no expectation of being able to prove apodeictically the absolute reality of space; for they are confronted by

---

*I can indeed say that my representations follow one another; but this is only to say that we are conscious of them as in a time-sequence, that is, in conformity with the form of inner sense. Time is not, therefore, something in itself, nor is it an objective determination inherent in things.

idealism, which teaches that the reality of outer objects does not allow of strict proof. On the other hand, the reality of the object of our inner sense (the reality of myself and my state) is, [they argue,] immediately evident through consciousness. The former may be merely an illusion; the latter is, on their view, undeniably something real. What they have failed, however, to recognise is that both are in the same position; in neither case can their reality as representations be questioned, and in both cases they belong only to appearance, which always has two sides, the one by which the object is viewed in and by itself (without regard to the mode of intuiting it—its nature therefore remaining always problematic), the other by which the form of the intuition of this object is taken into account. This form is not to be looked for in the object in itself, but in the subject to which the object appears; nevertheless, it belongs really and necessarily to the appearance of this object.

Time and space are, therefore, two sources of knowledge, from which bodies of *a priori* synthetic knowledge can be derived. (Pure mathematics is a brilliant example of such knowledge, especially as regards space and its relations.) Time and space, B 56 taken together, are the pure forms of all sensible intuition, and so are what make *a priori* synthetic propositions possible. But these *a priori* sources of knowledge, being merely conditions of our sensibility, just by this very fact determine their own limits, namely, that they apply to objects only in so far as objects are viewed as appearances, and do not present things as they are in themselves. This is the sole field of their validity; should we pass beyond it, no objective use can be made of them. This ideality of space and time leaves, however, the certainty of empirical knowledge unaffected, for we are equally sure of it, whether these forms necessarily inhere in things in themselves or only in our intuition of them. Those, on the other hand, who maintain the absolute reality of space and time, whether as subsistent or only as inherent, must come into conflict with the principles of experience itself. For if they decide for the former alternative (which is generally the view taken by mathematical students of nature), they have to admit two eternal and infinite self-subsistent nonentities (space and time), which are there (yet without there being anything real) only in order to contain in themselves all that is real. If they adopt the latter alternative (as advocated by certain metaphysical students of nature), and regard space and time as relations of appearances, alongside or B 57 in succession to one another—relations abstracted from experience, and in this isolation confusedly represented—they are obliged to deny that *a priori* mathematical doctrines have any validity in respect of real things (for instance, in space), or at least to deny their apodeictic certainty. For such certainty is not to be found in the *a posteriori*. On this view, indeed, the *a priori* concepts of space and time are merely creatures of the imagination, whose source must really be sought in experience, the imagination framing out of the relations abstracted from experience something that does indeed contain what is general in these relations, but which cannot exist without the restrictions which nature has attached to them. The former thinkers obtain at least this advantage, that they keep the field of appearances open for mathematical propositions. On the other hand, they have greatly embarrassed themselves by those very conditions [space and time, eternal, infinite, and self-subsistent], when with the understanding they endeavour to go out beyond this field. The latter have indeed an advantage, in that the representations of space and time do not stand in their way if they seek to judge of objects, not as appearances but merely in their relation to the understanding. But since they are unable to appeal to a true and objectively valid *a priori* intuition, they can neither account for the possibility of *a priori* mathematical knowledge, nor bring the propositions of experience into necessary agreement with it. On our theory of the true character of these two B 58 original forms of sensibility, both difficulties are removed.

Lastly, transcendental aesthetic cannot contain more than these two elements, space and time. This is evident from the fact that all other concepts belonging to sensibility, even that of motion, in which both elements are united, presuppose something empirical. Motion presupposes the perception of something movable. But in space, considered in itself, there is nothing movable; consequently the movable must be something that is found *in space only through experience*, and must therefore be an empirical datum. For the same reason, transcendental aesthetic cannot count the concept of alteration among its *a priori* data. Time itself does not alter, but

only something which is in time. The concept of alteration thus presupposes the perception of something existing and of the succession of its determinations; that is to say, it presupposes experience.

§ 8   General Observations on Transcendental Aesthetic

I. To avoid all misapprehension, it is necessary to B 59 explain, as clearly as possible, what our view is regarding the fundamental constitution of sensible knowledge in general.

What we have meant to say is that all our intuition is nothing but the representation of appearance; that the things which we intuit are not in themselves what we intuit them as being, nor their relations so constituted in themselves as they appear to us, and that if the subject, or even only the subjective constitution of the senses in general, be removed, the whole constitution and all the relations of objects in space and time, nay space and time themselves, would vanish. As appearances, they cannot exist in themselves, but only in us. What objects may be in themselves, and apart from all this receptivity of our sensibility, remains completely unknown to us. We know nothing but our mode of perceiving them—a mode which is peculiar to us, and not necessarily shared in by every being, though, certainly, by every human being. With this alone have we any concern. Space and time are its pure forms, and sensation in general its B 60 matter. The former alone can we know *a priori*, that is, prior to all actual perception; and such knowledge is therefore called pure intuition. The latter is that in our knowledge which leads to its being called *a posteriori* knowledge, that is, empirical intuition. The former inhere in our sensibility with absolute necessity, no matter of what kind our sensations may be; the latter can exist in varying modes. Even if we could bring our intuition to the highest degree of clearness, we should not thereby come any nearer to the constitution of objects in themselves. We should still know only our mode of intuition, that is, our sensibility. We should, indeed, know it completely, but always only under the conditions of space and time—conditions which are originally inherent in the subject. What the objects may be in themselves would never become known to us even through the most enlightened knowledge of that which is alone given us, namely, their appearance.

The concept of sensibility and of appearance would be falsified, and our whole teaching in regard to them would be rendered empty and useless, if we were to accept the view that our entire sensibility is nothing but a confused representation of things, containing only what belongs to them in themselves, but doing so under an aggregation of characters and partial representations that we do not consciously distinguish. For the difference

B 61 between a confused and a clear representation is merely logical, and does not concern the content. No doubt the concept of "right,"in its common-sense usage, contains all that the subtlest speculation can develop out of it, though in its ordinary and practical use we are not conscious of the manifold representations comprised in this thought. But we cannot say that the common concept is therefore sensible, containing a mere appearance. For "right" can never be an appearance; it is a concept in the understanding, and represents a property (the moral property) of actions, which belongs to them in themselves. The representation of a body in intuition, on the other hand, contains nothing that can belong to an object in itself, but merely the appearance of something, and the mode in which we are affected by that something; and this receptivity of our faculty of knowledge is termed sensibility. Even if that appearance could become completely transparent to us, such knowledge would remain *toto coelo* different from knowledge of the object in itself.

The philosophy of Leibniz and Wolff, in thus treating the difference between the sensible and the intelligible as merely logical, has given a completely wrong direction to all investigations into the nature and origin of our knowledge. This difference is quite evidently transcendental. It does not merely

B 62 concern their [logical] form, as being either clear or confused. It concerns their origin and content. It is not that by our sensibility we cannot know the nature of things in themselves in any save a confused fashion; we do not apprehend them in any fashion whatsoever. If our subjective constitution be removed, the represented object, with the qualities which sensible intuition bestows upon it, is nowhere to be found, and cannot possibly be found. For it is this subjective constitution which determines its form as appearance.

We commonly distinguish in appearances that which is essentially inherent in their intuition and holds for sense in all human beings, from that which belongs to their intuition accidentally only, and is valid not in relation to sensibility in general but only in relation to a particular standpoint or to a peculiarity of structure in this or that sense. The former kind of knowledge is then declared to represent the object in itself, the latter its appearance only. But this distinction is merely empirical. If, as generally happens, we stop short at this point, and do not proceed, as we ought, to treat the empirical intuition as itself mere appearance, in which nothing that belongs to a thing in itself can be found, our transcendental distinction is lost. We then believe that we know things in themselves, and this in spite of the fact that in the world of sense, however deeply we enquire into its objects, we have to do with nothing B 63 but appearances. The rainbow in a sunny shower may be called a mere appearance, and the rain the thing in itself. This is correct, if the latter concept be taken in a merely physical sense. Rain will then be viewed only as that which, in all experience and in all its various positions relative to the senses, is determined thus, and not otherwise, in our intuition. But if we take this empirical object in its general character, and ask, without considering whether or not it is the same for all human sense, whether it represents an object in itself (and by that we cannot mean the drops of rain, for these are already, as appearances, empirical objects), the question as to the relation of the representation to the object at once becomes transcendental. We then realise that not only are the drops of rain mere appearances, but that even their round shape, nay even the space in which they fall, are nothing in themselves, but merely modifications or fundamental forms of our sensible intuition, and that the transcendental object remains unknown to us.

The second important concern of our Transcendental Aesthetic is that it should not obtain favour merely as a plausible hypothesis, but should have that certainty and freedom from doubt which is required of any theory that is to serve as an organon. To make this certainty completely convincing, we shall select a case by which the validity of the position adopted will be rendered obvious, and which will serve to set what has been said in B 64 § 3 in a clearer light.

Let us suppose that space and time are in themselves objective, and are conditions of the possibility of things in themselves. In the first place, it is evident that in regard to both there is a large number of *a priori* apodeictic and synthetic propositions. This is especially true of space, to which our chief attention will therefore be directed in this enquiry. Since the propositions of geometry are synthetic *a priori*, and are known with apodeictic certainty, I raise the question, whence do you obtain such propositions, and upon what does the understanding rely in its endeavour to achieve such absolutely necessary and universally valid truths? There is no other way than through concepts or through intuitions; and these are given either *a priori* or *a posteriori*. In their latter form, namely, as *empirical* concepts, and also as that upon which these are grounded, the *empirical* intuition, neither the concepts nor the intuitions can yield any synthetic proposition except such as is itself also merely empirical (that is, a proposition of experience), and which for that very reason can never possess the necessity and absolute universality which are characteristic of all geometrical propositions. As regards the first and sole means of arriving at such knowledge, namely, in *a priori* fashion through mere concepts or through intuitions, it is evident that from mere concepts only analytic knowledge, not B 65 synthetic knowledge, is to be obtained. Take, for instance, the proposition, "Two straight lines cannot enclose a space, and with them alone no figure is possible," and try to derive it from the concept of straight lines and of the number two. Or take the proposition, "Given three straight lines, a figure is possible," and try, in like manner, to derive it from the concepts involved. All your labour is vain; and you find that you are constrained to have recourse to intuition, as is always done in geometry. You therefore give yourself an object in intuition. But of what kind is this intuition? Is it a pure *a priori* intuition or an empirical intuition? Were it the latter, no universally valid proposition could ever arise out of it—still less an apodeictic proposition—for experience can never yield such. You must therefore give yourself an object *a priori* in intuition, and ground upon this your synthetic proposition. If there did not exist in you a power of *a priori* intuition; and if that subjective condition were not also at the same time, as regards its form, the universal *a priori* condition under which alone the object of this outer intuition is itself possible; if the object (the

triangle) were something in itself, apart from any relation to you, the subject, how could you say that what necessarily exist in you as subjective conditions for the construction of a triangle, must of necessity belong to the triangle itself? You could not then add anything new (the figure) to your concepts B 66 (of three lines) as something which must necessarily be met with in the object, since this object is [on that view] given antecedently to your knowledge, and not by means of it. If, therefore, space (and the same is true of time) were not merely a form of your intuition, containing conditions *a priori*, under which alone things can be outer objects to you, and without which subjective conditions outer objects are in themselves nothing, you could not in regard to outer objects determine anything whatsoever in an *a priori* and synthetic manner. It is, therefore, not merely possible or probable, but indubitably certain, that space and time, as the necessary conditions of all outer and inner experience, are merely subjective conditions of all our intuition, and that in relation to these conditions all objects are therefore mere appearances, and not given us as things in themselves which exist in this manner. For this reason also, while much can be said *a priori* as regards the form of appearances, nothing whatsoever can be asserted of the thing in itself, which may underlie these appearances.

II. In confirmation of this theory of the ideality of both outer and inner sense, and therefore of all objects of the senses, as mere appearances, it is especially relevant to observe that everything in our knowledge which belongs to intuition—feeling of pleasure and pain, and the will, not being knowledge, are excluded—contains nothing but mere relations; namely, of locations in an intuition (extension), of change of location (motion), and of B 67 laws according to which this change is determined (moving forces). What it is that is present in this or that location, or what it is that is operative in the things themselves apart from change of location, is not given through intuition. Now a thing in itself cannot be known through mere relations; and we may therefore conclude that since outer sense gives us nothing but mere relations, this sense can contain in its representation only the relation of an object to the subject, and not the inner properties of the object in itself. This also holds true of inner sense, not only because the representations of the *outer senses* constitute the proper material with which we occupy our mind, but because the time in which we set these representations, which is itself antecedent to the consciousness of them in experience, and which underlies them as the formal condition of the mode in which we posit them in the mind, itself contains [only] relations of succession, coexistence, and of that which is coexistent with succession, the enduring. Now that which, as representation, can be antecedent to any and every act of thinking anything, is intuition; and if it contains nothing but relations, it is the form of intuition. Since this form does not represent anything save in so far as something is posited in the mind, it can be nothing but the mode in which the mind is affected through its own activity (namely, through this positing of its B 68 representation), and so is affected by itself; in other words, it is nothing but an inner sense in respect of the form of that sense. Everything that is represented through a sense is so far always appearance, and consequently we must either refuse to admit that there is an inner sense, or we must recognise that the subject, which is the object of the sense, can be represented through it only as appearance, not as that subject would judge of itself if its intuition were self-activity only, that is, were intellectual. The whole difficulty is as to how a subject can inwardly intuit itself; and this is a difficulty common to every theory. The consciousness of self (apperception) is the simple representation of the "I," and if all that is manifold in the subject were given by the *activity of the self*, the inner intuition would be intellectual. In man this consciousness demands inner perception of the manifold which is antecedently given in the subject, and the mode in which this manifold is given in the mind must, as non-spontaneous, be entitled sensibility. If the faculty of coming to consciousness of oneself is to seek out (to apprehend) that which lies in the mind, it must affect the mind, and only in this way can it give rise to an intuition of itself. But the form of this B 69 intuition, which exists antecedently in the mind, determines, in the representation of time, the mode in which the manifold is together in the mind, since it then intuits itself not as it would represent itself if immediately self-active, but as it is affected by itself, and therefore as it appears to itself, not as it is.

III. When I say that the intuition of outer objects and the self-intuition of the mind alike represent the objects and the mind, in space and in time, as they affect our senses, that is, as they appear, I do not mean to say that these objects are a mere *illusion*. For in an appearance the objects, nay even the properties that we ascribe to them, are always regarded as something actually given. Since, however, in the relation of the given object to the subject, such properties depend upon the mode of intuition of the subject, this object as *appearance* is to be distinguished from itself as object *in itself*. Thus when I maintain that the quality of space and of time, in conformity with which, as a condition of their existence, I posit both bodies and my own soul, lies in my mode of intuition and not in those objects in themselves, I am not saying that bodies merely *seem* to be outside me, or that my soul only *seems* to be given in my self-consciousness. It would be my own fault, if out of that which I ought to reckon as appearance, I made mere illusion. That does not follow as a consequence of our principle of the ideality of all our sensible intuitions—quite the contrary. It is B 70 only if we ascribe *objective reality* to these forms of representation that it becomes impossible for us to prevent everything being thereby transformed into mere *illusion*. For if we regard space and time as properties which, if they are to be possible at all, must be found in things in themselves, and if we reflect on the absurdities in which we are then involved, in that two infinite things, which are not substances, nor anything actually inhering in substances, must yet have existence, nay, must be the necessary condition of the existence of all things, B 71 and moreover must continue to exist, even although all existing things be removed—we cannot blame the good Berkeley for degrading bodies to mere illusion. Nay, even our own existence, in being made thus dependent upon the self-subsistent reality of a non-entity, such as time, would necessarily be changed with it into sheer illusion—an absurdity of which no one has yet been guilty.

IV. In natural theology, in thinking an object [God], who not only can never be an object of intuition to us but cannot be an object of sensible intuition even to himself, we are careful to remove the conditions of time and space from his intuition— for all his knowledge must be intuition, and not *thought,* which always involves limitations. But with what right can we do this if we have previously made time and space forms of things in themselves, and such as would remain, as *a priori* conditions of the existence of things, even though the things themselves were removed? As conditions of all existence in general, they must also be conditions of the existence of God. If we do not thus treat them B 72 as objective forms of all things, the only alternative is to view them as subjective forms of our inner and outer intuition, which is termed sensible, for the very reason that it is *not original,* that is, is not such as can itself give us the existence of its object—a mode of intuition which, so far as we can judge, can belong only to the primordial being. Our mode of intuition is dependent upon the existence of the object, and is therefore possible only if the subject's faculty of representation is affected by that object.

This mode of intuiting in space and time need not be limited to human sensibility. It may be that all finite, thinking beings necessarily agree with man in this respect, although we are not in a position to judge whether this is actually so. But however universal this mode of sensibility may be, it does not therefore cease to be sensibility. It is derivative (*intuitus derivativus*), not original (*intuitus originarius*), and therefore not an intellectual intuition. For the reason stated above, such intellectual intuition seems to belong solely to the primordial being, and can never be ascribed to a dependent being, dependent in its existence as well as in its intuition, and which through that intuition determines its existence solely in relation to given objects. This latter remark, however, must be taken only as an illustration of our aesthetic theory, not as forming part of the proof.

Conclusion of the Transcendental Aesthetic Here, then, B 73 in pure *a priori* intuitions, space and time, we have one of the factors required for solution of the general problem of transcendental philosophy: *how are synthetic a priori judgments possible?* When in *a priori* judgment we seek to go out beyond the given concept, we come in the *a priori* intuitions upon that which cannot be discovered in the concept but which is certainly found *a priori* in the intuition corresponding to the concept, and can be connected with it synthetically. Such judgments, however, thus

based on intuition, can never extend beyond objects of the senses; they are valid only for objects of possible experience.

Transcendental Doctrine of Elements   B 74

Second Part: Transcendental Logic
Introduction: Idea of a Transcendental Logic
I. Logic in General

Our knowledge springs from two fundamental sources of the mind; the first is the capacity of receiving representations (receptivity for impressions), the second is the power of knowing an object through these representations (spontaneity [in the production] of concepts). Through the first an object is *given* to us, through the second the object is *thought* in relation to that [given] representation (which is a mere determination of the mind). Intuition and concepts constitute, therefore, the elements of all our knowledge, so that neither concepts without an intuition in some way corresponding to them, nor intuition without concepts, can yield knowledge. Both may be either pure or empirical. When they contain sensation (which presupposes the actual presence of the object), they are empirical. When there is no mingling of sensation with the representation, they are pure. Sensation may be entitled the material of sensible knowledge. Pure intuition, therefore, contains only the form under B 75 which something is intuited; the pure concept only the form of the thought of an object in general. Pure intuitions or pure concepts alone are possible *a priori,* empirical intuitions and empirical concepts only *a posteriori.*

If the *receptivity* of our mind, its power of receiving representations in so far as it is in any wise affected, is to be entitled sensibility, then the mind's power of producing representations from itself, the *spontaneity* of knowledge, should be called the understanding. Our nature is so constituted that our *intuition* can never be other than sensible; that is, it contains only the mode in which we are affected by objects. The faculty, on the other hand, which enables us to *think* the object of sensible intuition is the understanding. To neither of these powers may a preference be given over the other. Without sensibility no object would be given to us, without understanding no object would be thought. Thoughts without content are empty, intuitions without concepts are blind. It is, therefore, just as necessary to make our concepts sensible, that is, to add the object to them in intuition, as to make our intuitions intelligible, that is, to bring them under concepts. These two powers or capacities cannot exchange their functions. The understanding can intuit nothing, the senses can think nothing. Only through B 76 their union can knowledge arise. But that is no reason for confounding the contribution of either with that of the other; rather it is a strong reason for carefully separating and distinguishing the one from the other. We therefore distinguish the science of the rules of sensibility in general, that is, aesthetic, from the science of the rules of the understanding in general, that is, logic.

Logic, again, can be treated in a twofold manner, either as logic of the general or as logic of the special employment of the understanding. The former contains the absolutely necessary rules of thought without which there can be no employment whatsoever of the understanding. It therefore treats of understanding without any regard to difference in the objects to which the understanding may be directed. The logic of the special employment of the understanding contains the rules of correct thinking as regards a certain kind of objects. The former may be called the logic of elements, the latter the organon of this or that science. The latter is commonly taught in the schools as a propaedeutic to the sciences, though, according to the actual procedure of human reason, it is what is obtained last of all, when the particular science under question has been already brought to such completion that it requires only a few finishing touches to correct and perfect it. For the objects under consideration must already be known fairly completely before it can be possible B 77 to prescribe the rules according to which a science of them is to be obtained.

General logic is either pure or applied. In the former we abstract from all empirical conditions under which our understanding is exercised, i.e., from the influence of the senses, the play of imagination, the laws of memory, the force of habit, inclination, etc., and so from all sources of prejudice, indeed from all causes from which this or that knowledge may arise or seem to arise. For they concern the understanding only in so far as it is being employed under certain circumstances, and to become acquainted with these circumstances experience is required. Pure general logic has to do, therefore, only with principles *a priori,* and is a *canon of understanding* and of reason, but only in respect of what is formal in their employment, be the content what it may, empirical or transcendental. General logic is called applied, when it is directed to the rules of the employment of understanding under the subjective empirical conditions dealt with by psychology. Applied logic has therefore empirical principles, although it is still indeed in so far general that it refers to the employment of the understanding without regard to difference in the objects. Consequently it is neither a canon of the understanding in general nor an organon of B 78 special sciences, but merely a cathartic of the common understanding.

In general logic, therefore, that part which is to constitute the pure doctrine of reason must be entirely separated from that which constitutes applied (though always still general) logic. The former alone is, properly speaking, a science, though indeed concise and dry, as the methodical exposition of a doctrine of the elements of the understanding is bound to be. There are therefore two rules which logicians must always bear in mind, in dealing with pure general logic:

1. As general logic, it abstracts from all content of the knowledge of understanding and from all differences in its objects, and deals with nothing but the mere form of thought.

2. As pure logic, it has nothing to do with empirical principles, and does not, as has sometimes been supposed, borrow anything from psychology, which therefore has no influence whatever on the canon of the understanding. Pure logic is a body of demonstrated doctrine, and everything in it must be certain entirely *a priori.*

What I call applied logic (contrary to the usual meaning of this title, according to which it should contain certain exercises for which pure logic gives the rules) is a representation of the understanding and of the rules of its necessary employment *in concreto,* that is, under the accidental subjective conditions which may hinder or help its application, B 79 and which are all given only empirically. It treats of attention, its impediments and consequences, of the source of error, of the state of doubt, hesitation, and conviction, etc. Pure general logic stands to it in the same relation as pure ethics, which contains only the necessary moral laws of a free will in general, stands to the doctrine of the virtues strictly so called—the doctrine which considers these laws under the limitations of the feelings, inclinations, and passions to which men are more or less subject. Such a doctrine can never furnish a true and demonstrated science, because, like applied logic, it depends on empirical and psychological principles.

II. Transcendental Logic

General logic, as we have shown, abstracts from all content of knowledge, that is, from all relation of knowledge to the object, and considers only the logical form in the relation of any knowledge to other knowledge; that is, it treats of the form of thought in general. But since, as the Transcendental Aesthetic has shown, there are pure as well as empirical intuitions, a distinction might likewise be drawn between pure and empirical thought of objects. In that case we should have a logic in which we do not abstract from the entire content of knowledge. This other logic, which should contain solely the rules of the pure thought of an object, would exclude only those modes of knowledge which have empirical content. It would also treat of the origin of the modes in which we know objects, in so far as that origin cannot be attributed to the objects. General logic, on the other hand, has nothing to do with the origin of knowledge, but only considers representations, be they originally *a priori* in ourselves or only empirically given, according to the laws which the understanding employs when, in thinking, it relates them to one another. It deals therefore only with that form which the understanding is able to impart to the representations, from whatever source they may have arisen.

And here I make a remark which the reader must bear well in mind, as it extends its influence over all that follows. Not every kind of knowledge *a priori* should be called transcendental, but that only by which we know that—and how—certain representations (intuitions or concepts) can be employed or are possible purely *a priori*. The term "transcen-

B 80

dental," that is to say, signifies such knowledge as concerns the *a priori* possibility of knowledge, or its *a priori* employment. Neither space nor any *a priori* geometrical determination of it is a transcendental representation; what can alone be entitled transcendental is the knowledge that these representations are not of empirical origin, and the possibility that they can yet relate *a priori* to objects of experience. The application of space to objects in general would likewise be transcendental, but, if restricted solely to objects of sense, it is empirical. The distinction between the transcendental and the empirical belongs therefore only to the critique of knowledge; it does not concern the relation of that knowledge to its objects.

B 81

In the expectation, therefore, that there may perhaps be concepts which relate *a priori* to objects, not as pure or sensible intuitions, but solely as acts of pure thought—that is, as concepts which are neither of empirical nor of aesthetic origin—we form for ourselves by anticipation the idea of a science of the knowledge which belongs to pure understanding and reason, whereby we think objects entirely *a priori.* Such a science, which should determine the origin, the scope, and the objective validity of such knowledge, would have to be called *transcendental logic*, because, unlike general logic, which has to deal with both empirical and pure knowledge of reason, it concerns itself with the laws of understanding and of reason solely in so far as they relate *a priori* to objects.

B 82

III. The Division of General Logic into Analytic and Dialectic

The question, famed of old, by which logicians were supposed to be driven into a corner, obliged either to have recourse to a pitiful sophism, or to confess their ignorance and consequently the emptiness of their whole art, is the question: What is truth? The nominal definition of truth, that it is the agreement of knowledge with its object, is assumed as granted; the question asked is as to what is the general and sure criterion of the truth of any and every knowledge.

To know what questions may reasonably be asked is already a great and necessary proof of sagacity and insight. For if a question is absurd in itself and calls for an answer where none is required, it not only brings shame on the propounder of the question, but may betray an incautious listener into absurd answers, thus presenting, as the B 83 ancients said, the ludicrous spectacle of one man milking a he-goat and the other holding a sieve underneath.

If truth consists in the agreement of knowledge with its object, that object must thereby be distinguished from other objects; for knowledge is false, if it does not agree with the object to which it is related, even although it contains something which may be valid of other objects. Now a general criterion of truth must be such as would be valid in each and every instance of knowledge, however their objects may vary. It is obvious however that such a criterion [being general] cannot take account of the [varying] content of knowledge (relation to its [specific] object). But since truth concerns just this very content, it is quite impossible, and indeed absurd, to ask for a general test of the truth of such content. A sufficient and at the same time general criterion of truth cannot possibly be given. Since we have already entitled the content of knowledge its matter, we must be prepared to recognise that of the truth of knowledge, so far as its matter is concerned, no general criterion can be demanded. Such a criterion would by its very nature be self-contradictory.

But, on the other hand, as regards knowledge in respect of its mere form (leaving aside all con-
B 84 tent), it is evident that logic, in so far as it expounds the universal and necessary rules of the understanding, must in these rules furnish criteria of truth. Whatever contradicts these rules is false. For the understanding would thereby be made to contradict its own general rules of thought, and so to contradict itself. These criteria, however, concern only the form of truth, that is, of thought in general; and in so far they are quite correct, but are not by themselves sufficient. For although our knowledge may be in complete accordance with logical demands, that is, may not contradict itself, it is still possible that it may be in contradiction with its object. The purely logical criterion of truth, namely, the agreement of knowledge with the general and formal laws of the understanding and reason, is a *conditio sine qua non,* and is therefore the negative condition of all truth. But further than this logic cannot go. It has no touchstone for the discovery of such error as concerns not the form but the content.

General logic resolves the whole formal procedure of the understanding and reason into its elements, and exhibits them as principles of all logical criticism of our knowledge. This part of logic, which may therefore be entitled *analytic,* yields what is at least the negative touchstone of truth. Its rules must be applied in the examination and appraising of the form of all knowledge before we proceed to determine whether their content contains positive truth   B 85
in respect to their object. But since the mere form of knowledge, however completely it may be in agreement with logical laws, is far from being sufficient to determine the material (objective) truth of knowledge, no one can venture with the help of logic alone to judge regarding objects, or to make any assertion. We must first, independently of logic, obtain reliable information; only then are we in a position to enquire, in accordance with logical laws, into the use of this information and its connection in a coherent whole, or rather to test it by these laws. There is, however, something so tempting in the possession of an art so specious, through which we give to all our knowledge, however uninstructed we may be in regard to its content, the form of understanding, that general logic, which is merely a *canon* of judgment, has been employed as if it were an *organon* for the actual production of at least the semblance of objective assertions, and has thus been misapplied. General logic, when thus treated as an organon, is called *dialectic.*

However various were the significations in which the ancients used "dialectic" as the title for a science or art, we can safely conclude from their actual employment of it that with them it was never anything else than the *logic of illusion.* It was   B 86
a sophistical art of giving to ignorance, and indeed to intentional sophistries, the appearance of truth, and by the device of imitating the methodical thoroughness which logic prescribes, and of using its "topic" to conceal the emptiness of its pretensions. Now it may be noted as a sure and useful warning, that general logic, if viewed as an organon, is always a logic of illusion, that is, dialectical. For logic teaches us nothing whatsoever regarding the content of knowledge, but lays down only the formal conditions of agreement with the understanding; and since these conditions can tell us nothing at all as to the objects concerned, any attempt to use this logic as an instrument (organon) that professes to extend and enlarge our knowledge can end in noth-

ing but mere talk—in which, with a certain plausibility, we maintain, or, if such be our choice, attack, any and every possible assertion.

Such instruction is quite unbecoming the dignity of philosophy. The title "dialectic" has therefore come to be otherwise employed, and has been assigned to logic, as a *critique of dialectical illusion.* This is the sense in which it is to be understood in this work.

IV. The Division of Transcendental Logic
B 87 *into Transcendental Analytic and Dialectic*

In a transcendental logic we isolate the understanding—as above, in the Transcendental Aesthetic, the sensibility—separating out from our knowledge that part of thought which has its origin solely in the understanding. The employment of this pure knowledge depends upon the condition that objects to which it can be applied be given to us in intuition. In the absence of intuition all our knowledge is without objects, and therefore remains entirely empty. That part of transcendental logic which deals with the elements of the pure knowledge yielded by understanding, and the principles without which no object can be thought, is transcendental analytic. It is a logic of truth. For no knowledge can contradict it without at once losing all content, that is, all relation to any object, and therefore all truth. But since it is very tempting to use these pure modes of knowledge of the understanding and these principles by themselves, and even beyond the limits of experience, which alone can yield the
B 88 matter (objects) to which those pure concepts of understanding can be applied, the understanding is led to incur the risk of making, with a mere show of rationality, a material use of its pure and merely formal principles, and of passing judgments upon objects without distinction—upon objects which are not given to us, nay, perhaps cannot in any way be given. Since, properly, this transcendental analytic should be used only as a canon for passing judgment upon the empirical employment of the understanding, it is misapplied if appealed to as an organon of its general and unlimited application, and if consequently we venture, with the pure understanding alone, to judge synthetically, to affirm, and to decide regarding objects in general. The employment of the pure understanding then be-

comes dialectical. The second part of transcendental logic must therefore form a critique of this dialectical illusion, and is called transcendental dialectic, not as an art of producing such illusion dogmatically (an art unfortunately very commonly practised by metaphysical jugglers), but as a critique of understanding and reason in respect of their hyperphysical employment. It will expose the false, illusory character of those groundless pretensions, and in place of the high claims to discover and to extend knowledge merely by means of transcendental principles, it will substitute what is no more than a critical treatment of the pure understanding, for the guarding of it against sophistical illusion.

First Division: Transcendental Analytic
B 89

Transcendental analytic consists in the dissection of all our *a priori* knowledge into the elements that pure understanding by itself yields. In so doing, the following are the points of chief concern: (1) that the concepts be pure and not empirical; (2) that they belong, not to intuition and sensibility, but to thought and understanding; (3) that they be fundamental and be carefully distinguished from those which are derivative or composite; (4) that our table of concepts be complete, covering the whole field of the pure understanding. When a science is an aggregate brought into existence in a merely experimental manner, such completeness can never be guaranteed by any kind of mere estimate. It is possible only by means of *an idea of the totality* of the *a priori* knowledge yielded by the understanding; such an idea can furnish an exact classification of the concepts which compose that totality, exhibiting their *interconnection in a system.* Pure understanding distinguishes itself not merely from all that is empirical but completely also from all sensibility. It is a unity B 90 self-subsistent, self-sufficient, and not to be increased by any additions from without. The sum of its knowledge thus constitutes a system, comprehended and determined by one idea. The completeness and articulation of this system can at the same time yield a criterion of the correctness and genuineness of all its components. This part of transcendental logic requires, however, for its complete exposition, two books, the one containing the *concepts,* the other the *principles* of pure understanding.

Book I. Analytic of Concepts

By "analytic of concepts" I do not understand their analysis, or the procedure usual in philosophical investigations, that of dissecting the content of such concepts as may present themselves, and so of rendering them more distinct; but the hitherto rarely attempted *dissection of the faculty of the understanding* itself, in order to investigate the possibility of concepts *a priori* by looking for them in the understanding alone, as their birthplace, and by analysing the pure use of this faculty. This is the proper task of a transcendental philosophy; anything beyond this belongs to the logical treatment of concepts in philosophy in general. We shall therefore follow up the pure concepts to their first seeds and dispositions in the human understanding, in which they lie prepared, till at last, on the occasion of experience, they are developed, and by the same understanding are exhibited in their purity, freed from the empirical conditions attaching to them.

B 91

Chapter I. The Clue to the Discovery of All Pure Concepts of the Understanding

When we call a faculty of knowledge into play, then, as the occasioning circumstances differ, various concepts stand forth and make the faculty known, and allow of their being collected with more or less completeness, in proportion as observation has been made of them over a longer time or with greater acuteness. But when the enquiry is carried on in this mechanical fashion, we can never be sure whether it has been brought to completion. Further, the concepts which we thus discover only as opportunity offers, exhibit no order and systematic unity, but are in the end merely arranged in pairs according to similarities, and in series according to the amount of their contents, from the simple on to the more composite—an arrangement which is anything but systematic, although to a certain extent methodically instituted.

B 92

Transcendental philosophy, in seeking for its concepts, has the advantage and also the duty of proceeding according to a single principle. For these concepts spring, pure and unmixed, out of the understanding which is an absolute unity; and must therefore be connected with each other according to one concept or idea. Such a connection supplies us with a rule, by which we are enabled to assign its proper place to each pure concept of the understanding, and by which we can determine in an *a priori* manner their systematic completeness. Otherwise we should be dependent in these matters on our own discretionary judgment or merely on chance.

Section 1. The Logical Employment of the Understanding The understanding has thus far been explained merely negatively, as a non-sensible faculty of knowledge. Now since without sensibility we cannot have any intuition, understanding cannot be a faculty of intuition. But besides intuition there is no other mode of knowledge except by means of concepts. The knowledge yielded by understanding, or at least by the human understanding, must therefore be by means of concepts, and so is not intuitive, but discursive. Whereas all intuitions, as sensible, rest on affections, concepts rest on functions. By "function" I mean the unity of the act of bringing various representations under one common representation. Concepts are based on the spontaneity of thought, sensible intuitions on the receptivity of impressions. Now the only use which the understanding can make of these concepts is to judge by means of them. Since no representation, save when it is an intuition, is in immediate relation to an object, no concept is ever related to an object immediately, but to some other representation of it, be that other representation an intuition, or itself a concept. Judgment is therefore the mediate knowledge of an object, that is, the representation of a representation of it. In every judgment there is a concept which holds of many representations, and among them of a given representation that is immediately related to an object. Thus in the judgment, "all bodies are divisible," the concept of the divisible applies to various other concepts, but is here applied in particular to the concept of body, and this concept again to certain appearances that present themselves to us. These objects, therefore, are mediately represented through the concept of divisibility. Accordingly, all judgments are func-

B 93

B 94 tions of unity among our representations; instead of an immediate representation, a *higher* representation, which comprises the immediate representation and various others, is used in knowing the object, and thereby much possible knowledge is collected into one. Now we can reduce all acts of the understanding to judgments, and the *understanding* may therefore be represented as a *faculty of judgment*. For, as stated above, the understanding is a faculty of thought. Thought is knowledge by means of concepts. But concepts, as predicates of possible judgments, relate to some representation of a not *yet* determined object. Thus the concept of body means something, for instance, metal, which can be known by means of that concept. It is therefore a concept solely in virtue of its comprehending other representations, by means of which it can relate to objects. It is therefore the predicate of a possible judgment, for instance, "every metal is a body." The functions of the understanding can, therefore, be discovered if we can give an exhaustive statement of the functions of unity in judgments. That this can quite easily be done will be shown in the next section.

B 95 *Section 2. § 9 The Logical Function of the Understanding in Judgments* If we abstract from all content of a judgment, and consider only the mere form of understanding, we find that the function of thought in judgment can be brought under four heads, each of which contains three moments. They may be conveniently represented in the following table:

I
Quantity of Judgments
Universal
Particular
Singular

II	III
Quality	*Relation*
Affirmative	Categorical
Negative	Hypothetical
Infinite	Disjunctive

IV
Modality
Problematic
Assertoric
Apodeictic

As this division appears to depart in some, though not in any essential respects, from the technical distinctions ordinarily recognised by logicians, the following observations may serve to guard against any possible misunderstanding. B 96

1. Logicians are justified in saying that, in the employment of judgments in syllogisms, singular judgments can be treated like those that are universal. For, since they have no extension at all, the predicate cannot relate to part only of that which is contained in the concept of the subject, and be excluded from the rest. The predicate is valid of that concept, without any such exception, just as if it were a general concept and had an extension to the whole of which the predicate applied. If, on the other hand, we compare a singular with a universal judgment, merely as knowledge, in respect of quantity, the singular stands to the universal as unity to infinity, and is therefore in itself essentially different from the universal. If, therefore, we estimate a singular judgment (*judicium singulare*), not only according to its own inner validity, but as knowledge in general, according to its quantity in comparison with other knowledge, it is certainly different from general judgments (*judicia communia*), and in a complete table of the moments of thought in general deserves a separate place—though not, indeed, in a logic limited to the use of judgments in reference to B 97 each other.

2. In like manner *infinite judgments* must, in transcendental logic, be distinguished from those that are *affirmative*, although in general logic they are rightly classed with them, and do not constitute a separate member of the division. General logic abstracts from all content of the predicate (even though it be negative); it enquires only whether the predicate be ascribed to the subject or opposed to it. But transcendental logic also considers what may be the worth of content of a logical affirmation that is thus made by means of a merely negative predicate, and what is thereby achieved in the way of addition to our total knowledge. If I should say of the soul, "It is not mortal," by this negative judgment I should at least have warded off error. Now by the proposition, "The soul is non-mortal," I have, so far as the logical form is concerned, really made an affirmation. I locate the soul in the unlimited sphere of non-mortal beings. Since the mortal constitutes one part of the whole extension of possible beings,

and the non-mortal the other, nothing more is said by my proposition than that the soul is one of the infinite number of things which remain over when I take away all that is mortal. The infinite sphere of all that is possible is thereby only so far limited that the mortal is excluded from it, and that the soul is located in the remaining part of its extension. But, even allowing for such exclusion, this extension still remains infinite, and several more parts of it may be taken away without the concept of the soul being thereby in the least increased, or determined in an affirmative manner. These judgments, though infinite in respect of their logical extension, are thus, in respect of the content of their knowledge, limitative only, and cannot therefore be passed over in a transcendental table of all moments of thought in judgments, since the function of the understanding thereby expressed may perhaps be of importance in the field of its pure *a priori* knowledge.

3. All relations of thought in judgments are (*a*) of the predicate to the subject, (*b*) of the ground to its consequence, (*c*) of the divided knowledge and of the members of the division, taken together, to each other. In the first kind of judgments we consider only two concepts, in the second two judgments, in the third several judgments in their relation to each other. The hypothetical proposition, "If there is a perfect justice, the obstinately wicked are punished," really contains the relation of two propositions, namely, "There is a perfect justice," and "The obstinately wicked are punished." Whether both these propositions are in themselves true, here remains undetermined. It is only the logical sequence which is thought by this judgment. Finally, the disjunctive judgment contains a relation of two or more propositions to each other, a relation not, however, of logical sequence, but of logical opposition, in so far as the sphere of the one excludes the sphere of the other, and yet at the same time of community, in so far as the propositions taken together occupy the whole sphere of the knowledge in question. The disjunctive judgment expresses, therefore, a relation of the parts of the sphere of such knowledge, since the sphere of each part is a complement of the sphere of the others, yielding together the sum-total of the divided knowledge. Take, for instance, the judgment, "The world exists either through blind chance, or through inner necessity, or through an external cause." Each of these

propositions occupies a part of the sphere of the possible knowledge concerning the existence of a world in general; all of them together occupy the whole sphere. To take the knowledge out of one of these spheres means placing it in one of the other spheres, and to place it in one sphere means taking it out of the others. There is, therefore, in a disjunctive judgment a certain community of the known constituents, such that they mutually exclude each other, and yet thereby determine *in their totality* the true knowledge. For, when taken together, they constitute the whole content of one given knowledge. This is all that need here be considered, so far as concerns what follows.

4. The *modality* of judgments is a quite peculiar function. Its distinguishing characteristic is that it contributes nothing to the content of the judgment (for, besides quantity, quality, and relation, there is nothing that constitutes the content of a judgment), but concerns only the value of the copula in relation to thought in general. Problematic judgments are those in which affirmation or negation is taken as merely possible (optional). In assertoric judgments affirmation or negation is viewed as real (true), and in apodeictic judgments as necessary. Thus the two judgments, the relation of which constitutes the hypothetical judgment (*antecedens et consequens*), and likewise the judgments the reciprocal relation of which forms the disjunctive judgment (members of the division), are one and all problematic only. In the above example, the proposition, "There is a perfect justice," is not stated assertorically, but is thought only as an optional judgment, which it is possible to assume; it is only the logical sequence which is assertoric. Such judgments may therefore be obviously false, and yet, taken problematically, may be conditions of the knowledge of truth. Thus the judgment, "The world exists by blind chance," has in the disjunctive judgment only problematic meaning, namely, as a proposition that may for a moment be assumed. At the same time, like the indication of a false road among the number of all those roads that can be taken, it aids in the discovery of the true proposition. The problematic proposition is therefore that which expresses only logical (which is not objective) possibility—a free choice of admitting such a proposition, and a purely optional admission of it into the understanding. The assertoric proposition deals with logical reality or

truth. Thus, for instance, in a hypothetical syllogism the antecedent is in the major premise problematic, in the minor assertoric, and what the syllogism shows is that the consequence follows in accordance with the laws of the understanding. The apodeictic proposition thinks the assertoric as determined by these laws of the understanding, and therefore as affirming *a priori*; and in this manner it expresses logical necessity. Since everything is thus incorporated in the understanding step by step—inasmuch as we first judge something problematically, then maintain its truth assertorically, and finally affirm it as inseparably united with the understanding, that is, as necessary and apodeictic—we are justified in regarding these three functions of modality as so many moments of thought.

B 102 *Section 3. § 10   The Pure Concepts of the Understanding, or Categories* General logic, as has been repeatedly said, abstracts from all content of knowledge, and looks to some other source, whatever that may be, for the representations which it is to transform into concepts by process of analysis. Transcendental logic, on the other hand, has lying before it a manifold of *a priori* sensibility, presented by transcendental aesthetic, as material for the concepts of pure understanding. In the absence of this material those concepts would be without any content, therefore entirely empty. Space and time contain a manifold of pure *a priori* intuition, but at the same time are conditions of the receptivity of our mind—conditions under which alone it can receive representations of objects, and which therefore must also always affect the concept of these objects. But if this manifold is to be known, the spontaneity of our thought requires that it be gone through in a certain way, taken up, and connected. This act I name *synthesis*.

B 103   *By synthesis*, in its most general sense, I understand the act of putting different representations together, and of grasping what is manifold in them in one [act of] knowledge. Such a synthesis is *pure*, if the manifold is not empirical but is given *a priori*, as is the manifold in space and time. Before we can analyse our representations, the representations must themselves be given, and therefore as regards *content* no concepts can first arise by way of analysis. Synthesis of a manifold (be it given empirically or *a priori*) is what first gives rise to knowledge. This

knowledge may, indeed, at first, be crude and confused, and therefore in need of analysis. Still the synthesis is that which gathers the elements for knowledge, and unites them to [form] a certain content. It is to synthesis, therefore, that we must first direct our attention, if we would determine the first origin of our knowledge.

Synthesis in general, as we shall hereafter see, is the mere result of the power of imagination, a blind but indispensable function of the soul, without which we should have no knowledge whatsoever, but of which we are scarcely ever conscious. To bring this synthesis *to concepts* is a function which belongs to the understanding, and it is through this function of the understanding that we first obtain knowledge properly so called.

Pure synthesis, *represented in its most general* B 104 *aspect*, gives us the pure concept of the understanding. By this pure synthesis I understand that which rests upon a basis of *a priori* synthetic unity. Thus our counting, as is easily seen in the case of larger numbers, is a synthesis according to concepts, because it is executed according to a common ground of unity, as, for instance, the decade. In terms of this concept, the unity of the synthesis of the manifold is rendered necessary.

By means of analysis different representations are brought under one concept—a procedure treated of in general logic. What transcendental logic, on the other hand, teaches, is how we bring to concepts, not representations, but the *pure synthesis* of representations. What must first be given—with a view to the *a priori* knowledge of all objects—is the *manifold* of pure intuition; the second factor involved is the *synthesis* of this manifold by means of the imagination. But even this does not yet yield knowledge. The concepts which give *unity* to this pure synthesis, and which consist solely in the representation of this necessary synthetic unity, furnish the third requisite for the knowledge of an object; and they rest on the understanding.

The same function which gives unity to the various representations *in a judgment* also gives unity to the mere synthesis of various representa- B 105 tions *in an intuition*; and this unity, in its most general expression, we entitle the pure concept of the understanding. The same understanding, through the same operations by which in concepts, by means of analytical unity, it produced the logical form of a judgment, also introduces a transcendental content into its representations, by means of the synthetic unity of the manifold in intuition in general. On this account we are entitled to call these representations pure concepts of the understanding, and to regard them as applying *a priori* to objects—a conclusion which general logic is not in a position to establish.

In this manner there arise precisely the same number of pure concepts of the understanding which apply *a priori* to objects of intuition in general, as, in the preceding table, there have been found to be logical functions in all possible judgments. For these functions specify the understanding completely, and yield an exhaustive inventory of its powers. These concepts we shall, with Aristotle, call *categories,* for our primary purpose is the same as his, although widely diverging from it in manner of execution.

B 106

TABLE OF CATEGORIES
I
Of Quantity
Unity
Plurality
Totality

II	III
Of Quality	*Of Relation*
Reality	Of Inherence and Subsistence
Negation	(*substantia et accidens*)
Limitation	Of Causality and Dependence
	(*cause and effect*)
	Of Community (reciprocity
	between agent and patient)

IV
Of Modality
Possibility—Impossibility
Existence—Non-existence
Necessity—Contingency

This then is the list of all original pure concepts of synthesis that the understanding contains within itself *a priori*. Indeed, it is because it contains these concepts that it is called pure understanding; for by them alone can it *understand* anything in the manifold of intuition, that is, think an object of intuition. This division is developed systematically from a common principle, namely, the faculty of judgment

(which is the same as the faculty of thought). It has not arisen rhapsodically, as the result of a haphazard search after pure concepts, the complete enumeration of which, as based on induction only, could never be guaranteed. Nor could we, if this were our procedure, discover why just these concepts, and no others, have their seat in the pure understanding. It was an enterprise worthy of an acute thinker like Aristotle to make search for these fundamental concepts. But as he did so on no principle, he merely picked them up as they came his way, and at first procured ten of them, which he called *categories* (predicaments). Afterwards he believed that he had discovered five others, which he added under the name of post-predicaments. But his table still remained defective. Besides, there are to be found in it some modes of pure sensibility (*quando, ubi, situs,* also *prius, simul*), and an empirical concept (*motus*), none of which have any place in a table of the concepts that trace their origin to the understanding. Aristotle's list also enumerates among the original concepts some derivative concepts (*actio, passio*); and of the original concepts some are entirely lacking.

B 107

In this connection, it is to be remarked that the categories, as the true primary concepts of the pure understanding, have also their pure derivative concepts. These could not be passed over in a complete system of transcendental philosophy, but in a merely critical essay the simple mention of the fact may suffice.

I beg permission to entitle these pure but derivative concepts of the understanding the *predicables* of the pure understanding—to distinguish them from the predicaments [i.e., the categories]. If we have the original and primitive concepts, it is easy to add the derivative and subsidiary, and so to give a complete picture of the family tree of the [concepts of] pure understanding. Since at present we are concerned not with the completeness of the system, but only with the principles to be followed in its construction, I reserve this supplementary work for another occasion. It can easily be carried out, with the aid of the ontological manuals—for instance, by placing under the category of causality the predicables of force, action, passion; under the category of community the predicables of presence, resistance; under the predicaments of modality the predicables of coming to be, ceasing to be, change,

B 108

etc. The categories, when combined with the modes of pure sensibility, or with one another, yield a large number of derivative *a priori* concepts. To note, and, where possible, to give a complete inventory of these concepts, would be a useful and not unpleasant task, but it is a task from which we can here be absolved.

In this treatise, I purposely omit the definitions of the categories, although I may be in possession of them. I shall proceed to analyse these concepts only so far as is necessary in connection with the doctrine of method which I am propounding. In a system of pure reason, definitions of the categories would rightly be demanded, but in this treatise they would merely divert attention from the main object of the enquiry, arousing doubts and objections which, without detriment to what is essential to our purposes, can very well be reserved for another occasion. Meanwhile, from the little that I have said, it will be obvious that a complete glossary, with all the requisite explanations, is not only a possible, but an easy task. The divisions are provided; all that is required is to fill them; and a systematic "topic," such as that here given, affords sufficient guidance as to the proper location of each concept, while at the same time indicating which divisions are still empty.

§ *11* This table of categories suggests some nice points, which may perhaps have important consequences in regard to the scientific form of all modes of knowledge obtainable by reason. For that this table is extremely useful in the theoretical part of philosophy, and indeed is indispensable as supplying the *complete plan of a whole science,* so far as that science rests on *a priori* concepts, and as dividing it systematically *according to determinate principles,* is already evident from the fact that the table contains all the elementary concepts of the understanding in their completeness, nay, even the form of a system of them in the human understanding, and accordingly indicates all the *momenta* of a projected speculative science, and even their *order,* as I have elsewhere shown.

The first of the considerations suggested by the table is that while it contains four classes of the concepts of understanding, it may, in the first instance, be divided into two groups; those in the first group being concerned with objects of intuition, pure as well as empirical, those in the second group with the existence of these objects, in their relation either to each other or to the understanding.

The categories in the first group I would entitle the *mathematical,* those in the second group the *dynamical.* The former have no correlates; these are to be met with only in the second group. This distinction must have some ground in the nature of the understanding.

Secondly, in view of the fact that all *a priori* division of concepts must be by dichotomy, it is significant that in each class the number of the categories is always the same, namely, three. Further, it may be observed that the third category in each class always arises from the combination of the second category with the first.

Thus *allness* or *totality* is just plurality considered as unity; *limitation* is simply reality combined with negation; *community* is the causality of substances reciprocally determining one another; lastly, *necessity* is just the existence which is given through possibility itself. It must not be supposed, however, that the third category is therefore merely a derivative, and not a primary, concept of the pure understanding. For the combination of the first and second concepts, in order that the third may be produced, requires a special act of the understanding, which is not identical with that which is exercised in the case of the first and the second. Thus the concept of a *number* (which belongs to the category of totality) is not always possible simply upon the presence of concepts of plurality and unity (for instance, in the representation of the infinite); nor can I, by simply combining the concept of a cause and that of a substance, at once have understanding of *influence,* that is, how a substance can be the cause of something in another substance. Obviously in these cases, a separate act of the understanding is demanded; and similarly in the others.

Thirdly, in the case of one category, namely, that of *community,* which is found in the third group, its accordance with the form of a disjunctive judgment—the form which corresponds to it in the table of logical functions—is not as evident as in the case of the others.

To gain assurance that they do actually accord, we must observe that in all disjunctive judgments the sphere (that is, the multiplicity which is contained in any one judgment) is represented as a whole divided into parts (the subordinate concepts), and that since no one of them can be contained under any other, they are thought as co-ordinated with, not subordinated to, each other, and so as determining each other, not in one direction only, as in a series, but reciprocally, as in an aggregate—if one member of the division is posited, all the rest are excluded, and conversely.

Now in a *whole* which is made up of *things*, a similar combination is being thought; for one thing is not subordinated, as effect, to another, as cause of its existence, but, simultaneously and reciprocally, is co-ordinated with it, as cause of the determination of the other (as, for instance, in a body the parts of which reciprocally attract and repel each other). This is a quite different kind of connection from that which is found in the mere relation of cause to effect (of ground to consequence), for in the latter relation the consequence does not in its turn reciprocally determine the ground, and therefore does not constitute with it a whole—thus the world, for instance, does not with its Creator serve to constitute a whole. The procedure which the

B 113 understanding follows in representing to itself the sphere of a divided concept it likewise follows when it thinks a thing as divisible; and just as, in the former case, the members of a division exclude each other, and yet are combined in one sphere, so the understanding represents to itself the parts of the latter as existing (as substances) in such a way that, while each exists independently of the others, they are yet combined together in one whole.

§ 12   In the transcendental philosophy of the ancients there is included yet another chapter containing pure concepts of the understanding which, though not enumerated among the categories, must, on their view, be ranked as *a priori* concepts of objects. This, however, would amount to an increase in the number of the categories, and is therefore not feasible. They are propounded in the proposition, so famous among the Schoolmen, *quodlibet ens est unum, verum, bonum.* Now, although the application of this principle has proved very meagre in consequences, and has indeed yielded only propositions that are tautological, and therefore in recent times has retained its place in metaphysics almost by courtesy only, yet, on the other hand, it represents a view which, however empty it may seem to be, has

maintained itself over this very long period. It therefore deserves to be investigated in respect of its origin, and we are justified in conjecturing that it has its ground in some rule of the understanding which, as often happens, has only been wrongly interpreted. These supposedly transcendental predicates   B 114 of *things* are, in fact, nothing but logical requirements and criteria of all *knowledge* of things in general, and prescribe for such knowledge the categories of quantity, namely, *unity, plurality,* and *totality.* But these categories, which, properly regarded, must be taken as material, belonging to the possibility of the things themselves [empirical objects], have, in this further application, been used only in their formal meaning, as being of the nature of logical requisites of all knowledge, and yet at the same time have been incautiously converted from being criteria of thought to be properties of things in themselves. In all knowledge of an object there is *unity* of concept, which may be entitled *qualitative unity,* so far as we think by it only the unity in the combination of the manifold of our knowledge: as, for example, the unity of the theme in a play, a speech, or a story. Secondly, there is *truth,* in respect of its consequences. The greater the number of true consequences that follow from a given concept, the more criteria are there of its objective reality. This might be entitled the *qualitative plurality* of characters, which belong to a concept as to a common ground (but are not thought in it, as quantity). Thirdly, and lastly, there is *perfection,* which consists in this, that the plurality together leads back to the unity of the concept, and accords completely with this and with no other concept. This may be entitled the *qualitative completeness* (totality). Hence it is evident that these logical criteria of the possibility of   B 115 knowledge in general are the three categories of quantity, in which the unity in the production of the quantum has to be taken as homogeneous throughout; and that these categories are here being transformed so as also to yield connection of *heterogeneous* knowledge in one consciousness, by means of the quality of the knowledge as the principle of the connection. Thus the criterion of the possibility of a concept (not of an object) is the definition of it, in which the *unity* of the concept, the *truth* of all that may be immediately deduced from it, and finally, the *completeness* of what has been thus deduced from it, yield all that is required for the construction of the whole concept. Similarly, the criterion of a hypothesis consists in the intelligibility of the assumed ground of explanation, that is, in its *unity* (without any auxiliary hypothesis); in the *truth* of the consequences that can be deduced from it (their accordance with themselves and with experience); and finally, in the *completeness* of the ground of explanation of these consequences, which carry us back to neither more nor less than was assumed in the hypothesis, and so in an *a posteriori* analytic manner give us back and accord with what has previously been thought in a synthetic *a priori* manner. We have not, therefore, in the concepts of unity, truth, and perfection, made any addition to the transcendental table of the categories, as if it were in any respect imperfect. All that we have done is to bring the employment of these concepts under general logical rules, for the agreement of knowledge with itself—the question of their relation to objects

B 116 not being in any way under discussion.

Chapter II. The Deduction of the Pure Concepts of Understanding

Section 1. § 13   The Principles of Any Transcendental Deduction   Jurists, when speaking of rights and claims, distinguish in a legal action the question of right (*quid juris*) from the question of fact (*quid facti*; and they demand that both be proved. Proof of the former, which has to state the right or the legal claim, they entitle the *deduction*. Many empirical concepts are employed without question from anyone. Since experience is always available for the proof of their objective reality, we believe ourselves, even without a deduction, to be justified

B 117 in appropriating to them a meaning, an ascribed significance. But there are also usurpatory concepts, such as *fortune, fate,* which, though allowed to circulate by almost universal indulgence, are yet from time to time challenged by the question: *quid juris.* This demand for a deduction involves us in considerable perplexity, no clear legal title, sufficient to justify their employment, being obtainable either from experience or from reason.

Now among the manifold concepts which form the highly complicated web of human knowledge, there are some which are marked out for pure *a priori* employment, in complete independence of all

experience; and their right to be so employed always demands a deduction. For since empirical proofs do not suffice to justify this kind of employment, we are faced by the problem how these concepts can relate to objects which they yet do not obtain from any experience. The explanation of the manner in which concepts can thus relate *a priori* to objects I entitle their transcendental deduction; and from it I distinguish empirical deduction, which shows the manner in which a concept is acquired through experience and through reflection upon experience, and which therefore concerns, not its legitimacy, but only its *de facto* mode of origination.

We are already in possession of concepts which are of two quite different kinds, and which yet agree   B 118 in that they relate to objects in a completely *a priori* manner, namely, the concepts of space and time as forms of sensibility, and the categories as concepts of understanding. To seek an empirical deduction of either of these types of concept would be labour entirely lost. For their distinguishing feature consists just in this, that they relate to their objects without having borrowed from experience anything that can serve in the representation of these objects. If, therefore, a deduction of such concepts is indispensable, it must in any case be transcendental.

We can, however, with regard to these concepts, as with regard to all knowledge, seek to discover in experience, if not the principle of their possibility, at least the occasioning causes of their production. The impressions of the senses supplying the first stimulus, the whole faculty of knowledge opens out to them, and experience is brought into existence. That experience contains two very dissimilar elements, namely, the *matter* of knowledge [obtained] from the senses, and a certain *form* for the ordering of this matter, [obtained] from the inner source of the pure intuition and thought which, on occasion of the sense-impressions, are first brought into action and yield concepts. Such an investigation of the first strivings of our faculty of knowledge, whereby it advances from particular perceptions to universal concepts, is undoubtedly   B 119 of great service. We are indebted to the celebrated Locke for opening out this new line of enquiry. But a *deduction* of the pure *a priori* concepts can never be obtained in this manner; it is not to be looked for in any such direction. For in view of their subsequent employment, which has to be entirely independent of experience, they must be in a position to show a certificate of birth quite other than that of descent from experiences. Since this attempted physiological derivation concerns a *quaestio facti,* it cannot strictly be called deduction; and I shall therefore entitle it the explanation of the *possession* of pure knowledge. Plainly the only deduction that can be given of this knowledge is one that is transcendental, not empirical. In respect to pure *a priori* concepts the latter type of deduction is an utterly useless enterprise which can be engaged in only by those who have failed to grasp the quite peculiar nature of these modes of knowledge.

But although it may be admitted that the only kind of deduction of pure *a priori* knowledge which is possible is on transcendental lines, it is not at once obvious that a deduction is indispensably necessary. We have already, by means of a transcendental deduction, traced the concepts of space and time to their sources, and have explained and deter-

B 120   mined their *a priori* objective validity. Geometry, however, proceeds with security in knowledge that is completely *a priori,* and has no need to beseech philosophy for any certificate of the pure and legitimate descent of its fundamental concept of space. But the concept is employed in this science only in its reference to the outer sensible world—of the intuition of which space is the pure form—where all geometrical knowledge, grounded as it is in *a priori* intuition, possesses immediate evidence. The objects, so far as their form is concerned, are given, through the very knowledge of them, *a priori* in intuition. In the case of the *pure concepts of understanding,* it is quite otherwise; it is with them that the unavoidable demand for a transcendental deduction, not only of themselves, but also of the concept of space, first originates. For since they speak of objects through predicates not of intuition and sensibility but of pure *a priori* thought, they relate to objects universally, that is, apart from all conditions of sensibility. Also, not being grounded in experience, they cannot, in *a priori* intuition, exhibit any object such as might, prior to all experience, serve as ground for their synthesis. For these reasons, they arouse suspicion not merely in regard to the objective validity and the limits of their own employment, but owing to their tendency to employ the *concept of space* beyond the conditions of sensible intuition, that concept also they render ambiguous;

and this, indeed, is why we have already found a transcendental deduction of it necessary. The reader   B 121 must therefore be convinced of the unavoidable necessity of such a transcendental deduction before he has taken a single step in the field of pure reason. Otherwise he proceeds blindly, and after manifold wanderings must come back to the same ignorance from which he started. At the same time, if he is not to lament over obscurity in matters which are by their very nature deeply veiled, or to be too easily discouraged in the removal of obstacles, he must have a clear foreknowledge of the inevitable difficulty of the undertaking. For we must either completely surrender all claims to make judgments of pure reason in the most highly esteemed of all fields, that which transcends the limits of all possible experience, or else bring this critical enquiry to completion.

We have already been able with but little difficulty to explain how the concepts of space and time, although *a priori* modes of knowledge, must necessarily relate to objects, and how independently of all experience they make possible a synthetic knowledge of objects. For since only by means of such pure forms of sensibility can an object appear to us, and so be an object of empirical intuition, space and time are pure intuitions which contain *a priori* the condition of the possibility of objects as appearances, and the synthesis which takes place in them   B 122 has objective validity.

The categories of understanding, on the other hand, do not represent the conditions under which objects are given in intuition. Objects may, therefore, appear to us without their being under the necessity of being related to the functions of understanding; and understanding need not, therefore, contain their *a priori* conditions. Thus a difficulty such as we did not meet with in the field of sensibility is here presented, namely, how *subjective conditions of thought* can have *objective validity,* that is, can furnish conditions of the possibility of all knowledge of objects. For appearances can certainly be given in intuition independently of functions of the understanding. Let us take, for instance, the concept of cause, which signifies a special kind of synthesis, whereby upon something, A, there is posited something quite different, B, according to a rule. It is not manifest *a priori* why appearances should contain anything of this kind (experiences cannot be cited in its proof, for what has to be established is the objective validity of a concept that is *a priori*); and it is therefore *a priori* doubtful whether such a concept be not perhaps altogether empty, and have no object anywhere among ap-

B 123 pearances. That objects of sensible intuition must conform to the formal conditions of sensibility which lie *a priori* in the mind is evident, because otherwise they would not be objects for us. But that they must likewise conform to the conditions which the understanding requires for the synthetic unity of thought, is a conclusion the grounds of which are by no means so obvious. Appearances might very well be so constituted that the understanding should not find them to be in accordance with the conditions of its unity. Everything might be in such confusion that, for instance, in the series of appearances nothing presented itself which might yield a rule of synthesis and so answer to the concept of cause and effect. This concept would then be altogether empty, null, and meaningless. But since intuition stands in no need whatsoever of the functions of thought, appearances would none the less present objects to our intuition.

If we thought to escape these toilsome enquiries by saying that experience continually presents examples of such regularity among appearances and so affords abundant opportunity of abstracting the concept of cause, and at the same time of verifying the objective validity of such a concept, we should be overlooking the fact that the concept of cause can never arise in this manner. It must either be grounded completely *a priori* in the understanding, or must be entirely given up as a mere phantom

B 124 of the brain. For this concept makes strict demand that something, A, should be such that something else, B, follows from it *necessarily and in accordance with an absolutely universal rule.* Appearances do indeed present cases from which a rule can be obtained according to which something usually happens, but they never prove the sequence to be *necessary.* To the synthesis of cause and effect there belongs a dignity which cannot be empirically expressed, namely, that the effect not only succeeds upon the cause, but that it is posited *through* it and arises *out of* it. This strict universality of the rule is never a characteristic of empirical rules; they can acquire through induction only comparative universality, that is, extensive applicability. If we were to

treat pure concepts of understanding as merely empirical products, we should be making a complete change in [the manner of] their employment.

§ 14 Transition to the Transcendental Deduction of the Categories There are only two possible ways in which synthetic representations and their objects can establish connection, obtain necessary relation to one another, and, as it were, meet one another. Either the object alone must make the representation possible, or the representation alone must make the object possible. In the former case, this relation is only empirical, and the representation B 125 is never possible *a priori.* This is true of appearances, as regards that [element] in them which belongs to sensation. In the latter case, representation in itself does not produce its object in so far as *existence* is concerned, for we are not here speaking of its causality by means of the will. None the less the representation is *a priori* determinant of the object, if it be the case that only through the representation is it possible to *know* anything *as an object.* Now there are two conditions under which alone the knowledge of an object is possible, first, *intuition,* through which it is given, though only as an appearance; secondly, *concept,* through which an object is thought corresponding to this intuition. It is evident from the above that the first condition, namely, that under which alone objects can be intuited, does actually lie *a priori* in the mind as the formal ground of the objects. All appearances necessarily agree with this formal condition of sensibility, since only through it can they appear, that is, be empirically intuited and given. The question now arises whether *a priori* concepts do not also serve as antecedent conditions under which alone anything can be, if not intuited, yet thought as object in general. In that case all empirical knowledge of objects would necessarily B 126 conform to such concepts, because only as thus presupposing them is anything possible as *object of experience.* Now all experience does indeed contain, in addition to the intuition of the senses through which something is given, a *concept* of an object as being thereby given, that is to say, as appearing. Concepts of objects in general thus underlie all empirical knowledge as its *a priori* conditions. The objective validity of the categories as *a priori* concepts rests, therefore, on the fact that, so far as the form of thought is concerned, through them alone does

experience become possible. They relate of necessity and *a priori* to objects of experience, for the reason that only by means of them can any object whatsoever of experience be thought.

The transcendental deduction of all *a priori* concepts has thus a principle according to which the whole enquiry must be directed, namely, that they must be recognised as *a priori* conditions of the possibility of experience, whether of the intuition which is to be met with in it or of the thought. Concepts which yield the objective ground of the possibility of experience are for this very reason necessary. But the unfolding of the experience wherein they are encountered is not their deduction; it is only their illustration. For on any such exposition they would be merely accidental. Save through their original relation to possible experi-
B 127   ence, in which all objects of knowledge are found, their relation to any one object would be quite incomprehensible.

The illustrious Locke, failing to take account of these considerations, and meeting with pure concepts of the understanding in experience, deduced them also from experience, and yet proceeded so *inconsequently* that he attempted with their aid to obtain knowledge which far transcends all limits of experience. David Hume recognised that, in order to be able to do this, it was necessary that these concepts should have an *a priori* origin. But since he could not explain how it can be possible that the understanding must think concepts, which are not in themselves connected in the understanding, as being necessarily connected in the object, and since it never occurred to him that the understanding might itself, perhaps, through these concepts, be the author of the experience in which its objects are found, he was constrained to derive them from experience, namely, from a subjective necessity (that is, from *custom*), which arises from repeated association in experience, and which comes mistakenly to be regarded as objective. But from these premises he argued quite consistently. It is impossible, he declared, with these concepts and the principles to which they give rise, to pass beyond the limits of
B 128   experience. Now, this *empirical* derivation, in which both philosophers agree, cannot be reconciled with the scientific *a priori* knowledge which we do actually possess, namely, *pure mathematics* and *general*

science of nature; and this fact therefore suffices to disprove such derivation.

While the former of these two illustrious men opened a wide door to *enthusiasm*—for if reason once be allowed such rights, it will no longer allow itself to be kept within bounds by vaguely defined recommendations of moderation—the other gave himself over entirely to *scepticism,* having, as he believed, discovered that what had hitherto been regarded as reason was but an all-prevalent illusion infecting our faculty of knowledge. We now propose to make trial whether it be not possible to find for human reason safe conduct between these two rocks, assigning to her determinate limits, and yet keeping open for her the whole field of her appropriate activities.

But first I shall introduce a word of explanation in regard to the categories. They are concepts of an object in general, by means of which the intuition of an object is regarded as determined in respect of one of the logical functions of judgment. Thus the function of the categorical judgment is that of the relation of subject to predicate; for example, "All bodies are divisible." But as regards the merely logical employment of the understanding, it remains undetermined to which of the two concepts the function of the subject, and to which the function of predicate, is to be assigned. For we can also say, "Something divisible is a body." But when the   B 129
concept of body is brought under the category of substance, it is thereby determined that its empirical intuition in experience must always be considered as subject and never as mere predicate. Similarly with all the other categories.

Section 2. Transcendental Deduction of the Pure Concepts of the Understanding. § 15   The Possibility of Combination in General The manifold of representations can be given in an intuition which is purely sensible, that is, nothing but receptivity; and the form of this intuition can lie *a priori* in our faculty of representation, without being anything more than the mode in which the subject is affected. But the combination (*conjunctio*) of a manifold in general can never come to us through the senses, and cannot, therefore, be already contained in the pure form of sensible intuition. For it is an act of spontaneity of the faculty of representation; and since   B 130 this faculty, to distinguish it from sensibility, must be entitled understanding, all combination—be we conscious of it or not, be it a combination of the manifold of intuition, empirical or non-empirical, or of various concepts—is an act of the understanding. To this act the general title "synthesis" may be assigned, as indicating that we cannot represent to ourselves anything as combined in the object which we have not ourselves previously combined, and that of all representations *combination* is the only one which cannot be given through objects. Being an act of the self-activity of the subject, it cannot be executed save by the subject itself. It will easily be observed that this action is originally one and is equipollent for all combination, and that its dissolution, namely, *analysis,* which appears to be its opposite, yet always presupposes it. For where the understanding has not previously combined, it cannot dissolve, since only as having been combined *by the understanding* can anything that allows of analysis be given to the faculty of representation.

But the concept of combination includes, besides the concept of the manifold and of its synthesis, also the concept of the unity of the manifold.
B 131   Combination is representation of the *synthetic* unity of the manifold.* The representation of this unity cannot, therefore, arise out of the combination. On the contrary, it is what, by adding itself to the representation of the manifold, first makes possible the concept of the combination. This unity, which precedes *a priori* all concepts of combination, is not the category of unity (§ 10); for all categories are grounded in logical functions of judgment, and in these functions combination, and therefore unity of given concepts, is already thought. Thus the category already presupposes combination. We must therefore look yet higher for this unity (as qualitative, § 12), namely in that which itself contains the ground of the unity of diverse concepts in judg-

---

*Whether the representations are in themselves identical, and whether, therefore, one can be analytically thought through the other, is not a question that here arises. The *consciousness* of the one, when the manifold is under consideration, has always to be distinguished from the consciousness of the other; and it is with the synthesis of this (possible) consciousness that we are here alone concerned.

ment, and therefore of the possibility of the understanding, even as regards its logical employment.

§ 16   *The Original Synthetic Unity of Apperception* It must be possible for the "I think" to accompany all my representations; for otherwise something would be represented in me which could not be thought at all, and that is equivalent to saying   B 132 that the representation would be impossible, or at least would be nothing to me. That representation which can be given prior to all thought is entitled intuition. All the manifold of intuition has, therefore, a necessary relation to the "I think" in the same subject in which this manifold is found. But this representation is an act of *spontaneity*, that is, it cannot be regarded as belonging to sensibility. I call it *pure apperception,* to distinguish it from empirical apperception, or, again, *original apperception,* because it is that self-consciousness which, while generating the representation "*I think*" (a representation which must be capable of accompanying all other representations, and which in all consciousness is one and the same), cannot itself be accompanied by any further representation. The unity of this apperception I likewise entitle the *transcendental* unity of self-consciousness, in order to indicate the possibility of *a priori* knowledge arising from it. For the manifold representations, which are given in an intuition, would not be one and all *my* representations, if they did not all belong to one self-consciousness. As *my* representations (even if I am not conscious of them as such) they must conform to the condition under which alone they *can* stand together in one universal self-consciousness, because otherwise they would not all without exception belong   B 133 to me. From this original combination many consequences follow.

This thoroughgoing identity of the apperception of a manifold which is given in intuition contains a synthesis of representations, and is possible only through the consciousness of this synthesis. For the empirical consciousness, which accompanies different representations, is in itself diverse and without relation to the identity of the subject. That relation comes about, not simply through my accompanying each representation with consciousness, but only in so far as I *conjoin* one representation with another, and am conscious of the synthesis of them. Only in so far, therefore, as I can unite a manifold of given representations in *one conscious-ness,* is it possible for me to represent to myself the *identity of the consciousness in [i.e. throughout] these representations.* In other words, the *analytic* unity of apperception is possible only under the presuppo-sition of a certain synthetic unity.*

B 134   The thought that the representations given in intuition one and all belong to me, is therefore equivalent to the thought that I unite them in one self-consciousness, or can at least so unite them; and although this thought is not itself the consciousness of the *synthesis* of the representations, it presup-poses the possibility of that synthesis. In other words, only in so far as I can grasp the manifold of the representations in one consciousness, do I call them one and all *mine.* For otherwise I should have as many-coloured and diverse a self as I have rep-resentations of which I am conscious to myself. Syn-thetic unity of the manifold of intuitions, as gener-ated *a priori,* is thus the ground of the identity of apperception itself, which precedes *a priori* all *my* determinate thought. Combination does not, how-ever, lie in the objects, and cannot be borrowed from them, and so, through perception, first taken up B 135   into the understanding. On the contrary, it is an affair of the understanding alone, which itself is nothing but the faculty of combining *a priori,* and of bringing the manifold of given representations un-

der the unity of apperception. The principle of ap-perception is the highest principle in the whole sphere of human knowledge.

This principle of the necessary unity of apper-ception is itself, indeed, an identical, and therefore analytic, proposition; nevertheless it reveals the ne-cessity of a synthesis of the manifold given in intu-ition, without which the thoroughgoing identity of self-consciousness cannot be thought. For through the "I," as simple representation, nothing manifold is given; only in intuition, which is distinct from the "I," can a manifold be given; and only through *com-bination* in one consciousness can it be thought. An understanding in which through self-consciousness all the manifold would *eo ipso* be given, would be *intuitive;* our understanding can only *think,* and for intuition must look to the senses. I am conscious of the self as identical in respect of the manifold of rep-resentations that are given to me in an intuition, be-cause I call them one and all *my* representations, and so apprehend them as constituting *one* intu-ition. This amounts to saying, that I am conscious to myself *a priori* of a necessary synthesis of represen-tations—to be entitled the original synthetic unity of apperception—under which all representations that are given to me must stand, but under which they have also first to be brought by means of a synthesis.   B 136

§ 17   *The Principle of the Synthetic Unity Is the Su-preme Principle of All Employment of the Understand-ing* The supreme principle of the possibility of all intuition in its relation to sensibility is, according to the Transcendental Aesthetic, that all the manifold of intuition should be subject to the formal condi-tions of space and time. The supreme principle of the same possibility, in its relation to understand-ing, is that all the manifold of intuition should be subject to conditions of the original synthetic unity of apperception.* In so far as the manifold repre-

---

*The analytic unity of consciousness belongs to all gen-eral concepts, as such. If, for instance, I think red in general, I thereby represent to myself a property which (as a characteristic) can be found in something, or can be combined with other representations; that is, only by means of a presupposed possible synthetic unity can I represent to myself the analytic unity. A representation which is to be thought as common to *different* representa-tions is regarded as belonging to such as have, in addition to it, also something *different.* Consequently it must previ-ously be thought in synthetic unity with other (though, it may be, only possible) representations, before I can think in it the analytic unity of consciousness, which makes it a *conceptus communis.* The synthetic unity of apperception is therefore that highest point, to which we must ascribe all employment of the understanding, even the whole of logic, and conformably therewith, transcendental phi-losophy. Indeed this faculty of apperception is the under-standing itself.

---

*Space and time, and all their parts, are *intuitions,* and are, therefore, with the manifold which they contain, sin-gular representations (*vide* the Transcendental Aesthetic). Consequently they are not mere concepts through which one and the same consciousness is found to be contained in a number of representations. On the contrary, through them many representations are found to be contained in

sentations of intuition are *given* to us, they are subject to the former of these two principles; in so far as they must allow of being *combined* in one consciousness, they are subject to the latter. For without such combination nothing can be thought or known, since the given representations would not have in common the act of the apperception "I think," and so could not be apprehended together in one self-consciousness.

Understanding is, to use general terms, *the faculty of knowledge.* This knowledge consists in the determinate relation of given representations to an object; and an *object* is that in the concept of which the manifold of a given intuition is *united.* Now all unification of representations demands unity of consciousness in the synthesis of them. Consequently it is the unity of consciousness that alone constitutes the relation of representations to an object, and therefore their objective validity and the fact that they are modes of knowledge; and upon it therefore rests the very possibility of the understanding.

The first pure knowledge of understanding, then, upon which all the rest of its employment is based, and which also at the same time is completely independent of all conditions of sensible intuition, is the principle of the original *synthetic* unity of apperception. Thus the mere form of outer sensible intuition, space, is not yet [by itself] knowledge; it supplies only the manifold of *a priori* intuition for a possible knowledge. To know anything in space (for instance, a line), I must *draw* it, and thus synthetically bring into being a determinate combination of the given manifold, so that the unity of this act is at the same time the unity of consciousness (as in the concept of a line); and it is through this unity of consciousness that an object (a determinate space) is first known. The synthetic unity of consciousness is, therefore, an objective condition of all knowledge. It is not merely a condition that I myself require in knowing an object, but is a condition under which every intuition must

B 137

B 138

stand in order *to become an object for me.* For otherwise, in the absence of this synthesis, the manifold would *not* be united in one consciousness.

Although this proposition makes synthetic unity a condition of all thought, it is, as already stated, itself analytic. For it says no more than that all *my* representations in any given intuition must be subject to that condition under which alone I can ascribe them to the identical self as *my* representations, and so can comprehend them as synthetically combined in one apperception through the general expression, "*I think.*"

This principle is not, however, to be taken as applying to every possible understanding, but only to that understanding through whose pure apperception, in the representation "I am," nothing manifold is given. An understanding which through its self-consciousness could supply to itself the manifold of intuition—an understanding, that is to say, through whose representation the objects of the representation should at the same time exist—would not require, for the unity of consciousness, a special act of synthesis of the manifold. For the human understanding, however, which thinks only, and does not intuit, that act is necessary. It is indeed the first principle of the human understanding, and is so indispensable to it that we cannot form the least conception of any other possible understanding, either of such as is itself intuitive or of any that may possess an underlying mode of sensible intuition which is different in kind from that in space and time.

B 139

§ 18 The Objective Unity of Self-Consciousness The transcendental unity of apperception is that unity through which all the manifold given in an intuition is united in a concept of the object. It is therefore entitled *objective,* and must be distinguished from the *subjective* unity of consciousness, which is a *determination* of *inner sense*—through which the manifold of intuition for such [objective] combination is empirically given. Whether I can become *empirically* conscious of the manifold as simultaneous or as successive depends on circumstances or empirical conditions. Therefore the empirical unity of consciousness, through association of representations, itself concerns an appearance, and is wholly contingent. But the pure form of intuition in time, merely as intuition in general, which contains a given

B 140

---

one representation, and in the consciousness of that representation; and they are thus composite. The unity of that consciousness is therefore synthetic and yet is also original. The *singularity* of such intuitions is found to have important consequences (*vide* § 25).

manifold, is subject to the original unity of consciousness, simply through the necessary relation of the manifold of the intuition to the one "*I think,*" and so through the pure synthesis of understanding which is the *a priori* underlying ground of the empirical synthesis. Only the original unity is objectively valid; the empirical unity of apperception, upon which we are not here dwelling, and which besides is merely derived from the former under given conditions *in concreto*, has only subjective validity. To one man, for instance, a certain word suggests one thing, to another some other thing; the unity of consciousness in that which is empirical is not, as regards what is given, necessarily and universally valid.

§ 19   *The Logical Form of All Judgments Consists in the Objective Unity of the Apperception of the Concepts Which They Contain* I have never been able to accept the interpretation which logicians give of judgment in general. It is, they declare, the representation of a relation between two concepts. I do not here B 141 dispute with them as to what is defective in this interpretation—that in any case it applies only to *categorical*, not to hypothetical and disjunctive judgments (the two latter containing a relation not of concepts but of judgments), an oversight from which many troublesome consequences have followed.* I need only point out that the definition does not determine in what the asserted *relation* consists.

But if I investigate more precisely the relation of the given modes of knowledge in any judgment, and distinguish it, as belonging to the understanding, from the relation according to laws of the reproductive imagination, which has only subjec-

tive validity. I find that a judgment is nothing but the manner in which given modes of knowledge are brought to the objective unity of apperception. This is what is intended by the copula "is." It is employed to distinguish the objective unity of given B 142 representations from the subjective. It indicates their relation to original apperception, and its *necessary unity*. It holds good even if the judgment is itself empirical, and therefore contingent, as, for example, in the judgment, "Bodies are heavy." I do not here assert that these representations *necessarily* belong *to one another* in the empirical intuition, but that they belong to one another *in virtue of the necessary unity* of apperception in the synthesis of intuitions, that is, according to principles of the objective determination of all representations, in so far as knowledge can be acquired by means of these representations— principles which are all derived from the fundamental principle of the transcendental unity of apperception. Only in this way does there arise from this relation a *judgment*, that is, a relation which is *objectively valid*, and so can be adequately distinguished from a relation of the same representations that would have only subjective validity—as when they are connected according to laws of association. In the latter case, all that I could say would be, "If I support a body, I feel an impression of weight"; I could not say, "It, the body, is heavy." Thus to say "The body is heavy" is not merely to state that the two representations have always been conjoined in my perception, however often that perception be repeated; what we are asserting is that they are combined *in the object*, no matter what the state of the subject may be.

§ 20   *All Sensible Intuitions Are Subject to the Cate-* B 143 *gories, as Conditions under which Alone Their Manifold Can Come Together in One Consciousness* The manifold given in a sensible intuition is necessarily subject to the original synthetic unity of apperception, because in no other way is the *unity* of intuition possible (§ 17). But that act of understanding by which the manifold of given representations (be they intuitions or concepts) is brought under one apperception, is the logical function of judgment (cf. § 19). All the manifold, therefore, so far as it is given in a single empirical intuition, is *determined* in respect of one of the logical functions of judg-

---

*The lengthy doctrine of the four syllogistic figures concerns categorical syllogisms only; and although it is indeed nothing more than an artificial method of securing, through the surreptitious introduction of immediate inferences (*consequentiae immediatae*) among the premises of a pure syllogism, the appearance that there are more kinds of inference than that of the first figure, this would hardly have met with such remarkable acceptance, had not its authors succeeded in bringing categorical judgments into such exclusive respect, as being those to which all others must allow of being reduced—teaching which, as indicated in § 9, is none the less erroneous.

ment, and is thereby brought into one consciousness. Now the *categories* are just these functions of judgment, in so far as they are employed in determination of the manifold of a given intuition (cf. § 13). Consequently, the manifold in a given intuition is necessarily subject to the categories.

B 144 § 21 *Observation* A manifold, contained in an intuition which I call mine, is represented, by means of the synthesis of the understanding, as belonging to the *necessary* unity of self-consciousness; and this is effected by means of the category.* This [requirement of a] category therefore shows that the empirical consciousness of a given manifold in a single intuition is subject to a pure self-consciousness *a priori*, just as is empirical intuition to a pure sensible intuition, which likewise takes place *a priori*. Thus in the above proposition a beginning is made of a *deduction* of the pure concepts of understanding; and in this deduction, since the categories have their source in the understanding alone, *independently of sensibility*, I must abstract from the mode in which the manifold for an empirical intuition is given, and must direct attention solely to the unity which, in terms of the category, and by means of the understanding, enters into the intuition. In what follows (cf. § 26) it will be shown, from the mode in which the empirical intuition is given in sensibility, that its unity is no other than that which the category B 145 (according to § 20) prescribes to the manifold of a given intuition in general. Only thus, by demonstration of the *a priori* validity of the categories in respect of all objects of our senses, will the purpose of the deduction be fully attained.

But in the above proof there is one feature from which I could not abstract, the feature, namely, that the manifold to be intuited must be given prior to the synthesis of understanding, and independently of it. How this takes place remains here undetermined. For were I to think an understanding which is itself intuitive (as, for example, a divine understanding which should not represent to itself given

objects, but through whose representation the objects should themselves be given or produced), the categories would have no meaning whatsoever in respect of such a mode of knowledge. They are merely rules for an understanding whose whole power consists in thought, consists, that is, in the act whereby it brings the synthesis of a manifold, given to it from elsewhere in intuition, to the unity of apperception—a faculty, therefore, which by itself knows nothing whatsoever, but merely combines and arranges the material of knowledge, that is, the intuition, which must be given to it by the object. This peculiarity of our understanding, that it can produce *a priori* unity of apperception solely by means of the categories, and only by such and so many, is as little capable of further explanation as B 146 why we have just these and no other functions of judgment, or why space and time are the only forms of our possible intuition.

§ 22 *The Category Has No Other Application in Knowledge Than to Objects of Experience* To *think* an object and to *know* an object are thus by no means the same thing. Knowledge involves two factors: first, the concept, through which an object in general is thought (the category); and secondly, the intuition, through which it is given. For if no intuition could be given corresponding to the concept, the concept would still indeed be a thought, so far as its form is concerned, but would be without any object, and no knowledge of anything would be possible by means of it. So far as I could know, there would be nothing, and could be nothing, to which my thought could be applied. Now, as the Aesthetic has shown, the only intuition possible to us is sensible; consequently, the thought of an object in general, by means of a pure concept of understanding, can become knowledge for us only in so far as the concept is related to objects of the senses. Sensible B 147 intuition is either pure intuition (space and time) or empirical intuition of that which is immediately represented, through sensation, as actual in space and time. Through the determination of pure intuition we can acquire *a priori* knowledge of objects, as in mathematics, but only in regard to their form, as appearances; whether there can be things which must be intuited in this form is still left undecided. Mathematical concepts are not, therefore, by themselves knowledge, except on the supposition that

---

*The proof of this rests on the represented *unity of intuition*, by which an object is given. This unity of intuition always includes in itself a synthesis of the manifold given for an intuition, and so already contains the relation of this manifold to the unity of apperception.

there are things which allow of being presented to us only in accordance with the form of that pure sensible intuition. Now *things in space and time* are given only in so far as they are perceptions (that is, representations accompanied by sensation)—therefore only through empirical representation. Consequently, the pure concepts of understanding, even when they are applied to *a priori* intuitions, as in mathematics, yield knowledge only in so far as these intuitions—and therefore indirectly by their means the pure concepts also—can be applied to empirical intuitions. Even, therefore, with the aid of [pure] intuition, the categories do not afford us any knowledge of things; they do so only through their possible application to *empirical intuition*. In other words, they serve only for the possibility of *empirical knowledge*; and such knowledge is what we entitle experience. Our conclusion is therefore this: the categories, as yielding knowledge of *things*, B 148 have no kind of application, save only in regard to things which may be objects of possible experience.

§ 23   The above proposition is of the greatest importance; for it determines the limits of the employment of the pure concepts of understanding in regard to objects, just as the Transcendental Aesthetic determined the limits of the employment of the pure form of our sensible intuition. Space and time, as conditions under which alone objects can possibly be given to us, are valid no further than for objects of the senses, and therefore only for experience. Beyond these limits they represent nothing; for they are only in the senses, and beyond them have no reality. The pure concepts of understanding are free from this limitation, and extend to objects of intuition in general, be the intuition like or unlike ours, if only it be sensible and not intellectual. But this extension of concepts beyond *our* sensible intuition is of no advantage to us. For as concepts of objects they are then empty, and do not even enable us to judge of their objects whether or not they are possible. They are mere forms of thought, without objective reality, since we have no intuition at hand to which the synthetic unity of apperception, which constitutes the whole content of these forms, could be applied, and in being so applied determine an object. Only *our* sensible B 149 and empirical intuition can give to them body and meaning.

If we suppose an object of a *non-sensible* intuition to be given, we can indeed represent it through all the predicates which are implied in the presupposition that it has none of the characteristics proper to sensible intuition; that it is not extended or in space, that its duration is not a time, that no change (succession of determinations in time) is to be met with in it, etc. But there is no proper knowledge if I thus merely indicate what the intuition of an object is *not*, without being able to say what it is that is contained in the intuition. For I have not then shown that the object which I am thinking through my pure concept is even so much as possible, not being in a position to give any intuition corresponding to the concept, and being able only to say that our intuition is not applicable to it. But what has chiefly to be noted is this, that to such a something [in general] not a single one of all the categories could be applied. We could not, for instance, apply to it the concept of substance, meaning something which can exist as subject and never as mere predicate. For save in so far as empirical intuition provides the instance to which to apply it, I do not know whether there can be anything that corresponds to such a form of thought. But of this more hereafter.

§ 24   *The Application of the Categories to Objects of* B 150 *the Senses in General*   The pure concepts of understanding relate, through the mere understanding, to objects of intuition in general, whether that intuition be our own or any other, provided only it be sensible. The concepts are, however, for this very reason, mere *forms of thought*, through which alone no determinate object is known. The synthesis or combination of the manifold in them relates only to the unity of apperception, and is thereby the ground of the possibility of *a priori* knowledge, so far as such knowledge rests on the understanding. This synthesis, therefore, is at once transcendental and also purely intellectual. But since there lies in us a certain form of *a priori* sensible intuition, which depends on the receptivity of the faculty of representation (sensibility), the understanding, as spontaneity, is able to determine inner sense through the manifold of given representations, in accordance with the synthetic unity of apperception, and so to think synthetic unity of the apperception of the manifold of *a priori sensible intuition*—that being

the condition under which all objects of our human intuition must necessarily stand. In this way the categories, in themselves mere forms of thought,
B 151 obtain objective reality, that is, application to objects which can be given us in intuition. These objects, however, are only appearances, for it is solely of appearances that we can have *a priori* intuition.

This synthesis of the manifold of sensible intuition, which is possible and necessary *a priori,* may be entitled *figurative* synthesis (*synthesis speciosa*), to distinguish it from the synthesis which is thought in the mere category in respect of the manifold of an intuition in general, and which is entitled combination through the understanding (*synthesis intellectualis*). Both are *transcendental,* not merely as taking place *a priori,* but also as conditioning the possibility of other *a priori* knowledge.

But the figurative synthesis, if it be directed merely to the original synthetic unity of apperception, that is, to the transcendental unity which is thought in the categories, must, in order to be distinguished from the merely intellectual combination, be called the *transcendental synthesis of imagination. Imagination* is the faculty of representing in intuition an object that is *not itself present.* Now since all our intuition is sensible, the imagination, owing to the subjective condition under which alone it can give to the concepts of understanding a corresponding intuition, belongs to *sensibility.* But inasmuch as its synthesis is an expression of spontaneity, which is determinative and not, like sense, determinable merely, and which is therefore able to determine
B 152 sense *a priori* in respect of its form in accordance with the unity of apperception, imagination is to that extent a faculty which determines the sensibility *a priori;* and its synthesis of intuitions, conforming as it does to the *categories,* must be the transcendental synthesis of *imagination.* This synthesis is an action of the understanding on the sensibility; and is its first application—and thereby the ground of all its other applications—to the objects of our possible intuition. As figurative, it is distinguished from the intellectual synthesis, which is carried out by the understanding alone, without the aid of the imagination. In so far as imagination is spontaneity, I sometimes also entitle it the *productive* imagination, to distinguish it from the *reproductive* imagination, whose synthesis is entirely subject to empirical laws, the laws, namely, of association, and

which therefore contributes nothing to the explanation of the possibility of *a priori* knowledge. The reproductive synthesis falls within the domain, not of transcendental philosophy, but of psychology.

* * *

This is a suitable place for explaining the paradox which must have been obvious to everyone in our exposition of the form of inner sense (§ 6): namely, that this sense represents to consciousness B 153 even our own selves only as we appear to ourselves, not as we are in ourselves. For we intuit ourselves only as we are inwardly *affected,* and this would seem to be contradictory, since we should then have to be in a passive relation [of active affection] to ourselves. It is to avoid this contradiction that in systems of psychology *inner sense,* which we have carefully distinguished from the faculty of *apperception,* is commonly regarded as being identical with it.

What determines inner sense is the understanding and its original power of combining the manifold of intuition, that is, of bringing it under an apperception, upon which the possibility of understanding itself rests. Now the understanding in us men is not itself a faculty of intuitions, and cannot, even if intuitions be given in sensibility, take them up *into itself* in such manner as to combine them as the manifold of its *own* intuition. Its synthesis, therefore, if the synthesis be viewed by itself alone, is nothing but the unity of the act, of which, as an act, it is conscious to itself, even without [the aid of] sensibility, but through which it is yet able to determine the sensibility. The understanding, that is to say, in respect of the manifold which may be given to it in accordance with the form of sensible intuition, is able to determine sensibility inwardly. Thus the understanding, under the title of a *transcendental synthesis of imagination,* performs this act upon the *passive* subject, whose *faculty* it is, and we are there- B 154 fore justified in saying that inner sense is affected thereby. Apperception and its synthetic unity is, indeed, very far from being identical with inner sense. The former, as the source of all *combination,* applies to the manifold of *intuitions in general,* and in the guise of the *categories,* prior to all sensible intuition, to *objects in general.* Inner sense, on the other hand, contains the mere form of intuition, but without combination of the manifold in it, and therefore so far contains no *determinate* intuition, which is possible only through the consciousness of the determination of the manifold by the transcendental act of imagination (synthetic influence of the understanding upon inner sense), which I have entitled figurative synthesis.

This we can always perceive in ourselves. We cannot think a line without *drawing* it in thought, or a circle without *describing* it. We cannot represent the three dimensions of space save by *setting* three lines at right angles to one another from the same point. Even time itself we cannot represent, save in so far as we attend, in the *drawing* of a straight line (which has to serve as the outer figurative representation of time), merely to the act of the synthesis of the manifold whereby we successively determine inner sense, and in so doing attend to the succession of this determination in inner sense. Motion, as an act of the subject (not as a determination of an object),* and therefore the synthesis of the manifold B 155 in space, first produces the concept of succession— if we abstract from this manifold and attend solely to the act through which we determine the *inner* sense according to its form. The understanding does not, therefore, find in inner sense such a combination of the manifold, but *produces* it, in that it *affects* that sense.

How the "I" that thinks can be distinct from the "I" that intuits itself (for I can represent still other modes of intuition as at least possible), and yet, as being the same subject, can be identical with the latter; and how, therefore, I can say: "I, as intelligence and *thinking* subject, know myself as an object that is *thought*, in so far as I am given to myself [as something other or] beyond that [I] which is [given to myself] in intuition, and yet know myself, like other phenomena, only as I appear to myself, not as I am to the understanding"—these are questions that raise no greater nor less difficulty than how I can be an object to myself at all, and, more particularly, an object of intuition and of inner

perceptions. Indeed, that this is how it must be is B 156 easily shown—if we admit that space is merely a pure form of the appearances of outer sense—by the fact that we cannot obtain for ourselves a representation of time, which is not an object of outer intuition, except under the image of a line, which we draw, and that by this mode of depicting it alone could we know the singleness of its dimension; and similarly by the fact that for all inner perceptions we must derive the determination of lengths of time or of points of time from the changes which are exhibited to us in outer things, and that the determinations of inner sense have therefore to be arranged as appearances in time in precisely the same manner in which we arrange those of outer sense in space. If, then, as regards the latter, we admit that we know objects only in so far as we are externally affected, we must also recognise, as regards inner sense, that by means of it we intuit ourselves only as we are inwardly affected *by ourselves*; in other words, that, so far as inner ituitionn is concerned, we know our own subject only as appearance, not as it is in itself.*

§ 25   On the other hand, in the transcendental B 157 synthesis of the manifold of representations in general, and therefore in the synthetic original unity of apperception, I am conscious of myself, not as I appear to myself, nor as I am in myself, but only that I am. This *representation* is a *thought*, not an *intuition*. Now in order to *know* ourselves, there is required in addition to the act of thought, which brings the manifold of every possible intuition to the unity of apperception, a determinate mode of intuition, whereby this manifold is given; it therefore follows that although my existence is not indeed appearance (still less mere illusion), the determination of my existence† can take place only in

---

*Motion of an object in space does not belong to a pure science, and consequently not to geometry. For the fact that something is movable cannot be known *a priori,* but only through experience. Motion, however, considered as the describing of a space, is a pure act of the successive synthesis of the manifold in outer intuition in general by means of the productive imagination, and belongs not only to geometry, but even to transcendental philosophy.

---

*I do not see why so much difficulty should be found in admitting that our inner sense is affected by ourselves. Such affection finds exemplification in each and every act of *attention*. In every act of attention the understanding determines inner sense, in accordance with the combination which it thinks, to that inner intuition which corresponds to the manifold in the synthesis of the understanding. How much the mind is usually thereby affected, everyone will be able to perceive in himself.
†The "I think" expresses the act of determining my existence. Existence is already given thereby, but the mode in

B 158 conformity with the form of inner sense, according to the special mode in which the manifold, which I combine, is given in inner intuition. Accordingly I have no *knowledge* of myself as I am but merely as I appear to myself. The consciousness of self is thus very far from being a knowledge of the self, notwithstanding all the categories which [are being employed to] constitute the thought of an *object in general*, through combination of the manifold in one apperception. Just as for knowledge of an object distinct from me I require, besides the thought of an object in general (in the category), an intuition by which I determine that general concept, so for knowledge of myself I require, besides the consciousness, that is, besides the thought of myself, an intuition of the manifold in me, by which I determine this thought. I exist as an intelligence which is conscious solely of its power of combination; but

B 159 in respect of the manifold which it has to combine I am subjected to a limiting condition (entitled inner sense), namely, that this combination can be made intuitable only according to relations of time, which lie entirely outside the concepts of understanding, strictly regarded. Such an intelligence, therefore, can know itself only as it appears to itself in respect of an intuition which is not intellectual and cannot be given by the understanding itself, not as it would know itself if its *intuition* were intellectual.

§ 26 *Transcendental Deduction of the Universally Possible Employment in Experience of the Pure Concepts of the Understanding* In the *metaphysical deduction* the *a priori* origin of the categories has been proved through their complete agreement with the general logical functions of thought; in the *transcendental deduction* we have shown their possibility as *a priori* modes of knowledge of objects of an intuition in general (cf. §§ 20, 21). We have now to explain the possibility of knowing *a priori*, by means of *categories*, whatever objects may *present themselves to our senses*, not indeed in respect of the form of their intuition, but in respect of the laws of their combination, and so, as it were, of prescribing laws to nature, and even of making nature possible. For B 160 unless the categories discharged this function, there could be no explaining why everything that can be presented to our senses must be subject to laws which have their origin *a priori* in the understanding alone.

First of all, I may draw attention to the fact that by *synthesis of apprehension* I understand that combination of the manifold in an empirical intuition, whereby perception, that is, empirical consciousness of the intuition (as appearance), is possible.

In the representations of space and time we have *a priori forms* of outer and inner sensible intuition; and to these the synthesis of apprehension of the manifold of appearance must always conform, because in no other way can the synthesis take place at all. But space and time are represented *a priori* not merely as *forms* of sensible intuition, but as themselves *intuitions* which contain a manifold [of their own], and therefore are represented with the determination of the *unity* of this manifold (*vide* the Transcendental Aesthetic).* Thus *unity of the synthesis* of the manifold, without or within us, and consequently also a *combination* to which everything B 161

---

which I am to determine this existence, that is, the manifold belonging to it, is not thereby given. In order that it be given, self-intuition is required; and such intuition is conditioned by a given *a priori* form, namely, time, which is sensible and belongs to the receptivity of the determinable [in me]. Now since I do not have another self-intuition which gives the *determining* in me (I am conscious only of the spontaneity of it) prior to the act of *determination*, as time does in the case of the determinable, I cannot determine my existence as that of a self-active being; all that I can do is to represent to myself the spontaneity of my thought, that is, of the determination; and my existence is still only determinable sensibly, that is, as the existence of an appearance. But it is owing to this spontaneity that I entitle myself an *intelligence*.

*Space, represented as *object* (as we are required to do in geometry), contains more than mere form of intuition; it also contains *combination* of the manifold, given according to the form of sensibility, in an *intuitive* representation, so that the *form of intuition* gives only a manifold, the *formal intuition* gives unity of representation. In the Aesthetic I have treated this unity as belonging merely to sensibility, simply in order to emphasize that it precedes any concept, although, as a matter of fact, it presupposes a synthesis which does not belong to the senses but through which all concepts of space and time first become possible. For since by its means (in that the understanding determines the sensibility) space and time are first *given* as intuitions, the unity of this *a priori* intuition belongs to space and time, and not to the concept of the understanding (cf. § 24).

that is to be represented as determined in space or in time must conform, is given *a priori* as the condition of the synthesis of all *apprehension*—not indeed in, but with these intuitions. This synthetic unity can be no other than the unity of the combination of the manifold of a given *intuition in general* in an original consciousness, in accordance with the categories, in so far as the combination is applied to our *sensible intuition.* All synthesis, therefore, even that which renders perception possible, is subject to the categories; and since experience is knowledge by means of connected perceptions, the categories are conditions of the possibility of experience, and are therefore valid *a priori* for all objects of experience.

* * *

B 162   When, for instance, by apprehension of the manifold of a house I make the empirical intuition of it into a perception, the *necessary unity* of space and of outer sensible intuition in general lies at the basis of my apprehension, and I draw as it were the outline of the house in conformity with this synthetic unity of the manifold in space. But if I abstract from the form of space, this same synthetic unity has its seat in the understanding, and is the category of the synthesis of the homogeneous in an intuition in general, that is, the category of *quantity.* To this category, therefore, the synthesis of apprehension, that is to say, the perception, must completely conform.*

When, to take another example, I perceive the freezing of water, I apprehend two states, fluidity and solidity, and these as standing to one another B 163   in a relation of time. But in time, which I place at the basis of the appearance [in so far] as [it is] inner *intuition,* I necessarily represent to myself synthetic *unity* of the manifold, without which that relation of time could not be given in an intuition as being *determined* in respect of time-sequence. Now this synthetic unity, as a condition *a priori* un-

der which I combine the manifold of an *intuition in general,* is—if I abstract from the constant form of *my* inner intuition, namely, time— the category of *cause,* by means of which, when I apply it to my sensibility, I determine *everything that happens* in accordance with the relation which it prescribes, and I do so *in time in general.* Thus my apprehension of such an event, and therefore the event itself, considered as a possible perception, is subject to the concept of the *relation* of *effects* and *causes,* and so in all other cases.

Categories are concepts which prescribe laws *a priori* to appearances, and therefore to nature, the sum of all appearances (*natura materialiter spectata*). The question therefore arises, how it can be conceivable that nature should have to proceed in accordance with categories which yet are not derived from it, and do not model themselves upon its pattern; that is, how they can determine *a priori* the combination of the manifold of nature, while yet they are not derived from it. The solution of this seeming enigma is as follows.

That the *laws* of appearances in nature must   B 164 agree with the understanding and its *a priori* form, that is, with its faculty of *combining* the manifold in general, is no more surprising than that the appearances themselves must agree with the form of *a priori* sensible intuition. For just as appearances do not exist in themselves but only relatively to the subject in which, so far as it has senses, they inhere, so the laws do not exist in the appearances but only relatively to this same being, so far as it has understanding. Things in themselves would necessarily, apart from any understanding that knows them, conform to laws of their own. But appearances are only representations of things which are unknown as regards what they may be in themselves. As mere representations, they are subject to no law of connection save that which the connecting faculty prescribes. Now it is imagination that connects the manifold of sensible intuition; and imagination is dependent for the unity of its intellectual synthesis upon the understanding, and for the manifoldness of its apprehension upon sensibility. All possible perception is thus dependent upon synthesis of apprehension, and this empirical synthesis in turn upon transcendental synthesis, and therefore upon the categories. Consequently, all possible perceptions, and therefore everything that can come to

---

*In this manner it is proved that the synthesis of apprehension, which is empirical, must necessarily be in conformity with the synthesis of apperception, which is intellectual and is contained in the category completely *a priori.* It is one and the same spontaneity, which in the one case, under the title of imagination, and in the other case, under the title of understanding, brings combination into the manifold of intuition.

empirical consciousness, that is, all appearances of nature, must, so far as their connection is concerned, be subject to the categories. Nature, considered merely as nature in general, is dependent upon these categories as the original ground of its necessary conformity to law (*natura formaliter spectata*). Pure understanding is not, however, in a position, through mere categories, to prescribe to appearances any *a priori* laws other than those which are involved in a *nature in general*, that is, in the conformity to law of all appearances in space and time. Special laws, as concerning those appearances which are empirically determined, cannot in their specific character be *derived* from the categories, although they are one and all subject to them. To obtain any knowledge whatsoever of these special laws, we must resort to experience; but it is the *a priori* laws that alone can instruct us in regard to experience in general, and as to what it is that can be known as an object of experience.

§ 27 *Outcome of This Deduction of the Concepts of Understanding* We cannot think an object save through categories; we cannot *know* an object so thought save through intuitions corresponding to these concepts. Now all our intuitions are sensible; and this knowledge, in so far as its object is given, is empirical. But empirical knowledge is experience. *Consequently, there can be no* a priori *knowledge, except of objects of possible experience.**

But although this knowledge is limited to objects of experience, it is not therefore all derived from experience. The pure intuitions [of receptivity] and the pure concepts of understanding are elements in knowledge, and both are found in us *a*

---

*Lest my readers should stumble at the alarming evil consequences which may over-hastily be inferred from this statement, I may remind them that *for thought* the categories are not limited by the conditions of our sensible intuition, but have an unlimited field. It is only the *knowledge* of that which we think, the determining of the object, that requires intuition. In the absence of intuition, the thought of the object may still have its true and useful consequences, as regards the subject's *employment of reason.* The use of reason is not always directed to the determination of the object, that is, to knowledge, but also to the determination of the subject and of its volition—a use which cannot therefore be here dealt with.

priori. There are only two ways in which we can account for a *necessary* agreement of experience with the concepts of its objects: either experience makes these concepts possible or these concepts make experience possible. The former supposition does not hold in respect of the categories (nor of pure sensible intuition); for since they are *a priori* concepts, and therefore independent of experience, the ascription to them of an empirical origin would be a sort of *generatio aequivoca*. There remains, therefore, only the second supposition—a system, as it were, of the *epigenesis* of pure reason—namely, that the categories contain, on the side of the understanding, the grounds of the possibility of all experience in general. How they make experience possible, and what are the principles of the possibility of experience that they supply in their application to appearances, will be shown more fully in the following chapter on the transcendental employment of the faculty of judgment.

A middle course may be proposed between the two above mentioned, namely, that the categories are neither *self-thought* first principles *a priori* of our knowledge nor derived from experience, but subjective dispositions of thought, implanted in us from the first moment of our existence, and so ordered by our Creator that their employment is in complete harmony with the laws of nature in accordance with which experience proceeds—a kind of *preformation-system* of pure reason. Apart, however, from the objection that on such a hypothesis we can set no limit to the assumption of predetermined dispositions to future judgments, there is this decisive objection against the suggested middle course, that the *necessity* of the categories, which belongs to their very conception, would then have to be sacrificed. The concept of cause, for instance, which expresses the necessity of an event under a presupposed condition, would be false if it rested only on an arbitrary subjective necessity, implanted in us, of connecting certain empirical representations according to the rule of causal relation. I would not then be able to say that the effect is connected with the cause in the object, that is to say, necessarily, but only that I am so constituted that I cannot think this representation otherwise than as thus connected. This is exactly what the sceptic most desires. For if this be the situation, all our insight, resting on the supposed objective validity of our judgments, is nothing but

B 165

B 166

B 167

B 168

sheer illusion; nor would there be wanting people who would refuse to admit this subjective necessity, a necessity which can only be felt. Certainly a man cannot dispute with anyone regarding that which depends merely on the mode in which he is himself organised.

Brief Outline of This Deduction The deduction is the exposition of the pure concepts of the understanding, and therewith of all theoretical *a priori* knowledge, as principles of the possibility of experience—the principles being here taken as the *determination* of appearances in space and time *in general,* and this determination, in turn, as ultimately following from the *original* synthetic unity of apperception, as the form of the understanding in its relation to space and time, the original forms of sensibility.

B 169

Refutation of Idealism

Idealism—meaning thereby *material* idealism—is the theory which declares the existence of objects in space outside us either to be merely doubtful and indemonstrable or to be false and impossible. The former is the *problematic* idealism of Descartes, which holds that there is only one empirical assertion that is indubitably certain, namely, that "I am." The latter is the *dogmatic* idealism of Berkeley. He maintains that space, with all the things of which it is the inseparable condition, is something which is in itself impossible; and he therefore regards the things in space as merely imaginary entities. Dogmatic idealism is unavoidable, if space be interpreted as a property that must belong to things in themselves. For in that case space, and everything to which it serves as condition, is a non-entity. The ground on which this idealism rests has already been undermined by us in the Transcendental Aesthetic. Problematic idealism, which makes no such assertion, but merely pleads incapacity to prove, through immediate experience, any existence except our own, is, in so far as it allows of no decisive judgment until sufficient proof has been found, reasonable and in accordance with a thorough and philosophical mode of thought. The required proof must, therefore, show that we have *experience,* and

B 275

not merely imagination of outer things; and this, it would seem, cannot be achieved save by proof that even our inner experience, which for Descartes is indubitable, is possible only on the assumption of outer experience.

Thesis

The mere, but empirically determined, consciousness of my own existence proves the existence of objects in space outside me.

Proof

I am conscious of my own existence as determined in time. All determination of time presupposes something *permanent* in perception. But this permanent cannot be an intuition in me. For all grounds of determination of my existence which are to be met with in me are representations; and as representations themselves require a permanent distinct from them, in relation to which their change, and so my existence in the time wherein they change, may be determined. Thus perception of this permanent is possible only through a *thing* outside me and not through the mere *representation* of a thing outside me; and consequently the determination of my existence in time is possible only through the existence of actual things which I perceive outside me. Now consciousness of my existence in time is necessarily bound up with consciousness of the condition of the possibility of this time-determination; and it is therefore necessarily bound up with the existence of things outside me, as the condition of the time-determination. In other words, the consciousness of my existence is at the same time an immediate consciousness of the existence of other things outside me.

B 276

Note 1. It will be observed that in the foregoing proof the game played by idealism has been turned against itself, and with greater justice. Idealism assumed that the only immediate experience is inner experience, and that from it we can only *infer* outer things—and this, moreover, only in an untrustworthy manner, as in all cases where we are inferring from given effects to determinate causes. In this particular case, the cause of the representations, which we ascribe, perhaps falsely, to outer things, may lie in ourselves. But in the above proof

it has been shown that outer experience is really
B 277 immediate,* and that only by means of it is inner experience—not indeed the consciousness of my own existence, but the determination of it in time—possible. Certainly, the representation "I am," which expresses the consciousness that can accompany all thought, immediately includes in itself the existence of a subject; but it does not so include any *knowledge* of that subject, and therefore also no empirical knowledge, that is, no experience of it. For this we require, in addition to the thought of something existing, also intuition, and in this case inner intuition, in respect of which, that is, of time, the subject must be determined. But in order so to determine it, outer objects are quite indispensable; and it therefore follows that inner experience is itself possible only mediately, and only through outer experience.

Note 2. With this thesis all employment of our cognitive faculty in experience, in the determination of time, entirely agrees. Not only are we unable to perceive any determination of time save through change in outer relations (motion) relatively to the permanent in space (for instance, the motion of the sun relatively to objects on the earth), we have
B 278 nothing permanent on which, as intuition, we can base the concept of a substance, save only *matter;* and even this permanence is not obtained from outer experience, but is presupposed *a priori* as a necessary condition of determination of time, and therefore also as a determination of inner sense in respect of [the determination of] our own existence through the existence of outer things. The

consciousness of myself in the representation "I" is not an intuition, but a merely *intellectual* representation of the spontaneity of a thinking subject. This "I" has not, therefore, the least predicate of intuition, which, as permanent, might serve as correlate for the determination of time in inner sense—in the manner in which, for instance, *impenetrability* serves in our *empirical* intuition of matter.

Note 3. From the fact that the existence of outer things is required for the possibility of a determinate consciousness of the self, it does not follow that every intuitive representation of outer things involves the existence of these things, for their representation can very well be the product merely of the imagination (as in dreams and delusions). Such representation is merely the reproduction of previous outer perceptions, which, as has been shown, are possible only through the reality of outer objects. All that we have here sought to prove is that inner experience in general is possible only through outer experience in general. Whether this or that B 279 supposed experience be not purely imaginary, must be ascertained from its special determinations, and through its congruence with the criteria of all real experience.

Editor's note: What follows is a long footnote Kant added to the Preface *explaining the argument of the* Refutation of Idealism.

The only addition, strictly so called, though one affecting the method of proof only, is the new refutation of psychological *idealism* (cf. p. 473), and a strict (also, as I believe, the only possible) proof of the objective reality of outer intuition. However harmless idealism may be considered in respect of the essential aims of metaphysics (though, in fact, it is not thus harmless), it still remains a scandal to philosophy and to human reason in general that the existence of things outside us (from which we derive the whole material of knowledge, even for our inner sense) must be accepted merely on *faith*, and that if anyone thinks good to doubt their existence, we are unable to counter his doubts by any satisfactory proof. Since there is some obscurity in the expressions used in the proof, from the third line to the sixth line, I beg to alter the passage as follows: "*But this permanent cannot be an intuition in me. For all grounds of determination of my existence which are to be met with in me are representations; and as*

---

*The *immediate* consciousness of the existence of outer things is, in the preceding thesis, not presupposed, but proved, be the possibility of this consciousness understood by us or not. The question as to its possibility would be this: whether we have an inner sense only, and no outer sense, but merely an outer imagination. It is clear, however, that in order even only to imagine something as outer, that is, to present it to sense in intuition, we must already have an outer sense, and must thereby immediately distinguish the mere receptivity of an outer intuition from the spontaneity which characterises every act of imagination. For should we merely be imagining an outer sense, the faculty of intuition, which is to be determined by the faculty of imagination, would itself be annulled.

*representations themselves require a permanent distinct
from them, in relation to which their change, and so my
existence in the time wherein they change, may be determined.''* To this proof it will probably be objected,
that I am immediately conscious only of that which
is in me, that is, of my *representation* of outer things;
and consequently that it must still remain uncertain
whether outside me there is anything correspond-
B xl ing to it, or not. But through inner *experience* I am
conscious of *my existence* in time (consequently also
of its determinability in time), and this is more than
to be conscious merely of my representation. It is
identical with the *empirical consciousness of my existence,* which is determinable only through relation
to something which, while bound up with my existence, is outside me. This consciousness of my existence in time is bound up in the way of identity
with the consciousness of a relation to something
outside me, and it is therefore experience not invention, sense not imagination, which inseparably connects this outside something with my inner sense.
For outer sense is already in itself a relation of intuition to something actual outside me, and the reality
of outer sense, in its distinction from imagination,
rests simply on that which is here found to take
place, namely, its being inseparably bound up with
inner experience, as the condition of its possibility.
If, with the *intellectual consciousness* of my existence, in the representation "I am," which accompanies all my judgments and acts of understanding,
I could at the same time connect a determination of
my existence through *intellectual intuition,* the consciousness of a relation to something outside me
would not be required. But though that intellectual
consciousness does indeed come first, the inner intuition, in which my existence can alone be determined, is sensible and is bound up with the condition of time. This determination, however, and
therefore the inner experience itself, depends upon
B xli something permanent which is not in me, and consequently can be only in something outside me, to
which I must regard myself as standing in relation.
The reality of outer sense is thus necessarily bound
up with inner sense, if experience in general is to be
possible at all; that is, I am just as certainly conscious that there are things outside me, which are in
relation to my sense, as I am conscious that I myself
exist as determined in time. In order to determine to
which given intuitions objects outside me actually

correspond, and which therefore belong to outer
sense (to which, and not to the faculty of imagination, they are to be ascribed), we must in each single
case appeal to the rules according to which experience in general, even inner experience, is distinguished from imagination—the proposition that
there is such a thing as outer experience being always presupposed. This further remark may be
added. The representation of something *permanent*
in existence is not the same as *permanent representation.* For though the representation of [something
permanent] may be very transitory and variable like
all our other representations, not excepting those of
matter, it yet refers to something permanent. This
latter must therefore be an external thing distinct
from all my representations, and its existence must
be included in the *determination* of my own existence, constituting with it but a single experience
such as would not take place even inwardly if it
were not also at the same time, in part, outer. How
this should be possible we are as little capable of
explaining further as we are of accounting for our
being able to think the abiding in time, the coexistence of which with the changing generates the concept of alteration.

Second Analogy

Principle of Succession in Time, in Accordance with the Law of Causality

All alterations take place in conformity with the
law of the connection of cause and effect.

Proof

(The preceding principle has shown that all appearances of succession in time are one and all only *alterations,* that is, a successive being and not-being of
the determinations of substance which abides; and
therefore that the being of substance as following on
its not-being, or its not-being as following upon its
being cannot be admitted—in other words, that
there is no coming into being or passing away of
substance itself. Still otherwise expressed the principle is, that *all change (succession) of appearances is*

B 233

merely alteration. Coming into being and passing away of substance are not alterations of it, since the concept of alteration presupposes one and the same subject as existing with two opposite determinations, and therefore as abiding. With this preliminary reminder, we pass to the proof.)

I perceive that appearances follow one another, that is, that there is a state of things at one time the opposite of which was in the preceding time. Thus I am really connecting two perceptions in time. Now connection is not the work of mere sense and intuition, but is here the product of a synthetic faculty of imagination, which determines inner sense in respect of the time-relation. But imagination can connect these two states in two ways, so that either the one or the other precedes in time. For time cannot be perceived in itself, and what precedes and what follows cannot, therefore, by relation to it, be empirically determined in the object. I am conscious only that my imagination sets the one state before and the other after, not that the one state precedes the other in the object. In other words, the *objective* B 234 *relation* of appearances that follow upon one another is not to be determined through mere perception. In order that this relation be known as determined, the relation between the two states must be so thought that it is thereby determined as necessary which of them must be placed before, and which of them after, and that they cannot be placed in the reverse relation. But the concept which carries with it a necessity of synthetic unity can only be a pure concept that lies in the understanding, not in perception; and in this case it is the concept of the *relation of cause and effect,* the former of which determines the latter in time, as its consequence—not as in a sequence that may occur solely in the imagination (or that may not be perceived at all). Experience itself—in other words, empirical knowledge of appearances—is thus possible only in so far as we subject the succession of appearances, and therefore all alteration, to the law of causality; and, as likewise follows, the appearances, as objects of experience, are themselves possible only in conformity with the law.

The apprehension of the manifold of appearance is always successive. The representations of the parts follow upon one another. Whether they also follow one another in the object is a point which calls for further reflection, and which is not decided by the above statement. Everything, every representation even, in so far as we are conscious of it, may be entitled object. But it is a question for deeper enquiry what the word "object" ought to signify in B 235 respect of appearances when these are viewed not in so far as they are (as representations) objects, but only in so far as they stand for an object. The appearances, in so far as they are objects of consciousness simply in virtue of being representations, are not in any way distinct from their apprehension, that is, from their reception in the synthesis of imagination; and we must therefore agree that the manifold of appearances is always generated in the mind successively. Now if appearances were things in themselves, then since we have to deal solely with our representations, we could never determine from the succession of the representations how their manifold may be connected in the object. How things may be in themselves, apart from the representations through which they affect us, is entirely outside our sphere of knowledge. In spite, however, of the fact that the appearances are not things in themselves, and yet are what alone can be given to us to know, in spite also of the fact that their representation in apprehension is always successive, I have to show what sort of a connection in time belongs to the manifold in the appearances themselves. For instance, the apprehension of the manifold in the appearance of a house which stands before me is successive. The question then arises, whether the manifold of the house is also in itself successive. This, however, is what no one one will grant. Now immediately I unfold the transcendental B 236 meaning of my concepts of an object, I realise that the house is not a thing in itself, but only an appearance, that is, a representation, the transcendental object of which is unknown. What, then, am I to understand by the question: how the manifold may be connected in the appearance itself, which yet is nothing in itself? That which lies in the successive apprehension is here viewed as representation, while the appearance which is given to me, notwithstanding that it is nothing but the sum of these representations, is viewed as their object; and my concept, which I derive from the representations of apprehension, has to agree with it. Since truth consists in the agreement of knowledge with the object, it will at once be seen that we can here enquire only regarding the formal conditions of empirical truth, and that appearance, in contradistinction to the representations of apprehension, can be represented as an object distinct from them only if it stands under a rule which distinguishes it from every other apprehension and necessitates some one particular mode of connection of the manifold. The object is *that* in the appearance which contains the condition of this necessary rule of apprehension.

Let us now proceed to our problem. That something happens, i.e., that something, or some state which did not previously exist, comes to be, cannot B 237 be perceived unless it is preceded by an appearance which does not contain in itself this state. For an event which should follow upon an empty time, that is, a coming to be preceded by no state of things, is as little capable of being apprehended as empty time itself. Every apprehension of an event is therefore a perception that follows upon another perception. But since, as I have above illustrated by reference to the appearance of a house, this likewise happens in all synthesis of apprehension, the apprehension of an event is not yet thereby distinguished from other apprehensions. But, as I also note, in an appearance which contains a happening (the preceding state of the perception we may entitle A, and the succeeding B) B can be apprehended only as following upon A; the perception A cannot follow upon B but only precede it. For instance, I see a ship move down stream. My perception of its lower position follows upon the perception of its position higher up in the stream, and it is impossible that in the apprehension of this appearance the ship should first be perceived lower down in the stream and afterwards higher up. The order in which the perceptions succeed one another in apprehension is in this instance determined, and to this order apprehension is bound down. In the previous example of a house my perceptions could begin with the apprehension of the roof and end with B 238 the basement, or could begin from below and end above; and I could similarly apprehend the manifold of the empirical intuition either from right to left or from left to right. In the series of these perceptions there was thus no determinate order specifying at what point I must begin in order to connect the manifold empirically. But in the perception of an event there is always a rule that makes the order in which the perceptions (in the apprehension of this appearance) follow upon one another a *necessary* order.

In this case, therefore, we must derive the *subjective succession* of apprehension from the *objective succession* of appearances. Otherwise the order of apprehension is entirely undetermined, and does not distinguish one appearance from another. Since the subjective succession by itself is altogether arbitrary, it does not prove anything as to the manner in which the manifold is connected in the object. The objective succession will therefore consist in that order of the manifold of appearance according to which, *in conformity with a rule,* the apprehension of that which happens follows upon the apprehension of that which precedes. Thus only can I be justified in asserting, not merely of my apprehension, but of appearance itself, that a succession is to be met with in it. This is only another way of saying that I cannot arrange the apprehension otherwise than in this very succession.

In conformity with such a rule there must lie in that which precedes an event the condition B 239 of a rule according to which this event invariably and necessarily follows. I cannot reverse this order, proceeding back from the event to determine through apprehension that which precedes. For appearance never goes back from the succeeding to the preceding point of time, though it does indeed stand in relation to *some* preceding point of time. The advance, on the other hand, from a given time to the determinate time that follows is a necessary advance. Therefore, since there certainly is something that follows [i.e., that is *apprehended* as following], I must refer it necessarily to something else which precedes it and upon which it follows in conformity with a rule, that is, of necessity. The event, as the conditioned, thus affords reliable evidence of some condition, and this condition is what determines the event.

Let us suppose that there is nothing antecedent to an event, upon which it must follow according to rule. All succession of perception would then be only in the apprehension, that is, would be merely subjective, and would never enable us to determine objectively which perceptions are those that really precede and which are those that follow. We should then have only a play of representations, relating to no object; that is to say, it would not be possible through our perception to distinguish one appearance from another as regards relations of time. For the succession in our apprehension would always be one and the same, and there would be nothing in B 240 the appearance which so determines it that a certain sequence is rendered objectively necessary. I could not then assert that two states follow upon one another in the [field of] appearance, but only that one apprehension follows upon the other. That is something merely subjective, determining no object; and may not, therefore, be regarded as knowledge of any object, not even of an object in the [field of] appearance.

If, then, we experience that something happens, we in so doing always presuppose that something precedes it, on which it follows according to a rule. Otherwise I should not say of the object that it follows. For mere succession in my apprehension, if there be no rule determining the succession in relation to something that precedes, does not justify me in assuming any succession in the object. I render my subjective synthesis of apprehension objective only by reference to a rule in accordance with which the appearances in their succession, that is, as they happen, are determined by the preceding state. The experience of an event [i.e., of anything as *happening*] is itself possible only on this assumption.

This may seem to contradict all that has hitherto been taught in regard to the procedure of our understanding. The accepted view is that only through the perception and comparison of events repeatedly following in a uniform manner upon preceding appearances are we enabled to discover a rule according to which certain events always B 241 follow upon certain appearances, and that this is the way in which we are first led to construct for ourselves the concept of cause. Now the concept, if thus formed, would be merely empirical, and the rule which it supplies, that everything which happens has a cause, would be as contingent as the experience upon which it is based. Since the universality and necessity of the rule would not be grounded *a priori*, but only on induction, they would be merely fictitious and without genuinely universal validity. It is with these, as with other pure *a priori* representations—for instance, space and time. We can extract clear concepts of them from experience, only because we have put them into experience, and because experience is thus itself brought about only by their means. Certainly, the logical clearness of this representation of a rule determining the series of events is possible only after we have employed it in experience. Nevertheless, recognition of the rule, as a condition of the synthetic unity of appearances in time, has been the ground of experience itself, and has therefore preceded it *a priori.*

We have, then, to show, in the case under consideration, that we never, even in experience, ascribe succession (that is, the happening of some event which previously did not exist) to the object, and so distinguish it from subjective sequence in our apprehension, except when there is an underlying rule which compels us to observe this order   B 242 of perceptions rather than any other; nay, that this compulsion is really what first makes possible the representation of a succession in the object.

We have representations in us, and can become conscious of them. But however far this consciousness may extend, and however careful and accurate it may be, they still remain mere representations, that is, inner determinations of our mind in this or that relation of time. How, then, does it come about that we posit an object for these representations, and so, in addition to their subjective reality, as modifications, ascribe to them some mysterious kind of objective reality. Objective meaning cannot consist in the relation to another representation (of that which we desire to entitle object), for in that case the question again arises, how this latter representation goes out beyond itself, acquiring objective meaning in addition to the subjective meaning which belongs to it as determination of the mental state. If we enquire what new character *relation to an object* confers upon our representations, what dignity they thereby acquire, we find that it results only in subjecting the representations to a rule, and so in necessitating us to connect them in some one specific manner; and conversely, that only in so far   B 243 as our representations are necessitated in a certain order as regards their time-relations do they acquire objective meaning.

In the synthesis of appearances the manifold of representations is always successive. Now no object is hereby represented, since through this succession, which is common to all apprehensions, nothing is distinguished from anything else. But immediately I perceive or assume that in this succession there is a relation to the preceding state, from which the representation follows in conformity with a rule, I represent something as an event, as something that happens; that is to say, I apprehend an object to which I must ascribe a certain determinate position in time—a position which, in view of the preceding state, cannot be otherwise assigned. When, therefore, I perceive that something happens, this representation first of all contains [the consciousness] that there is something preceding, because only by reference to what precedes does the appearance acquire its time-relation, namely, that of existing after a preceding time in which it itself was not. But it can acquire this determinate position in this relation of time only in so far as something is presupposed in the preceding state upon which it follows invariably, that is, in accordance with a rule. From this there results a twofold consequence. In the first place, I cannot reverse the series, placing that which happens prior to that upon which it follows. And secondly, if the state which precedes is B 244 posited, this determinate event follows inevitably and necessarily. The situation, then, is this: there is an order in our representations in which the present, so far as it has come to be, refers us to some preceding state as a correlate of the event which is given; and though this correlate is, indeed, indeterminate, it none the less stands in a determining relation to the event as its consequence, connecting the event in necessary relation with itself in the time-series.

If, then, it is a necessary law of our sensibility, and therefore a *formal condition* of all perceptions, that the preceding time necessarily determines the succeeding (since I cannot advance to the succeeding time save through the preceding), it is also an indispensable law of *empirical representation* of the time-series that the appearances of past time determine all existences in the succeeding time, and that these latter, as events, can take place only in so far as the appearances of past time determine their existence in time, that is, determine them according to a rule. *For only in appearances can we empirically apprehend this continuity in the connection of times.*

Understanding is required for all experience and for its possibility. Its primary contribution does not consist in making the representation of objects distinct, but in making the representation of an object possible at all. This it does by carrying the time-B 245 order over into the appearances and their existence. For to each of them, [viewed] as [a] consequent, it assigns, through relation to the preceding appearances, a position determined *a priori* in time. Otherwise, they would not accord with time itself, which [in] *a priori* [fashion] determines the position of all

its parts. Now since absolute time is not an object of perception, this determination of position cannot be derived from the relation of appearances to it. On the contrary, the appearances must determine for one another their position in time, and make their time-order a necessary order. In other words, that which follows or happens must follow in conformity with a universal rule upon that which was contained in the preceding state. A series of appearances thus arises which, with the aid of the understanding, produces and makes necessary the same order and continuous connection in the series of possible perceptions as is met with *a priori* in time—the form of inner intuition wherein all perceptions must have a position.

That something happens is, therefore, a perception which belongs to a possible experience. This experience becomes actual when I regard the appearance as determined in its position in time, and therefore as an object that can always be found in the connection of perceptions in accordance with a rule. This rule, by which we determine something B 246 according to succession of time, is, that the condition under which an event invariably and necessarily follows is to be found in what precedes the event. The principle of sufficient reason is thus the ground of possible experience, that is, of objective knowledge of appearances in respect of their relation in the order of time.

The proof of this principle rests on the following considerations. All empirical knowledge involves the synthesis of the manifold by the imagination. This synthesis is always successive, that is, the representations in it are always sequent upon one another. In the imagination this sequence is not in any way determined in its order, as to what must precede and what must follow, and the series of sequent representations can indifferently be taken either in backward or in forward order. But if this synthesis is a synthesis of apprehension of the manifold of a given appearance, the order is determined in the object, or, to speak more correctly, is an order of successive synthesis that determines an object. In accordance with this order something must necessarily precede, and when this antecedent is posited, something else must necessarily follow. If, then, my perception is to contain knowledge of an event, of something as actually happening, it must be an empirical judgment in which we think

B 247 the sequence as determined; that is, it presupposes another appearance in time, upon which it follows necessarily, according to a rule. Were it not so, were I to posit the antecedent and the event were not to follow necessarily thereupon, I should have to regard the succession as a merely subjective play of my fancy; and if I still represented it to myself as something objective, I should have to call it a mere dream. Thus the relation of appearances (as possible perceptions) according to which the subsequent event, that which happens, is, as to its existence, necessarily determined in time by something preceding in conformity with a rule—in other words, the relation of cause to effect—is the condition of the objective validity of our empirical judgments, in respect of the series of perceptions, and so of their empirical truth; that is to say, it is the condition of experience. The principle of the causal relation in the sequence of appearances is therefore also valid of all objects of experience ([in so far as they are] under the conditions of succession), as being itself the ground of the possibility of such experience.

At this point a difficulty arises with which we must at once deal. The principle of the causal connection among appearances is limited in our formula to their serial succession, whereas it applies also to their coexistence, when cause and effect are simultaneous. For instance, a room is warm while the outer air is cool. I look around for the cause, B 248 and find a heated stove. Now the stove, as cause, is simultaneous with its effect, the heat of the room. Here there is no serial succession in time between cause and effect. They are simultaneous, and yet the law is valid. The great majority of efficient natural causes are simultaneous with their effects, and the sequence in time of the latter is due only to the fact that the cause cannot achieve its complete effect in one moment. But in the moment in which the effect first comes to be, it is invariably simultaneous with the causality of its cause. If the cause should have ceased to exist a moment before, the effect would never have come to be. Now we must not fail to note that it is the *order* of time, not the *lapse* of time, with which we have to reckon; the relation remains even if no time has elapsed. The time between the causality of the cause and its immediate effect may be [a] *vanishing* [quantity], and they may thus be simultaneous; but the relation of the one to the other will always still remain determinable in time. If I view as a cause a ball which impresses a hollow as it lies on a stuffed cushion, the cause is simultaneous with the effect. But I still distinguish the two through the time-relation of their dynamical connection. For if I lay the ball on the cushion, a hollow follows upon the previous flat smooth shape; but if (for any B 249 reason) there previously exists a hollow in the cushion, a leaden ball does not follow upon it.

The sequence in time is thus the sole empirical criterion of an effect in its relation to the causality of the cause which precedes it. A glass [filled with water] is the cause of the rising of the water above its horizontal surface, although both appearances are simultaneous. For immediately I draw off water from a larger vessel into the glass, something follows, namely, the alteration from the horizontal position which the water then had to the concave form which it assumes in the glass.

Causality leads to the concept of action, this in turn to the concept of force, and thereby to the concept of substance. As my critical scheme, which is concerned solely with the sources of synthetic *a priori* knowledge, must not be complicated through the introduction of analyses, which aim only at the clarification, not at the extension, of concepts, I leave detailed exposition of my concepts to a future system of pure reason. Such an analysis has already, indeed, been developed in considerable detail in the existing text-books. But I must not leave unconsidered the empirical criterion of a substance, in so far as substance appears to manifest itself not through permanence of appearance, but more adequately and easily through action.

Wherever there is action—and therefore activity and force—there is also substance, and it B 250 is in substance alone that the seat of this fruitful source of appearances must be sought. This is, so far, well said; but when we seek to explain what is to be understood by substance, and in so doing are careful to avoid the fallacy of reasoning in a circle, the discovery of an answer is no easy task. How are we to conclude directly from the action to the *permanence* of that which acts? For that is an essential and quite peculiar characteristic of substance (as phenomenon). But while according to the usual procedure, which deals with concepts in purely analytic fashion, this question would be completely insoluble, it presents no such difficulty from the standpoint which we have been formulating. Action signifies the relation of the subject of causality to its effect. Since, now, every effect consists in that which happens, and therefore in the transitory, which signifies time in its character of succession, its ultimate subject, as the substratum of everything that changes, is the *permanent*, that is, substance. For according to the principle of causality actions are always the first ground of all change of appearances, and cannot therefore be found in a subject which itself changes, because in that case other actions and another subject would be required to determine this change. For this reason action is a sufficient empirical criterion to establish the substantiality of a subject, without my requiring first B 251 to go in quest of its permanence through the comparison of perceptions. Besides, by such method [of comparison] we could not achieve the completeness required for the magnitude and strict universality of the concept. That the first subject of the causality of all coming to be and ceasing to be cannot itself, in the field of appearances, come to be and cease to be, is an assured conclusion which leads to [the concept of] empirical necessity and permanence in existence, and so to the concept of a substance as appearance.

When something happens, the mere coming to be, apart from all question of what it is that has come to be, is already in itself a matter for enquiry. The transition from the not-being of a state to this state, even supposing that this state [as it occurs] in the [field of] appearance exhibited no quality, of itself demands investigation. This coming to be, as was shown above in the *First Analogy*, does not concern substance, which does not come to be, but its state. It is, therefore, only alteration, not a coming to be out of nothing. For if coming to be out of nothing is regarded as effect of a foreign cause, it has to be entitled creation, and that cannot be admitted as an event among appearances, since its mere possibility would destroy the unity of experience. On the other hand, when I view all things not as phenomena but as things in themselves, and as objects B 252 of the mere understanding, then despite their being substances they can be regarded, in respect of their existence, as depending upon a foreign cause. But our terms would then carry with them quite other meanings, and would not apply to appearances as possible objects of experience.

How anything can be altered, and how it should be possible that upon one state in a given moment an opposite state may follow in the next moment—of this we have not, a priori, the least conception. For that we require knowledge of actual forces, which can only be given empirically as, for instance, of the moving forces, or what amounts to the same thing, of certain successive appearances, as motions, which indicate [the presence of] such forces. But apart from all question of what the content of the alteration, that is, what the state which is altered, may be, the form of every alteration, the condition under which, as a coming to be of another state, it can alone take place, and so the succession of the states themselves (the happening), can still be considered *a priori* according to the law of causality and the conditions of time.*

If a substance passes from one state, a, to an-   B 253 other, b, the point of time of the second is distinct from that of the first, and follows upon it. Similarly, the second state as reality in the [field of] appearance differs from the first wherein it did not exist, as b from zero. That is to say, even if the state b differed from the state a only in magnitude, the alteration would be a coming to be of $b-a$, which did not exist in the previous state, and in respect of which it $=0$.

The question therefore arises how a thing passes from one state$=a$ to another$=b$. Between two instants there is always a time, and between any two states in the two instants there is always a difference which has magnitude. For all parts of appearances are always themselves magnitudes. All transition from one state to another therefore occurs in a time which is contained between two instants, of which the first determines the state from which the thing arises, and the second that into which it passes. Both instants, then, are limits of the time of a change, and so of the intermediate state between the two states, and therefore as such form part of the total alteration. Now every alteration has a cause which evinces its causality in the whole time in which the alteration takes place. This cause,

---

* It should be carefully noted that I speak not of the alteration of certain relations in general, but of alteration of state. Thus, when a body moves uniformly, it does not in any way alter its state (of motion); that occurs only when its motion increases or diminishes.

therefore, does not engender the alteration suddenly, that is, at once or in one instant, but in a time; so that, as the time increases from the initial instant *a* to its completion in *b*, the magnitude of the reality ($b-a$) is in like manner generated through all smaller degrees which are contained between the first and the last. All alteration is thus only possible through a continuous action of the causality which, so far as it is uniform, is entitled a moment. The alteration does not consist of these moments, but is generated by them as their effect.

That is the law of the continuity of all alteration. Its ground is this: that neither time nor appearance in time consists of parts which are the smallest [possible], and that, nevertheless, the state of a thing passes in its alteration through all these parts, as elements, to its second state. In the [field of] appearance there is no difference of the real that is the smallest, just as in the magnitude of times there is no time that is the smallest; and the new state of reality accordingly proceeds from the first wherein this reality was not, through all the infinite degrees, the differences of which from one another are all smaller than that between *0* and *a*.

While we are not concerned to enquire what utility this principle may have in the investigation of nature, what does imperatively call for investigation is the question how such a principle, which seems to extend our knowledge of nature, can be possible completely *a priori*. Such an enquiry cannot be dispensed with, even though direct inspection may show the principle to be true and [empirically] real, and though the question, how it should be possible, may therefore be considered superfluous. For there are so many ungrounded claims to the extension of our knowledge through pure reason, that we must take it as a universal principle that any such pretension is of itself a ground for being always mistrustful, and that, in the absence of evidence afforded by a thoroughgoing deduction, we may not believe and assume the justice of such claims, no matter how clear the *dogmatic* proof of them may appear to be.

All increase in empirical knowledge, and every advance of perception, no matter what the objects may be, whether appearances or pure intuitions, is nothing but an extension of the determination of inner sense, that is, an advance in time. This advance in time determines everything, and is not in itself determined through anything further. That is to say, its parts are given only in time, and only through the synthesis of time; they are not given antecedently to the synthesis. For this reason every transition in perception to something which follows in time is a determination of time through the generation of this perception, and since time is always and in all its parts a magnitude, is likewise the generation of a perception as a magnitude through all degrees of which no one is the smallest, from zero up to its determinate degree. This reveals the possibility of knowing *a priori* a law of alterations, in respect of their form. We are merely anticipating our own apprehension, the formal condition of which, since it dwells in us prior to all appearance that is given, must certainly be capable of being known *a priori*.

In the same manner, therefore, in which time contains the sensible *a priori* condition of the possibility of a continuous advance of the existing to what follows, the understanding, by virtue of the unity of apperception, is the *a priori* condition of the possibility of a continuous determination of all positions for the appearances in this time, through the series of causes and effects, the former of which inevitably lead to the existence of the latter, and so render the empirical knowledge of the time-relations valid universally for all time, and therefore objectively valid.

The Antimony of Pure Reason   B 455

First Conflict of the Transcendental Ideas

Thesis The world has a beginning in time, and is also limited as regards space.

Proof If we assume that the world has no beginning in time, then up to every given moment an eternity has elapsed, and there has passed away in the world an infinite series of successive states of things. Now the infinity of a series consists in the fact that it can never be completed through successive synthesis. It thus follows that it is impossible for an infinite world-series to have passed away, and that a beginning of the world is therefore a necessary condition of the world's existence. This was the first point that called for proof.

As regards the second point, let us again assume the opposite, namely, that the world is an infinite given whole of coexisting things. Now the magnitude of a quantum which is not given in intuition[1] as within certain limits, can be thought only through the synthesis of its parts, and the totality of such a quantum only through a synthesis that is brought to completion through repeated addition of unit to unit.[2] In order, therefore, to think, as a whole, the world which fills all spaces, the successive synthesis of the parts of an infinite world must be viewed as completed, that is, an infinite time must be viewed as having elapsed in the enumeration of all coexisting things. This, however, is impossible. An infinite aggregate of actual things cannot therefore be viewed as a given whole, nor consequently as simultaneously given. The world is, therefore, as regards extension in space, not infinite, but is enclosed within limits. This was the second point in dispute.

Antithesis The world has no beginning, and no limits in space; it is infinite as regards both time and space.

Proof For let us assume that it has a beginning. Since the beginning is an existence which is preceded by a time in which the thing is not, there must have been a preceding time in which the world was not, *i.e.* an empty time. Now no coming to be of a thing is possible in an empty time, because no part of such a time possesses, as compared with any other, a distinguishing condition of existence rather than of nonexistence; and this applies whether the

thing is supposed to arise of itself or through some other cause. In the world many series of things can, indeed, begin; but the world itself cannot have a beginning, and is therefore infinite in respect of past time.

As regards the second point, let us start by assuming the opposite, namely, that the world in space is finite and limited, and consequently exists in an empty space which is unlimited. Things will therefore not only be related *in space* but also related *to space*. Now since the world is an absolute whole beyond which there is no object of intuition, and therefore no correlate with which the world stands in relation, the relation of the world to empty space would be a relation of it to no *object*. But such a relation, and consequently the limitation of the world by empty space, is nothing. The world cannot, therefore, be limited in space; that is, it is infinite in respect of extension.[3]

Observation on the First Antimony

I. On the Thesis In stating these conflicting arguments I have not sought to elaborate sophisms. That is to say, I have not resorted to the method of the special pleader who attempts to take advantage of an opponent's carelessness—freely allowing the appeal to a misunderstood law, in order that he may be in a position to establish his own unrighteous

B 456 (margin)
B 457 (margin)
B 458 (margin)
B 459 (margin)
B 457 (margin)

---

[1] An indeterminate quantum can be intuited as a whole when it is such that though enclosed within limits we do not require to construct its totality through measurement, that is, through the successive synthesis of its parts. For the limits, in cutting off anything further, themselves determine its completeness.

[2] The concept of totality is in this case simply the representation of the completed synthesis of its parts; for, since we cannot obtain the concept from the intuition of the whole—that being in this case impossible—we can apprehend it only through the synthesis of the parts viewed as carried, at least in idea, to the completion of the infinite.

[3] Space is merely the form of outer intuition (formal intuition). It is not a real object which can be outwardly intuited. Space, as prior to all things which determine (occupy or limit) it, or rather which give an empirical intuition in accordance with its form, is, under the name of absolute space, nothing but the mere possibility of outer appearances in so far as they either exist in themselves or can be added to given appearances. Empirical intuition is not, therefore, a composite of appearances and space (of perception and empty intuition). The one is not the correlate of the other in a synthesis; they are connected in one and the same empirical intuition as matter and form of the intuition. If we attempt to set one of these two factors outside the other, space outside all appearances, there arise all sorts of empty determination of outer intuition, which yet are not possible perceptions. For example, a determination of the relation of the motion (or rest) of the world to infinite empty space is a determination which can never be perceived, and is therefore the predicate of a mere thought-entity.

claims by the refutation of that law. Each of the above proofs arises naturally out of the matter in dispute, and no advantage has been taken of the openings afforded by erroneous conclusions arrived at by dogmatists in either party.

I might have made a pretence of establishing the thesis in the usual manner of the dogmatists, by starting from a defective concept of the infinitude of a given magnitude. I might have argued that a magnitude is infinite if a greater than itself, as determined by the multiplicity of given units which it contains, is not possible. Now no multiplicity is the greatest, since one or more units can always be added to it. Consequently an infinite given magnitude, and therefore an infinite world (infinite as regards the elapsed series or as regards extension) is impossible; it must be limited in both respects. Such is the line that my proof might have followed. But the above concept is not adequate to what we mean by an infinite whole. It does not represent *how great* it is, and consequently is not the concept of a *maxi-*

B 460   *mum.* Through it we think only its relation to any assignable unit in respect to which it is greater than all number. According as the unit chosen is greater or smaller, the infinite would be greater or smaller. Infinitude, however, as it consists solely in the relation to the given unit, would always remain the same. The absolute magnitude of the whole would not, therefore, be known in this way; indeed, the above concept does not really deal with it.

The true transcendental concept of infinitude is this, that the successive synthesis of units required for the enumeration of a quantum can never be completed.[4] Hence it follows with complete certainty that an eternity of actual successive states leading up to a given (the present) moment cannot have elapsed, and that the world must therefore have a beginning.

In the second part of the thesis the difficulty involved in a series that is infinite and yet has elapsed does not arise, since the manifold of a world which is infinite in respect of extension is given as *coexisting.* But if we are to think the totality of such a multiplicity, and yet cannot appeal to limits that of themselves constitute it a totality in intuition, we

have to account for a concept which in this case cannot proceed from the whole to the determinate multiplicity of the parts, but which must demonstrate the possibility of a whole by means of the successive synthesis of the parts. Now since this synthesis must constitute a never to be completed series, I cannot think a totality either prior to the synthesis or by means of the synthesis. For the concept of totality is in this case itself the representation of a completed synthesis of the parts. And since this completion is impossible, so likewise is the concept of it.

II. On the Antithesis The proof of the infinitude of the given world-series and of the world-whole, rests upon the fact that, on the contrary assumption, an empty time and an empty space, must constitute the limit of the world. I am aware that attempts have been made to evade this conclusoin by arguing that a limit of the world in time and space is quite possible without our having to make the impossible assumption of an absolute time prior to the beginning of the world, or of an absolute space extending beyond the real world. With the latter part of this doctrine, as held by the philosophers of the Leibnizian school, I am entirely satisfied. Space is merely the form of outer intuition; it is not a real object which can be outwardly intuited; it is not a correlate of the appearances, but the form of the appearances themselves. And since space is thus no object but only the form of possible objects, it cannot be regarded as something absolute in itself that determines the existence of things. Things, as appearances, determine space, that is, of all its possible predicates of magnitude and relation they determine this or that particular one to belong to the real. Space, on the other hand, viewed as a self-subsistent something, is nothing real in itself; and cannot, therefore, determine the magnitude or shape of real things. Space, it further follows, whether full or empty,[5] may be limited by appearances, but appearances cannot be limited *by an empty space* outside   B 461

---

[4] This quantum therefore contains a quantity (of given units) which is greater than any number—which is the mathematical concept of the infinite.

[5] It will be evident that what we here desire to say is that *empty space,* so far as it is *limited by appearances,* that is, *within the world,* is at least not contradictory of transcendental principles and may therefore, so far as they are concerned, be admitted. This does not, however, amount to an assertion of its possibility.

them. This is likewise true of time. But while all this may be granted, it yet cannot be denied that these two non-entities, empty-space outside the world and empty time prior to it, have to be assumed if we are to assume a limit to the world in space and in time.

The method of argument which professes to enable us to avoid the above consequence (that of having to assume that if the world has limits in time and space, the infinite void must determine the magnitude in which actual things are to exist) consists in surreptitiously substituting for the sensible world some intelligible world of which we know nothing; for the first beginning (an existence preceded by a time of non-existence) an existence in general which presupposes no other condition whatsoever; and for the limits of extension boundaries of the world-whole—thus getting rid of time and space. But we are here treating only of the *mundus phaenomenon* and its magnitude, and cannot therefore abstract from the aforesaid conditions of sensibility without destroying the very being of that world. If the sensible world is limited, it must necessarily lie in the infinite void. If that void, and consequently space in general as *a priori* condition of the possibility of appearances, be set aside, the entire sensible world vanishes. This world is all that is given us in our problem. The *mundus intelligibilis* is nothing but the general concept of a world in general, in which abstraction is made from all conditions of its intuition, and in reference to which, therefore, no synthetic proposition, either affirmative or negative, can possibly be asserted.

B 462 ## The Antinomy of Pure Reason

B 463 ### Second Conflict of the Transcendental Ideas

Thesis Every composite substance in the world is made up of simple parts, and nothing anywhere exists save the simple or what is composed of the simple.

Proof Let us assume that composite substances are not made up of simple parts. If all composition be then removed in thought, no composite part, and

(since we admit no simple parts) also no simple part, that is to say, nothing at all, will remain, and accordingly no substance will be given. Either, therefore, it is impossible to remove in thought all composition, or after its removal there must remain something which exists without composition, that is, the simple. In the former case the composite would not be made up of substances; composition, as applied to substances, is only an accidental relation in independence of which they must still persist as self-subsistent beings. Since this contra- B 464 dicts our supposition, there remains only the original supposition, that a composite of substances in the world is made up of simple parts.

It follows, as an immediate consequence, that the things in the world are all, without exception, simple beings; that composition is merely an external state of these beings; and that although we can never so isolate these elementary substances as to take them out of this state of composition, reason must think them as the primary subjects of all composition, and therefore, as single beings, prior to all composition.

Antithesis No composite thing in the world is made up of simple parts, and there nowhere exists in the world anything simple.

Proof Assume that a composite thing (as substance) is made up of simple parts. Since all external relation, and therefore all composition of substances, is possible only in space, a space must be made up of as many parts as are contained in the composite which occupies it. Space, however, is not made up of simple parts, but of spaces. Every part of the composite must therefore occupy a space. But the absolutely first parts of every composite are simple. The simple therefore occupies a space. Now since everything real, which occupies a space, contains in itself a manifold of constituents external to one another, and is therefore composite; and since a real composite is not made up of accidents (for accidents could not exist outside one another, in the absence of substance) but of substances, it follows that the simple would be a composite of substances—which is self-contradictory.

The second proposition of the antithesis, that B 465 nowhere in the world does there exist anything simple, is intended to mean only this, that the existence of the absolutely simple cannot be established by any experience or perception, either outer or inner; and that the absolutely simple is therefore a mere idea, the objective reality of which can never be shown in any possible experience, and which, as being without an object, has no application in the explanation of the appearances. For if we assumed that in experience an object might be found for this transcendental idea, the empirical intuition of such an object would have to be known as one that contains no manifold (factors) external to one another and combined into unity. But since from the non-consciousness of such a manifold we cannot conclude to its complete impossibility in every kind of intuition of an object; and since without such proof absolute simplicity can never be established, it follows that such simplicity cannot be infered from any perception whatsoever. An absolutely simple object can never be given in any possible experience. And since by the world of sense we must mean the sum of all possible experiences, it follows that nothing simple is to be found anywhere in it.

This second proposition of the antithesis has a much wider application than the first. Whereas the first proposition banishes the simple only from the intuition of the composite, the second excludes it from the whole of nature. Accordingly it has not been possible to prove this second proposition by reference to the concept of a given object of outer intuition (of the composite), but only by reference to its relation to a possible experience in general.

B 466 ## *Observation on the Second Antimony*

B 467 *I. On the Thesis* When I speak of a whole as necessarily made up of simple parts, I am referring only to a substantial whole that is composite in the strict sense of the term "composite," that is, to that accidental unity of the manifold which, given as *separate* (at least in thought), is brought into a mutual connection, and thereby constitutes a unity. Space should properly be called not *compositum* but *totum*, since its parts are possible only in the whole, not the whole through the parts. It might, indeed, be called a *compositum ideale*, but not *reale*. This, however, is a mere subtlety. Since space is not a composite made up of substances (not even of real accidents), if I remove all compositeness from it, nothing remains, not even the point. For a point is

possible only as the limit of a space, and so of a composite. Space and time do not, therefore, consist B 468 of simple parts. What belongs only to the state of a substance, even though it has a magnitude, *e.g.* alteration, does not consist of the simple; that is to say, a certain degree of alteration does not come about through the accretion of many simple alterations. Our inference from the composite to the simple applies only to self-subsisting things. Accidents of the state [of a thing] are not self-subsisting. Thus the proof of the necessity of the simple, as the constitutive parts of the substantially composite, can easily be upset (and therewith the thesis as a whole), if it be extended too far and in the absence of a limiting qualification be made to apply to everything composite—as has frequently happened.

Moreover I am here speaking only of the simple in so far as it is necessarily given in the composite—the latter being resolvable into the simple, as its constituent parts. The word *monas*, in the strict B 470 sense in which it is employed by Liebniz, should refer only to the simple which is *immediately* given as simple substance (*e.g.* in self-consciousness), and not to an element of the composite. This latter is better entitled *atomus*. As I am seeking to prove the [existence of] simple substances only as elements in the composite, I might entitle the thesis of the second antinomy, transcendental *atomistic*. But as this word has long been appropriated to signify a particular mode of explaining bodily appearances (*moleculae*), and therefore presupposes empirical concepts, the thesis may more suitably be entitled to dialectical principle of *monadology*.

II. On the Antithesis Against the doctrine of the infinite divisibility of matter, the proof of which is purely mathematical, objections have been raised by the monadists. These objections, however, at once lay the monadists open to suspicion. For however evident mathematical proofs may be, they decline to recognize that the proofs are based upon insight into the constitution of space, in so far as space is in actual fact the formal condition of the possibility of all matter. They regard them merely as inferences from abstract but arbitrary concepts, and so as not being applicable to real things. How can it be possible to invent a different kind of intuition from that given in the original intuition of space, and how can the *a priori* determinations of space fail to be directly applicable to what is only possible in so far as it fills this space! Were we to give heed to them, then beside the mathematical point, which, while simple, is not a part but only the limit of a space, we should have to conceive physical points as being likewise simple, and yet as having the distinguishing characteristic of being able, as parts of space, to fill space through their mere aggregation. Without repeating the many familiar and conclusive refutations of this absurdity—it being quite futile to attempt to reason away by sophistical manipulation of purely discursive concepts the evident demonstrated truth of mathematics—I make only one observation, that when

B 469 philosophy here plays tricks with mathematics, it does so because it forgets that in this discussion we are concerned only with *appearances* and their condition. Here it is not sufficient to find for the pure concept of the composite formed by the understanding the concept of the simple; what has to be found is an intuition of the simple for the intuition of the composite (matter). But by the laws of sensibility, and therefore in objects of the senses, this is quite impossible. Though it may be true that when a whole, made up of substances, is thought by the pure understanding alone, we must, prior to all composition of it, have the simple, this does not hold of the *totum substantiale phaenomenon* which, as empirical intuition in space, carries with it the necessary characteristic that no part of it is simple, because no part of space is simple. The monadists have, indeed, been sufficiently acute to seek escape from this difficulty by refusing to treat space as a condition of the possibility of the objects of outer intuition (bodies), and by taking instead these and the dynamical relation of substances as the condition of the possibility of space. But we have a concept of bodies only as appearances; and as such they necessarily presuppose space as the condition of the possibility of all outer appearance. This evasion of the issue is therefore futile, and has already been sufficiently disposed of in the Transcendental Aesthetic. The argument of the monadists would indeed be valid if bodies were things in themselves.

B 471   The second dialectical assertion has this peculiarity, that over against it stands a dogmatic assertion which is the only one of all the pseudo-rational assertions that undertakes to afford manifest evidence, in an empirical object, of the reality of that which we have been ascribing only to transcenden-

tal ideas, namely, the absolute simplicity of substance—I refer to the assertion that the object of inner sense, the "I" which there thinks, is an absolutely simple substance. Without entering upon this question (it has been fully considered above). I need only remark, that if (as happens in the quite bare representation, "I") anything is thought as object only, without the addition of any synthetic determination of its intuition, nothing manifold and no compositeness can be perceived in such a representation. Besides, since the predicates through which I think this object are merely intuitions of inner sense, nothing can there be found which shows a manifold [of elements] external to one another, and therefore real compositeness. Self-consciousness is of such a nature that since the subject which thinks is at the same time its own object, it cannot divide itself, though it can divide the determinations which inhere in it; for in regard to itself every object is absolute unity. Nevertheless, when this subject is viewed *outwardly,* as an object of intuition, it must exhibit [some sort of] compositeness in its appearance; and it must always be viewed in this way if we wish to know whether or not there be in it a manifold [of elements] *external* to one another.

The Antinomy of Pure Reason   B 472

Third Conflict of the Transcendental Ideas   B 473

Thesis Causality in accordance with laws of nature is not the only causality from which the appearances of the world can one and all be derived. To explain these appearances it is necessary to assume that there is also another causality, that of freedom.

Proof Let us assume that there is no other causality than that in accordance with laws of nature. This being so, everything which *takes place* presupposes a preceding state upon which it inevitably follows according to a rule. But the preceding state must itself be something which has taken place (having come to be in a time in which it previously was not); for if it had always existed, its consequence also would have always existed, and would not have only just arisen. The causality of the cause through which something takes place is itself, therefore, something that has *taken place*, which again presupposes, in accordance with the law of nature, a preceding state and its causality, and this in similar manner a still earlier state, and so on. If, therefore, everything takes place solely in accordance with laws of nature, B 474 there will always be only a relative and never a first beginning, and consequently no completeness of the series on the side of the causes that arise the one from the other. But the law of nature is just this, that nothing takes place without a cause *sufficiently* determined *a priori*. The proposition that no causality is possible save in accordance with laws of nature, when taken in unlimited universality, is therefore self-contradictory; and this cannot, therefore, be regarded as the sole kind of causality.

We must, then, assume a causality through which something takes place, the cause of which is not itself determined, in accordance with necessary laws, by another cause antecedent to it, that is to say, an *absolute spontaneity* of the cause, whereby a series of appearances, which proceeds in accordance with laws of nature, begins *of itself*. This is transcendental freedom, without which, even in the [ordinary] course of nature, the series of appearances on the side of the causes can never be complete.

Antithesis There is no freedom; everything in the world takes place solely in accordance with laws of nature.

Proof Assume that there is freedom in the transcendental sense, as a special kind of causality in accordance with which the events in the world can have come about, namely, a power of absolutely beginning a state, and therefore also of absolutely beginning a series of consequences of that state; it then follows that not only will a series have its absolute beginning in this spontaneity, but that the very determination of this spontaneity to originate the series, that is to say, the causality itself, will have an absolute beginning; there will be no antecedent through which this act, in taking place, is determined in accordance with fixed laws. But every beginning of action presupposes a state of the not yet acting cause; and a *dynamical* beginning of the action, if it is also a first beginning, presupposes a state which has no *causal* connection with the preceding state of the cause, that is to say, in nowise follows from it. Transcendental freedom thus stands opposed to the law of causality; and the kind of connection which it assumes as holding be- B 475 tween the successive states of the active causes renders all unity of experience impossible. It is not to be met with in any experience, and is therefore an empty thought-entity.

In nature alone, therefore, [not in freedom], must we seek for the connection and order of cosmical events. Freedom (independence) from the laws of nature is no doubt a liberation from compulsion, but also from the guidance of all rules. For it is not permissible to say that the *laws* of freedom enter into the causality exhibited in the course of nature, and so take the place of natural laws. If freedom were determined in accordance with laws, it would not be freedom; it would simply be nature under another name. Nature and transcendental freedom differ as do conformity to law and lawlessness. Nature does indeed impose upon the understanding the exacting task of always seeking the origin of events ever higher in the series of causes, their causality being always conditioned. But in compensation it holds out the promise of thoroughgoing unity of experience in accordance with laws. The illusion of freedom, on the other hand, offers a point of rest to the enquiring understanding in the chain of causes, conducting it to an unconditioned causality which begins to act of itself. This causality is, however, blind, and abrogates those rules through which alone a completely coherent experience is possible.

Observation on the Third Antinomy   B 476

I. On the Thesis The transcendental idea of freedom B 477 does not by any means constitute the whole content of the psychological concept of that name, which is mainly empirical. The transcendental idea stands only for the absolute spontaneity of an action, as the proper ground of its imputability. This, however, is, for philosophy, the real stumbling-block; for there are insurmountable difficulties in the way of admitting any such type of unconditioned causality. What has always so greatly embarrassed speculative reason in dealing with the question of the freedom of the will, is its strictly transcendental aspect. The problem, properly viewed, is solely this: whether we must admit a power of *spontaneously* beginning a series of successive things or states.

How such a power is possible is not a question which requires to be answered in this case, any more than in regard to causality in accordance with the laws of nature. For, [as we have found], we have to remain satisfied with the *a priori* knowledge that this latter type of causality must be presupposed; we are not in the least able to comprehend how it can be possible that through one existence the existence of another is determined, and for this reason must be guided by experience alone. The necessity of a first beginning, due to freedom, of a series of appearances we have demonstrated only in so far as it is required to make an origin of the world conceivable; for all the later following states can be taken as resulting according to purely natural laws. But since the power of spontaneously beginning a series in time is thereby proved (though not understood), it is now also permissible for us to admit within the course of the world different series as capable in their causality of beginning of themselves, and so to attribute to their substances a power of acting from freedom. And we must not allow ourselves to be prevented from drawing this conclusion by a misapprehension, namely that, as a series occurring in the world can have only a relatively first beginning, being always preceded in the world by some other state of things, no absolute first beginning of a series is possible during the course of the world. For the absolutely first beginning of which we are here speaking is not a beginning in time, but in causality. If, for instance, I at this moment arise from my chair, in complete freedom, without being necessarily determined thereto by the influence of natural causes, a new series, with all its natural consequences *in infinitum,* has its absolute beginning in this event, although as regards time this event is only the continuation of a preceding series. For this resolution and act of mine do not form part of the succession of purely natural effects, and are not a mere continuation of them. In respect of its happening, natural causes exercise over it no determining influence whatsoever. It does indeed follow upon them, but without arising out of them; and accordingly, in respect of causality though not of time, must be entitled an absolutely first beginning of a series of appearances.

This requirement of reason, that we appeal in the series of natural causes to a first beginning, due

B 478

to freedom, is amply confirmed when we observe that all the philosophers of antiquity, with the sole exception of the Epicurean School, felt themselves obliged, when explaining cosmical movements, to assume a *prime mover,* that is, a freely acting cause, which first and of itself began this series of states. They made no attempt to render a first beginning conceivable through nature's own resources.

II. On the Antithesis The defender of an omnipotent nature (transcendental *physiocracy*), in maintaining his position against the pseudo-rational arguments offered in support of the counter-doctrine of freedom, would argue as follows. *If you do not, as regards time, admit anything as being mathematically first in the world, there is no necessity, as regards causality, for seeking something that is dynamically first.* What authority have you for inventing an absolutely first state of the world, and therefore an absolute beginning of the everflowing series of appearances, and so of procuring a restingplace for your imagination by setting bounds to limitless nature? Since the substances in the world have always existed—at least the unity of experience renders necessary such a supposition—there is no difficulty in assuming that change of their states, that is, a series of their alterations, has likewise always existed, and therefore that a first beginning, whether mathematical or dynamical, is not to be looked for. The possibility of such an infinite derivation, without a first member to which all the rest is merely a sequel, cannot indeed, in respect of its possibility, be rendered comprehensible. But if for this reason you refuse to recognise this enigma in nature, you will find yourself compelled to reject many fundamental synthetic properties and forces, which as little admit of comprehension. The possibility even of alteration itself would have to be denied. For were you not assured by experience that alteration actually occurs, you would never be able to excogitate *a priori* the possibility of such a ceaseless sequence of being and notbeing.

Even if a transcendental power of freedom be allowed, as supplying a beginning of happenings in the world, this power would in any case have to be outside the world (though any such assumption that over and above the sum of all possible intuitions there exists an object which cannot be given in any possible perception, is still a very bold one).

B 479

But to ascribe to substances in the world itself such a power, can never be permissible; for, should this be done, that connection of appearances determining one another with necessity according to universal laws, which we entitle nature, and with it the criterion of empirical truth, whereby experience is distinguished from dreaming, would almost entirely disappear. Side by side with such a lawless faculty of freedom, nature [as an ordered system] is hardly thinkable; the influences of the former would so unceasingly alter the laws of the latter that the appearances which in their natural course are regular and uniform would be reduced to disorder and incoherence.

B 480 ## The Antinomy of Pure Reason

B 481 ### Fourth Conflict of the Transcendental Ideas

Thesis There belongs to the world, either as its part or as its cause, a being that is absolutely necessary.

Proof The sensible world, as the sum-total of all appearances, contains a series of alterations. For without such a series even the representation of serial time, as a condition of the possibility of the sensible world, would not be given us.[6] But every alteration stands under its condition, which precedes it in time and renders it necessary. Now every condition that is given presupposes, in respect of its existence, a complete series of conditions up to the unconditioned, which alone is absolutely necessary. Alteration thus existing as a consequence of the absolutely necessary, the existence of something absolutely necessary must be granted. But this necessary existence itself belongs to the sensible world. For if it existed outside that world, the series of alterations in the world would derive its beginning from a necessary cause which would not itself belong to the sensible world. This, however, is im-

B 482

possible. For since the beginning of a series in time can be determined only by that which precedes it in time, the highest condition of the beginning of a series of changes must exist in the time when the series as yet was not (for a beginning is an existence preceded by a time in which the thing that begins did not yet exist). Accordingly the causality of the necessary cause of alterations, and therefore the cause itself, must belong to times and so to appearance—time being possible only as the form of appearance. Such causality cannot, therefore, be thought apart from that sum of all appearances which constitutes the world of sense. Something absolutely necessary is therefore contained in the world itself, whether this something be the whole series of alterations in the world of a part of the series.

Antithesis An absolutely necessary being nowhere exists in the world, nor does it exist outside the world as its cause.

Proof If we assume that the world itself is necessary, or that a necessary being exists in it, there are then two alternatives. Either there is a beginning in the series of alterations which is absolutely necessary, and therefore without a cause, or the series itself is without any beginning, and although contingent and conditioned in all its parts, none the less, as a whole, is absolutely necessary and unconditioned. The former alternative, however, conflicts with the dynamical law of the determination of all appearances in time; and the latter alternative contradicts itself, since the existence of a series cannot be necessary if no single member of it is necessary.

If, on the other hand, we assume that an absolutely necessary cause of the world exists outside the world, then this cause, as the highest member in the series of the causes of changes in the world, B 483 must begin the existence of the latter and their series.[7] Now this cause must itself begin to act, and its causality would therefore be in time, and so

---

[6] Time, as the formal condition of the possibility of changes, is indeed objectively prior to them; subjectively, however, in actual consciousness, the representation of time, like every other, is given only in connection with perceptions.

---

[7] The word "begin" is taken in two senses; first as *active*, signifying that as cause it begins (*infit*) a series of states which is its effect; secondly as *passive*, signifying the causality which begins to operate (*fit*) in the cause itself. I reason here from the former to the latter meaning.

would belong to the sum of appearances, that is, to the world. It follows that it itself, the cause, would not be outside the world—which contradicts our hypothesis. Therefore neither in the world, nor outside the world (though in causal connection with it), does there exist any absolutely necessary being.

B 484 ## Observation on the Fourth Antinomy

B 485 *I. On the Thesis* In proving the existence of a necessary being I ought not, in this connection, to employ any but the *cosmological* argument, that, namely, which ascends from the conditioned in the [field of] appearance to the unconditioned in concept, this latter being regarded as the necessary condition of the absolute totality of the series. To seek proof of this from the mere idea of a supreme being belongs to another principle of reson, and will have to be treated separately.

The pure cosmological proof, in demonstrating the existence of a necessary being, has to leave unsettled whether this being is the world itself or a thing distinct from it. To establish the latter view, we should require principles which are no longer cosmological and do not continue in the series of appearances. For we should have to employ concepts of contingent beings in general (viewed as objects of the understanding alone) and a principle which will enable us to connect these, by means of mere concepts, with a necessary being. But all this belongs to a *transcendent* philosophy; and that we are not yet in a position to discuss.

If we begin our proof cosmologically, resting it upon the series of appearances and the regress therein according to empirical laws of causality, we must not afterwards suddenly deviate from this mode of argument, passing over to something that B 486 is not a member of the series. Anything taken as condition must be viewed precisely in the same manner in which we viewed the relation of the conditioned to its condition in the series which is supposed to carry us by continuous advance to the supreme condition. If, then, this relation is sensible and falls within the province of the possible empirical employment of understanding, the highest condition or cause can bring the regress to a close only in accordance with the laws of sensibility, and therefore only in so far as it itself belongs to the temporal series. The necessary being must therefore be regarded as the highest member of the cosmical series.

Nevertheless certain thinkers have allowed themselves the liberty of making such a *saltus* (μετάβασις εἰς ἄλλογένος). From the alterations in the world they have inferred their empirical contingency, that is, their dependence on empirically determining causes, and so have obtained an ascending series of empirical conditions. And so far they were entirely in the right. But since they could not find in such a series any first beginning, or any highest member, they passed suddenly from the empirical concept of contingency, and laid hold upon the pure category, which then gave rise to a strictly intelligible series the completeness of which rested on the existence of an absolutely necessary cause. Sine this cause was not bound down to any sensible conditions, it was freed from the temporal condition which would require that its causality should itself have a beginning. But such procedure is entirely illegitimate, as may be gathered from what follows.

In the strict meaning of the category, the contingent is so named because its contradictory opposite is possible. Now we cannot argue from empirical contingency to intelligible contingency. When anything is altered, the opposite of its state is actual at B 488 another time, and is therefore possible. This present state is not, however, the contradictory opposite of the preceding state. To obtain such a contradictory opposite we require to conceive, that in the same time in which the preceding state was, its opposite could have existed in its place, and this can never be inferred from [the fact of] the alteration. A body which was in motion (= A) comes to rest (= non-A). Now from the fact that a state opposite to the state A follows upon the state A, we cannot argue that the contradictory opposite of A is possible, and that A is therefore contingent. To prove such a conclusion, it would have to be shown that in place of the motion, and at the time at which it occurred, there could have been rest. All that we know is that rest was real in the time that followed upon the motion, and was therefore likewise possible. Motion at one time and rest at another time are not related as contradictory opposites. Accordingly the succession of opposite determinations, that is, alteration, in no way establishes contingency of the type represented in the concepts of pure understanding;

and cannot therefore carry us to the existence of a necessary being, similarly conceived in purely intelligible terms. Alteration proves only empirical contingency; that is, that the new state, in the absence of a cause which belongs to the preceding time, could never of itself have taken place. such is the condition prescribed by the law of causality. This cause, even if it be viewed as absolutely necessary, must be such as can be thus met with in time, and must belong to the series of appearances.]

II. On the Antithesis The difficulties in the way of asserting the existence of an absolutely necessary highest cause, which we suppose ourselves to meet as we ascend in the series of appearances, cannot be such as arise in connection with mere concepts of the necessary existence of a thing in general. The difficulties are not, therefore, ontological, but must concern the causal connection of a series of appearances for which a condition has to be assumed that is itself unconditioned, and so must be cosmological, and relate to empirical laws. It must be shown that regress in the series of causes (in the sensible world) can never terminate in an empirically unconditioned condition, and that the cosmological argument from the contingency of states of the world, as evidenced by their alterations, does not support the assumption of a first and absolutely originative cause of the series.

B 487   A strange situation is disclosed in this antinomy. From the same ground on which, in the thesis, the existence of an original being was inferred, its non-existence is inferred in the antithesis, and this with equal stringency. We were first assured that *a necessary being exists* because the whole of past time comprehends the series of all conditions and therefore also the unconditioned (that is, the necessary); we are now assured that *there is no necessary being,* and precisely for the reason that the whole of past time comprehends the series of all conditions (which therefore are one and all themselves conditioned). The explanation is this. The former argument takes account only of *the absolute totality* of the series of conditions determining each other in time, and so reaches what is unconditioned and necessary. The latter argument, on the other hand, takes into consideration the *contingency* of everything which is determined in the temporal series (everything being preceded by a time in which the

condition must itself again be determined as conditioned), and from this point of view everything un- B 489 conditioned and all absolute necessity completely vanish. Nevertheless, the method of argument in both cases is entirely in conformity even with ordinary human reason, which frequently falls into conflict with itself through considering its object from two different points of view. M. de Mairan regarded the controversy between two famous astronomers, which arose from a similar difficulty in regard to choice of standpoint, as a sufficiently remarkable phenomenon to justify his writing a special treatise upon it. The one had argued that *the moon revolves on its own axis,* because it always turns the same side towards the earth. The other drew the opposite conclusion that *the moon does not revolve on its own axis,* because it always turns the same side towards the earth. Both inferences were correct, according to the point of view which each chose in observing the moon's motion.

The Antinomy of Pure Reason   B 490

Section 3: The Interest of Reason in these Conflicts

We have now completely before us the dialectic play of cosmological ideas. The ideas are such that an object congruent with them can never be given in any possible experience, and that even in thought reason is unable to bring them into harmony with the universal laws of nature. Yet they are not arbitrarily conceived. Reason, in the continuous advance of empirical synthesis, is necessarily led up to them whenever it endeavours to free from all conditions and apprehend in its unconditioned totality that which according to the rules of experience can never be determind save as conditioned. These pseudo-rational assertions are so many attempts to solve four natural and unavoidable problems of reason. There are just so many, neither more nor fewer, owing to the fact that there are just four series of synthetic presuppositions which impose *a priori* limitations on the empirical synthesis.

    The proud pretensions of reason, when it strives to extend its domain beyond all limits of

experience, we have represented only in dry formulas that contain merely the ground of their legal
B 491 claims. As befits a transcendental philosophy, they have been divested of all empirical features, although only in connection therewith can their full splendor be displayed. But in this empirical application, and in the progressive extension of the employment of reason, philosophy, beginning with the field of our experiences and steadily soaring to these lofty ideas, displays a dignity and worth such that, could it but make good its pretensions, it would leave all other human science far behind. For it promises a secure foundation for our highest expectations in respect of those ultimate ends towards which all the endeavors of reason must ultimately converge. Whether the world has a beginning [in time] and any limit to its extension in space; whether there is anywhere, and perhaps in my thinking self, an indivisible and indestructible unity, or nothing but what is divisible and transitory; whether I am free in my actions or, like other beings, am led by the hand of nature and of fate; whether finally there is a supreme cause of the world, or whether the things of nature and their order must as the ultimate object terminate thought—an object that even in our speculations can never be transcended: these are questions for the solution of which the mathematician would gladly exchange the whole of his science. For
B 492 mathematics can yield no satisfaction in regard to those highest ends that must closely concern humanity. And yet the very dignity of mathematics (that pride of human reason) rests upon this, that it guides reason to knowledge of nature in its order and regularity—alike in what is great in it and in what is small—and in the extraordinary unity of its moving forces, thus rising to a degree of insight far beyond what any philosophy based on ordinary experience would lead us to expect; and so gives occasion and encouragement to an employment of reason that is extended beyond all experience, and at the same time supplies it with the most excellent materials for supporting its investigations—so far as the character of these permits—by appropriate intuitions.

Unfortunately for speculation, though fortunately perhaps for the practical interests of humanity, reason, in the midst of its highest expectations, finds itself so compromised by the conflict of opposing arguments, that neither its honour nor its security allows it to withdraw and treat the quarrel with indifference as a mere mock fight; and still less is it in a position to command peace, being itself directly interested in the matters to dispute. Accordingly, nothing remains for reason save to consider whether the origin of this conflict, whereby it is divided against itself, may not have arisen from a mere misunderstanding. In such an enquiry both parties, per chance, may have to sacrifice proud claims; but a lasting and peaceful reign of reason B 493 over understanding and the senses would thereby be inaugurated.

Concluding Note on the Whole Antinomy of Pure Reason
B 593

So long as reason, in its concepts, has in view simply the totality of conditions in the sensible world, and is considering what satisfaction in this regard it can obtain for them, our ideas are at once transcendental and cosmological. Immediately, however, the unconditioned (and it is with this that we are really concerned) is posited in that which lies entirely outside the sensible world, and therefore outside all possible experience, the ideas become transcendent. They then no longer serve only for the completion of the empirical employment of reason—an idea [of completeness] which must always be pursued, though it can never be completely achieved. On the contrary, they detach themselves completely from experience, and make for themselves objects for which experience supplies no material, and whose objective reality is not based on completion of the empirical series but on pure *a priori* concepts. Such transcendent ideas have a purely intelligible object; and this object may indeed be admitted as a transcendental object, but only if we likewise admit that, for the rest, we have no knowledge in regard to it, and that it cannot be thought as a determinate thing in terms of distinctive inner predicates. As it is independent of all empirical concepts, we are cut off from any reasons that could establish the possibility B 594 of such an object, and have not the least justification for assuming it. It is a mere thought-entity. Nevertheless the cosmological idea which has given rise to the fourth antinomy impels us to take this step. For the existence of appearances, which is never self-grounded but always conditioned, requires us to look around for something different from all appearances, that is, for an intelligible object in which this contingency may terminate. But once we have allowed ourselves to assume a self-subsistent reality entirely outside the field of sensibility, appearances can only be viewed as contingent modes whereby beings that are themselves intelligences represent intelligible objects. Consequently, the only resource remaining to us is the use of analogy, by which we employ the concepts of experience in order to form some sort of concept of intelligible things—things of which as they are in themselves we have yet not the least knowledge. Since the contingent is not to be known save through experience, and we are here concerned with things which are not to be in any way objects of experience, we must derive the knowledge of them from that which is in itself necessary, that is, from pure concepts of things in general. Thus the very first step which we take beyond the world of sense obliges us, in seeking for such new knowledge, to begin with an enquiry into absolutely necessary being, and to derive from the concepts of it the concepts of all things in so far as they are purely intelligible. This we propose to do in the next chapter. . . .

B 595